DATE DUE

12-20-04			

Demco No. 62-0549

HEARST OVER HOLLYWOOD

Power, Passion, and Propaganda in the Movies

FILM AND CULTURE
JOHN BELTON, EDITOR

FILM AND CULTURE
A SERIES OF COLUMBIA UNIVERSITY PRESS
EDITED BY JOHN BELTON

HEARST OVER HOLLYWOOD

Power, Passion, and Propaganda in the Movies

Louis Pizzitola

COLUMBIA UNIVERSITY PRESS
NEW YORK

Columbia University Press

Publishers Since 1893

New York   Chichester, West Sussex

Copyright © 2002 Louis Pizzitola

Library of Congress

Cataloging-in-Publication Data

Pizzitola, Louis.

Hearst over Hollywood : power, passion,

and propaganda in the movies /

Louis Pizzitola.

p. cm. — (Film and culture)

Includes bibliographical references (p.)

and index

ISBN 0–231–11646–2 (cloth : alk. paper)

1. Hearst, William Randolph, 1863–1951.

2. Motion picture producers and directors—

United States —Biography.

3. Publishers and publishing—

United States—Biography.

4. Motion picture industry—California—

Los Angeles—History. I. Series

PN1998.3.H43 P59   2002

791.43'023'092—dc21

[B]   2001047230

∞

Columbia University Press books are

printed on permanent and durable

acid-free paper.

Printed in the United States of America

c 10 9 8 7 6 5 4 3 2 1

For my mother and Spence

Contents

Preface

During my research for *Hearst Over Hollywood*, I interviewed the late Edward L. Bernays, a nephew of Sigmund Freud and widely recognized as the father of public relations. Bernays, who was over one hundred years old when I spoke with him, had spent a lifetime developing techniques of persuasion and creating publicity schemes that promoted corporate America and sold the public on things they never knew they needed. While some might have seen a dubious honor in being known as the creator of spin, Bernays proudly called himself a propagandist. Apparently, Bernays was never close to William Randolph Hearst, but he did work for the Hearst organization, and he was close at least in spirit to Hearst's brand of communication.

In the 1920s Bernays was hired as a consultant to Hearst's *Good House-keeping* and *Cosmopolitan* magazines and for a corporation called Inter City Radio that was Hearst's initial attempt to form a network of radio stations that would enable him to channel his political ambitions into the nation's largest urban centers. As early as the 1910s Bernays enjoyed yellow journalism as a medium of information and entertainment. He visited the Hearst newspaper offices in New York and looked on in amusement as the paper's drama department made sure that "publicity a play received matched the amount of advertising [it purchased]." Over the years Bernays formed friendships with a number of Hearst associates. A Hearst reporter named Karl Von Weigand told Bernays over dinner in 1933 that he had just seen a copy of the spin master's book *Crystallizing Public Opinion* on Joseph Goebbels's "propaganda library" shelf and that he believed the Nazi Party was using Bernays's theories to guide their policies aimed at the destruction of the Jews.

In his autobiography, Bernays described the film industry as "a crude, crass, manufacturing business, run by crude, crass men," but he never dismissed its significance. He immediately understood my interest in exploring Hearst's impact on American culture through Hollywood—how and why the man, the film medium, and the film industry were so intrinsically related. Because of Bernays's advanced age, my interview with him was brief, but there was a hint of his earlier enthusiasm for his work when he closed our conversation with a question for me. Bernays was eager to know what title I had chosen for my book. When I told him, he responded like a true public relations counsel. "That's good," he said, "it sounds like power."

While Hearst appears to be a man of unfathomable contradictions when viewed in the context of journalism, as a force in and of Hollywood his life is a more constant marriage of passion, action, and meaning. In an interview with biographer William Swanberg in the late 1950s (never included in his book *Citizen Hearst*), Hearst's widow, Millicent, summed up her husband in these words: "He was a showman, like his mother." Indeed, Hearst, always something of petulant child, was a master of show-and-tell. In the 1890s, as an adult, his passion for putting on a show and telling a story took a leap toward the cinema with experiments in photography. Hearst took hundreds of photographs, developing some as stereopticon images to be projected on a screen and others to be looked at through a stereo viewer that suggested images in three dimensions. Even as late as the 1940s Hearst was still viewing (moving) images onscreen or, as one visitor to San Simeon recalled, retreating from his Hollywood guests to view 3-D scenes of Bad Nauheim, Venice, and Nuremberg through the black peepholes of a darkly stained stereopticon.

The earliest sections of *Hearst Over Hollywood* explore the relationship between Hearst's burgeoning communications empire and the development of film. As the story unfolds, Hearst's exploits with the novelist Stephen Crane, his drama-driven exploitation of the Spanish-American War, his connections to Tammany Hall politics and vice, and his perfection of dubious advertising practices take on an increasingly profound meaning. In yellow journalism, Hearst found a showplace to satisfy his desire to re-create for others the sensations he experienced. His newspapers became print moving-picture screens, and in turn the movies in the nickelodeons and storefronts became a reflection of Hearst newspapers. As cinema became the dominant medium of the twentieth century, Hearst latched on to it with gusto, knowing that he had found a new way to expand his power over the masses. He used film to entertain himself and to explore fantasies and myths about women, history, and religion. Hearst also used film as a weapon against those he feared, those he believed stood in opposition to his way of life and those against whom he held petty grudges.

It is a common myth—perpetuated by parallel situations in the film *Citizen Kane* and even by recent biographies—that Hearst became and remained a film producer mainly to boost the career of his mistress, Marion Davies. This romantic but myopic view does disservice to both Davies and Hearst and is certainly not how Hearst's relationship to Hollywood was always perceived. In 1916, two years before Davies appeared in a Hearst film production, a San Francisco journal called *The Lantern* was already drawing attention to Hearst's deepening film influence, describing how he was "employing the cinema as a means of moulding [*sic*] public opinion." This was a whole year before Hearst took virtual control of the Committee on Public Information, the film unit of the government's World War I propaganda machine, and nearly two decades after Hearst first utilized film to promote his political agenda.

In *A Million and One Nights* (1926), one of the earliest and most comprehensive film histories, author Terry Ramsaye heralded Hearst journalism as the muse of the film medium and Hearst as a multifaceted producer. The film historian made only a couple of passing references to Marion Davies. Although Davies played an important role in Hearst's life, her career was often a glamorous show window for the more complicated inner workings of Hearst's film ventures. She was only part of his Hollywood legacy. Hearst's influence cast a much wider net, helping to shape cinema into a popular medium and Hollywood into an industry of publicity, prejudices, artifice, and excess that was a mirror image of his interests and a vehicle serving his personal and political desires.

My goal in writing this book is to tell a story about Hollywood's first fifty years while simultaneously telling Hearst's life story from a Hollywood perspective. *Hearst Over Hollywood* does not purport to be a definitive biography of Hearst or a comprehensive history of the cinema but perhaps more of a biography of Hollywood and a journey into the essential Hearst. While this book will include analyses of many of the scores of films produced by Hearst and other films that he influenced but did not produce, its primary focus is the impact and context of films and film genres. I will avoid burdening the reader with my own opinions on the artistic or lasting value of individual films. After all, it was Hearst himself who believed that movies were not art so much as passing entertainment, a powerful propaganda tool and a form of storytelling.

One of the largely unsung pioneers of the pre-cinema era—the period when *Hearst Over Hollywood* begins—was Alexander Black. In the early 1890s the Brooklyn-born Black was a celebrity, known nationally for lectures—what he called "picture talks"—that focused on the subject of photography and were accompanied by glass slides projected on a screen by a stereopticon. His most popular talk was "Ourselves as Others See Us." Out of this lecture, Black developed an idea to present to audiences a screen story made up of 250 individual slides that when photographed and projected in a certain way would imply or indicate real motion. Black's trick was to subdivide his 250 pictures into groups of two to four images. Each sequence would show an actor in the process of making a motion, such as entering a room and sitting down in a chair or taking a revolver from his pocket and shooting a victim. Black took the pictures in each smaller group from the same precise camera angle against a single background. The only "movement" came from the actor, who was actually photographed at the start and finish of his movement. The slide pictures were projected by a stereopticon that kept each image frozen onscreen for about ten seconds before slowly dissolving it into another. In such "slow motion" a feature-length story, just under two hours, was eventually told.

Black believed the vehicle for telling a story in pictures to the masses was secondary to the actual storytelling. Audiences accepted the convention of his "picture plays," filling in the missing movements in their minds. The first, entitled *Miss Jerry*, premiered in October 1894 before an invitation-only gathering of press and literary friends in the studio of wealthy art photographer and Stanford White cohort James Lawrence Breese, located on West Sixteenth Street in New York City. One of the picture play's first sequences involves Jerry, the story's adventurous young reporter heroine, who seems to come to life when Black has her "step" outside her gilded frame.

Over the next few years Black produced three other picture plays. They were all feature length and included montage, crosscutting, flashbacks, closeups, and other techniques that would not become standard in film for decades. To give his screen stories an extra dimension, Black used realistic studio sets and actual outdoor locations. He was the proverbial one-man band, taking the photographs with his own camera, writing the picture scenarios, and presenting each show in person as he recited the dialogue for all the characters from the wings of the stage. He even added a touch of politics and celebrity to his pictures, inducing President Grover Cleveland to "act" for a series of dissolving slow-motion shots in a picture play he called *A Capitol Courtship*. When Black's first picture play premiered, film as we know it had already been invented, but it was unavailable to most people except in brief sequences viewed through the lens of a peepshow machine.

In 1913 Hearst hired Alexander Black as art director for his newspaper feature service, soon renamed King Features Syndicate. Black's responsibility was to coordinate the visual aspects of King Features, a key unit of the Hearst organization that distributed cartoons, photographs, illustrated feature articles, and other picture and entertainment-oriented items for inclusion in local Hearst publications as well as competitor clients' newspapers. That same year marked the start of an uninterrupted twenty-seven years of film production for Hearst: his planning for the serial *Perils of Pauline* began in late 1913. Perhaps it was only a coincidence, but the heroine of *Pauline*, played by Pearl White, begins her adventure in the serial in a fashion remarkably similar to Black's picture play character Jerry, emerging from a still photograph in a magazine.

Details about Black's working relationship with Hearst are unknown, although he visited San Simeon on a few occasions and the Hearst Corporation employed him for twenty-two years. When Black wrote his autobiography in the 1930s, he discussed Hearst only briefly, most tellingly in a passage where he compared Hearst to his other employer, the newspaper publisher Joseph Pulitzer. Both Hearst and Pulitzer were vigorous exponents of yellow journalism, but Black saw a clear distinction in their concerns. Pulitzer's real affinity was with words. Hearst was a picture man, "always acutely concerned [with] clearness that eyes encountered." This passion for telling stories with pictures was a strong link between Hearst and Black. When Black started working for Hearst, some of his more erudite friends were surprised. But one who knew him better than most was not. "Black," he said, "is the yellowist of them all."

The metaphor of the stereopticon, used by Black in his picture plays and long enjoyed by Hearst, may be a useful guide for readers making their way through this book. In *Hearst Over Hollywood*, two pictures are presented in relationship to each other. One is a portrait of William Randolph Hearst, and the other reveals the culture of Hollywood and the history of the film industry during his lifetime. When these two pictures of Hearst and Hollywood meet in a dissolve, as they so often did during the twentieth century, a third picture comes into view. This picture—"an illusion of reality," as Alexander Black used to call the effects in his picture plays—is perhaps more revelatory of both Hearst and Hollywood than might otherwise be possible.

Acknowledgments

Over the years, so many people were helpful to me in completing this book. Some knew Hearst, some knew one or more who were associated with Hearst, and some had done their own work in areas related to Hearst. Others simply responded to my interests with enthusiasm that went beyond perfunctory professional courtesies, and they took the extra step to point me in right direction. I will always be grateful for their willingness to share their time and their times.

Bruce Abrams of the Municipal Archives (NYC), Joe Adamson, Jana Allison, Jane Ardmore, Mike Barrier, Blaine Bartell of the UCLA Film Archives, Pat Culver Battle, Bill Berkson, Eleanor Lambert Berkson, Brigid Berlin, Edward Bernays, Linton von Beroldingen, Jean Willicombe Bissantz, the family of Alexander Black, Bill Blackbeard, Mary Carlisle Blakely, William Block, Patricia Bosworth, Sean Patrick Brady, Suzanne Brent, Roy Brewer, Ben Brewster of the Wisconsin Center for Film and Theater Research, Kevin Brownlow, John Canemaker, Jack Casserly, Igor Cassini, Larry Ceplair, Anthony Champagne, Michael Ciepley, Taylor Coffman, Robert Cole, Judy Coleman, Ned Comstock of USC, Mrs. Frank Conniff, Joseph V. Connolly Jr., Adrian Consentini, Tim Considine, Donald Crafton, Daniel Czitrom, Susan Darer, Luther Davis, Walter de Hoog, Harvey Deneroff, Martin Dies Jr., Bill Doyle, Angela Fox Dunn, Daniel Mark Epstein, Richard Fenton, Phil Frank of the Sausalito Historical Society, James Frasher, Tina Friedrich, Doris Gale, Dewitt Goddard, Mrs. Dean Goodsell, Milton Gould, Walter Gould, Lita Grey, Fred Guiles, Barbara Hall of the Academy of Motion Picture Arts and Sciences Library, Michael Hall, Egon Hanfstaegl, Nils Hanson of the Ziegfeld Club, Charles Harris, Will Hays Jr., William Randolph Hearst Jr., Robert Herzstein, Joseph J. Hovish of the American

Legion, the family of Joseph Hubbell, the family of Martin Huberth, Vicky Jones of the University of Oregon, Elizabeth Kendall, Heather Kiernan, Laird Kinnaird, Sigrid Kleinschmidt, Helmut W. Klinner, Cindy Knight of the State Historical Society of Wisconsin, the family of Gregory LaCava, Richard Lamparski, Frances Langford, Walter Lantz, Anne Miller Lopez, Pare Lorentz, Jerry Luboviski, Tex McCrary, Dorothy Mackaiil, Luke McKernan of the National Film Archive of the British Film Institute, the family of Victor MacLaglin, Paul McNamara, Dr. Rolf McPherson, Leonard Maltin, Kenneth Marx, Sam Marx, Martin Matthews, Ruth Matthews, Marsha Miner, Joel Montigue, the family of Colleen Moore, Whitney Moore, Henry Morgenthau III, Joan Munkacsi, Tibor Munkacsi, Kay Murray of the Author's League of America, Robert C. Pavlik, Ginny Payette, Darwin Payne, Grace Matthews Pressman, Jane Preston, Col. Edson Raff, Barbara Reid, John Reidy, Virginia Jenkins Roach, Caren Roberts-Frenzel, James Rogers, Elaine St. Johns, Mac St. Johns, Roberta McPherson Salter, Robert Samuels, Spencer Samuels, Nora Sayre, Frederick Schlink, Georganne Scheiner, Ralph Schoenstein, George Seldes, the family of Parker Sercombe, Pittman Shay, Sheila Fitzmaurice Shay, the family of Winfield R. Sheehan, Charles Silver of the Museum of Modern Art, Helen Munkacsi Sinclair, Anthony Slide, Jack C. Smith of the *Los Angeles Times*, Liz Smith, Pete Steffens, George Stevens Jr., Gloria Hatrick Stewart, Edward Stratton, William Swanberg, Truman Talley Jr., Dace Taube of the Regional History Center (LA), John Taylor of the National Archives (Washington, D.C.), John Tebbel, Patty Tobias, Ted Troll of the Hearst Corporation, Gretl Urban, Patrick Watson, Thor & Elynor Willat, Greg Williams of the Rutgers University Consumer Research Archive, Jean Wood, Eugene Zukor, and James Zukor.

Also deserving of special thanks for helping to make this book not only a history of Hearst and Hollywood but a story for readers are my editors Jennifer Crewe and Sarah St. Onge.

Above all others, for their love and kindness, I want to thank my family, Marleen Schuss, the Halperin family, Maria Messina, Carla Wynn, Billy McKay, Thor Case, Alison Bond, and Patrick Mulcahy.

HEARST OVER HOLLYWOOD

Power, Passion, and Propaganda in the Movies

Behind the Scenes

1880s–1890s

THE TAMMANY MODEL

In the 1930s a writer described Hollywood as "the creature and the wish-fulfillment of the mob on which Hearst has played all his life." William Randolph Hearst, he said, "will not be understood by those who miss his personal preference for the gaudy features that sold his papers along the Fourteenth streets of the land, and who suppose that he consciously and sardonically stooped to a plane below that which he lived."

When these observations were made, Fourteenth Street was still fondly remembered by many New Yorkers as its first Great White Way, a gaslight rialto, the cradle of the modern entertainment industry. For several decades before the turn of the twentieth century, this long wide street at the edge of the Tenderloin district and overlooking Union Square was home for the city's most important music and stage periodicals, its most popular actors' hotels, and even show business's most celebrated legends: the offices of the William Morris Agency, located between Third and Fourth Avenues. Some of the "gaudy features" of Fourteenth Street most likely recalled were the embarrassment of brothels, pool halls, and saloons often owned by ex-prize-fighters or local politicians. The street—dubbed "the line" because it stood at the junction of the densely immigrant populated Lower East Side—was also famous for its beer gardens. Its most popular were on the south side of the street: Theiss's music hall and Luchow's restaurant and hotel, a rendezvous for celebrated opera singers and less renowned show people from the nearby Bowery dives. Next door to Luchow's was Huber's Dime Museum, a theme park of raucous entertainment. Huber's was most famous for its German brass bands and circus freak show performers. Because its guttural sounds carried well beyond its walls, Huber's was partly responsible for making Thirteenth Street (where it had a second entrance) one of the more affordable places in the city to rent a flat.

With its reputation for welcoming less established entertainment and less established entertainers, Fourteenth Street was a natural location for the motion picture show to take root. By the late 1890s most vaudeville houses on the street included short films on their programs, and theater managers and stage performers were doubling as part-time film presenters. William Fox became one of the most famous of these theatrical chameleons. He started as a boy selling umbrellas on the sidewalk outside the Clarendon Music Hall on Thirteenth Street, moved inside as one half of a comedy duo, and eventually went on to become owner or part owner of theaters on Fourteenth Street and elsewhere. After saving enough money from his real estate ventures, he went into film distribution and film production, setting up an office in Union Square. By the early twentieth century, the future movie mogul Fox had been joined by the Hungarian-born Adolph Zukor, who presented movies at a penny arcade on Fourteenth Street years before he founded Famous Players–Lasky and Paramount Pictures. Directly across the street from Zukor in those early days was the Biograph Company, where David W. Griffith established himself as a leading film director of the silent era.

One theater that incorporated film into its lineup of vaudeville acts was in a unique position to play both sides of the respectability game on Fourteenth Street. Tony Pastor's Theater, located on the opposite side of the street from Luchow's, was perhaps the most popular vaudeville house in the entire city in the late nineteenth century, home to rising stars like Sophie Tucker and Harrigan and Hart and a singing waiter it employed named Irving Berlin. In his day Tony Pastor, the theater's impresario and a singer himself, was famous for his knack for finding talent and the quick pacing of his acts, which emphasized comedy and music popular with immigrants. Today, Pastor is best known for being a leader in moving vaudeville into the mainstream by making his shows suitable for men accompanied by their wives. This legend about Pastor seems almost certainly to have been in part a product of press agentry. One of his theater's film presenters in the late 1890s was the pioneer movie producer Albert Smith, who later described how Pastor established a squeaky clean reputation without completely breaking the ties to vice that supported the entertainment business: "It wasn't easy to break down public prejudice. Tony had to entice respectable people into his dingy little theater in Tammany Hall. And he did it by calling in nightly a bevy of damsels wearing conservative dress and soft manners not generally associated with their professions. Properly escorted, these easygoing ladies took seats here and there about the theater. The decoy worked."

No doubt being located on the ground floor of Tammany Hall, the headquarters for political power for generations, gave Pastor a reason to put the best face on his theater. Tony Pastor's was the official show window for Tammany, but by no means the only popular amusement doubling as a deception.

Photographs of Tammany Hall in the 1890s show a nondescript building with its upper stories usually bathed in bright sunlight. The commonplace presentation of red brick and marble hardly mirrored the building's inner workings; in fact, Tammany was an oversized octopus that countless editorial cartoonists drew to depict its slippery, untouchable influence. Its dark shadow tumbled down its half-dozen front steps and into the facing street, spreading in all directions, through surrounding tenements, music halls, beer gardens, and brothels. Years before the term came to be universally associated with the Mafia, the Reverend Charles Parkhurst likened Tammany to an "organization of crime." Tammany's weapons were the weapons of gangsters: extortion, intimidation, and worse. There was no aspect of city life that Tammany did not touch and often control. Saloonkeepers, building contractors, fire inspectors, the public transportation authorities, theaters, and hotels all paid handsome and regular tribute to Tammany. Tammany leaders—who were often saloon, theater, or other property owners themselves—made a strange distinction between graft and "good graft." They implied that any alleged excesses and any surplus of money that filled their pockets was excused by the greater good of improving the lot of those citizens who had previously been ignored by everyone, especially the government. But in reality Tammany leaders were mostly interested in enriching themselves, and the poor among them remained poor despite the crumbs cast their way. Tammany Hall played a pivotal role in city, state, and national politics for generations, from the vice presidency of Aaron Burr to the presidencies of Martin Van Buren and Franklin D. Roosevelt, but it was equally influential in shaping business practices and popular culture. Its power was maintained by organized fear and through an expert understanding of the pleasure-seeking masses. It became a model system for those who would create new entertainment arenas successfully linked to political forces and vice.

Parkhurst, whose widely publicized sermon in 1892 began the first major assault on Tammany and its notorious connections, compared the political machine to Rockefeller's Standard Oil. Tammany, he declared, is a business enterprise that is in the business of coddling and controlling urban criminality. "The material from which it draws prolific dividends," he said, "is crime and vice, such as flourishes in gambling resorts, disorderly houses and corner groceries." Tammany, the master, knew that for it to exist and prosper, its servants had to be kept relatively comfortable. Madams, saloonkeepers, theater owners, and others were provided with protection. Later, as nickelodeon owners sprang up, the same Tammany reward and protection system applied to these new captains of amusement. They enjoyed licensing advantages and escaped the city's fire, liquor, and building rules. And those who did not play Tammany's game found themselves overburdened with regulations or simply denied the chance to build their businesses. In typical monopolistic fashion, Tammany discouraged independent businessmen and encouraged big business, which was always able to provide larger kickbacks and political contributions.

In the nearby saloons, pool halls, and storefront peep show arcades, whose walls were lined with a photographic hodgepodge of local pugilists, prize horses, and pretty girls, pictures of Tammany politicians competed for the eyes' attention. And outside these venues, like awnings covering the streets, canvas poster-sized pictures or cartoons of candidates for mayor, district leader, sheriff, or even national offices were often strung from banners. One usual destination for these political banners was a theater directly across the street from Tammany Hall. The Dewey Theater was linked to Tammany in more ways than one. Because it was owned by one of the city's most powerful bosses, Timothy D. Sullivan, it had the distinction of being the unofficial entertainment center of Tammany Hall. Tony Pastor's may have been a show window, but the Dewey Theater was the real thing.

Sullivan—known by constituents as "Big Tim"—was born in 1863, the same year as Hearst, in a tenement on New York City's Greenwich Street. Unlike Hearst, Sullivan lived a childhood in extreme poverty. When Tim was four years old his father died, leaving a young widow to raise four young children. Things went from bad to worse when Tim's mother remarried an Irish immigrant named Lawrence Mulligan, an alcoholic who was physically abusive. Barely seven years old, Tim Sullivan had to quit school and look for a job. He worked as a shoeshine boy in a police station and later as a manual laborer bundling newspapers and loading delivery wagons in Park Row, the great publishing hub in lower Manhattan. Over the next ten years, he gradually worked his way up to becoming a manager overseeing newspaper distribution for a number of different publishers.

During this period and while still a teenager, Sullivan made his first connection with Tammany Hall. Along with scores of others, he was hired by a district leader shortly before election day and instructed to go from one saloon to another registering voters under different, fictitious names. On election day, Sullivan and his fellow "repeat voters" cast their votes "early and often." Sullivan earned about two dollars per vote, or the equivalent of more than a week's pay loading newspapers. As a young adult, Sullivan was an impressive figure—he was over six feet tall and barrel-chested—but he was also clever and outwardly emotional in manner and speech. He was a good storyteller, fluent in Boweryese, and his best stories were always about his humble upbringing and his innate love of humanity. While he was still working in the wholesale newspaper distribution business, Sullivan made the acquaintance of certain higher-level Tammany men, who must have recognized the bond of devotion that existed between Sullivan and his fellow Lower East Siders and saw in him a modern politician in the making. Picking Sullivan from the anonymous ranks of repeat voters, they hired him to transport protection money and engage in some small-time spying on political opponents. Possibly with some help from or as a reward for helping Tammany, Sullivan opened a saloon near the Bowery in 1885.

In the late nineteenth century, owning a saloon was an established stepping-stone to political influence, mainly because the system of kickbacks required a saloonkeeper to maintain friendly relations with Tammany. In addition, the saloon itself functioned as a political meeting place, especially among the economically disadvantaged. Evidence that Sullivan was on a fast track to power was indisputable: over the next four years Sullivan became the owner of three more saloons on the Lower East Side, one in a prime location directly across the street from the Tombs police court on Centre Street. During this period, Sullivan was elected to the state assembly. In 1892 he became a district leader under Tammany boss Richard Croker, a former street thug and accused murderer. It was Croker who once tried to elevate Tammany and its nefarious connections by comparing it to Wall Street and other established institutions. "Everything is business," he told Lincoln Steffens, then a reporter for the *New York Evening Post*.

Sullivan actively courted press coverage, and most newspaper reporters found that Sullivan was colorful copy. In private, he enjoyed the company of newspapermen, who, almost to a man, fell in line with his liberal attitudes toward drinking, gambling, and sexuality. With few exceptions, the press became his willing accomplice, always playing up the genuinely good aspects of his nature and his various philanthropic works. Press accounts about massive annual shoe giveaways for the poor and regular beer and chowder fests and musical outings to Sulzer's Harlem River Park Casino (future site of Hearst's Cosmopolitan motion picture studio) helped Sullivan to establish a populist persona. At these events, Sullivan's celebrity image was promoted through the sale of his picture, which citizens were encouraged to bring home and hang on their tenement walls.

Sullivan was not the first to interweave the public's interest in cheap amusements with the corrupt maintenance of political power, and New York was not the only corrupt city. Sullivan's reign, however, occurred at a time and place where sensational journalism and mass entertainment met with explosive force and enormous potential for propaganda. Sullivan's own skill at manipulating these happy accidents cannot be underplayed. When, in rare instances, Sullivan was directly accused of wrongdoing, the press had been well trained to focus on his tearful responses and his homilies about mother and sacrifice. Melodramatic displays and extravagant diversions were simply too tempting for editors interested in selling newspapers.

The Lexow Committee investigations of 1894 into police corruption exposed a darker side of Sullivan. According to testimony before the committee, very early in his elective career "Big Tim" was seen ordering his cousin Florrie and some other men to severely beat a poll watcher who was resisting Tammany pressure. Along with the threat of violence, Sullivan created a repeat voter system that was cleverly designed to minimize double-crosses. At the time, voters were provided with a choice of ballots to deposit in boxes. Sullivan had the pro-Tammany ballots dabbed with a gum solution mixed with the recognizable scent of sassafras. The repeater was sure about which ballot to choose, and a district leader who got a whiff of a paid repeater afterward was sure his man had chosen correctly. (Sassafras had other Tammany connotations as well: it was an ingredient in drinks prostitutes ordered instead of whiskey to fool their clients into thinking they were drinking alcohol, and it was used by some as a cure for venereal diseases and to induce abortions.)

Repeaters often doubled as bouncers at saloons, theaters, and brothels, and they were the men who collected protection money from these same establishments during nonelection periods. A madam or a theater owner who wanted to remain in business had little choice but to pay Tammany, and the corrupt system was supported by an abundance of participating allied enterprises, such as preferred brewers, cigarette and cigar manufacturers, clothing and laundry services, newspaper classified pages for soliciting customers, abortionists, and performers to provide entertainment for theater and brothel patrons. James Watson Gerard Jr., who was closely associated with Tammany during this period and went on to become Hearst's attorney, ambassador to Germany during World War I, and a power broker in the

Democratic Party for decades, remembered the eve of an election being called "Dough Day." As chairman of the campaign committee, Gerard personally delivered bags of cash—collected in various shakedowns—to district leaders who in turn paid gang members. Sullivan's men were groomed to be some of the most notorious gangsters at the turn of the century: Paul Kelly and his brother "Jimmie" (Italians posing as Irish who mentored Lucky Luciano and Al Capone), "Monk" Eastman, and Arnold Rothstein all rose from the ranks of Sullivan's vote repeaters and strong-arm enforcers.

One ritual of urban life where Tammany's system of vice and entertainment synergy flourished was the theater. In the theater men and women commingled, the sale of liquor was permitted, darkness provided a modicum of privacy and titillation, and the performances of attractive actors and actresses on the stage played to the audiences' desire for fantasy. The stage shows themselves often included material that promulgated Tammany as the people's friend. Perhaps the most flagrant demonstrations of the theater and prostitution alliance occurred in the so-called third tier. This was a gallery of seats located in the uppermost area of a theater, above the dress and family circles, that was reserved for prostitutes and clients. The convention was first established in the middle of the eighteenth century and commonplace in major American cities by the early 1800s. Theater owners, who sometimes built a special separate stairway in their houses just for prostitutes, encouraged the arrangement. Individual prostitutes (and sometimes an entire brothel) arrived at a theater about an hour before curtain time to avoid meeting other audience members on the street. Liquor was made available for the ladies and their visiting clients at a bar in the rear of their section. From here, the prostitutes made arrangements with men for sexual rendezvous later in the evening at nearby brothels or hotels, although sometimes they used the third tier itself for such sexual encounters.

By the mid-nineteenth century, under pressure from reformers, many theater owners quietly discontinued the lucrative practice. But, like Willie Sutton, who robbed banks because that was where the money was, prostitutes continued to frequent the places where their clients were. Presumably, a significant number of prostitutes still remained scattered among the audience—the higher-priced women called "stars"—but more often other locations in the theater or nearby the theater became their domain. Frequently, the setting for sexual encounters was the actors' dressing rooms or the greenroom, so called because it was situated in the rear of the theater's scene room where decorative foliage was stored. This arrangement gave rise to the coinage "behind the scenes," used even today, frequently in association with show business, to connote a hidden truth. These in-house provisions for prostitution did not supplant the brothel. There was usually at least one brothel within a block of every theater in New York City, and some, like the brothel in the rear of the Park Theater in Theater Alley, were actually connected to theaters by short hallways, a flight of stairs, or a courtyard. This particular setup was a more elaborate version of the "behind-the-scenes" arrangements and had connections to Sullivan and Hearst as well.

For nearly a decade, beginning in 1895, Hearst was one of the most prominent allies of Tammany Hall. In turn, the official organ of the organization, the *Tammany Times*, praised his brand of journalism as a populist medium. Tammany's rule of Fourteenth Street and the other streets that stretched beneath its shadow became a model for Hearst, both in his publishing business and in the communications-entertainment industry he was about to help create. The origins of Hearst's affinity with Tammany and its ways almost certainly went back to his formative years, when he learned about the power of putting on a show and the rewards of having a father with powerful friends.

Two of Hearst's favorite amusements as a child were of a theatrical nature. In a playroom crammed with books, watercolor sets, and mechanical toys, the pièce de résistance was a miniature theater where Hearst could hover over Lilliputian actors, tiny stage sets, and precious dressing rooms. Another, larger theater was for his Punch and Judy shows. From behind its stage, Hearst invisibly controlled a pair of lunatic puppets engaged in a strange mix of comedy and brutality. No doubt Hearst's flashy toys made him a celebrity among his neighborhood friends, and he may have first caught the showman bug from the experience.

The San Francisco where Hearst was born in 1863 was a rough-and-tumble Punch and Judy show itself, where politics, vice, and entertainment were deftly mixed and political violence shared the stage with sexual bawdiness. The city's earliest female settlers were prostitutes and surprisingly well respected because of their closeness to men in power. Just a few years before Hearst's birth, newspapers regularly presented the San Francisco politician as a rogue or romantic figure; dramatic duels seem to have been an annual event. Like any native son of San Francisco, Hearst would have been acquainted with the Tammany-style bossism that dominated the post–Civil War era. But Hearst had more than a mere acquaintance with such trends because he was not just any son of San Francisco. He was the son of George Hearst, and he never knew a time when his father wasn't interested in politics and political alliances.

When Hearst was young, Christopher Buckley was the West Coast counterpart to what "Big Tim" Sullivan would become. Buckley actually grew up in New York City, departing for San Francisco on the eve of Boss Tweed's notorious reign at Tammany Hall. Like so many political bosses in the making, Buckley began his career in a saloon, working at the age of seventeen as a bartender at Tom Maguire's San Francisco Snug Saloon. Maguire had also come from New York, where he rose in the entertainment business in the late 1840s as a third-tier bartender at the Park Theater in New York. He parlayed this position into an association with Tammany, and one of its bosses became his partner in a prominent saloon near city hall. Associated at times with producer David Belasco, Maguire became one of the most famous theater personalities in the second half of the nineteenth century. He owned theaters in San Francisco and Sacramento, as well as in the mining town Virginia City. Maguire's Snug Saloon was perhaps the foremost gathering place in San Francisco for politicians, actors, and businessmen.

Like his boss, Chris Buckley moved effortlessly from bartender to saloon owner. Over the next twenty years, forming alliances with other saloon owners, influential district leaders, and municipal department officials, Buckley delved deeply into politics and successfully managed the campaigns of a number of Democratic Party candidates in San Francisco. His winning qualities echoed those of the Tammany Hall bosses: he knew how to run a tight political machine (which meant perfecting the patronage and repeat voter systems), and he understood the people's need for cheap amusement. In San Francisco, under Buckley's influence, entertainment in the form of circuses and clambakes became a way of life just as chowder parties and clothing giveaways were Tammany's rewards.

In 1882, while young Hearst was enrolled at Harvard University, his father, increasingly interested in politics, made plans to capture the Democratic Party nomination for governor. George Hearst's financial war chest must have certainly been attractive to Buckley, but in addition the miner and rancher was a newspaper publisher, having purchased the *San Francisco Examiner* a few years earlier solely to serve as a Democratic Party mouthpiece. Buckley had befriended George Hearst during this period, and in the race for the Democratic nomination he became one of his political managers.

Having failed to secure the nomination, Hearst and Buckley nevertheless remained allies over the next few years, as both men's power steadily increased. It was mainly due to Buckley's backing and the propaganda value of the *Examiner* that George Hearst in 1886 was appointed by the governor to the seat in the United States Senate that became open with the death of Senator John Miller. From this position and with the continuing support of Boss Buckley, Senator Hearst was elected a year later to a full six-year term.

Hearst's election, and the ultimate usefulness of his *Examiner*, coincided with his son's expulsion from Harvard University. Shortly before March 4, 1887, when he was sworn in as senator, Hearst apportioned his political power by turning over ownership of the *San Francisco Examiner* to his son. Young Hearst would not be content simply to maintain the political agenda of his father's newspaper. Under his stewardship, the *Examiner* made sudden and sweeping strides in circulation and notoriety by presenting what might be called "cheap news," counterpart of the cheap amusements of the masses.

THE HOUSE BEHIND THE DEWEY THEATER

On March 12, 1893, the Reverend W. R. Huntington spoke to his congregation at New York City's Grace Church. With considerable regret, he informed them that the church's chapel, which was located only a few blocks north, on East Fourteenth Street, was being forced to relocate to an area several blocks east. Grace Chapel, he said, evoking little surprise from his audience, was surrounded by the merchants of vice. "Churches have to compass their ends by spiritual rather than political means, and there are vested rights which do not yield to sermons. The law which forbids the placing of a saloon within so many feet of the threshold of a school or of a church, gives you but slender help in ejecting a bad neighbor when he has once established himself, and the name of the bad neighbors who hedge in Grace Chapel is legion."

In appearance, Grace Chapel was a typical wooden structure when it was built in 1875, but it was an anomaly on irreligious Fourteenth Street. Huber's Dime Museum was located a few doors west, and Theiss's music hall a few doors east. As early as 1884, when Theiss's was erected, the church had complained to the city's board of excise about the music hall's proximity to worshipers. Theiss's, which served liquor seven days a week, featured what was advertised as a "monster orchestrion," an automated pipe organ and percussion instrument machine that later became a popular sound effects device in silent film theaters. The music hall was an immense structure that included "the only sliding roof in the world," a billiard parlor, bowling alleys, an oyster bar, a restaurant, and theater space. Theiss's attracted hundreds of patrons a night, and according to reports a significant number of them were prostitutes or men seeking prostitutes. Like many other music halls, Theiss's offered its customers an upper floor of hotel rooms for privacy. To make matters worse for the Grace Chapel, Theiss's had an outdoor courtyard that wrapped itself around the narrow property at the rear of the church. Patrons exiting Theiss's this way had easy access to disorderly houses and other amusements that fronted on the less conspicuous Thirteenth Street. In the eyes of Reverend Huntington and Bishop Henry Codman Potter, the rector of Grace Church, Thirteenth Street wasn't any better than Fourteenth Street. Clarendon Hall at 116–118 East Thirteenth Street had a reputation similar to Theiss's, and there were numerous brothels running up and down the street. Police dockets for 1896, like most other entries for the decade, are mostly filled with petty crimes and cases of women being arrested for "disorderly conduct." In August, for instance, a prostitute appearing in court named Maggie Brown gave her address as 123 East Thirteenth Street, a building directly across the street from the Clarendon.

In July 1896, when Martin Huberth, a young agent for Folsom Brothers Real Estate, sold the Grace Chapel, Reverend Huntington's sermon came full circle, and the last vestige of conventional respectability in the area vanished. Huberth's $1,000 commission for the sale of Grace Chapel was part of a package deal that included the sale of three four-story houses on East Thirteenth Street, numbers 123, 125, and 127. The properties on Thirteenth Street were only a dozen feet to the rear of the church and Theiss's music hall. The lots on Fourteenth Street and Thirteenth Street were technically sold to John B. Smith, an unknown party who was apparently standing in for a much better known figure. By the mid-1890s, "Big" Tim Sullivan had already launched a new career in real estate and show business that would grow over the next decade to include several vaudeville houses and nickelodeons (sometimes in partnership with William Fox) and (in partnership with John W. Considine) a theater circuit that controlled some forty houses nationwide. In 1896 Sullivan turned the old Grace Chapel into a music hall or concert theater. For several months Sullivan's place was called Volks Garden; in 1897 he renamed it the Dewey Theater.

Sullivan, who managed the theater with George and David Kraus, father-and-son music hall owners, didn't publicize his ownership at first, and Tammany kept its distance across the block, but both parties were interested in the theater's success from the start. At first Sullivan made few obvious alterations to his building's exterior beyond the removal of church steeples and the reconfiguration of windows. Inside, a small musical stage replaced a church altar. Bars were set up in convenient corners, and rows of inexpensive tables and chairs were installed to increase the seating capacity to fourteen hundred. The various political banners, lithographs, and emblems that were placed over the rows of liquor bottles behind the bars and on the walls of the box office were a confirmation and a reminder of Tammany's unofficial support of Sullivan's enterprise. Tammany also helped Sullivan circumvent bureaucratic building and fire code requirements, so that he could make speedy renovations. In one of his more consequential legal dodges, Sullivan had his builders construct a narrow passageway behind the performing stage that connected his theater to the attached buildings at 123 and 125 East Thirteenth Street. Almost overnight a literal link between political power and vice had been accomplished, and the Dewey's doors—both front and back—were open to those who prospered by such connections.

About twelve years before the Dewey opened its doors, Hearst was away at Harvard, invariably tempted by the less cerebral activities that lurked around the corners of Boston's cheap amusement district. Shunning entertainment of a classical nature, he rushed to a minstrel show, a music hall, almost any sort of vaudeville sketch and enjoyed closing the night drinking beer at some risqué party thrown in the outskirts of town.

One performer who personified Hearst's taste in entertainment during this period was a native of Massachusetts whose specialty "eccentric dancing" is now largely forgotten. During the early 1880s, George Leslie had some local triumphs playing Keith's Boston Theater and other nearby playhouses. Leslie's dancing and performing style was best demonstrated years later by actor and dancer Buddy Ebsen and Wizard of Oz star Ray Bolger. Its trademark was a long-legged high kick, to which Leslie added lowbrow jokes and "coon songs." Leslie was never a headliner, but he was hardworking, sometimes performing ten shows a day. His appearance—rail-thin and dressed in a tight-fitting plaid suit and white top hat—was a variation on the dandy look, which Hearst himself favored at the time. Eccentric dancing was something Hearst's rebellious side could identify with: it poked holes in the formalities of proper society. It is not known whether Hearst first saw Leslie's act in Boston, but about a dozen years later Hearst introduced the performer to showman Tony Pastor in New York. Sometime between his Harvard days and the late 1890s, Hearst had struck up a friendship with Leslie, whose real name was George Willson.

Millicent Willson Hearst was hard to pin down about her past. She recalled her father, George, as a printing press inventor not a vaudeville performer. Publicly she never mentioned her mother at all. Hannah Willson was born Hannah Murray in Portland, Maine, on Christmas Day, 1858, the daughter of Patrick, an Irish-born waiter who likely worked at the Fairmouth Hotel, Portland's popular center of political and theatrical life. After her father's death, Hannah, along with two or more siblings and their widowed mother, moved to Manhattan's Lower East Side. In New York Hannah met and married George Willson, a struggling actor who worked in a nearby theatrical prop shop. The Willsons had two daughters, born a few years apart, Anita being the elder. When his children were still toddlers, George Willson began to try out his eccentric dance routine. He took his act on the road and adopted a stage name, possibly to cash in on the notoriety of George Leslie, a period folk hero sometimes called the King of the Bank Robbers. Although Willson was away for months at a time, touring theaters in the Southwest and New England, his eccentric dancing never amounted to more than a novelty and certainly offered no sure path to financial security for his family. Back home, with the pressure to make ends meet, Hannah Willson took in laundry, as did her mother, and she bided her time until Anita and Millicent were old enough to help with the bills.

Millicent was no more forthcoming about her first meeting with Hearst than she was about her parents. From limited sources Hearst biographers have concluded that Hearst met his future wife during her run in a Herald Square Theater production called *The Girl from Paris* that opened in 1896. Considering how things turned out, the show's premise was ironically appropriate: its lead character is a rich rascal who leads a double life, maintaining one home for his wife and another for his mistress. Surviving playbills suggest that Millie Willson's contribution to the production (which starred Clara Lipman and Louis Mann) was minimal: she did a dance routine along with eight other lacy-legged "Bicycle Girls," one of whom was her older sister, Anita.

Millicent never discussed her stage career in any detail, and in one account she claimed to have met Hearst at an Irish fair in Manhattan. Millicent and Hearst probably both attended this event, which occurred in May 1897, since the *New York Journal*, Hearst's latest newspaper acquisition, publicized the event, and the cast of *The Girl from Paris* were highlighted in his paper. It seems likely, however, that the first meeting between Hearst and Millicent occurred earlier, at least three months before the Irish fair, when the *Journal* held a benefit concert, publicizing the Willson sisters' show in conjunction with it. Even before this benefit concert, the *Journal* was publicizing *The Girl from Paris*. It was in fact the only paper other than the *Tammany Times* to take real notice of the show.

By 1895, when the Willson girls were teenagers, their mother, Hannah Willson, had herself listed in the city directory as keeper of a boardinghouse at 123 East Thirteenth Street. A preponderance of circumstantial evidence indicates, however, that the Willson house was not really a boardinghouse, except as the term was loosely defined at the time. An alternative version of the life of the Willson family is sketched in a 1913 one-sheet broadside published by anonymous foes of Hearst who wanted to dampen his continuing political ambitions. It is not known if the broadside was widely circulated, but a copy was saved by James Gerard, the Hearst friend and attorney who had early connections with Tammany Hall. The broadside (it has no title) declares Hearst to be unfit for present or future political office. This was hardly an unusual charge by Hearst opponents, but what sets the document apart is the evidence it submits to back up its charge. According to the broadside, at the turn of the century, the Willson's house—which is specifically mentioned as being located on East Thirteenth Street in the rear of Theiss's beer garden—was actually a "resort," or what most would understand to be a brothel. Furthermore, it implies, the Willson house was not an insignificant brothel but a popular place patronized by an "enthusiastic" and elite clientele that included the monopolist John D. Rockefeller's "Standard Oil crowd." The broadside is dripping with arch sarcasm about Hearst's aspirations, his "conspicuous ability" and his "statesmanlike qualities." The most scornful lines are saved for the Willsons and their so-called resort. In one ironic passage, Millicent is described as being of "distinguished lineage." In another passage, a not-so-veiled reference to either George Willson's or Hearst's sexual orientation is made: "A dozen years ago all then clamored for her and her mother's seductive and lascivious attentions as young boys clamored for his."

Throughout the late 1890s and early twentieth century, the Dewey Theater had a reputation as low if not lower than that of any theater on the Fourteenth Street rialto. Nevertheless, despite the occasional jabs it received in some anti-Tammany newspapers, it continued to be immune from building laws and regulations. Meanwhile, Martin Huberth, the real estate agent who handled the sale of the Willson house along with the Grace Chapel, was soon employed by Hearst and quickly climbing his way up the corporate ladder. By 1913 Huberth was Hearst's chief real estate adviser, involved in the purchase of numerous properties for Hearst, including some buildings around Columbus Circle that even the mayor suspected of being houses of prostitution. Huberth negotiated the purchase of the Clarendon apartment building on Eighty-sixth Street and Riverside Drive where Hearst set up residence with Millicent several years after their marriage in 1903, along with sister Anita and parents George and Hannah Willson. Eventually, the enterprising Huberth sat on the board of directors of the Hearst Corporation and was named an executor of Hearst's will.

Until shortly before his marriage to Millicent, Hearst was seen in the company of both Willson sisters. Hearst's "decided penchant for chirpies," as one newspaper put it, had resulted in the purchase of "a private and well-equipped cab" to escort his girlfriends. Rumors persisted that Hearst was infatuated with both sisters, who were increasingly "at loggerheads about him." Around 1900 Millicent and Hearst began living together (in a house with separate quarters for sister Anita). Some have suggested that political realities were a key factor in Hearst's decision to marry Millicent in 1903, but one source who was close to the couple claimed it was an unplanned pregnancy that cinched the wedding plans.

News of Hearst's marriage caused the old *New Yorker* magazine to publish two short articles—"Sacrificed the Presidency?" and "The New Arrival"—that added fuel to the rumors about the Willsons and speculated on how they might impact on Hearst's political future. The *New Yorker* expressed bemusement that Bishop Potter—who was recognized as a campaigner against the evils of vice—had officiated at the Hearst wedding ceremony at his landmark Grace Church. They made no mention of the fact that Potter also oversaw the Grace Chapel on Fourteenth Street, located in front of the Willsons' resort. Some accounts claimed that Potter was a friend of the Willson family and close enough to Hearst's wife to name the motorboat at his Adirondack residence *Millie*, after her. The *New Yorker*'s choicest remarks seem to substantiate the claims that would be made in the 1913 broadside against Hearst and the Willsons, and they even anticipate the "Candidate Caught in Love Nest" scene in the 1941 film about Hearst, *Citizen Kane*. With his marriage to Millicent, the *New Yorker* wrote that Hearst "has signed his political death warrant." Whether Millicent's past is known "outside a comparatively small circle of New Yorkers, no one knows exactly," but if Hearst saw marriage as "morally rehabilitating" to his own reputation, "he would have been better advised [than] to marry one of the so-called 'Sassafras Sisters.'" In conclusion, the *New Yorker* suggests that if "by any unheard-of chance Hearst were to blackmail his way to a presidential nomination, it would take only about three weeks for the cold facts to be brought by the opposition managers to the consciousness of every voter in the country." Just such a scenario suggested by the *New Yorker* takes place in *Citizen Kane* when the Hearst character, Charles Foster Kane, finds his political hopes dashed when his rival in a race for governor threatens to expose his affair with a common girl whom he met outside a boardinghouse. In the film, the candidate for governor seals his fate by standing by his mistress and eventually marrying her.

What detrimental effect, if any, marriage to Millicent may have had on Hearst's political career is hard to assess, since his path to power was as unconventional as his romantic relationships. It is possible that fear of exposure about Millicent and her family may have kept Hearst's grander political ambitions in check. The possibility exists, however, that Hearst's connection to Millicent and her connections to politicians like Sullivan and religious leaders like Potter made her an invaluable ally and confidential emissary. A year before the Hearst marriage in 1903, "Big Tim" Sullivan played a prominent role in raising Hearst's political viability by handing him a nomination as the congressional candidate from a Tammany-controlled Manhattan district. Hearst easily won the election and was reelected two years later, or one year after his wedding.

Sullivan entered Congress the same year as Hearst. In some congressional memoirs, Hearst was linked to Sullivan, not because of their mutual connections to prostitution but because the two men had the worst attendance records in Congress. To be sure, stages other than the workaday world of legislation and committees were better suited to Hearst's circuitous personality. From his father and from Sullivan, Hearst had learned firsthand that backroom politics often held more clout than elective office. With Tammany, the Tenderloin, and his own carnival brand of journalism as models, Hearst was setting the stage for a new combination of politics and entertainment from which he would control the show from behind the scenes.

2

The Artist Journalist
1895–1898

> He is intelligent, you know. Not many careers have been so
> planned, so intelligent, so firmly managed as his. A work of
> art, that man's life has been, and conscious. . . . I wish Mr.
> Hearst would be again an artist-journalist.
>
> —*Lincoln Steffens on Hearst, 1935*

NOVELETTES

On an afternoon in September 1896 Hearst came hurtling around a stairwell of a building in lower Manhattan's Printing House Square. Somewhere
between the ground floor and third floor where his *New York Journal* newspaper was headquartered he ran into his editor, Henry R. Haxton. Hearst
considered the British-born Haxton a kindred spirit who saw journalism as
a competitive entertainment, or what Hearst called a "glad sport." Like
everyone else who knew Hearst's habits in those days, Haxton was used to
seeing his boss in quick spurts. The young publisher was in constant—however imprecise—movement; a man nicknamed GUSH by his chief publishing rival at the time, Joseph Pulitzer. On the steps of the stairwell, Hearst laid
out the bullet points for a series of articles to run in the *Journal*. He wanted
the feature articles to be written by the much-sought-after novelist Stephen
Crane. He wanted them written in "dramatic form," not quite fiction but
not quite reportage. He wanted to advertise the Crane pieces as "novelettes."

Hearst directed his newspaper staff with the same effortless determination with which he entered the publishing field. After his father turned over

the *San Francisco Examiner* to him, Hearst remade his present into a laboratory for the development of a brand of sensationalist human-interest journalism that borrowed liberally from publishers James Gordon Bennett,
Charles A. Dana, and Pulitzer. It was on the new *Examiner* that editor Haxton was first engaged by the young publisher and enthralled by his penchant
for drama. During a stormy night in 1890, Haxton literally took a dive for
Hearst—into the San Francisco Harbor. Hot on the trail of a news bulletin
about a group of fishermen who were spotted shipwrecked on a rock,
Hearst commandeered a tugboat and set out to make news. He gathered up
some of the younger members of what he called his "adventure squad," a
small group of reporters that included Haxton and Edward Townsend, a
humor writer whose Chimmie Fadden stories would later be illustrated by
the Yellow Kid cartoons. From the relative safety of the tug, Hearst directed
a quite willing Haxton, long rope in hand, to swim out to the surviving
men, who were desperately clinging to a slippery rock. Haxton swam to the
rock for one man and then back for another, and eventually a few fortunate
men were pulled aboard the tug. Later, in the warm offices of the *Examiner*,
the fishermen got hot coffee, food, and blankets; they were photographed
with Haxton, happy by all appearances to have been creatively saved by
Hearst. Although—as one competitive newspaper noted—an unknown
number of men lost their lives that night, the Hearst story the next day
played up Haxton's brave trips to rescue the few.

Six years later, Hearst and Haxton were still together hatching new
adventures. The *New York Journal*, a preexisting daily whose readership, it was
whispered, was mostly comprised of men looking for escorts in the person-
als, became Hearst's second newspaper and a near carbon copy of his first,
with a good portion of Pulitzer's *New York World* thrown in as well. The lowbrow reputation of the *Journal* appealed to Hearst, but he was not content
to settle for a faithful but finite audience. He knew that in a city that prided
itself as the center of action, he must work overtime to attract attention. He
instructed his staff to visualize the news before they wrote it. The *Journal*
crew was told to be bold and to model their first page on the natural phenomenon of a sudden thunderstorm.

In 1896 the *Journal* was only a year old but well into a series of bitter battles with Pulitzer's equally sensational *World*. To most observers, the *World*
seemed to be in a safe position; its circulation remained high and, in contrast
to the new kid on the block, its owner was well respected, even a bit stodgy.
The *World*'s headquarters seemed to be a tangible demonstration of invin-
cibility: it was located in a gold-domed building erected in 1890, while
Hearst only leased space in the building that housed another newspaper

rival, the *New York Tribune*. But in large part because of Hearst's more experimental visual sense, his millions, and his willingness to spend them, things were about to change. Always a fiend for advertising, Hearst trumpeted his *Journal* in the mass communication medium of the day, the billboard, and hardly a train station, street corner, or potential newspaper reader escaped Hearst's self-promotion. Hearst's money also enabled him to hire the most talented reporters and writers, often luring them away from Pulitzer's *World*. Hearst was performing a sleight of hand with the public. In terms of sensationalism, the look of the *Journal*—except for the masthead—was an almost exact duplicate of the *World*. But when Hearst reduced the price of the *Journal* to a penny and forced the *World* to do the same, the public was conditioned to view the two newspapers as interchangeable and not to see Hearst as a mere copycat. Hearst needed only to outdo Pulitzer in dramatic fashion and on a regular basis to differentiate his newspaper and ensure a steady increase in circulation and advertising.

Hearst's cordial relationship with Tammany Hall was one way to draw a contrast with Pulitzer. In 1896 the *Tammany Times*, the Hall's official organ, rarely missed an opportunity to attack the *World*. The newspaper, it declared, was "a regular self-praise sheet. The World is completely ignored. It's all Josef [*sic*] Pulitzer." While Pulitzer saw Tammany as an insidious force that worked against the people's interests, Hearst was more willing to overlook immorality for the sake of setting himself apart. No doubt he also saw Tammany as a way to extend his political power and make some money on the side as well. As he did for the *Examiner* with San Francisco's political chiefs, Hearst made a lucrative deal with Tammany for the *Journal* to acquire the exclusive rights for municipal printing jobs. Tammany, in turn, regularly applauded Hearst's "new journalism," and it became the first organization to promote the publisher as a potential presidential candidate.

Stephen Crane probably first met Hearst in the spring of 1896, when the writer began contributing articles to the *Journal*. He was already a bona fide celebrity: his classic *The Red Badge of Courage* had been published a year earlier, and his newspaper pieces about poverty, alcoholism, and drug addiction, sketched with an absence of sentimentality uncommon for the era, made him the talk of literary circles. Those who knew Crane or saw him regularly at his favorite haunts (he was fond of the Hearst newspaper hangout Jack's Restaurant), found him to be a gentle but nervous man, always smoking and always observing. Contemporaries who paid close attention to Crane's writing style struggled to explain it in traditional literary terms. They spoke about movement in the language and a rhythmic editing of scenes. They drew comparisons to painting and photography. A *New York Times* critic said

Crane's work had accomplished the "effect of a photographic revelation," bringing to mind the motion picture experiments of the photographer Edward Muybridge in the late 1870s and early 1880s.

Crane's *Maggie: A Girl of the Streets*, a novel he actually completed before *The Red Badge*, was published in hardcover by D. Appleton and Company in 1896. Widely reviewed during the summer, *Maggie* told the story of a lower-class Irish girl who turns to prostitution after her fantasy of escaping to the world of the theater collides with the hard realities of parental abuse, poverty, and inhumanity. The *New York Times*, as it had in its review of *The Red Badge of Courage*, compared Crane's writing to another medium, saying the story was "shown with such vivid and terrible accuracy as to make one believe [it is] photographic." In the *San Francisco Wave*, critic Frank Norris described Crane's writing with words that seem to reach beyond the medium of still photography to cinema. Norris said the work was like "scores and scores of tiny flashlight photographs, instantaneous, caught, as it were, on the run."

Moments after Henry Haxton met Hearst in the stairwell to discuss a *Journal* project for Crane in September 1896, the *Journal* editor sent the writer a "confidential" letter. "I am sure that if you read the police news in next Sunday and Monday mornings' papers and go to Jefferson Market Police Court on Monday morning," he wrote, "you will get the material for a good Tenderloin story to start with." It was Hearst's intention, Haxton informed Crane, that the story appear over a period of weeks in his sensationalist illustrated Sunday supplement section, popular with the public but much denounced by the pulpit. "A good Tenderloin story" from a jailhouse point of view meant only one thing. The Tenderloin was a district of midtown Manhattan heavily populated by houses of ill repute that extended as far south as East Fourteenth Street, where Tammany Hall was conveniently located. The district was well known as an area where police and politicians alike shared prime cuts of the commercialized sex business—hence the name Tenderloin.

Crane's "The Tenderloin as It Really Is," the first of a series of *Journal* features, appeared on October 25, but the unofficial start of the series was September 17. On that day *Journal* readers first learned about Crane's adventures on the city's streets, and a seminal chapter in Crane lore was written. According to the *Journal*, early on the morning of September 14, Crane met a Hearst reporter at Shanley's bar in lower Manhattan, and the two men departed for the Jefferson Market Courthouse. On the evening of the next day, for additional research, Crane met with two chorus girls in a "Turkish Smoking Parlor" on West Twenty-ninth Street. The threesome left immediately for another brothel on Thirty-first Street (located quite near *Journal* editor Haxton's apartment), where a prostitute named Dora Clark joined them. At two o'clock in the morning all four left the brothel, and as Crane helped one of the chorus girls into an uptown Broadway trolley he became momentarily unaware of the two remaining women behind his back. Suddenly, he noticed two men walking briskly away from the scene and a third man violently grabbing the arms of the women. From his actions and language, Crane quickly realized this man was a plainclothes police officer, subsequently identified as Charles Becker, a notoriously corrupt cop, and years later executed for complicity in the murder of his partner, the gambler Herman Rosenthal. Before Crane's eyes, Becker was arresting Dora Clark and the chorus girl for prostitution. In all the excitement and in an attempt to save her reputation, the chorus girl told Becker that Crane was her husband. Crane backed up the girl's story, but Becker persisted. Soon, Crane and his female friends were all hauled off to court. After considerable indecision, Crane gathered enough courage to confront the court and proclaim Clark's innocence. The accusation of solicitation against Clark was false, he said; the young woman was being arrested for having been a prostitute and not for committing any specific act of prostitution at the time of her arrest.

Other city newspapers had similar reports to those in the Hearst-Crane narrative, but none reached the *Journal*'s level of dramatic lyricism. Ostensibly, the *Journal* story was a news article, but its form anticipates the short films that would soon be the staple of nickelodeon screens. The story is a first-person account by the drama's hero (Crane), who begins by declaring Dora Clark's innocence. All the story's characters are described as dramatic types. The novelist-hero, whom one officer—significantly—confuses for an actor, is vibrant and strong. Clark is young and very pretty. The court's magistrate is stern and impatient. The court's audience (a dramatic device introduced for *Journal* readers to identify with) is portrayed as a circle of hard and "pitiless" eyes that slowly soften as they observe Clark's "desperate glance." The police, always cold and insulting to Clark, are the chief villains of the piece. Almost certainly by design but also through an instinctive knack for seizing the moment, *The Red Badge of Courage* met "the journalism that acts," and Hearst, Haxton, and Crane turned their Tenderloin adventure into a well-publicized entertainment with a message.

Stephen Crane continued to work for Hearst off and on until the turn of the century (he died in 1900 from lung disease probably complicated by yellow fever and a botched medical procedure; he was not quite twenty-nine years old). In 1899, shortly after completing a number of war correspondent assignments for the *Journal*, Crane became the first well-known writer to create a fictional character modeled on Hearst. His novel *Active Service* includes among its characters a newspaper publisher named Sturgeon who owns a newspaper Crane called *The Eclipse*. Like Hearst, publisher Sturgeon is a rich and powerful man whose erratic and egocentric behavior is somewhat offset by his benevolence and creativity. Crane describes Sturgeon as a man with "light blue eyes afire with interest—[and] some kind of poet using his millions romantically, spending wildly on a sentiment that might be with beauty or without beauty, according to the momentary vacillation."

ARTS AND ENTERTAINMENT

While the Crane and Clark story was entertaining New Yorkers, Hearst was entertaining himself in a style that fit right into the life of the Tenderloin but was actually a carryover from his younger days. Hearst arrived in New York in 1895 accompanied by a woman he had already been involved with for nearly a decade. Theresa M. Powers, known as Tessie, was a young waitress in Cambridge during the years that Hearst was a student at Harvard University. According to Anne Apperson Flint, a cousin of Hearst, the two met when Hearst's friend Jack Follansbee was no longer interested in keeping her as a mistress. There is little firsthand information about Tessie Powers beyond Hearst's cousin's description of her as a pretty country girl. It was said that she was referred to as "Dirty Drawers" or "The Harvard Widow." (The second term was applied to women who made something of a career of being kept by young wealthy students, the implication being that these women were prostitutes.)

Soon after Hearst was expelled from Harvard in 1887—after flaunting his affair with Powers and causing other trouble on campus—the two young lovers lived together in Sausalito and traveled abroad like husband and wife. Hearst's years in Sausalito would become the subject of wild rumors, some even suggesting that Powers was only one of many mistresses and that orgies were commonplace. The precise nature of Hearst's life in Sausalito may never be known. If Hearst was a callous playboy, as some claimed, his cousin Ms. Flint never saw the evidence. To the contrary, despite her disgust over many of his moral choices, she thought he was always less promiscuous than imagined and truly committed and kind to the women in his life.

As close as Hearst may have been to Powers during this period, she must have often taken second place to his work. When Hearst took over the *Examiner*, he wanted the newspaper to get noticed and to cause public comment, rejecting the idea of making improvements in degrees.

He hired men decidedly younger than past employees, and he cleaned up the look of the paper, reducing the number of columns from nine to five or six. In a move to distance himself at least superficially from his father, Hearst began to mask some of the more obvious political bias that had permeated the news reporting. Most of all, he focused his attention on illustrations and sensationalist reporting.

Even when Hearst was home in Sausalito, he occupied himself with a new interest that would have a profound affect on his newspaper publishing and the media empire he would eventual rule. Probably while he was at Harvard, Hearst met George Pancoast, an expert at printing presses and printing processes who worked for a publishing house called the Cambridge Press. Soon after they met, Pancoast settled into the role of Hearst's personal secretary, and he eventually became a highly paid consultant on printing press construction matters. More important, he taught Hearst about photography.

During the six years before he became occupied with printing presses, Pancoast toured the country's vaudeville houses as a song and dance man; in fact, his familiarity with show business was a plus with Hearst. There is no indication that Pancoast had any artistic training in photography. Still, with his encouragement, Hearst soon became so obsessed with photography that he converted the entire second floor of his home, Sea Point (leased from a liquor distiller, the monthly bills charged to a Hearst holding firm, the Piedmont Land and Cattle Company), into a darkroom and picture gallery. Hearst took dozens of photographs in and around San Francisco Bay, and in the early 1890s, with Pancoast and Powers by his side, he traveled to Europe and Egypt, taking pictures all the while. The party spent several weeks in Egypt, armed with valises of expensive cameras and wet plates, where they found the Valley of the Kings an especially compelling sight.

Previously the tombs had only been photographed in available light. Venturing deep into the chambers of Luxor and Karnak, Hearst and Pancoast decided on the bright but explosive flashlight powder then in use among amateur photographers. Later, an authorized study of Hearst's life reported that the flashlight frightened the native Egyptians, who had never been exposed to modern technology. It was more likely that damage or potential damage to the tombs from the corrosive chemicals caused the British government, then in power in Egypt, to demand that the Hearst party leave the area and to ban flash photography at the sites. Hearst was personally insulted by this, which he saw as an overreaction by the British, but he rounded up his small photography party and traveled to the Hotel Wagram in Paris. There, he instructed the Levy Company of France to make colored stereopticon slides from the boxes of Egyptian negatives, processing the pictures to be viewed through stereopticon peepholes and projected on screens by similar devices. Eager to impress others with his emerging talent, Hearst made over a section of his estate into a sort of screening room, where magic lantern shows became a ritual. In photography, Hearst found a vehicle for his showmanship that was reminiscent of the toy theaters of his childhood and the adult entertainment he had previously experienced only in lowbrow theater shows. Photography was no mere diversion; he immediately recognized its potential for reaching the masses and its ability to capture action and tell stories in ways that broke the boundaries of traditional publishing.

Like his passion for vaudeville melodrama, Hearst's enthusiasm for photography quickly showed up in his newspaper during this period. Illustrations derived from photographs were increasingly prominent features of the paper, used to stimulate the imagination and increase circulation. In 1892 Hearst instituted photographic giveaways to boost the newspaper's readership. Significantly, one of the first prints to be sent out to lucky readers was a photograph of an actress, Fanny Davenport. Apparently, however, only a small circle of friends and associates ever saw the hundreds of photographs that Hearst took during this period—his entire collection was reportedly destroyed in the great San Francisco fire of 1906—nevertheless, considering how he liked to have a hand in all aspects of his work, it is possible that at least some of the illustrations published in the *Examiner* in the 1890s were etched from his photographs.

While Hearst and Powers were living at Sea Point, they made plans to build a larger estate. But, except for a retaining wall, there would be no Hearst castle in Sausalito. Neither was there any acceptance of the couple's relationship. The closest Hearst and Powers ever got to the prestigious Sausalito Yacht Club was the house that overlooked it. Once the locals found out about his live-in relationship with Powers, the invitation to become a member customarily offered to prominent new residents never arrived. Exactly how Hearst reacted to this slight and others, such as the silence Powers met whenever she ventured into town, is not known. But judging from his future pattern of behavior, it is likely that this rejection served to harden his disdain for the pretensions of his own class.

Although initially Hearst hid his relationship with Powers from his mother—it was said that whenever Phoebe Hearst visited Sausalito, Powers was put onboard the Hearst's yacht, the *Aquilla*—eventually he told her all. If Hearst was seeking his mother's approval, she was not moved by his honesty. She continued to share the belief of others that Powers was a prostitute with no possibility of reform. Sometime after Hearst and Powers returned from their photographic tour abroad, Phoebe Hearst began to use her strongest weapon—her money—to put an end to her son's affair. By some accounts she paid Powers tens of thousands of dollars to promise that she would stop seeing Hearst. If this is true, it had no lasting effect: he was back with Powers by the time he moved to New York. His decision to move there in 1895 may have caused his estate plans to be shelved, or possibly, as some have suggested, his mother's rejection of his lifestyle and the snubs of the town fathers of Sausalito hastened his departure.

After making a deal to purchase the *New York Journal* late in the summer of 1895, Hearst moved into the Hoffman House, on Broadway overlooking Madison Square, where he furnished his four-room suite with paintings and tapestries, conducted interviews with prospective employees, and engaged in other newspaper business. The Hoffman House had a magnetic pull on Hearst even before his move. In 1889 he wrote a letter to his mother from the Hoffman telling her about his dream of someday owning a New York City newspaper. During another visit to the Hoffman, Hearst became so impressed with a headwaiter named George Thompson that he hired him on the spot as his personal valet. The Irish-born Thompson, who lived on Twenty-eighth Street near Lexington Avenue, picked up his few personal belongings and moved in with Hearst for the next twenty years.

The Hoffman House was a hub of lusty indulgence during the Gilded Age. Its public rooms, which included two cafés, a number of luxurious parlors, a billiard room, and a reading room, were densely furnished with Victorian trappings. One Hoffman room in particular attracted more visitors than any other: the barroom with its adjoining art gallery. A moose head hung on one wall, there were plush red sofas nearby, sculptures of Eros, plaster cupids scattered here and there, and bronze spittoons and majolica buckets everywhere. The artwork—such as it was—communicated male power and female eroticism, suggesting a sort of high-class bordello. Some of the paintings were overtly political, with prominent portraits of the hard-drinking General Grant and the party boss Roscoe Conkling. The Hoffman House was especially popular among Tammany politicians, who enjoyed its atmosphere of personal liberty and made it the official Democratic Party campaign headquarters for a number of electoral races in the late nineteenth century.

The Hoffman bar was the scene of continuing chic scandal because of its painting by W. A. Bouguereau titled *Nymphs and Satyr*, a whimsical evocation of temptation in all its glory, which depicts the mythological character of Pan in a shady brook, surrounded and tugged at by a group of voluptuous nymphs. According to observers, the nymphs' ample, bare skin seemed to be in motion, almost palpitating. Hung on a velvet curtained wall, dramatically framed in gold, and lit by a brilliant crystal chandelier, the eight-by-ten-foot painting resembled a stage or screen presentation. Its prominence in the room was further enhanced by its placement opposite a large mirror above the bar.

Nymphs and Satyr exemplified what customers came to look for and look at in the pre-cinema era, when the less-than-fine-art paintings in saloons were about to be supplanted by risqué moving pictures in theaters. Much like corner saloons were doing on a smaller scale, the Hoffman bar made titillating imagery available for different classes. The lineage of visual delights from the saloon to the theater was clearly demonstrated in the way film was first screened for audiences. Edison's vitascope films of flimsily dressed dancers at the Koster and Bial Music Hall in April 1896 were projected into the center of a huge gilded picture frame that rested against a velvet curtain.

No sooner had Hearst set up residence in the Hoffman than he decided to live elsewhere, the idea of being just another tenant in a large hotel being entirely foreign to his makeup. As early as 1894, when his primary residence was still in California, Hearst had leased an apartment in a small New York building, probably the Worth House, where he lived for an extended period. The Worth House was located at 7 West Twenty-fifth Street around the corner from the Hoffman and was actually considered an annex to that grand hotel. By late 1895 Hearst was occupying the entire third floor and wasting no time in creating a home that reflected his image. For his apartment's remodeling, he hired the prominent California architect A. C. Schweinfurth, who had worked on his mother's Hacienda ranch in Pleasanton, California. There, among other things, the architect had constructed a small theater with dressing rooms and a musician's gallery. Now, he was employed to bring the Spanish, West Coast style that Hearst loved so much to his "little" New York apartment. Using Pancoast as a go-between, Hearst instructed his architect, who in turn drew sketches for his boss's approval. Soon, beamed ceilings were being installed, the floors were tiled, and the walls were paneled in stained poplar. Schweinfurth had few New York commissions, but the Worth House was not the only project he took on for Hearst. On St. Valentine's Day, 1896, with Pancoast again taking care of the details, Tessie Powers was set up in a townhouse located at 119 Lexington Avenue. The architect quickly got to work, modernizing windows, moving stairways, and constructing a doorway for a less conspicuous entrance on a side street. At the time, the Powers home was in an area of Manhattan with rows of elegant townhouses but a reputation only marginally better than the Tenderloin's. Interestingly, it was located only two doors and a short courtyard away from a townhouse that Hearst would buy a few years later and live in with his wife Millicent during the early years of their marriage.

Information about Powers's whereabouts after the turn of the century is almost nonexistent. By all accounts, Hearst was already seeing other women before the end of 1896. According to Hearst's cousin Mrs. Flint, when the relationship between Hearst and Powers finally ended (it was more than a decade old), the former "Harvard Widow" suffered a nervous breakdown. By 1900 there is no record of Powers living in New York City, and quite possibly, as Flint suggests, the young woman spent her remaining years (she was said to be alive as late as the 1930s, supported by Hearst) in upstate New York. New York State census records for the period list two women named Theresa Powers, although it is impossible to know for sure whether either is actually the women in question. One became an "inmate" at an asylum for "feeble women" in Arcadia, New York, called the Newark State School, around 1900 and lived there as late as 1920. But her age as recorded by the census keeper suggests that she was too young to be Hearst's Tessie Powers. The other woman, according to the records, lived in the 1920s in a remote upstate New York community with a child she had given birth to in Canada around 1900. Her age matches that of Hearst's Tessie Powers, and her son's name is listed as William.

Between his romantic encounters and his newspaper and political conferences at the Hoffman House, Hearst could often be found in some of the more respectable art galleries of Manhattan. Hearst's impulse to collect art on the scale he did, which began in the late 1880s, may be understood in psychological terms as a symbol of his grandiosity. His wife saw it as an obsession that acted as a substitute for deeper satisfactions. It was both, but it was also a tangible way for him to capture the things that delighted him visually and to preserve them for himself and others. Two of Hearst's favorite haunts in the 1890s were the Hanfstaengl shop and the American Art Galleries. The German-born Edgar J. Hanfstaengl opened a branch shop on Fifth Avenue in the 1880s that dealt almost exclusively in prints. Its flagship store was located in Munich, and there were other branch stores in London and Paris. Hearst knew the shop's owner and his American-born wife fairly well, and a quarter of a century later he would get to know their son even better. Ernst Hanfstaengl, nicknamed "Putzi," was only eight years old in 1895. By 1909 the Harvard-educated Hanfstaengl—known for his wit, ambition, and talent for musical composition—was already moving in exclusive circles, close to the rich and powerful, friends with rising politicians such as Congressman Hamilton Fish and Franklin D. Roosevelt. His own son, Egon, would later describe his father as a man who used "all of his gifts and the sheer weight of his personality with brazen insistence." Hearst probably first got to know Putzi Hanfstaengl through his family's print shop; they were friends by the 1920s. In the 1930s their encounters were less frequent, as Hanfstaengl was living in Germany. There, as he later boasted, he refashioned the football chants he learned at Harvard into "Sieg Heils" for the man his family fortune now financed, Adolf Hitler.

On the evening of November 19, 1895, the American Art Galleries on Madison Square South was the site of an auction of paintings and drawings by Frederic Remington. A copy of the catalog kept by Remington indicates that Hearst attended the auction and bought a drawing called *The Box of the Ranch Coach* and a painting called *Coming to the Rodeo*. Over the years, Hearst would continue to buy other Remington works, including bronzes and a painting he commissioned of the Hearst family estate in Mexico. Remington was one of the few, and certainly one of the most famous, contemporary artists, American or not, whose works Hearst purchased in a lifetime of intense collecting. Remington kept himself informed of the art trends of his day and studied briefly at Yale University and the Art Students League in New York City. His genius for capturing realistic movement was inspired by the medium of photography. His horses with all four legs off the ground show the influence of Eadweard Muybridge and the motion picture experiments he conducted for George Hearst's friend and ally, Senator Leland Stanford. The horses in Muybridge's photograph series galloped from left to right, but in a number of Remington's paintings and drawings the artist turned his horses around so that they seemed to be moving directly towards the viewer.

One historian noted that Remington had "a taste for dramatic narrative and highly-charged scenes of physical action, portrayed in a style whose realism was well adapted to the technical inheritance and popularly-based social location of the new medium." The new medium referred to here is the cinema, and not only did Remington anticipate it, he helped launch Hollywood's most enduring genres, the western. In the process of familiarizing the public with notions of the West (much as his contemporaries Teddy Roosevelt, writer Owen Wister, and Hearst did), Remington infused his work with moving images of courage, dignity, and physical strength that resonated in enduring, popular myths. Well into the twentieth century, one master of the western genre, director John Ford, readily admitted copying the artist for his film *She Wore a Yellow Ribbon*. "I tried to get his color and movement," Ford would say, "and I think I succeeded partly."

Hearst was well acquainted with the subject matter Remington explored in his work. Although his life was rooted in privilege, his father's loyalty to rough mining friends familiarized Hearst with the types Stephen Crane called "straight out-and-out, and sometimes hideous, often braggart westerners." Hearst's boyhood travels on the Transcontinental Railroad had taken him through western states and territories and made him a witness to the waning days of the wide-open plains. Remington's romanticizing of western life had an instinctual attraction for Hearst. Remington once said he wanted to paint so viewers "would feel the details and not *see* them." It was the emotional vibration in Remington's work—echoing with Monet and Muybridge influences—that pulled Hearst in completely.

Two years after the American Art auction, during the Spanish-American War, the names of Hearst and Remington would be linked again, and more permanently, through an exchange of telegrams that have never been fully documented. As the story goes, during an inactive period of the war in Cuba, Remington, assigned by Hearst's *Journal* to draw battle illustrations, wired his boss: "Everything is quiet. There is no trouble here. There will be no war. I wish to return." According to legend, Hearst shot back: "Please remain. You furnish the pictures and I'll furnish the war." With time, these alleged messages have developed allegorical dimensions, representing a marriage of journalism and art and the meshing of melodrama and heightened reality. *Citizen Kane's* writers Orson Welles and Herman Mankiewicz thought the telegrams were so revealing of the ego and originality of their Hearst character, Charles Foster Kane, that they included a slight variation on them in their script. The communications between Hearst and Remington, the Russian film director Sergei Eisenstein would later write, may be apocryphal, but they are "more truthful as 'human' documents than numerous historical documents." They seem to have been created, he wrote, "with the single goal of serving as material for future description."

LIVING PICTURES

In his first public declaration of note, which appeared in 1888, Hearst was already speaking about news in terms of entertainment and vigorously defending himself against any potential critics. "If a sensation is true, of course it is a great deal better than any other sort of news, from the mere fact that it is a sensation,—that is to say, news of extraordinary interest," Hearst wrote. "No one knows better than the intelligent newspaper man that truth is stranger than fiction. Indeed, this is the great reason why the newspaper holds its own against the novel and play."

Critics who questioned Hearst's genuineness claimed that most of what appeared as fact in his publications was faked. Exaggerations and outright lies did appear in Hearst publications; however, it would be more accurate to say that news was conceived and produced with the eye in mind and often reshaped to conform to a dramatic presentation. Newspaperman Arthur Brisbane, whom Hearst lured from Joseph Pulitzer's *New York World*, became one of the editor's closest friends and the first of Hearst's camp to totally embrace yellow journalism publicly. Brisbane's simple, direct style of writing attempted to defuse critics by glorifying yellow journalism as the champion of the masses and the most modern form of communication. He lectured on its uses as a "safety valve" for the inarticulate and powerless, whom he claimed were being educated and looked after by Hearst. "I am a yellow journalist," he once said, "and proud of it. The great modern newspaper is the sole amusement for many a hard working man, besides being at the same time to him what vaudeville is to higher classes. It has its comic parts, its excitement and its pathos. Not an act is missing." Brisbane was making an important point about the accessibility of both yellow journalism and film. For the lowest economic classes a daily dose of vaudeville was beyond their means. The yellow journal—a penny or two during the week and a nickel on Sundays—was their most affordable entertainment before the arrival of the nickelodeon.

Screen entertainment in the form of movies as we know them today began in earnest around 1896, when technology made possible the celluloid printing and commercial projection of images that appeared to move. Like the movies that became intertwined with it, yellow journalism was also characterized by imagery for the masses, produced at breakneck speed, widely circulated, easily digested, and quickly discarded. Yellow journalism appealed to many of the same groups who would flock to the movies—the lower classes and immigrants—and some of its strongest critics were the same as those who later opposed the movies: conservative politicians and religious leaders. Significantly, both yellow journalism and the movies were described in loathsome terms more commonly reserved for the saloon and the brothel. Yellow journalism—a term that has been used primarily to disparage Hearst—was actually one he embraced. It represented, even in its catchy, colorful naughtiness, the thing that attracted him to publishing. It told dramatic, human-interest stories, presented pictorially, in an active present tense. Hearst believed that yellow journalism was the only brand of news reporting that was both entertaining and capable of stirring emotions to action, the only medium with such potential with the exception of film.

Most media historians credit Ervin Wardman, editor of the *New York*

Press, with coining the term *yellow journalism* in response to the circulation battle between Hearst and Pulitzer most comically exemplified by the publishers' months-long tug-of-war over a cartoon covering the exploits of a character known as the Yellow Kid. As the story goes, one of the first of the *New York World*'s star employees to make the move to Hearst's *Journal* was a cartoon artist named Richard Outcault, famous for his goofy-looking bald-headed Yellow Kid character, who was the ringleader of a cast of lowlife misfits on the Lower East Side. Outcault called the cartoon character Mickey Dugan when he drew him for Pulitzer. But as the man-child character's long yellow nightshirt became his prominent feature—the artist used it as a billboard to make subversive comments—Mickey under Hearst acquired the nickname of the Yellow Kid. After Outcault's departure, Pulitzer continued to publish the cartoon, replacing the original artist with the Ash Can School painter George Luks. Thus in the fall of 1896 Hearst and Pulitzer had equally talented artists drawing identical-looking characters who inhabited the identical tenement tapestries. Pulitzer, increasingly burdened by blindness and stress, shrank from these circulation shenanigans, but Hearst was energized by the attention-getting conflict.

The story of the Yellow Kids is a journalism mainstay, but it may have had nothing to do with the origin of yellow journalism. During the first five-month double appearance of the Yellow Kid, there is no documented use of the term *yellow journalism*. It didn't even surface when, as prepublicity for his hiring of Outcault, Hearst used what he called "Yellow Fellows"—cyclists dressed from head to toe in yellow—as mascots for a transcontinental bicycle race. From late 1896 through early 1897, Hearst's use of sensational illustrations, his personality-driven coverage, and his blaring headlines were under almost constant attack from the established press. Still, it was the adjectives *freak, fake,* and *vaudeville* that the old guard used to describe what Hearst continued to call "new journalism." Rival newspapers and other critics compared Hearst journalism to a house of prostitution and to diseases, but they did not use the term *yellow journalism*. As late as March 1897 a preacher connected with Anthony Comstock's Society for the Suppression of Vice was still using Hearst's own term but clearly against him: "New Journalism indeed! It is as old as the nameless vice of buried Pompeii, old as Noah's shame. The man who allows it in his family opens a connection between the cradle and the sewer, the nursery and the swamp, and is inviting the germs of moral typhoid."

The use of the word *yellow*—as a notorious mark—predates Hearst journalism by centuries. Jews knew the yellow badge (and later the yellow Star of David) as a emblem of oppressive distinction with roots in medieval times. By the nineteenth century, *yellow* was part of street slang, invariably preceded by the word *dirty*. A yellow dog was considered a rabid dog, and crowded tenement families, among others, lived in fear of the uncontrollable disease called yellow fever, thought by some to be caused by filth. Associations of *yellow* with immorality and prostitution were also apparent by the late 1800s. The scandalous playwright Oscar Wilde, whose *Salome* was illustrated by the equally scandalous Aubrey Beardsley, was usually pictured in newspaper cartoons sporting a huge yellow sunflower in his lapel and yellow kid gloves on his hands. In czarist Russia at the turn of the century, a woman was forced to carry a "yellow ticket" or "yellow passport" to identify her as a prostitute. The *Yellow Book*, a London periodical of drawings, short stories, and poems, founded in 1894, is said to have defined the nineties as the Decadent Decade. The book's founders, artist Beardsley and novelist Henry Harland, deliberately used the color yellow in their title and on their cover to suggest the popular yellow paperback French novels considered sexually explicit for the period. Critics of the *Yellow Book* drew attention to the covers and the drawings within the book, most prominently Beardsley's black ink drawings on a yellow background depicting prostitutes, lesbians, and transvestites. There is some evidence to suggest that for purposes of identification houses of prostitution in New York City in the late nineteenth century were frequently painted yellow, the most infamous being the notoriously glowing Haymarket resort in the Tenderloin.

The phrase *yellow journalism* first appeared on January 9, 1897, in a promotional advertisement for the *New York Press*'s Sunday supplement. In the ad, the *Press* proudly announced that its upcoming Sunday supplement would not "yield to any of the new newspaper maladies" and (in even bolder type) that it would contain "No Yellow Jaundice." For two weeks, there was no follow-up to this yellow allusion; there were only continuing uses of "new journalism" and even an occasional use of "nude journalism." By the end of January, however, a shift occurred in the characterization of Hearst's journalism. In expectation of Hearst's coverage plans, the *Press* on January 28 editorialized against the upcoming championship fight between James J. "Gentleman Jim" Corbett and his challenger Bob Fitzsimmons. The paper called Carson City, Nevada—where the March 17 bout was scheduled to take place—an appropriate site for the loathsome and corrupting sport, referring to that region of the country as the "Tenderloin of America." Three days later, with the upcoming Corbett-Fitzsimmons fight very much in the air, *Press* editor Ervin Wardman wrote a column that took a jab at Hearst by pretending to offer advice to aspiring newspaper reporters. Starting off with a passing nod to "my young and enthusiastic friend William R.

Hearst" (the two men actually were friends: they went to Harvard and worked together on the *Lampoon*), Wardman quickly gets to the point. Anyone who wants to start at the bottom, Wardman writes, couldn't "possibly start lower than by obtaining employment in Yellow Journalism." In this context, not the Yellow Kid war, the catchphrase was born.

Terry Ramsaye, a pioneer cinema historian, saw the film of the 1897 fight between Corbett and Fitzsimmons, and the hoopla surrounding it, as the start of a long love affair between film and lowbrow entertainment. Hearst did not produce his own film about the fight, which occurred shortly after he made films of President McKinley's inauguration, but his involvement with the event proved to be equally cinematic. He made a deal for exclusive rights for photographs and certain accounts of the fight. Day after day, beginning in early 1897, the Hearst press, surpassing all other media, orchestrated interest in a rather minor event for the sole purpose of elevating its importance, which in turn elevated their obsessive coverage of it. Every minor detail about the celebrity fighters' training sessions, their personalities, and their family lives became big news. Hearst hired combatant Fitzsimmons as a correspondent weeks before the fight took place, and he sent photographers, illustrators, and other reporters to the remote fight location to keep readers posted on the relatively little that was happening.

The period leading up to the fight had all the classic characteristics of what historian Daniel J. Boorstin later termed a "pseudo-event." Through the medium of his newspapers, Hearst was providing a print version of a movie trailer enticing future audiences with unrelenting edited flashes of fluff, gore, and excitement. Hearst's unique presentation of the fight "news" excited the public to flock to screenings of the Corbett-Fitzsimmons fight film. The film was widely discussed, and its box office sales were huge. Human interest stories in Hearst's newspapers that preceded the fight and the realism of the fight film itself (some thought this was best demonstrated by the two young pugilists' scanty boxing shorts) helped attract the first significant wave of female filmgoers. This aspect of the film was not missed by budding filmmakers. It proved that diverse audiences could be enticed to sit through a feature-length film. At the same time, the widespread acceptance of a "brutal" actuality or news film caused the defenders of moral propriety to condemn such amusements and state legislatures to introduce bills calling for a ban on all future fight films.

The first denunciation of film occurred simultaneously with the first published use of *yellow journalism* as an attack on Hearst. On February 19, 1897, the *New York Daily Tribune* joined the *New York Press*, which was just beginning its own regular use of the new term. The *Tribune* editorial, titled "The

Yellow War," did not focus on the cartoon rivalry or even on the increasing prospects of war in Cuba. According to the *Tribune*, possibilities of a real war "seem just now somewhat blurred and indefinite," but Hearst's "word-painters, fiction writers, and inspired artists" had headed off to another more pictorial event, west to Nevada, where "the odds are about 16 to 1 that a fight between the yellows will be more blood-curdling and heart-rending than the fight between the gladiators." During the same month, the *Press* compared Hearst's "yellow journal" on several separate occasions to a "disorderly dive" and to yellow fever and disease. For most of the first half of 1897 the phrase was repeated in the *Press* dozens of times and in dozens of different ways, far more often than in any other contemporary publication. The *Press* made many connections between *yellow* and vice and illness—including a large front-page cartoon of a rabid "yellow dog" as a symbol of the new journalism—but there was not one mention of the Yellow Kid cartoon.

In the spring of 1897, yellow journalism began to face a pattern of suppression and censorship that would become increasingly associated with film. The newspaper assaults were led by the *New York Press*, which at one point covered an entire page with quotations from a score of religious leaders pontificating on the yellow evil. Criticism was so intense that organizations were formed demanding the removal of Hearst's papers—and Pulitzer's paper to a lesser extent—from libraries and clubs, and there were calls for a general boycott. Morality crusader Anthony Comstock and newspaper editorialists condemned the "graphic" subject matter of Hearst's newspaper realism, which, they said, presented "scandals of all sorts in high life and low life, in the great houses and the slums, or spread abroad in display type the prurient gossip of the concert halls and the stage."

Comstock's language about Hearst and yellow journalism proved to be identical to what he and others used in their assault on the Corbett-Fitzsimmons film and future films. The social reformers who would soon point to movie theaters as dens of sex slavery had initially aimed their arrows at the yellow newspaper publishing house that printed personal ads that were frequently nothing more than published platforms for prostitution. Before religious leaders cited the popular Sunday movie show as undermining the Christian Sabbath, these same critics railed against Hearst's most colorful and feature-filled supplement section, which was published on Sundays.

Hearst's self-proclaimed "art of presenting" the Nevada fight did more than provoke criticism of his journalism. On one occasion, still early in the life of yellow journalism and film, the *New York Press* seemed to be specifically linking these two mediums of entertainment. In his book *A History of the American Film Industry from Its Beginnings to 1931*, historian Benjamin B.

Hampton repeatedly used the term "Living Pictures" to describe moving pictures in early 1897, when the infant industry was said to have experienced a slump. A British periodical in late 1897 used the same term when it dismissed predictions that the musical halls and vaudeville entertainments of the preceding winter would be a passing novelty. According to Hampton, "Living Pictures" were given their first big boost by the Corbett-Fitzsimmons fight film. On April 10, 1897, a *Press* editorial appeared titled "Just Living Pictures." As with the term *yellow journalism*, the use of "Living Pictures" summoned more than one association. It was used to describe both the silent and motionless stage presentation called tableaux vivants, as well as Alexander Black's picture play experiments. But at the precise moment that the *Press* editorial appeared, it seems likely that their editorial writer had movies on his mind as well. In his mailbox was a letter to the editor, which he published on the same opinion page on the following day, that called the fight film "obscene." The "Just Living Pictures" editorial of April 10 demonstrates how Hearst's yellow journalism was interlocked with an emerging communications-entertainment medium from the start. It is reprinted here for the first time:

> Where the editors of Yellow Journalism made a mistake was in not understanding the difference between stimulated growth and healthy growth. They were poor judges of American character in supporting that the public would tolerate Yellow Journalism any longer than it tolerated living pictures; for Yellow Journalism is nothing but living pictures.

A Short-Lived Craze

> When the living picture craze struck New York we "had it bad" for awhile. You couldn't go to any sort of amusement place without having to look at living pictures. They were dragged from the vaudeville into melodrama, to opera, even tragedy. The people didn't mind it for a time, but [all] of a sudden the living picture business collapsed. Six months after it had been in its glory you couldn't fill a 20-by-30 concert hall with spectators at five cents a head to look at living pictures. So with the living pictures of Yellow Journalism. First the public, which always will look at a novelty, showed an interest in Yellow Journalism. Then it got bored with it. Then it got disgusted with it. Then it got mad with it. And that was the end of Yellow Journalism. The Yellow editors have been turned to the wall with the living pictures.

The last line finds an interesting way to bring out a previously mentioned hidden connotation of yellow journalism. It recalls a popular song of the period called "The Picture That Is Turned Toward the Wall," which was a sentimental lament of an "unforgiving" father disowning his daughter, who has left home for the city; she is a fallen girl and "gone beyond recall." Once again *yellow*, attached to both journalism and film, is also meant to remind us of unspoken immorality.

Putting on a Popular Show

While his papers stirred up excitement for the Corbett-Fitzsimmons fight, Hearst found an opportunity to make his own film, not in Carson City but in Washington, D.C. Coinciding with the emergence of Hearst's "new journalism" was the administration of the last president of the nineteenth century and the first president of the twentieth, William McKinley. Already adept at still photography, Hearst apparently began experimenting with a movie camera at this time. In an often-overlooked passage of the earliest Hearst biography, author John Winkler says that Hearst made an unpublicized debut as a movie cameraman, perhaps assisting the main cameraman, at McKinley's inauguration. While primary documentation on Hearst's personal role may be forever lost, a careful reading of the *Journal* and *Examiner* coverage of the March 1897 inauguration suggests there is truth to Winkler's story.

A story in the Sunday supplement of the *New York Journal* on March 7 was headlined "The New Journalism at 106 Miles An Hour." Most of the page is taken up with illustrations, but the total effect demonstrates Hearst's linking of yellow journalism and film. The images the Hearst publications used to depict the events in Washington were not reproductions of any filmed sequences. Instead, across the top of the newspaper page was a large pen-and-ink cross-section drawing of the *Journal* train chartered to take Hearst's staff to and from the inauguration. Below the illustration, the text tells the story behind the story, of a "wild ride," a high-speed race returning from Washington to New York with the news pictures. Another prominent illustration shows the train heading straight for the viewer and tilted at a cinematic angle. The picture is a preview of images in Hearst's movie serial of the 1910s, *The Perils of Pauline*, and countless other action genre films to come.

In each flag-draped car of the cross-sectioned train is pictured the inner workings of the new journalism. In the lead car, a reporter dictates his story into a phonograph dictation device. Further back in the car, one artist draws the outlines of the inauguration ceremony; another fills in the details. A still photographer develops pictures in a makeshift darkroom in another train car. Standing in the train's caboose, with a very visible, very cumbersome vitascope in hand, is a silhouette representing the new cinema century. As the text explains, a movie cameraman is taking pictures from the open rear section of the train, and the resulting footage is a view of tracks receding into the distance. According to the same account, the young cameraman is L. Edson Raff, the stepson of Norman Raff of the Raff and Gammon Company, film manufacturers for Thomas Edison. Pictures of trains and tracks would be a highlight of many early films. Shots that probably resembled Raff's were used in shows like Hales Tours, presented by Adolph Zukor on Fourteenth Street around 1905 in a storefront fitted with a train car and designed to suggest a depot station.

Several companies made films of McKinley at the moment he was sworn in, but Hearst's *Journal* made no claim to such specific scenes. It does appear to be true, however, that they shot footage from the window of Hearst's Washington Bureau building of McKinley and the outgoing president, Grover Cleveland, riding side by side in a horse-drawn carriage parade. Film views taken from such a perch—and later stored among Hearst newsreel archives—are among the little footage that survives from the day. Winkler's assertion that Hearst personally took these pictures would make Hearst's Washington-Hollywood connection uniquely bittersweet: the first moving pictures of a president may have been taken by the man who would spend decades trying to win that office.

In Hearst's news version of the inauguration events, the evolutionary track of information travels side by side with entertainment, told with distinct pictures and prose to match the visual excitement. The reader is able to come up close to the scene through the picture Hearst presents. Hearst anticipates and manipulates the reader by infusing a "gee-whiz" feeling into every sentence and every picture. Not only are readers seeing the image, they are present at the making of the image and taken behind the scenes. This piece of yellow journalism created the mold for countless movie marketing schemes, *People*-type magazines, and television shows of the *Entertainment Tonight* variety to come. In capping its inauguration coverage, Hearst's *Journal* gave a final boost to its film accomplishment, declaring that "it proved that the principle of the vitascope could be adapted to photograph accurately any animated scene and preserve it forever."

In 1925, years before he revolutionized the art of motion picture documentaries, the Scottish-born filmmaker John Grierson visited the United States to give a a series of lectures on the subject of "popular appeal" and its relationship to film box office. Grierson would later say that it was during this period of his life that he focused his ideas about the documentary, a word that he coined. Grierson surprised some of the movie theater managers in the audience of one of his speeches by calling Hearst "the greatest newspaper genius of them all." In contrast to the usual attacks on Hearst and his methods, the filmmaker heaped praise on yellow journalism. Grierson was aware that his point of view on Hearst's "dramatic approach" might be seen as a rejection of highbrow art in favor of lowbrow entertainment. But Grierson believed that Hearst was "putting on a popular show" that "gave the people something real where idealism only too often finishes by giving them nothing at all."

Hearst's "genius," he declared, was his understanding of the essence of cinema's power and appeal. Grierson suggested that film industry insiders use Hearst's brand of journalism as their guide. "A newspaper article or a photoplay," Grierson said, "isn't going to be a bit of use unless it has something the average public can catch on to, a theme familiar enough and simple enough for them to follow, a point of human interest that connects with their own lives. The first thing about an audience anywhere is that the people in it are more interested in themselves than in anything else in the world."

The "yellow medium" (it was never really journalism) was especially appealing to the less sophisticated because it downplayed established methods of reporting news and editorializing. It continued to tell the news and to crusade for causes, but through bold, active language and heightened accounts of everyday realities. It spoke with pictures—first pen-and-ink drawings and then halftones—that were carefully arranged on the page. Alongside yellow headlines the visuals were said to appeal to the senses and to make the newspaper vibrate. It may have been for these reasons that it was called "live" journalism by some contemporaries, "nude" journalism by others, and "kinetic, motion-pictorial journalism," by one early perceptive film historian. Even later historians who have given short shrift to Hearst have come to describe the earliest period of film as the era of the "visual newspaper."

Stories survive of how Hearst began a typical midnight task of page makeup in his *Journal* pressroom. During the early days, he arrived from an evening at a vaudeville theater where a short film was becoming a regular "act" on almost every bill. Often arm in arm with his girlfriend, Millicent, and her sister, Hearst hopped from his hansom cab with the flickers still in his eyes and literally danced through the composing of his newspaper page.

Employees have recalled Hearst, at some distance from a mock-up of a dou-
ble-truck page, doing a sort of Irish jig while he played with headlines,
exclamation points, space, and half-toned images. Others who met with
Hearst in his home observed the same eccentric work process. He would
spread out early versions of a newspaper page on one of his Persian carpets
and stand over it looking from some distance as he moved the cutout images
and headlines this way and that with his toes. Hearst's true believers—his fellow yellows—were remarkably like their counterpart fans at the nickelodeons and future screen presentations. Lured by all the melodrama Hearst
saw fit to print, their impressionable eyes gazed into the stereopticon, the
peepshow, and the movie screen that his opened newspaper resembled. Cutting an aperture into the light and putting the rest of the world in darkness,
they were not only readers, they were spectators.

Film News

1898–1906

STILL REMEMBERING THE MAINE

In November 1911 advertisements began appearing for the release of *The Mystery of the Maine*. The film was what historians today call an actuality, a term that emphasizes the absence of manipulation of real events in a film (the term was not widely used in 1911). Ads at the time of the picture's release called *The Mystery of the Maine* a feature film although it was only two reels long. The film showed views of the wreckage of the battleship U.S. *Maine*, whose sinking in Havana Harbor in 1898 sparked the Spanish-American War. With the cooperation of the War Department, which was trying to identify the cause of the *Maine*'s sinking and recovering the remains of about seventy servicemen still entombed in the wreckage, a Cuban cameraman named Diaz working for an American firm had filmed the greatest engineering marvel of its day. Diaz translated the nine-month-long project of building a huge cofferdam that lifted the ship above the water's surface into a dramatic twenty-minute film.

Notwithstanding the film's title and some shots of gaping holes in the ship's hull, there was little exploration of hard evidence in *The Mystery of the Maine*. The producer seemed more interested in resurrecting the sensations of war fever that swept the nation in 1898. As huge sections of the ship became recognizable, Diaz's camera focused on the barnacle-encrusted cabin of the ship's captain, where remarkably a washstand faucet still seemed to be in working condition. Shots of skeletons and bone fragments were avoided, but grim reminders of the losses were captured in the pictures of the crew's belongings and a brass bugle and a poignant shot of the ship's lieutenant's simple gold ring.

The Raising-The-Maine Film Company—a New York City concern headed by a young producer named Jack Parker Read Jr.—pulled out all the jingoistic stops to market its film. "Remember the *Maine*," a battle cry of the Spanish-American War, was now the catchphrase for a campaign promoting the film to exhibitors and audiences. Parker—later associated with director Thomas Ince and a Hollywood producer in his own right—was banking on the public's collective and conflicting memories. The war in Cuba that came and went so swiftly had created a near hysteria of patriotism and left a trail of lingering doubts about its causes and purpose.

Ever since the *Maine* went down in February 1898, Americans had generally believed that a mine placed by a Spanish submarine or by Cuban insurgents beneath the ship was the cause. Some critics, however, found the mine theory inconclusive at best. A thorough inquiry done after the raising of the *Maine* in 1911 left open the possibility that the ship had sunk as the result of a spontaneous internal combustion. The belief in an enemy mine had less to do with hard evidence than a rush to judgment by those who saw war with Spain as the way to achieve independence for Cuba. For years, uncertainties about the events of 1898 remained, like the *Maine*, mostly below the surface, and a majority of Americans continued to view the war as a noble adventure.

History records no one more devoted to the mine theory and the cause of war than Hearst. But in 1911 his reputation for single-handedly starting the Spanish-American War was less fixed in the public's mind and less associated with selfish motives. Hearst had been advocating for Cuban independence long before most and long before the *Maine* sank. Under his leadership the *San Francisco Examiner* called for intervention in Cuba as early as 1893. Within days of the *Maine* explosion, Hearst was exceedingly impatient with the U.S. government's response. With great publicity, he engaged a team of divers from Key West and dispatched them to take underwater photographs of the sunken ship. His enthusiasm for the dramatic undertaking was only slightly dampened when Spain denied all access to the ship. When Hearst spoke to his staff after war was declared, he referred to the conflict in Cuba as "our war." Eagerness for war came from other quarters—among newspaper publishers, chief rival Joseph Pulitzer was particularly strident—but for the most part the others followed Hearst's lead.

The man who Hearst and Pulitzer most wanted to bend to their side apparently felt regret for eventually being so malleable. In 1912, years after his death, a story circulated that President William McKinley wished he had held out a little longer for a peaceful settlement, believing that home rule in Cuba as a step toward complete independence was just around the corner. He criticized the yellow press for arousing the country and pressuring him, but he put most of the blame on Theodore Roosevelt, assistant secretary of the navy turned Rough Rider. When McKinley's inner feelings were alleged, the press asked Roosevelt for a response. The man who had succeeded McKinley after an assassin struck him down in 1901 brushed the comments aside. With the *Maine* tragedy fresh in the public's mind because of the recent raising, Roosevelt joked, "I might as well now confess that I was the man who blew up the *Maine*; and I am ready to confess also that I introduced the serpent into the Garden of Eden."

Hearst was largely responsible for keeping his warmonger reputation anchored in the murky waters surrounding the *Maine*. While he often obsessed over political events and controversial issues and then quickly discarded them like day-old newspapers, the story of the Spanish-American War was different; he couldn't seem to let it go. To some, Hearst's fixation suggested that he had a direct hand in plotting and causing the *Maine* tragedy. Hearst's pattern of skirting moral and legal boundaries to create news fueled the rumors about him. In December 1897, months before the *Maine* blew up, his own paper reported a story that Cuban police were accusing one of his reporters of hatching a plan to dynamite the U.S. consulate in Cuba. The implication was that Hearst would then pin the crime on the pro-Spain party there and move the American people to war. It was also speculated that he had business interests tied up in Cuba that might benefit from war. Many years after the war, one writer implied that Hearst wanted Cuba annexed so that it could become America's tropical playground, a kind of floating Fourteenth Street.

It may be a stretch to say that Hearst was willing to sacrifice American lives for money, but clearly his desire to boost newspaper circulation colored his compassion for the Cuban cause, and a detached business proclivity exploited the tragedy. Within days of the sinking of the *Maine*, he began a well-publicized campaign to raise funds for the "*Maine* martyrs." The project went on for years, keeping Hearst's name closely associated with the war. On a morning in November 1911, a private screening of *The Mystery of the Maine* was presented to representatives of his *Maine* Monument Committee, Mayor Gaynor, and other invited guests at Oscar Hammerstein's Victoria Theater. Film trade magazines indicated the audience gave the film an enthusiastic reception. A *New York Times* article about the picture—which was excerpted in a blurb in the film's ad campaign—said *The Mystery of the Maine* was exhibited as an adjunct to Hearst's fund-raising efforts for a memorial. The necessary funds to erect a monument were soon collected, and after considerable haggling with city officials a location—at the edge of New York City's Central Park, near what became Columbus Circle—was agreed on. Hearst's thirteen-year project to commemorate his highly personalized war in Cuba had finally come to an end. The remains of the battleship itself were ceremoniously tugged out to sea, filmed again, and sunk one final time. Audiences in 1911 who experienced *The Mystery of the Maine* and its promotion may well have undergone a myriad of emotions related to the war. They might have remembered the days of the Spanish-American War as being their first encounter with war and the link to their first exposure to film. They might even have been able to see behind the images of sacrifice and sadness imbedded in a once glorious ship's twisted steel a man who made this war his stage.

PICTURE DRAMA

Between 1896 and 1912 Hearst's forays into film may best be described as experiments. He had yet to create a permanent organization for producing films, and his primary interest remained newspaper (and eventually magazine) publishing. However, as film continued to develop as an industry and audiences for this phenomenon widened, Hearst was clearly evaluating the new medium's uses, especially as they related to education, politics, advertising, and propaganda. His relationships with the movers and shakers of the film industry were solidifying, and he refined his own special contribution to the film medium, developing it as a communications and storytelling medium, as an entertainment rather than an art form.

About five months before the battleship *Maine* exploded, Hearst found a less politically earthshaking but potentially more dramatic human-interest story to set the stage for his sales pitch for war. The story of Evangelina Cisneros—the eighteen-year-old niece of a rebel leader imprisoned in Cuba by Spanish authorities—has been examined before in the context of Hearst's political involvement, but it also exemplifies Hearst's skill at molding facts and fictions into entertainment to create cinematic propaganda. Under Hearst's direction, the Cisneros story had all of the elements appropriate to yellow journalism—the dime novel melodrama and the anticipation of cinema—and it even echoed the recently dramatized adventures of Stephen Crane and the prostitutes in the Tenderloin. According to Spanish authori-

ties, Cisneros had been arrested (along with her sister) for seducing a Spanish military commander and luring him to her home, where accomplices
were waiting to murder him. Her "crime" was further demonstrated by the
nature of the jail where she was being kept, a prison housing mostly prostitutes. The *Journal* claimed that the charges against Cisneros had been
trumped up. She was simply a loving daughter fighting for the release of her
father, imprisoned as a rebel insurgent. The *Journal* insisted that the military
commander had forced himself on Cisneros, and she later turned to sympathetic friends, who on their own tried to kill her attacker. Pulitzer's *World*,
picking up on the story only after Hearst was already running with it, gave
credence to the version offered by Spanish authorities, who vehemently
denied any mistreatment of their prisoner.

The truth about Cisneros, her imprisonment, and her treatment by the
authorities has never been convincingly established. Hearst's accounts
focused on Cisneros's malnutrition and the hardships she endured in jail and
less on her possible crimes. The possibility that Cisneros was a prostitute was
never mentioned by the *Journal*, although it was rumored that an underground system existed in Havana and other Cuban cities whereby prostitutes were important allies of the rebels. They engaged in sexual activities
with Spanish military personnel of all ranks and were paid not in pesos but
in boxes of Mauser cartridges. A rebel friend would arrive after the fact with
some items of interest to the women—wine, wood, or sugarcane—and leave
with the much-needed supplies of ammunition. It was a form of payment
profitable to all sides that resembled corrupt systems in many U.S. cities.

At Hearst's direction, Karl Decker, a reporter in the *Journal*'s Washington
bureau, traveled secretly to Cuba and rented a house located a plank's length
away from Cisneros's prison cell. According to the *Journal*, Decker wrenched
Cisneros's prison bars apart, and the girl was whisked to a waiting carriage;
then, dressed in boy's clothes, she was smuggled aboard a launch that took
her to the steamer *Seneca*. As Roy L. McCardell—a journalist who in 1898
would have the distinction of becoming the first person to be hired specifically as a screenwriter—would later describe the Cisneros affair: "They
make motion pictures of matter much less melodramatic." Years later a former *Journal* employee, Willis Abbot, remembered the Cisneros story differ-
ently from the way it was presented. Hearst was deadly serious about the
plight of Cisneros and imagined himself a modern-day Sir Galahad, but his
staff viewed the whole affair from beginning to end as a mere stunt. As for
Cisneros and Decker, Abbot suggested there was more playacting than
courage in their actions: the guards and officials at the prison, he claimed,
had been bribed with Hearst money and allowed the girl to escape.

As he had done with the Crane and Clark story, Hearst presented Cisneros's rescue as a drama played out by a hero, a heroine, and other dramatic types. There was another parallel. Hearst realized that a story with a female lead character might expand his readership. When he first broke the story of Cisneros's imprisonment, he had his reporter James Creelman gather and publish a long list of distinguished women who demanded action for her release. After Cisneros's escape, Hearst approached the same group of women for their gleeful responses and worked the *Journal*'s column-after-column reportage into a "woman's story." While most of Hearst's rival newspapers in New York ignored the Cisneros drama even as thousands gathered in the city to welcome her to American shores, the story resonated nationwide, carried by the Associated Press Wire Service.

Cisneros's triumphant arrival in the United States proved to be as much of a Hollywood production as her rescue. At the Waldorf-Astoria and Delmonico's restaurant, banquets were held in Cisneros's honor and attended by hundreds, while even larger crowds, whipped to a frenzy by the *Journal*'s full-page stories, waited outside to greet the celebrity. For an added attraction, the *Journal* presented Cisneros and Decker, in pictorial and text accounts, as a romantic couple (Decker was in fact married, but his wife kept her distance). In one long article in the *Journal*, the reception for Cisneros took the form of a series of glass slide tableaux. "Here," the *Journal* reported, "like one of those dissolving views of a stereopticon, the picture fades away in a confusion of lights and loud shouts; there ensues the wild interval of a triumphant procession through the street, noisy and bewildering, and then it all brightens up again and another picture stands out—and now this picture, too, fades and darkness follows." The *Journal* filled its pages with illustrations of Cisneros and her prison breakout that also resembled filmstrips. In a comfortable hotel room, shortly after arriving in New York, an unruffled Cisneros reenacted the key moments of imprisonment and escape for a photographer hired by Hearst. The action shots were then published in the *Journal*, lined up in a series that approximated film stills.

Later that same year Hearst showed a clear awareness that film was becoming the dominant visual medium. He made arrangements with David Belasco—described by one writer as a producer who "carried existing staging methods to a cinematic level"—to present a stage drama expressly for a *Journal* photographer. A special performance of the play *The Crime of the Boulevard*, a detective drama that starred Nat Goodwin and Anna Held, was photographed by a "flashlight" cameraman in the Garden Theatre. The photographic stills that were used in the *Journal*'s serialization of the play were similar to those taken of Cisneros. The screen was already pulling the eye away from the stage.

The daylong celebration for Cisneros climaxed with a huge fireworks display that supplemented Hearst's pseudofireworks. The *Journal* later described Cisneros as "the star of the night." Torches lit up the side of the *Journal* building, where crowds gathered, and an "electric transparency" read "Journal wants bring quick results." Hearst was undoubtedly chiefly responsible for the over-the-top production, although he remained behind the scenes, a brief handshake with Cisneros being his only public participation in the events. His exploitation of Evangelina Cisneros whet the country's appetite for war and for his own future dramatizations of war. For months following Cisneros's arrival in New York, the *Journal* kept the affair alive by serializing her story. Shortly after the series ended, the story in book form—with illustrations by Frederic Remington—was readied for publication. Then, as if on cue, the *Maine* sank. Two months later, on April 19, 1898, a war resolution narrowly passed in the Senate and overwhelmingly succeeded in the House of Representatives.

SENDING PICTURES

In 1898 two companies—the Edison Manufacturing Company and the Biograph Company (first called the American Mutoscope Company)—dominated filmmaking in the United States. Their success can be traced to their cinematic interpretation of the year's biggest news event, the Spanish-American War. What these film companies and others learned about interpreting news events in story form—and stories in terms of sensational entertainment—can be traced directly to Hearst and his brand of communications. When the war came, he literally escorted filmmakers to the war zone with a patriotic fervor that helped send the first wave of Americans to the movies.

Edison was the most well known film company in large part because of its prestigious association with Thomas Alva Edison, a folk hero of the late nineteenth century. Although Edison had little involvement in the technical aspects of their development, the concept of motion pictures came to him as early as 1888, when Edison became aware of Eadweard Muybridge's motion picture experiments. The following year Edison instructed one of the key members of his inventing team, William Kennedy Laurie Dickson, to find a way of combining the phonograph (an invention Edison personally worked on) and a moving-picture machine like one used by Muybridge for projecting his sequential image photographs.

For two years the Edison film project met with one disappointment after another, and Dickson's work often took a backseat to other projects in the famed West Orange, New Jersey, laboratory. But soon after a visit with a Frenchman named Etienne Jules Marey who was having success in photographing images on filmstrips, Edison's interest in film was renewed. He provided Dickson with some new ideas based on Marey's work as well as an assistant named William Heise. Dickson and Heise created a peephole machine for viewing films in 1891. The first images that were shown were moving pictures of Dickson taking a well-deserved bow. In 1893 Dickson designed a forty-eight-foot-long tar-covered studio at the Edison lab specifically for making movies. Dickson called it the "Kinetograph Theatre," but it was quickly nicknamed the "Black Maria" because its odd shape resembled a paddy wagon of the same name used by police for transporting prostitutes and other criminals. With a moving-picture camera and studio in place, Dickson produced the first copyrighted films, a minute or less in duration and intended for use in peephole kinetoscopes.

Work in various quarters in the United States and Europe was accelerating during this time to create a projector capable of screening films for audiences. Thomas Armat and C. Francis Jenkins of Washington, D.C., created just such an invention in 1895. Agreeing with Edison associates that the Edison name would provide prestige and capital for his invention to flourish, Armat swallowed his pride and concluded negotiations that established the Edison vitascope. On April 23, 1896, the vitascope debuted for the public at Koster and Bial's Music Hall in Herald Square, New York.

Edison's success at grabbing publicity and moving himself to the front and center of his experiments was something Hearst could relate to. Before Koster and Bial's was remodeled in 1893, the music hall's Corkroom saloon, located in the basement below the stage, was a gathering place of politicians, newspapermen, and writers. One of its attractions was the special electric lighting installed by Edison. The light fixtures on the walls were bronze brackets in the shape of arms holding white glass globes shaped like champagne bottles. It was a sign of the inventor's sense of showmanship and of his own importance that he used a mold of his own arm to cast the bronze fixtures and made sure the press knew about it.

Even before Edison introduced the vitascope, he had established a cordial relationship with Hearst and his *San Francisco Examiner* and *New York Journal*. Hearst greatly admired Edison, likening the inventor to a religious leader whose inventions were nourishing the capitalist system and thereby elevating the living standard of the masses. As a historical figure of importance, Hearst would later write, Edison was without equal, for no one else had done "so much to the health and wealth, to the material and spiritual progress of mankind."

Like Edison, Hearst had an ego to match his imagination, but both men were surprisingly modest in personal encounters. Edison's reserve may have been a result of his near deafness. Hearst's problem, some said, was his wispy speaking voice. He was also painfully shy, once telling a newspaper editor that even addressing a staff meeting gave him "stage fright." Unlike Edison, there were limits to Hearst's power over the press as a whole. Despite his enormous stature as a publisher, Hearst often found himself in a defensive posture, surrounded by rivals falling all over themselves to cut him down. His skill as a publicist was unparalleled when it came to others, but it was a double-edged sword when it came to publicizing himself as Edison did. Hearst seemed to fumble badly when he had a chance to be the hero or exploit his positive qualities. In 1896, for example, when a flying machine successfully glided over a hillside in Staten Island, New York, a gathering of onlookers saw two brave souls inside the rickety device: its forgotten inventor and Hearst. The *Journal* was directed by Hearst to cover the event, and they published articles for two days. One piece was accompanied by a large drawing. There wasn't a mention of Hearst in either article. Since the flight was dramatic but of no lasting impact, Hearst's newspaper competition felt no obligation to report the event. Needless to say, they must have felt even less compulsion knowing Hearst was involved. An authorized biography of Hearst in the 1930s furnishes the only mention of Hearst's participation in the flight.

Hearst and Edison did manage to share some of the public spotlight in 1896. On February 5, in a telegram to Edison, Hearst suggested as a "favor to the *Journal*" that the inventor make "a cathodograph" or X-ray of the human brain. An exchange between the two that followed might imply that Hearst was personally interested in being the subject. He told Edison he was available any day of the week except Tuesday and Wednesday, and Edison told Hearst that he intended to conduct "a number of experiments" related to the X-ray and that he would let him know by phone when he should come out to his laboratory. (Precisely what Hearst might have been looking for in an X-ray of the brain is a mystery, as talk about X-rays of the body during this period usually focused on finding lodged bullets and other objects. A *Journal* article published later in 1896 may offer a clue. Hearst's paper touted "an extraordinary discovery" from France: researchers had supposedly created a device that could penetrate the skull and "photograph" dreams.) Whether or not Hearst meant to have his own brain X-rayed, his proposal stimulated Edison, who was just beginning to focus more intensely on developing his own X-ray machine. Some of Hearst's rivals in the press were quick to ridicule the proposed brain experiment. The public, however, followed news of the X-ray with great interest, and for most of 1896 stories about the technology—many of which appeared in Hearst's *Journal* and his *San Francisco Examiner*—appeared to be at least as popular with readers as advances in film. Edison made progress in his experiments, but he was unable to meet Hearst's specific challenge of X-raying the brain (the thickness of the skull proved to be too great an obstacle until a Portuguese scientist met with success in 1927).

Another association sprang up between Hearst and Edison in April 1896, when the inventor was approached with the idea of developing and promoting what was dubbed a "picture telegraphing machine." Hearst's representative on the project was Paul Latzke, a man who in 1899 served as secretary of the *Maine* Monument Committee organized to build a memorial to the *Maine* victims. Latzke and Edison agreed to work on an invention that might be especially valuable in newspaper publishing. According to an account that appeared later in the *New York Journal*, Hearst wanted to know if pictures, like words, could be sent over telegraph wires. Edison was quick to respond that he had been working on just such a device for years and had nearly perfected it. His problem, he said, was that there seemed to be no commercial profit in sending pictures over wires since newspapers rarely published photographs. That was of course before pictorial or yellow journalism. "Newspapers," a *Journal* reporter told Edison, "were less enterprising than they are now."

With this enticement, Edison instructed one of his electrical experts, Patrick Kenny, to complete the work they had begun years earlier, and a letter of agreement outlining the arrangement with Hearst was drafted. In the document, Hearst was given exclusive use of the Autograph-Telegraph system for a period of one year. Hearst would pay for all test expenses, including materials and personnel necessary to carry out the experiments at the Edison lab. For the amount of $25,000, Edison would be willing to "sell and transfer" all interest in the patents and machinery they developed after a successful long-distance demonstration was completed. As no document other than this draft letter has surfaced, it is not known for certain how far the points in this arrangement between Edison and Hearst were taken; however, a version of Edison and Kenny's Autograph-Telegraph was successfully demonstrated in the pages of Hearst's *Journal* on October 25, 1896. In a headline that ran across a full page of the Sunday supplement, the *Journal* announced, "Here Are the First Pictures Ever Telegraphed." The newspaper called it a "joint invention" of Edison and Kenny, but the slant of the coverage implied that Hearst's *Journal* was crucially involved, if not an equal partner in the venture.

The *Journal*'s Autograph-Telegraph issue was published only a few days before the presidential election, which gave Hearst the opportunity to merge his two primary interests: communications and politics. Two of the first pictures transmitted by the new device were of Hearst's preferences in the election, Democrats William Jennings Bryan and his running mate, Arthur Sewall. The candidates' telegraphed images were placed prominently at the top of the *Journal*'s full-page coverage. So as not to short-change the celebrity-inventor himself, an artist's rendering of Edison standing proudly at the side of his device was placed in the center of the page. The *Journal* also published a telegraphed picture of Edison, but unlike Hearst's candidates, it was below the fold and alongside two other pictures that seem to have been chosen for their special appeal to Hearst readers. One picture was of female music hall dancers. The other was a wired image of the Yellow Kid cartoon character.

In the late nineteenth century, the amusement business was almost entirely run by and catering to men. When motion pictures began, most film companies were eager to continue established practices. They became extensions of venues that were proven draws, from music halls and vaudeville houses to less accredited moneymakers such as saloons, the pornographic picture postcard business, and houses of prostitution. The Edison Company and other film companies created films that embraced the interests of men. Sex and violence, most obviously seen in boxing films and dancing girl films, were common subjects of the peepshows because they evoked the dance halls and barrooms that men frequented. Filmmakers discovered that the sensationalist press could be a natural promotional ally; after all, it was already borrowing its imagery and point of view from the same sources as the film medium.

Thomas Edison exploited sensationalism in popular culture and sensationalism in the popular press to spread publicity about himself and his work. In 1894, when he set up his first peepshow kinetoscope parlor, Manhattan was chosen as its location for more than one reason. New York was obviously the center of entertainment, but it was also the capital of news dissemination. A success in New York would mean that his success would spread. Edison made sure his kinetoscope parlor dovetailed with established amusements. He hired a pretty female ticket taker to sit at the entrance and located the parlor on Broadway, in the Tenderloin. It was just a matter of time before the prevailing culture absorbed the new entertainment medium. Saloons and even some houses of prostitution would absorb the film medium as well, installing peepshows adjacent to their player pianos and their stacks of graphic newspapers.

Edison, working through an outside marketing group, soon had kinetoscope parlors set up in Chicago and San Francisco. These initial locations were significant: at the turn of the century New York, Chicago, and San Francisco were the most populated cities in the country, and venues of entertainment and communication were successfully commingled in all three. This factor was not inconsequential in Hearst's decision to make these cities the locations for his first newspapers.

Sex appeal was the angle that Hearst played up when the vitascope was demonstrated for the press during the evening of April 3, 1896. The next day's *Journal* published the most provocative of all the newspaper accounts of the two-hour press show. It publicized the event with a series of suggestive headlines that gradually decreased in size. The largest type was saved for the words "Skirt Dancers," followed by the somewhat smaller "In Gauzy Silks They Smirk and Pirouette At Wizard Edison's Command." The alluring imagery refers to film of dancing girls that was screened, but in the *Journal* account even Edison, who acted as host for the press gathering, is placed in a sexual context:

> The figure of a girl dressed for a skirt dance was thrown upon the screen. The delicate colors of the shimmering silk were shown as distinctly as though a calcium light were being thrown upon a living dancer on a real stage. Mr. Edison watched the effect with much interest. Then he walked close to the screen to note more precisely the effect of the draperies and the flesh tints on the arms and face of the young woman. As the graceful figure showed now and then when the yards of silk were sent floating high in the air Edison smiled.

In their account of the press preview, the *Journal* also made a point of recognizing film's potential: "Not only is it possible with the new machine to show life-size figures in every detail of movement with every tint of costume and change of expression, but groups of as many as fifty figures can be reproduced perfectly. With a background copied from the scenes of some theatre this will enable an entire play to be shown exactly as it is given by actors themselves."

The press debut of the vitascope was as important as the public theater presentation that occurred a few weeks later. From the moment he began working with Edison in the Autograph-Telegraph venture, Hearst had become a factor in the elevation of motion pictures and the elevation of the Wizard of Menlo Park. For their part, Edison and his associates, masters at working the press, understood that newspapermen—especially those in the yellow press—had an obsession with simplifying stories for the masses and creating celebrities. By remaining silent about the origins of the motion picture projecting machine, the Edison team did more than simply redirect attention from the work of other motion picture pioneers; together with their friends in the press, they crafted a myth of Edison as film's sole inventor. It is a myth that lived on well after Edison's death in 1931.

CREATING THEMES

Of all the film companies that sprang up in the late 1890s and survived into the twentieth century, Hearst was most closely associated with the Biograph Company. The Biograph offices and rooftop studio were in an area of Manhattan well known to Hearst. Located at Broadway and Thirteenth Street, they were just around the corner from the strip of Fourteenth Street where Tammany Hall faced the Dewey Theater. They were less than a block away from the house run by his future in-laws, the Willsons, and next door to the offices of the Folsom Brothers, where Hearst's new friend and future real estate chief, Martin Huberth, worked. Biograph had a long-term presence in the Fourteenth Street area; except for one four-month period between 1897 and 1905, Biograph films ran continuously at the Union Square Theater.

It is unknown what role, if any, these circumstances played in Hearst's decision to favor Biograph. Probably the most important factor was that Biograph had developed a projector in late 1896 that produced an onscreen image that was larger and clearer than its rivals. Biograph's achievement even caused Edison's vitascope operation to go into decline. The Edison Company would rebound, however. It began selling films overseas through its agents, Maguire and Baucus, and developed its own projecting machine. Edison would remain a powerful force in the film industry through the turn of the century, primarily by driving many competitors out of business in a series of patent infringement lawsuits.

The American Mutoscope Company, later Biograph, was founded by Henry Marvin in 1895 as a manufacturer of the Mutoscope, a peepshow machine that flipped photograph cards, giving images the appearance of moving. From its inception, Biograph was a company with healthy financial backing and strong political connections. Its major stockholder was Abner McKinley, the brother of Ohio Republican William McKinley. Among its other stockholders was former president Benjamin Harrison, also a Republican. Biograph did not have a completely adversarial relationship with the Edison Company, which shared its political affiliation and actually produced a few films that were blatantly pro-Republican and anti–Tammany Hall. Edison inventor William Dickson helped Biograph to develop a camera that led the company away from flip cards to film presentations onscreen. Biograph's first public film presentation occurred on October 12, 1896, at Hammerstein's Olympia Music Hall, in New York City. By then, savvy theater producer Oscar Hammerstein was also on the list of Biograph stockholders.

By late 1896 audiences were beginning to accept motion pictures as a novelty analogous to other entertainment novelties they enjoyed. Still, audiences were relatively small and composed for the most part of paying customers at urban vaudeville houses. The film experience, such as it was, had not reached the level of public discourse. It was not the fad that, for instance, bicycling had become at the time; there were no constant mentions of motion pictures in the press or specific publications to publicize the medium. That Hearst himself was a regular paying customer at variety shows is clearly demonstrated by an event he produced in New York City on the evening of the 1896 presidential election. For days leading up to election, night readers were told how the *Journal*'s resources would provide them with the best, most up-to-date election result news. This wasn't the half of it. At various outdoor locations in Manhattan, Brooklyn, and even Jersey City, Hearst staged extravagant programs that mixed stereopticon slide shows, band music, fireworks displays, block-long illuminated maps to chart election results, and high-flying balloons that provided color-coded versions of the same results. Motion pictures were prominent in this mix of entertainments, projected on fifty-foot-wide outdoor screens scattered around town. Even in what the *Journal* itself characterized as a three-ring circus, film was a unique feast for the eyes. It had not yet entered the center ring, but by the evening's end Hearst seemed determined to move it closer.

Arrangements were made with the Biograph Company and Koster and Bial's Music Hall, their current theater venue, for the loan of several films. Two were political films made earlier in the year. One, filmed by cameramen William "Billy" Bitzer and William Dickson, showed William McKinley on the lawn of his Canton, Ohio, home reenacting his nomination notification. The other showed views of William Jennings Bryan giving a speech from the rear of a campaign train. Hearst also secured the use of a Biograph film called *The Empire State Express*, which was screened purely for its entertainment value. This classic film, which showed a simple scene of an approaching train, was a huge hit when it was first presented in theaters, but it so startled some audience members that they jumped from their seats screaming in fear that they were about to be run over.

Hearst was also able to get J. Austin Fynes, manager of Keith's Union

Square Theater, to loan a number of Lumière Brothers films that had been made in and around Paris and debuted at his theater in June. Fynes was an important association for Hearst. The manager has been credited with being a major influence in getting other vaudeville impresarios to accept the motion picture as a credible act on their variety bills. Oscar Hammerstein agreed to allow the *Journal* to use the huge front of the Olympia Theater to screen other films and slides. Risqué turns by the dancing Barrison Sisters and Loie Fuller were screened between satirical stereopticons of Homer Davenport's political caricatures and Outcault's Yellow Kid.

According to the *Journal*, Woodville Latham provided stereopticons for the evening. It is possible that Latham and his sons, Gray and Otway, also provided films, since they were then pioneers in the new medium. The Lathams first came to New York in 1894, following the failure of their pharmaceutical business in Nashville, Tennessee. In New York the Latham sons took jobs at various drug companies and at a firm owned by Samuel Tilden Jr., the son of the onetime governor of New York (Otway became plant manager). From the Bartholdi, a Tenderloin district hotel they called home, the handsome young brother regularly ventured into the night for evenings in the company of actresses and dancers they met at the cheaper amusements of Broadway and Fourteenth Street. On some of these excursions an old friend and recent engineering graduate, Enoch Rector, accompanied the Latham sons. A chance visit by the Lathams and Rector to the Edison Kinetoscope parlor at 1155 Broadway sparked an interest in the business opportunities of the motion picture medium. Gray and Otway passed along their excitement to their father, who until then had no particular expertise in motion pictures (he was primarily a chemist, with only a limited knowledge of photography). Soon afterward, the Lathams became Edison Kinetoscope licensees, opening their own parlor on Nassau Street, near Newspaper Row in lower Manhattan. With employer Tilden and friend Rector they also formed an outside company to develop longer peepshow films, suitable for showing boxing matches. Rector would go on to film the Corbett-Fitzsimmons fight. Through Edison, the Lathams came to know William Dickson, who shared their belief that the future of motion pictures was outside the peepshow box and up on the screen. Meanwhile, the Latham sons' playboy lifestyle became useful to Edison's film company. Through the young men's coaxing, a number of chorus girls they had known in Manhattan briefly left the stage for a ferry ride to New Jersey, where they went through their motions in Edison's Black Maria, becoming some of the earliest film subjects.

In the spring of 1895 Dickson left Edison in part to assist the Lathams in developing a motion picture projecting machine (Dickson was also working at this time on the Mutoscope). When the Lathams exhibited a projector they called the eidoloscope, Edison's remaining film specialists doubled their efforts to produce their own projector. As previously mentioned, they were unsuccessful until Armat and Jenkins came along with their projector—originally called the phantoscope—and Edison's vitascope was introduced.

Hearst was likely to have been aware of the Lathams' kinetoscope parlor, since the *Journal* was also located nearby on Nassau Street. He may even have crossed paths with Otway and Gray on Broadway or at one of their famous dinner parties at the Hoffman House. His use of the Lathams' stereopticons for his election night celebration also involved the promotion of the Latham name in the next day's *Journal* coverage. Earlier that same year, in the May 24 issue of his *San Francisco Examiner*, Hearst had given an even bigger boost to the Lathams by publishing a full-page article about a Latham film titled *Bull Fight*. Besides being an especially prominent article, the page is taken up almost entirely by line drawings reproducing sequential frames from the film; the slight degree of change in each successive frame gave readers a basic sense of how motion pictures work.

Crusading for William Jennings Bryan in 1896 had its rewards for Hearst. As the only major newspaper in the East to support Bryan, the *Journal* became the de facto campaign headquarters for the Democratic Party soon after the nominating convention. Pro-Bryan material began appearing in the *Journal*'s columns. Soon Hearst dreamt up an even more effective propaganda tool: he had he *Journal* publish a weekly freestanding campaign extra for campaign field operatives that was devoted exclusively to boosting Bryan. To reinforce his commitment and strengthen his influence, Hearst personally donated tens of thousands of dollars to the Democratic Party.

Hearst paid in other ways for supporting Bryan, whom many considered a radical. Social clubs looked down their noses at Hearst and his staff. Many of the well-established businesses began to cancel their advertising contracts with his newspapers. These advertising losses were compounded when other companies became increasingly leery of associating with a newspaper that had little track record, courted controversy, and embraced a brand of journalism that was almost daily being compared to a house of prostitution. Publicly, however, Hearst never showed concern over the consequences of his controversial stand for Bryan.

Hearst saw the entertainer in the politician Bryan, a strikingly handsome man who could have been a matinee idol. The race for the presidency became Hearst's blood-and-thunder variety show. "Bryan was Punch and McKinley became Judy in the *Journal*'s bid for readers," wrote Hearst biographer Ferdinand Lundberg. With Hearst's approval, Richard Outcault's Yellow Kid character made a mockery of the presidential election in several of the *Journal* comic *Mcfadden's Row of Flats* tableaux leading up to the election. In one, the Yellow Kid is seen leading a band of misfits through the East Side. One dead-end scamp holds a placard that declares: "WHY NOT ELECT EM BOTH AN LET EM FIGHT IT OUT BETWEEN EM?" In another cartoon the Yellow Kid's East Side turf looks more than a little like Fourteenth or Thirteenth Street. He parades through cartoon character Tim McFadden's (Tim Sullivan's?) flats, where a sign hanging from a political clubhouse (Tammany Hall?) reads: "HERES HEADQUARTERS OF DE JUVENILE POLITICAL CLUB WE ARE OUT FER BRYAN AND MCKINLEY (A FINE TICKET)." Standing out among Outcault's colorful East Side crowd are the "naughty" Riccadonna Sisters. The girls are dressed like ballet dancers but are clearly meant to suggest prostitutes as they stand outside a boardinghouse where a sign reads: "COUCHE-COO DANCING COME EARLY AND AVOID THE CROWD."

Hearst's exciting coverage of the race brought a boost to Hearst readership that defied the criticism and eventually brought back the advertisers. Close to one million copies of the *Journal*'s postelection issue were sold (more than one-and-a-half million if one includes his morning, evening, and German-language editions), breaking all previous circulation records.

In his postelection coverage, Hearst segued effortlessly from political defeat to self-congratulation by shifting his focus from Bryan to the *Journal*'s sensational party for the masses, its "marvellous Election Day display and wonderful pictures." In column after column Hearst continuously commented on the huge crowds that had gathered for the *Journal* (if not for William Jennings Bryan). He noted that the throngs included many "enthusiastic, up-to-date women" and that they and others particularly "relished the treat" of the film shows. In fact, it seemed as if Hearst was declaring the *Journal* and their motion pictures to be the real winners of the day. "The success of the *Journal*'s election return bulletins was in a great measure due to the animated picture machines, which were engaged to amuse the throngs that gathered on Tuesday night to gain the first news of the results of the great vote." The success of the election displays showed Hearst how the right balance of facts and fancy, human-interest–based news, and controlled hullabaloo could captivate the public. In an editorial that appeared in the *Journal* four days later, Hearst made a confident declaration that some would see as his credo and might also be seen as the hallmark of communication in the century to come. "The public," he said, "is even more fond of entertainment than it is of information."

MOVING PLATFORMS

Those who hoped that Hearst would go down in the same crashing defeat as his candidate were sadly disappointed. His sensational form of communication had made its mark, and he seemed empowered. Still, Hearst's audacious business methods and his anything but circumspect lifestyle invited criticism. Joining the sniping editorialists from rival newspapers were the preachers who were particularly inflamed by the success of Hearst's Sunday newspaper section (one minister called publishing newspapers on Sunday a "violation of divine law"). They compared it to the lascivious Sunday shows at music halls, which they believed were making the Christian Sabbath no different from any other day. By 1897 the term *yellow journalism*, with all of its connotations, was in full usage.

Hearst's personal behavior at this time—he had just become involved with the Willson family—demonstrated a cavalier attitude toward society, but he was not entirely averse to public image building. As some began to identify him with his Yellow Kid cartoon, he embraced the nonthreatening association. More than this, he took note of the cartoon's amazing marketing power. The image of the funny-looking street urchin, sometimes with his dancing girl sidekick, began to appear on buttons, cigarette boxes, toys, and calendars. Songs and theatrical productions based on the cartoon began to appear. On the evening of November 28, 1896, a performer named Silas Johnson played a Yellow Kid character for an opening night sketch at "Big" Tim Sullivan's Volks Garden (later Dewey Theater). The Lubin Film Company of Philadelphia released a short film at the end of 1897 that capitalized on the cartoon by using "Yellow Kid" in its title. At Hammerstein's Olympic Theater roof garden, the *Journal*'s ballet girl and yellow kid—actors made up like the cartoons—were the opening act for an elaborate dance production. This particular connection recalls a remark that the observant Stephen Crane made at the time: "Nobody understands the popular mind as well as Oscar Hammerstein, unless it's Willie Hearst. I see no difference between the *Journal* and Hammerstein's roof garden. You get the blonde with the tin can in her gullet and the comic speaker and the song about mother's wayward boy in both shows."

Hearst introduced a new entertainment to his readers in 1897 that further acknowledged the interest of Hearst and the public in motion pictures, when a cartoon titled *The "Journal" Kinetoscope, Taken at the Rate of a Million a Minute*, began appearing regularly. The cartoon strip was positioned vertically along one entire side of the newspaper's humor page and drawn with perforated edges like the frames of a filmstrip. But as much as Hearst loved the funnies, he was eager to find something of more weight to establish his brand name. Even in his early days in San Francisco, Hearst peppered his newspaper with "true" stories of the news that touched on issues of privilege. Now the struggle between the privileged and the underprivileged would be a theme to dominate his stories and illustrations. Hearst developed a platform for his papers; he would later call it "an American internal policy" that championed public ownership of public franchises, a graduated income tax, and the popular election of senators. The trusts—gas, sugar, ice, and a score of other business monopolies—came in for particularly harsh treatment in his papers. Hearst's approach to domestic issues was to use yellow journalism's human-interest approach and to tell stories framed by the theme of privilege. The crusades were unmerciful and short on facts at times but generally progressive in their thrust. They were sometimes effective at changing policy but even more effective at building a loyal following.

Hearst journalism borrowed from the bread-and-circus methods perfected by Tammany Hall and "Big" Tim Sullivan. In what became a predictable pattern, Hearst would expose an inequity or tragic circumstance in society, claim that his reporting had improved the situation, and then with great flair celebrate victory by throwing a party for the people and for his crusading newspaper. The year 1897 began with an event the *Journal* sponsored at Oscar Hammerstein's ever-friendly and -available Olympia Theater. This time Heart put on a vaudeville show as a benefit concert to aid those recently made homeless by a Manhattan tenement fire. Another "monster operatic, dramatic and vaudeville performance" was held at the Metropolitan Opera House on February 9, "in aid of the destitute of this city." The stars of the evening were Lillian Russell, May Irwin, and Anna Held. Seats and boxes for the event were auctioned off at the Garrick Theater a few days before the event. Two of the more famous auctioneers at the Garrick were actors Louis Mann and Clara Lipman. They were then appearing in the show *The Girl from Paris*, which also featured Hearst's new companions, Millicent and Anita Willson. Hearst's skillful elevation of celebrity worship was also demonstrated in the *Journal*'s stories about a society ball in February. His coverage of the gala made points about the excesses and snobbery of the rich. The overall trust of the piece, however, emphasized pleasure and opulence that tempted his readers: it was a five-page-long newspaper version of the peepshow. Hearst had discovered that even those who loved to hate the rich loved to read about them just the same.

The poor children of New York City came in for a dose of Hearst largesse when the *Journal* began to paint a contrasting picture of summertime in the city. On one side were healthy children of privilege whose parents could afford for their own a season of joy frolicking in the cooling waves of the ocean. On the other side were the children of poverty, who knew no joy and whose only hope, the *Journal* would later boast, was "the paper which was temporarily making their lives worth living." Beginning in June, the *Journal* announced its plan to send scores of city kids—between the ages of six and fourteen—on day trips to Coney Island. The trips took place between the first weeks of July and September. Nearly every day during this period, the *Journal* published illustrated articles promoting its seaside outings, which included ice cream, baseball games, and visiting actors and actresses putting on impromptu shows. While there were no newspaper reports that the *Journal* arranged for the filming of these Coney Island excursions, films of a similar *Journal* outing in the summer of 1900 have been documented. At that time, the Biograph Company took motion pictures of children riding the rails to Coney Island and others of the children amusing themselves on carousel rides. The films, which were exhibited nationwide, were taken, Hearst said, because "pictures will be the best proof of the great good the *Journal* is accomplishing that could be presented."

Biograph did collaborate with Hearst in July 1897 on a youth program called the *Journal* Junior Republic. In a camp nestled in a farming community in Rockland County, New York, the program—which resembled the Boy Scouts—offered kids a refuge from the city and an opportunity to experience activities and responsibilities that prepared them for adulthood. To help finance the charity, Hearst threw a gala event on July 24 at a hotel in Sheepshead Bay, Brooklyn, with entertainment provided by more than a dozen vaudeville stars, including comedienne Marie Dressler. A Biograph crew filmed at least three scenes at the Junior Republic with camera equipment weighing some two tons. One shows a group of boys working the farm like adults, and another shows youngsters interacting in a pint-size version of the American judicial system; a final scene shows the boys on parade. In its coverage of the films, the *Journal* again emphasized the power of film to spread their good work:

> The fame of the *Journal* Junior Republic is spreading. Up at Keith's they are showing the Biograph pictures of actual scenes at the Republic. The gem of the lot is a court scene taken in the open air at the farm. A chicken thief was convicted on wing testimony. One of the hens flew out of his coat and tiny chickens fluttered down from their cozy hiding place in the culprit's hat. Then there is a series of illustrations showing the boys helping to load hay. Lastly, the evening parade and review are presented in a way to make a Seventh Regiment man

at the State camp green with envy. These pictures are also to be shown in London—films will also be sent to Australia—exhibited at Keith's in Boston and Philadelphia and at theatres in Toledo, Chicago and Asbury Park—Three times a day these biograph scenes prepared by the best artists and mechanics of the American Mutoscope Company will be shown.

Hearst also explored his theme of privilege in his coverage of international issues. He quickly shifted the nation's attention from McKinley and Bryan to Cuba and its struggle for independence from Spain. In the winter of 1896 Hearst sent dashing celebrity journalists like Richard Harding Davis and Frederic Remington to gather and present war news to his readers. Both men were exceedingly talented and narcissistic, a combination Hearst found, at least for limited periods of time, irresistible. He believed that men who were convinced of their own importance gave weight to any story they covered and that the power of their celebrity could carry their stories when there was no real news to report.

Hearst was determined to provide his readers with "illustrations of the news," even if it meant he needed to create the news personally. After artist Remington returned from Cuba in January 1897 empty-handed—no war pictures and no war—Hearst considered going to Cuba himself. On February 15, reports circulated that Hearst would soon be arriving in Jacksonville, Florida, a bawdy port that was a gathering place for reporters and arms smugglers working for Cuban insurgents. The press speculated that Hearst would board his 138-foot yacht the *Buccaneer* in Jacksonville and then head south for Cuba. The purpose of a trip was unclear; would his steamer be used for running guns, or was he planning to expose some fresh atrocity in Cuba?

There were no published sightings of Hearst in Jacksonville, but Stephen Crane was seen in town. Since December 1896—close to the time Hearst first met the Willsons—Crane had been having an affair with Cora Stewart, the thirty-one-year-old madam of the Hotel de Dream, one of Jacksonville's high-class brothels. In January 1897 Crane secured a passport to travel to Cuba. On February 15, as Hearst's yacht arrived in Jacksonville, Crane told fellow reporters who were flooding the town in anticipation of war news that he would soon be traveling with Hearst's party to Cuba. When the *Buccaneer*'s captain, Theodore Hilborn, was asked to comment, he implied that Crane was talking nonsense. According to Captain Hilborn, Hearst was simply planning "a pleasure trip" to the West Indies. Reporters who knew the habits of Hilborn's boss must have recognized the disingenuousness of this response, since Hearst often mixed business with pleasure. With Crane still reeling from his involvement with the prostitute Dora Clark and his troubles with the police, Hearst may not have wanted to publicize a trip or a relationship of any kind. But rumors of Hearst's own private life were surfacing at this time, and a nervous Crane—who was generally discreet—may have felt the same way. Hearst's reputation was being discussed openly in the nation's Capitol in early 1897. A California congressman who had previously been assailed by the *San Francisco Examiner* gave a long speech on the floor of the House of Representatives outlining Hearst's "licentious" ways. He even went so far as to say that Hearst was known to frequent "haunts of vice" located "in every city in the globe."

Precisely what happened to Hearst and Crane between the middle of February and the middle of March when they returned to New York is not known. If a Hearst-Crane trip to Cuba occurred, it may have turned out as unproductive as Frederic Remington's, for it wasn't discussed for publication. On March 11 Crane wrote his brother that having spent nearly a month "among the swamps further south wading miserably to and fro in an attempt to avoid our derned U.S. Navy," he had lost all enthusiasm for reporting on Cuba. Returning to New York, Crane decided to take Hearst up on his latest offer: sailing to Crete and reporting on the Greco-Turkish War. By late March Crane shipped off to Europe. Crane's mistress, Cora Stewart, also made the trip. She was temporarily out of the brothel business and, writing under the byline of "Imogene Carter," was working for Hearst as one of two female war correspondents. Dispatches from Cora were telegraphed back to the *Journal* until the summer of 1897, when Hearst turned his attention to another woman with a dubious past—Evangelina Cisneros—whose tale would round out the remainder of the year.

Hearst was more prepared than anyone else to cover the war when hostilities commenced following the *Maine* explosion on February 15, 1898. He was not only the first newspaper publisher to send dispatch boats to Cuba; he eventually had a flotilla of ten yachts and tugboats in the area, twice as many as any other newspaper or press association. A number of these vessels provided more than transportation for Hearst's writers and correspondents. Movie cameras were set up on their decks, and the ships became moving platforms for filming scenes on the sea and shore.

By early March Hearst had a yacht named the *Anita*, which he had recently chartered, heading for Havana. The *Anita* was stocked with liquor, cigars, and other amenities for an excursion of congressmen he was hosting. On its fact-finding mission, the *Anita* first stopped in Newport News, Virginia. It then stopped in Key West, Florida, for two days before making its way to Cuba. The trip was thoroughly covered by the *Journal* and milked for every ounce of useful pro-war propaganda. When a congressmen's wife who had accompanied her husband on the Anita trip died suddenly from a heart attack, the *Journal* used her death as proof of the horrors of starvation and disease in Cuba that she had reportedly just witnessed. The congressional mission did not have the desired affect Hearst had hoped for, however; a war declaration still was not forthcoming. By late March the *Anita* had returned to Key West, met there by Hearst's larger yacht the *Buccaneer*. Increasingly impatient for war to begin, Hearst created some artificial excitement in his *Journal* office, making a public bet with an associate that hostilities in Cuba would be under way within a week. Hearst lost $15,000 on the wager, but his employees were suitably impressed with his zeal.

Between the time of the *Maine* explosion and April 10, the Biograph Company had two cameramen in Cuba. Billy Bitzer and Arthur Marvin, a brother of a Biograph executive, took films in late February showing Cubans herded together in concentration camps and scenes from the shore of divers working on the sunken battleship. While the cameramen were on their filming mission, the Biograph Company screened a film in New York theaters that they claimed to show the battleship *Maine* before it sank (in fact, the ship wasn't the *Maine* but a similar-looking battleship, the U.S. *Massachusetts*). In mid-March the Edison Company also released so-called war films that were hits with audiences. Shot in a studio, they showed brief glimpses of the American flag and the Cuba Libre flag blowing in the breeze. After returning to New York, Bitzer worried that his own static films—however truthful—would pale in comparison to the hoaxes Biograph and Edison had successfully put over on the public. To the contrary, audiences who were being primed for war by Hearst and Pulitzer greeted even Bitzer's less-than-riveting films with enthusiasm.

The propaganda success of the Biograph and Edison films pushed Hearst further into the movie field. When Edison's selling agents F. Z. Maguire and Co. approached him about sending a cameraman to Cuba to make real films of the war, he jumped at the offer. Cameraman William C. Paley became an Edison licensee after receiving serious radiation injuries working as an X-ray exhibitor. In early 1898 Paley achieved considerable notoriety with the New York City screening of his *Passion Play*, a series of twenty-three shorter films that were strung together and based on events leading up to the crucifixion of Christ. In accord with an agreement with Hearst, Paley traveled to Key West in late March. There he met the *Journal*'s rescue reporter Karl Decker, and the two men made plans for a Hearst-sponsored film junket.

Burial of the Maine *Victims*, the first film Paley made in Key West, was of a funeral procession. Groups of soldiers and young black boys lead a line of nine coffins, each draped in the American flag. Military officers, carriages, and a large crowd follow the coffins and their accompanying pallbearers. Reporter Decker played a small but significant onscreen role in two other Paley films. One film showed Decker and other correspondents on the deck of Hearst's yacht the *Buccaneer* as it cut through the waters. The other film, called *War Correspondents*, was something of a lighthearted view of yellow journalism. The film shows a group of eager reporters running toward the camera, pretending to be hurrying to file their dispatches at the Key West telegraph office. Decker, always the star reporter, arrives last in the comfort of his hansom cab.

In Havana harbor the team of Paley and Decker took other films, among them, *Wreck of the Battleship "Maine"* and *"Morro Castle," Havana Harbor*. These two films in particular made practical use of Hearst's traveling yacht. With his bulky camera secured on the deck, Paley was able to capture a panorama pan shot that was novel for the time. The films were first shown at Manhattan's Eden Musee Theater on April 18 and well publicized by Hearst as "Journal Pictures" when they were shown on April 25 at Proctor's Theater. Paley had returned to New York with his package of films shortly before war was declared. By the time his films debuted at Proctor's, he had returned to Florida. Still traveling under the auspices of Hearst and Edison, he remained in Tampa for almost two months, taking several films of troops as they disembarked from railroad cars and set up camp. The film *Roosevelt's Rough Riders Embarking for Santiago* was taken by Paley on June 8.

Hearst's interest in photographing the Cuban conflict was no less pronounced than his interest in putting it on film. In April 1898 George Palmer—the *San Francisco Examiner*'s art director, who had recently transported his talents to the *Journal*—held a brief meeting in his office with a young friend from the Manhattan-based Byron Photography Company. Byron was well known for its pictures of stage personalities and stage sets. In fact, the stationery of the company read "The Stage Is My Studio." Many of the Byron photographs were published in the Hearst papers, possibly including a series taken of posed actors that was used to illustrate a David Belasco and Hearst venture, called a "flashlight play," that was published in the *Journal* in 1897. Palmer asked Percy Byron, the son of the company's founder, if he would be interested in traveling with an upcoming Hearst junket to Cuba. Byron was agreeable, and he quickly packed his bags of photography equipment; Palmer wanted him to catch a train to Tampa,

Florida, the very next day. Arriving in Tampa, Byron was told that he and his fellow passengers would be traveling on Hearst's *Buccaneer*. Dragging his heavy suitcases of cameras and developing chemicals along its deck, Byron noticed that the ship seemed to be especially prepared for combat: along the railings flint-fire pistols were positioned where pins were normally placed to hold the halyards. No sooner had Byron unloaded his equipment than he was told there had been a change of plans. The Hearst party of photographers and reporters would now be taking the nearby *Anita*. That vessel was commandeered by *Journal* city editor Joe Qual. Karl Decker was also onboard, along with several reporters from other non-Hearst newspapers who had paid a fee to travel with the group. The magazine *Frank Leslie's* was represented by illustrator Dan Smith and a reporter named Edwin Emerson. In an arrangement that may have been similar to the one he had with Edison, Hearst also hired the Biograph Company's motion picture cameraman Arthur Marvin to join the *Anita*'s voyage.

During this period, the *Buccaneer* would make several trips to the war zone, although its missions were not always publicized. In late April and early May, a *Journal* reporter named Sidney G. Tovey was sending dispatches from the *Buccaneer* when a bloody confrontation between Spanish gunboats and American torpedo boats occurred in the nearby harbor of Cárdenas. He was also on the yacht when it traveled the waters near Kingston, Jamaica, in search of a Cuban fleet that was rumored to be heading for the U.S. mainland. Hearst seems to to have had enormous trust in young Tovey's abilities, even though he was a newcomer to the *Journal* and to journalism. The British-born Dublin University graduate's previous experience was as a Kansas schoolteacher and as an actor, with a role in the Willson sisters' 1897 show *The Girl from Paris*.

Cameraman Billy Bitzer was making local news films in Boston in late April when he received a telegram from Biograph executive Wallace McCutcheon Sr. indicating that the Hearst organization wanted him to cover the war in Cuba. Bitzer, who had only returned from the area a week or so before, was told that he would be part of a team of Hearst reporters and two still cameramen. In his memoirs Bitzer says that he arrived in Siboney, Cuba, on April 21 and proceeded to take films from the beach of American troops landing from the battleships *Yale* and *Harvard*. At some later point, Bitzer writes, he was taken by tugboat to the Hearst yacht *Sylvia*, which was anchored in the harbor. Onboard the *Sylvia* were Hearst's old theater cronies George Pancoast and Jack Follansbee, as well as "two pretty young ladies who were sisters," apparently Millicent and Anita Willson. Champagne was made available for all, including cameraman Bitzer, served by the undisputed host of the Spanish-American War himself. Hearst had finally made his official personal entrance into Cuban waters.

The *Sylvia* was Hearst's second choice for traveling to Cuba. The plan had been to make himself available to become a commissioned officer in command of his yacht the *Buccaneer*. On June 14 Hearst went to Washington for what he thought would be a cakewalk. Reporter Edwin Emerson was in an outer office when the secretary of war rebuffed Hearst's offer. He reportedly told Hearst, "The thing to do with a dirty sheet was to wash it." The government was happy to make use of Hearst's *Buccaneer*, but they had no use for its owner. Hearst quickly readied the *Sylvia*, which had been chartered a month before from the Baltimore Fruit Company. On June 15 Hearst was onboard the *Sylvia* with a party of friends, photographers, and illustrators, headed for Kingston, Jamaica, and points south.

Still photographer John C. Hemment later recalled that he was approached to join the *Sylvia* party by *Journal* correspondent James Creelman: "He told me that my path would be a mighty thorny one; that while he [Hearst] had made a great effort in that war to obtain good photographic material, had employed the best of men, and given them every facility, they had absolutely failed from one cause or another to give him practical results—Mr. Hearst's intention was to depict and describe to his fellow-citizens the events at the seat of war with all the vividness and accuracy possible to camera and pen."

For the Hearst trip, Hemment brought along almost as many medical supplies as he did equipment for taking photographs. Acetate of lead was carried for mosquito bites, petroleum jelly for sunburns, and rhubarb pills and cholera drops for the expected assaults on the bowels. At Hearst's direction, the *Sylvia* was equipped with cameras and developing chemicals that might adequately furnish a small photography shop. Containers of ice, which was necessary for developing film in the unfriendly climate, were picked up in Kingston, Jamaica, on the way to Cuba. During the brief stopover, Hearst and his party visited a racecourse, where several ponies were bought for the war adventure.

The *Sylvia* arrived in Cuba on June 18, and the Hearst party disembarked for a leisurely sightseeing trip to the outskirts of Santiago de Cuba. The Willson sisters got dressed up in sailor uniforms to safeguard their identity, if not their lives. Hemment began taking photographs almost immediately. Two spacious dining rooms on the *Sylvia* were converted into a darkroom, the cabin's windows covered with red muslin and an electric fan installed. Hearst interviewed Admiral Sampson, General Shafter, and General Garcia. A Cuban house near Clara Barton's Red

Cross compound was turned over to the *Journal*. It became a crowded headquarters as a dozen or more reporters and artists, including Frederic Remington and actor-journalist Burr McIntosh, arrived via the dispatch boat *Simpson* and an army transport.

The Hearst party, with its ample supply of ice, cool drinks, and youthful gaiety, was a welcome sight to Bitzer. His memoir's chronology of events suggests that he had been in Cuba for nearly two months before Hearst arrived. If this is accurate, he shot very little film during such a long stay. Possibly Bitzer arrived in Cuba when he claimed but returned to New York before making his third trip back. There seems to be no question, however, that he did meet up with the Hearst party. The detail about the "ladies who were sisters" being onboard is something not many would have known, and it is a story confirmed in a 1950s interview with Hearst's cousin. In addition, a repository of Billy Bitzer papers held by the Museum of Modern Art, in New York, contains a rare item from the Hearst trip to Cuba: Bitzer's brittle souvenir copy of an issue of Hearst's *Journal* dated July 10, 1898. This edition wasn't published in New York but in Cuba, printed for the troops from "on board the *Journal* dispatch steamer *Sylvia* off Santiago." The Cuban edition of the paper was also a souvenir of one of the few films Bitzer took in Cuba: footage of Hearst reporters and printers putting out the special newspaper below the deck of the *Sylvia*.

In addition to the Edison and Biograph companies, the Vitagraph Company, founded by J. Stuart Blackton and Albert E. Smith, also discovered ways to exploit the public's interest in seeing the war they read so much about. Blackton and Smith met around 1894 and were primarily stage entertainers during the first years of their association. Blackton, who was born in England, was a fine sketch artist who worked for Pulitzer's *World*, and Smith, who was also English, was a magician. Appearing on the Lyceum circuit, they entertained audiences with a variety show that consisted of sleight-of-hand tricks, "lightning" cartoon drawings, and magic lantern slide shows narrated by Blackton. While on assignment for the *World*, Blackton visited Edison's Black Maria and appeared in three films doing his comic chalk sketches. An 1896 Edison film, *Inventor Edison Sketched by World Artist*, showed Blackton exhibiting his sketching talents. It was particularly successful, no doubt in part because of its well-known subject.

Blackton was becoming famous through his connection with Edison and film, and along with Smith he was increasingly interested in finding ways to tell stories through projected images. The two were particularly inspired by Alexander Black's stereopticon "picture play" presentations, which projected dissolving images that suggested motion and told feature-length stories.

Around February 1897 Blackton and Smith purchased a motion picture machine for taking and projecting films, and one month later they formed a copartnership with Edison called the Edison Vitagraph Company. By the end of 1897 Blackton and Smith had formed a new company that made advertising films for various New York manufacturers. The two partners began producing films for themselves in 1898.

There is controversy over whether Blackton and Smith ever set foot in Cuba, let alone made films of the conflict there. Smith claimed that he and his partner made the trip to Cuba on the same ship as Teddy Roosevelt and that footage was taken near the famous Battle of San Juan Hill. A history of the Vitagraph Company that was serialized in the *Motion Picture News* magazine in 1925 retells Smith's story, adding that Blackton and Smith's desire to go to Cuba was fueled by Hearst's journalism. According to the serialization, when word reached the partners that Hearst planned to cover the war personally, Blackton used his influence with "his many newspaper friends," and the cameramen boarded the *Buccaneer* for Cuba. An article in the George Eastman house journal *Image* repeats the story in a condensed version and even reproduces frames from what is alleged to be the film they took titled *Fighting with Our Boys in Cuba*. No copyright has been located for a film with this title, and recent film historians dispute Smith's claim of taking films in Cuba. Author Anthony Slide has written of an interview with Blackton's daughter in which she maintains that her father and Smith never went to Cuba. Slide also interviewed Smith's widow, but he did not ask her about her husband's claims.

Some of the suspicion about Smith and his Cuba story can be traced to a fake film he made with Blackton that has become a legend of film history. As the story goes, Smith and Blackton wanted to make a film that would rouse the patriotic fervor of the public. Because they never got to Cuba, as most historians believe, or because the film they shot in Cuba was dull, as Smith and others claim, the Vitagraph duo staged a battle scene in their office building at 140 Nassau Street, in Manhattan. First, they turned a table upside down and filled it with a few inches of water. A painted background, puffs of cigar smoke, and a few paper-cutout boats dabbed with gunpowder were brought in to complete the illusion: the Battle of Santiago Bay was filmed. Although this film demonstrated Blackton and Smith's capacity for fakery, it should be noted that they acknowledged their hoax before they were discovered. They never renounced their story about going to Cuba to make films.

Film historian Charles Musser has been able to account for Smith and Blackton's whereabouts during the summer of 1898, but for little more than a week. Mostly in New York and sometimes in Massachusetts, the Vitagraph partners could conceivably have traveled to Cuba and returned between late June and early July. This is a significant week for them to be missing: the Battle of San Juan Hill took place on July 1, and Hearst was in Cuba during this time. A Spanish-American War veteran's memoir—never quoted in this context—provides further corroboration of the Vitagraph cameramen's story. Just as the most famous battle of the war was about to begin, army private Charles Johnson Post recalled seeing a man atop a horse whom he recognized as Hearst. Several others recognized Hearst as well, and a chorus of "Hey Willie! Hey Willie!" broke out among the soldiers. According to Post, Hearst remained "always poker-faced, he never cracked a smile." It was Post's impression that Hearst seemed unsure whether the men were greeting or mocking him. Post noticed Hearst was wearing a "scarlet-banded hat" as he rode alongside reporter James Creelman and followed the troops into battle. Shortly after the *Journal* editor and reporter headed down a trail and passed from view, Post saw three other civilians headed in the same direction. "One of them," he wrote "was J. Stuart Blackton of the Vitagraph Moving Picture Company, who was going to make a real picture of a real battle. His two men carried a black box about one-half the size of a steamer trunk. How far they got, I don't know, but in one minute they came out again—Mr. Blackton was very wise to come out immediately; had he stayed in, his black-box camera would have become a sieve."

A PASSION MOTION PICTURE PLAY

With perfect theatrical timing—just as the Fourth of July approached—the long anticipated war in Cuba came rapidly to a close. The battle for the San Juan Heights—or the Battle of San Juan Hill, as it came to be known—began at 6:30 A.M. on the morning of July 1. Fighting paused for about an hour between 10 and 11 A.M. and then resumed. At 3:45 P.M. the Americans occupied El Caney, and the firing stopped. On July 3 the Spanish fleet of six warships, which was attempting to flee Santiago harbor, was encircled by the U.S. fleet under Commodore W. S. Schley's command. Before the day was over, the war in Cuba was essentially over.

The Hearst party spent a couple of days visiting smoldering battleships and taking still photographs at the harbor. Photographer Hemment took a memorable profile shot of Hearst as he was snapping away taking his own pictures. The *Sylvia*'s darkroom would be in full use traveling back to Siboney and points north. Hemment's small team found themselves in a semicomic struggle to keep their developing plates from flying out of their chemical trays as they plowed through rough waters. In Port Antonio Hearst and Hemment's photograph prints were put onboard a steamer for faster delivery to the *Journal* office in New York. Victory for the United States, for the Cubans, and for the war's insurgents at home and abroad had come fast. It was a splendid little war, they would later say. Hearst was clearly euphoric, but what lasting effect the war had on him can only be surmised. Many years later, he spoke of it as the great adventure of his youth (he was actually thirty-five years old in 1898). Shortly after the war, however, in a letter written to his mother, he speaks of personal failure and strayed opportunities. He stands convinced that he had "brought on the war," but unlike Teddy Roosevelt he was never rewarded for his efforts. He wallows in self-pity and exhibits self-loathing. His mood is depressed, with all of the bluster gone from his words.

Physical suffering came to those who had passionately carried Hearst's banner of modern war and modern communications. At least two *Journal* reporters, Edward Marshall and James Creelman, were wounded by gunshot during the conflict, but both survived. When the *Sylvia* returned to Siboney, Creelman was carried to a cabin across a narrow hallway from Billy Bitzer. The Biograph cameraman was in a sickbed himself, feeling the symptoms of what would later be diagnosed as typhoid malaria, one of the potentially more deadly aftereffects of a tropical war. Bitzer later recalled being in a twilight state as the yacht departed for New York City on July 15. Concerned about the contagious nature of his illness, Hearst and the crew kept their distance from Bitzer, who only occasionally ventured on deck for fresh air. The only sounds he remembered hearing were the laughter of the carefree Willson sisters and the clacking of their high heels against the wooden decks as they raced back and forth. On July 17 the *Sylvia* landed in Baltimore. Fearing that Bitzer's condition might cause the group to be quarantined, Hearst ordered the cameraman to disembark. Leaving his camera equipment onboard, Bitzer made his way to a railroad station for a journey to Hoboken, where he caught a ferry for the final leg of his trip to New York City. He was gravely ill by the time he reached the city and was lucky to find the Post-Graduate Hospital within walking distance. He collapsed on the steps of the hospital and remained ill for several months.

Cameraman William Paley's health while in Cuba and after his return was similar to Bitzer's. Correspondent and fellow *Anita* passenger Edwin Emerson remembered Paley—"the Vitascope man," as he called him—as being constantly nauseated during the trip. Paley was "spouting like a whale," and the *Anita* crew nicknamed him "grampus" after the mammal. Paley's ill-ness—probably yellow fever—caused the cameraman to take an early leave from filming in the war zone. Before his voyage home, however, he mustered enough strength to convince the *Anita*'s captain to make a side trip to St. Thomas so that he could purchase a supply of cheap liquor, which presum-ably he added to the Hearst expense account.

Paley left for New York on May 16 but apparently returned to Cuba in June or early July. On July 14 a reporter spotted the cameraman departing from Cuba on the *Seneca*, a hospital ship. While Paley would ultimately regain his health, on this return trip to New York, the fever came back and nearly killed him.

While Paley and Hearst were still in Cuba, the *Journal* presented Paley's early 1898 film hit *The Passion Play* as a *Maine* Monument Committee fund-raiser. For one week beginning in late June, the film was shown three times a day on a twenty-five-by-thirty-five-foot screen on the fourth floor of the Siegel-Cooper Company department store, which was located on Ladies Mile, on Sixth Avenue, between Eighteenth and Nine-teenth streets. The film about the death of Christ was screened at a time when thoughts of death and dying were on the minds of many Ameri-cans. A *Journal* article that gave a synopsis of all its twenty-three scenes predicted the Paley film would "do a great deal toward making the peo-ple realize and comprehend some of the great mysteries connected with the life and death of the Redeemer." Screening a film at Siegel-Cooper's—dubbed "The Big Store"—was somewhat unusual but entirely fitting. The department store's opening in 1896 was covered like a the-atrical event. Some 150,000 people arrived for the occasion, and the Byron Company, the theater photographers, photographed the landmark building. The seven-story store, which offered tearooms, music concerts, and cooling water fountains along with clothing, furniture, and even .38-caliber revolvers for young boys and girls, became an overnight sensation: it was a recreation center for the masses. Siegel-Cooper's entertainment concept gelled perfectly with Hearst journalism, which moved quickly to sign the store on as a major advertiser.

Screening a dramatic, "uplifting" film at The Big Store acknowledged that modern methods of entertainment, education, and advertising were inter-twined. A *Journal* advertisement for Hearst's fund-raiser announced, "The famous 'Passion Play of Oberammergau' is reproduced life size and so per-fectly that every one who sees it will have enjoyed a performance just as fine as those who traveled thousands of miles to Oberammergau to see it. The admission will be but 10 cents, but all the net proceeds will go to the *Maine*

Monument Fund." Another *Journal* ad that promoted the department store
and included a promotion of *The Passion Play* was modeled on a vaudeville
bill: "These happenings are varied—no two days are ever alike, so we are
perfectly safe in saying that at any time of the day or season there is bound
to be—somewhere in this Big Store—something which will prove interesting and profitable to you. Below we give a programme of the events now
transpiring, just as they do at the theatre."

Reporter Sidney Tovey, who had been entrusted to send dispatches
from the *Buccaneer*, returned home from his Cuban war tour of duty in the
middle of August 1898. The Hearst favorite did not fare nearly as well as
cameramen Bitzer and Paley. Shortly after returning to New York, the
would-be actor and would-be journalist developed a fever from typhoid
malaria. Within days he was taken to New York Hospital, but his condition
rapidly declined. During the night of August 26, Tovey died. His prominent obituary in Hearst's paper included a photograph of the twenty-six-
year-old taken aboard the *Buccaneer*. The *Journal* story closed with a touching note: the young Tovey had recently been engaged to be married. When
doctors at New York Hospital gave up hope of saving Tovey's life, they
called for Hearst. In what must have been a surprising gesture to those
who imagined him as a cold and ruthless warmonger, Hearst came to the
hospital to stay by Tovey's bedside. If Hearst felt any guilt in bringing
about a war that had brought such grief, it was never mentioned. The *Journal* explained the reporter's death as "war's sacrifice." Tovey's body was
taken to 76 West Twelfth Street for a funeral wake. The house was not
Tovey's but a three-story brownstone rented by George Willson for his
wife and daughters. One of those daughters, Anita, was apparently the girl
Tovey was engaged to marry, for in her moment of sorrow, she took his
last name as her own.

On October 26, 1899, the *Evening Journal* published an editorial said to
have been inspired by a letter written to Hearst by the newspaper's newest
recruit, a cartoon artist named Frederick Opper. The artist, it seems, had gotten his boss's attention not only by drawing the humorous Happy Hooligan
and Alphonse and Gaston but by making thoughtful observations about
human nature. Opper's letter to Hearst was about remembering and moving on. It was only a year after the Spanish-American War, and the war cry
"Remember the *Maine*" and the novel news films about the conflict were
still fresh in many minds. The *Journal* editorial quoted Opper: "If every generation is to keep on remembering things for the purpose of vengeance,
what progress can be made toward a state of universal peace or anything
approaching it. It seems to me that what the world needs is less 'remember-

ing' and more forgetting." The editorialist, who may have been Hearst or at the least reflected Hearst's sentiments, thought Opper's philosophy was "interesting" but believed there was an intrinsic value to recording the past, regardless of motives. "The whole strength of man to-day," the editorialist wrote, "lies in his memory—even 'remembering' in the sense of vengeance is sometimes necessary, although perhaps morally deplorable."

Medium for a New Century

1900–1907

DIVERSIONS

On November 1, 1899, Hearst departed for a long trip abroad, accompanied by the Willson sisters and their parents. Hearst and his party spent the month of November in London, Paris, and seaside villages in Italy. For most of the remaining months of the trip—from December until early April 1900—Hearst took a slow cruise up the Nile River, making stops in Cairo and Luxor. The trip generated the type of gossip that would become a hallmark of Hearst's life. Some said that he went abroad to live in a harem and dropped out of sight because he suffered from venereal disease. The rumors recalled earlier accusations, such as those of a U.S. congressman who claimed that that Hearst traveled on the Nile to restore his health "from loathsome disease contracted only by contagion in the haunts of vice." The only clues to the state of Hearst's health during his travels in late 1899 and early 1900 are in the letters he sent back home to his mother in which he made references to a stomach ailment and a nonspecific "nervousness."

While Hearst and his future in-laws were abroad, changes were made to the adjoining Dewey Theater and Willson's resort just below Fourteenth Street. On or close to October 24, 1899, when a new building code affecting theater construction was adopted, certain major alterations were made on "Big" Tim Sullivan's properties. In court records related to a later use of the properties, transcripts contain no specific documentation that the Willson resort was a brothel; they only refer to a past "use of that Thirteenth Street building for certain purposes" in connection with the Dewey Theater. They do indicate, however, that Sullivan (acting without a permit) had had the walls separating the Dewey and the resort torn down. The two building structures were "brought into and made part of the said theatre." According to sworn testimony, around the same time key documents related to the Dewey Theater and the Willson property were surreptitiously removed from the New York City Building Department.

Also while Hearst was out of the country, the Mazet Committee of New York State's Republican-controlled legislature held an investigation charged with uncovering municipal waste and inefficiency. It wasn't long before issues related to Tammany Hall dominated the proceedings, producing in the end the most comprehensive account to that point of the synergistic relationship between political power and the cheap amusements of the city. But even though the corruption exposé was a huge story for the metropolitan area, involving politicians, the police, brothel owners, and saloon and theater owners, Hearst's New York papers paid little attention to it, except to ridicule it. From April until November they presented the investigation as a hapless comedy. News articles about the chairman and his counsel implied they were engaged in a stunt, and cartoons accompanying these pieces caricatured Mazet as a buffoon with a long, snooping nose that ran all the way from Albany to the rear entrances of Manhattan's neighborhood saloons.

On November 1, the first day of Tammany boss Richard Croker's second round of testimony (he had first testified in April 1899) and the same day that Hearst and the Willsons boarded the Pacific and Orient steamer for Europe, the tone and intensity of the Hearst coverage changed. Using huge headlines, the *Journal* presented the Tammany boss as a strong and confident leader. The headline of the November 2 issue of the *New York Journal* screamed, "Croker Faces Mazet!" On the following day, the *Evening Journal*'s banner headline declared "Croker Tells, Under Oath, Mazet He Lies!" On the same page a caption over a drawing of the Tammany boss announced "Croker Challenges Mazet." A few weeks later a favorable *Evening Journal* editorial was titled, "Mr. Croker, the City Looks to You." In fact, Croker was more bumbling than defiant. During one particularly long and damaging stretch of questions and answers from a lawyer for the committee, he was asked about kickbacks and whether they were filling his pockets. Croker barked back, "All the time; the same as you."

The Mazet Committee wound up its investigation while Hearst was abroad. There is no evidence that Hearst thought he might have become involved in any charges or countercharges, although he may have been concerned about the Willsons. It wasn't until December 1900 that the Mazet Committee issued a final report, and when it was published—by coincidence or convenience—Hearst and the Willsons were off again on another European and Egyptian holiday. If Hearst was really worried, he needn't have been: Mazet provided the public with five juicy volumes on the inner workings of Tammany and vice, but the shakeup was far short of a fatal blow to either interconnected industry.

During his travels in late 1899 and early 1900, Hearst's image underwent a major transformation. The playboy who came from the West to shake up the eastern establishment was retired or, like one of his favorite stereopticon views, dissolved into a man who could be considered morally fit for public office. Some said they first noticed a change in his dress. The dandy look was gone, his customary loud, plaid suits and brilliant neckties replaced by dark, drab colors. But a more dramatic change was occurring in his newspapers, which were suddenly pointing the finger at the darker side of mass entertainment.

In October 1899 Hearst hired Ella Wheeler Wilcox, a poet who lived in grand style at the Hoffman House, to write three consecutive page-one theater reviews exposing theater immorality. The plays Wilcox chose to write about were lowbrow comedies, entertainment Hearst was known to enjoy personally. Wilcox showed her distaste for the material in the plays, but her reviews were not nearly as negative as advertised. A bold headline over both pieces declares: "Worst Plays on New York's Immoral Stage Justly Chastised." The reviews are punctuated with subheadings such as "Devoid of Sense or Morality" and "Lowers Our Ideals of Humanity." The subheadings are actual quotes from the text; that Wilcox also found elements in the plays to praise one would never know from a quick glance at the page. Wilcox took a swipe at something rather close to Hearst when discussing a French actress named Fougère who was appearing in one of the plays: "We must not take it for granted that the better classes of men and women in Paris go to hear and applaud such 'actresses' as Fougère. They do not, any more than the best class of New Yorkers go to the Dewey Theatre or the Bowery Playhouses." The inclusion of this unexpected judgment on the Dewey may have simply missed the editor's eye, but more likely it is an example of the degree of immunity figures like Hearst (and Sullivan) could have.

By early 1900 the Hearst press had widened its stage crusade. Cabinet officials, congressmen, clergymen, and out-of-state police officials were called on for comments that might convince law officers in New York that the play *Sapho* should be closed. The drama, about a French prostitute who posed for a sculpture of the lesbian poet Sappho, was repeatedly attacked as "vulgar" and "a menace to morality." In February, largely because of Hearst's efforts, the play was closed, and its star performer, Olga Nethersole, was put on trial. On April 4 the *Evening Journal* announced in bold headlines "Sudden Close of the 'Sapho' Case." The next day, Nethersole was acquitted of committing "a public nuisance," and soon afterward the play reopened. Despite this setback to his cause, Hearst continued to warn other plays and playwrights that "we expect the police to forbid on stage what they would forbid in streets and low resorts."

The duplicity of Hearst's public stands for morality resulted in some curious editorials. In one of his many attacks against the "indecency" of the stage, he began by absolving theater managers of responsibility because they "feel that they need and must have the money to be got by selling indecency at $2 a peep." The Hearst paper declared: "The public alone is responsible; the public has grown evil-minded. The public has created the demand, which the panders of the stage willingly supply." Hearst even threatened to become a roving moral vigilante if necessary. "I may decide to print the names of individuals of any standing who attend indecent performances and to discourage by very energetic critical measures actors who lend themselves to the debauchery of the public mind."

Ever since the movies began, a few films, such as *The May Irwin Kiss* of 1896 and the Corbett-Fitzsimmons fight film of 1897, had raised protests from various quarters. The criticisms had focused on individual films, but the attacks were fleeting and did not receive extensive press notice. In October 1899 Hearst launched his own "picture crusade." He targeted no specific film but rather a class of films that were being shown in motion picture slot machines located at various sites in New York City. Hearst enlisted the support of civic leaders, the clergy, and the police, and, as expected, his crusade was highly publicized. It appears to have been the first concerted effort to censor film.

Hearst was called to action by the Reverend John Josiah Munro, the chaplain of the Tombs Prison, on Centre Street in lower Manhattan. Munro provided one of Hearst's reporters with a list of objectionable picture shows on the Lower East Side and on 125th Street. Hearst was quick to grab Munro's list and run with it. Munro's "dives," as Hearst later called them, were penny slot machine parlors that were showing "indecent" films. Within hours of conducting a cursory investigation of its own, Hearst's newspaper hit the streets, calling for the immediate closing of eighteen resorts on the Bowery, Broadway, Eighth Avenue, and at other Manhattan locations. One downtown arcade that the Hearst press specifically sited was The Fair, located next door to the Dewey Theater on a strip of Fourteenth Street that within a few years would be one of the world's most heavily concentrated areas of motion picture theaters. Throughout the reporting and publicizing of its budding crusade, the *Journal* made no mention of individual film titles, nor did it make very specific objections. There is only a suggestion that the films contained female nudity or at least women in various stages of undress.

Reverend Munro's precise motivation in providing Hearst with ammunition is unknown. He may have been acting independently, but his ministry at the Tombs would have made him close to the police and Tammany Hall, possibly skewing his selection of "objectionable" sites. By its own account, the *Evening Journal* claimed that it "worked hand in hand" with Chief of Police William Devery (a man notoriously indifferent to vice and someone Hearst himself would later accuse of bribery). According to the *Journal*, Chief Devery ordered scores of detectives to accompany Hearst reporters combing suspected sites. To legitimize its effort further, Hearst papers published supportive statements from officials of the Salvation Army and the Young Men's Christian Association. Manhattan's superintendent of schools, John Jasper, came forward to say that he was happy to do what he could to aid Hearst's crusade, and the Hearst press repeated his charge that pictures were "causing the moral contamination of boys and girls in all parts of the city."

Perhaps Hearst's most influential ally was the Women's Christian Temperance Union, a rapidly growing reform organization in the late 1890s that worked for a number of goals in addition to prohibition. The WCTU had previously spoken out against the Corbett-Fitzsimmons film, and as early as 1895 it functioned as a lobby group with its own department of legislation headquartered in Washington, D.C. Hearst's combine of educators, Christian reformers, and law enforcement agents, propelled by a sensationalist press, was a precursor to organized film censorship as it evolved in the twentieth century.

Only four days after the start of the "picture crusade," the Hearst press declared its mission accomplished and congratulated itself for its "great work for morality." It claimed total victory in eliminating every offensive film being shown in New York. Either the extent of "immorality" or Hearst's claim of victory was greatly exaggerated, since in the end the police were said to have made only a handful of arrests. Two men arraigned in the Essex Market Police Court, Joseph Belder and Jacob Katz, were not even movie men but cigar store owners who had slot machines in their shops. In total, six arcades were closed, and motion picture machines from other locations were also confiscated. As the Hearst press virtually ignored the issue once the crusade was over, it is unknown how many of these arcades were permanently closed. The *Evening Journal* noted that many suspected arcades had avoided prosecution by removing any offensive films they rented or simply keeping them out of sight of investigators.

One of the side issues that Hearst raised in his campaign for morality was that moving-picture resorts acted—figuratively and literally—as anterooms to other vices. The *Evening Journal* reported: "The evil results of the immoral pictures shown in the slot machines have not been at all overestimated. Many of the pictures were incentives to immorality. Through their agency debauchery was dressed in tempting spangles and glitter." Hearst also highlighted the fact that a number of slot machine arcades had back rooms where roulette wheels and possibly other games of chance took place. Hearst's focus on gambling as a vice became a staple of the Hearst press for decades. In 1900 an *Evening Journal* editorial cautioned citizens not to confuse morality and legality. "Laws may make gambling legal, as they do in some countries," the paper declared "but they can never make it moral."

At first glance, Hearst's censorship efforts of 1899 seem to be inconsistent with his documented appreciation of film and other lowbrow entertainment. Only weeks before the crusade began, for instance, the *Evening Journal* published an article publicizing a film made in Asbury Park, New Jersey, of one of boxer Jim Jeffries's training session. Alongside the boxing article were two photographs of Jeffries's upcoming opponent Tom Sharkey registering a punch, the pictures taken in sequence to resemble film frames. On November 11 the *Evening Journal*'s sports page gave further publicity to the film medium when it published three enlarged frames from Biograph's film of the Jeffries-Sharkey fight. Clearly, Hearst was not interested in crushing the burgeoning structure that was the moving-picture industry; he was more intent on creating a good name for himself and his drive for moral respectability. Just as his November picture crusade made no attacks on specific filmmakers or films, it was also careful not to offend unduly the leaders of the industry or the big-time theater managers. Some of them were his friends, and all of them were valuable or potentially valuable advertisers. The slot machine crusade seems to have been an example of Hearst's clever diversionary tactics. By intimidating the vulnerable upstarts and separating them from the mainstream film business, Hearst was able to prove himself a formidable ally of the film establishment.

The first clear indication that Hearst had an ulterior motive for his new strident moral stands came in 1900. Shortly after he returned from his overseas trip, Hearst made a deal to set up a newspaper in Chicago as a political organ in exchange for the presidency of the National Association of Democratic

Clubs. This political position was highly visible, and Hearst used it to build a network that would facilitate his ambition to hold office. Not incidentally, it also paved the way for a truly national communications empire. Phoebe Hearst called her son's idea of creating a third newspaper an "expensive scheme." In May 1900 she protested that his requests for money were more like demands, but as she almost always did, she later gave in. Hearst certainly needed loads of cash and energy to build a paper on such short notice. Unlike his *San Francisco Examiner* and *New York Journal*, which had preexisting building structures and certain staff members already in place when Hearst took ownership, the *Chicago American* had to be built from scratch.

Although Hearst would never spend as much time in Chicago as he did in New York or San Francisco (or later in Los Angeles, for that matter), he was there for days at a time during the newspaper's early months. A building for the *American* was found on a dark and drab stretch of Madison Street. Hearst's paper made little positive impact on the neighborhood, but it did give it life; now the sound of mammoth futuristic printing presses that had arrived via luxurious Pullman cars could be heard behind the howling newsboys, and electric lights in rows of office windows lit up the night.

The *Chicago American*—especially in the period from its inception until 1907—became the most sensational of all Hearst papers. Geography was the reason Hearst focused on crime stories, according to Moses Koenigsberg, who started on the *Chicago American* in 1901, left for two years, and later returned. "The city was a hub of highways and secret trails leading from the penitentiaries of five adjacent states. It was the center of operations of ex-convicts numerous enough to crowd the largest penal institution extant. Homicide was commercial." A new era in Chicago journalism was dawning—a fast-talking, wacky, and sometimes violent time that would later be immortalized in a slew of theater potboilers and Hollywood screwball comedies.

Historians who have studied Chicago newspapers point to the 1910s as a period of bloody warfare waged by henchmen working at the behest of Hearst and his rivals. Some newspapermen and bystanders were beaten and some killed, but because all sides in the rivalry suppressed news about their own misdeeds and firsthand accounts were scarce, a complete story of what happened may never be known. Circumstantial evidence suggests, however, that violence plagued the newspaper rivalries from the inception of Hearst's *American*. As early as 1900 Hearst told a reporter that his rivals had hired "an army of thugs" to prevent newspaper boys and news dealers from selling the *American*. He acknowledged that he had directed the *American* to fight back. "If the *American* was to be compelled to make a physical fight for its existence," he said, "why the only thing to be done was to put up the best possible battle, and abide by the result. All of the broad shouldered, big fisted men in Chicago had not been given employment by the opposition. There were a few others, and some of them were soon drawing pay from me. It was hardly fighting the devil with fire, but was meeting force with force."

The battles between Hearst's *Chicago American* and his rivals centered on circulation and advertising disputes (one fight was apparently touched off after the *American* won a prized contract to have its posters plastered over the city's ubiquitous trash cans). The clashes also had a political component, for Hearst's foes must have realized a quid pro quo was involved in the *American*'s creation. They were also aware of Hearst's rapid rise to power in New York City, in the face of the powerful Pulitzer and political forces there. They weren't eager for Hearst to establish another power base in their town.

Hearst's Chicago entrance paralleled his New York arrival, as he quickly made hay of the political and cultural system he found, a near duplicate of the one maintained by Tammany Hall. Chicago's newspaper battles resembled the street fights and wars of intimidation instigated by "Big" Tim Sullivan during election periods. Discussing the future of the *Chicago American* in 1900, Hearst predicted the violence would end and that his newspaper would succeed on its merits, no matter how many critics focused on his "ultra-yellow methods."

Hearst won his bet, and within six weeks the *Chicago American* was up and running. As the Democratic Party was about to nominate William Jennings Bryan for president for a second time, Hearst sent hundreds of copies of the *American* by rail to Kansas City to be distributed among delegates in the convention hall. Shortly before the election of 1900, Boss Croker urged Democrats "to congregate about the polling places on the evening of election day, count noses, and then, if the election returns for Bryan don't tally with their count, to go into the polling places and throw those fellows in charge of the returns into the street." But Hearst's best efforts and even Tammany's pressure couldn't win the election for Bryan, who nevertheless remained a crowd-pleasing public figure for many years to come.

Hearst's reward—leadership of the National Association of Democratic Clubs—gave him the opportunity to form a sort of party within a party. Max F. Ihmsen, one of Hearst's trusted Washington correspondents, was selected to beef up the association's membership and turn it into a publicity machine for his boss's political ambitions. Ihmsen conducted an extensive campaign that enrolled over one million new members and announced a convention to take place in Indianapolis in October 1900. An attack of stage fright caused Hearst to miss the opening of his own convention, but he reached out to the theater world and enlisted actor-turned-playwright Augustus Thomas to replace him as a key speaker. At the convention, Thomas announced that Hearst would match dollar for dollar any contribution that was made to the Bryan campaign.

Thomas was an apt choice to represent the theatrical Hearst. In 1900 he achieved considerable fame with his play *Arizona*, which along with his other plays of the period has been called a transitional work that bridged "marshmelodrama" and realism. Later, Thomas would become one of the first successful playwrights to enter the field of motion pictures. He directed a movie version of *Arizona* in 1913 and was both screenwriter and director of the film version of a novel by Richard Harding Davis, one of Hearst's correspondents during the Spanish-American War.

Torn from Today's Headlines, Cartoons, and Illustrations

New York Journal editor Arthur Brisbane and business manager Solomon Carvalho, whose New York Nassau Street office adjoined Hearst's, were sent to Chicago to do most of the organizing of the *Chicago American. Journal* cartoonist Homer Davenport was also sent. Davenport was extremely popular with the public, his name a household word. He was also popular in the Hearst organization—most of the time. Hearst enjoyed Davenport's biting artistry, especially those cartoons that attacked corporations and corruption. He paid the cartoonist well, but on occasion the two men clashed. They parted ways for a period after Hearst demanded that Davenport attack Teddy Roosevelt with more venom than the artist thought the politician deserved. Hearst's wishes were not easily denied. He had a driver take him to Davenport's home in Morris Plains, New Jersey, assuming that his unexpected and imposing presence on the artist's doorstep would be pressure enough to change Davenport's mind. The tactic usually worked for Hearst, but he apparently met his match in Davenport: the impulsive artist left the Hearst organization for a rival newspaper. Before he was lured back into the Hearst camp again, he made an extensive lecture tour in which he spiced up his performance by telling risqué anecdotes about Hearst's womanizing. The stories got back to Hearst, but he may have been immune to the cartoonist's biting satire by then. Davenport had started mimicking Hearst as far back as the Spanish-American War, when he drew a pen-and-ink drawing showing him in a loud plaid suit smiling a Cheshire cat smile and sitting cross-legged in a chair like an oversized kid. It was a relatively gentle ribbing, but in the right-hand corner of the cartoon Davenport inserted a toy boat interpretation of Hearst's famous wartime yacht, the *Buccaneer*. This particular sly comment on the childish nature of the publisher's war exploits must have offended some, if not Hearst himself: the image of the yacht was excised from all subsequent reproductions that have appeared in numerous books and periodicals.

In a development that must have enhanced his popularity, Davenport became the subject of two Biograph films in September 1900. Cameraman Arthur Marvin made the films in a New York studio soon after the artist returned from his work on the new *Chicago American*. In one film Davenport is seen drawing a caricature of Teddy Roosevelt. In the other he draws his trademark "dollar sign" cartoon of Senator Marcus A. Hanna, President McKinley's close adviser and financial backer. The Biograph films of Davenport were probably the earliest taken of a yellow journalism celebrity.

The turn of the century was the heyday for cartoonists such as Davenport, Frederick Opper, Windsor McCay, and Rudolph Dirks. Historian John Fell believes that the novel and imaginative use of color in these early cartoons was a key reason for their attraction. "Just as movement was the element which drew nickelodeon audiences to the feats of the Lumières, Edison, and Méliès, color helped to insure strip cartoons their 'readers.'" Hearst and the Biograph Company conceived of a novel approach to combining the magic of film and cartoons in the fall of 1903. Cartoon characters Alphonse and Gaston (Opper), the Katzenjammer Kids (Dirks), and Happy Hooligan (Opper) were among the dozen stars of short films shot by Biograph's principal cameramen Billy Bitzer and A. E. Weed. The cartoon films were transferred to small paper cards called "thumb books," which, bound by a rubber band or staple, gave the appearance of movement when flipped. Simultaneous with the release of these moving-picture thumb books, given away as premiums by the *New York Journal*, Hearst advertised the sale of "five funny forty-page—10 x 15 [inch]—picture books of wit, humor and satire" that featured the work of the *Journal*-Biograph cartoonists and others.

On October 24, 1900, the *Evening Journal* published an editorial simply entitled "Yellow Journalism" that fully embraced the term. The editorial, written by Brisbane, begins with what seems like an endorsement from God. Hearst's active approach—"the journalism that acts"—is likened to a passage from the Bible: "But be ye doers of the Word, and not hearers only." In his trademark punchy prose, Brisbane presents a list of yellow journalism's accomplishments. His prime examples are Hearst's "freeing" of Evangelina Cisneros and the U.S. intervention for Cuban independence. Domestically, Brisbane offers two more recent examples: the 1899 kidnapping and safe return of baby Marion Clark and the relief efforts for the victims of the Galveston flood of 1900. Like Cisneros and Cuba, the Clark and Galveston stories are noteworthy for their cinematic components.

Returning from his stint setting up the *Chicago American*, Brisbane settled back into his role as Hearst's chief editorial writer. At the same time, he actively sought ways to increase readership and advertising revenues. One of his innovations was establishing the back page of the Hearst paper as an especially dense page of entertainment and information, crammed with editorials, cartoons, and other humorous fables and philosophical jottings. The result was that a reader might spend a considerable time reading this one page. And as the reader walked down the street or waited for a trolley, he or she became an unpaid advertiser, forced to hold outward for others to see the front page with its Hearst masthead and its bold headlines.

Brisbane's editorials leaned to variations on themes related to philosophy, literature, and science. The subject of babies—especially their care and their brain capacity—interested Brisbane. It offered him an opportunity to espouse a variety of half-baked theories on love and evolution. Coupled with regularly featured snapshots of baby beauty contest winners and other pseudonews stories, Brisbane's baby writings were appeals to female readers, appeals to sentimentality, and ultimately appeals for circulation. Baby images and stories became a regular feature of the Hearst press, culminating in its media and cinematic exploitation of Canada's Dionne quintuplets in 1936. Film historian Charles Musser has written that filmmaker Edwin Porter of the Edison Manufacturing Company found the Hearst papers' baby obsession of the turn of the century so appealing it influenced the making of two of his films, *Heavenly Twins at Lunch* and *Heavenly Twins at Odds*, both released in 1903.

On the afternoon of May 21, 1899, an eighteen-month-old girl named Marion Clark vanished. The nurse who had taken the child in her carriage for a stroll in Central Park was also gone. Within hours the baby's parents received a ransom note: "If the matter is kept out of the hands of the police and newspapers you will get your baby back safe and sound." Hearst did more than simply ignore the kidnapper's request for discretion; he made the crime a huge story in his newspaper. He took it on himself to teach the kidnappers that "they had something more than the police to deal with."

The *Journal* turned itself into a wanted poster, with offers of a $2,000 reward and the baby's picture churned out in numerous extra editions. Hearst also published drawings lined up in strips (like filmstrips) depicting what he believed were the series of events leading up to the crime—or perhaps what he believed to be the most visual possibilities. The *Journal* plas-

tered every available fence, every elevated train station, and scores of building exteriors with photographs of the missing child. Theaters were encouraged to screen slides of the baby between vaudeville acts and films. From the
day baby Marion disappeared until she was safely recovered about a week
later (the *Journal* chartered a train to rush the child home), the story was so
sensationalized that the *New York World* suggested Hearst had stolen the child
himself simply to create a news story.

Within twenty-four hours of baby Marion Clark's return to her parents,
Keith's Theater was screening a Biograph film of the child "sitting on her
mother's lap, playing with her doll . . . and kissing her hand to the audience."
At the same time, the *Journal* presented its own "interesting" photographic
image—remarkably similar to the film—the baby "posed prettily" sitting in
a chair and fondling a doll. Another section of the same day's *Journal* showed
a strip of drawings of the happy child held by her mother, playing with her
toys, and viewed from behind waving to the crowds outside her window.
The *Journal* photograph, the "filmstrip" drawings of baby Marion, and the
Biograph film: each was an extensions of the other.

The Hearst press held up the coverage of baby Clark as an illustration of
the positive uses of yellow journalism, but it was more than this. As a writer
in *Leslie's Weekly* magazine noted, until the Clark story the primary motivation behind the taking of nonfiction film or any footage shot of real events
was its usefulness as a record for posterity; its newsworthiness was not so
apparent. Clark proved that film subjects could be drawn from everyday life
and be as varied as the subjects appearing in the popular press. The Clark
story (which was by and large Hearst's story of the Clark story) had shown
how the mediums of yellow journalism and film could work "hand in
hand," augmenting each other in a rivalry for the same "contemporaneous
interest."

While the safe return of baby Marion Clark gave the *Journal* a chance to
gloat over its power to outwit the police, *Leslie's* magazine saw the Clark
story as a reason to rejoice in film's ability to provide a release of emotions.
Film, it said, had given the Clark parents an opportunity to acknowledge the
public's outpouring of emotion. It gave the public a chance "to behold the
object of their solicitude." The journalism–film pairing had clearly demonstrated that film, like yellow journalism, could be in the present tense: active
and sensational. But even beyond this it had the power to be interactive, or,
in the words that Brisbane used to describe Hearst journalism, to act as "a
safety valve for public indignation." A Frederick Burr Opper cartoon published in the *Journal* in 1901 predicts how interactive film might one day be
used. Entitled "Peeps Ahead—As It May Be in 1950," the cartoon shows a

shocked husband viewing a large screen image of his wife on a couch embracing another man. As a sleazy-looking man in futuristic costume works the contraption, a sign above the screen reads: "Telepathic Biographic Camera, See What Your Distant Friends Are Doing For 25 cents."

On the night of August 30, 1900, a huge crowd that included the kings of political power and the entertainment business gathered at Madison Square Garden. From the theater world were Abe Erlanger, Tony Pastor, and Joe Weber (of Weber and Fields). Tammany stars Richard Croker, "Big" Tim Sullivan, and "Honest" Tom Kelly were in attendance as was Martin Engel, the district leader who owned numerous houses of prostitution, including one on East Sixth Street that doubled as a meeting place for the Democratic Club. The stage was set for a boxing match between James J. Corbett and Charles "Kid" McCoy. It was a festive night, something like Mardi Gras, for the repeal of the Horton law was about to put a ban on all prizefights in the city. No one really believed they were seeing their last fight. Tim Sullivan, who was well connected to fighting establishments in Brooklyn, told a reporter that night, "This may be a wake, but I've an idea there will be many more like it—and not far from New York. Boxing bouts never hurt anybody." In the stands at the Garden were cameramen from the Lubin Company who were hoping to record the main event for film. As the lights dimmed, however, the Lubin crew realized that the available lighting was inadequate. Forced to abandon their plans to film the bout, Lubin opted for the next best thing; representatives of Hearst's *Journal* were approached to facilitate the filming of a staged fight. Within a few days Corbett and McCoy traveled to Lubin's Philadelphia studio to make what the *Journal* announced on September 4 were "the only authorized pictures in existence."

Hearst was in Chicago on September 9 when newspapers around the country first learned that a deadly hurricane and flood had hit Galveston, Texas, the night before. By September 10 he was already organizing a relief effort from the offices of the *Chicago American*. A Texas doctor named William L. Crosthwait happened to be visiting the newspaper offices at the time, and he found himself suddenly drafted by the publisher to head a medical team that included five other doctors and eleven nurses. After conferring with Crosthwait on the best train routes to Texas, Hearst took to the telephone, ordering the fastest train from the Santa Fe railroad company. He put a newspaper manager in charge of the relief train and gave him a check reportedly in the amount of $50,000 for expenses. Meanwhile, never one to overlook every conceivable angle, Hearst called New York to see if Biograph executive Wallace McCutcheon Sr. had a movie cameraman who could be sent to Galveston from New York. McCutcheon assigned Billy Bitzer, who had long ago recovered from his Cuban War adventure with Hearst. After a brief meeting with Hearst's relief team at the *Journal* office, Bitzer packed a relatively lightweight deluxe Biograph camera onboard the train for the trip south. The *Journal* train arrived in Texas City on September 13, and Bitzer shot some footage there on the fourteenth and fifteenth. On September 25 Bitzer took films in the Galveston area, including *NY Journal's Relief Corps at High School*, *Galveston Men at Work on Debris*, and *Galveston Men Going to Commissary*.

While Bitzer and the *Journal* relief team were on the nightmarish scene—it is estimated that eight thousand died and damages totaled $30 million—Hearst was back in New York putting on vaudeville shows for surviving victims. On September 13 Hearst presented fund-raisers at no less than six Manhattan theaters. A week later another event was held at Tony Pastor's, and a show at the New York Theater on September 21 featured actress Anna Held, boxer "Bob" Fitzsimmons, and cartoonist Homer Davenport. In what was becoming a regular method of publicity and subtle coercion, the names of charity contributors and their donation amounts were prominently printed in the Hearst papers. Hearst was always at the top of these charity lists, his name in the boldest type and his pledge the largest. It is doubtful that he followed through on all his public pledges, however. Once, when an accountant working at his *Chicago American* newspaper wondered why Hearst's check was not forthcoming, she was told to consider the amount as an advertising expense. "You see, Mr. Hearst is giving a lot of valuable space in his paper to this matter, and so he should not be expected to give money, too."

On the morning of September 28 the *Journal* train and Bitzer returned to New York. Bitzer had not been the only cameraman in Galveston—Edison, Lubin, and Vitagraph had sent representatives—but, according to Bitzer, Hearst was the first to consider exploiting the event.

In the early years of the twentieth century a number of films appear to have been made while their directors and cameramen were peering over the shoulders of Hearst readers. One director in particular, Edwin Porter of the Edison Company, looked inside the *New York Journal* to find out what might interest his audiences. In early February 1901 a *Journal* photograph of a saloon wrecked by a temperance zealot inspired the film set, and cartoons in the same paper suggested the film plot for Porter's *Kansas Saloon Smashers* (1901). A cartoon that appeared in the *Journal* on February 4, 1901, lampooning Teddy Roosevelt—the vice president–elect is seen traveling with

A stagestruck Hearst (*right*) in a student production at Harvard University circa 1884.

Tammany Hall on 14th Street, the Rialto where politics, entertainment, and vice intermingled.

Hannah Willson, eventually Hearst's mother-in-law, ran a popular and politically connected "resort" on 13th Street. (Bancroft Library, University of California, Berkeley)

Mrs. Willson with her two daughters Millicent and Anita. (Bancroft Library)

Hearst's film of the 1897 inauguration of William McKinley.

Biograph camera-
man Arthur Marvin
filming from Hearst's
yacht the *Anita* near
Cuba in 1898.
(Museum of the
City of New York)

PUCK

THE CLEANSING OF NEW YORK.
WHY NOT MAKE A CLEAN JOB OF IT WHILE WE 'RE AT IT?

Originally, yellow journalism was synonymous with prostitution and other vices (detail, *below*).

Hearst brought entertainment journalism to Los Angeles in 1903, several years before the moviemakers arrived. (Regional History Center)

To counteract attacks on his own morality, Hearst launches a crusade against small-time movie exhibitors in 1899.

JOURNAL'S SEARCHLIGHT CLOSES DIVES.

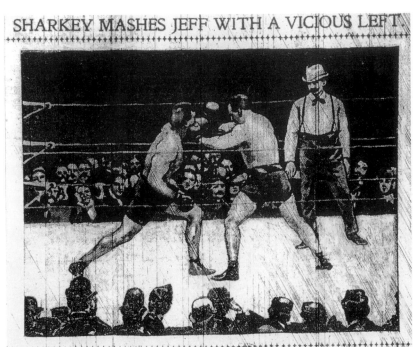

SHARKEY MASHES JEFF WITH A VICIOUS LEFT.

At the same time, Hearst boosts Biograph and other big-time film companies.

(Copyright, 1899, by the American Mutoscope and Biograph Company.)
The sailor was here making one of his mad rushes in the ninth round. Every two or three seconds there was the inevitable mix-up and clinch. Sharkey had rushed the big fellow into the open and, breaking

Hearst's cliff-hanger serial *The Perils of Pauline* (1914) became an instantly referenced movie icon.

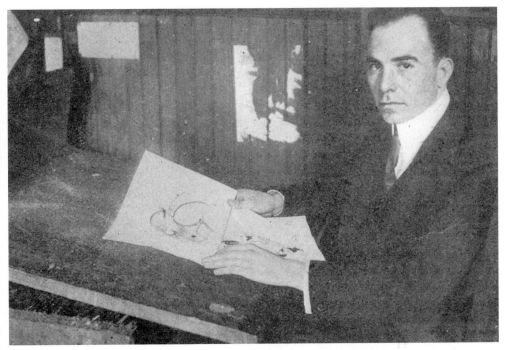

Future feature film director Gregory La Cava ran Hearst's animation studio in the late 1910s.

Hearst's International Newsreel is inaugurated with a film of Woodrow Wilson's inauguration in 1913.

Vol. II, No. 23—July 14th, 1915   Price 5 Cents

THE
Fatherland
A Weekly
(Title Reg. U. S. Pat. Off.)

WILLIAM RANDOLPH HEARST

HE LED THIS COUNTRY INTO ONE WAR—HE HAS HELPED TO KEEP IT OUT OF ANOTHER

THE BUSINESS OF THE TOOLS OF DEATH
By GEORGE SYLVESTER VIERECK
IN THIS ISSUE

★

Germany considered Hearst an ally during WWI, while the film unit of America's propaganda efforts was also under his control.

The volatile Ivan Abramson became Hearst's partner in the Graphic Film Company in 1917.

Hearst and his wife Millicent at San Simeon in the 1910s.

Marion Davies in Hearst's *Cinema Murder* (1919).

Hearst's Cosmopolitan film studio in Manhattan, formerly a Tammany casino. (Bison Archives)

An interior view of the Cosmopolitan studio. (Bison Archives)

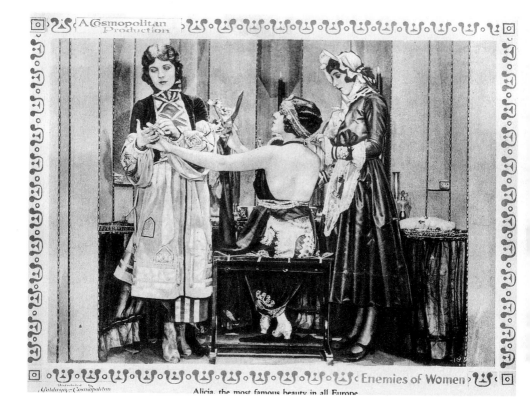

A lobby card for *Enemies of Women* (1923), starring Alma Rubens and Lionel Barrymore, shows set designer Joseph Urban's Wiener Werkstätte influence.

Cosmopolitan's *Yolanda* at Hearst's Cosmopolitan Theater in Columbus Circle in 1924. (Regional History Center, LA)

Hearst is prominent at a dinner welcoming movie czar Will Hays (*far left*) in 1922. Also on the dais (*left to right*) are Secretary of Labor John J. Davis and Mayor John Hylan. (Bancroft Library)

Hearst's yacht the *Oneida* was at the center of Hollywood's most enduring unsolved mystery after the death of director Thomas Ince in 1924. (Courtesy of Whitney Moore)

In 1925, Hearst and Millicent (*seated at center*) host a party in New York for Will Hays and guests, including a woman (*at far right*) believed to be actress Mae Murray. (Indiana State Library)

Marion Davies clowns with costars on the set of *Show People* (1928).

Hearst's studio liaison Ed Hatrick with the "MGM lion" after the formation of Metro-Goldwyn-Mayer in 1924. (Regional History Center)

Hollywood power-brokers (*left to right*) Joseph Schenck, Irving Thalberg, A. H. Giannini, Nicholas Schenck, Louis B. Mayer, and Hatrick. (Regional History Center)

The Urban-designed, Hearst-owned Ziegfeld Theater.
Hearst films often paid homage to the Follies. (Regional
History Center)

San Simeon's movie theater. (Regional History Center)

Expanding internationally, Hearst financed Germany's *Graf Zeppelin* flight of 1929 in exchange for the movie rights. (Regional History Center)

In 1927 he sent Moses Koenigsberg (*center, left*) to Rome for a meeting with Mussolini soon after a film exchange agreement had been signed with the dictator.

his own personal photographer as he hunts wild animals—"provided the storyboard" for Porter's *Terrible Teddy, the Grizzly King* (1901). In Porter's spin-off of Hearst's cartoon, the publicity-hungry Roosevelt takes aim at a common house cat as two men stand nearby, one wearing a sign saying "My Photographer" and the other, one saying "My Press Agent."

In 1902 the story of two handsome brothers, Jack and Ed Biddle, convicted of murder and then smuggled out of prison by the warden's wife, Katherine Soffel, was ripe for pictorial journalism and the cinema. A drawing on the front page of the *New York Journal*'s February 2 issue sparked director Porter's film *Capture of the Biddle Brothers* (in 1984, the story was told in the film *Mrs. Soffel*). A scene of Mrs. Soffel and the fugitives on a sleigh being attacked by a sheriff's posse—which a *Journal* artist had drawn "from a telegraphic description"—is nearly identical to one filmed by Porter. In 1902 violent scenes in films, such as the police attack in *The Capture of the Biddle Brothers*, did not generate criticism from Hearst. In fact, an editorial appearing in the *Journal* on February 26, 1902, seems to offer an ancillary enticement to moviegoers. The editorial, entitled "The Strange Fascination of Crime," makes the case for acceptance of crime news, saying that it is human nature to be interested in crime.

According to film historian Charles Musser, Hearst's "disparate array of mimetic techniques" in covering the Russo-Japanese War in the spring of 1904 was also mimicked by filmmakers. When the Edison Company produced news films of the war, for example, it incorporated a similar mix of real and staged footage. Hearst journalism continued to serve as a template for filmmakers in 1906 and 1907, as the public obsessed over the century's first great story of love and murder. The Hearst press swung into action the instant it learned that the famed architect Stanford White was killed by Harry Thaw in a jealous rage over White's past affair with Thaws's wife, Evelyn Nesbit. As details emerged the story of White, Thaw, and Nesbit offered a glimpse into the world of the Tenderloin among the rich and famous. Hearst's own proximity to this world might suggest a reason for him to stay clear from focusing on the story. The opposite held: he circled the story, part vulture and part carrier pigeon, clawing at the remains while he brought the news to the people. White's murder had no affect on Hearst's personal life, except for offering him the chance to bid successfully on a $3,000 dining-room ceiling that was put up for sale by the architect's estate. Men like Hearst had no reason to believe that, short of a criminal trial, their private lives would ever be exposed. Even District Attorney William Travers Jerome had a young mistress at the very moment he was prosecuting Thaw.

As he had done before, Hearst looked for the story angle in the White-

Thaw case and ways to visualize it for his readers. Most of the dramatic elements were quite apparent. White was an internationally known celebrity with erotic tastes. His shooting took place in public as he watched a performance in the rooftop theater of Madison Square Garden. Thaw was a rich man from a prominent family, and Evelyn's sexual past had its own abundance of riches (including a 1902 dalliance with John Barrymore, the future movie star who was then working as a cartoonist for Hearst's *Journal*). Parker H. Sercombe, a Chicago journalist who published *To-morrow, For People Who Think*, a small magazine of poetry, opinion, and health, had previously applauded the "ethical concept and constructive morality" of Hearst's press. The Thaw–White coverage changed Sercombe's mind, inspiring in him an antagonism toward Hearst that would grow stronger over the years. Sercombe saw no harmless showmanship in Hearst' remolding of truth to suit a preconceived script:

> The sex affairs of three people, and the shooting of one of them, in its relation to our population, is insignificant; but the bringing of the two living figures in the drama into the limelight of publicity, as the greatest hero and heroine of our times, as examples for emulation, by millions of young people—printing photographs in a thousand poses; misrepresenting testimony; making up daily page upon page of news when no news existed; anticipating occurrences and in cold blood attempting, for pay, to form public opinion so as to force the court to free Thaw, is a crime so stupendous as to place the original shooting scrape entirely out of the same class. If the crime of Thaw was killing one man, the crime of Hearst is the killing of five hundred thousand.

Apparently, film companies that produced motion pictures related to the Thaw–White case saw nothing but inspiration in Hearst's rendering of the events. Biograph and cameraman Billy Bitzer were first out with *The Thaw–White Tragedy*. The thirty-foot-long film, a one-scene depiction of White's murder, was shot only two days after the murder, when the public had just begun to gobble up the sensational news. Whether Bitzer got any of his ideas about shooting the film from Hearst's newspapers cannot be documented, but Hearst was his usual source for news and subject matter. Earlier in 1906 Bitzer was the cameraman for a Biograph film called *The Critic*. The film's lead character is named Dalan Ale, an obvious jumbling of Hearst's drama critic Alan Dale's name. In a final scene of the film that takes place at a newspaper office, Bitzer inserts an extreme close-up of the critic's newspaper column.

The Biograph/Bitzer film about the White shooting was screened primarily in penny arcades, and even though it only suggested a more licentious story that was still unfolding, authorities in several cities banned it. *The Unwritten Law* (1907), a Lubin-produced film, made shortly before Thaw was convicted, may have also been influenced by the Hearst press, which had kept up an active campaign during the trial encouraging an unwritten law that justified a jilted husband's act of murder. A *Journal* reporter, Charles Sommerville, was a friend of Thaw's, and the slant of his reports favored Thaw's acquittal. When Thaw was found not guilty by reason of insanity in 1908, Sommerville and the *Journal* arranged for a private railroad car stocked with whiskey to take him to an asylum. *Variety* said the film was made with "an eye to [the case's] sensational points," and according to film historian Kevin Brownlow, it was as well crafted as an early D. W. Griffith film.

Despite its relative authenticity, the film was considerably less graphic than the newspaper coverage, which regularly published lengthy and often explicit testimony transcripts from the Thaw trial. As Brownlow has written, "those familiar with the yellow press could fill in the rest." But not all the yellow journalism and pseudonews stories in Hearst publications that were duplicated for the cinema dealt in kidnapping, floods, and murder. Sometimes pure fluff gave filmmakers material for the screen. A Charles Chaplin film for Mack Sennett was inspired in part by a series of Hearst editorials. As Sennett recalled, "Late in 1914 newspapers, magazines, and Arthur Brisbane's editorials created a flurry of popular interest in mankind's Stone Age origins. Our response with Chaplin was two reels called 'His Prehistoric Past,' in which Chaplin played a thin-muscled cave man in a derby hat."

MOVING PICTURES OF HEARST

Hearst's marriage to Millicent Willson on April 28, 1903, seems like the closing chapter of his "rescue" of the "sassafras" girl from Thirteenth Street and of a three-year effort to rehabilitate himself as well. His mother, a world traveler, did not make the trip to New York for the wedding ceremony. When word of Phoebe's reaction reached Hearst, he sent her a letter with his own words of defiance. "Our wedding was cheerful," he wrote, "and not to be mistaken for a funeral." During a honeymoon stop in London, Hearst gave an interview with a newspaper reporter that seems to reflect an attempt to deflect attention from the contradictions in his life. In the end, his words betray a man who remains attracted to both highlife and lowlife:

I certainly think that a journalism which employs the power of its vast audience to accomplish beneficial results for all the people is the journalism of the present. I cannot imagine why any one should want to print a newspaper except for that purpose. I myself don't find any satisfaction in sensational news, comic supplements, dress patterns and other features of journalism, except as they serve to attract an audience to whom the editorials in my newspapers are addressed. You must first get your congregation before you can preach to it and educate it to an appreciation and practice of the higher ideals of life.

In 1902 Hearst was given a new platform from which to use his power to benefit a "vast audience" when "Big" Tim Sullivan handed him a nomination as Democratic Party candidate for Congress. Although he was running in a safe Tammany district on the east side of Manhattan and victory was a foregone conclusion, Hearst gave his public the theatrical experience they were coming to expect from him. Posters and celluloid buttons carrying his picture were seen everywhere. The *Journal* published a series of voter interviews—a certain percentage undoubtedly faked—with a wide variety of demographic groups pledging their support for Hearst. The fake interview was perfected by Hearst and used again and again over the years, in his own campaigns and for and against other candidates. In October Tammany predicted certain victory for their new favorite son, thanks in large part to his "damned picture, pen, and ink show." Hearst in fact won the election with the largest majority ever received by a candidate for Congress in New York City, and his dizzying election night celebration near Madison Square Garden promised to outdo any previous Hearst extravaganza. At the moment, however, that a huge stereopticon image of Hearst's face with its deep-set eyes flashed on an outdoor screen, the crowd's attention was directed elsewhere. At first they must have thought that the thunderous fireworks explosion they heard was just part of the act. It would have been had it not turned into an accidental chain reaction. In the end, the Hearst election show left eighteen people, including some children, dead.

The voters in Hearst's district were apparently satisfied with the job he did and reelected him two years later. In 1904 Hearst ran well ahead of the Democratic ticket in his district. Almost immediately after winning, he announced that with the completion of his term he would not seek office again, "because I think my political work will be less subject to misrepresentation and consequently more effective, if I am not myself a candidate for any office whatever." It was said that as Hearst announced his intentions he was actually conferring with William Jennings Bryan and Thomas E. Watson, the southern populist, and laying the groundwork for a third party.

During the first decade of the new century, Hearst formed the Municipal Ownership League, the Independence League, and the Independence Party, all for the purpose of giving himself a platform to seek higher office. Despite attempts over the next three decades to become president, senator, governor, and mayor, his earlier pledge involuntarily came true, and he never held public office again. The closest Hearst ever came to winning office again was in 1905, as a candidate of the Municipal Ownership League for mayor of New York City. Ironically, Hearst probably won the election, but victory was denied him by elements of Tammany Hall (apparently not including Sullivan) who now opposed him.

It was around this time that Hearst began to use the grander "William Randolph Hearst," as opposed to the more modest "William R. Hearst." One magazine noted that Hearst was engaged in "the exploitation of himself as persistently as if he were a brand of soap or baking powder in this age of advertisement." Tammany leader Charles Francis Murphy was increasingly resentful of Hearst's ability to hog the political spotlight. Another claw in Tammany's side was the fact that although Hearst spent enormous sums of money on his election campaigns, contrary to established practice he did little to fill Tammany's pork barrel. Even a week before the 1905 election, when Murphy followers allegedly dumped thousands of pro-Hearst ballots in the river, dooming his chances, they were conducting a covert operation against the candidate, directing a huge mailing to potential voters that contained "defamatory" comments about Hearst's character. The specific contents of the postcards sent to voters are unknown, but the postal authorities deemed them sufficiently obscene to confiscate hundreds of thousands of them.

In 1906 Hearst managed to reach an accommodation with Boss Murphy that aided his last significant political race, as a candidate of the Independence League and Democratic Party for governor of New York. In a comment on the tight bond that once again existed between Hearst and Murphy, a cartoon in the *New York Herald* on October 16 showed the two men caught surprised in a lover's embrace (Murphy is drawn wearing a dress) behind a "moral screen." A caption reads: "The Hypocrite Exposed," and the imagery seems meant to suggest the common saloon practice of permitting commercialized sex behind screens.

Up until the closing days of the campaign, the race between Hearst and Republican candidate Charles Evans Hughes—a progressive who shared many of Hearst's antitrust views—remained tight. Then, at the eleventh hour, Hearst saw his chances fade, as President Theodore Roosevelt instructed his secretary of state, Elihu Root, to give a speech in which he would relay Roosevelt's long-held antipathy for Hearst. Secretary Root's dramatic speech for Hughes painted Hearst and his yellow journalism as forces of evil that were as guilty as the assassin Leon Czolgosz was in the murder of President McKinley in 1901. The race was over for Hearst.

A communications innovation that was a precursor to the modern political commercial proved to be the highlight of Hearst's campaign for governor. Looking for a way to reach voters in remote upstate areas without having to make any nerve-racking public appearances, Hearst turned to Arthur Brisbane for advice. Brisbane, who regularly recorded his editorials on cylinders to be played back and transcribed by his staff, suggested that Hearst visit a "talking machine place" in Manhattan. Soon afterward, along with some of his political advisers, Hearst drove downtown—probably to the Columbia shop at 155–57–59 Broadway—where he made twelve soft wax "graphophone" cylinders. The recordings completed, the shop electroplated and molded the cylinders to increase their volume and longevity for use before public gatherings. Hearst's "canned" speeches, as the cynics called them, often began with the candidate's typical high-pitched greeting, "My friends," and proceeded with blistering attacks on the ticket of Republican Party candidates (he called one a "cockroach" and another a "rat"). Hearst's operatives distributed the cylinders to town halls and sometimes paired them with stereopticon slides made from Frederick Opper cartoons. Other recordings were delivered to libraries or general stores so that voters who owned their own talking machines could borrow them as they might a library book. In addition to the "My friends" opening, Hearst's speeches seem to foreshadow President Franklin Roosevelt's celebrated radio addresses; as the *New York Times* reported, "By utilizing these agencies Mr. Hearst will be able to reach the very fireside with his speeches."

An even more novel approach to modern campaigning than the "canned speeches" was an idea to combine Hearst's cylinder recordings with films of Hearst in the process of denouncing his opponents. Some of the films were taken of Hearst at the Broadway cylinder shop as he recorded his antitrust speeches. Footage of Hearst arriving at rallies was thrown in as well. Excited campaign workers made plans to send their film-and-sound packages to theaters and halls in more than a dozen towns, and stories about the device were distributed to the press. News of Hearst's new method of campaigning reached as far as London, where a music hall manager thought they would be a clever addition to his vaudeville bill. But what was meant as a compliment in England was turned to ridicule in the United States. Press critics quickly dubbed the campaign device "Hearst's vaudeville show." The negative publicity coupled with the crudeness of the presentations—the sound and film were not properly synchronized—caused crowds to find the shows more amusing than electrifying. Hearst's managers were forced to cancel many engagements and ship their cylinders and films back to Hearst's campaign headquarters in Manhattan. The very nature of the novelty seemed to reinforce the consensus that Hearst was a "political self-seeker who, though he often leads good causes, seldom if ever prefers his cause to himself." In 1906 voters were not willing to embrace a political showman who campaigned as a remote-control candidate.

It Pays to Advertise

1907–1915

I won't say that I was successful, because I don't know whether I was successful or not. I don't think anybody actually knows that, that's up to box office. And according to Mr. Mayer and Warners, they had no complaints about box office on that score. But they couldn't attribute it to my talent particularly because they could have said it was publicity. And the old saying—it pays to advertise—I suppose that's all right. I used to think maybe it's publicity, used to feel I had too much. But one is no judge of that because if the producers gain by it, then why say I was over-publicized? If I was over-publicized, it would only hurt me. It did not hurt the picture.

—*Marion Davies*

ZIT'S DAY AT THE RACES

Just one decade into the twentieth century, the moving pictures were a commonly accepted and addictive diversion. Only the saloon and the yellow press—film's closest rivals—managed to merge and entertain such diverse elements as the rich and the poor, the educated and the undereducated. Despite the enormous popularity of the movies—especially among the newest immigrants and lower classes—the establishment media was slow to embrace them. Most serious journalists, who made their living with words, thumbed their noses at the mass-appealing pictures, or "flickers," as they were sometimes called, considering them a product of fringe elements.

Around 1907 Hearst established a policy for his newspapers that cornered the easy-spending class of theatergoers who were seeing movies as often as plays. The plan was based on two principles that always guided Hearst's operations: it gave the public the behind-the-scenes glimpse at the world of entertainment they craved, and it charged the entertainers for the publicity they craved. To oversee his new drama department policy, Hearst hired Carl Florian Zittel, a man everyone in show business called Zit. Hearst called Zittel his dramatic editor, but the thirty-one-year-old go-getter was really a director of advertising. Like Hearst, Zittel had an early interest in film. In 1898, the same year Hearst was sending cameramen to cover the war in Cuba, Zittel was attuned to the business side of film and learning methods he would later employ with Hearst. In the back of the Ehrich Brothers' Drygoods Store, at the corner of Sixth Avenue and Twenty-third Street in New York, Zittel set up a small moving-picture theater. Curious movie patrons weren't charged a fee; putting on the film program, which changed daily, wasn't expensive, and the Ehrich Brothers found that films filled their store and increased their sales. "We made it pay," Zittel recalled, "and that is the purpose of all business."

Immediately before he joined Hearst, Zittel was working part-time in his family's real estate business while simultaneously writing for the *New York Morning Telegraph*. The *Telegraph*, which was for a time owned by the debonair former gunslinger William "Bat" Masterson, had a peculiar distinction and even a symbolic link to Eadweard Muybridge's pioneering photographs of horses in motion. It was the only daily paper that was almost equally divided between theatrical news and horse-racing news. When Hearst hired Zittel in 1907, he made him a feature writer under the paper's dramatic editor Ashton Stevens and the editorial czar Arthur Brisbane. Stevens, originally from Chicago, had been brought East from Hearst's *San Francisco Examiner*, where he had gained a reputation as a respected critic of serious music and theater. Stevens's chief concession to popular entertainment was banjo playing, and in his spare time he gave lessons to Hearst.

If Stevens was the brains to bring esteem to the Hearst masthead, the bespectacled jokester nicknamed Zit was the muscle to pump in the excitement and the money. Zittel was full of his own ideas and ways of implementing the ideas of his boss. "Don't make the mistake of trying to show your employer how to save money," Zittel once said. "Teach him how to spend money and thereby make more money.... He employs you for your department because you know more about it than he does. When you make money for him he will never question the fact that it cost the initial investment."

The sporting-life concept of the *Telegraph* was an appropriate starting gate for Zittel. On the *New York Journal* he gained prominence with the general public for "Zit's Vaudeville Racing Chart," which turned the entertainment world into a real horse race. Published weekly, Zittel's dramatic page displayed intricate charts of plays, performers, stage acts, and movies and pitted various productions and personalities against each other. Every Saturday Zit announced his subjective evaluation of the odds of success or failure. As one of Zit's contests between comediennes Eva Tanguay and Vesta Victoria went: "It was Tanguay at the start, Tanguay at the half, Tanguay into the stretch and Tanguay at the finish. Victoria had no more chance of winning from Tanguay than a Twenty-eighth Street horse car could beat the Twentieth Century Limited." Zittel's chart quickly became a household term; honored in verse, it was unquestionably respected and feared by the leaders of the entertainment industry.

Behind Zittel's diverting racing chart was a simple extortion plan. Theatrical managers paid the *New York Journal* newspaper five hundred dollars for a half-page or a thousand dollars for a full-page advertisement of their productions. In return for payment, a stage production received a well-placed advertisement in one of the best-circulated newspapers or, better still, a plug in a Brisbane editorial, called "constructive criticism" by Hearst but really just another form of paid advertisement. A glowing boost on Brisbane's well-read opinion page could give "Little Mary" Pickford or a new production at the Hippodrome as much significance as an editorial on a revolution in Mexico. Producers able to spend a little extra money might receive a bonus: a photograph, often taken at the Hearst-owned Campbell Photography Studio on Fifth Avenue, or an elaborately illustrated drawing by a Hearst artist might accompany the solicited plug.

Zittel's deal with Hearst was certainly one of the most lucrative arrangements for a newspaperman during this period, even though he worked without a contract and never received a fixed salary. Instead, Hearst guaranteed him 40 percent of all the advertising business he brought to the paper. "Never accept a contract," Zittel once said, "for the man who demands one admits his weakness by wanting to have his freedom tied up." It was years before Hearst's advertising practice was publicly called into question, since the gentlemen's agreements between Zittel and producers were financially beneficial to all concerned—all, that is, who had money to begin with. Like Zittel's own commission salary, advertising payments were always in cash and exchanged without written contracts. When questions were eventually raised, it was assumed that "constructive criticism" and the rest were the brainchild of Brisbane or Zittel, but in a 1915 directive to his editors, Hearst established his underlying role:

As you know I am wholly averse to old style dramatic criticism and believe merely in dramatic reviews and interesting accounts of dramatic performances with only kindly and considerate criticism of performance. I would not want any one on paper who would not adopt our style dramatic article. In other words I don't want dramatic critic. I want dramatic reporter who will give entertaining account of performance, quote bright lines and consider on the whole the viewpoint of public rather than perverse view of a blase critic.

Zittel had another special perk in his position on the *Journal*. Hearst allowed him to take a salary from producers who used Zittel as their press agent. His lists of clients was long, including such rising stars as film producer Adolph Zukor and comedienne and singer Eva Tanguay, whose act and trademark rendition of "I Don't Care" profited greatly from almost weekly plugs in the *Journal*. Film mogul Marcus Loew was said to have had a close relationship with Zittel and an exclusive advertising deal with the *Journal*, spending in excess of $1,000 a week, an amount at least equal to what had been spent by all producers combined in the days before Hearst and company's scheme. Will Gordon, who along with Mike Connelly was an assistant to Zittel, remembered being at a lunch once with his boss and Marcus Loew: "While Mr. Loew was never a talkative person, nevertheless, in so many words he told me he offered Zit a percentage of the entire circuit, which was still young if he would change from the Hearst papers and assist him in the running of his entire business. But Zittel was a loyal person. . . . The motion picture business was then in its infancy, Adolph Zukor, William Fox, Schwalbee [*sic*], Selznick and several other companies were just starting and it was Zittel's aid that launched these companies."

Arthur Brisbane had quickly replaced Ashton Stevens on the editorial side of Hearst's adverting scheme, when the critic balked at the shenanigans and threatened to leave the organization. Brisbane, however, voiced no qualms about the direction of Hearst's advertising policy, although his background might not have predicted such a path. Brisbane was educated in France and Germany, fluent in several languages, and surrounded as a child by the freethinkers of his time. In the mid-nineteenth century, his father, Albert, became a convert to a temperate French socialist movement called Fourierism, and he established the experimental commune of Brook Farm. In the United States in his day, Albert was considered a first-generation communist. In 1848, in an attempt to convert the masses, Albert bought front-page advertising space in Horace Greeley's *New York Tribune*, where three times weekly he railed against unrestricted private property rights. Young Arthur Brisbane's life took him on a course far afield of his father's radicalism; however, he did inherit a streak of his old man's powers of persuasion. The newspaper editor, who helped turn Pulitzer's *New York World* into a yellow journal, was an old hand at getting the public's attention and changing their minds by the time he came to Hearst's *Journal*. Brisbane would boast that while working for Hearst, he wrote the first advertisement for Corn Flakes, which appeared in a July 1906 issue of the *Ladies Home Journal*. The breakfast food baron W. K. Kellogg claimed that the full-page ad was responsible for increasing sales of the toasted cereal from 33 to 2,900 cases per day.

Brisbane seemed to have an instinctive taste for advertising, which was perfectly attuned to Hearst's new selling strategy. He thought that advertising needed four essential ingredients to be successful; it had to be seen, it had to be read, it had to be understood, and it had to be believed. Large-type newspaper headlines and bold illustrations—which were first employed by Brisbane and the Sunday newspaper editor Morrill Goddard when they worked on Pulitzer's *New York World*—met the standards for the first three elements of successful advertising and came close enough to meeting the fourth. When Hearst lured Brisbane and Goddard away from the *World*, those sensational and eye-catching headlines and pictures were utilized more regularly and to even greater advantage, and they quickly became associated with the Hearst newspapers. Newspaper boys also found the headlines, as well as the expanded use of newspaper photography, appealing to customers. They would often wrap a layer of the eye-catching Hearst papers around the bundle of newspapers they were hawking on street corners. But the newsies' unsolicited circulation boost for the Hearst paper was frequently offset; many New Yorkers, embarrassed to be seen carrying the *Journal*, would often buy a more sedate newspaper to wrap around the Hearst paper.

Some of the illustrations that accompanied Brisbane's "constructive criticisms" were delicately romanticized pen-and-ink drawings by a twenty-nine-year-old artist and writer named Nell Brinkley. Brinkley was a cartoonist for several Denver newspapers when she caught the eye of Brisbane, who snatched her up for the *Journal*. In real life, the self-taught artist resembled the waiflike women she drew, and the comparison made her as recognizable and celebrated as her work. The Ziegfeld Follies of 1909 featured a group of dancers called the Nell Brinkley girls. Many young women copied Brinkley's appearance—a head of voluminous curls framing a pale white face accented by pursed lips—and the look came to typify the fragile female form of the preflapper era. Brinkley's near-anemic image was so indelible that one wan and scantily dressed sixteen-year-old girl was picked up wandering in the bitter cold of Perth Amboy, New Jersey, speaking incoherently except to claim with certainty that she was Nell Brinkley.

In addition to Hearst's team of Zittel, Brisbane, and Brinkley, two of the dramatic department's best workhorses were the duo of J. Wesley Hamer and Victor Watson. The two men were inseparable. Because Hamer was slight in appearance and Watson somewhat stocky, they were often referred to as "Mutt and Jeff," a reference to the cartoon of the same name. Some who observed them prowling the theater districts and the nickelodeon parlors making deals for valuable advertising considered them more sinister and called them "the undertakers." While Hamer seemed to leave no lasting impression, he did become a part-time secretary to Hearst after his work for Zittel. During his twenty-five years with the organization, he was also a dramatic editor and political writer. Coincidentally, Hamer died on the very same day in 1944 as artist Nell Brinkley. One coworker remembered Hamer's sidekick, Victor Watson, as a tenderhearted man with a fatal streak of paranoia. "Though I regard Watson as one of the best editors of our day," he said, "I have never met a man so easily disposed to conjure up fancied grievances, to attribute motives where there were none, to create feuds where there was no reason for them." In a long career with Hearst, Watson became the dramatic editor of Hearst's *American* and was at one time that paper's associate publisher and managing editor. In later years, however, even Hearst grew tired of Watson's dark side; he was shunted and relegated to trifling assignments. (Some said this was Hearst's way: unable to deal with completely severing himself from an employee, he would set him or her adrift.) In the twenties Watson hired and then married a *Journal* photographer—one of the first female news photographers—named Katherine Nolan de Sarno. But the Watson marriage was stormy. In 1938, despondent over his estranged wife's decision to marry theater producer Sam Harris and with a family history of suicide, Watson checked into the Abbey Hotel in New York and leapt from an eleventh-floor window.

In 1909 Nicholas Schenck hired Zittel to promote the Palisades Amusement Park in New Jersey. Nick and his brother, Joe, had begun as New York newsies and drugstore errand boys. In American dream fashion, they eventually bought the drugstore where they worked. The Schenck brothers continued buying drugstores until they stumbled on an idea of Ferris wheels and roller coasters. The site of their first amusement park was in Manhattan at Fort George. But the Schencks real claim to fame came in carving their names in the jagged cliffs of the Palisades on the other side of the Hudson

River. In a 1914 newspaper column, Zittel wrote that the Schenck brothers "took hold of Palisades Park, which was at that time an unknown quantity ... losing thousands every summer. Nicholas Schenck went there and personally patented and built every ride and device and amusement enterprise on the grounds."

Almost immediately after meeting Zittel, the Schencks and the Hearst press made an exclusive contract. Zittel later recalled that "the *New York Evening Journal*, through its advertising columns, made for Palisades Park over $80,000 the first year, and it has gone higher every year since. It was then that the Schenck Brothers became known the world over as park owners." The Schenck brothers, Zittel wrote, "say their success is due entirely to the *New York Evening Journal*," and the two brothers, destined to be major power brokers in the film industry, concurred with Zittel's story. In the special Christmas 1915 section of the *Journal*—an annual celebration of the theater and the movies—the Schenck brothers paid for another advertisement: "TO 'ZIT' WHO MADE PALISADES PARK FAMOUS."

Cliff-hanging

The Perils of Pauline, Hearst's first full-scale film production, was probably the first film title to become a catchphrase. Soon after the film's release in March 1914, the twenty-part adventure series, propelled by massive publicity, was a smash hit around the nation. Its daring scenes of actress Pearl White dangling from a precipice made New Jersey's Palisades the most recognizable early film location and introduced the word *cliff-hanger* into the English language. Its simple but sensational plots gave its star worldwide hero status. Like almost every successful film to follow, it is a perfect circular melding of star, action, and promotion.

Hearst not only came up with the alliterative title of the series but conceived the story and organized the film's wide distribution. Around Christmas 1913 he summoned the younger brother of Morrill Goddard, his paper's Sunday supplement editor, to his Clarendon apartment building on New York's Riverside Drive. Charles Goddard was a successful playwright, having cowritten *The Ghost Breaker* and *The Misleading Lady* with his brother-in-law, Paul Dickey. Morrill told Charles about his boss's passion for producing a movie with "a background of wealth and power, melodrama with a suspense hangover carrying into the next installment."

Movie serialization was relatively new, but the concept in general was well established. Charles Dickens—a writer Hearst idolized and whose blending of journalism and art he tried to emulate—had perfected the continuing serial idea in the penny press years before the freshman film producer was born. *What Happened to Mary*, an Edison release of 1912, was the prototype of the movie serial. Although not a serial in the true sense—most of its episodes were self-contained—it was the first to link film with serializations published in newspapers and magazines: an abridged story of each episode appeared in monthly installments of the *Ladies World* magazine. William Selig's *Adventures of Kathlyn*—the first real continuing series—was near but far from dear to Hearst. On December 29, 1913—while *Perils* was still in the works—the Selig Company film series was released and serialized in the *Chicago Tribune* newspaper, a Hearst competitor. Moses Koenigsberg, Hearst's chief Chicago newspaper editor and manager of his wire services, was particularly exasperated by news of Selig's production. As early as 1905 Koenigsberg had toyed with the idea of a newspaper-movie tie-in and said as much to Selig, who was considered a friend, and to his Hearst associates. But in the ensuing years, despite Koenigsberg's labors, it was the concept of a newsreel that really excited the Hearst organization, and the movie serial idea was shelved for others to grab.

At Hearst's direction, Edgar Hatrick had been hard at work since the early 1910s to establish a pictorial news-gathering organization that would ultimately lead to the creation of a Hearst newsreel. By 1913 Hatrick had successfully combined the Hearst News Syndicate and the Hearst News Photo Syndicate into a single unit and simultaneously set up Hearst news bureaus, staffed with news photographers, in key cities around the country. Sensing a certain "nose for news" weakness among the successful French film films working in the United States (Pathé, Lumière, and Gaumont), Hearst instructed Hatrick to train his divisional news cameramen in the art of taking moving pictures. To demonstrate the effectiveness of the burgeoning Hearst operation, Hatrick sent a cameraman named Louis de Lorme to film the inauguration ceremony of Woodrow Wilson in March 1913. The Hatrick operation was competing with about eight established film firms taking pictures at the event, but de Lorme's eight hundred feet of film, which required an expenditure of $298 for the negative film stock, quickly netted over $3,000 after it was distributed to theaters by Harry Warner's United Film Exchanges. With this successful experiment under his belt, Hatrick went to Thomas Edison with a proposal that he join forces with Hearst to create a fully American newsreel organization. For some unknown reason, the inventor declined the offer. Wasting no time, Hatrick struck a deal with William Selig.

In late 1913, while the *Chicago Tribune* and Selig prepared to present their serial collaboration, Hearst and Selig were organizing a newsreel they called the *Hearst-Selig News Pictorial*. The first of the reels was announced for February 27, 1914, to be distributed by General Film Corporation, a trust company that owned practically every licensed film exchange in the United States. The forthcoming Hearst-Selig reel would be the most significant rival to the *Pathé Weekly Review*, which was established in 1911 as the first newsreel in America and was also distributed by General Film.

While the newsreel negotiations progressed, Hearst became increasingly convinced of the viability of the serial idea. He quickly tried to make up for lost time, contacting Edward A. McManus and French film pioneer Charles Pathé. McManus was the brains behind the 1912 *Whatever Happened to Mary* series, and he knew firsthand the ins and outs of the marketing end of the serial business. He was employed to supervise the various elements of the *Perils* production, advertising, and distribution.

During the early winter of 1913 filmmaker Pathé was in New York, finalizing the severing of his relationship with the General Film Corporation. Like other independent-thinking producers, Pathé had thought for some time that General Film was an incompetent giant, uninterested in producers' interests and eager to cut into a large slice of Pathé's profits. In April 1913 Pathé had set up a company called Eclectic as an importer of films, with an eye toward creating his own distribution unit. News of General Film's plan to distribute the Hearst newsreel was the final straw. Pathé established the Pathé-Eclectic Company as an exchange system later that year. He was always more of a film manufacturer and businessman than a showman. Around the same time that Pathé created his distribution company, the bankers Merrill, Lynch, and Company bought the production end of Pathé in America. Soon afterward, the Wall Street bankers joined forces with French Pathé to make an alliance with the Dupont chemical manufacturers of Delaware to produce raw film in direct competition with the stock film trust of Eastman Kodak.

Cut out of the Selig deal for a movie serial, Hearst went to Pathé for the distribution system he needed to advance the ambitious project to be known as *The Perils of Pauline*. Pathé's deal with Hearst was a sweet one for the film company, part of a broader arrangement whereby Pathé releases were heavily promoted in the Hearst press, with many productions serialized in the same manner as *Perils*. When Pathé released a film based on Emile Zola's *Germinal*, the *New York American* ran installments of the story in the morning, and the readers were urged to see the photoplay in the afternoon or evening. The paper's headlines declared that Hearst and Pathé were collaborating "in a Plan to Amuse, Entertain and Educate New York."

With these plans behind him, Hearst was set for his script meeting with writers Charles and Morrill Goddard in late 1913. At ten o'clock in the morning, a nervous and bleary-eyed Charles, who preferred to work in his own home away from people, picked up his brother, who lived a few blocks from Hearst's apartment at Eighty-sixth Street and Riverside Drive. With only one day's notice, Charles had put together a brisk five-hundred-word outline. Early in the hour meeting, Charles was put at ease by Hearst's surprising talent for coming up with cinematic story ideas and characters. Hearst approved Goddard's outline but made some suggestions to move the plot along and at the same meeting came up with the film's famous title. Within a few weeks, with Hearst's continuing input, the twenty-chapter script was completed.

Actress Pearl White—a marketing dream name that Hearst had no part in creating—was relatively new to film when she starred in *The Perils of Pauline*. Only a few years before her famous serial, she had been a circus performer, worked as a stewardess on an ocean liner to Cuba, entertained audiences at a café in Buenos Aires, and played bit parts in forgettable one- and two-reelers. Because of her natural charm onscreen and the Hearst publicity to support her, White became a bigger star with each chapter release of her serial. Photographs of Pearl White from *Perils* appeared sometimes daily in the Hearst press, and publicists wrote about her with an eye toward making her an ideal for young women. Repeatedly, they wrote about her daring stunts, her modest but stylish dresses designed by Lady Duff-Gordon, and her long curly eyelashes grouped together in what screenwriter Charles Goddard described as "that starry effect, like Nell Brinkley's girls."

The opening scene of the first episode of *Perils* shows the clear influence of Hearst and his synergistic advertising methods. In the story, Pearl White's character, Pauline Marvin, is the ward of a wealthy automobile mogul named Stanford Marvin, who is trying to match her up with his son, Harry. But the independent-thinking Pauline isn't interested in marriage. "Someday, maybe," she tells Stanford, "but first I must see the world [so] that I may progress with my writing." Stanford is skeptical, amused by Pauline's ambitions. She rushes off and quickly returns with a copy of Hearst's *Cosmopolitan* magazine. The camera takes in a close-up of an illustrated article with Pauline Marvin's byline. Slowly one of the half-tone illustrations—a fire onboard an ocean liner—fades into screen action, and its two-dimensional figures come to life. In the first reel of his first serial Hearst is already constructing a bridge between his world of publishing and his world of film.

A new episode of *The Perils of Pauline* was released weekly during the spring of 1914. Paul Panzer as the villain and Crane Wilbur as Harry Marvin, Pauline's love interest, became nearly as well known as Pearl White. The twenty episodes had a number of credited and uncredited directors, including George Seitz, George Fitzmaurice, Louis Gasnier, and Donald MacKenzie. Its chief cameraman was Arthur Miller (no relation to the playwright).

Through his newest venue of 1913, Hearst acted without hesitation to make *Perils* and its formulaic lowbrow qualities a vehicle for entertainment and propaganda. His heroine was much more than a mere descendant of theater's long line of melodramatic ladies. With an emphasis on autonomy and strength, both physical and cerebral, the serial and its star, through great popularity, created a new female film hero. Hearst had an early and genuine sensitivity to women's issues, especially influenced by his own mother's prominence and strongly held views. Phoebe Hearst plodded slowly toward a public declaration for a woman's right to vote. But as early as 1896, in an unpublicized meeting with Susan B. Anthony, the recently widowed heir to an array of business fortunes quietly voiced her understanding of women's urgent need for political power. By 1913, the year that *Perils* was first planned, Phoebe—no longer speaking in private—took the lead from her son, who through his own venues was increasingly clear and vocal on the subject of woman's suffrage. If *The Perils of Pauline*, like most early film, seems quaint to modern eyes, Hearst's message of female independence appears to have resonated at the time of the series' initial release. As Pearl White's personal publicist Victor Shapiro put it in public relations lingo, " 'A girl's best friend was herself' was the moral of the serial."

Perils came out slightly too late to compete directly with the Selig–*Chicago Tribune* serial, but its enormous success and its wide Pathé distribution surpassed that serial and all others that came before it. Under the supervision of the clever Edward McManus, 147 prints were sent to exchanges across the country; the norm was fewer than 30. In addition to the "continued next week" serializations, the Hearst newspapers offered weekly prizes of $1,000 for readers who could guess the intricate plot twists waiting just around the corner. Even a popular song, "Poor Pauline," was quickly rolled out to celebrate the film's heroine and perpetuate the film's box office success. Carl Zittel and Hearst's advertising staff announced to would-be clients that "Pauline Pulls People." And it was true. *The Perils of Pauline* became nearly as popular in China and Russia as it was in the United States, creating one of the first international film stars.

In addition to the location of Pearl White's cliff-hanging, Zittel's business friendships with the Schencks had at least one conspicuous effect on *Perils*. In a scene introducing Pearl's death-defying ride on a huge sabotaged balloon, we see the villain plotting with an amusement park worker in charge of the ride. In two separate shots, Arthur Miller's camera lingers significantly on the wooden gateway. A large sign in bold print advertises: "THE SCHENCK BROS.—PALISADE AMUSEMENT PARK."

PAPERHANGING

Around the same time that Hearst produced *The Perils of Pauline*, he began a ritual of screening movies at home and taking home movies. Aware of her husband's new interest in film, Millicent surprised Hearst with a special gift at Christmastime 1913. She gave him a film taken of herself and their three sons only a few days earlier at the Vitagraph Studios. Apparently, the film, which is lost, was personal but professionally produced, containing some ten different scenes. One showed the Hearst boys playing football on the studio's lawn. Another scene delighted Hearst most of all with its use of trick photography that magically animated a group of framed Hearst family portraits. Hearst's film-watching passion would soon become a habit that he would never break. As one of Hearst's employees and biographers later noted, "[Hearst] was projecting crude, flickering pictures upon a screen in his home long before Charlie Chaplin came to America and pantomimed an intoxicated spectator in a vaudeville sketch called 'A Night in an English Music Hall.'" Between 1914 and 1920 Hearst produced, directed, wrote, and starred in an elaborate home movie that costarred his wife, Millicent. *The Lighthouse Keeper's Daughter*, which was thirty-eight minutes long, titled, and color-tinted but never intended for audiences beyond Hearst's circle of friends, was an obvious tongue-in-cheek reference to his earlier movie serials. Many of the film's titles (some illustrated with cartoons drawn by Hearst) included clever comical asides about the clichés of filmmaking and the film industry. Millicent plays the *Perils of Pauline* role in a series of thrilling adventures filmed at San Simeon and set against a backdrop of bootlegging. In the end, as expected and frequently forewarned by the film's title writer, the heroine is rescued by her hero (Hearst).

Hearst's personal involvement—financial and otherwise—in the entertainment field caused some cracking in the advertising structure at his newspapers. With the arrival of Hearst films, other producers found they were no longer simply vying with each other for valuable advertising space. On the other side of the equation, advertisements for Hearst films in Hearst publications were being sold at a loss. In Hearst's exchange system between the entertainment producers and the entertainment exploiters, men like Zittel had become wealthy being employed by both parties to the bargain. As Zittel himself boasted, his motto was, "Live well, dress well, act the part of the millionaire. Be your employer's equal; try to be his partner." Once Hearst entered the advertising picture as a producer, however, Zittel, Watson, and Hamer had no special financial incentive to boost his films, since they would be promoted in Hearst's papers regardless of their input.

For Hearst, becoming a player in show business demanded that he perform a delicate balancing act. He needed to advertise himself vigorously, since few of his newspaper rivals would, but he had to be careful not to antagonize his film producer competitors, whose advertisements he still needed. Although Hearst had a genuine passion for the film industry, from a purely business standpoint he would have had no alternative but to embrace it and its producers. In 1914 Robert Grau, a theater producer and one of film history's first historians, wrote that the *New York Journal* "was one of the very first newspapers in the country to emphatically endorse the new art and its productivity. In fact, to this day no more helpful contribution to film progress may be pointed to than the editorials which appeared in all of Mr. Hearst's newspapers in 1913. The 'New York Evening Journal' has for over a year reviewed photoplays with as much seriousness as the spoken play." Grau displayed insight about Hearst in his writings, but careful observers might have noted that he was not exactly an unbiased observer. As a theater manager, Grau was undoubtedly tied to and benefiting from Hearst advertising. He even managed to get several plugs for his film history book in Zittel's column before and after its publication.

The start of World War I in 1914 transformed the nature of news, advertising, and publicity. Hearst's system of "gentlemen's agreements" in the world of entertainment was edging close to the new field of public relations that was engulfing the gathering and reporting of hard news. As an editor of the *New York World* remembered:

> [The war] played havoc with the lucrative "space" system—except for the lads who covered the Liberty Loan Drives, in which three and four columns or more per day were [a] "must." They used such large quantities of the material given out by Liberty Loan Headquarters, that they were called "paperhangers—not reporters." . . . The war brought the handout system, organized publicity, government press releases, long speeches and statements to fill up columns. Formerly the newspapers had to send out their men to hustle for news, but after the war it poured in upon them in floods and the big problem was what to do with it all. The war took the edge off accuracy. It introduced propaganda.

Although Zittel and Watson were still in charge of their newspapers' show business sections in 1914, Hearst hired a dramatist, translator, and journalist named Charles Henry Meltzer to write film and music criticism. By engaging the Oxford-educated, long-haired Meltzer—who began his career in Paris as a music and literary reporter for James Gordon Bennett's *Herald* newspaper—Hearst was acknowledging the cultural significance of film and, to some extent, the shortcomings of a purely commercial link between criticism and advertising. Hearst must have sensed as well that the selling strategy that was known and begrudgingly accepted by the trade was becoming too well known to the public—and to his competition. The procedure was no longer unique to his own publications. Hearst must have cringed at the thought that he was becoming one of the crowd, when a July 1914 issue of *Variety* reported:

> The policy practiced by the *Evening Journal* for several years of favorable write-ups for liberal advertisers, with $1,000 a page the price for favor, the publishers of other papers have at last taken cognizance of officially, and in three cases the rival sheets are preparing to do likewise, eliminating the dramatic chair entirely and replacing its incumbent with a reporter pure and simple whose pen must never seethe. "The papers that are pursuing the policy are adding about $25,000 yearly to their receipts," the publishers are now saying, "and the public seem to like the treacle, and if so, why not give them what they want?"

By late September 1914 Hearst's advertising strategy was entangled in public controversy. The playwright George H. Broadhurst sent Hearst an urgent letter asking him to replace the *American*'s longtime critic Alan Dale as reviewer of Broadhurst's play called *Law of the Land*, set to open at the Forty-eighth Street Theater. Somehow Broadhurst got wind of Dale's intention to write a "critical" and therefore negative review of the play. In the relative calm of Hearst's system of friendly dramatic reviewing, Dale became Hearst's lightning rod.

The British-born Dale (whose real name was Henry Cohen) worked under Victor Watson writing theater and film criticism. He had a notorious mean streak, repeatedly targeting actors and playwrights he disliked. At the *Journal*, where he engaged in frequent office quarrels, he had a highfalutin attitude, often boasting that he cared little for "the whole shooting match of the theatrical profession." On one occasion he brought out the meanness of a fellow critic, who compared the diminutive Dale to a character from a

Hearst Sunday supplement's cartoon and talked of his striding the theater aisles with the gait of a hyena while his bald birdlike head invoked the image of a woodpecker. The legendary reporter Richard Harding Davis once said, "Dale accounts as his highest achievement in dramatic criticism the writing of a line, which will make a poor little chorus girl cry when she wakes up in the morning and reads it." Despite his abrasive qualities or because of them, Dale was popular with the public. Hearst found Dale's personality amusing, and he saw a quality in his freewheeling and sarcastic writing style that must have reminded him of the writer Ambrose Bierce, a favorite enfant terrible of the early *San Francisco Examiner* days.

In his preemptive note to Hearst, Broadhurst wrote that theater managers and producers didn't deserve Dale's harsh treatment, when so much time and money went into staging their productions (and, needless to say, into Hearst advertising). Hearst, who had a reputation for being loyal to a fault when it came to his employees, was forced to make a business decision. On October 1, the morning after Broadhurst's play opened, the *American*, as requested, carried a noncritical review that was written by a substitute writer named Ada Patterson. A few weeks later Alan Dale, who had written reviews for Hearst for nineteen years, aired his disagreements in the competitive *New York Times* and announced that he was quitting Hearst. "It seems to me that an era of commercialism in journalism has set in and I do not want to be in it." Hearst tried to stay above the fray. He issued a statement by one of his editors that avoided the significance of Dale's statement to the press and asserted that his paper "never has had any dissatisfaction with Mr. Dale." Despite Dale's very public protest, Hearst didn't appear to be seriously worried. He knew that one day, with the right offer, he could get Mr. Dale back again. And within a few years he did.

It is unknown what Hearst really thought about Dale's remarks on a new era of commercialism, but it is known that he never completely retired the system that he, Zittel, and Brisbane had mastered. As late as 1937 a Labor Relations Board hearing in Washington disclosed that Hearst's tabloid newspaper in New York, the *Daily Mirror*, was carrying on the thirty-year-old tradition of Carl Zittel's pay-for-play racing chart. According to sworn testimony, the *Mirror's* entertainment, music, food, and travel writers were still simultaneously receiving sizable salaries and sizable commissions for advertising. The basic structure of Hearst's advertising methods can be seen even today in the film practice known as product placement and even in newspapers and magazines when a good review or a puff piece about a film is published perilously close to a full-page ad for the same film.

In late 1914 Hearst made an alliance with Vitagraph, the Brooklyn-based film company that ten months earlier had produced his wife's Christmas gift to him and had first gained prominence in 1898 with the Spanish-American War films of its founders, J. Blackton and Albert E. Smith. In December Hearst and Vitagraph cosponsored what was to become for a number of years an annual Christmas tree celebration. The event—which predated the Rockefeller Center tree lighting by nineteen years—was billed as a charity event that included children's parties, coffee and sandwich giveaways, and beds for the night for the homeless. Trees were set up in three Manhattan locations: Columbus Circle, city hall, and Madison Square Garden. In the evening benefit performances by Vitagraph stars, bands, Hearst cartoonists, opera singers, and chorus girls, sponsored and heavily promoted by the *New York American*, were held at the Vitagraph Theater at Broadway and Forty-fourth Street. The highlight of the charity events was saved for the evening when Vitagraph film comedies were projected on outdoor screens for thousands who gathered in the streets.

Hearst and Vitagraph signed another contract on October 29, 1915, to begin releasing newsreels shortly after the New Year. Film trade papers reported that a staff of some fifty-six salaried cameramen was being employed by the film partners to comb the country, and they predicted that "the distribution of this pictorial would be the widest ever obtained by a film of this character." Stories on the operation may have been exaggerated, but the *Hearst-Vitagraph News Reel*—or *News Pictorial*, as it was sometimes called—did manage to score some important scoops. Two exclusives involved the screening of footage from recent war disasters at sea: the sinking of the British battleship *Audacious* in late 1914, which Hearst had covered with some controversy in his newspapers, and the loss of the German battle cruiser *Blücher* and a crew of nine hundred in early 1915.

Perhaps the most important of the Vitagraph arrangements with Hearst was the one tied to the Star Company, a subsidiary of the Hearst organization. In April 1915 Vitagraph had significantly increased its strength in the industry with the incorporation of Vitagraph-Lubin-Selig-Essanay, Inc. Soon known as V-L-S-E, the new organization had been formed to release feature-length films made by these member pioneer film studios. Vitagraph's Albert Smith was V-L-S-E's president and William Selig was treasurer, but the day-to-day operations were handled by its general manager Walter W. Irwin, an attorney and Hearst's brother-in-law, who had just recently married Millicent's sister, Anita. Through his Star Company deal, Hearst oversaw an extensive exploitation program for Vitagraph films. The joint venture was a big moneymaker for Hearst because it was primarily connected with advertising. According to the accountants Price Waterhouse, whose deposition surfaced later, all eight newspapers of the Hearst chain—including the *San Francisco Call* and the secretly owned *Los Angeles Herald*—contracted to run full-page advertisements and serializations in return for a 50 percent share of the gross profits. Apparently all the dozens of Vitagraph films produced during the approximately one-year period of the partnership were involved in this arrangement.

With an unprecedented flood of publicity for their productions, Vitagraph seemed as happy as Hearst over the arrangement. When actress Anita Stewart—the star of two films made during this arrangement, *The Girl Philippa* and *The Goddess*—announced plans to leave Vitagraph, the company's president, Albert Smith, reminded her of the personal relationship he had with Hearst. "By using my friendship with Mr. and Mrs. Hearst to get them interested in you personally," Smith told Stewart, "I succeeded in getting you a great deal of free advertising in all the Hearst newspapers." In a legal proceeding that followed Stewart's departure, Smith, somewhat defensively, continued to point out the uniqueness of his Hearst deal:

> [We explained to Miss Stewart] the great benefit which she derived from the publicity given her in the Hearst papers resulting from the financial arrangements existing between the so called Hearst organization and the Vitagraph Co. The fact that the payment for such advertising took the form of an agreement to permit the advertiser to share in the gross profit instead of provision being made for payment in cash, is, I am advised, entirely immaterial and did not remove such payment from the category of legitimate expenses.

After Anita Stewart left Vitagraph she signed up with a young, virtually unknown exhibitor who had made a small fortune in New England distributing D. W. Griffith's *Birth of a Nation*. Stewart starred in his first production, a film called *Virtuous Wives*, which was based on a magazine story with the same title. The film's producer paid the magazine's publisher approximately $15,000 for the film rights, and he made a subsidiary advertising arrangement as well. The magazine where the film story originated was Hearst's *Cosmopolitan*, and the film *Virtuous Wives* would receive the typical full-blast treatment in the Hearst press. The *Virtuous Wives* deal was another stepping-stone for Hearst on his unusual path to Hollywood and quite a leap for the film's producer, the future head of MGM and a future producing partner of Hearst, Louis B. Mayer.

6

When Men Betray

1915–1918

DEFECTS

In the spring of 1918—three years after the Great War began in Europe—the Germans made an assault on British and French forces on the western front. The U.S. commander, General "Black Jack" Pershing, asked President Woodrow Wilson for a quick call-up of young doughboys to assist the Allies. It was the beginning of the first major infusion of American troops since Wilson had declared war one year before. The intensity of the fighting and the need for reinforcements would fluctuate over the next few months. But it wasn't until late July that the Germans would be put on the defensive, and not before the loss of nearly ten thousand American lives. At New York State's Camp Upton, a frightened draftee, on getting wind of Pershing's plan, ditched the rifle he had barely learned to clean and in the middle of the night fled for his young life. He didn't get very far. He was picked up by the military police, arrested, and charged with treason. If convicted—which was likely—he would be shot. Desperate to save the young man's life, his relatives went to the only family member who had anything more than a modicum of influence.

Ivan Abramson, a cousin of the deserter, was the idol of the family. In 1918, approaching the age of fifty, he still carried the heavy accent of his native Lithuania, which he had left as a child. Through a combination of energy, talent, and gall, Abramson established a name for himself in the

United States, successively if not always successfully, as a newspaperman, opera impresario, theater manager, and movie producer. Despite the affection in which his family held him, Abramson's outspokenness, his intractable personality, and an ever-swelling ego made it difficult for him to make friends. Luckily for his cousin, one of Abramson's few friends—a man with similar traits—was William Randolph Hearst.

Hearst was Ivan Abramson's equal partner in a movie-producing company they formed in 1917, the Graphic Film Corporation. With a giant eye encircled by the letter G as its logo, Graphic leased a suite of offices in the newly built seventeen-story Godfrey Building. At 729 Seventh Avenue and Forty-ninth Street in Manhattan and still standing today, the Godfrey was then the East Coast equivalent of Hollywood. During the film industry's earliest years, it was home to Mary Pickford, Charlie Chaplin, Lewis Selznick, and Adolph Zukor, as well as dozens of other lesser-known producers.

When Graphic was incorporated, Hearst's primary film-producing company, the International Film Service, was just three years old, but Hearst already encompassed a newsreel business and an animation studio and was producing several popular movie serials in conjunction with the Pathé film company.

Aside from sharing the Graphic company expenses, Abramson and Hearst coproduced, selecting projects and casting their films together. Abramson directed and wrote all the films, and the Hearst press provided bundles of publicity. It was the first time Hearst had ever made such an equal financial venture in the film business. It would also to be the last.

Abramson went to Hearst with his cousin's dilemma. Abramson was fairly certain that Hearst would give the case a sympathetic ear. After all, during this period Hearst was burned in effigy, his newsreels were heckled, and his newspapers boycotted over his war views. In the years preceding the April 6, 1917, declaration of war on Germany—when the United States was supposedly committed to a strict nonpartisan policy—Hearst waved a banner of what he called Americanism. Others thought his proud stance was a thin disguise for Anglophobia, or, worse still, they thought him subversively pro-German.

Hearst struggled between neutrality and inner prejudices. In 1914 he fell under the spell of a mysterious but articulate editorial writer named Philip Francis, who had once worked for George Hearst on the old *San Francisco Examiner*. During the summer of 1918 Francis spent weeks at a time with Hearst in California, and they traveled by train back to New York plotting editorial strategies. Francis's views were decidedly anti–President Wilson, pro-German, and pro-Irish. The Justice Department surmised Francis was a German agent. Even fellow Hearst writers were suspicious. It was discovered some thirty years later—possibly even to Hearst's surprise—that Francis had changed his name from Diefendorf, a fact that, if it had been known earlier, would have most certainly fueled criticism of Hearst during the war.

Hearst spoke of the war as essentially a financial call to arms, an unprecedented bloodbath instigated by Wall Street barons such as J. P. Morgan and Company that would be the main beneficiaries of war loans. Hearst lambasted these titans as international bankers acting as fiscal agents of foreign powers. Ferdinand Lundberg, the most critical of Hearst's biographers, remained wary of the Hearst papers' multifarious motives, describing Hearst's connections with German-American bankers and brewers and shared copper and mining interests with J. P. Morgan. But in an otherwise unrelenting treatise against the Hearst press, Lundberg acknowledges that "almost everything [the Hearst Press] said about the nature of the war as a gigantic slaughter for the benefit of financial and industrial groups was literally true."

Pondering Ivan Abramson's problem with his cousin, Hearst immediately enlisted the services of a powerful political crony. Senator John Hollis Bankhead II was the patriarch of a powerful southern dynasty, first elected to the Senate in 1907, the last year of Hearst's second and final term in Congress. The senator's brother, William, was a congressman, as was his son, Will, who was elected in 1916. The senior senator from Alabama, at seventy-six years of age, was the senior man in the Senate and the last veteran of the Confederate Army to hold office in Congress.

In 1916 Senator Bankhead held what Hearst considered a critical position as chairman of the Senate's Post Office Committee. The U.S. Postal Service oversaw the interstate transportation of newspapers, magazines, and films. Bankhead was particularly friendly to Hearst and other media moguls, introducing legislation to repeal laws that required publishers and editors to submit lengthy biannual data reports on circulation, personnel, and stockholders.

Perhaps most pivotal to Abramson and his cousin, Bankhead was close to the War Department's secretary, Newton D. Baker, who was, to a lesser degree, friendly with Hearst as well. Aside from his obvious military duties, Baker became an enthusiast for the modern field of communications. The secretary was the first cabinet official to hold scheduled news conferences, and he enjoyed talking to reporters about everything from war policy to an interest in horticulture. Baker was one of the first officials to advocate government-sponsored propaganda films, suggesting in 1916 that movie cameramen join reporters and photographers with U.S. troops stationed in Mexico. When war with Germany was declared, he promoted an organization to oversee censorship problems and methods of propaganda. A week later Wilson created the Committee on Public Information (CPI), appointed George Creel its chairman, and made Baker an executive board member. The five-foot-tall Baker—who was respected by his generals but derisively nicknamed "pansy" by critics—was an old friend of Creel, and they worked together closely. Baker lent Creel the services of a young major and organizational wizard named Douglas MacArthur while continuing a hands-on involvement with the CPI, especially its most effective film division.

After an initial contact from Bankhead, Secretary of War Baker arrived at Hearst and Abramson's film office on Seventh Avenue. Spoken or unspoken, understandings were reached at this unpublicized meeting. No doubt there was talk about press relations and the war for which Hearst had shown so little eagerness, for soon after the Godfrey office meeting Victory Bond rallies were held in New York City and given a huge publicity splash in the Hearst papers. Then Baker, who also held the wartime title of chairman of the Council of National Defense, made an unusual statement denouncing government criticism of the press. Stranger still, considering the well-known antagonism between Hearst and President Wilson, the secretary of war went out of his way to condemn criticism of the Hearst press.

The non-Hearst press was suspicious of this seemingly singular unsolicited advertisement for Hearst. One critic complained in the *New York Times* that Secretary Baker's recent flattering remarks were proof "that Hearst was a favorite with certain bureaus and departments in Washington." Baker's chief field officer, James Scherer—an outspoken critic of Hearst—felt Baker's prepared comments were aimed specifically at him. He resigned his post in protest. At first, Baker maintained that his statements about treating the press fairly were not partial. "I don't care if it is a Hearst paper or anybody else's," he declared. But later he inadvertently acknowledged that he had been persuaded to speak out by "a representative of one of the Hearst papers."

As if all this wasn't enough, around the time of his meeting with Hearst and Abramson, Secretary Baker also spoke out in favor of leniency toward military defectors. Teddy Roosevelt, a longtime Hearst nemesis, wondered why suddenly the Wilson administration was tolerating Hearst's antiwar activities. Roosevelt believed that "Hearst has kept in mind only the interests of Germany. He has been (violently) fundamentally anti-American."

According to those close to Abramson, Senator Bankhead made it clear to the Graphic partners that he wanted a small kindness from Hearst and

Abramson in return for his help in Abramson's cousin's case. Bankhead said he had a granddaughter who was living in New York and hopelessly stagestruck. The girl's father, Will Bankhead, through his own connections with the theater-producing Shuberts, had secured for her a small role in a play called *The Squab Farm*. "I think she's nuts," the senior Bankhead confessed to Hearst, but he thought that perhaps if Hearst and Abramson's Graphic Film Corporation could put her in a movie she might finally realize that she could never be a good actress. To Hearst this was a modest request.

Back at the army stockade, Abramson's cousin was reclassified as a conscientious objector, and all charges against him were dropped. In the lobby of New York's Algonquin Hotel, where famous Barrymore family members and Talmadge sisters mingled, a tiny redheaded sixteen-year-old was relaxing between performances when she received a calling card. Tallulah Bankhead's memories of that day would be hazy; she later recalled the short-but-sweet summons had come from a Mr. Abramson, who she thought was "electrifying" but identified only as a Russian director. Abramson told Miss Bankhead that he was casting a film called *When Men Betray*, a melodramatic tale of adultery and wild parties that he planned to release that summer. He had come to the Algonquin to find the actress to play the supporting role of Alice Edwardes, a rape victim.

When Men Betray, a six-reeler, was completed in fourteen days. Although the film was still not a star vehicle for the teenager, it was the first film in which her qualities as the "Southern Belle of Vamp" captured the public's attention and the critics.' It is worth noting that her positive notices extended beyond the expected raves of the Hearst press. Years later, Bankhead did remember the release of *When Men Betray* as a crossroads in her career. It was the moment she first felt like a self-sustaining actress.

Senator Bankhead and Secretary Baker could open doors, but Hearst was independently familiarized with Washington corridors. The incongruent coupling of Abramson's cousin and actress Bankhead constituted one episode in a film exchange of favors, but it was also a sign of things below the surface—and things to come.

GRAPHIC

The partnership of Ivan Abramson and Hearst originated, at least in spirit, in 1898. It was in that year that they both found their voices and their power in sensationalism. Born in Vilnius in 1869, Abramson left Lithuania for the

United States as a youngster and, after a minor brush with formal education, built a thriving business in New York City selling Singer sewing machines. By the end of the century Ivan had married Lizzie Einhorn, a Romanian opera singer, and settled in Greenwich Village. With the money he saved from his sewing machine business, Abramson took advantage of a real estate boom and bought up buildings and parcels of land in the Bronx. He befriended a journalist named John Paley and at his new friend's urging pooled his burgeoning income to back the establishment of a New York City newspaper.

By the late 1800s Abramson owned and managed the *Teglikhe Presse (Jewish Daily Press)*. New York's second-largest Yiddish newspaper, the *Teglikhe* was a liberal offshoot of Paley's orthodox *Tagelblatt*, the first Yiddish daily anywhere. In the first months of its operation, Abramson's newspaper had a disappointing circulation of less than twelve thousand. (During 1905 Hearst also owned a Yiddish newspaper in New York City, called *Der Amerikaner*. The paper, which was edited by both a Jewish scholar and translator named Jacob Pfeffer and a number of non-Jews, was unsuccessful and closed within a year.)

During the time of Abramson's *Teglikhe*, Hearst had two New York newspapers, the *New York Journal*, which he had bought from publisher John McLean in 1895, and the German-language paper *Das Morgen Journal*, which he acquired as a bonus in the McLean deal. Although Hearst's New York papers were doing much better than Abramson's Yiddish paper, they were still in a fierce uphill circulation battle with Joseph Pulitzer's *New York World*.

Fortunately for both Hearst and Abramson and their instincts for theatrics, 1898 was the year of the newspaper-driven Spanish-American War. In the midst of a climate of heightened patriotism, Abramson worried that, being foreign-born, his loyalty might be questioned. Always impulsive, he considered enlisting in the army and closing down his struggling newspaper. Perhaps Abramson thought that by joining Teddy Roosevelt's fighting brigade of Rough Riders he could erase any lingering doubts about his Americanism, or perhaps like many others he was swept up by the "splendid little war" and saw it as an escape from the weariness of trying to keep his poor little newspaper alive. Years later Abramson remembered a meeting at the *Teglikhe*'s downtown office when his entire staff lobbied him to stay. They suggested that he could better serve the war effort by using his newspaper to excite and unite his readers. The gloomy meeting quickly turned into a pep rally, and before long Abramson rose to his feet and spoke to his staff with a new sense of mission: "We must bring down to a minimum all petty news, all petty daily topics. . . . I want all of us to influence the young

Jewish generation to enlist in the army and navy. We must fill the hearts of the Jewish youth with the cry, 'Glory or the Grave!' "

Overnight, Abramson put his passion into printer's ink. With its large dramatic etchings and bold headlines, the *Teglikhe Presse* began to echo the dynamic look of the Hearst press. A publisher with a similar flamboyant style and a corresponding liberal attitude, Abramson was likely to have met Hearst during the period of the Spanish-American War. Almost certainly it was then that Abramson first came to believe in Hearst. To an impassioned man with humble beginnings like Abramson, Hearst was the master at speaking to the emotions of the "common man." Although it was mocked by more established newspapers, Hearst's new journalism was like a beacon to many others who were tired of tradition for tradition's sake and hungry for action, even if only for action's sake. With his unremitting crusades for the downtrodden, Hearst not only spoke to Abramson but also helped him to uncover his own powers of popular persuasion.

While it was true that Hearst was one of the first American men of great wealth to speak to and for the poor and disenfranchised and champion their causes in a consistent and effective way, it was also true that he was a businessman attuned to his own interests. Whatever the crusade, he never seriously risked his financial security. Nevertheless, Hearst's frequent editorials advocating reform of a myriad of institutions and his newspaper's daily menu of headlines and political cartoons attacking monopolies and money barons did not endear him to his class. But his acquiescence to this ostracism was not entirely self-sacrificing either. He may have believed there was no one better to look after the poor and powerless than a rich powerful man of compassion, but by appointing himself the people's watchdog his narcissistic traits often overpowered his capacity to do good for those most in need of help. He was much like a Tammany boss, except that he had a growing audience they could only reach in their dreams.

Hearst's disgust with trusts was largely in the abstract, while Abramson felt similarly repelled through personal experience. When the Spanish-American War ended, Abramson's publishing venture had the wind knocked out of it, and his momentarily thriving venture went into an irrevocable decline. Once again Abramson decided on a new path. Unloading the *Teglikhe Presse* and most of his Manhattan property, he put his resources into opera. In a decision of heart over mind, Abramson set out to engage a group of artists to create what he called an American grand opera.

To differentiate his troupe, Abramson made a commitment to presenting his opera performances at popular prices for ordinary people who lived outside the privileged Manhattan cliques. Proudly calling his company the Ivan Italian Grand Opera, he employed a chorus, a ballet, and an orchestra of forty-eight musicians under the direction of maestro Geotano Merola. He announced a top ticket price of $2.50 (a summer opera ticket at New York's West End Theater could be had for as little as 75 cents and for 50 cents at a Bowery theater). He cleverly planned his touring schedule to open in New York before the more flashy opening of the Metropolitan Opera, timing his road tour to end with a reprise performance in New York after the Met closed for the season.

By 1909, after a few years of more good intentions than financial success, the same old frustrations again plagued Abramson. His persistent crusade for a "People's Opera" was met by audience apathy. With increasing resentment, Abramson charged that the business of opera in the United States constituted a trust: "Grand Opera has been called a fashionable rather than a popular entertainment. Why? Simply because grand opera patrons have been taxed for the wide advertisement of so-called stars who possess personality rather than voice. A voice nearly as good as Caruso's will serve the purpose just as well as Caruso's voice, but because the possessor of the nearly-as-good voice has not been made famous or notorious through costly advertising he is given little chance to get ahead."

Abramson called the powers of the industry "dictators" and "grand opera czars." Their enormous wealth, he said, was controlling an art form and preventing opera from expanding beyond the cloistered environment of Manhattan. Abramson maintained that hundreds of good singers as well as numerous independent producers like him were being prevented from a fair chance at competing. In the end, the objects of Abramson's challenge were unmoved, and his experiment in popular opera went bankrupt, his company of artists unpaid.

Opera moved too slowly for Hearst. He was more likely to be cramming his pear-shaped two-hundred-pound body into a front row seat of the New Amsterdam Theatre and enjoying the Follies. But in 1909, speeding toward a third-place loss in a race for mayor of New York City, Hearst continued to use his newspaper chain as a political platform, editorializing on the evils of monopolies, striking out against nationwide trusts in insurance, coal, sugar, railroads, and oil. In Detroit he railed against the brick trust. New York came in for special assaults, including attacks on everything from the milk trust to the bathtub trust.

For all their fury about monopolies, both Hearst and Ivan Abramson were relatively silent and seemingly unfazed by one newly established monopoly: the Film Trust. In 1909, after months of negotiation, ten film manufacturers came together to form the Motion Pictures Patents Company. It was so named because each member, including Thomas Edison, George Kleine, Harry N. Marvin, and Albert Smith, owned a crucial patent linked with the filming or projecting of motion pictures. Strangely, the Patents Company was not immediately viewed as a dangerous monopoly. As film historian Benjamin Hampton wrote, "although the corporation was regarded as an 'airtight trust,' its lawyers declared that its formation was entirely legal." One year later, while the public's attention remained elsewhere, the Motion Picture Patents Company established an all-powerful distribution branch called the General Film Company. In short order and with little resistance, the Patents Company had begun a concerted effort to destroy competition from independent film producers.

Between 1910 and 1914, following the failure of his opera company, Ivan Abramson struggled to take hold of his career. Although he managed actor Jacob Adler, the father of the Yiddish theater, and staged productions of *Hamlet*, *King Lear*, and Leo Tolstoy's *The Living Corpse*, he found the business end of the theater dissatisfying. In 1914, while trying to write a Yiddish-language play of his own, he was approached by friends in the Union Square area to promote a foreign film about Jewish life in Palestine called *Life in the Holy Land*. Although this was basically another business assignment, Abramson found the film medium whet his appetite for screenwriting. Tired of his recent unhappy stretch of working for others, Abramson put his energies into writing, producing, and directing his own films. With the guidance of an attorney and friend, Moses A. Sachs—who also helped to mend the ragged edges of his broken English—Abramson formed Ivan Productions.

Abramson's titillating film titles announced melodramas that reflected his modern thinking as well as his risky showmanship. Usually five reels long and opulently designed, the films tackled such taboo subjects as common-law marriage, divorce, seduction, and illegitimacy. With their concern for people in unconventional relationships caught up in extraordinary events, they were unique for their day. Always the moral crusader, Abramson declared his intention was to make films that "point out an evil in life through one character and at the same time show the manner in which that evil might be cured through another character." His first film, *The Sins of the Parents*, featured a rare starring role by theater actress Sara Adler, the wife of Jacob, his former associate. The names of many of his other films—for example, *Should a Woman Divorce* and *Forbidden Fruit*—showed that Abramson had learned something about the value of shock as well as the merits of moral teaching.

Shock value was double edged. In late 1916 Abramson's *Sex Lure* opened. Early in 1917 the film brought Abramson to court and to the closer attention of his future partner. By order of the State Supreme Court of New York, the exhibition of *Sex Lure* was banned. But in an unusual ruling the court, under Judge Clarence J. Shearn, found nothing objectionable about the film's content. What the judge found legally unacceptable was the racy title and the producer's advertising. Shearn declared that the movie's producer "was inviting the public to the theater upon false pretenses, and seeking to capitalize whatever degenerate interest there may be created by the use of this name and the posters that go with it."

Hearst was naturally drawn to this case that was making legal history. He had known Judge Shearn since 1900, when he retained him as an attorney to fight his legal battles against the ice trust (Shearn would later become a Hearst executive, and in 1937 he took financial control of the Hearst organization when it teetered on the edge of bankruptcy). And the judge's censure of Abramson must have been most particularly intriguing to Hearst, as he had faced similar attacks on his own sensationalism and his advertising methods. It was at this time that Hearst and Abramson began discussing the possibilities of an independent film movement.

Hearst shared Abramson's view of film as an uplifting and penetrating force, with enormous attention-getting potential for communication with the masses. Working in the new medium came easy for Hearst, who saw film as an "extension" of publishing, specifically his own brand of publishing. He was convinced that the techniques he used in making up newspapers and magazines—his headlines and sensational illustrations shooting across the page like firework displays and his advertising methods that were more like a barter system—could be successfully applied to film. While many in the industry considered Abramson's types of films prurient, Hearst viewed Abramson's approach as the film equivalent of yellow journalism. He ignored Abramson's critics as he did his own. If some were offended by Abramson, many others would be drawn to the attractions.

Still, the businessman in Hearst was not about to throw all caution to the winds. While Hearst gave each Graphic Film production his attention and abundant publicity, he remained a silent partner in the enterprise. Abramson seemed to have no problem with this arrangement. He enjoyed the persona of a struggling independent. He seemed happy to be a sort of barker for the Graphic film shows. Abramson's ego swelled, knowing that he was an equal partner with a man he had admired for so long. With an affectionate bit of ribbing that recalled well-known political losses, he called Hearst "the Governor," and he later referred to Hearst as "noble by heritage."

Abramson convinced himself that Hearst was the perfect ally to produce films for the independent market in the climate of the rapidly developing film monopolies. As Abramson later wrote: "[Hearst was] a man whose great influence was like a vein of water flowing underground, hidden, but secretly nourishing the soil. . . . His name gave the independents new hope and strength in the battle for commercial freedom, and his presence in the industry was regarded as a panacea for all the evils from which the independents were suffering."

Abramson's high-energy showmanship and high-minded propaganda were often a refuge for personal disappointments. After years as an independent, struggling in an industry headed for conglomeration, Abramson had come to Hearst for the kind of clout, he later said, he needed "to save my business from destruction." Abramson saw Hearst as the savior of independent filmmakers. He had no idea how the road to Hearst would lead him into further disrepute and total disintegration.

BLUEPRINTS FROM THE GODFREY BUILDING

In 1917, as he organized the Graphic Film Corporation with Abramson, Hearst was already engaged in a myriad of film ventures. Headquartered on William Street, in lower Manhattan, was the Hearst newsreel run by the charming and perceptive Edgar Hatrick. Like many Hearst men, Hatrick's career started in advertising and publicity. A native of Pennsylvania, he claimed that one of his earliest stunts was getting the robust and publicity-seeking Teddy Roosevelt to pose and spar with a client who was a Japanese jujitsu expert. Hatrick worked briefly in the executive offices of the Associated Press but was soon wrested away. In 1908 Hearst put Hatrick in charge of the Hearst news photo service. Like his new employer, Hatrick foresaw film as a storyteller for news. With Hearst's encouragement, Hatrick created for himself the post of Hearst newsreel czar, in which he helped to invent the modern newsreel business, utilizing the best technology of the period and filling his organization with first-rate news gatherers.

Following a succession of *The Perils of Pauline* episodes in 1914, Hearst directed the production of a string of alliteratively titled cliff-hangers including *The Exploits of Elaine* and *The Mysteries of Myra*. Hearst also produced *Beatrice Fairfax* under the guidance of former magazine editor Edward McManus, who in 1912 originated the idea of tying a movie serial to its newspaper serial equivalent. With actress Grace Darling in the title role, *Beatrice* presented the continuing adventures of a Hearst lovelorn columnist and was filmed by the Wharton Brothers, successful serial directors and producers in Ithaca, New York.

By 1916 Hearst's International Film Service presented half-reel nature studies filmed by Edward Curtis, the pioneer photographer, best known for his dreamlike photographs of Native Americans. The Hearst newspapers praised Curtis as a "master of light and shade" and called his views of the Yosemite Falls and the Canoe Indians of Alaska "pictures of sublime beauty." These nature studies made up half of what was called a "split reel," or "motion picture cocktail." They were screened biweekly, alternating with filmed fashion shows staged especially for the IFS cameras. Hearst publicity gave the fashion half-reels equal play with the Curtis films. One group of popular International Film fashion stars that included well-known actresses like Olive Thomas and the singing and dancing Hungarian Dolly sisters (the Gabor sisters of their day) also included a newcomer. Dressed in a gown by Lucille, the teenager Marion Davies made her celluloid debut. The other half of the reel was a cartoon produced by Hearst's animation studio at the Godfrey Building at 729 Seventh Avenue.

On the fifteenth floor of the Godfrey, Gregory La Cava managed a staff busy animating the cartoons of the Hearst Sunday newspaper supplement. The Hearst Animation Studio was an eerie space. Window shades drawn, tireless cartoonists worked their magic over the glow of light boxes casting expressionist shadows on the ceiling. La Cava had a small office in a partitioned section of the floor where a shelf held a thick stack of cartoon scenario manuscripts. (To create a greater sense of fluidity and realism in his cartoon characters, La Cava instructed his artists to increase the number of drawings for an average cartoon from 2,000 to 3,500 and to discontinue the distracting use of "bubble" titles.) In the middle of the studio's largest space, some twenty young women sat at desks tracing artist sketches onto thin sheets of celluloid. A separate area was set aside for Hearst newspaper cartoonists; elder statesmen of newspaper cartooning like George Herriman (*Krazy Kat*) and George McManus (*Bringing Up Father*) would meet there to exchange ideas with the film animators of their cartoons. The end of the production line at Hearst's fun factory was a room where a stationary motion picture camera was placed directly over a table to take pictures of celluloid drawings clamped to a light box, one exposure at a time.

When Hearst and Abramson's Graphic Film Corporation was incorporated on December 3, 1917, their suite of offices, combined with the International Film Service offices, occupied the top two floors of the Godfrey Building. The two-floor layout included a choice corner office for Abramson, Graphic's president, director, and chief scenarist, as well as an office for advertising zealot Carl Zittel—who was now the film company's general manager—in addition to business and exchange offices and nitrate film storage vaults. A large projection room was constructed for the executives on the sixteenth floor. One floor below, another larger theater, richly paneled in the neoclassic Adam style, seated fifty people.

Hearst's similarly paneled office was rarely used. The 1915 blueprints for the Godfrey Building included plans for a simple rooftop apartment that would become Hearst's headquarters. The first tenant of the penthouse was Earl Carroll, an enterprising young showman whose glamorous girls would soon make attempts to rival Flo Ziegfeld's. When the Godfrey went up, Carroll was a songwriter, and it was in this penthouse that he wrote a hit song called "Dream of Long Ago," with music by Enrico Caruso, as well as some of his earliest musical comedies. When International and Graphic moved into the Godfrey, a few changes were made to the compact apartment. But to Hearst's delight it had already been designed in his beloved tile-roofed California bungalow style by Arthur Loomis Harmon, the building's architect, who some fifteen years later was part of the architectural team that contributed to the design of the Empire State Building.

One of the Godfrey's three elevators rode express to the penthouse. Hearst's apartment, some twenty-six by twenty-eight feet, took up less than half the roof space but included a kitchen, bath, bedroom, dining room, and comfortable living room with a fireplace. A window in the bedroom opened on a manicured Japanese garden, where one of Hearst's antique fountains was installed, sprinkling a gentle mist. A Japanese butler was on duty twenty-four hours a day.

Next door to the main entrance of the Godfrey Building, on Seventh Avenue, was a new hangout for the moving-picture crowd. In keeping with the new tenor of the neighborhood, Billie's Restaurant changed its name, becoming the Film Cafe. In its front window were displayed photographs of the latest movie stars. One of the most popular actresses in the Film Cafe's window and on screens around the country was Clara Kimball Young. The dark-haired Young was the jewel of Lewis Selznick's World Film Company. Selznick—a friend of Hearst and Abramson—was as well known for his film publicity as for his films. The former jewelry shop owner was one of the first to arrange banquets at hotels where the press could screen prereleased films. Copying an idea coined by theater promoters, he set up huge electric signs to advertise his films and the Selznick name. When World Film's financial backers grew tired of what they perceived to be Selznick's endless self-promotions, they eased him out. But, to the Wall Street owners' dismay, Selznick took Young with him and incorporated a company in her name. When the Godfrey opened in 1916, Selznick was its first film company tenant. He moved from the Hotel Claridge, where he had been headquartered, and named the entire seventh floor of the Godfrey the Clara Kimball Young Film Corporation executive offices.

At five o'clock on most afternoons, on the sidewalks outside the Godfrey, Hearst and Abramson would meet with their bookmakers, who were then more politely called betting commissioners. Horse racing became a passion for Hearst, as it had been for his father, George. Three or four times a week a limousine waited at the curb to whisk the Graphic Film partners away on an hour drive to the racetrack at Belmont Park on Long Island.

Isaac E. Chadwick, a young executive at Graphic, was often Hearst and Abramson's racetrack companion. The British-born Cornell University graduate had previously been a U.S. agent for the French Pathé Frères film company and had organized the Merit Film Corporation. Chadwick was an elegant gentleman, as interested in books as in film. While climbing the ladder of the film industry, he devoted much of his time to his own book-bindery, printing books with expensively tooled bindings. (Years later, Chadwick established a film studio complex in Hollywood at Gower and Sunset, in the center of which he managed an office for the distribution of his fine books. Over the years he sold Hearst hundreds of rare editions.) Sometimes these afternoon trips to the racetrack required the use of several cars. Along with Chadwick and Abramson's two grandchildren—who were plucked from their school—Marion Davies, who was a popular Ziegfeld Follies girl but not yet a film actress, often escorted Hearst. And Abramson was also likely to bring a girlfriend along. More often than not it was Clara Kimball Young, whom his grandsons assumed to be his mistress.

Returning to the top of the Godfrey, Hearst, Abramson, and their guests were presented with a panoramic view of Times Square at sunset. Stretching out below them was the illuminated roof garden of the Astor Hotel and the not-too-distant Hudson River. Below, on Forty-seventh Street, hurdy-gurdy men could still be spotted playing the popular songs of the day. The Seventh Avenue trolley passed the celebrity-filled restaurant of former police captain Jim Churchill and swung past Rectors's restaurant on Forty-eighth Street, where a "special $1.50 table d'hôte dinner" was served in a magnificent seven-hundred-seat ballroom, while showgirls costumed in creations by Madame Sherri entertained the crowd.

In their two-year partnership, Hearst allowed Abramson free rein in choosing story material for the Graphic films. The first film, directed by Abramson and completed in February 1918, was called *Moral Suicide*. (According to an unresolved plagiarism suit later that year, Abramson had, at least unconsciously, reached back to a turn-of-the-century Yiddish play called *The Wild Man* for the film's storyline and characters.) The film starred

Anne Luther, a twenty-five-year-old Fox star. With camera work by the no-frills cameraman Henry Conjager—nicknamed "One Take"—*Moral Suicide* was a roller-coaster ride pinned to the exploits of a cold-hearted vamp named Fay Hope whose extravagances are bankrupting her much older businessman husband. In the course of seven reels, infidelity and betrayal are played against a backdrop of secret service intrigue.

Moral Suicide, distributed by the Pathé Exchange, was shown at the Broadway and Empire theaters as well as the theaters of the Loews circuit. The Hearst papers gave the film and the Graphic Film Corporation an appropriate send-off. Hearst in particular was excited by the finished film. "He was so enthused over my story and direction," Abramson remembered, "that he gave an order to one of his most famous writers, Nell Brinkley, to novelize the story, and to have it printed daily in New York, and syndicated it in his papers all over the country."

The release of *Moral Suicide* was the peak of Abramson's working relationship with Hearst, who serialized the scenario and provided flattering reviews in his newspaper chain. Hearst support, Abramson said, had "created a great demand for our productions." Abramson's public optimism about his relationship with Hearst was probably more self-promotion than self-assurance. Soon enough, ideals about independent filmmaking would be abandoned, trusts would be betrayed, and the egotism and volatility of both men would bring the partnership to a fiery end.

Perils of Passion
1915–1918

THE GOSSIP

As the summer of 1918 neared, a small item appeared at the bottom of a
page of movie and Broadway gossip in the New York magazine *Town Topics*:

> The town is plastered with Lithos and other flamboyant advertising
> material of Marion Davies, who has been making movie appearances
> here recently. This advertising, which must have cost a fortune, is
> reported to have been done by William Randolph Hearst, who is
> deeply interested in the movie business and believed that in Miss
> Davies he had another Pickford. Last winter the Hearsts entertained
> the Davies girl in Palm Beach, together with the Dolly Sisters, and no
> one will be more disappointed than the newspaper magnate at the fail-
> ure of his new star to impress the critics and enthuse the audiences.

The column was ghostwritten by Lady Duff-Gordon, a British society
matron, fashion guru, and sister to Elinor Glyn, author of the sensational
novel *It*. While submitting her fluffy pieces, Duff-Gordon was also employed
as a part-time writer for the Hearst publications.

For many years the slogan pinned to every Hearst newsroom bulletin
board was "Get It First." It wasn't until much later that a directive on accuracy was posted. Hearst was in love with high-speed communication, and he

relished being the first to know the news. Recognizing that gossip often turned out to be fact, he held a special place for those among his employees and friends who could supply him with information—no matter how fragmentary—about the rich and famous, millionaires or movie stars, just about anyone he deemed important or interesting. Often there was no distinction: if they were interesting they became important. It was said that at his San Simeon estate guests at the long dining table of the Refectory found themselves moved farther away from their host seated at its center the longer they stayed at the hilltop "ranch." These guests were not being permanently shunned; they had simply used up their supply of stories, rumors, and gossip. It was time for them to move on and be replaced.

While Hearst enjoyed hearing about others and seeing his own name given prominence in print, he wasn't eager to spread accounts of his private affairs. But he was reckless and not always able to intercept the gossip that was being generated about his own life. Fortunately for Hearst freelancer Lady Duff-Gordon, her *Town Topics* filler wasn't seen by her boss until several months after it first appeared, for despite some inaccuracies, the chatty lines came dangerously close to revealing the beginnings of Hearst's secret passionate liaison. If Hearst's wife, Millicent, saw the piece, the revelation that "the Hearsts entertained the Davies girl" must have hit her like a slap in the face. It was true that William Randolph Hearst had vacationed in Palm Beach—but his wife, Millicent Hearst, had been alone in New York that winter.

Although Marion Davies would later claim she was born several years into the twentieth century, she was in fact born Marion Douras on January 3, 1897, only a few blocks from the docks and saloons scattered along Brooklyn's waterfront. Although Marion's grandparents on her mother's side of the family may have been wealthy (she later said they owned numerous properties between Twelfth and Fourteenth streets in Manhattan), her father, Bernard Douras, was only a moderately successful lawyer and a heavy drinker. His battle with alcoholism caused him and Rose, Marion's mother, to separate frequently. One of the longer separations began in 1905 and was probably also impelled by the sudden drowning death of the Douras's only boy, Charles. In the wake of the tragedy, Rose left Bernard and took her children to live in an apartment at 218 East Twentieth Street, a few blocks from Union Square, where vaudeville houses and music halls were steadily being replaced by movie theaters and cheap dives. Whether Rose moved to this part of town because her parents owned real estate there or because it was close to the rialto area is not known, but the locale may have made the adjustment easier for the all-female household. Rose's older daughters in particular thoroughly enjoyed the fast-paced city and the opportunities open to women, especially pretty young women, on the stage.

A likely catalyst to the girls' quick advancement was Rose's constant refrain that they stood a better chance of bettering their lives by getting well connected with well-connected men. Reine, a brunette beauty who was considered the most talented of the singing and dancing Douras daughters, was able to please her mother and make an important show business association for herself when she met and married the leading vaudeville producer of the time, George Lederer. Another chapter in the transformation of Rose's daughters occurred after Reine passed by a memorable billboard. There on the side of a Manhattan building was an advertisement for the J. Clarence Davies Company, a well-known real estate firm, whose name dangled on the shingles of properties all over town. As Reine and her two other sisters, Ethel and Rose, prepared to join the music hall and vaudeville circuit of Keith-Orpheum, the three young women changed their last name to Davies. And their youngest sister, Marion, soon followed their lead.

Theater producer Charles Dillingham was a sort of lucky charm for Hearst, Millicent, and Marion Davies. Before he went into the theater, the well-loved Dillingham was a hotel reporter for the *Chicago Tribune*, writing pieces on celebrities and politicians who were passing through town on their way to New York or California. In the course of his work in Chicago and Washington, Dillingham became friendly with Hearst's father, the gregarious Senator George Hearst. In 1887 the senator told Dillingham that his young son would soon be arriving in Chicago on his way West to take ownership of the *San Francisco Examiner*. Senator Hearst suggested that Dillingham speak to his son: "I have a laugh for you. My son Will wants me to buy him a San Francisco newspaper. He is my son and I'm going to do it, but he hasn't any chance at all with those hard-boiled San Francisco publishers. They'll have his paper in six months. . . . Ask him what he is going to do with the newspaper."

Two weeks later the twenty-four-year-old Hearst granted his first interview to Charles Dillingham. Years later Hearst remembered feeling "elated" and "pretty much inflated" by the flattering experience. The day of that interview was especially etched in Dillingham's mind for another reason. As he recalled in his unpublished memoirs, after meeting with Hearst he met with another young journalist at the Richelieu Hotel, in Chicago. Whether it was a coincidence is not known, but Hearst's future editor Arthur Brisbane wound up giving his first interview on the very same day to Dillingham.

Years later, looking back on Broadway's first years during the new century, producer Dillingham had a nostalgic recollection of the era's irreplaceable images. In a letter he wrote to Millicent Hearst in 1915, he recalled the sights of "Paderwiski's [*sic*] long hair, Anna Held's bath of consommé soup," and "W.R.'s big hats." The composer's bohemian look may have been as contrived as Held's beauty regimens, but Hearst's look was the genuine article. At six feet plus, with his Stetson hat and a penchant for spontaneous tap dancing, Hearst was a press agent's inspiration. Dillingham remained friends with Hearst and his family for most of his adult life. He and his wife were much-welcomed guests of Phoebe Hearst's in 1915. During their weekend stay in California they watched Hearst family home movies. One film, made by cameraman Joe Hubbell, showed a camera-shy Phoebe squinting in the sunlight and surrounded by her family. Dillingham was particularly fond of Millicent, and in one of the playful letters he exchanged with her he suggested that it was time she put her on her dancing slippers and return to the stage. Millicent played along with Dillingham's flatteries and hinted that she was seriously considering his offers. But there was no chance that Hearst's wife would return to her former life, and she signed her note to Dillingham, "The Hesitating Hearst." In 1933, at the end of his life in the theater, Dillingham was forced to file for bankruptcy. Only a few who remembered their bond to the show business legend came to his rescue with loans that were never repaid. One of them was Millicent, and the other was Marion Davies.

One of the first of the rich and powerful men whose names Rose Douras may have planted in her daughter's mind was William Randolph Hearst. Sometime before 1910, on Halloween, when Davies was still Douras, Marion and her friends went trick-or-treating to 123 Lexington Avenue, just a few blocks from the Douras household. At the time, Hearst and Millicent were still living at the townhouse. Although the couple may not have been home when Marion and her girlfriends arrived, their butler was, and he found himself on the wrong end of a bag of rotten fruits and vegetables. Later, when the police came to chase Marion away and send her home to her mother, she learned about the famous man who lived inside the house that was a target of her childhood mischief.

A Charles Dillingham production that opened in late 1914 may have been the backdrop for the first face-to-face meeting between the fifty-one-year-old Hearst and the seventeen-year-old Davies. At that time, except for political functions or charity events, when Millicent was usually by his side, Hearst spent most evenings with friends like newspaper publisher Paul Block, editors Arthur Brisbane and Carl Zittel, or some other crony who would keep him company at a Broadway musical or comedy show. Sometimes Hearst would take a large group of friends and associates to the theater, and at other times, according to legend, he would purchase only two seats, one for himself and one for his wide-brimmed hat.

The gossip columnist Hedda Hopper, who became a close confidante of Davies's, claimed Hearst met his mistress on the opening night of the 1914 stage production of *Queen of the Movies*. The title of the play makes it seem almost too fitting a background for the start of the Davies–Hearst relationship, and Hopper's story has never been corroborated. Correspondence among the surviving papers of the show's producer, Charles Dillingham, indicates, however, that Hearst did intend to go to the opening night of *Queen of the Movies*. On January 7, 1914, Victor Watson, Hearst's friend and drama critic on the *New York American*, sent a telegram to the show's producer: "Will it be possible for me to purchase fifteen good seats well down front for the opening of the 'Queen of the Movies' for Mr. W. R. Hearst personally please advise at once so I can get busy with the speculators if you cannot accommodate Mr. Hearst."

On the same day the telegram was sent, Dillingham responded to Watson, saying that although the order was large, Hearst would have the tickets. But Hearst soon realized that a previous appointment in Canada, where he had newspaper pulp business, would prevent him and his friends from attending the show's first night. Unfortunately for fans of Hopper's romantic story, Watson was forced to send off a handwritten note to Dillingham with Hearst's apologies. "He has asked me to return the box which you so kindly sent to him." Of course, given the regularity with which Hearst attended the theater, it is more than likely that he saw *Queen of the Movies* and Davies soon after he returned from Canada. Indeed, Hopper may be essentially correct about their first meeting.

Like her sisters, Marion Davies faithfully abided by her mother's program for success. Even as a young teenager she was filled with ambition to be a performer and fueled by a desire for adventure, material things, and attachments with wealthy and dynamic older men. Romantic encounters for Davies—some more serious than others—seemed to be as frequent as the twirls she performed on the musical stage. With each turn she moved closer to the spotlight, closer to acclaim, and closer to the wealthiest and most dynamic man she would ever know. Hearst never recorded his memories about his first meeting with Davies. Davies's recollections were a jumbling of dates, people, and places that may be the deliberate evasions of a woman who was "the other woman" or possibly the confusion of an actress who spent the early years of her life in the pursuit of accomplished men and promising acting roles. The memories of others are not definitive either, but they do provide a portrait of the lives Davies and Hearst lived in the late teens of the twentieth century.

One surviving story that turns up with slight variations has Davies being brought to Hearst as what is euphemistically called an escort. An associate of Hearst during those days claimed that an obscure figure named Leo Taub, who had something of a reputation for finding girls for rich men, worked his magic between Hearst and Davies and was later handsomely rewarded with an executive position in the film industry. Others suggest that Zittel— who was better known for soliciting advertising for Hearst—was the go-between, this possibility offering one logical explanation for the soft spot Hearst had for the less than loyal employee. Still another scenario has Paul Block, the publisher, acting as a stepping-stone between Davies and Hearst. Davies's biographers, Fred Guiles and Kenneth Marx, and the screenwriter Anita Loos, who knew Davies well, were convinced that Block and Davies were involved in an affair just before Hearst entered the picture. They imply that the otherwise happily married Block came to his senses and "passed her on" to Hearst. In her posthumous memoirs, culled from a series of often insightful, sometimes rambling interviews, Davies seems barely able to recognize Block's name.

The extent of this early relationship between Block and Davies is uncertain, but witnesses to their affair claim it was a romance that the couple took little trouble to hide. Block, Davies, and Hearst remained close friends right through the 1940s. Block helped secure newspapers in Pittsburgh and elsewhere for Hearst, and he also served as an advertisement adviser to his friend. He took his children on some of the numerous visits he paid to Hearst and Davies at San Simeon and their Wyntoon estate in northern California. Block and Hearst were not only early rivals for Davies's affections. In 1934, while both men were traveling in Germany, they tried to scoop each other with an exclusive interview with Adolf Hitler. Hearst won the race, and Block settled for a low-level Nazi official.

Even before she met the wealthy Block or the Svengali-like Hearst, Davies's sexy but friendly qualities were attracting attention. Like many other chorus girls who have romanticized their way of life, she would later brag about the expensive gifts she received and the numerous proposals she turned down. The names Astor, Duke, Wanamaker, and Vanderbilt were often mentioned, and letters and invitations to after-theater parties from some of these men do survive. Some of Davies's admirers were wealthy men who were unknown to her but had become infatuated by her stage performances. After World War I broke out and Davies was just starting her film career, a soldier from a wealthy Boston family, a nephew of J. P. Morgan, who was now a lonesome ambulance driver stationed at the front, wrote the actress from "somewhere in France":

My dear Miss Davies:

Possibly this letter will seem rather peculiar to you. I am at the Front in France and wanted to know whether you would send me your photograph with your signature as I am one of your most ardent admirers and have seen you act many times. It is absolutely impossible to procure or buy your photograph over here, so I thought if it wasn't too much to ask you, you would send me one. Hoping not to have bothered you too much

When the young soldier wrote his fan letter to Davies, he was relatively unknown. But by the end of the 1920s Harry Crosby was a bohemian poet and publisher of the Black Sun Press, a handsome, reckless, and extravagant icon who would come to represent the Jazz Age. At the very end of that decade, two months after the great stock market crash, Crosby's peculiar thoughts about worshiping the sun became intertwined with a dark foreboding and haunting memories of loss and youth at the front. Lying in a bed in a borrowed loft in New York's Hotel des Artistes, Crosby shot his mistress to death, two hours later took the same gun to himself, and on the following morning made headlines that eclipsed those of most movie stars.

A Test

At the Crystal Studio, on Claremont Avenue in the Bronx, on a weekend in early April 1918, Tallulah Bankhead was being filmed by Hearst's Graphic partner Ivan Abramson for a scene in *When Men Betray*. Near the end of Bankhead's last scene for the day, Marion Davies arrived at the same studio for her first screen test. Only a few months earlier, Hearst had seen a prerelease screening of Davies's first feature film, a forgettable gypsy love story called *Runaway Romany*. The picture seemed to represent some of the forces that had advanced Davies's career and simultaneously fulfilled her mother's prophecy. It was written in part by a Hearst newspaperman named Clarence Linder (Davies herself may have contributed to the screenplay) and produced for the Pathé Company by Davies's ex-brother-in-law, George W. Lederer, who had recently gone into motion pictures. A substantial chunk

of the picture's financing—the now ridiculously low figure of $23,000—
came from Davies's former lover, Paul Block.

Davies's arrival at the Crystal Studio was announced by Ella "Bill"
Williams, a telephone operator, gatekeeper, and notorious busybody. Miss
Williams ushered Davies into the office of Zittel, general manager of
Hearst's film interests. In the main studio, a French cameraman named Mar-
cel A. Le Picard was setting up his equipment for Davies's anxiously awaited
screen test. Le Picard, who was said to have an extraordinary eye for light,
would eventually work on D. W. Griffith's *America*. In the late teens he
worked almost exclusively for Abramson. While waiting for the test to begin,
Davies and Zittel discussed her limited film experience and her future. Sitting across from her, Zit was his usual blunt self. "I've seen your picture," he
told Davies, referring to the Lederer production, "and it rather stinks."
Davies, who was always as skeptical about her own talents as her harshest
critic, must have surprised and charmed Zit when she pretty much agreed
with his assessment. But what Zittel, or Davies, or anyone else thought of
Davies as an actress meant little compared to what Hearst thought. He had
summoned Davies to his studio not to see what she looked like on film but
for the purpose of formally introducing her to his film partner. From the
moment he began to see Davies as a movie actress, Hearst began to conceive
of Abramson's supervising her in the sumptuous and seductive style that had
brought him some raves and considerable notoriety.

Hearst and Abramson were planning to make a film called *Ashes of Love*
after completing *When Men Betray*. The film tells the story of an unfaithful
woman named Ethel who marries Arthur Woodridge, a much older wealthy
philanthropist, so that she can care for her lonely live-in mother. Ethel's
ongoing tryst with her cousin's husband reaches its climax, cinematically
represented by a thunderstorm that leads to pneumonia and death for Ethel.
Arthur, grieving and still naively trusting in the memory of Ethel, eventually finds some solace in marrying his dead wife's mother. Hearst had Davies
in mind to play Ethel. But it was not to be. When Abramson finished directing Tallulah Bankhead's scene, Davies was called to the set. Abramson's
grandson, Milton Gould, a child actor at the time who would later become
a well-known New York attorney, remembered visiting the studio that day,
as well as Abramson's recollections about what transpired:

> I went over—I think it must have been a weekend—with Ivan to the
> studio and watched them take the screen tests of Marion Davies. She
> was terrible according to him. I certainly had no judgement. . . . But I
> remember that the screen tests didn't go well. And that there then

ensued some bitter arguments between Abramson and Hearst, in which Ivan—who was feeling his oats, you know he was getting drunk on his own liquor, even thought he was a great artist—he kept telling Hearst that she was no good. That she would never be an actress, and that he didn't want to direct her, didn't want to use her.

Unbeknownst to Abramson, even before the test camera rolled, Davies and Zittel had already discussed the five-hundred-dollar weekly salary that Hearst was planning to pay her. A contract was waiting for Davies, and the screen test and the meeting with Abramson were a mere formality.

Hearst did allow Abramson to make *Ashes of Love* without Davies. The film was released in September 1918, with its lead parts filled by stage actors Ruby De Remer and James K. Hackett. One reviewer, who was unlikely to have known the backstory of the picture, called it a "much involved sex mess" and observed that "the cast was satisfactory considering what they had to go through." Graphic, a company that was heralded as starting a new independent film movement, made only two more films: *Echo of Youth* and *Life or Honor*, the second apparently never released. By early 1919 Hearst was seeking new alliances, Abramson bought out Hearst's half share, and Graphic ceased operations. Afterward, Hearst and Abramson remained outwardly cordial, but their quarrels over Davies had a lasting effect. According to Ivan Abramson's grandson, "from then on they were enemies." The screen test was an equally important marker in the partnership of Davies and Hearst: the actress had passed the test of the man who would provide her with an emotional commitment and the basis for the career she had long planned.

8

Trader

1914–1918

WIRELESS

In the fall of 1914, through the auspices of the International News Service, the Hearst newspaper chain published a dramatic photograph of a capsized British battleship, the S.S. *Audacious*, that had been wrecked by a German torpedo. Until that moment, England, maintaining a strict control of war news because of its virtual monopoly on cable communications, had repeatedly denied that the sinking had occurred. It was now confronted with the black-and-white newsprint truth, and it was humiliated. The British-born George Allison, Hearst's INS man in London since 1912, had obtained the pictures of the H.M.S. *Audacious*. Allison was charged with keeping a steady flow of illustrations going to the New York office. "There was a wild scramble for photographs of anything appertaining to war," he recalled, "soldiers, weapons, ships, aircraft and the rest of the panoply. I contacted every photographic agency in London and asked them to submit photographs."

Later, Allison acknowledged that the *Audacious* photographs came to him more through "luck and chance" than through hard work. One day, at the bar of London's Press Club, Allison struck up a conversation with a man who was waiting for an appointment with a Belfast newspaper editor. Several drinks later Allison realized there was no sign of the editor. Allison's companion suggested that one possible reason for the delay was his editor friend's indecision about what to do with a just-received package of pictures showing the sinking of a British battleship off the north coast of Ireland. The pictures, he told Allison, had been taken by a tourist from a nearby ocean liner named the *Olympia*.

Allison could barely contain himself, as rumors about the *Audacious* had been spreading in London all week long. By the end of the day, he had made a deal with the Belfast editor and sent the prized pictures off to International's New York office. Coincidentally, another passenger from the *Olympia*, unrelated to the amateur photographer, arrived in New York the same day as the parcel of *Audacious* photographs. As Allison recalled: "He rushed, strangely enough to one of our New York newspaper offices, burning to tell and sell his story. The paper was skeptical. It feared that it might be a phoney yarn. While the doubts were being expressed my pictures arrived."

The Hearst papers scooped their rivals, put the story and the pictures together, and blew the official British denials right out of the water. Over the next two years Hearst's criticism of Great Britain steadily increased. He believed that British banking interests and arms manufacturers were driving the world toward war, and he resented their technological stranglehold on news communication. During 1916 Hearst editorialized in praise of Sir Roger Casement, a British diplomat accused of treason. On the eve of Easter, Casement was arrested as he exited a U-boat that was traveling from Germany. He had been in secret negotiations with various German officials, including Ambassador to the United States Count von Bernstorff, hoping to garner military support for an Irish rebellion for independence. Through the weeks of Casement's arrest and trial, Hearst led America's most vocal attack against Britain and in defense of Casement and Ireland, publishing numerous articles about Casement and presenting glowing images of him in the Hearst newsreels. When Casement was convicted and hanged that August, the Hearst papers carried a full-page tribute to him bordered in black.

On October 9, in the retaliatory and vindictive style at which Hearst himself excelled, England boycotted the Hearst wire services and Hearst newsreels, forbidding them to secure news by disallowing their use of the mails and cables running from Great Britain. On October 29 France followed Britain's lead, and on November 11 Canada was nudged to do the same. Before the end of the year Australia, Portugal, and Japan had joined the ban. With the list of boycotts growing, financial losses piled up alongside Hearst's already punctured pride and active prejudices, but he would not be suppressed. Not surprisingly, he turned to guerrilla news-gathering methods and was further drawn into Germany's sphere of influence. It was later learned through a landmark case on the "ownership" of news that Hearst's INS was actively pilfering news from the Associated Press and sending it out to its own affiliates "sometimes with slight verbal alterations, in many cases verbatim." Often, because of their advanced telegraphic communications technology, the Hearst wire services were even able to publish AP-obtained news before the AP did.

Soon a new opportunity for Hearst to make himself a player in the field of communications arrived. In October of 1916—seven months before the U.S. declaration of war and two years after direct radio communication between the United States and Germany had been inaugurated—Hearst struck a deal with Germany for the use of the wireless station it owned and operated at Sayville, Long Island. At the time, the Sayville station was one of the largest licensed centers in the United States for the sending and receiving of messages, capable of communication with the German wireless headquarters at Nauen, a suburb of Berlin, more than four thousand miles away. But although the German wireless station was considered a practical means for communicating news and information, it operated on a weak circuit.

Indications are that Hearst saw his deal with the Germans as just the beginning of a much wider arrangement. On October 21 one of his International News Service correspondents, Bayard Hale—who was also being financed by Germany—wrote Hearst from his office in Berlin: "View British news blockade would you consider enlarged internews service connection important agencies here. Have already obtained temporary working understanding, including larger accommodation wireless. Full understanding only waits your authority.... Believe large possibilities open great European news service." Hale hustled the negotiations with the Germans and was able to reduce the wireless rate for Hearst to eight cents a word. His telegram later that same day convinced Hearst to move toward the new arrangement with Germany: "Can perfect arrangements International News Service and agencies here if given authority. Believe can obtain valuable connection for you, thus making possible greatly expanded International News Service. Service would include photograph, films. You should come yourself or give authority me and nobody else." Hearst soon began to send wireless payments to Stuttgart through the New York bankers Schultz and Ruckgaber.

Despite his repeated and very public displays of hostility toward Great Britain, Hearst was a practical businessman. He maintained close and useful ties to the publishing magnate Lord Northcliffe as well as to others in the British government. Soon after the British boycott, Hearst secured a place in British army intelligence for his newsreel cameraman Ariel Varges. As early as 1914, while in London covering society news, Varges made friends with the tea merchant and international yachtsman Sir Thomas Lipton, who had previously been a social acquaintance of Hearst and his wife. During the spring of 1915 Lipton converted his yacht, the *Erin*, into a hospital ship and brought a group of Red Cross doctors and nurses with medical supplies to Serbia, which was in the midst of a typhoid epidemic. He became a folk hero to the Serbians, who with affection called Sir Thomas "Tchika Toma" (Uncle Tom). On his mission of mercy, Lipton brought along his friend Varges, who had just finished an assignment for Hearst filming the effects of a major earthquake in Avezzno, Italy.

Edgar Hatrick, the Hearst newsreel chief, later confirmed the arrangement with the British and remembered Varges as his most adventurous cameraman:

After "covering" the earthquake he returned to Marseilles, France, where he rejoined the *Erin* and started to Serbia. His experiences there were horrible and thrilling. At that time a Typhus was raging throughout the country, and the people were dying by the thousands. Varges was taken down with the fever, but his good condition managed to pull him through. He returned to London in June 1915 and here he received permission to join the British forces at Salonica, being the only American photographer permitted to work with the British Army. He worked on this front for a year, making a number of remarkable films.

During the period when Varges worked side by side with the British, he was still a cameraman for Hearst. Despite the fact that they were clamping down on the Hearst wire services, in the fall of 1916 the British asked permission of the International Film Service to take Varges on as a captain in their intelligence department. George Allison also continued to be of help to Hearst during the troubles with Britain. He remained Hearst's representative in London while being "attached officially" to the British War Office and the admiralty. In the fall of 1916 Allison arranged the making of a film called *Two Wrecked Zeppelins in England*. The admiralty gave permission to make the film and in exchange bought the British rights (the film was shown for the benefit of naval charities). On September 29 Allison wrote Ed Hatrick in New York, "I had to break off my vacation to get back to look after this new development but it was worth it after what I have been able to achieve. I know you will give the film a big show as that is eminently desirable from many viewpoints."

Meanwhile, although an agreement came close, Allison was unable to secure a Hearst distribution deal for the war films of Charles Urban, a pioneering American-born producer who had moved his film company to England following patent disputes with Edison. Urban had little confidence in Hearst's stated desire to give his film *The Battle of the Somme*—the first in a series of British propaganda films—a "big show." With a widespread distrust of Hearst on his side, Urban's U.S. agent nixed the deal by convincing the director that it was Hearst's intention to buy up British films simply to shelve or destroy them. In his autobiography, Allison scoffed at the idea that his American boss's anti-British attitude was harmful to the Allied cause:

> The propaganda pictures which I put out officially were mostly taken by Hearst cameramen operating on all fronts. Propaganda pictures went into his chain of newspapers across the United States. I had the Hearst system publicizing pictorially the cause of Britain and her Allies. . . . There were two-way scoops, like the one which was lapped up by the Admiralty this side and by our organization on the other. One of my newsreel men [A. E. Wallace] returning from the Hook of Holland in the *Batavia III*, a Dutch ship, was sitting in his cabin when he heard something of a commotion. His professional instinct told him to fix his movie camera. From a porthole he took what was the first picture ever seen by authorities in England of a German submarine in action. The cameraman was an American, the U.S. was not yet in the war, and the German boarding-party allowed him to carry on. Back in London I had the film rushed to the developing tanks and advised the Admiralty. For some days naval experts had the film run through and through to study these pictures. It was about that time that I placed my personal services and those of our professional staff at the disposal of the Admiralty.

With orders from the Hearst office in New York, Allison sent an unknown Belgium movie cameraman (who also carried a German passport) to film newsreels of the ruins of the Belgian city of Louvain, which had been leveled by the German army. Shot in late August or early September 1914, the footage was sent to New York, edited down to 650 feet, and shown a month later in the *Hearst-Selig News Pictorial*. Universal's London representative John D. Tippett claimed that these films were the only early war pictures of consequence. According to Tippett, everything else that made it to the States at that stage of the war was "old faked-up junk." The Belgian cameraman with two passports returned to his native country to secure more film for Hearst but was never seen again. "We saw him no more," Allison remembered. "The Kaiser's secret service, we heard later, caught up with him, and who knows his fate?"

ENTANGLEMENTS

For Hearst, Germany was barely a foreign country. He sentimentally remembered spending summers there in 1877 and 1878, when he enjoyed the sights in the shadow of his doting mother. He returned to Germany as a young man and gravitated to the brightly festooned beer gardens, the women of the Café Luitpold and the Bierkellers, and the secessionist artists of fin-de-siècle Munich. He continued to make yearly pilgrimages, visiting his old friend the eccentric-looking painter Orrin Peck, who was still living in Germany in the days before the war. But sentimentality was only one factor affecting his perception of Germany. As always, his emotions were closely connected to his business interests. The Allied stories about atrocities in Germany—some true and some part of a propaganda campaign—had little hope of penetrating Hearst's romantic notions of Germany when those notions involved the possibility of lucrative news and film deals.

Hearst editorialized that the war in Europe was "a crime against civilization" and "a reversion to barbarism," but even during the early days of American neutrality he encouraged production and expansion of foreign markets. There could be profit in an emergency situation: "People who formerly bought foreign goods will now buy American goods. On the other hand the greater part of our foreign markets will remain untouched. We can still export our products to England, France, Italy, Spain, and many other European countries, to all of South America and to the Orient." Noticeably missing from Hearst's list was Germany, a country where he clearly hoped for a favored relationship.

Hearst gave valuable newspaper space to the writings of the fiery Hudson Maxim, who had gained fame as the inventor of a smokeless powder explosive and as the brother of Sir Hiram Stevens Maxim, a machine gun inventor. Hudson Maxim's book on war preparedness was published by Hearst's International Library and turned into 1915's popular film *The Battle Cry of Peace*. In an August 1914 article for the *New York American*, Maxim echoed Hearst's repeated calls for the establishment of a merchant marine and urged the United States to take advantage of the war. While European countries were preoccupied, Maxim suggested that America rush to capture the more than one-billion-dollar South American market, where, not insignificantly, Hearst already had important copper interests in the Cerro de Pasco region of Peru, still dominated at the beginning of the war by British banking interests.

Like other men interested in film, Hearst understood the medium's importance as a trading product. As W. Stephen Bush wrote in the *Moving Picture World* magazine of September 1914: "Never before in the history of motion pictures have conditions in the international film market been more favorable for American producers than at this time." According to Bush, Germany was third in line after France and Italy in its hold on the world's film market: "Whether the country is a victorious one or whether it must be numbered among the vanquished it will have to look for its films without its borders. There is but one country which can offer the supply needed and that country is the U.S.A."

Hearst understood the importance and urgency of being well positioned in the competition for the expanding film market. In July 1914, two years before he changed his name to Goldwyn, Sam Goldfish, then general manager of the Jesse L. Lasky Company, returned from an extensive trip through Europe. While in Germany he finalized a distribution deal with the Duesseldorfer Film Company and made similar arrangements in England. "The men on the other side are begging for good stuff," Goldfish told eager film executives in New York. "I feel we have the materials and the organization to give them what they want."

When President Wilson declared war on Germany in April 1917, Hearst's sudden burst of patriotic spirit was rightly suspect. Many Americans, remembering his attacks on Great Britain and his kid-glove treatment of Germany, were convinced that Hearst was secretly working for the enemy. It became almost a right of passage for a non-Hearst reporter to uncover some new and damaging piece to the puzzle that pictured Hearst entangled with German plots and propaganda. An often-told story maintained that before the United States entered the war, Hearst held numerous meetings with Count von Bernstorff, the German ambassador to the United States, as well as a French publisher named Paul Bolo Pasha, who was later convicted of spying for Germany. The ambassador, among others, led a concerted pro-German indoctrination effort in United States through various means, including the purchasing of newspapers and the distribution of propaganda films. Bolo Pasha, with his publishing and paper mill connections in America, acted as a well-connected henchman. Hearst never denied that he had met von Bernstorff. The meeting was no secret, he said, the ambassador was a well-known diplomat and had also met with a *New York Times* editor and other prominent New Yorkers. Anyway, Hearst pointed out, the United States was not at war at the time.

In truth, Hearst had more than a few meetings with von Bernstorff and other well-placed Germans, beginning as early as 1915. According to Justice Department files, on June 24, 1915, Hearst met in person with Dr. Heinrich Albert, of the German Department of the Interior. Albert, whose office was in the Hamburg-American Building at 45 Broadway, was Germany's commercial attaché and charged with overseeing the expenditures of tens of millions of dollars for propaganda and sabotage purposes. A few months after their June meeting, Albert received a letter from Hearst related to Hearst's interest in sending a movie cameraman to Germany. On December 13, 1915, Hearst sent a letter to von Bernstorff, again on the subject of getting a cameraman into Germany: "I am very glad to hear that the moving picture matter can be arranged, so that we can expect German pictures. Of course you know that I am anxious to do this for every reason. I have a moving picture man in Holland [A. E. Wallace], whom I can send promptly to Berlin, or if desirable, on account of letters of introduction, passport, etc., I can send you one of our best men immediately from here."

At the time of the questionable meetings, it was not known that Bolo Pasha was betraying his native country. And Ambassador von Bernstorff's secret dealings had not been divulged. Nevertheless, Hearst's obvious sympathy for Germany between 1915 and 1917 prompted the United States government to focus part of its investigation into German propaganda directly on Hearst's activities. Hearst files in various government departments grew thick as Attorney General Thomas Watt Gregory and future justice head A. Mitchell Palmer ordered—under legal cover—the interception of Hearst's mail, secret service infiltration of his businesses, and monitoring of his telephone conversations.

During a Senate hearing following the government's investigation, Bruce Bielaski, a Justice investigator, produced fourteen selected telegrams written by Hearst to his editors over seven separate days from his Palm Beach winter vacation home of 1917. A larger number of telegrams exchanged between staff members and written to Hearst were added to the mix. It would seem that these telegrams—photographic copies furnished by the Naval Intelligence Service—were the best evidence Justice had. All in all they show a publisher acutely interested in circulation—he makes specific instructions on political cartoons, typographical composition, and the use of patriotic flags on the banner head—but also a man disturbed by the increasing power of the presidency and the threat of war. Hearst may have been sincere in this regard, since he likely had no reason to believe that what he said in confidence to employees would be stolen by the government and eventually disseminated to the press and published in newspapers across the country.

A March 2 telegram written by Hearst to S. S. Carvalho, editor of the *New York American*, had nothing to do with German propaganda, but it must have really peeved the Justice Department. The first subject of the telegram is the veracity of the so-called Zimmermann note, purportedly written by Arthur Zimmermann, Germany's foreign affairs secretary to Mexico, intercepted by British Intelligence in February 1917 and passed along to President Wilson shortly thereafter. Zimmermann offers Mexico assistance in the recovery of Texas, Arizona, and New Mexico, if Mexico will agree to attack the United States if and when it declared war against Germany. Commenting on the Zimmermann disclosure in his telegram, Hearst declared his belief—shared at the time by many in the Wilson administration—that the note was a hoax, meant to create an atmosphere for war. It was what Hearst then wrote to editor Carvalho that was so pointed. "In all probability [the note was]," he said, "[an] absolute fake and forgery, prepared by a very unscrupulous Attorney General's very unscrupulous department." Hearst went on to call federal agents "the most reckless concoctors of evidence," specifically accusing Attorney General Gregory of being "a spy fancier and plot conceiver." Hearst further expressed his faith in the intelligence of the American public if presented with all points of view. "The people," Hearst said, "should neither be deceived by the machinations of a tricky Attorney General nor deceived of their rights to decide a question of war or any other momentous question."

As the investigation into Hearst's disloyalty stretched into the Christmas holiday season of 1918, the tenacious Bruce Bielaski was still trying to link Hearst with von Bernstorff and Bolo Pasha. He produced affidavits from five chauffeurs and three elevator boys, a doorman, a janitor, and a switchboard operator from Hearst's Clarendon apartment building in New York. One elevator boy declared under oath that von Bernstorff and Bolo Pasha had been regular visitors of either Hearst or his wife. Von Bernstorff and Bolo Pasha, whom the Clarendon staff nicknamed the "Duke de la Brew" and the "Duke de la Caw," had such privileged status, he declared, that they could be escorted to Hearst's apartment door unannounced. Hearst dismissed the charges as the hallucinations of disgruntled employees and claimed that powerful federal agents had manipulated the workers.

The general testimony about visits from von Bernstorff and Bolo remained inconclusive. None of the witness affidavits could establish specific dates or patterns in the timing of the visits. And none could in any way determine the nature of the visits; the employees' observations of the visitors never went farther than the Clarendon's elevator gates.

Some of the stories circulated by government investigators strained credulity. They said that Hearst was sending secret messages to German U-boats in the Hudson River by means of color-coded lights from a top floor of the Clarendon, on Riverside Drive. But the mysterious signals turned out to be chandelier bulbs flickering through Hearst's extensive collection of Tiffany stained glass. Claims were made that a roof bridge had been constructed to connect the Clarendon with an adjoining building on Eighty-sixth Street, for the easy passage of German spies. But it was never explained why such recognizable figures as Bolo Pasha and von Bernstorff would need a secret passageway, since according to the employees' depositions the spies already felt free to enter and exit through Hearst's front door. Martin Huberth, Hearst's real estate manager, said the accusations about the wrought-iron roof bridge were ludicrous. It was nothing more than a much-needed fire escape from a penthouse enclosure that included a rooftop swimming pool for Hearst's sons.

Another important focus of the Senate investigation in 1918 was an attempt to establish a tie between Hearst and Germany in the use of film to wage a propaganda war against the Allies. Investigators claimed that an alliance had been formed as early as 1914, when war broke out in Europe and the established methods of newspaper reporting and news film taking had been interrupted. Hearst's well-known sympathy for Germany would have given him a jump start on any other American newsreel man who was being lured by the propagandists, and it is entirely conceivable that he seized the opportunity that presented itself to him. In September 1914 the German Information Service was organized, ostensibly to offer features and news articles portraying a positive image of German and German policies to U.S. news agencies. The financial operations of the organizations were run by Dr. Karl Fuehr. It was revealed in 1918 that the editorial chief of the German Information Service was Dr. William Bayard Hale, Hearst's International News Service's Berlin correspondent. While Hale was working for the German Information Service, he was advising Hearst on the operation of a small publishing house in New York. Hearst's Deutschland Library operated briefly in 1916, publishing books and other literature with a decidedly pro-German slant. As a hands-on publisher, Hearst undoubtedly knew that the Information Service distributed up to one dozen pro-German and bitterly anti-British articles every day. He may have also known that the German service was having only limited success through the print media. By 1915 the propagandists were already searching for new ways to gather favorable stories and present their version of the news more persuasively.

In April, under the guidance of Matthew Claussen, a publicist for the Hamburg-America shipping line, the Germans incorporated the American Correspondent Film Company, a propaganda vehicle organized with an emphasis on the widest possible circulation of its films rather than the greatest financial profits. Dr. Fuehr of the German Information Service became the film company's secretary. In its one-year lifetime, the company produced a dozen or so documentaries on the Danube River, Zeppelin travel, and scenes of battle in Europe from an explicitly German point of view. On the eve of the formation of the German-owned film company, Arthur Zimmermann had wired von Bernstorff: "As propaganda through pictures has shown itself to be remarkably effective in neutral foreign countries, it seems expedient to place this work of publication on a greater basis than heretofore."

While Hearst's association with Dr. Hale, Ambassador von Bernstorff, and others suggests an affinity with German propagandists, the precise nature of his relationship with the German Information Service or the American Correspondent Film Company is not known. One section of an internal German Information Bureau report, introduced at the Senate investigation in late 1918, is intriguing but somewhat ambiguous. The most incriminating evidence against Hearst appears in a short paragraph that expresses regrets at "the shipwreck of our combination with Hearst." The report submits that the "combination" with Hearst had to do with "circulation of our films." The "circulation" may refer to Hearst newspaper publicity for the films, but this is something the Germans were likely to secure regardless of any secret agreement. More likely the Germans wanted help from Hearst in setting up distribution and theaters to exhibit their films. Another reference to the "shipwreck" implies that the Hearst "combination" had only been in the planning stages and was never concluded. Perhaps for these reasons, the investigators did not pursue the pieces of the puzzle with the most potential damage. Bruce Bielaski and the other Justice officials seemed perfectly satisfied to leave the Senate and the public with tantalizing traces of Hearst's unproven disloyalty. The Justice Department may also have realized that whatever the true nature of Hearst's arrangement with the American Correspondent Film Company, it was extremely short lived and therefore of little consequence. The report that noted the termination, or "shipwrecking," of the Hearst connection was written on November 14, 1915, only a few months after the film company's incorporation.

If Hearst was directly involved with the American Correspondent Film

Company, he saw nothing wrong with attaching himself to a film venture seemingly at odds with the aims of German propagandists. In late 1915 a film rivalry that echoed the Hearst–Pulitzer newspaper circulation wars of a generation earlier began in earnest when the general manager of the *New York World* approached John Wheeler of the Wheeler Syndicate. The *World's* manager reported that a correspondent named E. Alexander Powell had gotten his hands on some interesting battle films from France as a reward for his agreeable reporting. The French government was looking for an American newspaper to promote the footage and a producer to distribute it. Powell had been chosen to give lectures to accompany the pictures. The *World* was approaching Wheeler to make a deal with Powell and the theater impresario Morris Gest.

Wheeler met Gest at the producer's lavish office, where, according to Wheeler, "the carpet was so thick you would sink in up to your ankles and the lighting so dim you couldn't read the fine print in a contract." Gest apologized to his friend Wheeler: the *World's* offer had come a day too late. Gest had been up until three in the morning at the Clarendon screening the same films for Hearst, and he had agreed to back them. Wheeler bounced back from the disappointment: " 'You know he has the reputation of being pro-German,' I answered. 'You'll make a great hit with the French I guess if *he* is connected with them.' "

This was enough to talk Gest out of the deal with Hearst. The next day, over lunch, Wheeler mentioned his coup to the reporter Frederick Palmer. Palmer said he knew all about the French films, that in fact no one had exclusive use of them. "The French give them away for publicity," he told Wheeler, "I have some I am going to use with my lecture." Sure that the Hearst organization had already gotten wind of this too, Wheeler struggled to move Gest more quickly to set up a theater for the *World's* "exclusive" battle films. But it wasn't until a two-page advertisement in the *American* appeared for the quickly edited and titled *Fighting for France* that Gest really woke up. According to Wheeler, while Gest dawdled, Ed Hatrick "found out where we were having our prints made and bribed one of the hands to make a duplicate negative." Hearst's *Fighting for France* made it to the George M. Cohan Theater six hours before the *New York World's Fighting in France* opened at the Fulton Theater. But despite the neck and neck race, the two film presentations were identical except for their advertisements.

As the Senate investigation into Hearst's activities came to a close in December 1918, chief investigator Bielaski surprised many by announcing that no criminal charges would be made against Hearst. "Hearst was well advised," Bielaski told the press. "He did many things before we entered the war that he refrained from doing thereafter, and he did many things before the enactment of the espionage law that he did not do after that." Almost in passing, he indicated that in his opinion Hearst was most eager to establish a friendly relationship with Germany to obtain an exclusive wireless arrangement. In the end, Bielaski seemed to be saying, Hearst had skirted the law and the standards of patriotism during war. Hearst wanted a jump on the emerging international communications market; his loyalty was to his own business interests: German and American interests were secondary.

Further evidence that Hearst saw a new, exciting, and lucrative world of communications over the horizon need not be gleaned from confiscated telegrams; it is there in his own publications. In 1916, while Hearst was eagerly watching developments in Germany on devices for high-speed wireless transmission of news and pictures, his New York newspapers had joined forces with radio and television pioneer Lee DeForest to broadcast election results in the metropolitan area. DeForest's Harlem River station was connected by a special line to the seventh floor of the *New York American*'s printing plant, near the Brooklyn Bridge. There is no suggestion that the inventor's experimental tie-in with Hearst had anything to do with Germany's propaganda campaigns or the war in general. It did, however, give a hint of things to come in the field of communication, such as television and facsimile transmissions. DeForest called the experiment the "first Wireless Telephone Newspaper." In thanking Hearst for his cooperation, DeForest predicted that "the time will come when from large wireless telephone stations scattered throughout the country, literally hundreds of thousands of listeners provided with a simple receiver, will be able to get the latest news, combined with music and entertainment, in their homes."

The Perils of Propaganda
1917–1918

FILM BY COMMITTEE

On the evening of June 23, 1918, a sign went up outside New York's Broadway Theater warning late arrivals that a film called *The Yanks Are Coming* would not be coming. In bold yellow letters, the makeshift poster ordered by a furious film producer declared that the showing had been: "STOPPED BY THE CREEL-HEARST COMMITTEE."

It is unlikely that more than a handful of moviegoers coming to the Broadway Theater to see the short documentary about aircraft preparedness, filmed by the Universal Film Manufacturing Company at the Dayton-Wright Airplane factory, would have any notion of what the sign meant. Those already in the theater sat in silence as James M. Sheen, counsel for Universal, took the stage and explained the reason for the ban. The film was being stopped, Sheen said, because something called "the Committee" had maintained that the film was missing an appropriate permit and that it might in some way divulge military secrets. At the risk of bringing on a Justice Department investigation and possible criminal action, Sheen said, the theater had decided to cancel the screening. Finally, Sheen got specific, and he laid the blame for the banning of *The Yanks Are Coming* on the "Creel Committee" and its cozy relationship with William Randolph Hearst.

The "Creel Committee" was the Committee on Public Information (CPI), the United States' first ministry of propaganda, headed by George

Creel. A little more than a year before *The Yanks Are Coming* controversy and one week after a declaration of war was approved, President Wilson appointed the Missouri-born Creel to lead an unprecedented mission to persuade Americans to transform an accepted policy of neutrality into readiness and willingness for war. To rally the country's spirit it was necessary to convince the public that Germany—"the Hun"—was a ruthless incorrigible enemy and that America was a land of inherent virtue and invincible military strength. Creel came to work for the government with a reputation as a fine journalist, but his seemingly sudden conversion of principles caused him to be attacked as a turncoat by his former colleagues. Many regarded him as a censor of freedom more than a propagandist for freedom. From his new cabinet-level post Creel spent as much time fending off his critics as he did coordinating propaganda efforts with the secretaries of state and the navy, and especially War Secretary Newton Baker, whose Council of National Defense supervised the nationwide distribution of war films.

Creel would later say about his job at the CPI that it was nothing less than the advertising and selling of America. It was not surprising, considering his mission, that in his earlier profession, Creel had encountered Hearst, one of America's most successful advertisers and salesmen. The two men had known each other since the late 1890s, when Creel was a humor writer on the *New York Evening Journal* and its Sunday comic supplement. Creel would later recall that period of his life with fondness, especially Hearst, whom he remembered as a man dashing here and there "very Western in his black, broad-brimmed Stetson." Their relationship continued in the years between the Spanish-American War and the First World War. Creel published articles in Hearst's *Cosmopolitan* magazine, and in 1914 his successful book on the evils of child labor, *Children in Bondage*, was published by Hearst's International Library. As late as 1916 Creel was still occasionally employed as a freelance writer for Hearst. And like Hearst Creel also had connections with the film industry. He was married to Blanche Bates, an actress who appeared in *The Girl of the Golden West* and *The Seats of the Mighty*, this last a 1914 production of the World Film Corporation, headed by future Committee on Public Information executives William Brady and Jules Brulatour, a salesman of raw film stock for the Eastman Kodak Company. Creel even did some acting himself and dabbled in scenario writing.

A film division for the CPI was a natural offshoot, and its formation was officially announced in the fall of 1917, several months after Creel's appointment. But its first months, dominated by the involvement of Brady of the World company, were marked by financial and distribution problems, conflicting interests, and rumors of kickbacks on the part of Creel's friend Jules Brulatour. The division remained haphazard, and only a few films of significance were produced. It wasn't until about February 1918, when Creel named Charles Hart to run the film unit, that motion pictures became a vital factor in the government's program. Hart made the film division so strong that many commercial filmmakers feared he was working with Creel to encroach and possibly take over their industry. Some of their fear was likely related to the fact that Hart was even closer to Hearst than Creel was. Hart had no experience in film before coming to work for Creel. For the seven years prior to the government assignment, he had been the advertising manager of *Hearst's Magazine*, a pictorial weekly of fiction and politics. It was Hart's success at that job that piqued Creel's interest. With the urging of the CPI's associate director, Carl Byoir, and another assistant, named Edgar Sisson, Creel nominated Hart to head a totally restructured film unit. Their advice had considerable weight. Byoir had been previously employed as the circulation manager and Sisson as the editor of Hearst's *Cosmopolitan* magazine.

On the day following attorney Sheen's theater speech about *The Yanks Are Coming* and fueled by a press release issued by Robert H. Cochrane, a cofounder of Universal and a former advertising man, New York City newspapers detailed the Creel-Hearst story with notable enthusiasm on their front pages. The papers reported the names of the Hearst men who worked for the committee and disclosed details about Hearst's most recent influence on the film division. A week before Universal's aircraft factory film was suppressed, apparently, concerns over sensitive military secrets had been overlooked, and the Hearst-Pathé newsreel screened a film similar to the Universal picture.

It was also one week before *The Yanks Are Coming* episode that Universal's vice president, Patrick A. Powers, appeared in Washington before representatives of the House Ways and Means Committee, which had been convened to discuss proposed tax increases on movie theater admissions. During the hearing, Powers shifted the subject of his testimony to make an attack on Creel and Hearst. According to Powers, the Creel Committee was actively engaged in stamping out competition in the newsreel industry. As Powers told Congress, Creel and his right-hand man, Charles Hart, had ordered all filming of war pictures, formerly under the loose control of the Red Cross, to be put under the direction of Army Signal Corps personnel and cameramen. Ed Hatrick, the Hearst film vice president, had been ordered to France, where from a room at the Grand Hotel in Paris, nursing a life-threatening bronchial condition, he oversaw the film division's reorganization. Joe Hubbell, Hearst's favorite cameraman at the time, was also sent to Europe to join Hatrick. Hubbell and a small group of reporters and cameramen went first to Neufchâteau and thence to other points where they began taking pictures to be sent home primarily for the CPI's own newsreel called *Official War Review*. A good deal of Hatrick and Hubbell's film footage was incorporated into a feature-length Creel Committee film entitled *America's Answer*, which after successful showings at theaters in Europe premiered in the United States on July 29, 1918. *America's Answer* purported to be patriotic propaganda, but it also presented a more subtle message that war itself might be more horrible than the Hun. Many of the scenes lacked the expected rabble-rousing, focusing instead on more mundane aspects of the war effort: the clearing of land for roads and the like. One of the more striking sequences is quite bleak: it features a young, lost-looking soldier nearly shrouded by a huge pile of discarded army boots.

While Hearst men were being given certain advantages in obtaining film of the war, real war footage was still hard to come by. Cameramen were weighed down with heavy equipment and forced to stay back from the action. Often the idea of a war scene was infinitely more vivid than an actuality. Cameraman Hubbell later recalled how filming often required a certain "stretching" of reality: "Our idea was to make up propaganda films to show what we were doing. On one occasion they had hospital trains near us that could run up to the front and bring back the wounded. We took a company of men, bandaged them up and laid them out in the sun on stretchers and loaded the train. I was brought up on charges that I was faking it. Well, that wasn't a good word. I was just representing an occasion that you wouldn't take the chance with a lot of wounded men. And it looked just the same."

The charges against Hubbell apparently didn't stick. Soon after, near the German border, he thought of another representation to glorify the power of the Allied army. "I had a couple of companies of men marching past the borderline into Germany," Hubbell would later say, "which was good propaganda. They simply went across the border and around the city square and crossed the border. After doing that a half dozen times we had a pretty good picture of thousands of men going into Germany."

Within a few months, Ed Hatrick's organization of cameramen and film editors made the Signal Corps a small but competitive operation that rivaled the commercial news film industry. Creel strictly forbade film concerns other than official Signal Corps cameramen from going abroad and obtaining pictures. And while no film company was restricted from volunteering the services of its cameramen, the top decision-making level was controlled by Hatrick and Hearst.

The most cunning aspect of the Creel-Hearst operation was how it pretended to be even-handed in its approach to other newsreel companies. According to Creel, some duplicate and inferior films rejected for the CPI's *Official War Review* newsreel would be sent back home and made available to commercial newsreel concerns. But what actually happened was that the choice film material went to the so-called highest bidder, which just happened to be Pathé, a film exchange in partnership with Hearst. Not surprisingly, this favored relationship with Pathé meant that a number of key Pathé officials—from J. A. Berst (an executive with the organization since 1896) to its vice president, Paul Brunet—rose to the top of the CPI's film division, working side by side with Hearst's hand-picked film lieutenants.

"Out of the entire industry," Universal's Pat Powers told Congress in his testimony, "they have selected one particular concern to make a contract with for the exclusive distribution of the war pictures and the pictures of the boys at the front."

"So that the men who had the say about the monopoly and who should have the monopoly were formerly in the Hearst-Pathé service and now under the Creel Bureau?" asked Representative Treadway of Massachusetts.

"Yes, sir," replied Powers.

The committee's protestations over the revelation regarding a Hearst-Creel alliance came swiftly, but they were clumsy. In the matter of the *Yanks Are Coming* ban, Creel claimed that Universal had not been issued a permit to film a military installation, while Carl Byoir, Creel's associate director, claimed it had. Paul Brunet and others with Pathé stated there was not nor had there ever been any connection between their company and Hearst. But of course Hearst was associated with Pathé as early as 1914, engaged in the highly publicized *Perils of Pauline* deal. Its entire film product had been distributed through Pathé exchanges since January 1917. And the Hearst-Pathé News did not split until the end of 1918.

Hearst felt it was necessary for him to respond personally to the accusations of a Creel alliance by publishing a letter he had written to the CPI chairman in 1917, only weeks after the appointment of his employee Charles Hart. In the widely circulated letter, Hearst describes himself as "greatly disturbed" about losing such an important man as Hart to Creel's Committee. The use of the letter was duplicitous; surely if Hearst had not agreed to the "loss" of Hart and others it would not have happened. "I felt ashamed of myself," Hearst said in expounding on his letter, "after having written such a letter and replied again to Mr. Creel, telling him to take anyone he liked." Clearly, it was no real "loss" to have Hart or any of his men working for Creel when he would be having an important say in their operation and also receive a percentage of the profits of the "government's" films.

Although they turned out to be unwarranted, there were real worries in the summer of 1918 that after the war Creel's division of film might become a formidable film industry unto itself. Some suspected that Hearst had this in mind when he agreed to lose some of his key executives to the new government agency. Universal executive Robert Cochrane was one who had no doubts about the motives of Creel and Hearst:

> [Creel] is so completely under the Hearst control and so surrounded with Hearst influences that he will take advantage of his official position in the exploitation of pictures in any way dealing with Government propaganda. In other words, Mr. Hearst practically controls the Creel Committee so far as films are concerned. If Mr. Hearst can secure control of the screen in this way, he has created for himself the biggest political weapon ever wielded by any one man in the history of the United States. With Hearst control of the screen through the Committee of Public Information, Mr. Hearst has more power than he would have if he controlled all of the newspapers in the United States. He would have a bigger daily audience, no matter how many of his newspapers were burned every day in hundreds of cities. He could elect his own President, he could direct his own Governors, and he could be his own Czar.

In making his cautionary statement to the press, Cochrane may have recalled some prophetic comments Hearst had made two years earlier. In a letter to one of his newspaper writers that was published in a film trade magazine, Hearst declared that film was "the most modern form of presentation" of ideas. "That which is shown in moving pictures," Hearst wrote, "impresses itself upon the mind with a force not equaled in any other way."

PATRIA

Although Hearst had friends in high places, Woodrow Wilson was never one of them. Their antipathy toward each other, already simmering because of Hearst's attitudes toward Germany and Great Britain, burgeoned into outright rivalry with the making of the 1917 movie serial *Patria*. From the start, Hearst saw this film as an incredible opportunity to combine propaganda with box office appeal, and when Wilson got wind of the project he saw it as a chance to embarrass and maybe even neutralize Hearst. As their battle behind the scenes unfolded, the rescue-and-adventure series became the focus of a seminal clash of politics and cinema that turned a president into a movie censor and a producer into a power in the film industry.

In early 1915 the correspondent Edward Lyell Fox was dispatched to Germany by the Wildman News Syndicate to write feature-length articles on the war. Unbeknownst to Wildman, Fox at the same time was in the pay of Germany as editorial chief of the German Information Service and hired by the American Correspondent Film Company to give lectures to accompany the company's pro-German propaganda films. Meanwhile, while in Germany in the spring of 1915, Hearst's Berlin bureau chief Gustav Schweppendick made an arrangement with Fox to write articles for the Hearst syndicate. Hearst may not have known that Germany was financing Fox when this deal was struck, but his views certainly harmonized with Fox's writings, which were critical of the British, soft on German aggression, and cautionary about a vague Japanese menace. In April 1915 Fox excited the Hearst editors by writing an article for Hearst's *New York American* and his *Deutsches Journal* entitled "Professor Stein, Greatest Peace Apostle, Warns United States of Japanese Perils." Fox was encouraged by Schweppendick to continue to play up "the Japanese stuff."

The Germans were well aware of Hearst's antipathy toward Japan, an ally of England in 1915. Fox wrote a memorandum to Captain Fritz von Papen of the German Information Service, intercepted by the Justice Department, which discusses in detail how an organized fear campaign against Japan could divert attention from the European conflict and how Hearst and other "peace promoters" could be used as unwitting agents in this enterprise: "An examination of the files of the Hearst newspapers will show their bitterness toward Japan. No chance has been passed by them to warn people against the Japs and to foment trouble in California. . . . Any anti-Japanese move would have the complete support of Mr. Hearst. He is a native of California and in the past has done his utmost against them."

The same memo discusses how Hiram Moe Greene, a playwright and editor-in-chief of the *Illustrated Sunday Magazine* and the *Literary Magazine*—Sunday supplements partially owned by Paul Block, possibly acting as a stand-in for Hearst—could be approached to write anti-Japanese articles and fiction on a weekly basis. Considered by Fox to be pro-German, Greene was in 1914 the scenarist for a Universal movie serial called *Lucille Love, Girl of Mystery*. Fox suggests to von Papen that Greene's dramatic talents made him an ideal candidate to write a film infused with anti-Japanese sentiments "to be shown in weekly installments that synchronize with a continued story to be syndicated in the same cities the pictures appear." Fox goes on to discuss the specific costs of such a venture, including amounts to be paid for a manuscript and for a completed production. The memo stressed the likelihood that Greene could be contacted directly, without a need to approach the better-known Block. Speaking in the third person, Fox assures Von Papen that "Fox can arrange the entire matter."

Greene later vehemently denied that he had ever been approached to write Japanese propaganda. Fox admitted to writing the memo; however, he said it was really the bluster of a fired-up, overzealous writer. He also claimed that the memo was actually penned to extort money from von Papen. In his strange vision of an anti-Japanese press and film combination, Fox saw Hearst playing a passive but receptive role. The memo emphasizes that "Mr. Hearst must not know that this is fermenting. When the trouble breaks out he will rush into it quickly enough."

Production on *Patria* commenced in the late summer of 1916. Writers Louis Joseph Vance and Charles Goddard—author of *Pauline*—were hired to write various episodes of the series. Their specific contributions are unknown, but surviving production records indicate they were closely following Hearst's instructions and developing plot lines that followed German notions of propaganda films. A 1917 magazine article discussed the film in terms of other propaganda tools of the period. The author of the article makes it clear that the film is propaganda, but he is reticent about drawing a straight line from the Germans to Hearst. "I understand that the offer to write the motion picture drama came to him [the screenwriter] direct from the Hearst organization and that he accepted it in good faith."

In June 1916 Hearst began pulling out all the stops for *Patria*, which he described as "the film we consider most essential." Hearst's most elaborate production to date was expected to be, after *The Perils of Pauline*, his biggest box office hit. *Patria* starred Irene Castle, the tempestuous half of the popular dancing couple (sometimes referred to in publicity and in the film's titles as Mrs. Vernon Castle) and Warner Oland, a Swedish-born actor in the role of a sinister Japanese. Hearst had known Castle socially for a number of years, possibly from the time when she lived across the street from him on Lexington Avenue. In 1914 the Castles were invited to the Hearst home at the Clarendon to give dancing lessons to both Millicent and Hearst. According to William Randolph Hearst Jr., his father also may have been carrying on a brief romance with Irene Castle around the time of *Patria*.

Patria was billed as a serial about war preparedness or, rather, the lack of it. It was also a fast-moving tirade against Japan and Mexico, framed within opulent sets and threaded by elegant fashion shows. While Pearl White's character in *The Perils of Pauline* was the girl next door as feminist, Castle played Patria Channing as a chic version of the heroine type. But much like her sister of the previous serial, Patria is mixed up in a series of breathtaking adventures that include train wrecks, airplane crashes, automobile chases, and a munitions plant explosion. Unlike Pearl White and many other actresses appearing in films at the time, Castle boasted a thin figure and, thanks to her training, was exceedingly graceful in her movements (mostly, dancing, running, falling, or being carried by the hero). She had few illusions about her talents in this frequently death-defying part. "Fortunately," Castle would write in her autobiography, "I wasn't called on for any acting except to look terrified occasionally, and on those occasions I didn't need to act. I was."

Hearst executives assigned to the project included newsreeler Ed Hatrick, movie serial pioneer Edward McManus, and a young business manager named Walter Wanger, who negotiated Castle's deal with Hearst. (In the 1930s Wanger would become a highly sought-after film producer who would play a future role in Hearst's efforts to produce a propaganda film.) *Patria* was directed by Paul Dickey, Leopold Wharton, and Jacques Jaccard. The fifteen-part series was filmed in various locations, including Ithaca, New York, and the San Gabriel Canyon and the Universal ranch near Los Angeles. In this last, director Jacques Jaccard created an entire Mexican town of streets, stores, and adobe houses. Some three thousand extras were hired to play cowboys, Indians, Japanese soldiers, and U.S. cavalry. On Hearst's instructions, other footage of the Ziegfeld Follies in Manhattan was also filmed for inclusion in *Patria*. Hearst found the scattering of film locations an opportunity to begin what would become a long tradition of sending detailed directions by mail. The famous art nouveau poster artist and book designer Will Bradley was temporarily relieved of his art direction duties at Hearst's *Good Housekeeping* magazine and appointed set designer of Patria. The job title was somewhat misleading. In addition to his dramatic scenic work, Bradley was on numerous occasions a surrogate director for Hearst.

In one letter to Bradley, Hearst gave instructions for "retakes and improvements" that showed him to be a hands-on producer and something of a screenwriter and set designer as well: "Make these scenes high spots of beauty and interest. . . . The close ups in the [airplane] machines should be taken with the use of electric fans or blades to give some appearance of wind and action. If we can't have genuine adventure as in the Jockey of Death [another film released by Hearst] we must at least have realistic and convincing imitation."

Patria's romantic interest and the serial's hero is a secret service agent named Dan, but Patria as played by Castle is always her own woman. In the course of the installments, she inherits one hundred million dollars, which she uses to reorganize the army. With herself in command, Patria beats back the forces of Japanese and Mexican aggression. One of the film's more dramatic scenes and obvious propaganda pieces is the dynamiting of a warehouse, a "torn-from-today's headlines" episode inserted into the serial after the real Black Tom Island terrorism disaster that occurred on the New Jersey coast near Ellis Island during the summer. Hearst, with his beveled window view on current affairs, structures the narrative of *Patria* to manipulate the audience into believing that blame for the deadly crime of sabotage should be placed on Japan and not—as the real facts indicated—on Germany. Hearst's film direction to artist Bradley was strikingly similar to his legendary directives to newspaper editors. For the scene based on the Black Tom disaster, Hearst instructed Bradley:

> One explosion should follow the other in quick succession in several great blasts and earth and dirt and smoke should be projected into the air in overwhelming volume if we are to get adequate effect of a great number of ammunition stores being exploded.... In this connection some moving pictures should be taken from an aeroplane over the scene as well as from cameras on the ground. In this way we will show what Patria and Dan saw of the death of the Jap and the destruction of the Japs ammunition warehouses....We must have variety and individual thrills.... Every thriller must really *thrill*.... Angles of vision should be taken and the people in the aeroplane should act as if they *were in one* looking down and over the side and getting blown about and thrown about in more realistic manner.... The few close ups which must be faked should be convincingly faked.

For another scene, Hearst suggests ways to present labor unrest without defeating the purpose of the propaganda: "There is one small point in these scenes I would like to make. The leader of the strikers must not be shot down in cold blood by the secret service agent. That is the kind of thing which is denounced in strike troubles and it would prejudice the audience against our hero's side. The striker must be knocked down or if he is shot it must be under great provocation and to save the life of Dan or something of that kind."

Whatever questions regarding *Patria*'s authorship remain unanswered, there is no doubt that the yellow peril message of the film was an idea that had been floating around for years and seized upon by Hearst and the German propagandists. In the foreword to the first installment of the series, which appeared on a title card, *Patria*'s screenwriter, Louis Joseph Vance, thanked both the film's star and its producer: "The inspiration for 'Patria,' then, was Mrs. Vernon Castle; its sponsor, in whose mind originated the scheme to preach 'preparedness,' painlessly through the medium of the cinema, William Randolph Hearst."

Colonel E. J. Chambers, chief movie censor of Canada—still following the general British boycott of Hearst news services—pronounced *Patria* objectionable soon after its general release in January 1917. Around the United States there were a few rumblings about the film, but it was generally well received and seemed a likely hit. But when President Wilson saw an episode of *Patria* at Keith's Theater in Washington in the spring of 1917, he was troubled. Soon afterward Wilson received a letter from his secretary of commerce, William Redfield:

> Possibly your attention has already been called to the "Patria" film which has been exhibited in various parts of the country and which I am told has been stopped in several places. My attention has been called to it and I have seen it for myself. It purports to show a joint invasion of the United States by combined Mexican and Japanese forces and puts stress upon the Japanese participation in the matter. . . . I know that it has caused a great deal of feeling on the part of Japanese and it seems to me a very improper thing to show it at a time when in a sense Japan is our ally. The matter was brought up at the Council of National Defense and I think all the members agreed that the film was unwise, especially at this time. I should be glad to have any steps taken which would stop its use. . . . It seems to me that a request from you would stop the further use of the film and that this should be done although I am informed it cost three-quarters of a million to get it up.

On June 4, within days of receiving Secretary Redfield's letter, President Wilson had tracked down Pathé's general manager, J. A. Berst:

> Several times in attending Keith's Theatre show I have seen portions of the film entitled "Patria," which has been exhibited there and I think in a great many other theatres in this country. May I not say to you that the character of the story disturbed me very much? It is extremely unfair to the Japanese and I fear that it is calculated to stir

up a great deal of hostility which will be far from beneficial to the country, indeed will, particularly in the present circumstances, be extremely hurtful. I take liberty, therefore, of asking whether the Pathé Company would not be willing to withdraw it if it is still being exhibited.

Between June and October 1917, while he mourned the death of his wife and conducted the United States' entry into the war, Woodrow Wilson remained occupied with Hearst's *Patria*. Pathé's Berst responded to Wilson on June 8. He said he was aware of the criticisms in some quarters and had taken steps as early as the middle of April to eliminate "several scenes portraying Japanese and Japanese flags." He had already informed the counsel for the State Department, Frank Polk, about the changes. The letter from Wilson, Berst contended, was the first official objection that Pathé had received. Berst pleaded with the president to modify his request: "A great deal of money has been invested in the making, advertising and marketing of this picture by the International Film Service and by our Company and should we have to withdraw it at present from the public it would place these two companies in serious financial embarrassment not counting on the fact that very likely many motion picture exhibitors of this country who have advertised and started this picture would suffer and bring suit for damages against us."

Wilson immediately wrote Polk to find out what changes had been made on *Patria*. Polk claimed that he had sent Berst a letter in April, requesting that he voluntarily withdraw the film from circulation. A meeting was then held between Polk and Hearst's Boston attorney, Grenville S. McFarland. McFarland, according to Polk, agreed to make alterations on the film but refused to pull it from the theaters. The changes were the same ones demanded by the Canadian censors: elimination of Japanese names and all reference to Japan, both in the film itself and in the advertisements. But McFarland, as Polk reported to Wilson, had barely kept his promise: although the lead villain was given a Mexican name, he is seen at the end of the episode committing hara-kiri.

Although the administration was determined to stop the showing of *Patria*, the State Department's attorney cautioned the president that no federal legislation made the production or exhibition of this film in any sense unlawful. In late June attorneys Polk and McFarland met again. Later that summer all thirty-one reels of *Patria* were shown to a representative of the State Department and the Japanese embassy. Polk wrote the president that new modifications were still "inadequate." The leading Japanese conspirator, who was now supposedly Mexican, still wore a Japanese kimono. Will Bradley's interior settings were still "entirely Japanese." And Japanese regiments in Japanese uniforms were still invading the United States from Mexican soil. "As now shown," Polk wrote, "the picture is calculated to stir up prejudice and race hatred against the Japanese." In closing his letter to Wilson, a frustrated Polk made it clear that despite the fact that there was nothing unlawful about *Patria*, "I shall be glad to endeavor through the channels available to have its exhibition made impossible."

On August 16 Pathé's general manager, Berst, wrote the president that the International Film Service had called a conference of its officers. They agreed to make additional changes in *Patria*, including the elimination of the kimono and the Japanese uniforms. Japanese-style interior fittings were dropped. But, contending that the movie's villains no longer carried a "stamp of nationality," the producers had retained the rousing scenes of invasion, pillaging, and the abuse of women. McFarland claimed that the editing had meant the cutting of some three million feet of film and the shooting of seventy-five thousand feet of new film. Half-chastised and half-haughty, he wrote Wilson in words that Hearst himself must have inspired:

> We make these changes at any cost because you take the responsibility of asking for it in the present critical juncture of public affairs. We make the changes entirely upon your request and without prejudice as to the merits of the propaganda of the play, which you helpfully avoided characterizing. Those who disapprove [of] the propaganda, I would remind [them] of the very respectable Athenian citizens who denounced Demosthenes for attempting to disturb the amicable relations of Athens with the friendly power of Macedonia.

By early September Secretary of State Robert Lansing was actively engaged in the administration's *Patria* obsession. Although he found the requested changes an improvement, Lansing still thought the film "engenders ill feeling and race hatred, causes unrest and incites mob violence, and in no way, as I see it, contributes to the welfare of the country." Lansing offered no proof that *Patria*, in its eight months of exhibition, had actually caused any real harm, but he went so far as to pass on the suggestion of a Japanese embassy official that, short of eliminating at least the last ten reels of the serial, the title be changed to obliterate any public awareness of the film's content.

On September 21, soon after a face-to-face meeting with Wilson, McFarland sent the president a handwritten note from his room at the Willard

Hotel. In a friendly but forceful manner, he reminded the president. "Apropos our recent conversation," he wrote, "how much the organs of publicity, with which I am associated, are helping the Great Cause." Attorney McFarland went on to list the Hearst efforts on the part of the administration, including the positive Hearst-Pathé newsreel coverage, Ambassador James Gerard's anti-German articles, supportive editorials, and so on. He was holding out an olive branch, with roots very much attached. In a tone that carried as much threat as promise, McFarland wrote the president, "I hope that this tendency will grow into a steady policy."

In a letter to his secretary, Wilson revealed his own frustration: "I confess myself very much mixed up about it. I am afraid there are a number of things still in the film which are objectionable, but it is true that they could hardly be eliminated now without destroying the whole thing, and I am inclined to think that we cannot fairly insist upon more than has been done."

Wilson was slowly getting the picture. He knew the battle over *Patria* was not worth making a long-term enemy of Hearst. On October 1, Wilson wrote his secretary: "Please intimate to the Department of State that I think probably we have compelled these people to do as much as it is fair to compel them to do in the circumstances, and that I think we had better inform them to that effect."

Although attendance never lived up to Hearst's expectations, and extensive editing, retakes, and distribution delays significantly cut into the profits, *Patria* was a modest hit for Hearst. The stylish adventure story was praised by the critics, and the series's message proved its producer to be a worthy propagandist. However, the experience of making and remaking *Patria* may have been more exasperating than anything else for at least one member of his production team. Twenty years later, *Patria* was still on Ed Hatrick's mind during discussions about the prospects of producing another film with an anti-Japanese viewpoint *The Pride of Palomar* (the 1922 film would also star Warner Oland playing a Japanese villain) and trying to get it past government officials and film censors: "I hate substituting nationalities, especially Japs, owing to past experiences. We made a picture one time in which a Jap was the heavy. It happened during the war. We were stepped on by the War Department and the Japanese Embassy. We substituted a Mexican and were promptly stepped on by the Mexican government. However, the brutal tragedy was that the American public did the worst stepping—they wouldn't go to see it."

IO

Fits and Starts

1917–1919

A MOTHER AND SON'S WILL

It may only have been his experience with the film *Patria* that kept Hearst a safe distance from another film project that resulted in a film producer being sent to prison by the United States government. In April 1917 Robert Goldstein, a Los Angeles costume rental company owner turned motion picture entrepreneur, completed his first film, called *The Spirit of '76*. Goldstein's Revolutionary War period production, written by him and directed by George Siegmann, was most notable for its lurid depictions of British atrocities. It was set in the eighteenth century, but it resonated with modern audiences whose government was now allied with Great Britain in a war against Germany. As *The Spirit of '76* included many scenes filmed on elaborate and expensive sets, Goldstein spent much of the production schedule searching for financial backers. Those backers undoubtedly reflected his own interests: some were pro-German, some were anti-British, and others were presumably most interested in making a quick buck in the movie business. On the eve of the film's Chicago release (set for early May), the struggling Goldstein hatched a plan to offer Hearst a certain percentage of the film's profits in exchange for his nearly priceless publicity. According to a report written by Military Intelligence officials who were watching Goldstein closely and already suspicious of Hearst's motives, a man connected with the *Los Angeles Examiner* "was of the opinion that Hearst had an interest in the production and had full knowledge of the nature of the motion picture play." The military report went on to claim:

> [The *Examiner* informant] stated that he was sent to witness a private presentation of the film, immediately after it was finished for the purpose of writing a confidential report on the film from a dramatic or artistic standpoint. Informant stated that he reported adversely, pointing out that it was a poor production from a dramatic and artistic standpoint, and also pointing out that it was over-drawn and distorted from an historical viewpoint and would have a most certain result of provoking hatred and ill-will toward the English at [a] time when the hearty co-operation and good-will between the American and English people is essential to a successful prosecution of the war. Not withstanding this report informant states, which was in the hands of Mr. Hearst's local representative some months ago, the Examiner and other Hearst papers gave the play much favorable publicity.

Elsewhere in the intelligence files related to *The Spirit of '76* was a copy of a letter written by Goldstein on April 19, 1917, and sent to the German-born managing editor of the *Los Angeles Examiner*, M. F. Ihmsen. In the letter Goldstein informs Ihmsen that he can arrange a private screening of his film in Chicago for Hearst in early May, when presumably the publisher would be visiting the city. "We would like to make Mr. Hearst a special proposition and give him an interest in the picture," Goldstein writes, "as we believe that the publicity which he could give us would increase the income of the picture several fold." Whether Hearst actually saw the film, as Goldstein proposed, is unknown. When Chicago censors threatened to ban the picture for its alleged pro-German slant, however, Hearst's *Chicago Examiner* published a long editorial attacking the censor.

Although substantial cuts were made in Goldstein's film in Chicago and in other cities around the country, the picture was largely intact when it was screened in Los Angeles on November 28, 1917. Two days after the film opening, the authorities, alerted to the picture's content, confiscated the print and arrested Goldstein for violation of the Espionage Act. During Goldstein's trial government lawyers made attempts to bring Hearst's name into the proceedings, but they were mostly unsuccessful, and no press reports linked Goldstein to Hearst. In his defense Goldstein denied having any financial deal with Hearst. In the hysteria of the times, Goldstein, who had none of Hearst's wealth and influence, was convicted and sentenced to ten years in jail. After his release, the disheartened and friendless Goldstein left the United States to live in Germany.

Despite the fact that Hearst's actions and the actions of his staff at his corporation and his household were being monitored by the Justice Department and there was a real possibility that the Espionage Act of 1917 and the Sedition Act of 1918 might be used against him, it was not until late 1918 that Hearst began to reconstruct his public image. Then, with the armistice in sight, Hearst instructed his operatives to help in the distribution of Liberty Loan posters, flag-waving broadsides that also contained not-so-subtle advertisements for the *New York American*. Hearst had newsreel footage taken of a Fifth Avenue army parade, but the cameraman (at Hearst's insistence, or to his delight, or both) panned the crowd so as to linger a little longer on the image of Hearst in the reviewing stand. Hearst's boost of *America's Answer*, the film Ed Hatrick had produced for the Committee on Public Information, helped make it the most financially successful of three feature-length films made by George Creel's propaganda organization. Its mixed messages of war as an event both glorious and horrifying proved enormously popular among movie audiences. It opened in New York on July 29, and nationwide distribution began in the middle of October—its run cut short only by the influenza epidemic, which caused the closing of many theaters. In another concession to the prevailing patriotic fervor, Hearst imitated an idea that director Thomas Ince had presented on the West Coast. He made films of soldier's families that consisted almost entirely of the bittersweet smiles of women and children whose husbands and fathers were far away. While the film subjects waited their turn to be filmed, they were entertained by the comedy antics of Hearst's veteran newspaper cartoonist Harry Hershfeld. Later, Hearst publicized the films in his newspapers and sent reels overseas for viewing by the homesick doughboys.

A few days following the public allegations of Hearst's ties to the German ambassador, von Bernstorff, and his operative, Bolo Pasha, Hearst recommended in an editorial that New York City's mayor, John Hylan, declare a Hero's Day to commemorate the war's casualties. Although he was never seriously wounded by scandal, Hylan was considered a puppet of Hearst, and he was hounded by some of the same rumors of disloyalty. For a time, feeling short of friends, Hearst and Hylan grew very close. A casual suggestion by Hearst in his evening paper often become a Mayor Hylan proclamation by morning. Within days of the newspaper editorial, Hearst and Millicent were throwing a Hero's Day celebration at the Hippodrome for wounded soldiers and the mothers of the war dead. Hearst personally designed a medal—a gold star on an altar surrounded by a laurel wreath—

to present to the grieving mothers. Later the same week the Hearsts gave a grand dance at the Clarendon for young Brazilian and Argentine officers. For one evening there were no somber images or suspicions, and the war at home and abroad faded away in Hearst's private world. Ballroom tables were decorated with blue and white flowers for Argentina and yellow and green for Brazil. In the center of each table were giant glass bowls stocked with goldfish and with tiny wooden battleships floating on the surface of the water.

In a shrewd move, Hearst engaged former ambassador to Germany James W. Gerard to fight the court battles against the various city injunctions that were attempting to ban Hearst papers for being pro-German. The Hearst and Gerard families had been friendly for years, going back to an 1880s mining partnership between Gerard's father-in-law, Marcus Daley, and George Hearst. When James Gerard returned to the United States from Germany with the outbreak of war, he used the Hearst press to parlay a short but highly profitable career in film. In the summer of 1917, three relatively unknown film-producing brothers noticed a promotional advertisement for a continuing series in Hearst's *Los Angeles Examiner*. Gerard's memoirs of his years as ambassador, called *My Four Years in Germany*, were to be serialized throughout the Hearst chain of newspapers. Gerard's autobiographical account of his service in Germany was a call to arms against Hun aggression and deceit. On July 23 film producer Jack Warner wrote Ambassador Gerard: "We note by the HEARST papers that you are to publish a series of articles written by you, entitled 'My Four Years in Germany.' Please advise us if there would be a possibility of arranging with you for the exclusive right to produce your articles in motion picture form. We are in a position to produce the subject on an elaborate scale, which at this time, would create much thought and comment, and would have a telling effect on the American public."

After a bidding war, Gerard signed with Jack Warner and his three brothers. The filming of Gerard's story took place on the East Coast—the Warner Bros.'s New York office was in the Godfrey Building—and Hearst remained peripherally involved in the production when Arthur Brisbane lent a few of his New Jersey acres to the production team. The fantastic Bavarian-style village Brisbane had already constructed on his property for his own enjoyment was a great savings to the Warner Bros. art department. (In the summer of 1918, no doubt as a move to garner positive publicity for his boss, he donated the same property to the U.S. government to be used as an army training camp.) *My Four Years in Germany* was a smash, playing to capacity audiences well into 1918. Years later, Harry Warner would credit Gerard's film as "the foundation of our success."

In 1918, at perhaps his lowest point in terms of public acceptance—some even demanded that he be jailed as a traitor—Hearst was growing increasingly attached to Marion Davies. Hearst's cousin Anne Flint remembered their mutual friend Orrin Peck, a bohemian portrait painter, telling her in 1918 that what would become one of the century's most famous May-December romances was a serious affair of the heart. Hearst, he said, was "desperately in love." Mrs. Flint, who had seen Hearst in the company of a number of women, including his wife, Millicent, would later say: "I think the love of his life was Marion Davies. . . . He was very much attracted right from the beginning, and wanted to marry her." It was easy to see how Hearst's new mistress might distract him from his troubles. She was young and physically beautiful, she was witty and earthy, and she admired Hearst with something approaching worship. Something of what Davies saw in Hearst was expressed in an incident that occurred in 1928, when Davies's mother, Rose Douras, died suddenly at the age of fifty-six (Hearst's age in 1918). For the mother of a major movie star who was surrounded by publicity, Rose had managed to stay far from the spotlight. But because Hearst believed she deserved it, Davies's mother was given a Hollywood-style funeral. Scores of Hearst and Davies's industry friends were invited, and mountains of flowers arrived for the funeral mass. Charlie Chaplin was a pallbearer. It was all a blur to the grieving Davies, but she never forgot how Hearst turned to her during one of her darkest moments and whispered, "May I be a mother to you?" Those words, she said, were "the sweetest thing."

For reasons not entirely clear, Hearst was unable to separate from his wife, and he began to lead a stimulating though sometimes maddening double life. Anita Loos, the screenwriter who would eventually work for Hearst and Davies, remembered being invited to dinner at the Beaux Arts Building, near Bryant Park, where Hearst had set up a hideaway apartment for himself and Davies. Loos and Davies had been seated to Hearst's right and left. "Now it so happened," Loos recalled, "that I'd been asked by W.R.'s wife Millicent, to dine the very following evening at the legitimate home on Riverside Drive. When dinner was announced I was embarrassed to find myself again seated next to W.R." Hearst was able to cut the tension, Loos felt, with a twinkle "in those pale eyes of his." Hearst turned to his returning dinner companion and whispered, "Well, Nita, we seem to be meeting under rather different circumstances, don't we?"

Although Hearst was generally indifferent if not rebellious toward convention, he was not one to flaunt his mischief in public. He almost never appeared out on the town alone with Davies for instance; friends or business associates were usually there as well to act as chaperones. Nevertheless, some of Hearst's closest friends must have taken his generally relaxed persona as an excuse to be indiscreet themselves about his comings and goings. One, the painter Orrin Peck, apparently told Phoebe Hearst all about the affair with Davies in 1917. Phoebe reacted as only a controlling mother with millions could.

Since her husband's death in 1891, when she had inherited his entire fortune—$20 million, tax free—Phoebe often came to her son's rescue to relieve him of one financial difficulty or another. On one level, Hearst was undoubtedly pleased to receive his mother's money, but he was also deeply resentful. In the late nineteenth century it was unusual for a father with an adult son to leave his fortune to his wife. Phoebe's niece, Mrs. Anne Flint, who was as close as a daughter, remembered the repercussions in the Hearst family at the reading of George Hearst's will. "Phoebe said she felt WR was not only annoyed but embarrassed over this." Mrs. Flint recalled. "She thought it not quite fair, so in very few years she gave him half. He just went through it . . . borrowed several times from her. He never repaid. He hadn't the faintest money sense." Presumably, Phoebe hoped that by doling out her money piecemeal she could control her son financially and perhaps in other ways as well.

Phoebe was well versed in her son's past affairs going back as far as Tessie Powers in the 1890s. She was particularly annoyed in 1895 to discover that Hearst and Powers were living in her home, the Hacienda, in Pleasanton, California, while she was traveling abroad. Phoebe was even more deeply disturbed when her son courted and eventually married Millicent. Her distaste for the Willson girl was somewhat suppressed when Millicent made her a grandmother and began to show signs of having the social ambitions that Phoebe believed to be appropriate to a woman of her position, but her feelings about the rest of the Willson family were another matter. For a while, Phoebe hoped the pressures of public scrutiny—a career as a politician perhaps—might force her son to lead a more respectable life. Some said she even urged their mutual business associates to promote him for office for just such reasons. As she would soon learn, however, Hearst's commitments to her were fleeting; the more powerful and prominent he became, the freer he felt he was to do what he wanted.

By 1911, the year she first wrote her will, Phoebe was close to despair over her son's ways. So, with pen in hand, she managed to get a verbal agreement from Hearst that if he gave up all his mistresses she would on her death leave him her entire estate. But while Hearst felt his mother had a great deal of money that he deserved, he was almost obsessively interested in the possibility of returning to the Hacienda, where cherished times with Tessie Powers had taken place. Phoebe seems to have been concerned about this; in a twenty-two-page testament in 1911 she willed this home to her grandchildren and not to her son. On May 14, 1917, Phoebe made another more decisive change in her will. In a short codicil that contained some inconsequential money bequests to friends, Phoebe decided to leave her estate at Wyntoon to her favorite niece, Mrs. Flint, and to stipulate that the Hacienda be sold at her death. Thus, having heard the news about Marion Davies, Phoebe was going on record that no mistress of her son's would ever live under her roof. If Hearst wanted to pursue his way of life, he would have to make his own place of enchantments.

Star

Cecilia of the Pink Roses, Marion Davies's first film for Hearst, was a Graphic production in name only. Ivan Abramson, barely on speaking terms with Hearst, had nothing to do with it. *Cecilia* was directed by Julius Steger. Like Abramson, Steger enjoyed making controversial films. But unlike Abramson, Steger was a moneymaker. The year before Hearst selected the director for Davies's film, Steger had made a popular film called *Redemption*, starring Evelyn Nesbit, the leading lady of the Stanford White murder of 1906 and murder trial of Harry Thaw of 1907. The plot and publicity for *Redemption* contained just enough thinly veiled references to Nesbit's sensational past to make it a box office hit. On May 26, 1918, shortly after *Cecilia of the Roses* opened, the movie trade paper *Wid's Daily* said that "the publicity given this production by the Hearst organization has brought it into the limelight to such an extent that there is certain to be business awaiting it everywhere the Hearst papers reach." The paper's reviewer was polite but cautious about the talents of the film's star: "Miss Davies is a very beautiful girl and has been lighted sufficiently well to be most attractive. Fortunately the character did not call for any heavy 'emoting' and she got over all that was required in every scene without hitting any false notes."

Cecilia was a trial-run picture in Hearst's new distribution deal with Lewis Selznick's Select Films. By the middle of June it was announced that Select would release five pictures starring Marion Davies within the coming year. Select was also making star vehicles for the opera singer Anna Case and the sisters Norma and Constance Talmadge. Conveniently for Hearst Selznick occupied a suite of offices on the fourteenth floor of New York's Godfrey Building, where Hearst was also based.

The period following his break with the often volatile Abramson was a difficult one for Hearst, but he found great comfort in being with Davies.

They began to see each other and talk on the telephone almost every day, and one by one Davies shed her other boyfriends. Her natural optimism rekindled Hearst's, and her potential as an actress became his focus. He sent her to acting coaches and dance classes and delivered boxes of his favorite books by Dickens and Thackeray to their hideaway apartment. Hearst wanted audiences to feel what he felt for Davies. Huge posters and the delicately tinted image of Davies on a giant moving-picture screen were not enough for Hearst. At the premiere of *Cecilia of the Pink Roses*, he directed the theater's staff to perfume the audience with the scent of hundreds of real roses, which had been propped in front of large electric fans.

Hearst's first Select release with no connections to Graphic was *Burden of Proof*, a romance starring Davies. Filmed on location in Washington, D.C., and incorporating Hearst newsreel footage, *Burden* opens with a flag-waving promise of patriotism. But it quickly turns into an excuse for Hearst to thumb his nose at his detractors. The film is most notable for what it reveals about Hearst's knowledge of the secret investigations whirling around him. Davies plays Elaine Brooks, the wife of a cabinet officer's son who works in the U.S. Justice Department. Elaine's mother is working as a gossip columnist for a newspaper subsidized by Germany when Elaine herself becomes unwillingly involved in a German spy plot. Hearst's film presents the government's Department of Intelligence as a company of bunglers who carelessly leave vital documents lying around for the enemy to snatch. Knowing the full extent of Hearst's place at the center of the government's intelligence operations, the film can be seen as a picture show of pure audacity. But ironically the critics who found Davies's performance pleasing found the plot implausible.

In early October 1918 it was announced that the *Hearst-Pathé News Weekly* would go out of existence on Christmas Day. The rumor was that the Creel Committee controversy about Hearst and Pathé were troubling the film distributors. There were other reports that theater audiences, fed by the stories of Hearst's pro-German policies, were booing the screen when the Hearst-Pathé title came up. The agreement with Pathé had been one of Hearst's longest, but International seemed to be prepared for the break. Only a month after Pathé cut itself loose, Ed Hatrick was instructed to purchase the *Screen Telegram* from the Mutual Company and the *Universal Animated Magazine* and *Universal Current Events* newsreels from Universal. This new arrangement meant that Hearst's newsreels would now be distributed through Universal.

Hearst treated his newsreels much as he treated his newspapers: they were used to present sensational news events; they told colorful human-interest stories; and they promoted Hearst's ancillary business ventures. As examples, Hearst newsreels showed International's serial star, Grace Darling, in a baseball dugout at the Polo Grounds; the flyer B. A. Kendrich was seen shaking hands with *Beatrice Fairfax* leading man Harry Fox; and *Cosmopolitan* magazine illustrator Howard Chandler Christy was filmed hard at work in his studio. When the crew of Antarctic explorer Sir Ernest Shackleton was reported stranded on Elephant Island in August 1916, Hearst dispatched newsreel cameraman Tracy Mathewson to the scene. But before Mathewson departed another Hearst cameraman filmed him kissing his wife good-bye and receiving a letter written by Hearst to be delivered to Shackleton. The letter, reprinted in the *New York American*, read in part: "This letter will be presented by Mr. Tracy Mathewson, who is sailing to-day to represent the International News Service with the British Relief Expedition. You have the heartiest sympathy of the Americans with you in your noble efforts to rescue the survivors of your expedition to the Antarctic." The *American* pointed out that the Hearst letter was handed over to Mathewson by Eleanor Woodruff, an actress who had the leading role in the forthcoming International Film Service production entitled *Jaffrey*.

Ironically, given all the Sturm und Drang about the newsreels, only a small percentage of the news films from the 1910s survives to this day. What did not disintegrate through time and neglect was often sifted for much-needed silver during war shortages. Newsreels were considered to be of even less historic value than feature films, something like yesterday's newspaper and even more combustible. Once they were screened, news films were essentially up for grabs at the International Film Service office. Morrill Goddard's son Dewitt remembers his father, who was treasurer of IFS at the time, bringing footage home to their apartment on Riverside Drive, where the youngster spliced out the fashion sequences but left in the war-related scenes to entertain his friends on a miniature motion picture projector.

As infatuated as Hearst was by Davies, he was not completely oblivious to her limitations as an actress. While she filmed her third film for him, *The Belle of New York*, Hearst was considering other stars to lead his budding film company. Irene Castle and Olive Thomas, a sister-in-law of Mary Pickford and future Goldwyn star, were both serious contenders. Actually the girl Hearst was most after was the one with the long golden curls: the Canadian-born American Sweetheart. Hearst and Mary Pickford probably first made eye contact in the lobby of Los Angeles's Alexandria Hotel in early 1910. Pickford and a troupe of D. W. Griffith's Biograph players on their first West Coast shoot were using the hotel—a block from Hearst's *Examiner*—as their dressing area. Most likely Hearst had recognized Pickford from her recent one-reelers made in New York, and he probably had known Griffith since the heyday of Fourteenth Street. Passing each other at the hotel elevator, Hearst caught Pickford's attention with his best stage whisper, "I wonder who that pretty girl is." That evening, in the Alexandria dining room, after long looks over his glass of beer, the towering Hearst gathered the courage to ask Mary Pickford to dance. They chatted about the film business, but in the years following their waltz they rarely saw each other. Pickford became a star, and Hearst became a movie producer. Six years later, in 1916, during Pickford's contract negotiations with Adolph Zukor, Hearst sought her out again, hoping he could produce her pictures. Pickford's agent, Cora Wilkening, arranged for a meeting between Hearst and Pickford at Wilkening's New York office. Pickford's agent was playing it both ways. Knowing of Hearst's king complex when it came to business, she flattered him with the lie that it was really Pickford who desired the meeting: Pickford had a deal to propose. Wilkening told Pickford the reverse: it was Hearst who was eager to meet her with a deal he intended to propose. Agent Wilkening never shared her plan with her own client, however, and the shell game of egos backfired. "I never make propositions to business men but merely do my best in my pictures," Pickford claimed to have told Hearst. Once again their dance was over. As one film historian later wrote, "Hearst wanted a proposition. Pickford wanted an offer. It did not come to figures." The man who would be king had met the reigning queen of the movies.

MONEY

The real horrors of the battles abroad reached the shores of the United States in the form of the Spanish influenza epidemic of 1918. Like typhoid outbreaks following the Spanish-American War of 1898, returning soldiers brought the virus home. But unlike typhoid this flu was often deadly, and by the fall it reached worldwide epidemic proportions. Often forgotten today, during its yearlong rampage around the globe the plague left twenty million dead, twice as many as had been killed in the war itself. In some countries, such as Tahiti, nearly an entire generation was wiped out within a few months. The film business was hard hit by the influenza. The lung disease that often proved fatal struck several prominent film exchange executives. Although no famous national figure had died from the epidemic, it was creeping its way through the nation's subconscious. In a short time it seemed that everyone knew someone who had caught it. As fears about contamination spread, theater attendance dropped dramatically. In reaction to this and to prevent future losses, film production that was not already in progress was suspended for the month of October. Many movie theaters were forced to shut their doors during this period, and some even closed permanently, unable to sustain the losses.

In the midst of uncertain times, Adolph Zukor was one man who was thinking clearly. From the vantage point of a lifetime that would reach beyond one hundred years, Zukor in 1918, at forty-five years, had just reached middle age, and his stamina and bare-knuckled ambition made him seem almost a kid. Ivan Abramson, drawing from his bitter personal observations, would later record his memories of Zukor and his partner, Jesse Lasky, when they rose to power between 1916 and 1917:

> [They] conceived the idea of combining the three branches of the motion picture industry into one, so that they could more easily dominate the industry, suppress its freedom, and divert its enormous revenues into their own pockets. . . . The ambitious design of Zukor to dominate the industry has ruined thousands who were engaged in the production and distribution of motion pictures all over the country. The effect of his different mergers, combining the functions of production, distribution, and exhibition, has been to submit eighteen thousand exhibitors to his unjust and cruel demands. He has robbed the industry of its independence, destroyed the market of the independent exchanges, made janitors of thousands of successful exhibitors. He has even betrayed some of the men who helped him achieve his ambition.

It wasn't until his 1929 autobiography that Abramson for the first time publicly revealed the original reason he and Hearst had joined forces:

> After I had pointed out to Mr. Hearst the dangers of monopoly, he said that he had never had a partner in any of his undertakings, but for the purpose of helping the new art to remain independent, he would invest with me a large sum of money, and permit me to tell the trade that he was my partner. . . . My connection with this influential man greatly disturbed the trust. They feared that if we did not receive proper consideration and bookings from the theatres they controlled, Mr. Hearst might build his own theatres in competition with theirs.

Theaters were the cornerstone of the film industry. In a business where so much—an actor, a performance, a story—was a gamble, the motion picture theater was the only tangible. It has been romanticized as a palace of dreams, but it was always first and foremost real estate. Especially in 1918 this was something that bankers understood. Already a successful producer and distributor, Zukor realized that the future of his and all film expansion was tightly hinged to theater ownership and theater expansion. With the promise of a ten-million-dollar infusion from the bankers Kuhn, Loeb, and Company, Zukor set out to prepare a comprehensive study of conditions in the industry. His point man in this inquiry was Hearst's brother-in-law, the attorney Walter W. Irwin.

Zukor had known Irwin fairly well since at least 1916, when they were both executive committee members of the newly formed National Association of the Motion Picture Industry (NAMPI), a precursor to Will Hays's film industry organization. Irwin would eventually become vice president of NAMPI, which was established to fight political forces that were advocating the imposition of restrictive legislation on the industry. NAMPI worked hard for political candidates who were friendly to movie producers and against proponents of taxation and state censorship and those who held views they considered oppressive. Between 1915 and 1916, while still holding a position with NAMPI, Irwin was the general manager of Vitagraph-Lubin-Selig-Essaney, Inc. (V-L-S-E), organizing it into a highly successful releasing company.

Sometime late in 1918 Zukor sent Irwin to several major U.S. cities to evaluate current prospects for movie theater competition. In effect, Irwin was scouting for the best sites for Zukor to build his Paramount theaters. A few years later, Irwin claimed to have come up with the idea that

Paramount could destroy First National [a circuit of independent exhibitors] if it would go into each one of the First National cities and build, or threaten to build, the finest and largest theater in the city, as the industry had been through the influenza period, in which all exhibitors had lost money and many of the houses entirely closed for many weeks. ... If Zukor's representative went to these cities and threatened to build theaters the banker would be very likely to call the First National member in and ask that man why he was engaging in a fight with a very large and very strong corporation.... The banker would tell the depositor that he had better make a substantial reduction in his loan the next time it became due. Such action by bankers would cause disruption.... In any event it would not be necessary for Zukor to build more than a few theaters to frighten the First National members.

Contemporary press accounts pointed to Irwin's legal expertise—he almost single-handedly revitalized the Vitagraph Company and in 1915 was made lead counsel to the Thomas A. Edison Company in a General Film lawsuit against producer William Fox—as the reason he was chosen by Zukor to guide Famous Players through the minefield of trust-busting Sherman and Clayton statutes. Irwin's relationship to Hearst was never noted. When Anita Willson Tovey married Irwin on February 21, 1914, she found herself, like her sister, living with a man in the film industry. Hearst seems to have had a high regard for Irwin's talents or certainly appreciated the attorney's ability to make important contacts in the film business. On one occasion Hearst tried to get his brother-in-law to be the studio manager of his film company, but Irwin decided to stay with Zukor. Although there is no evidence that Irwin officially worked for any Hearst film company, he was keenly aware of the power and influence of both Hearst and Zukor and likely served as a valuable conduit between them.

After theaters or real estate, the most bankable element of the film industry was the story property. Developing a plan for the creation of a reservoir of readily available literary works with screen potential was a constant concern of early film producers. At the very dawn of motion pictures, Thomas Edison—the first great industrialist of motion pictures—actually fretted over whether the well of story ideas might soon run dry. Adolph Zukor personified the new movie mogul with his proverbial American dream story. He was a poor immigrant who came up the hard way but quickly in the new world of nickelodeons and screen shows. Zukor was also clever enough to promote himself as a maverick, but, like most successful businessmen of the twentieth century, he was conservative. And like most men who find sudden money, he preferred to take chances on sure things.

A safe bet for a producer who was looking for profits and expansion was to build on an already profitable product. Zukor was ahead of the pack in realizing that the future of motion pictures would find its foundation in plays and published fiction—a matter of common sense today. Zukor's approach helped change the industry. To do justice to theatrical and literary sources meant longer multiple reels of film. A process of survival of the most adaptable' began, as famous stage players and famous fiction writers moved to the new medium. And encouraged by the press, especially the Hearst press, the public would come to demand increased complexity in their films and star qualities in their actors. In a 1912 *New York Journal* two-column article, probably written by Carl Zittel, his part-time press agent at the time, Zukor said:"It seemed to me that something more was necessary to improve the standard of pictures as an amusement enterprise, and about a year and a half ago the idea first came to me to persuade the greatest actors and actresses of our time to perform before the camera in their best plays." Zittel plugged Zukor as an Everyman with a mind like Napoleon's. Zukor, he said, was "the elevator of moving pictures," who could rightfully claim credit for the "colossal" idea of "giving to people accurate, graphic reproductions of the great plays produced in the costliest theatres at a price within reach of the slender purse."

Zukor fully understood the assets Hearst brought to film. Before plunging into film, one of Hearst's most lucrative enterprises had been his magazine empire. While Zukor sent Walter Irwin off to plot a prominent role in the expansion of movie theaters, he encouraged his own son, Eugene, to establish connections with Hearst and his publishing ventures. Gene Zukor didn't have to look any further than his own best friend.

In late 1918 Gene and his schoolmate Carl Florian Zittel Jr. were trying to figure out what to do with the rest of their lives. After a wartime job of carrying top-secret messages to Secretary of the Navy Franklin D. Roosevelt (who, impressed by the Zukor name, confessed a secret penchant for screenwriting), Gene worked as an executive in one of his father's New York exchange offices. The extroverted Zit Jr. also seemed fated to follow in his father's footsteps. In fact, Gene Zukor remembers his friend as almost a carbon copy of Zit Sr.: "Hearst was very fond of Junior, because Junior had the same personality as the father. They were very entertaining. . . . The father and the son were very amusing and they had the same voice. When you would call on the telephone you didn't know which one you were going to get. They would imitate each other." Sometime around Christmas 1918 Gene and Zit Jr. began to discuss ways they could work together, establish their independence, and at the same time take advantage of their advantages. "Zit [Junior] had the idea," Gene Zukor would recall, "that he could get Hearst into the rights to properties, literary properties that Hearst had developed for his magazines and newspapers, Edna Ferber and Robert Chambers and people like that who were popular authors of the time, and that they would then be able to use those properties in films."

Hearst was excited by the boys' idea of forming a corporation solely for the purpose of expediting the process of turning the Hearst story materials into films. He gave Gene and Zit Jr. use of his penthouse apartment at the Godfrey to work out the details. By 1919 they were meeting with Hearst editors and magazine publishers like Ray Long and George d'Utassy. Hearst, his arms full of bundles—he did the grocery shopping for his apartment himself—would sometimes poke his nose in to see how the boys were doing and offer his own suggestions. To take advantage of Hearst's successful magazine business—and its star publication—the new film corporation was called Cosmopolitan Productions.

As late as February Hearst was still not completely over Ivan Abramson and their dreams of an independent film movement. He struggled with a way to link the International Film Service to the still-existing Graphic Film Corporation as a unit through which the Hearst fiction would be funneled and developed. Edward A. McManus, the magazine man who joined Hearst in 1914 to produce the popular International movie serials, was now working with a director named Burton King. Most likely on McManus's advice King was interviewed for a position at Graphic as a counterbalance to Abramson. But no decision was made. Hearst was more interested in building his own studio, perhaps in Davies's name, and he even considered the possibility of becoming a movie theater owner. As wealthy as Hearst was, he knew he needed to attach himself to a stable and well-financed production and distribution structure. He knew he needed a Zukor, or someone like him, to achieve his costly dreams. Zukor was amenable to a deal with Hearst, but as his son later confirmed, he wanted no part of the Graphic partner, whom he referred to as "pornographer."

Soon after the turn of 1919 there were rumors that Hearst was planning to join forces with the Rockefellers in a multimillion-dollar film–producing / film-releasing combine. When Zukor was asked to comment, he brushed the story aside but hinted that the New Year would hold many changes by saying "nineteen nineteen is too young yet." Actually, in early January Hearst reasoned that if he were able to sign up enough big talent it would be possible to set up his own distribution company. Charlie Chaplin was the most obvious film talent of the day. Zittel, never hesitating to emphasize his own role, remembered: "Mr. Hearst and myself were looking out the window up here. We're on the 16th floor and have considerable vision. The idea developed that we should handle the proposition. Why not? We have all the money that would be needed, millions if necessary, and brains enough, I believe to take care of the business. Besides, Chaplin and I have been friends for many years—way back in the days when he was in vaudeville." For weeks the trade papers were full of talk that the so-called Big Five—Charlie Chaplin, Mary Pickford, Douglas Fairbanks, D. W. Griffith, and William S. Hart—were actively shopping around for a releasing company. But it wasn't until January 21 that Hearst sent a telegram to Chaplin, quickly followed by duplicates to the other four. Signed by Zittel, the identical telegrams said:

> Naturally have heard of proposed combination of big five. Wiring you each individually same telegram in hopes you will take up with your attorneys. There is no organization in the world that can be of the

benefit to you as the Hearst institution with its wonderful chain of newspapers and magazines. Would you mind extending to the International your proposition? You know we can finance same plus the tremendous publicity. We are ready to negotiate if you are willing to talk business with us. Please wire.

Chaplin thanked Hearst and Zittel for their telegram. And he indicated he was considering the offer, since "we have not yet fully formulated our plans." Although it had not yet been announced, a few days before Chaplin and his four partners had already formed United Artists (UA). How Chaplin could possibly be keeping his options open after having signed a deal or why he might have been toying with the Hearst organization is not known. Clearly Hearst and Zittel, with their "considerable vision," had missed the boat.

United Artists was the first film company run by film artists created to produce and distribute their own films. The four partners of UA (Hart soon dropped out) were doggedly independent and seasoned creators but would essentially need on-the-job business experience. As one film executive observed, "The lunatics have taken charge of the asylum." The official announcement of UA's formation was released to the press on February 3. William G. McAdoo, UA's general counsel, a former treasury secretary and son-in-law of President Wilson, issued a statement saying in part that the five artists were "determined not to permit any trust to destroy competition or to blight or interfere with the high quality of their work. They feel that it is of the utmost importance to secure the artistic development of the moving picture industry and they believe that this will be impossible if any trust should get possession of the field and wholly commercialize the business." This was a thinly veiled swipe at Zukor, who would have loved to unite those artists under his huge Famous Players–Lasky umbrella, which now included his recently merged Paramount and Artcraft companies.

On the heels of the Big Five's rebuff of Hearst, the last Abramson-directed film for Graphic, called *The Echo of Youth*, was released in early February. Except for the Hearst press, reviews were universally poor. One reviewer said, "Ivan Abramson is so deadly serious," and referred to *Echo* as "decidedly unwholesome." Hearst had finally decided to sever all ties with Abramson and Graphic. As Abramson would remember:

After much persuasion by the trust, although Mr. Hearst was reluctant to leave me and the independents to our struggle to prevent the spread of monopoly, extraordinary circumstances arose which severed our connection. . . . Because they feared the power of this great man, the monopoly succeeded in luring Mr. Hearst away from me. At that time Mr. Hearst was planning to produce elaborate pictures on a very grand scale. No sooner did the trust learn that he was eager to secure a market for these costly productions, then they commenced to blind him with all kinds of flattery, with large offers.... Although they knew that these elaborate productions were bound to result in a financial loss, they guaranteed Mr. Hearst one hundred per cent distribution and an advance of one hundred and fifty thousand dollars for each picture that he would produce, however costly.

On March 12, 1919, it was learned that the ideas hatched in Hearst's penthouse apartment at the Godfrey Building could be used to do more than simply provide jobs for two rich kids. It was left for the famous fathers of Zit Jr. and Gene to do the talking. Zit Sr. spoke for Hearst when he announced: "The specials produced by us and distributed through Famous Players–Lasky will be known as 'The Cosmopolitan Productions.' This year we will produce nine feature pictures and possibly two spectacles. Next year and the years thereafter we will produce 12 feature pictures and possibly 3 spectacles. The spectacles which we contemplate, will set a new record in that phase of the industry and will consist of from eight to twelve reels."

The deal between Hearst and Zukor was said to involve an infusion of $5 million. *Variety* called the arrangement "probably the largest single deal ever made for picture material." And *Wid's Daily* pointed out that in addition to the wealth of story material, the film productions would have "the publicity obtainable through the Hearst publications, the circulation of which is said to reach a quarter of the population of this country." Zukor was asked to issue his own statement on the deal. His response must have thoroughly pleased Hearst. It recognized Hearst's uniqueness and how his stature had grown, and it suggested an even wider pervasion to come:

Personally, I am very much satisfied to know that Mr. Hearst not only can publish the works of our most eminent authors, but also can put them into pictures. This meets a public demand. It makes possible the producing of pictures that could come only with the aid of Mr. Hearst. I know that the efforts Mr. Hearst will make will spare no expense to make pictures worthy of the authors and worthy of their stories. I am glad, not alone from the standpoint of business, but for many other reasons that mean the uplifting of the film business as never before, that we have the distribution of these pictures.... I am confident that we can do justice to the undertaking.

II

Over Production

1919–1922

> Wealth is production. There may be prospective wealth, puta-
> tive wealth, potential wealth, in the soil, in the ore veins, in
> various latent forms—but actual wealth is only that which
> has been produced into things men require. The more there
> is of production, therefore, the more there is of wealth.
>
> —*William Randolph Hearst*

CITIZEN SUPPRESSION

Phoebe Hearst spent her last Christmas and New Year's with her son and his family in New York City. At the Clarendon apartment in December, mother and son talked about the expanding Hearst empire. Phoebe felt that Hearst was in bad financial straits and would soon be in need of major bank loans. She told him she intended to release him of any obligation to settle the debt of millions he had amassed since the year of his father's death. Phoebe's gift to her son had one condition. Of the total debt, she wanted her son to pay back to her $300,000 over the next three years, which she would put toward the construction of a museum in Berkeley to house her vast collection of art and antiques. Hearst would be giving Phoebe money that was her own, but through this arrangement she had found a way to force him son to follow in her footsteps by becoming a philanthropist. She hoped she might be able to generate some genuine altruism. Once before, when Phoebe had lobbied her son to contribute money to one of her interests, he had balked. "What would I get out of it?" Hearst asked her. "You know, I believe in advertising."

While the holidays were a time of forgiveness for Phoebe, disappointments decked the Clarendon's halls. The son she had hoped would be the apple of the public eye was a notorious figure. Friends tried to hide from her the newspapers that reported the winding down of the Senate investigation of German propaganda. But there was one encouraging article they might have hoped she would see. With something much less than a thud the Senate hearings were closing. The Justice Department's A. Bruce Bielaski suddenly declared Hearst had not broken any laws and that there would be no criminal charges against him.

Hearst's momentary vindication was buried among pages of newspaper Christmas advertisements. Soon after the holiday, while his mother was still visiting, Hearst was the subject of a parody at a victory dinner at the Waldorf held by a group of political writers who called themselves the Amen Corner. One of their skits played off the news reports that Mayor Hylan had picked Hearst to be part of a committee formed to welcome returning American doughboys. The story had received considerable attention in the press because hundreds of invited guests had dropped out of the event after hearing of the Hearst appointment. Scores of letters were sent to Hylan calling Hearst a traitor. Hylan was a steadfast supporter of his friend, but in the end he defused the protests by putting Hearst in a less visible position: head of the patriotic celebration's entertainment committee. Hearst was in charge of organizing an evening at the Ziegfeld Follies, as well as film entertainment for the soldiers. The Hearst parody at the Waldorf took the real controversy one step further. In its fictional scenario Hearst's fellow committee members were Germany's propaganda chief Dr. Dernburg, German agent and Hearst correspondent William Bayard Hale, and convicted saboteur Franz von Rintelen. Such was the atmosphere in New York shortly before Phoebe returned to her home in California.

Two weeks after the announcement of his deal with Zukor, Hearst received a telegram from the Hacienda. Hearst's mother, who had been unable to shake a cold for months, had developed pneumonia. Phoebe's doctor thought it was time for Hearst to make the trip west. Hearst hesitated. He was busy with plans for Cosmopolitan Productions and lending advice on the decoration of a townhouse at 331 Riverside Drive he had recently bought for Marion Davies and her family. In the middle of March 1919, a few days before Hearst received word of his mother's worsening health, he pleaded with her to hire a round-the-clock nurse. She reluctantly gave in, and there were hopes for improvement. But a lesion in Phoebe's lung made her condition grave. As Hearst and Millicent and their son William Jr. headed west, it was apparent that the end was coming for the seventy-six-year-old

Phoebe Hearst, the country's latest and most prominent victim of the Spanish influenza.

By the time Hearst arrived at the Hacienda on March 31, 1919, his mother knew she was dying. Anne Flint, who had been at her aunt's side since her condition had worsened, thought the mother-and-child reunion had revived Phoebe's spirits, but the break in mood was only momentary; the deeper resentments that had plagued their last years were soon on display. For two weeks, as she lingered near death, Phoebe said her good-byes to her relatives and friends.

Between his visits with his mother, Hearst maintained an active business and social life. Hearst and Millicent enlisted local friends as dinner companions and overnight guests. Employees, probably from the *Examiner*, were also installed to churn out the endless stream of telegrams that held his communications empire together. On some days, with his mother bedridden upstairs and Millicent downstairs making arrangements for the next coterie of guests, Hearst journeyed into San Francisco to visit his newspaper staff and to confer with Julia Morgan, his mother's right-hand architect and soon to be his own.

Hearst's self-absorption was a reflection of his mother's. Even as she lay dying, Phoebe could still muster the strength to maintain her matriarchy and her end of an emotional tug-of-war with her next of kin. For years she had carefully cultivated a circle of admirers. More than one of her dearest friends had usurped her son's place as the center of her universe. Her niece, Anne, was for all intents and purposes her beloved daughter. The Peck family, who were witnesses to most of the trials and triumphs of Phoebe's life in California, were constant, intimate friends. Their artist son, Orrin Peck, had come to share confidences Phoebe no longer entrusted to her son. He was described by one historian as being "closer to her than her own son." Even Phoebe's grandchildren—who spent nearly half their childhood's at the Hacienda in her care and far from their parents—were increasingly groomed as guardians of the Hearst legacy. Phoebe no longer believed her son capable of fulfilling her dreams, but she was twisted by a disappointment she could not put to rest. She lashed out to the very end. In one of her final and most severe acts of scorn toward her son, Phoebe banned Millicent from visiting her deathbed.

"Rosebud," as Orrin Peck nicknamed Phoebe Hearst, according to one of her biographers, died in the late afternoon of April 13. By the following morning, every Hearst newspaper was rolled out in borders of black mourning, and Hearst readers were supplied with extensive coverage of Phoebe's life and death. On April 16, the day of Phoebe's funeral in San

Francisco, federal office buildings across the nation lowered their flags to half-staff; the first time such a tribute was paid to a woman. Even rival newspapers gushed with words of respect and admiration for Phoebe's philanthropic contributions to the arts, her founding of the PTA, and her support for women's rights. A day after the funeral, the reading of Phoebe's will took place. Hearst had received the bulk of her estate: according to later estimates, Phoebe had made her son $11 million richer. Hearst turned the news of his mother's will into an advertising coup for the Hearst name, especially himself. He ordered his newspapers to carry the story as a news event, including long verbatim passages of the will. The publication of this document was in sharp contrast to the coverage of his father's: when George Hearst left his fortune to his wife and not his only male son, a furious Hearst ordered his staff to ignore the story.

Presumably, Hearst was aware of the Amen Corner parody at the Waldorf in late 1918 linking him to enemy propagandists, since accounts of the entertainment were published in the New York papers. He made no public comments about the event, and one suspects he took the high road, believing a stage routine that came and went in one night would soon be forgotten. But a few months later, when the forum for parody was the more far-reaching medium of film, Hearst would not be so magnanimous.

The biographical motion picture—in either the "true to life" format or the thinly veiled portrait—was not a brand-new genre in 1919. *The Life of Big Tim Sullivan* (1914), produced shortly after the death of the Tammany boss, was one of the earliest examples of a multiple-reel biopic. The film was produced by the New York–based Gotham Film Company and made with the assistance of Sullivan's secretary, Harry Apelbaum. A number of exterior scenes were filmed on the Bowery, and the film's director cast a distant cousin of Sullivan to portray the powerbroker in his middle years. Sullivan is shown as a force for both good and evil. Scenes showed his notorious voter-repeating system in action, as well as his acts of kindness to the poor at Christmastime. Another popular politician of the turn of the twentieth century, Teddy Roosevelt, was the subject of the film *Fighting Roosevelts* in 1919. Producers advertised their film as being "authorized." A character in D. W. Griffith's classic film *Intolerance* (1916) was apparently based on John D. Rockefeller. In Griffith's feature, the oil titan is portrayed as a hypocrite, fighting for censorship while secretly connected to vice rings. The connection is curious on the surface, but just such an accusation was implied in the broadside against Hearst in 1914 that claimed Mrs. Willson's brothel had enjoyed "the enthusiastic patronage of the Standard Oil crowd." Such biting film parodies were rare, for filmmakers feared that such invasions of privacy would encourage censorship and further vilification of their craft. Their reluctance to make such movies also demonstrated a growing recognition on the part of the film industry and the public that film had an unparalleled impact. Its ability to mirror the physical world had taken it far beyond the limits of stagecraft, and its power to reach a mass audience and possibly future generations was viewed as both a wonder and a danger.

Probably the first dramatic work to include a character based on Hearst was *The Power of Money*, a play that opened at the American Theater in New York City in 1906. *The Power of Money* was written by Owen Davis, a dramatist with a long and prolific career that included a Pulitzer prize award in 1923 for his play *Icebound* and a 1926 theatrical version of F. Scott Fitzgerald's novel *The Great Gatsby*. Owen thought his plays were quite similar to early cinema. They are "practically motion pictures," he wrote, "as one of the first things I learned was that my plays must be written for an audience who, owing to the huge, uncarpeted, noisy theatres, couldn't always hear the words, and who, a large percentage of them having only just landed in America, couldn't have understood them in any case." Owen was a protégé of Augustus Thomas, the playwright who was picked by Hearst to speak at the convention of the Associated Democratic Clubs in 1900 and also a friend of "Big Tim" Sullivan. Around 1902, as Owen would later recall, he accompanied Sullivan around town—around Sullivan's town—for a chance to see "plenty of things that would make good stories." Owen makes no mention in his autobiography of knowing Hearst, but he seems to have been something of an admirer. The *New York Dramatic Mirror* called Owen's *The Power of Money* "a genuine political melodrama." In the last act of the play, an unknown actor playing Hearst champions the workingman as he chomps on a huge cigar. For some unknown reason (the play is lost) Owen has the Hearst character aligned with another equally vigilant trust-busting character that is clearly based on Theodore Roosevelt. *The Power of Money* opened at the American Theater during Hearst's run for governor of New York. The *Dramatic Mirror* implied that Owen's Hearst characterization was a positive one and suggested that the candidate "could not do better than distribute free seats to the wavering voters."

Hearst may also be thinly disguised in a film based on the novel *The Fall of a Nation*, written by Thomas Dixon Jr., whose book *The Clansman* was the source of Griffith's film *Birth of a Nation*. Directed by Bartley Cushing and released in 1916, the film version's main character is Virginia Holland, a women's rights advocate who finds support for a crusade for universal disarmament in a multimillionaire named Charles Waldron. As the film story unfolds, Waldron becomes an increasingly dictatorial figure with sinister motives. He lives in a palatial New York home surrounded by equally menacing associates from an unspecified European nation. Waldron betrays his friendship with Holland and his own country by becoming the willing puppet of a foreign power. He declares himself the governor general of the "Provinces of North America" and oversees a military attack by airplane on New York City. In the end, Waldron is killed, and America is saved by an underground movement led by the now-militant Holland and others who formerly opposed her. Waldron, whose occupation is described as a banker-newspaperman, seems to have been at least in part modeled on Hearst, and elements of the story are strongly suggestive of Hearst's pacifist and pro-German leanings. There is no record of Hearst's reaction to this film.

Three years later another film flavored by the country's preoccupation with war and espionage was produced and ready to be released. It too contained a character with treasonous motives. *Enemies Within* was unquestionably about Hearst, and *Variety* acknowledged as much in an article that reported Hearst's swift response to the apparent affront:

> The Pathé release, "Enemies Within," featuring Fanny Ward, has been suppressed. It was virtually a rewrite of the old Pathé picture "At Bay." The new film has Edwin Stevens in support and George Fitzmaurice director. In some manner Mr. Stevens [was] made up to look like W. R. Hearst. A showing was given of the picture last week and the story as well as a description of Mr. Stevens's make up reached Mr. Hearst. The feature made the part played by Mr. Stevens that of a newspaper owner, pro-German. Paul Brunet was interviewed by Hearst's representatives. Mr. Brunet passed the buck to George Fitzmaurice, with the picture withdrawn.

Although no evidence of Fitzmaurice's film exists aside from this brief *Variety* notice, the outlines of its story can be pieced together. Evidently *Enemies Within* was based on a play by the same name that had a short run in the summer of 1918. The play was written and staged by A. H. Van Buren and based on a story written by two press persons, Kilbourn Gordon and E. H. Culbertson. Gordon was a press representative for theater and movie producer William A. Brady, and Culbertson was a former newspaperman on Hearst's *Washington Times* and an editor on the *Universal Weekly*, a newsreel also associated with Hearst. The play opened on tour in Hartford, Connecticut, and as a review in a local newspaper indicates, it was based on at least three famous people and a widespread rumor of the day:

The story is laid in Washington—the wartime Washington—and opens in the Lafayette Square home of Thomas Dawes, Assistant Secretary of War. Here you find Dawes, his daughter Marion, his son Gilbert, and their guests, Olaf Hansen, and his sister Nora. Hansen, an intimate friend of the Dawes family, is the representative of various Scandinavian pulp wood interests. . . . There comes to see Hansen, one Brunell, a representative of the Mid-Western Publishers' Association and it develops that the two are in reality enemy agents. . . . [Hansen] has been the active head of German Spy work and propaganda in this country. . . . "Enemies Within" is the only play of the day laid in the best advertised city in the world and it is further unusual in that it is the only spy play in which not a German appears. It is a well known fact that the most effective enemy agents operating in America today are not of German birth and rarely of German descent.

If the name Marion Dawes seems calculated to conjure up the name of Marion Davies, then it seems likely that Brunell is Brisbane and Hansen is Hearst. Few audience members who read the daily papers in 1918 and 1919 needed to be reminded which leading citizen with publishing interests was suspected of being a German agent. One can only speculate about what a film version of *Enemies Within* might have added to the play's portrait of Hearst and his associations. The film's star, Edwin Stevens, did bear an uncanny resemblance to Hearst, and he had a reputation that must have brought a certain edge to his role in *Enemies Within*. Stevens, a San Francisco native like Hearst, was well known in 1919 for playing villains. It was said that he had been especially compelling playing the title role in a play called *The Devil*.

MODELS, ARTISTS, AND MOVIE RIGHTS

Hearst had enjoyed the Ziegfeld Follies ever since their inception in 1907, and he may have even been a financial backer of some of the shows as early as 1915. He was on friendly terms with Flo Ziegfeld for many years, and in the 1920s they were associated in a venture to erect a more permanent pleasure dome to house their mutual obsession: the Ziegfeld Theater. As late as 1930, two years before Ziegfeld's death, Hearst and Davies were still thinking of their friend and collaborator. They gave the down-in-his-luck impresario and his family the use of their mansion on the beach in Santa Monica while his stage musical *Whoopee* was being translated to film.

Hearst was more than a financial supporter and friend to Broadway's most famous impresario: if Ziegfeld can be credited with "Glorifying the American Girl," then Hearst deserves credit for glorifying Ziegfeld's Follies. In a sense, both Ziegfeld and Hearst discovered the inspiration for the Follies at the same time. Anna Held was a twenty-three-year-old singer of little note when Ziegfeld first laid eyes on her at the Palace Theater in London. Before they set sail for the States, Held had become his lover, and by the time they reached New York Held was fast on her way to being his star. The chief attraction of the rather average-looking Held—at least as highlighted by Ziegfeld through his imaginative management of the press—was her naughtiness. Early on she became identified with a song called "Won't You Come and Play With Me?" which she sang in a German accent that anticipated the actress Marlene Dietrich. Ziegfeld came up with a visual gimmick to match Held's seductive words; he told the press that his star's beauty regimen was a daily bath in milk and then happily invited reporters to witness the ritual from a safe but tantalizing distance. These backstage theatrics quickly caught Hearst's attention, and by 1896 he was eager to incorporate Held's act into the pages of yellow journalism. Held was hired to give out prizes to bicyclists in a "Yellow Fellow" race that he sponsored in the fall of 1896. Around the same time, Held became attached to a story frequently told to illustrate Hearst's appetite for sensationalism and self-promotion. In an episode that would become a ritual for the Hearst press, drama critic Alan Dale interviewed the performer in her dressing room paying particular attention to her dress—or lack thereof. The public was effectively shocked and hooked by the stunt.

The Hearst press was unquestionably the chief publicist for the Follies throughout their lifetime. Every Ziegfeld production received a buildup that went a long way toward ensuring its success. Beyond the promotion of individual shows, Hearst frequently published news stories and fiction pieces that offered the chorus girl as the representative of a host of challenges faced by the modern woman. In these pieces the Ziegfeld girl was presented not only as a great beauty but also as a heroic figure; her struggle to make it and to rise above her humble beginnings had made her world-weary and vulnerable at the same time. The Ziegfeld chorines became barometers of fashion trends; they were indicators of working conditions and were on the frontlines of the nation's evolving morality. Intrinsically, Hearst knew how to mold the Ziegfeld girl to fit his cherished "damsel in distress" motif; in her rags-to-riches story, her insinuation of prostitution, and her fairy-tale rescue by a wealthy patron, she was Cuba's Evangelina Cisneros, the chic Irene Castle, and the independent Pearl White all rolled into one and wrapped in oscillating ostrich feathers.

The early years of the Follies reflected the transition that was occurring in visual entertainment. As motion pictures became an acceptable and competitive entertainment, Ziegfeld introduced eye-popping cinematic effects to his shows. Starting with the very first Follies edition of 1907, Ziegfeld hired Frank D. Thomas, who had an office in the Gaiety Theatre in New York City, for his patented "Kinetoscenes"; the first effect used was a combination of motion pictures and painted scenery for a surf bathing scene.

Much of the symbolism Hearst had attached to the Ziegfeld Follies and their showgirls became closely associated with Marion Davies once he met and fell in love with her. With his decision to make Davies a movie star, Hearst refocused his Follies vision into a cinematic one. Theater personnel were enlisted to work at various levels of his company. Along with Davies, Hearst announced that he had signed on celebrated Ziegfeld stars Mae Murray, Justine Johnstone, and Olive Thomas.

Although Davies's employment with Flo Ziegfeld's company had lasted little more than a year, for the rest of her life she was identified as a former Follies girl. This was the power of Hearst publicity, and in the process of building up Davies's past Hearst also secured an enduring place for the Follies in U.S. culture.

Hearst was not only interested in putting Ziegfeld girls on the screen; he wanted the screen to approximate a Ziegfeld Follies stage setting. On February 19, 1920, Hearst hired Joseph Urban, Ziegfeld's visual illusionist, to be his film production designer, and a contract was signed guaranteeing the Austrian native an unprecedented salary of over $1,200 a week. Urban quickly became a production designer in the modern sense, working side by side with directors, cinematographers, and scenarists to create a unified screen work. Urban's forte on the stage (he was also a set designer for the Metropolitan Opera) had been his impressionistic use of color. But through an expert use of lighting and experiments with photographing in black and white, his films achieved a depth and richness unusual for the period. Soon after Urban came onboard, he moved to infuse his own staff with his sensibility by screening for them a copy of the German avant-garde film *The Cabinet of Dr. Caligari*. He also brought in woodcarvers, sculptors, and other artisans from Europe to oversee technicians and set builders. Gretl Urban, the designer's daughter, who was fresh out of art school and hired to be Cosmopolitan's costume designer, remembered much initial confusion among her father's crew over just what her father was trying to achieve. Eventually, however, Urban's team came to respect their teacher and live up to his demands for artistic excellence.

Urban made his motion pictures more than lush. Drawing on his background in the Hagenbund and Wiener Werkstätte movements—art, design, and architecture movements of turn-of-the-century Vienna—and Hearst's seemingly endless bank account, Urban became one of the most prominent messengers of European modernism in the United States. Cosmopolitan films such as *Enchantment* (1920), *The Wild Goose* (1921), *The Young Diana* (1922), and *Enemies of Women* (1923) became showcases for Urban's interpretation of modern design. In subtle but significant ways— in the stylized checkerboard-patterned furniture of a bedroom or the sleek curves of a lobby—Urban's set designs for Hearst anticipated the art deco and art moderne styles that became closely associated with films of the 1930s and 1940s.

By obtaining Urban's services and exploiting other Ziegfeld Follies associations, Hearst's films automatically achieved notice for their visual qualities. But, as Hearst had already learned through yellow journalism, the look was less impressive without a story to back it up. Not only did he understand the storytelling power of film, he saw his own potential to be a story-selling power in the film industry.

Days before he moved into the Hearst magazine offices to take up his position as editor and consultant in December 1918, Ray Long was already working unofficially for his new boss to secure the film rights to the well-known fiction writer James Oliver Curwood:

> *Dear Jim:*
>
> I shall be through here in a week now, and go down East to take up my duties as editor of *Cosmopolitan* and consulting editor of the other magazines of the International Magazine Company.... You are already famous as a writer, and you are already receiving the sort of prices for your work of which there are only about ten men in the country with whom you can compare. By the time we get through, I do believe there will be [not] one man in the country who can compare. One of my very deep regrets in this new field is that you tell me that it is impossible, at least for the present, for the motion picture interests which are allied with the International Magazine Company to have your motion picture rights. I do not think I am going beyond my authority when I say that if it were possible for them to get those rights, you could command practically any figure within reason for them. If at any time it should become possible for this subject to be reopened, I want you to let me know.

In 1918 Curwood was primarily known as a novelist and short story writer who wrote adventure tales that were often set in the cold and rugged outdoors of the Canadian northwest, a genre Hearst thought naturally lent itself to cinematic interpretation. But Curwood was highly in demand in 1918, having already signed with Ernest Shipman's film company at the time Long approached him. After nearly a year of on-again, off-again negotiations Hearst and Long were able to reach an agreement with Curwood to film one of his stories, entitled *River's End*. Hearst financed the film and closely followed its production. (Hearst maintained his ties with Curwood over the years and filmed two more works that were presented as Cosmopolitan Productions: *The Valley of the Silent Men* [1922] and *The Flaming Forest* [1926].) Long had wanted Curwood to direct the film, but the assignment went to the established director Marshall Neilan. On October 27, 1919, Long wrote Curwood:

I, too, would prefer to have you do "River's End" for us, but that simply cannot be worked out. From all I hear, Nielan [*sic*] is doing a magnificent job. He is not trying to get through in any six weeks,—as a matter of fact, I shall be delighted if he gets through in six months. He is going to Canada for much of his material, and we are not stinting on money or anything else. While I haven't had time as yet to go into the details of how much your name will be displayed, you may rest assured that it will get real prominence because it is as much to our interest as it is to yours.

When *River's End* was released (by First National) in early 1920, it was not presented as a Cosmopolitan production or identified in any direct way as a Hearst film. Because Hearst had a financial stake in *River's End*'s success, however, the film did receive a considerable amount of publicity from his organization. In addition to positive newspaper reviews and feature articles, the Hearst subsidiary Cosmopolitan Book Corporation published a new edition of the book to accompany *River's End* and sent out 1,200,000 circulars to book readers as a tie-in to the film's release. The filming of *River's End* was an early example of Hearst's practice of reaping financial benefits in the lucrative but often unpublicized business of buying and selling and speculating in film rights.

In the spring of 1919 Hearst held a conference with his corporation's treasurer, Joseph Moore, and Ray Long. He expressed his concern that authors who wrote for his magazines were greater beneficiaries of publicity than were the magazines in which they appeared. "We are, as Brisbane puts it, advertising something that belongs to somebody else instead of advertising something that belongs to ourselves." Hearst argued further that the situation was the same with motion pictures. Unless advertising was redirected toward the International Film Service "or some individual that we have under contract," Hearst said, the authors whose work was adapted to the screen would only demand more money for their next story.

In a letter written to Moore on May 13, Hearst directed his magazine editors to consider authors' submissions for their literary value but equally "to make sure that every story will be fit for moving pictures." Hearst suggested a systematic approach. He wanted someone hired at the magazines "with ample experience in the moving picture field to sit in on such discussions." If the preliminary work was done, Hearst suggested, "there would then not be any question of whether a magazine story would be adaptable to moving pictures. It would be adapted not after it was written and printed but while it was being written and before it was printed."

On February 15, 1920, in an article publicizing Cosmopolitan Productions, the *New York American* pointed to the unique resources available to a film organization associated with Hearst:

> What makes it easier for this company to carry out a policy of this nature than it would be for any other company in the world is the fact that it has first option on the motion picture rights of the works of all the authors writing for the Hearst magazines. It is an acknowledged fact the *Cosmopolitan*, Hearst's *Good Housekeeping*, *Harper's Bazaar* [*sic*], and other Hearst publications, control the writings of the world's greatest authors—men and women who bring human beings to life in stories that are real—and the effort being made by Cosmopolitan Productions—more successfully so with each picture it makes—is to place on the screen exactly what was in these authors' minds when they wrote the stories.

The *New York American* article was referring to a company Hearst had formed at this time for the purpose of obtaining and speculating on the motion picture rights to books, short stories, and plays. The International Story Company, as it was called, was located at 145 West Forty-fifth Street in New York City. Much of the material bought up by the International Story Company had appeared in or was excerpted in one of the Hearst magazines, but the library apparently also contained other works that had no previous association with Hearst. According to Raymond Gardner, the publisher of

Hearst's *American Architect* magazine, by the mid-1920s "the inventory was over $2,000,000 and represented every cat and dog that had ever been in type."

Hearst's control of motion picture rights became a public controversy in 1921, when protests were organized by a number of famous authors who were allied with the Authors' League of America. In February the Authors' League issued a resolution that decried the Hearst magazines' refusal to purchase fiction "unless they are at the same time permitted to acquire an option on the motion picture rights in such fiction on terms dictated by the purchaser." According to the league, the International Story Company was in the business of speculating on literary works, acquiring material "at prices usually below ruling market values and offered for sale at terms paying good profits to the holder of the option, but not to the author, and the sales being made before that option price has been paid to him." The league declared that this practice, which was not followed by other "higher-class periodicals," was "dangerous to that which is best and most inspirational in American literature."

On February 27 Hearst responded to the criticisms with an editorial reprinted in the *New York Times* that spoofed the high-mindedness of the Authors' League's resolution. The editorial denied charges that the Hearst organization was refusing to buy stories unless they could also purchase the film rights to those stories:

> William Randolph Hearst, being duly assembled, considered the following resolutions with care and passed them unanimously. . . . Whereas these magazines do merely endeavor to buy the moving picture rights of certain stories which are desired to be made into moving pictures and . . . Whereas neither the above magazines nor any one connected with the above magazines, directly or indirectly, have any interest in the International Story Company . . . Resolved, That its fulminations are unworthy of serious consideration.

Based on his correspondence with Joseph Moore and others, Hearst was clearly avoiding the truth in his response to the Authors' League. His statement about the International Story Company was a blatant lie and could have been proven so by any enterprising journalist who checked the company's incorporation records. Documents show clearly that the president of International Story Company had a very direct connection to Hearst and his film company; she was none other than Reine Davies, the sister of Hearst's leading lady and mistress.

By the summer of 1921, after continuing bad publicity, the Hearst organization agreed to endorse and accept the standard rights agreement formulated by the Authors' League. Editor Long sent the league a written promise to the effect that from now on, if Hearst did not produce a film from an
author's work within two years of its purchase, then it would have to offer
the author the opportunity to buy back his or her rights. In the event that
an author chose not to purchase his rights back, Hearst could sell the film
rights to another producer but would have to pay the author 50 percent of
all sums realized in the sale.

To the very end Long maintained that Hearst had never been in the business of speculating in motion picture rights and was only interested in making motion pictures. Addressing the other aspect of the protests against
Hearst's practices, Long returned to the discredited public response previously made by Hearst. "This company," Long told the Authors' League, "has
never tried to influence any Author to build his stories so that they might
make better films and it has no intention of doing so."

The protests against Hearst had little lasting effect on his determination
to control story material for films. In 1924, when Hearst began talks leading
to an alliance with Metro-Goldwyn-Mayer, his story holdings became one
of the most attractive assets he brought to the negotiation table.

Production Costs

It was not long after signing a production deal with Famous Players–Lasky
(the company was soon more commonly known as Paramount Pictures, the
name of its distribution branch) that Hearst expressed dissatisfaction with
the relationship and began to pursue new alliances. On a social level he
remained cordial to Famous Player's top executives, occasionally inviting
both Zukor and the company's vice president, Jessie Lasky, for small dinner
parties at his Clarendon apartment. Hearst was increasingly convinced, however, that the business methods of Famous Players were unethical and that
the hierarchy of the organization was not to be trusted. On the issue of personal trust, Hearst's prejudices appear to have been encouraged by his adviser
Joseph Moore's anti-Semitism. As an example, in the spring of 1919 Joseph
Moore was lobbying Hearst to make director Allan Dwan the president of
International Film Service, with a substantial interest in net profits and a
five-year contract to make films. In addition to making Dwan the president,
Moore suggested that he, meaning Moore, move into the position of Cos-
mopolitan's business manager and that magazine editor Long head the film

company's story department. To complete the new shakeup, Moore urged Hearst to fire Carl Zittel, the longtime Hearst crony who was particularly close to Adolph Zukor and his son, Eugene. In making his case to Hearst, Moore said that Zittel, who was Jewish, was just like a lot of "tricky Jews who do not know the first living thing about real, proper business methods." Moore also pointed out to Hearst that in his opinion Dwan was being "maligned" by Jews that he encountered during his career (Moore may have been referring to Zukor as one of Dwan's encounters). Hearst told Moore that he too wanted to hire Dwan at "any price" but that he was not about to relinquish his own title as company president. In responding to Moore's slur on Jews, Hearst made no attempt to distance himself. In fact, he seemed to be of the same mind as his adviser, adding that there were very few "honorable gentlemen" in Hollywood; the choice of the word *gentlemen* having some significance since it was used at the time euphemistically to refer to Jews.

Beginning in 1920 and throughout 1921, Hearst's communications with his chief financial officer Joseph Moore frequently dwelled on the raw deal he believed his own good-faith efforts were receiving from Paramount. He accused the company of juggling its books to perpetuate an erroneous assessment of Cosmopolitan pictures' profitability. He suggested there were "sleight-of-hand" arrangements that the company had with exhibitors, coercing theater owners to make deals that benefited Zukor at Cosmopolitan's expense. Hearst was particularly angered by Paramount's method of lumping together Cosmopolitan pictures with other Paramount pictures in a binding package. The method of booking in a block—high-quality pictures with less desirable pictures—and signing deals to engage theaters for a period of from three months to a year was a near-foolproof way of marketing all of Paramount's product while simultaneously stifling its competition. Such block booking was not uncommon in the film business. But Paramount's dominance in the field of production and distribution and its unparalleled ownership of first-class theaters in major cities throughout the United States and even in a number of foreign locations had put it in a unique position. Its power in the industry was an almost certain guarantee that an exhibitor would sign an agreement that was primarily in the best interests of Paramount. When Paramount's subtle or not so subtle intimidation of an exhibitor did not do the job, one of Zukor's field representatives would inform the local exhibitor that Paramount intended to erect their own theater across the street or around the corner.

How deeply concerned Hearst was over Paramount's monopolistic growth is unknown, but he was unquestionably disturbed about the impact their practices had on his own film enterprises. He repeatedly complained to those in his inner circle that Famous Players never fully appreciated the uniqueness of its alliance with the Hearst organization. The Hearst press was not only paying to promote its own feature films, but it was making a major contribution to the advertisement of all Paramount pictures. Hearst wondered why this contribution was not factored into the advances for production costs or an accounting of profits. He wondered why his higher-quality productions were being lumped with poorer-quality Paramount productions. Frustrated, Hearst requested that Zukor put a Hearst man in the Paramount organization hierarchy to keep an eye on the books. Moore informed Hearst that Zukor was agreeable, but months passed without any obvious effort to implement the plan. When Moore informed him that Zukor found the requests for larger advances unrealistic because of the instability of the film industry, Hearst was thoroughly convinced that he was being made a scapegoat for Paramount's malfeasance. He strongly suspected that the profits on his films were being diverted to prop up Paramount's box office failures or perhaps to finance other ventures, such as their massive theater expansion. (By 1926 the Famous Players–Lasky Corporation had a controlling interest in 368 theaters in the United States alone.)

Hearst's objections to Paramount were remarkably similar to those in a Federal Trade Commission complaint issued against Zukor, Paramount, and others affiliated with them on August 30, 1921. The landmark complaint set off an investigation and a series of court decisions that extended for decades and produced seventeen thousand pages of testimony. The case's first milestone was a 1927 cease and desist order. It then journeyed through the U.S. Circuit Court of Appeals, where certain FTC bans were reversed in 1932. A second major suit against Paramount in 1938 resulted in a consent decree. Paramount was under fire again in the 1940s when an investigation of business practices was reactivated and a lower court decision unfavorable to Paramount was affirmed by the Supreme Court. All subsequent investigations of Paramount stemmed from the FTC complaint of 1921, which mirrored Hearst's complaints: Paramount was engaged in a coercive practice of block booking that was linked to its systematic control of the country's first-run theaters. Zukor quickly moved to defend himself against the charges, comparing Paramount to any other wholesale business that needed to secure a market for its products. The government was not swayed by the analogy, however, and pursued its claim that Zukor's company had routinely intimidated exhibitors and caused its competition to be unduly hindered. The practices that Zukor called standard and fair were alleged to have been designed "to create for said organization and its affiliated companies a monopoly in the motion-picture industry in the greater part of the United States."

The gist of the FTC action was widely believed to have originated with one or more disgruntled exhibitors, but evidence also suggests that Hearst played an important role in propelling the government investigation. *Variety* seemed to be speculating as much when it published the following in one of its more gossipy columns on September 23, 1921:

> Curiosity is existent in picture circles as to the source of the pressure that brought about the complaint before the Federal Trade Commission against the Famous Players et al. Several guesses have been made, but without any carrying enough assurance to guarantee accuracy. Two or three picture people have been reported of recent months harboring grievances against the Paramount group. One or two were strong enough politically to have accomplished an end in the commencement of the Federal Trade action. One particularly, reported to have believed he had been unfairly treated, stands big enough to start almost anything politically, state or national.

Even as late as early 1923, when Cosmopolitan had completely severed its ties with Zukor, *Variety* seemed to be implying Hearst was working behind the scenes against Paramount when it said that a motion picture producer with a large news-gathering operation was investigating certain "conditions" in the film industry that might lead to a larger exposé.

In the late spring of 1921, about three months before the FTC complaint was issued, Hearst directed a concerted effort to cozy up to exhibitors. He had an advertisement—several pages long—published in the May 21 issue of *Exhibitors Herald* magazine that touted the merits of his film enterprise. The ad, which was an open letter to exhibitors, made no mention of Famous Players, and it was illustrated with what resembled a campaign photograph of Hearst. A confident Hearst made the case for his films. "Cosmopolitan Productions," Hearst declared, "have scored more successful pictures than any other producing organization in the moving picture business." He reminded exhibitors that Cosmopolitan pictures were quality pictures because they had the great resources at the Hearst organization at their command—"the raw material in fiction"—and "everywhere power and agency work hand in hand for the highest success in production and exploitation."

Soon after the advertisement appeared, Hearst organized an event that was covered in the same trade magazine and designed to win over exhibitors further. Fifty New York City exhibitors and their wives and friends were invited to the Cosmopolitan film studios for a tour of the facilities. The group crowded into a screening room to view the recently completed film *The Woman God Changed* and was later guided onto one of the stages for a peek at Frank Borzage's film *Back Pay*, then in production. The exhibitors gave the director a round of applause when they were told he was the director of *Humoresque*, a surprising hit with exhibitors in 1920. To mark the exhibitors' studio visit and to flatter their egos, Hearst had a still cameraman take pictures to give out as souvenirs, and a motion picture cameraman filmed the group for a newsreel that would later flash their images across the country.

At the same time, Hearst put his newly appointed studio manager, George Van Cleve, in charge of coordinating a well-publicized fight against a proposed high tariff on foreign films and raw film stock, an issue close to exhibitors' hearts. Although Van Cleve had virtually no experience in film or politics, he had a background in advertising and had recently married Marion Davies's sister Rose; this was enough qualification for Hearst. Together, Hearst and Van Cleve waged their antitariff campaign in the Hearst newspapers and behind the closed doors of Washington, D.C. The issue was presented as a battle between the George Eastman celluloid monopoly and the interests of the people. Hearst's political operative from Chicago was contacted by Van Cleve and given his marching orders to influence President Warren G. Harding on the tariff issue by lobbying Fred Upham, the former treasurer of the Republican National Committee and a current Harding poker crony. Hearst's attorney, William de Ford, was drafted to make a personal appeal to Senator James A. Reed, a Hearst supporter who was a member of the Senate Finance Committee. Debate over the tariff legislation became a hot topic of the film trade magazines, with the *Exhibitors Herald* coming out strongly against it. The magazine backed up its opinion with the results of a survey of exhibitors that showed 60 percent opposed a high tariff on foreign films. In conducting his antitariff campaign, Hearst was aware that he was siding with the theater men. In fact, Van Cleve sent Hearst a letter on June 17 that reported to him that exhibitors had been wiring congressmen at the urging of the Hearst press. He suggested that the Hearst newspapers publish the sentiments of the exhibitors because the thrust of the campaign was "to prove to the exhibitor that Mr. Hearst is the motion picture exhibitor's friend."

A few weeks after Hearst published his advertisement in the *Exhibitors Herald*, Zukor placed a plea for support in the pages of the magazine. Accusations against Zukor's business practices were already showing up in trade magazine columns, and the mogul decided it was time to sign his name to a public defense of his reputation: "The attacks upon me are an effort to make the exhibitors believe that we are attempting to drive them out of business ... that we do not value their good will. I want every thinking exhibitor to know that we are primarily a producing and distributing organization and our only thought is to please the exhibitor."

Zukor dismissed the stories circulating that his agents had "harassed" or "embarrassed" exhibitors. Using language that at the time was usually reserved for radicals like the Bolsheviks, Zukor claimed the dissenting theater managers were far more dangerous than his own organization: "I feel that it is deplorable that for selfish reasons men will work to tear apart an industry and to create dissension instead of building good-will between component parts of our business: the exhibiting, the distributing and the producing branches. Now, of all times, too, we need a united force to fight the agitators who are attacking us from the outside."

By the summer of 1921, Hearst had reached the boiling point with Zukor. In his harshest language to date, he wrote a letter to adviser Moore on June 30 that fortified his previous grievances with a threat:

> If we cannot come to a proper agreement between ourselves, I will take the matter to the courts: first, because that is the most conclusive way of arbitrating; second, because I think the public ought to know what kind of practices the Famous Players indulge in; third because I think the Government ought to be apprised of the character of the Famous Players combination. And I propose asking the Attorney General to help us get at the facts in the case. I think I can be as pleasant as anybody when I am being treated right, and as disagreeable as anybody when I am not.

In concluding his letter to Moore, Hearst indicated that although he was open to a meeting with Zukor to discuss the matter further, he wearily declared that he had "the facts" about Famous Players at hand. "And I have taken the trouble since I left you this afternoon," he wrote Moore, "to go into them more thoroughly than I ever did before."

Hearst wrote his threatening letter from the Copley Plaza hotel in Boston, where he had been for the past week or so conducting real estate business related to his newspapers there. His temporary residence would soon figure in a controversy that would have serious ramifications for the film industry. In late May 1921 Massachusetts attorney general J. Weston Allen brought a court action against Nathan A. Tufts to remove the Middlesex County district attorney from office. It was Allen's contention that Tufts had taken $100,000 from various film executives to cover up a potential scandal resulting from an incident that had occurred some four years earlier. As testimony over the summer of 1921 revealed, on the evening of March 6, 1917, a banquet was held at the Copley Plaza under the auspices of Famous Players–Lasky to welcome their newest contract player, Roscoe "Fatty" Arbuckle. Following the event, some of the film executives, including Adolph Zukor, Paramount president Hiram Abrams, vice president Jesse Lasky, and several others, were driven to the nearby town of Woburn and more specifically to a brothel called the Mishawum Manor, run by a madam named Brownie Kennedy. Arbuckle was not among the midnight revelers. Everything seemed to have gone as planned. A few weeks later, however, Boston mayor James M. Curley was told that a number of the prostitutes at Kennedy's place—some married and some underage—were talking about the affair. There were rumors that the husbands of some of these women might bring charges against the partygoers. District attorney Tufts was investigating the matter when several of the film men involved went to see him. Between them, $100,000 was raised—in cash and in Famous Players stock—and through one of the film men's attorney presented to the DA. No hint of the scandal reached the press or any investigating official until 1921.

With a Federal Trade Commission investigation looming, there could not have been a worse time for a story linking political payoffs and prostitution to Zukor and the top brass at Famous Players–Lasky. The scandal was also likely to make Wall Street investors nervous about being linked to what appeared to be an unstable industry. With this in mind, after the scandal became public Zukor looked into the possibility of hiring Herbert Hoover as head of a proposed organization that would act as a buffer between the government and the film industry. As Harding's secretary of commerce, the department that would have the most influence in FTC matters, Hoover was a logical choice. When Hoover declined the offer, Zukor went elsewhere: on August 8, while the Tufts trial was proceeding in Boston, Zukor held the first of a series of conferences in New York with Will Hays, postmaster general in the Harding administration. Over the next weeks and months Zukor and Hays would continue to meet, sometimes in the company of Harry B. Rosen, a man *Variety* dubbed the "finance king of films." Rosen was well connected to the Harriman National Bank and other Wall Street bankers and well known in Hollywood for writing enormous insurance policies for movie moguls and movie stars to protect bank loans. Some of his clients included producer Lewis J. Selznick, Famous Players–Lasky actress Olive Thomas, and Adolph Zukor (who had taken out a life insurance policy for $5 million in August 1921, at the time he began meeting with

Hays). By late 1921 Hays's meetings with Zukor would come to include other leaders of the film industry. He also discussed the film industry with Thomas Lamont, the CEO of J. P. Morgan. In October and November Hays had several discussions with Arthur Brisbane. Brisbane and Hays had grown close during the presidential election of 1920, when Hays ran the Harding campaign and Brisbane produced a series of advertisements for the Republican ticket that were published in the Hearst press and elsewhere. An additional bond to their relationship was Courtland Smith, who was Hays's closest aide at the post office and Brisbane's brother-in-law.

On December 9 Hays was called on by Lewis Selznick and Saul Rogers, attorney for William Fox, and offered an opportunity to head a motion picture producers' organization that would function primarily as a lobbying group in Washington protecting the interests of the film industry. The movie men also hoped that Hays would present an image of stability to an industry mired in scandals. On December 28, after meeting insurance agent Rosen at the Harriman Bank, Hays met with a larger group of movie men that now included Sam Goldwyn, Carl Laemmle, and Fox. Hays had already made his decision to head what was formerly known as the National Association of the Motion Picture Industry and now being called the Motion Picture Producers and Distributors Association (MPPDA). In the vernacular of the day, Hays was the new movie czar.

Hays, who had worked closely with the film industry during the election of 1920, was well versed in the political applications of film. In fact, the selection of Hays to head the MPPDA must have seemed preordained to those close to him and the Hollywood moguls. In August 1920, in the midst of the Harding campaign, Robert G. Tucker, a former newspaperman and a Republican National Committee official, wrote Hays about the importance of establishing a close relationship with the movie producers. Tucker's letter reads like a blueprint for what happened in the fall of 1921:

> I called today on Lewis J. Selznick head of the Selznick Pictures Corporation. As I suspected not enough attention is being paid to the men at the head of this industry. Mr. Selznick was frank enough to say that he would like some recognition—not financial—in return for active cooperation in giving your candidate and cause publicity through his news weeklies. . . . If Selznick goes to Marion [the city in Ohio where Harding's campaign was headquartered] it won't be difficult to get the rest of the big men in line—and at heart they are for your ticket on account of financial conditions. What should be done is to arrange to have some one high up in your organization keep in closer touch with

these motion picture producers. Their editors of course must carry out their orders. No money is required to deal with them but they are anxious for recognition and I think they also look to the future. Make them understand that your vast organization recognizes their vast publicity resources and not only is grateful but that it looks for their help during the next four years. These men can be made your enduring friends by a little recognition on your part. . . . As soon as you arrange for Selznick to see Harding wire me and I will take time off to run over their [*sic*] and see that things go right. You must deal the rest of the way from the top of this moving picture industry—arrange for the dealing yourself through Ralph or some one on whom you rely and see that whatever is done to encourage this industry is done in such a manner that its heads will turn to you. This is important.

On January 15, 1922, it was announced that Hays's life had been insured for $2 million, payable in the event of his death to the motion picture organization he had agreed to head. Three days later, Hays privately signed a $100,000 a year contract with the film industry. Shortly after the real signing, Hays marched over to the Fox Film studio at Tenth Avenue and Fifty-fifth Street. Along with the industry's leading producers and on a makeshift film set, Hays reenacted the contract signing for a newsreel camera. Lined up behind him were his new associates. It should have been an easily acted scene, but Hays appeared ill at ease before the motion picture camera, his big ears and prominent front teeth making him a very unlikely screen personality. Within a few minutes a news film for the news weekly was completed. Hays was about to leave to join his colleagues at a private celebration when suddenly something caused him to return to the stage set where the hot lights had just been dimmed. The paper he had left on the table and attached his signature to was a seemingly meaningless document, but Hays seemed concerned; could someone fill in the blanks at some later date to make it look like Hays had signed his name to something he really hadn't? Quickly and deliberately, Hays ripped his name from the bottom of the page, discarded the movie prop, and followed his new associates to a late dinner at Delmonico's. Waiting for Hays at the restaurant were a couple of dozen other interested parties, including Courtland Smith, who was preparing to move from his post office position to join Hays at the MPPDA, and Arthur Brisbane, who was there representing Hearst, and invited to gave a short welcoming speech.

Ten days after Hays officially opened his Manhattan office, a "love feast," as he would later recall it in his autobiography, was held in his honor at the

Hotel Astor. Over one thousand attended the dinner for Hays, and among the guests were Joseph Urban, Hearst attorney Nathan Burkan, and future Hearst columnist Louella Parsons. Among a dozen or so on the dais with Hays were Adolph Zukor, Secretary of Labor John J. Davis, U.S. Shipping Board chairman Albert D. Lasker, and New York City mayor John Hylan. The Hearst organization was well represented as well, with Brisbane and Hearst himself only a couple seats away from Hays.

Mayor Hylan was one of the first to speak to the gathering, and he hastened to acknowledge that this film industry celebration was something of a political rally as well. Hylan thanked the motion picture industry and especially Hearst for his own good fortune on election day 1921, "when that great majority was rolled up." Turning to Hays, he joked, "And I am glad to welcome Mr. Hays, who has told us that he is no longer in politics. If he will leave his mid-Western home and come to this city to live I will see that he has the opportunity to join Tammany Hall in the near future!"

The evening's toastmaster, screenwriter John Emerson (who along with wife, Anita Loos, had penned the 1919 Cosmopolitan film *Getting Mary Married*) introduced Hearst, who had politics on his mind as well: "Speaking as a motion picture producer and as a Democrat like my friend Mayor Hylan, I am glad to see the Honorable Will H. Hays taken out of the Republican Party and put in as a manager of motion pictures. I have seen that gentleman at work and I know how efficient, how painfully efficient he is. . . . Now my friends, it seems to me that successfully managing a big industry is not so different from managing a big party." Then, addressing an unspecified criticism of the motion picture industry, Hearst said, "Most of the criticism of the moving picture industry has been due to prejudice, the prejudice that always awaits something new." Hearst told the film industry audience that jealousy of wealth and fame was also a factor in the criticism of some. "But I do not see why anybody should envy the motion picture producer. They do not make any money." As the crowd began to laugh at his remarks, Hearst closed with a joke that has long been considered apocryphal: "All the money I have been able to make out of newspapers I have sunk in motion pictures. I feel like the racing man who was asked if there was any money in horse racing and who replied: 'Sure, all my money.' When anybody asks me if there is any money in motion pictures, I say: 'You bet your life! All mine!' "

Albert Lasker, Hays's longtime friend and the advertising guru of the Harding campaign, spoke in a lighthearted and political vein as well. Before welcoming Hays to his new position, he thanked "that good Republican William Randolph Hearst" for defeating the League of Nations and helping to elect Harding and a Republican Congress. Speaking of Hearst, he said, "You know he is a Republican as often as he is a Democrat." In his address, Arthur Brisbane told Hays that he should try to emulate Hearst in his new job: "If you will make the same kind of a fight that Mr. Hearst makes when he thinks he is right—for the motion picture is nothing but a newspaper in another form—and make it aggressively instead of sitting down and wondering what you can do, you'll get results." In the end, it was Adolph Zukor's brief speech that got down to the bottom line. Making a not too subtle reference to the recent scandals associated with Paramount Pictures and the obvious concern that he and other producers felt, Zukor seemed to be delivering marching orders to Hays. "You will not permit our enemies," Zukor said, "to malign us on account of the actions of any individual."

In the fall of 1921 Hearst began making plans for *When Knighthood Was in Flower*. The film turned out to be a double-edged sword for Hearst: it made Davies a movie star and legitimized her as an actress, but it also cemented Hearst's reputation in the movie industry as the king of excess in production costs and advertising. *Knighthood* was an adaptation of an 1898 novel by Charles Major that had a previous incarnation as a film in 1908. The earlier film version was titled *When Knights Were Bold* and was most noteworthy as the only film to star D. W. Griffith and his wife, Linda Arvidson. Hearst's *Knighthood* was a natural vehicle to highlight Davies's talents; her role as Mary Tudor could showcase her beauty and her relatively untapped talent for easily shifting from light comedy to melodrama and back again. It is also safe to assume that Hearst was excited by the cinematic possibilities of the character of Mary Tudor. As eventually played by Davies, the character spends part of her screen time in elegant feminine costumes hoping to be rescued from a loveless marriage; in another story line, while disguised as a young man, she duels her way to the rescue of her true love, a handsome commoner.

Following its New York opening, Hearst made preparations to arrange and publicize *Knighthood*'s wide release and to do battle against another big budget film, the Douglas Fairbanks's *Robin Hood*, that was expected to open simultaneously in close to a dozen major cities. In Chicago Hearst organized a particularly intense effort to trounce his competition. Starting a month before *Knighthood*'s early October premiere, Hearst's *Chicago Herald-Examiner* and the *Chicago Evening American* published advertisements to whet the public's appetite. On learning that *Robin Hood* and *Knighthood* were slated to open on the very same day, Hearst made a series of telephone calls to Zukor, Marcus Loew, and the theater owners Balaban and Katz. He persuaded the Paramount and Loews chiefs and the prominent exhibitors to remove the Metro picture *The Prisoner of Zenda* from the downtown Roo-sevelt Theater, opening up a slot for *Knighthood*. The swift move, which was likely to have been eased by the greasing of several palms, would place Hearst's film in Chicago five days before Fairbanks's picture, scoring a sig-nificant advantage in what the press had dubbed a "Battle of the Hoods."

With a new date set for *Knighthood*, Hearst arranged to have a railroad carload of scenery and a thirty-piece orchestra dispatched to Chicago for a special stage presentation to envelop the film screening, the last-minute con-struction to be directed by scenic designer Urban. Hearst made calls to the Liggett and Myers tobacco firm and the Dodge automobile company and hurriedly secured 650 billboards for the purpose of advertising the film. Some three hundred spaces on elevated train platforms were also rented in Chicago and its surrounding areas.

On the day of the *Knighthood* premiere in Chicago, less than an hour after the box office opened, two lines, each a dozen abreast, had already extended the length of two city blocks. Hearst news photographers were sent to the scene snapping pictures for the next day's newspaper coverage. Even the somewhat more reserved *Variety* declared that "the opening of the 'Knight-hood' picture was an epoch."

In another *Variety* article on *Knighthood*—which must have particularly pleased Griffith-admirer Hearst—the film was called "the best bet that has come along since the 'Birth of a Nation.' " But although most observers declared *Knighthood* a financial success, it is difficult to assess the extent of that success because Hearst poured so much undisclosed money into the film's promotion. It has been often been reported that the film cost $1.5 mil-lion, a figure that presumably includes advertising expenditures. In her book about the early film industry and her work with Griffith, *When the Movies Were Young* (1925), Linda Arvidson discusses Hearst's *Knighthood* and states that the total cost of the film was $1,221,491.20. Arvidson's figure is so pre-cise that it has the ring of truth, although it is unclear how she came by this information. Whatever the exact figure, it was certainly an extraordinarily costly film for the period. Still, even with Hearst's excesses, the film was apparently quite profitable. In November *Variety* reported that the film's gross "is figured to top anything touched by any feature production released in the history of filmdom." As 1922 came to a close, *Knighthood* had been in the theaters for three months and was still doing strong business nearly everywhere it played.

With the success of *Knighthood* few could dispute that Hearst and Davies were at the peak of their collaboration. The industry respect that Hearst and Davies had desperately sought was finally bestowed on them. Yet there were rumblings among some critics and exhibitors. *Knighthood's* box office triumph caused Hearst to suffer from temporary amnesia regarding Paramount's previously criticized block booking methods. He was now comfortable taking advantage of the system that gave exhibitors a program of Cosmopolitan pictures that included the good with the bad. Exhibitors who had balked at Zukor were now turning the heat on Hearst as well. Marion Davies too was paying a price for the hoopla surrounding her most notable film to date. Hearst's heavy-handed advertising campaigns had gotten the public and critics to consider Davies seriously, but those who were suspicious about the depth of Davies's talent were given the ammunition they needed when the Hearst press stories about her often focused on the dazzling electric signs springing up to promote her name in major cities around the country. A Hearst paper in Boston reporting on a fur thief's having been shot down in the street by the police managed to allude to Davies's dazzling qualities in its lead paragraph. "He staggered," the paper reported, "and fell under the electric light sign on the Park theatre advertising 'When Knighthood Was in Flower.' " Even Will Rogers was heard joking that Marion Davies's next film would be called *When Electric Light Was in Power.*

Some of the excesses associated with *Knighthood* may derive from the fits and starts that had occurred over another Hearst and Davies film less than a year earlier. At the moment in the fall of 1921 when Hearst was looking to secure Griffith as a director for *Knighthood*, he was anticipating the opening of his film *Enchantment.* The outlines of a publicity campaign had already been discussed for weeks, and treasurer Joseph Moore was keeping Hearst updated on the costs of movie posters and the possibilities of newspaper serializations. Hearst sent Moore telegrams to remind him "about special publicity for star." Increasingly, Hearst and his staff referred to Davies not as "a star" or "the star" but simply as "star."

Although it was his impulse to pull out all the stops on the Davies film, Hearst was somewhat more circumspect with *Enchantment.* He informed Moore that he would inaugurate a newspaper serialization of the Cosmopolitan production *Get Rich Quick Wallingford* rather than *Enchantment.* There would be plenty of other opportunities for advertisements in the Hearst and non-Hearst press, including the movie sections of the *World*, the *Times*, the *Tribune*, and the evening editions of the *Sun*, the *Globe*, and the *Mail.* As the date of *Enchantment's* premiere at the Rialto Theater in New York neared, Hearst remained in Los Angeles, focused but relatively confident. He was ecstatic to hear that most New York critics had highly praised the film or at least recommended it. On the same day that he read the reviews, he received word that the woman he knew to be Davies's harshest critic had spoken her mind as well.

For several years Millicent Hearst had been a salaried consultant on some of the Hearst magazines. Apparently through her own connections she learned about the promotional plans for Davies, which were likely to exceed anything that had done before for the young actress. Shortly after learning about the campaign and before the Rialto opening of *Enchantment*, she demanded from Moore that the campaign plans be curtailed. Moore was quick to inform his boss that Millicent was upset. Apparently Hearst decided to communicate with his wife through Moore; he responded coolly and asked his adviser to do his best to calm her down. Tell her, Hearst suggested, that such leading lady publicity campaigns were customary and done merely "to comply with Paramount's requirements." Considering Hearst's on-the-record reluctance to comply with almost anything that Paramount required, this was truly a cagey remark. At a loss, Hearst told Moore, "I want Millicent to be satisfied." Moore suggested that Hearst allow Paramount to direct the advertising for Davies and *Enchantment*. Possibly, he told Hearst, they should put the campaign in the hands of a regular advertising agency. Moore must have known how Hearst would respond to such a suggestion. Hearst was still smarting over Paramount's "past offences," and he told Moore that he was "vehemently opposed and unwilling to submit to any further plunderings."

Millicent was not appeased by Hearst's line about customary practices, and she instructed Moore to redirect their advertising campaign to focus on the film and not the star. Caught between an estranged wife and her fidelity-divided husband, Moore asked Hearst what he should do. Hearst told Moore that they couldn't scrap the Davies publicity in their own papers when space in the competition's papers was already bought. "Advertising in our paper different from other papers," Hearst telegrammed Moore, "would cause unpleasant comment in scandal sheets." At the same time, he also suggested to Moore that he use Walter Irwin, Millicent's brother-in-law and a former Paramount insider, as a sounding board on the advertising plans. At Irwin's recommendation, or Millicent's urging, or perhaps a combination of both, Moore decided to pull back on the Davies promotion in the Hearst papers. All seemed fine until a few days had passed. Hearst, now on a tour of Mexico with Davies, got his hands on one of his newspapers. Flipping the pages quickly he turned to the movie section to see barely a mention of his star. Without delay Hearst sent off a blistering telegram to Moore. "I thought I made clear," he wrote, "that advertisement [sic] in our paper were to be the same as in other paper. . . . I cannot allow anybody to run my business but myself. I do not care what the results may be. I intend to manage my own affairs my way."

In what was becoming a typical behavior pattern, Hearst bombarded Moore with as many apologies as accusations. He followed up his first telegram with another that made him sound weary and characterized the advertisements for *Enchantment* as being "utterly emasculated." He still had some blame to throw around, but now he pointed his finger at his brother-in-law, Irwin, and mostly at himself. In a final message on the subject of *Enchantment*'s sabotaged publicity, Hearst told Moore to retain a copy of his letter of forgiveness for future reference. If he acted like this again to Moore, he was ready to be reminded. It was clear that Hearst would need no further lessons to deal with his wife's jealousy. He vowed that any future "interference from anyone" would not be tolerated.

Fire and Smoke
1922–1925

THE GOLDWYN-COSMOPOLITAN DEAL

In January 1923 a brief letter marked "Personal" was sent to Will Hays by John Eastman, a journalist from the *Chicago Daily Journal*: "Your January 24 letter has been received. I am almost inclined to ask what will be your plan when the Marion Davies scandal breaks. I assume you are aware that it is imminent, and that when the 'blow-off' comes it will create a bigger sensation than many of the meretricious doings at Hollywood."

The meaning of the letter is unknown. There is no correspondence elsewhere in the Will Hays papers—including the January 24 letter mentioned here—to indicate what "scandal" Eastman had in mind. Marion Davies's comings and goings in January and early February do not seem to be particularly unusual. In January she was busy working on her latest Cosmopolitan picture, *Little Old New York*. She took a break to visit New York radio station WEAF, as a guest of the Rankin advertising agency, to give a ten-minute talk called "How I Make Up for the Movies." After plugging Cosmopolitan Productions and a product called Mineralava, Davies offered a free autographed photograph to listeners and the radio station was bombarded with hundreds of requests. In early February, just days after Eastman wrote Hays, *Variety* reported that Davies was forced to halt work at the film studio and remain at home for several days after a fellow actor accidentally fell on top of her during a stunt. Was Davies's sudden seclusion related to

Eastman's unspecified charge? Was there even any validity to that charge? In the realm of Hearst and Hollywood, this would not be the first and certainly not the last time that a rumor of scandal and a suspicion of cover-up became inseparable elements of mysteries.

Davies had returned to work in early February 1923 for only a brief time when another much more serious interruption occurred. During the night of February 18, a massive fire of unknown origin practically wiped out the Cosmopolitan studio at 126th Street and Second Avenue, as well as a unit of the Hearst newsreel company operating out of the same building complex. Marion Davies's apartment at the studio, designed by Joseph Urban in shades of pink, was totally destroyed. The costumes and scenery for the ongoing production of *Little Old New York* were now tattered, burnt embers. Although Hearst had insurance to cover most of his losses, the fire destroyed irreplaceable artwork and antiques that Hearst had intended to use in the film. Among the items destroyed or damaged beyond repair were paintings by Sir Joshua Reynolds and Sir Francis Cotes, a highboy once owned by John Quincy Adams, and two mugs belonging to Washington Irving. From February 1923 until January 1924, most of the Cosmopolitan productions were filmed at four metropolitan studios. *Little Old New York*—which was three-quarters completed at the time of the fire—was completed at the Tilford Studio on Forty-fourth Street and the Jackson Studio in the Bronx. The film was ready for release in early June, and it had its premiere in London, reportedly the first time a Hollywood film was screened abroad before it was shown in a U.S. theater.

In late 1922, still unhappy with his Zukor arrangement, Hearst directed his energies toward forging a new distribution deal. In December, he wrote treasurer and adviser Joseph Moore requesting data about the Vitagraph Company: its income and expenses and the state of its distribution organization. He told Moore that he might buy Vitagraph or Universal "or some such concern with a distributing agency attached—and put our Cosmopolitan pictures out through that agency." While Hearst was still gathering information on various film companies and their distribution possibilities, he had Moore draft a contract with the Goldwyn organization. Apparently there was some haggling over specifics, but by February 1923 the contract was signed, and the Goldwyn-Cosmopolitan Distributing Company was formed. The organization replaced the preexisting Goldwyn Distributing Company but was separate from the producing companies of both Cosmopolitan and Goldwyn. The new distribution company was owned 50 percent by the Goldwyn Producing Company and 50 percent by Cosmopolitan. In addition, the creation of a new distribution company gave Hearst a foreign affiliation: Lord Beaverbrook, the British publisher, film producer, and owner of a controlling interest in 80 percent of the first-run movie theaters in England, had been half owner of the English Goldwyn Distributing Company. The two media moguls had something of a mutual admiration society, Hearst being inspired by the layout of Beaverbrook's *Daily Express* tabloid newspaper, and Beaverbrook later calling Hearst "one of the great American figures of the age." Hearst and Beaverbrook were friends as well, and during the summer before the Goldwyn agreement Hearst and Millicent spent the weekend at Beaverbrook's country estate, Leatherhead, in the Surrey Hills. According to Arthur Brisbane, it was the friendship with Beaverbrook beginning in the late 1910s that lessened Hearst's prejudices against Great Britain, which had caused such a tempest during World War I.

Soon after the deal with Goldwyn was closed, *Variety* opined that Hearst was finally achieving his longtime desire to be on an equal footing with other Hollywood moguls:

> During the last year the Hearst picture organization has made tremendous strides in the productions that they have been turning out, and for the first time since Hearst embarked in the motion picture game it began to look as though he was going to get a break in the matter of returns. This is particularly in regard to his "Knighthood" production, which within the next few weeks will have returned the cost of production and be on the road to a substantial profit. . . . Those who have been in on the conferences which led to the signing of the contracts between Hearst and Goldwyn state that the arrangement calls for an almost immediate activity on the part of the Hearst organization to furnish production for the releasing organization.

Between the few pictures still being readied under the existing Paramount contract and the new ones made with Goldwyn, the 1923–1924 film season was one of the more prolific periods for Cosmopolitan. In addition to *Little Old New York*, seven other feature films were produced and released. The Davies vehicles *Yolanda*, a medieval epic, and *Janice Meredith*, a production set during the American Revolution, were two of Hearst's costlier productions. Both films were plagued with production problems, as Hearst searched for bank loans to finance his extravagances. When Joseph Urban's expanding design practice seemed be adding to his financial worries, Hearst sent Moore a telegram: "Understand 'Yolanda' held up somewhat by sets not being ready is it possible that Urban is again doing outside work please investigate this carefully perhaps we should have a second art director for emergencies please see the 'Bright Shawl' let me know what you think of Everett Shinn's work."

Everett Shinn, a famed artist of the Ashcan School and an illustrator on several Hearst magazines, did wind up replacing Urban on *Janice Meredith*. Shinn was excited at first when he was called to Hearst's office and offered the commission. During the interview, while Hearst was called away on a telephone call, Shinn imagined designing sets with a minimum amount of frills for scenes depicting the bleak winter when Washington crossed the Delaware River and the rolling farms of Lexington and Concord:

> I was thrilled at the prospect of seeing it all come to life again until Mr. Hearst placed the telephone on its cradle and turned to me. In one sentence he had sunk my buoyant hopes for the picture's success under the ponderous weight of his final order. "I wish to spend a million dollars." Mr. Hearst's thin voice had high pitched that desire. "Yes, 'Janice Meredith' should make a very inspiring picture and I wish to spend a million dollars on it." His pale gray blue eyes moved slowly upward from under the tentlike flap of his slanting lids and rested, perhaps, on a visionary completion of that wish that would cost him a million dollars, but, how vastly different his mental picture must have been from mine. A million dollars. Where could it be spent? On what incident. No, no, Mr. Hearst must not dare to gold plate the homely pewter.

Despite his reservations, Shinn accepted the job. As he walked from Hearst's office, he came on the studio where another Cosmopolitan production, a historical costume drama called *Under the Red Robe*, was under way:

> I had wandered down the back stairs and found myself on one of the vast stages. There, sumptuousness was in the making, the throne room of a French King. . . . Here was the place for splashing about a million dollars. . . . Heavy in spirit I walked down the steps of the rich carpeted dais having flopped in my assumed assurance of a Dauphan's [*sic*] prerogative and dreamily contemplated a great ornate circle set in the marble floor. The seal of France, a masterpiece of carving with deep intaglio, glistening, sharp recessed the patient work of four expert German wood carvers. In the love of their labor they had cut, gouged and scraped into this six inches of black gutta percha and had achieved a wonder work, six feet in diameter. I was told that they had worked six weeks on it at a salary of eighty dollars a week per man.

Later, Shinn watched as a Cosmopolitan cameraman panned the elaborate seal without pausing, going straight for a close-up shot of the king's face. "The seal," Shinn wrote, "shunted to the piled up discards in the yards."

Urban was the designer of *Under the Red Robe*, which was directed by Alan Crosland and starred Alma Rubens, an actress whom the Cosmopolitan publicity department falsely trumpeted as a relative of the famous artist. The last Hearst film released as a Paramount picture was *Enemies of Women* (1923), and it was also directed by Crosland, with Rubens as the female lead and Lionel Barrymore as the male lead. According to an article in the *New York American*, the film marked the first time that an entire American film troupe was sent to Europe to make a picture. Director Crosland, the film's actors and crew, and Urban, once again the set designer, were in Monte Carlo for six weeks, where scenes of the casino and the palace of the prince of Monaco were filmed. A number of the interior studio sequences, especially of Rubens's exotic villa, are in the Wiener Werkstätte style that Urban pioneered in both Vienna and New York. The film included what was something of a trademark for Hearst films since *Patria*: a bevy of beautiful young women as extras drawn from the chorus lines of the Ziegfeld Follies and the Greenwich Village Follies. It was reported that Hearst planned to spend $25,000 on an advertising campaign for *Enemies of Women*. The movie's world premiere was on Easter Sunday, April 1, 1923, at the Central Theater, a Broadway house revamped by Urban for the occasion. "Urban will use all of his artistry," the *New York American* reported, "in designing a fitting setting for the presentation of 'Enemies of Women.' This coming week he will supervise the redecorating of the theatre. For the presentation there will be an augmented orchestra of thirty-six pieces which will render the special musical score composed by William Frederick Peters, who composed the operatic score for 'Knighthood.' "

Enemies star Lionel Barrymore also appeared in the 1923 Cosmopolitan release *Unseeing Eyes* (originally entitled *Snowblind*). The film, which was directed by E. H. Griffith (a distant relative of D. W. Griffith), with Seena Owen in the female lead role, was an adaptation of a story that had appeared in *Hearst's International Magazine*. Like the short story, the picture is set in the Canadian Rocky Mountains, and much of it was actually shot on location around Castle Rock in the Columbia Valley and in the vicinity of Quebec City. According to a Capitol Theater program for *Unseeing Eyes*, the picture made dramatic use of airplanes and extreme close-ups taken at great altitudes. During a portion of the filming, Hearst joined his production team at their headquarters, the landmark Hotel Frontenac in Quebec City. Gretl Urban, who was the costume designer on the picture, remembered the only trouble on the shoot, besides the cold weather, was the effort expended on keeping tabs on the unpredictable Barrymore, who was suffering from drug addiction at the time.

Frank Borzage, who had achieved a box office hit with *Humoresque* in 1920, directed the 1923 Cosmopolitan production *The Nth Commandment*. The film, which starred Colleen Moore and was supervised by Frances Marion, did not approach the success of Borzage's earlier work for Hearst, but it had some noteworthy attractions. A department store interior was re-created in a studio down to the minutest detail, and another scene showed a movie within a movie. "Motion picture fans," a publicity sheet explained

> will have an opportunity to see the psychological effect of pictures on themselves and how they quickly react to the emotions they are witnessing in one of the most striking scenes of "The Nth Commandment," Fannie Hurst's splendid story which the Cosmopolitan Corp. picturized at the Thomas Ince studio in Culver City, Cal. . . . The scene depicts the interior of a motion picture theatre and the audience which breathlessly watches a pulsating romance unfolded. It brings into play all the elements which go in the making of a motion picture audience, including the happy family who read titles out loud, the man who sneezes and makes everybody jump and the young lovers who hold hands in the dark.

In another scene, a Broadway supper club was reproduced with unusual authenticity. The room included a domal ceiling—sixty feet in diameter and fifty feet above the floor—suspending a gigantic chandelier. The set, designed by another Urban replacement, Stephen Goosson, appears to have been the first ever constructed with a ceiling. Ironically, Goosson would go on to design the sets for *The Lady from Shanghai* (1946), a film directed by Orson Welles, often credited as the first director to film a room with a ceiling, in *Citizen Kane*.

In late May 1923 executives, district branch heads, and salesmen of the Goldwyn and Cosmopolitan companies held a convention in Atlantic City, formally announcing that their merger (which included a third entity, called Distinctive Pictures, Inc.) constituted a combine valued at $25 million. Cosmopolitan had put $8 million into the new organization, Goldwyn $10 million, and Distinctive $7 million. The Goldwyn-Cosmopolitan Company was well positioned to compete against the Famous Players–Lasky Corporation, and news reports were in agreement that Hearst was primarily responsible for the merger. Hearst attended the Goldwyn-Cosmopolitan convention with

Arthur Brisbane and Joseph Moore. "The public has been played down to long enough," Hearst told the gathering in his keynote speech. "I have even heard in the moving picture business," Hearst said, "the difference drawn between a good picture and a good box office picture. I don't think there is any such distinction; the best picture is the best box office picture." A few weeks later Hearst issued a statement about his plans for Cosmopolitan, further explaining his motivation for making films. On the surface, Hearst's statement seemed to contradict his previous pragmatic approach to making films, but it was actually an expression of self-confidence, paternalism, or both; he knew, perhaps even better than the public itself what it wanted and what it needed in pictures. "No phase of tense interest," Hearst said, "no possibility of dramatic action or emotion will be neglected; but to interest will be added instruction in the hope of making the picture not only the enlivening but the uplifting force that it should be in the community."

While the Goldwyn–Cosmopolitan merger was one of the biggest news stories of the film industry in 1923, it was almost completely overshadowed a year later with the formation of Metro-Goldwyn-Mayer. This new film company had been in the making since shortly after the creation of Goldwyn-Cosmopolitan, and it was in part an outgrowth of that merger. In October 1923 Frank J. (Joe) Godsol, president of Goldwyn (Samuel Goldwyn had been deposed as company head in 1922, although he continued to hold a substantial financial interest), issued a statement to the press. The three-page document emphasized the soundness of his organization while addressing the shakiness of the industry as a whole. As Godsol laid out his solutions to rising film production costs, he seemed to suggest that only greater mergers could address the fundamental problems of the industry and that his company, because of its strength, should lead the way to such mergers:

> All of these unsound conditions can be remedied if three or four distributing companies, or more if others should choose to join, distribute as one. Joint distribution would put an end to the dictation of prices by exhibitors. If a sufficient number of pictures were in the hands of one distributing agency, exhibitors who persisted in their present strangling methods would soon find themselves facing a shortage of good pictures and they would then be willing to deal on a fair basis. . . . Mine is not a cry of personal distress. In fact, I feel that with the warm personal friendships of many leading exhibitors and with the powerful cooperation of Mr. W. R. Hearst, Goldwyn Cosmopolitan is better able to cope with the situation than some of the other companies.

In truth, the Goldwyn-Cosmopolitan Company was in bad financial shape by late 1923. Although it had important assets—in addition to its Hearst association it had a half-interest in the Capitol Theater in New York and it owned the Culver City studio formerly owned by Thomas Ince—its stock was low, and its investments were heavy. Hearst meanwhile continued to struggle to finance his expensive projects. In his correspondence with Joseph Moore he tried to put a positive spin on his film company's situation, but increasingly the focus is on more efficient production methods, new schemes to shift funds from one division of the corporation to another, and plans to secure additional bank loans. In April 16 Hearst wrote Moore and his Committee on Finances:

> Our present plan of proceedure [*sic*] up there is to finance our operations by borrowing from banks the amount spent—or approximate the amount spent—on our negative and hypothecating the negative until the income clears off the indebtedness. I think during the last year our production has been profitable or approximately so. I do not mean that the institution has been profitable in the last year, but that the pictures produced in the last twelve months indicate, as far as they are sold, that the pictures will be—on the average—profitable. That is to say, those that are profitable will make a sufficient profit to more than compensate those that are not.

On July 25, Moore wrote Hearst: "Some new plan of financing film company will have to be evolved immediately.... They may possibly be able to borrow on 'Under the Red Robe' but I doubt it."

Hearst replied to Moore on July 26: "We must get advances on completed pictures or else postpone further production until sales receipts come in. We should get five hundred on 'Red Robe.' It ranks with 'Enemies of Women' and 'Knighthood' and actually cost seven fifty. It should gross two million."

From San Simeon, Hearst sent Moore a telegram on August 4: "Understand [George] d'Utassy has not had control expenses of film organization gave him absolutely authority and want it immediately restored otherwise can't hold him to account for expenses and budget have ordered all work suspended on pictures until sane budget is prepared and approved after which Utassy must hold organization to that budget or promptly hand in resignation."

Later that same day Hearst sent Moore another telegram: "Please try very hard get money on 'Red Robe' in New York believe bank here will make advance on another picture when 'Enemies' paid off its well to keep them continually financing one picture and get other banks each to keep financing one picture thus we will have a dependable system."

THE INEVITABLE AND THE ILL-FATED DEAL

In November Hearst traveled to Havana, Cuba, before making his way north to Key West and Jacksonville, Florida. He was in New York in late January 1924 and invited to speak before a luncheon at the Hotel Astor given by the Theater Owner's Chamber of Commerce. The event proved to be an important moment, both for what Hearst had to say and for what others had to say about him. Speaking on the issue of film censorship, Hearst returned to a familiar theme:

> I know that this is an exhibitors' luncheon pure and simple, but I see members of the press here and I would like to say just a word on this matter of censorship. It is far wider in its significance, I think, and I imagine you do too, than merely an attempt to interfere with the fundamental rights of this particular motion picture industry. If it should be successful in this instance, if it should extend to other States, if it should become a recognized interference and an established evil, there is no reason at all why it should not be extended.

As other guests took to the podium, the luncheon turned into something like the love feast for Will Hays two years earlier, with several speakers pointing out Hearst's value to the film industry. Courtland Smith, assistant to Will Hays and brother-in-law of Arthur Brisbane, thanked Hearst for his help in defeating censorship legislation, especially in Massachusetts in 1922, and film executive I. G. Chadwick, formerly associated with Hearst's Graphic Film company, pointed out to the crowd that Hearst was an important exhibitor as well as a producer. One of the founders of the Theatre Owners' group, William Brandt, was the most effusive about Hearst: "Today, many of the men who owned nickelodeons now have the finest buildings in the world. We feel that we owe much of this to Mr. Hearst, who has never failed to give us his aid in measures that he thought were worthy of his support and in treating motion pictures in a dignified manner. His support and friendship has [sic] meant more to us than he himself realizes."

While many theater owners may have agreed with Brandt's praise for Hearst's elevation of the film industry, they were not always pleased by Hearst's uneven-handed approach to publicity. In February, in the *San Fran-*

cisco Examiner, so much space was taken up by publicity for the latest Cosmopolitan picture, *The Great White Way*, that other movie exhibitors had to depend on small ads and word of mouth to fill their theaters. A *Variety* article hinted at the downside of Hearst's excesses by titling an article on the theater owners complaints "Too Much Hearst."

Hearst was back in Florida in February, vacationing in Palm Beach with Millicent. Meanwhile, Marion Davies remained in New York. The actress was busy working on *Yolanda*, which was released in late February and selected for a long run at the Cosmopolitan Theater, to be followed by a general release (although unexpectedly Hearst pulled the picture from his theater when its run was up and ordered major retakes). Goldwyn head Joe Godsol was also in Palm Beach around the same time as Hearst, and so was Marcus Loew, the movie theater magnate and owner of the producing and distributing company called Metro since 1920. Godsol met with Hearst and Loew in Florida in February 1924, although it is not known if all three men met together. Apparently, Godsol offered both Hearst and Loew an opportunity to buy the controlling stock of the Goldwyn Company, and both men turned him down. Loew was not interested in an outright purchase of Godsol's company, but he did begin to consider seriously a possible merger with Goldwyn and with Louis B. Mayer, who owned an independent producing company that had a preexisting distribution deal with Metro. Loew directed his theater chief Nicholas Schenck to pursue the matter with both parties. Apparently, Schenck's efforts in pushing for a merger were paramount. "Negotiations for the purchase of Goldwyn," Schenck told film historian Bosley Crowther, "were started in 1923. Marcus Loew and I started this. . . . It was felt that the combination of the two products—Metro and Goldwyn—would strengthen the total product in output as well as quality. Output was important."

By late February, even before Loew had left Palm Beach, it was rumored that Hearst was dissatisfied with his distribution deal with Goldwyn and looking to tie up with Loew. Hearst denied the story, as did Loew a few weeks later, but by March 26 Hearst's attorney, Nathan Burkan, a former Tammany district leader, acknowledged that his client was being kept abreast of the negotiations among Metro, Goldwyn, and Mayer. The assets that Hearst brought to MGM were substantially increased with the rebuilding of the Cosmopolitan studio in upper Manhattan in early 1924. And Hearst had plans to build additional film stages in New York as well. When they were completed it was predicted that Hearst would own the largest film facility on the East Coast. In January he had told the *Exhibitors Herald* that he still found New York the ideal city for making motion pictures. His views were no doubt colored by his real estate investments, but he was also selling himself to his fellow filmmakers, reminding them of his importance. "There is an enormous advantage in making motion pictures in New York City." Hearst said.

> One of the most important of these is that the city is the center of stage play production. . . . It is folly to minimize the screen's need of the best artists on the stage in the casts of its worthiest productions. For this and other obvious reasons, Cosmopolitan Corporation decided some time ago to make all its pictures in New York City. We prefer to produce our pictures in studios with artificial lighting, rather than to depend on uncertainty and varying degrees of sunlight, a condition from which no part of this country is at all seasons exempt.

After months of speculation *Variety* reported on April 9 that an MGM merger was imminent. The only sticking points, according to the trade journal, were the size and circumstances of the financial payoff that would have Goldwyn severing his ties to every part of the company except for his name and a decision as to what role Hearst would play in the new organization. These points were presumably resolved by mid-April, when it was widely reported that MGM had been formed (its official incorporation occurred on May 16). Mayer was chosen as vice president under Loew, and Irving Thalberg was made a second vice president and production supervisor. It was later learned that 20 percent of the company's profits were guaranteed for Mayer, Thalberg, and Robert Rubin, MGM's secretary, with Mayer getting 10 percent and Thalberg and Rubin getting 5 percent each. Loew had bought out Joe Godsol's $750,000 interest in Goldwyn and paid Sam Goldwyn a million dollars.

The *New York American* gave a more detailed account of the MGM merger than most daily newspapers did, but it avoided any mention of Hearst's involvement. By late April it was reported that Hearst's films would be released through the new company. The first two Cosmopolitan-MGM releases would be *Janice Meredith* and the newly revamped *Yolanda*. Throughout the negotiations leading to the agreement, Hearst's name had been prominent in the gossip, but in the end even Hollywood insiders were unsure what his role had been in the formation and the formative days of MGM. Hearst was not on the board of directors of the new company, and neither were any recognizable names from his organization. Louis B. Mayer's biographer, Charles Higham, speculates that Hearst was an unofficial board member of MGM and that he was guaranteed a sizable chunk of the company's profits in return for the publicity he would shower on MGM. In this context, it is noteworthy that Louella Parsons, the movie critic and Hollywood tattler, became a syndicated columnist for Hearst shortly after the merger, bringing her distinctive brand of ballyhoo to both Hearst and MGM.

For further evidence of what Hearst could do to boost a film that interested him, an industry leader needed only go to the local theater in April and watch a Hearst newsreel. To publicize *Janice Meredith* Hearst got the colonel of the Twenty-sixth Regiment in Plattsburgh, New York, where scenes for the historic epic were taken, to bestow the title of "honorary colonel" on Marion Davies and then instructed the *International Newsreel* to film the actress as she reviewed her troops. The scenes were a quintessential Hearst marketing scheme that was only slightly dampened when an irate newspaper in Vermont alerted the War Department to the newsreel, causing Secretary of War John W. Weeks to issue an order that discontinued the short-lived practice of giving honorary military titles to "actresses or others."

One suspects that the idea of keeping Hearst's involvement with MGM unofficial was the inspiration of both Hearst and the new company's principal founders. Although there is every indication that Hearst and Marcus Loew were friends, an element of caution must have guided both men. On April 9 *Variety* seemed to be hinting at Hearst's reputation for unpredictability when it reported, "Hearst would be welcomed into the combination but there are several stories around of Hearst and his probabilities in further picture producing." As a hands-on producer, Hearst was unlikely to have entered a binding production agreement with such controlling forces as Mayer and Thalberg without considerable hesitation. MGM story editor Samuel Marx has written that even after Hearst decided to establish a more official relationship with MGM, he resisted relocating his operations to the MGM lot because of the close proximity and possible intrusion of Mayer and Thalberg. This was one of the reasons, according to Marx, that in the fall of 1924 Hearst considered setting up his headquarters in the nearby lot of the talented but less threatening independent director Thomas Ince.

In early July Hearst secured the rights to a picture play from Famous Players entitled *Zander the Great*. By mid-July Marion Davies and scenarist Luther Reed were in Los Angeles in rehearsals for the film, the first Cosmopolitan picture under Hearst's new production arrangement with MGM. In *Zander* Davies plays an atypical, unglamorous role, a character named Mamie, an orphan girl searching for a sense of family. She comes to live with a foster mother (played by future columnist Hedda Hopper) and her young son, Alexander, nicknamed Zander. Mamie raises the boy when illness strikes his mother, and the story involves a number of narrow escapes and rescues as Mamie and Zander travel west and get mixed up with bandits and bootleggers. The production on *Zander*, which was written by Frances Marion and directed by Marion's husband, George Hill, stretched on for months, and the picture was not released until May 1925. Joseph Urban, whose salary had recently risen from $100,000 to $125,000 a year, had very little to do with the film since it was set mostly in the desert, but he did create an adobe-style camp house for one scene that attracted some attention. Although a long shot of the house flashed on the screen for only a few seconds, it was long enough to get a Texas millionaire to commission Urban, an equally talented architect, to build it as a real home in Dallas.

When Hearst was not on the *Zander* set—sometimes with his legs wrapped in puttees and a megaphone strapped around his neck like a caricature of a director—he was screening and editing the film at San Simeon. Hearst sent long telegrams with instructions for retakes to Davies, who was living at her home in Beverly Hills, and to other Cosmopolitan executives. In early September Hearst gave Davies suggestions that were inspired by his film idol D. W. Griffith:

We fade out on Mamie and apparently hopeless situation then fade in on Dawn in camp and with first rays of light comes sandstorm. This must be big effect like Griffith's "[Orphans of the] Storm," the sand flies, the trees bend and break, the men's blankets and things are blown away, the cattle are blinded and start to stampede, men rush to save the cattle they have stolen and their things and Mamie's opportunity to escape arrives. . . . The thing I dread in this picture is that it will be commonplace. We have not big sets and gorgeous costumes to make scenes and we have got to make them out of drama. Escape of Mamie in sandstorm should offer opportunity for big Griffith effect.

Two months later, frustrated by the lack of progress on *Zander*, Hearst sent a letter to Daniel Carson Goodman, the production manager of Cosmopolitan, that he copied in a telegram to Davies: "Just waded through an interminable number of reels covering very few incidents in which long shots, semi long shots, medium and semi medium shots close ups and exaggerated close ups were taken from dozen different angles. Have not time to go through so many reels, rushes or money enough to pay for picture taken in this extravagant manner." After he had that off his chest, Hearst's telegram continued for an additional seven pages with a dozen scene ideas and camera angles suggestions.

When Hearst was not sending Davies directorial instructions, he was dashing off jealous letters. "You're running around with all your old beaux," Hearst wrote Davies in November, "and a lot of new ones. I know *all about you*." Hearst's suspicions appear to have been justified. It was widely rumored in Hollywood that Davies was having an affair with Charles Chaplin during the filming of *Zander*, and she may indeed have been involved with other men. When Hearst felt a little better about Davies, he once again used her as a sounding board for his film plans. In November 1924 he had more than one discussion with director Thomas Ince about forming a producing partnership. A film version of "The Enchanted Isle," a story owned by Cosmopolitan, was being considered as the first of a series of film projects. "I had a talk with Ince last night," Hearst wrote Davies, "and we agreed that we would agree on something but didn't decide what the exact terms would be. We are to talk it over further when I get to Los Angeles." As Mrs. Thomas Ince would later recall, the events in mid-November seemed to be leading up to a deal between the two men: "So, they planned to get together and discuss their plans. We were invited for a weekend on the Hearst yacht, on its way to San Diego. At the last moment, one of our boys was taken quite ill, so I was unable to accompany Mr. Ince on this trip." As Hearst planned it, the weekend trip would include a celebration of Ince's forty-second birthday onboard his luxury yacht, the *Oneida*.

Like San Simeon and *Citizen Kane*, the yacht called the *Oneida* has become a Hearst icon, a resonating symbol of his extravagance and audacity as well as an emblem of Hollywood mythmaking. But before the third weekend of November 1924, when Ince joined Hearst and Davies and a dozen or so others for a business and pleasure cruise that ended in death, the *Oneida* was far from notorious. Hearst's yacht was his floating castle, a magnet for the Hollywood crowd, much like that other enchanted castle on the hill. From the figurehead Indian chief with outstretched arms at its bow all 215 feet to its stern, the *Oneida* spelled luxury Hearst-style. Hidden from most visitors was an engine room two stories high and quarters for a crew of thirty-five. In the ship's white-tiled galley, an up-to-date refrigeration system enabled long-distance cruises that were said to include such exotic points as Tahiti and the Amazon. On the open-air decks were scattered oversize pillows, wicker tables, and chaise lounges (where, it was said, Greta Garbo preferred to sleep at night). A large blue plaid woolen throw onboard must have come from someone with a sense of humor and been meant for San Simeon, for it had a label reading "For the White House in California."

Kept in storage below deck were crates of the finest wines and liquors, fine crystal, and barrels of Tiffany china, all white and trimmed in gold, marked with the ship's name. There were many rooms on the *Oneida*, among them a dining room with seating for twelve, and five guest staterooms with their own bathrooms fitted with gold-plated faucets. A wood-paneled lounge was appointed with plush purple sofas, card tables, and a setup for screening films. The lounge also held other interesting artifacts. It has been erroneously said that Hearst's yacht was the same vessel where President Grover Cleveland was taken in 1893 for a secretly performed operation for throat cancer. In fact, there were two different *Oneida*s, and Hearst's yacht was not built until 1897. Apparently, Hearst believed the story, or liked others to believe it, because he kept a set of turn-of-the-century surgical instruments on display.

Near the front of the ship, below deck, were separate quarters for Hearst and Davies. Hearst's room was tastefully decorated with built-in furniture and oil seascapes on the curved walls. The Davies room was designed in shades of rose, the actress's favorite color. Among its furnishings were a dressing table, needlepoint chairs, and a cut velvet couch customized with dozens of tiny gold *M*'s for "Marion" scattered over a rose-colored background. Located across the hallway from Hearst's bedroom was another room that served as an office for his secretary, Joe Willicombe. In Willicombe's room, unbeknownst to most, there was a secret doorway for making quick and unnoticed exits from the yacht. Between the Hearst and Davies rooms, at the foot of a central stairway leading above deck, was a prominent display: a glass case for a collection of rifles and pistols.

Everyone who was on the *Oneida* at the time and willing to talk about it later insisted there was nothing suspicious about the Thomas Ince trip of November 1924. By all accounts, the director had become suddenly ill during the cruise from what appeared to be a heart ailment from which he would die two days later. One of the most talkative about the Ince trip was Gretl Urban, who was onboard with her father, Joseph Urban, and his wife, Mary, as the three had been many times before. Until the day she died in 1998, a few months shy of her one-hundredth birthday, Urban maintained that she saw nothing shady during the trip and that Ince had died from natural causes. She also acknowledged, however, that whatever initially happened to Ince occurred while she was sleeping and that she was awakened during the middle of the night by Ince's moans and told by her father that the director was having a heart attack. Although she claimed to have seen Ince being taken from the *Oneida*, she admitted she was never that close to the director during the events. While the witnesses appeared to be in agreement that there was no foul play involved in Ince's death, it sometimes seems that everyone who has ever heard the story is firmly convinced that Ince was shot or stabbed to death by Hearst. To this day, the story has become a legend of Hollywood's "unsolved mysteries." Among the most popular theories concerning Ince's "murder" was that Hearst killed the director in a jealous rage after seeing him making love to Davies outside her stateroom, so conveniently located near the ship's weapon display. Other variations on the story have Hearst discovering fellow passenger Charlie Chaplin in an embrace with Davies, upon which, in an attempt to shoot Chaplin, Hearst shot Ince by mistake. There is little dispute over the facts of the story from this point on. Ince was placed on a motorboat (the *Oneida* carried two) by Cosmopolitan studio manager, Daniel Goodman, and Joe Willicombe and taken to San Diego, the nearest town. From there a train was expected to take Ince to Los Angeles, but en route Ince's condition deteriorated. When the train stopped in Del Mar, Ince was taken to the Del Mar Hotel, and Mrs. Ince was telephoned about her husband's turn for the worse. Accompanied by a Dr. Glasgow, Mrs. Ince drove to Del Mar and brought her husband back to their home in Beverly Hills. In the early morning hours of November 19 Ince died, surrounded by his family. The official cause of death was given as heart failure, and a funeral, attended by Marion Davies and Chaplin, was held on November 21. Hearst did not attend the service; he had traveled to Salinas, California, and then on to San Simeon after Ince's death.

It is an indication of Hearst's reputation in the United States that so many people were ready to believe the worst of him. Even without hard evidence a story tying Hearst to Ince's death fit perfectly into the picture of a power so great as to be capable of and able to get away with murder. Rumors about Ince's supposed murder seem to have surfaced almost immediately after his death. They were fueled in part at least by the clumsy reaction of the Hearst press, which offered accounts with contradictions and omissions (some said that Ince had actually died at Hearst's San Simeon estate, and many others made no mention of Hearst or his yacht at all). Overall, the Hearst newspapers were subdued in their coverage of Ince's death, a factor that in itself must have made many suspicious. Here were presumably a dozen or more witnesses (including Hearst himself) to Ince's falling ill, and not one of the ship's passengers was made available to speak to either the Hearst or non-Hearst press.

Within a few years of Ince's death, the murder story seems already to have been fairly well established. In 1932, when the *Oneida* was sold with almost its entire contents intact to Elisha Goodsell, the entrepreneur used it as a ferryboat and offered tourists an opportunity to see the place where Hearst had done the dastardly deed. By the early 1930s the FBI was receiving unsolicited information on the *Oneida*–Ince matter (they apparently made no substantive inquiry of their own). Hearst's FBI files contain detailed letters (mostly hearsay) from an Ince associate and a prominent journalist who both made demands that Hearst be charged with murder. These accusers suggested that Hearst had paid off everyone from Los Angeles District Attorney Asa Keyes to the outspoken and flamboyant Los Angeles evangelist Aimie Semple McPherson to prevent them from telling the truth. While it was true that Keyes was later accused of taking bribes and that a Hearst reporter became one of McPherson's personal managers during a controversy of her own, the link between these public figures and Hearst and Ince remains titillating but sketchy.

The murder theory aside, the most likely trigger to a Hearst cover-up was the volatile issue of alcohol consumption and distribution during the era of Prohibition. Although it is rarely noted by historians, a brief investigation into Ince's death in early December 1924 that ruled out murder by gunshot or any other weapon also raised the possibility of another causal factor, a theory that came from Ince's own lips. According to the *New York Times*, at least two medical personnel had been called to attend to Ince while he was at the Del Mar Hotel, where the director lay dying but still able to communicate. Dr. T. A. Parker of La Jolla informed the inquiry that Ince had told him he had drunk heavily on the *Oneida*. A nurse named Jessie Howard who also spoke to Ince at the time said that the producer believed his illness was caused by "bad liquor." Years later Miss Howard confirmed her statement to the wife of Joe Willicombe, one of the men who apparently accompanied Ince on the train to Del Mar.

One can certainly see why Hearst would be reluctant to encourage an investigation if there was a suggestion that he had served liquor—good or bad—that may have caused a man's death. The liquor motive is supported by other information not known by the public. At the time of the fateful *Oneida* cruise, the U.S. Justice Department was looking into allegations that Hearst was engaged in a bootlegging operation on the West Coast. According to Justice Department documents, a motorboat owned by Hearst called the *Skedaddle* was alleged to have been rum-running in and around San Francisco Bay between the months of May and November 1924. Reportedly the *Skedaddle* was ferrying bootleg liquor to various ports from a British steamship called the *Quadra*. It appears that stories about the activities of the *Skedaddle* made their way to the Justice Department via government informants employed by Hearst. For several years, the case of the *Skedaddle* was discussed at high levels of the Justice Department, under the watchful eye of Assistant Attorney General Mabel Walker Willebrandt. The inquiry seems never to have found its way into the press, and although Willebrandt had a reputation for being strongly pro-Prohibition, there is no evidence to suggest that she seriously pursued Hearst's connections to bootlegging. Possibly she was too close to her subject. Willebrandt spent her formative years in California before coming to Washington during the Harding administration (she retained her prominent position in the Justice Department into the Coolidge years). Willebrandt met Louis B. Mayer in late 1924, and according to Mayer biographer Charles Higham, the two became "intimate" friends at this time. After Willebrandt left the Justice Department in 1929 and returned to private practice, she became Washington counsel for Metro-Goldwyn-Mayer, protecting the film company's interests with regard to tax problems and government inquiries. In addition to Mayer, her clients in the 1930s included such movie stars as Charles Chaplin, Jean Harlow, and Clark Gable. By the 1940s Willebrandt was still interested in the film industry and a forceful advocate for uncovering Communism in Hollywood.

A week after Ince's funeral, Hearst was in San Francisco. Even though he had been on the verge of launching a film partnership with Ince, he made no comment to the press on the director's life or death and would never publicly discuss the matter for the rest of his life. The only hint that something was troubling Hearst is suggested in a brief telegram he sent on November 28 to Marion Davies, who was still in Beverly Hills, but it is uncertain if he was referring to Ince: "Have considered matter carefully. Am sure better go east soon as possible. Situation here unsatisfactory."

The death of Thomas Ince had one certain effect on Hearst. After briefly considering setting up production at Joseph P. Kennedy's FBO (later RKO) studio and even buying the studio from Kennedy, Hearst abandoned his search for an independent filmmaker with whom to align his production company. Since early November Hearst's production manager, Daniel Goodman, had been in discussions with MGM officials about the prospects of a production deal. Now Hearst instructed Goodman to pursue the matter vigorously. Meanwhile, on the stages of the United Studios where two Cosmopolitan films were still in production, there were continuing delays and friction. Convinced that the *Zander the Great* team was taking advantage of his largesse, Hearst fired director Clarence Badger and replaced him briefly with scenarist Luther Reed (who only directed one scene) and then permanently with George Hill, a contract director at Harry Cohn's Columbia Pictures. It was reported that $75,000 worth of footage shot by Badger was scrapped by Hearst after he viewed a nearly completed film. Hearst reacted in a similar fashion when he saw the rushes on his film *Never the Twain Shall Meet*: he cut some 140,000 feet from the South Seas drama based on a novel by Peter Kyne and sent the film's leading actors, Anita Stewart and Bert Lytell, back into the studio for retakes. When both productions were essentially completed in mid-December, Hearst fired nearly the entire Cosmopolitan staff of technicians and executives with the exception of Joseph Urban, Goodman, and the production assistant, Harry Poppe. Hearst decided he would postpone all productions until at least February 1925.

On December 17, 1924, the page one headline of *Variety* announced, "W. R. Hearst Quits Movies." It was an attention-getting banner but thoroughly misleading: Hearst was by no means taking himself out of the picture. He was simply closing down his Cosmopolitan studios in New York for a period of time while he launched a production alliance with MGM. *Variety* noted that MGM would produce six pictures a year based on stories and plays owned by Hearst. Although Hearst would receive no money up front for his material, he would get 50 percent of the net profits on the pictures known as Cosmopolitan Productions. The deal (on a considerably larger scale) was similar to the one Hearst had been hoping to strike with Thomas Ince.

It was not until March 1925 that Hearst and MGM finally signed the contract that brought them together as producing partners. The delay was apparently caused by Hearst's insistence that he play a direct role in supervising the Cosmopolitan-labeled films at MGM, both those starring Marion Davies and those in which she did not appear. MGM was reluctant to give Hearst the same open-ended control as he had wielded at his New York studio. The company was also concerned that Hearst's promotion of Davies's career would have a demoralizing effect on other MGM stars, who were not likely to receive such loving attention. As he had done during the original MGM merger process in early 1924, Nick Schenck entered the negotiations between Hearst and Mayer to resolve the matter. In the end MGM decided that the benefits of linking up with Hearst outweighed the disadvantages. It was decided that Davies would receive a straight salary from MGM with no direct share in her pictures' profits. Davies still received a second salary from Cosmopolitan, however, and as a stockholder in that company she received an indirect financial benefit when Cosmopolitan productions were financially successful. As to the matter of Hearst's participation in the production of Cosmopolitan pictures, MGM announced that Harry Poppe, Goodman's assistant, would act as Hearst's representative at MGM; however, it was clear to most insiders that Hearst would remain the overlord of his productions.

In a sign of his permanent move to Hollywood and his break from his New York production ties, Hearst contracted M. S. Epstein, an associate of

Nick Schenck's brother, Joseph, and sent him east to tie up loose ends at the Cosmopolitan Studios. Soon afterward First National became the first film company to rent the Manhattan facilities from Hearst, making a picture there called *Chickie* (1925). In late March a meeting was held in Los Angeles between Hearst and Joseph Urban, who had two years left on his contract. Soon afterward, when Urban returned to New York and his home at the Plaza Hotel, he was called on by Ed Hatrick. The Hearst executive threw a lavish dinner party for Urban that climaxed with the presentation of a wad of crisp one-thousand-dollar bills that amounted to some $100,000. Urban, who was anxious to revive his somewhat stifled architectural career, was happy to take Hearst's going-away present. At around the same time, it was noted in the press that Marion Davies's home on Riverside Drive in Manhattan had been put up for sale. Also in late March the $20,000 bungalow with the Roman-style sunken bathtub, which Urban had built for Davies on the United lot, was being hauled over to Culver City, the new home for Cosmopolitan productions.

The idea of a deal between Hearst and Louis B. Mayer must have caused Hollywood veterans to roll their eyes. People who knew both men were well aware of their mutual needs to be in control and similar habits of demonstrating that control for others to see. Although in politics their growing conservatism made them compatible, on a personal level their self-absorption and attention-getting theatrics (though Mayer was considerably more outwardly melodramatic) gave their partnership a potential for volatility not seen since Hearst worked with producer Ivan Abramson. Director Clarence Brown, who was close to both men, thought their differences were softened by their similar approaches to business:

> When Hearst got his first newspapers, he wasn't an editor or a reporter, and he didn't know shit about the newspaper business. But he had ideas and this inborn sense of what the American public wanted to read. He was also smart enough to know that there were some things he didn't know, so he hired the best newspaper corps in America, stole them away from other papers. Mayer did exactly the same thing. Of course he wasn't exactly green when he took over at MGM, but still he had his weak spots, and he got the right people to fill them in. Like Hearst and Henry Ford, he was an executive genius.

However alike Hearst and Mayer's personalities may have been—some even described the two as father and son—their decision to work together was pragmatic. For his part, Hearst had no qualms about manufacturing a familial relationship with Mayer if that facilitated a better working relationship. Some proof of this manipulation can be found in correspondence about Mayer and with Mayer that began with a chat editor Arthur Brisbane had with the studio mogul in November 1926. Shortly afterward Brisbane wrote a letter to his boss describing the contact and offering some suggestions:

> I had a long talk with Mr. Mayer at Culver City after I talked with you on the telephone. . . . Mr. Mayer is not easy to keep on a subject that happens to interest YOU, because he has so many subjects that interest himself. But I think that my visit may be of some use. . . . I said to Mayer, "If you would take some clever young Jewish boy that understands pictures, let him concentrate on nothing else, make his success and future absolutely dependent on the star's [Davies's] success, you could build a great asset for yourself." I intend to take up the matter with him again when I come out and also with Thalberg. And meanwhile, I shall try to do or write some things to put those gentlemen in a mood to oblige me and really INTEREST THEMSELVES, if I can. They are so frightfully wrapped up in themselves, in their own great responsibilities, the fact that their work is killing them, etc., etc., etc., that it is hard for them to think of anything else. Those gentlemen can stand everything but prosperity. By the way I would suggest that nothing could be more important than to please the wife and daughters of my friend Mr. Mayer. When anybody gives a dinner, especially for somebody with a title like that young Englishman, the other night. They are extremely presentable, ten times more real than most picture people. To do anything to bring them into a good "gentile" atmosphere, would be extremely wise. Mr. Mayer and his family at this moment are just as important to that future, as Nathan Strauss and his family were important to the advertising of the "Evening Journal" in the old days.

Apparently, Hearst was quick to follow Brisbane's advice and quite consciously set out to ingratiate himself with Mayer and his family. As Mayer's daughter, Irene Mayer Selznick, would later recall in her memoirs, Hearst and his editor Arthur Brisbane became a strong presence in the Mayer house in the 1920s. As a mere youngster, she obviously saw no reason to suspect her guests' attentions: "Of all my father's friends, it was these two men, from far afield, who took the trouble to find out what I was thinking. Mr. Brisbane would come fifteen minutes earlier than he was bidden to 'have a little talk with Irene.' . . . Almost the best part was watching my father's pleasure when he joined us. But my strongest relationship, though less personal, was with Mr. Hearst, known to me as Uncle William."

In October 1927 Mayer sent a telegram to Hearst that seems to indicate that he was a willing participant in Hearst's seduction plans: "Received your interesting wire. Believe we should discuss further when you return New York. Don't believe you and I far apart, but needs clarifying. Hope you are well. Girls wish to be remembered to Uncle William. . . . Look forward to seeing you in New York. All will be well in our happy family."

A week later Hearst was fawning over Mayer, suggesting that he build a "bungalow" on the MGM lot that was big enough to match his stature as studio head and as impressive as his own Cosmopolitan headquarters: "Gosh man don't you realize that you are one of the big fellows of the country making a product that more people are interested in than in anything else presented to the public. Everybody of distinction from all over the world comes to Los Angeles and everybody who comes wants to see the studio and they all want to meet you and do meet you so put on few airs son and provide the proper atmosphere." Hearst signed his letter "Uncle William."

Despite their ups and downs, Hearst and Mayer remained partners from 1924 until 1934. It was the longest-lasting association with a film producer that Hearst ever had.

It was not very long after the Cosmopolitan-MGM deal that Mayer saw evidence of Hearst's value to his new film studio. The first Marion Davies film under the new contract, *Lights of Old Broadway*, did poorly at the box office initially, but it became a moneymaker through word of mouth. Before the box office upturn, Hearst and Irving Thalberg, the picture's producer, had blamed each other for the failure. Hearst suggested that his talents for picking stories had been ignored in the process. "I didn't select this story or like it." Soon after the picture opened, he wrote Davies, "The play had been a failure. Picture was not a star vehicle in my humble opinion. However, I did best I could to promote it and will continue to do so but nothing can be promoted to great success unless it has definite elements of success." From Thalberg's point of view the picture had been overpublicized by Hearst, creating expectations that could not be met. Looking at the box office receipts, Mayer was happy to see that both men were wrong. "Mayer moved quickly to congratulate Hearst and Thalberg," MGM story editor Sam Marx recalled, "for getting off to such an excellent start in their mutual endeavors. He predicted greater success ahead. Hearst wired his appreciation and Thalberg went to work preparing a half-dozen new Davies films."

Within the next few years, Davies made two of her most critically acclaimed films: *The Patsy* (1928) and *Show People* (1928). Both were directed by King Vidor, and both showcased Davies's comedic talents.

Other non-Davies films produced by Cosmopolitan helped establish MGM's reputation as a studio of stars. In 1925 Hearst owned the rights to two novels by Vincente Blasco Ibañez, *The Torrent* and *The Temptress*, that were translated to the screen by writer Dorothy Farnum. They were the first two American films for a Swedish actress that America would soon know as Greta Garbo. Actress Joan Crawford's first important film, *Our Dancing Daughters* (1928), was also a project developed through Cosmopolitan. In this picture, which was directed by Harry Beaumont, Crawford established her luminous and appealing screen image, equally believable as a reckless flapper or a woman of substance. As the decade of the twenties and the era of silent films came to an end, Cosmopolitan productions were at the forefront of the technical and psychological changes occurring in the industry. The popularity of three Hearst films in particular—director W. S. Van Dyke's *White Shadows in the South Seas* (1927), MGM's first all-talking *The Voice of the City* (1929), and the musical *Broadway Melody* (1929)—is considered by many historians to be largely responsible for the widespread acceptability of sound films. But the question naturally arises, besides supplying story material to MGM and promoting the finished product, how much involvement did Hearst have in the above-mentioned Cosmopolitan productions? Unfortunately, production records for the early Garbo and Crawford films, as well as for many of the other Cosmopolitan pictures of this period, are sparse at best, with scant evidence to confirm or contradict Hearst's direct involvement. Since Hearst's film production methods were often circuitous, however, the absence of documentation does not necessarily mean that he was an absentee landlord over his pictures. As *Variety* pointed out after the Cosmopolitan-MGM merger, Hearst would not have made this deal "unless he was permitted to have a representative as well as himself, supervise the casting, adaptation of the scenario and cost of the pictures."

Industry
1925–1929

The Bigger Picture

In mid–April 1925, through a setup between the American Telephone and Telegraph Company and publicists at MGM, Marion Davies became the first film celebrity to have her image transmitted over telephone wires. The grainy photographic image of Davies being handed a film makeup bag by Louis B. Mayer was published afterward in the Hearst newspapers with a caption noting that Davies's next production for MGM would be *The Merry Wives of Gotham* (later titled *The Lights of Old Broadway*). At the same time the Davies demonstration was made, Hearst and Loews executive Nicholas Schenck were working on plans to erect a chain of radio stations across the country. If successful, the chain would be a national delivery system for what Hearst called "inexpensive information and entertainment" and presumably also serve as a vehicle for promoting MGM films. Another aspect of Hearst and Schenck's radio plan was the development of a facsimile system for transmitting text and imagery similar to what was achieved with the Davies wire photograph. Over the next year, however, the project became bogged down in litigation over facsimile patents and other cost considerations. It was completely abandoned when Hearst decided to build a more loosely connected radio network on his own by buying up mostly preexisting stations over a more extended period of time.

Later in April 1925 the long-delayed *Zander the Great* opened in Los

Angeles. It was a gala event, with practically every major Hollywood star in attendance. Hearst did not appear at the premiere, but during the previous week he had worked tirelessly with Nick Schenck to make sure it went off without a hitch. Reviews for *Zander* were lukewarm at best, although Davies did receive generally good notice for her work in the film. The Hearst press, as expected, promoted Davies and the film as if their merits surpassed all others. Hearst's overkill operation was already becoming a distraction if not a cliché that was well noted by Hollywood insiders. On the day after the premiere Sam Goldwyn's secretary, Valeria Belletti, overheard Goldwyn studio head Abraham Lehr discussing the *Zander* premiere with Mrs. Goldwyn on the telephone. "Of course," Lehr was heard saying, "daddy had to show off his little girl, and there's nothing too good for her. Daddy wants everybody to think his little girl is wonderful, and he'll spare no expense to convince them."

In June Charlie Chaplin's film *The Gold Rush* premiered at Grauman's Egyptian Theater. If Hearst was still fuming over Chaplin's affair with Davies, it was not apparent; he attended the opening night ceremonies with his mistress by his side. After the screening Hearst, Davies, Louella Parsons, Elinor Glyn, theater man Sid Grauman, and dozens of other film luminaries attended a celebration of Chaplin's success at Sam Goldwyn's home. Goldwyn's secretary handled all the details for the party, including the making of arrangements with "all of the reliable bootleggers in town." A few weeks earlier, Hearst had shown another sign of friendship to Chaplin. He gave the actor the use of his yacht, the *Oneida*, so that his sixteen-year-old bride, Lita, could avoid the press as she gave birth to their first child. Still, as late as August 1925 *Variety* hinted at a continuing romance between Davies and Chaplin: "Sunday the New York 'Graphic' carried a story linking the names of Marion Davies and Charlie Chaplin. It is said that Chaplin is trying to overcome his fondness for Miss Davies, and that people on the coast did not understand when Chaplin was frequently seen with Marion how it happened he suddenly married his present wife."

Hearst made considerable efforts to ingratiate himself with the film industry in 1925. His estate at San Simeon—seemingly always in a state of construction and reconstruction—began to move from being primarily a home for his family and a small circle of friends into an entertainment theme park for the industry. Nineteen twenty-five was the clear starting point in the creation of Hearst's Hollywood on the hill. Animals were being collected for a proposed private zoo, gardens were being laid out, and large oak trees were being moved to make room for a north wing extension to the Casa Grande, the estate's main building, where the movie theater would eventually be constructed. On the grounds, 1925 saw the beginning of an extension to San Simeon's swimming pool, a luxury near and dear to the Hollywood crowd. When the Neptune pool reached its ultimate stage of completion ten years later, it was one hundred feet in length and surrounded by columns and other Roman ruins. With movie folk added to the picture, it looked, in the words of historian Sara Holmes Boutelle, like "a series of exquisitely engineered stage sets for hedonism." Another plan Hearst worked on in 1925 would never get off the drawing board. In correspondence with his architect Julia Morgan, Hearst spoke of his "sort of romantic" notion of building an observatory building on the grounds of his estate to house a big up-to-date telescope. Ostensibly, Hearst envisioned his movie industry guests studying more distant stars.

Meanwhile, in Los Angeles, architect Morgan had been hired to design a building to serve as a residence for women who were struggling for acting roles in the film industry or those working as secretaries and readers or in other supportive positions at the studios. The Hollywood Studio Club, which was completed in 1926 and would eventually house such film luminaries as Marilyn Monroe and Donna Reed, was the brainchild of Will Hays and in his own significant words located "in a respectable neighborhood" of Los Angeles. Since becoming the movie czar in 1922, Hays had been somewhat obsessed with the negative, "ladies of easy virtue" connotations associated with film actresses. The club was established, like his own position as movie czar, as a way to communicate to the world that Hollywood was making a concerted effort to disassociate itself from vice connections that extended as far back as the infamous third tier of the nineteenth-century theater. Another important force in the actress housing project was the wife of director Cecil B. DeMille, a man who had prospered greatly in the 1920s by casting scantily clad actors and actresses in epic productions that might be described as sex exploitation films. Although documentation is sketchy, one suspects that through their connections with Morgan, Davies and Hearst played some behind-the-scenes role in promoting the film industry's housing and public relations project attempting to rescue the image of the actress.

As he had frequently done before, in 1925 Hearst used his publishing empire to make friends with the film industry. In April the *New York American* sponsored what it called a "Coast-to-Coast party," a train trip from New York to California, with stops such as Niagara Falls and the Grand Canyon along the way. Hollywood was the final destination for a passenger willing to pay between $535 (for an upper berth) and $600 (for a drawing room). "Not only will the party be guided through the vast studios but, through the courtesy of [the] Metro-Goldwyn-Mayer unit, an invitation has been extended to the *American*'s party to witness the 'shooting' of actual scenes!" When the *American*'s tour group arrived in Hollywood in July, it was taken to Culver City to watch Davies filming scenes from *Lights of Old Broadway*. According to an article in the *American*, members of the tour actually appeared as extras in the Hearst film. In another promo, a reader who clipped three coupons from the *New York American* and sent nineteen cents to the Hearst newspaper could receive one "Movie Star Spoon" from a set of twelve. Thousands of movie fans sent in for the spoons that (coincidentally) were put out by the Oneida Community company. Each silver-plated spoon was embossed with the signature and likeness of a star such as Mary Pickford or Marion Davies. The spoons became something of a craze in 1925 and are still popular among movie memorabilia collectors today.

One of the bigger movie-related campaigns of the Hearst press occurred in late September and early October. For weeks, the *American* filled entire pages with advertisements for the contest topped with banner headlines reading, "Will the next baby movie star be your child?" Pictures of applicants between the ages of two and seven were sent in by the bushel. Louis B. Mayer became personally interested in the campaign, and he traveled to New York to see firsthand what progress the *American* was making. Speaking to a reporter, Mayer declared that the contest was open to all and that "nationality is no bar to a child." In the end, the chosen child was a boy with a Dutch-boy haircut, named Edwin Hubbell. It was not disclosed that the boy happened to be the son of Joe Hubbell, Hearst's senior newsreel executive.

By 1926 Millicent Hearst's visits to San Simeon had become infrequent, and Davies was becoming the reigning host. The actress was also increasingly visible in the role of movie industry booster at this time. When MGM was worried about securing exhibitors for director King Vidor's film *The Big Parade* because of its antiwar theme, Davies was enlisted to hold a private screening of the picture at her home in Santa Monica, a house where she lived before the construction of her much larger estate on the beach. Among the small group of Hollywood heavyweights invited to the Davies home was Joseph Schenck, who was reported (by the Hearst press) to be so excited by the screening that he expressed an interest in buying the picture from MGM for $1.5 million. The Davies screening was a clever method of generating interest and acceptance of the film. Soon afterward the film (which stayed with MGM) was booked at the prestigious Sid Grauman theater and on its way to becoming one of the highest-grossing films of the silent era. The movie made a star out of actor John Gilbert, who had just completed work in Erich von Stroheim's yet-to-be-released film *The Merry Widow*. Out of the experience of promoting *The Big Parade*, a friendship grew between King Vidor and Hearst and Davies. In 1928 the director made two pictures with Davies, *The Patsy* and *Show People*. *The Big Parade* remained an all-time favorite of Hearst, and he decided to remake it as a musical. That picture, which starred Davies and was released in 1929, was titled *Marianne*.

With the completion of their more permanent beach house in Santa Monica in 1926—a 110-bedroom, three-story mansion that cost nearly $7 million to build—Hearst and Davies had formally supplanted Douglas Fairbanks and Mary Pickford as Hollywood's top host and hostess. Located within fairly close proximity to the film community, the Santa Monica beach house may have been Davies's favorite of all the homes she shared with Hearst. Because of its colonial style of architecture and its early American furnishings, Helen Hayes nicknamed the estate "Mount Vernon by the sea." She would later recall the life that Hearst and Davies invented for themselves in Santa Monica as something out of F. Scott Fitzgerald's 1922 short story about the excesses of wealth and privilege, called "The Diamond as Big as the Ritz."

For several years following his feature film merger with MGM, Hearst continued to release his weekly *International Newsreel* through Universal. After 1927 MGM distributed the *MGM News*, "a newspaper of the screen," which was produced by the Hearst organization. The mid-1920s saw an increased interest among the public for aviation advances, a trend that Hearst newsreels were quick to exploit. Aerial moving pictures became the rage as International's cameramen captured the high-wireless balancing act of upside-down airplane demonstrations, bird's-eye views of natural disasters, and the rare solar eclipse of 1925.

The eclipse special was an example of competing newsreel operations working together, and Ed Hatrick of International and Emanuel Cohen of Pathé joined forces to capture the event from every conceivable angle. Cameramen from both companies were dispatched to an observatory at Yale University, in New Haven, where they took pictures of a big telescope and added a long-focus lens to their newsreel camera to duplicate the scientific view for the audience. A Hearst camera crew was sent to the streets and parks of New York to observe the public's reaction to the event, and fifteen Pathé cameramen were scattered between the Atlantic seaboard and Minnesota. With the cooperation of the Navy Department, a Hearst newsreel took pictures of the eclipse from the dirigible *Los Angeles* as it hovered over Montauk Point, Long Island. Within hours of the solar eclipse, audiences in many theaters were watching the most comprehensive pictorial coverage of such an event to date.

Although from news reports the views filmed by International and Pathé in early 1925 appear to have been indistinguishable, the U.S. government seems to have found a distinction. They formed a cooperative relationship with the Hearst newsreel in the mid-1920s that was reminiscent of the arrangement with the Committee on Public Information during World War I. In September 1924 the Army Air Service (precursor to the Army Air Force) made International's specialist in aerial photography, John A. Bockhorst, the government's official photographer, assigned to cover the first flight around the world, conducted by four Douglas World Cruisers, each with a crew of two. For this aviation event and others, Bockhorst was assigned to make historical films to be deposited in the army's archives. In July 1925 the government took its relationship with Hearst a step further. "Impressed by the remarkable results achieved by International Newsreel in aerial photography," the *New York American* reported, "Major-General Mason H. Patrick, Chief of the Army Air Service, has arranged with editors of International for the training of Air Service motion picture operators for the Government." According to the *American*, at least five government cameramen were attached to the New York and San Francisco offices of the *International Newsreel* to work as assistants for several weeks. Major H. Arnold, Army Air Service chief of information, told the Hearst press that he had sent his men to train with the Hearst newsreel in order to give them a more rounded experience in motion picture taking. "I asked the International Newsreel to undertake their training," Arnold was quoted as saying, "because I believe, from observation and experience with newsreels, that the International has a staff of cameramen superior to any other newsreel and that it is superior in every other respect."

During his first year with MGM, Hearst proved himself to be an ally of all the major players in the American film industry as they sought to dominate the market in Germany. In 1921 Germany lifted the embargo on film imports that had been in place since 1919 and replaced it with a quota system. When the U.S. film industry—goaded by the American Legion and other film trade associations based in Hollywood—responded by imposing a quota of its own, the Germans adjusted their rules and put in place a plan allowing one American film for each German film export. Since many German exhibitors were actually benefiting from the popular American movies, however, the so-called contingent plan was never fully enforced, and by late 1924 American films were flooding the German market. German filmmakers continued to demand more control over their own product and tougher laws against foreign competition. By early 1925 Germany had been able to achieve some balance between opposing camps within its own film industry and to establish a system that would keep imports at or close to 50 percent of the film market. The American film companies were not satisfied with either the contingent plan or the fifty-fifty system. Guided by Will Hays and his foreign relations advisers Frederick L. Herron and Oscar N. Solbert, this last recruited from his post as junior aide to President Coolidge, the American film majors began to advocate for a tariff system, knowing they could well afford to pay any financial sanctions imposed by Germany. In the late spring Hays's operatives were sent to Germany to deliver thinly veiled threats to officials of the country's leading film company Ufa. In June 1925 Oscar Solbert sent a letter to his boss describing a meeting he had just concluded with the Ufa producer, Eric Pommer, in Berlin:

> Pommer immediately began to defend the contingent system by all the well known arguments that have already been put into the reports that have been sent in. . . . Pommer kept harping back in every one of his arguments to the fact that the American film producers had not played fair on the German market and had consistently kept German films from being shown in America. This chat with Pommer gave me an excellent opportunity to hint at the combined strength of the American producers in our organization, *their influences with the American press* [italics added] as well as their control of a large part of the key theaters in the United States. I also let him know that we are well aware to what extent American money is supporting German industries and amongst them, directly or indirectly, the German film industry. . . . I very diplomatically hinted to the great disadvantage Ufa might be under if we were forced to keep their films off the American market and to more actively fight them in neutral countries. I also pointed out what it meant to the German Government and German industries in general if American people and American banks ceased to supply finances to German industries.

When the Germans rejected the tariff plan, the Americans launched a more aggressive program to exert their influence. But self-interest and competitiveness hampered individual efforts. When the Universal Film company offered much-needed loans to Ufa in exchange for unfettered distribution, Paramount and MGM responded by threatening to build their own chain of movie theaters to screen their own film products. By the late summer of

1925, Hays was being advised by Solbert in Berlin to take a more active hand in uniting the American film majors and reaching a solution that was beneficial to the film industry as a whole.

"What astonishes me most," Solbert wrote Hays on July 2,

is why have not the producers at home understood something of affairs here and heeded your advice long ago to let you make an investigation of the European situation and recommend ways and means of holding this market before it is too late. . . . Here are at present four foreign managers or their equivalent. One company (you can't blame it under present conditions) sells a bloc of pictures to the enemy (Ufa) and thus strengthens that monopoly. (I should like to state this is damned embarrassing for me in the middle of my fight to solve this situation.) The others get wind of this transaction and immediately rush to the scene to do the same or scramble for what is left. (Further may I say that if another big company sells its productions to Ufa the fat is in the fire and Ufa may get such a strangle hold on the market that it will be difficult to get a look in under the most favorable circumstances.) The tactics and counter tactics to beat the other fellow would be most amusing if not so tragic to our general cause. Of course I know my part is not to mix in the competitive end of the game, but under the circumstances it is my duty to report and apparently your duty to act when so much is at stake.

By the end of 1925 Hays had apparently done the trick, and the American film majors were ready to come together to ensure a greater U.S. film industry presence in Germany. As Nick Schenck later told film historian Bosley Crowther, the solution involved an infusion of money into the Ufa company that would make the German film industry financially dependent on Hollywood:

As I recall it, it brought about a distributing company in Germany called Parufamet. The stock was owned ⅓ by Paramount, ⅓ by Ufa and ⅓ by Metro. That distributing company had a contract with the two American companies to distribute their product in Germany. At the time the contract was made, Paramount and Loews each loaned to UFA $2,000,000 which was subsequently repaid. One of the conditions of the deal was that 75 percent of the playing time of the Ufa theatre was to be made available for the pictures distributed by Parufamet.

What role Hearst played in the arrangements between Ufa and the American film companies in late 1925 has not been documented, but there is nothing to indicate that he was anything but an enthusiastic supporter. In fact, while the high stakes wrangling over bank loans, tariffs, and contingent plans was going on, Hearst was doing what he did best to advance MGM's efforts and the industry in general: he was intimidating. In July 1925 Hearst and Millicent threw a dinner party at the Ritz-Carlton Hotel in New York, their temporary residence while the Clarendon was undergoing extensive renovations. Hearst's guests for the evening included Will Hays and a group of New York bankers and lawyers. No movie stars were invited except for one, former Ziegfeld Follies girl and now MGM star Mae Murray.

The actress, who was known for her lipstick-painted bee-stung lips as much as she was for her vamp acting, was a highly sought-after guest in 1925. The industry was abuzz over her performance in the soon-to-be-released picture *The Merry Widow*. She was also getting her name in the paper because of reports that she was about to jump ship from MGM. Shortly after completing her work on *The Merry Widow*, Murray had traveled by ocean liner for a vacation in Europe. Onboard ship she met with representatives of Ufa. Later, in Berlin, Murray was wined and dined by Ufa executives and movie star Emil Jannings. Shortly after meeting with producer Pommer, Murray was offered a three-year contract to star in a series of Ufa productions. As a gift bonus Ufa offered Murray a check for $75,000. The actress signed the contract.

News that Murray had signed a deal with Ufa and was preparing to begin her first movie for them in September was met with deep concern by MGM. They had high hopes of grooming the actress as one of their own stable of moneymaking stars, and they had no interest in helping the German film industry without some benefit to themselves. While Murray was in Hollywood working on her next picture for MGM, she began to get pressured by Irving Thalberg and Nick Schenck to call off her Ufa deal. Unsure about what she should do next, Murray picked up and left for New York. No sooner had she arrived than she received a telephone call from Louella Parsons, along with an invitation from her boss to attend a Ritz-Carlton dinner party that was said to be held in her honor. Since Hearst was only in New York briefly in July, the dinner must have been put together quite quickly.

During dinner, Murray soon realized the point of Hearst's gathering: "Louella tells me," Hearst said, "you're leaving for Europe. . . . We'd have to boycott those films over here. You're too big box office Mae, we couldn't allow the money to go out of the country. Pictures you make for Ufa will not be shown in America. We won't release them, Mae. . . . You're not just one star in a heaven of your own; you're part of an industry. . . . They're our competitors."

Then Will Hays chimed in: "Did it ever occur to you that going over there is not very patriotic, Miss Murray? That you'd be working against your country's business interests, enhancing another country's rival industry?"

Murray's decision was made for her. Ufa allowed the actress to break the contract when it realized it would have no hopes of distributing her films in the United States. Murray was politely asked by Ufa to return her gift bonus.

In 1926, following its agreement with Ufa, MGM delivered $2 million—its portion of Hollywood's loan—to Germany. A few years before the MGM merger, Metro produced a World War I drama called *Four Horsemen of the Apocalypse* (1921), a vehicle for matinee idol Rudolph Valentino based on a novel by Vincente Blasco Ibañez. The film was a box office hit in the United States, but it caused considerable consternation in Hollywood when the German press strongly protested its portrayal of the German army as barbarians. This early lesson about criticizing Germany would resonate as the financial futures of Berlin and Hollywood became more interlocked in 1926. For more than a decade following the agreement, no films were produced by MGM that might be perceived as being anti-German. In 1936, for example, MGM was preparing to produce a film based on Sinclair Lewis's *It Can't Happen Here*, the story of a Hitler-like dictator's rise in the United States. On learning of the project Will Hays and Louis B. Mayer summarily canceled it. Some said that German government representatives in Hollywood had also voiced their concern over the project.

Hollywood's deference to Germany did not apply to feature films alone. During the Berlin Olympics of 1936, Hitler demanded and received a written assurance from American newsreel companies attending the sports event that they would allow German documentary filmmaker Leni Riefenstahl to direct their cameramen and that they would ultimately turn over control of their footage to the propagandist. She used the U.S. newsreel films when she put together her classic film *Olympia*. It would not be until nearly the end of the 1930s, when it was quite apparent that the United States was being forced out of the German market, that MGM and the others majors felt themselves free to produce pictures with themes that were critical of Germany.

In May 1928 Hearst became interested in collaborating with Germany's Zeppelin Company on an airship still under construction in Friedrichshafen called the *Graf Zeppelin*. At that time, Karl von Wiegand, Hearst's foreign correspondent stationed in Berlin, began negotiations with Dr. Hugo Eckener, a well-known airship pilot who would eventually head a crew of thirty men in the *Graf*'s first transatlantic trip. From the start of these negotiations, Hearst's willingness to help finance the airship—at a cost of $175,000—was made contingent on the securing of motion and still picture rights to the proposed flight. In early June von Wiegand concluded his meetings with Eckener, and he reported the results to Hearst editor T.V. Rank, who passed along the good news to Hearst: "Have following cable from Wiegand quote Tell Chief subject to his approval closed deal with Eckener one hundred seventy five thousand dollars including newsreel stop wanted thirty thousand dollars for newsreel but got him down to fifteen stop details following stop get answer quickly as possible because *Times* man on way to Friedrichshafen unquote. This would indicate one hundred sixty thousand dollars for newspaper rights and fifteen thousand dollars for motion picture rights."

Hearst's interest in aviation (he was sponsoring a flight over Antarctica at the same time as the *Graf* flights), his love for a good cinematic story, and his partiality for all things German were the obvious motivating factors in his desire to become involved with the Zeppelin Company. From the German point of view, the flight was a demonstration of the reliability of passenger air travel and a furthering of ongoing plans for a regular air service between Europe and South America. No doubt the Zeppelin Company, which was always closely tied to the German government, saw Hearst as its own hovering vehicle to spread word of its aviation accomplishments and foster better relations throughout the United States. Another factor in Hearst's *Graf Zeppelin* association was likely to have been the fostering of good feelings between MGM and Ufa. One of several firsts associated with the *Graf Zeppelin*, as pointed out by the American press, was that on its transatlantic flight in 1928, the airship carried a copy of Fritz Lang's film *Spies*, recently acquired by Irving Thalberg for distribution in the United States. This was said to be the first motion picture to cross the ocean by air, a milestone that was celebrated with an appearance of the *Zeppelin* crew on the stage of the Capitol Theater.

The *Graf Zeppelin* collaboration between Hearst and Germany unfolded for the public in two stages. In October 1928 the *Graf Zeppelin* made a transatlantic voyage from Germany to the United States, and in late 1929 the airship made another even more highly publicized flight around the globe. In its second flight the *Graf Zeppelin* passed over a number of American cities, and its flight plan even included a special nighttime pass over Hearst's San Simeon. Later, after a stop in Los Angeles, Commander Eckener and his crew were the honored guests at a gala hosted by Hearst, who in a speech compared the journey he had sponsored to the voyage of Magellan.

Some twenty passengers were on the 1928 flight, several members of the German Reichstag and several Hearst correspondents, von Wiegand, and a contributing writer named Lady Drummond Hay being among the most prominent. The only news cameraman on board—said to be the first news cameraman ever to make a transatlantic flight—was Robert Hartman, Hearst newsreel representative in Berlin. Hartman was also the official film photographer of the 1929 *Graf* flight, which produced extensive newsreel footage and a separate short film released by MGM entitled *Around the World with the Graf Zeppelin*. On September 7, 1929, in purple prose that seemed to tap into the public's genuine excitement over the aviation achievements, the *Exhibitors Herald-World* described the *Graf Zeppelin* from a film perspective, focusing on Hearst's cameraman on the scene:

> Hartman has been on the huge dirigible every moment it has been in the air; the test flights over England and the continent, the first trans-Atlantic flight and return, the flight to Egypt, and last the unprecedented globe-circling flight. The motion pictures which Hartman made of that first trans-Atlantic flight which appeared in the MGM News, as did those of his other exploits, are particularly vivid memories. From on board the *Graf Zeppelin* he recorded in pictures the entire story of the trip, over the cities and villages of Europe, the Atlantic, the Azores, and through the terrific hurricane that all but brought disaster. Hartman risked his life to climb to the top of the ship to make pictures while members of the crew were engaged in their heroic task of repairing the damaged fin. . . . Throughout the history-making world flight of the *Graf Zeppelin* just completed, Hartman was the only cameraman on board the ship. His exclusive pictures of the first leg of the journey from New York to Friedrichshafen have already appeared in *MGM International Newsreel*. His succeeding pictures of the flight across Europe and Asia, the history making conquest of the Siberian wilds, the triumphant landing at Tokio [*sic*], the unprecedented flight over the Pacific, the soul-stirring arrival at Los Angeles and on across the United States to New York comprise the final graphic chapters of the greatest flight in history.

THE EFFECTS OF SOUND

Although as early as 1906 Hearst had made a "talking picture" of himself to use in his race for governor of New York, it was not until the mid-1920s that he recognized sound film as much more than a mere novelty. By 1927 Hearst was convinced that sound movies were here to stay. Homer Watters, a *Los Angeles Herald-Express* man, remembered Hearst calling him at the newspaper repeatedly that year inquiring about a 24-by-110-foot rug he had ordered from a New Jersey factory. Sometime passed before the rug arrived at Hearst and Davies's Santa Monica beach house, and when it did Hearst had forgotten he had ordered it. Taking his cue from Hearst, Watters shipped the carpet back to the manufacturer. It got as far as Albuquerque before Davies had reminded Hearst that the huge carpet was meant for the second floor of their beach estate where, after a wall was temporarily removed, it was installed in the couple's screening room to improve the acoustics.

The evolution of Hearst's interest in sound film closely reflected the major developments in the medium over the early years of the twentieth century. In 1907 Lee De Forest invented a detector, oscillator, and amplifier device called the Audion tube that enabled wire and wireless transcontinental telephone service and led to important developments in sound recording, reproducing, and amplifying. A year later he was broadcasting both live voices and phonograph records through a Pathé "talking machine" set up on the Eiffel Tower. Hearst may have seen De Forest's wireless demonstrations in San Francisco at the 1915 Panama Pacific Exposition. A year later he and De Forest joined forces to broadcast the presidential election. In November 1916 De Forest's Wireless Telephone Laboratories, located on the Harlem River, broadcast the latest voting trends, which had been wired from Hearst's *New York American* newspaper headquarters.

De Forest's attention-getting demonstrations and his high-profile work for Hearst secured for him the title of "father of radio." In truth a number of pioneers were working on wireless telegraphy, including important figures such as Guglielmo Marconi, Thomas Edison, and Reginald. A. Fessenden of the Westinghouse Electric and Manufacturing Company of Pittsburgh. By 1919, however, De Forest was a clear leader in the field, having taken out over 120 U.S. and foreign patents on radio telephony or systems and devices for transmitting sound between distant stations. In addition to his work in radio development, De Forest became engaged in inventing a practical sound-on-film system. Here, too, he was not working alone. In the 1880s Thomas Edison's organization had a staff member experimenting with sound and film, and shortly after the turn of the twentieth century inroads were made on sound-picture recording devices in Germany and England.

Owing to amplification problems and other difficulties—including World War I—progress on a number of fronts was slowed during the 1910s. In 1920, however, De Forest met another inventor, Theodore Case, and they began to explore their mutual interests in sound recording. Allied with a sound camera inventor named Earl I. Sponable, who was already working with Case, De Forest and Case developed a camera and a projector for recording and screening sound-on-film, calling the process "Phonofilm." In 1923 press and public demonstrations of several Phonofilms were presented at the Rivoli Theatre, in New York City, and Keith's Palace Theatre, in Cleveland, Ohio. By early 1924 the De Forest Phonofilm Corporation was actively seeking financial backing and looking for ways to garner publicity for its experiments. Private demonstrations were held for businessmen such as Martin Egan, a former news correspondent who was now a public relations executive with J. P. Morgan and Co. More sound films were produced, including a drama entitled *Love's Old Sweet Song* and a news film taken in July of President Calvin Coolidge reading a speech from notes outside the White House. The Coolidge film was exhibited throughout the country, with the president fully cooperating with the enterprise in the hopes that the novelty film would aid his presidential campaign. For their part De Forest and Case were hoping that the association with Coolidge would be good publicity for their new company, Phonofilms, Inc. Coolidge, it turned out, won the election in spite of the Phonofilm, which suffered in comparison to the more technically evolved and established silent film.

To enhance prospects for Phonofilm, De Forest reestablished his relationship with the Hearst organization in late 1924 or early 1925, and plans were made for a demonstration guaranteed to pack a wallop. Beginning in 1921 Moses Koenigsberg, president of King Features, presided over an annual luncheon and entertainment show for reporters and publishers at the Friars Club in New York that came to be known as "The Lark." The 1925 Lark was held during the afternoon of April 21 and attended by prominent politicians and some five hundred newspeople from around the country, with a heavy emphasis on Hearst employees. Hearst's twenty-one-year-old son George, who was interested in photography, stood in for his father, and Senators Arthur S. Capper of Kansas and Royal S. Copeland of New York were also in attendance. A lineup of Broadway luminaries and Hearst newspaper favorites such as George M. Cohan, Eddie Cantor, and Sophie Tucker was joined by chorus girls from the Ziegfeld Follies and a group of actors performing scenes from the current musical show *Louis the 14th*, whose sets had been designed by Davies's costume designer, Gretl Urban.

Traditionally, Koenigsberg's programs were capped with some special entertainment or innovation (the 1927 event, for instance, would include a demonstration of the ultranew communications medium called television). The specialty for 1925 was the Phonofilm, which was projected on a screen at the end of the banquet hall. Once again, President Coolidge was the subject of the new sound film invention, having been filmed a week before the Friar Club event reading a speech, much as he did for the first film on the White House lawn. The Coolidge film followed a fairly long line of presidential motion picture exploitations going back as far as Alexander Black's precinema picture play of Grover Cleveland and the films of William McKinley's inauguration in 1897.

As the room was darkened, Koenigsberg was able to give a double introduction for the president of the United States: the head of King Features was standing there in the hall and present in the opening sequence of the Phonofilm before the president spoke. The filmed Koenigsberg told his audience that this scientific breakthrough had an added bonus because it was connected to another relatively new medium: "The address you will hear will be lifted from the Phonofilm—just as these words of explanation are now being lifted—and projected by radio to hundreds of thousands of receivers. Thus this occasion marks the first time in history that the human voice has been broadcast from a motion picture. That achievement is being accomplished by the Radio Corporation of America."

Two radio stations, WJY and WRC, carried the Phonofilm broadcast, and subsequent newspaper reports on the presentation made as much fuss about the radio tie-in as they did about the demonstration of combining film and sound. Some suggested that since the broadcast was sent over the airwaves to Washington, D.C., President Coolidge himself might even have listened to himself on film on radio. Perhaps the flaws in De Forest's system had been worked out for this second film of Coolidge or maybe reporters were simply seduced by Koenigsberg's showmanship, but the Phonofilm demonstration of 1925 met with unanimous approval in both the Hearst and non-Hearst press.

De Forest's passion for sound films seemed to dissipate quickly after the King Features event. A few weeks after the demonstration, he came in for public ridicule when it was discovered he had been selling stock in his company by using a reproduction of Coolidge's Phonofilm image. The president, who had never authorized such an endorsement but seemed happy to use the invention to help him win elections, was outraged at De Forest's actions and at the Hearst organization for apparently aiding the gimmick. He even called on the FBI to investigate the matter. (While it was true that the Hearst papers had been involved in recruiting salesmen to sell Phonofilm stock, the film image in question had actually come from the first Phonofilm of the president taken a year before any Hearst participation.)

By the end of 1925, when their contract expired, De Forest and Case severed their ties. Case remained interested in sound films and continued with-

out his partner. To those who experienced De Forest's temperamental personality, the breakup of the partnership was not surprising, but the possibility exists that he was squeezed out of sound technology, as some of De Forest's patents were quickly swallowed up by the radio giant RCA.

After their break with De Forest, Case and Sponable pursued other partnerships, turning first to Western Electric, which was already aligned in a
sound development deal with Warner Bros., and then to a representative of
the Keith-Albee circuit, who simply saw no future in sound films. In late
1925 Case was approached by an assistant to Courtland Smith, who was now
with William Fox after having been assistant to Will Hays in charge of news-
reel-related matters. Smith was also keenly aware of developments in sound
films. It is likely that his interest grew as a result of the Hearst-sponsored and
well-publicized demonstration of Phonofilm. It is not known if he attended
the Friar's Club function, but he could not have been unaware of it, especially with his inside track to Arthur Brisbane.

By the 1920s Arthur Brisbane was a leading cheerleader of the movies,
although he never had an official role in the film industry. Hearst's editor had
long-standing associations with movie men such as Fox and Marcus Loew (in
1916 Brisbane sold Loew property he owned on 125th Street, in Manhattan,
that became Loew's Victoria movie house), and he frequently wrote editorials that ballyhooed the educational value in movies and gushed over the latest technical innovations. In 1926 Brisbane was inspired to write an editorial
about film's importance after seeing a statement by Rudyard Kipling that
"fiction is truth's younger sister": "If Fiction is Truth's younger sister, the
moving picture is the real teacher for Truth and History—not merely a sister. 'The Iron Horse,' 'The Birth of a Nation,' 'The Big Parade' are as far
above the average written history in their power to teach history as Paganini's
violin was above a South African tomtom in its power to interpret music."

Brisbane also shared his brother-in-law Courtland Smith's enthusiasm for
sound experiments. A great admirer of Thomas Edison, Brisbane became a
champion of the inventor's Dictaphone devices and used them religiously
to record his editorials. It was probably Brisbane's early interest in sound
recording that moved Hearst to make "canned" speeches in 1906. Later, during the silent film days, he convinced Hearst to utilize Dictaphones during
rehearsals and filming. Directors dictated their actor's movements into the
Edison contraption as a guide for subsequent film editing. As the film activities of Hearst, Fox, and Smith became more intertwined, Brisbane, who was
close to all three men, acted as a behind-the-scenes adviser and liaison.

An article written in the 1930s about Courtland Smith's role in developing sound newsreels points out the similarities between the newsreel pro-

ducer and the editor of a newspaper, both positions dealing with the tasks of selecting topics and making decisions on emphasis through placing and repetition. "In our news reels and in news reels in general, you see only the mirror, the record of the times," Smith is quoted as saying. "Our traffic is in satisfying the same emotions, curiosities, perplexities and other human feelings that a newspaper appeals to. The office is almost exactly parallel except that we deal in a medium appealing to two senses instead of one. We have sound as well as sight." The same article also makes reference to Smith's relationship to Brisbane and ponders its significance: "Smith is not unaware of the policies, features, and general characteristics of Mr. Hearst's papers and makes occasional conversational references to them."

In January 1926, shortly before he left the Hays organization, Smith received a call from William DeFord, an attorney who represented Hearst's film interests. DeFord—or "Billy," as Smith referred to him—wanted to discuss what role he might play in pushing for legislation that would repeal a newsreel censorship bill in New York State. A few days after the call Smith sent Hays a memorandum that argued for the Motion Picture Association to collect moneys from its newsreel members (and from Pathé, not a part of the Hays organization) to retain DeFord's services to file a brief on behalf of the newsreels. Such a brief, Smith explained, might not be necessary to repeal the latest censorship bill, but it might be useful for the future should other states seek similar restrictions on newsreels. In closing his memo, Smith reminded Hays that he had already established important relationships in the industry. "If you decide to do this," he wrote, "I know it will please Mr. Hearst and Mr. Fox."

Hays needed no one to remind him how important it was to placate Hearst and feed his ego whenever possible. Knowing how Hearst coveted close connections with presidents, Hays used his own relationship with Coolidge, which began during the Harding administration, to assure Hearst that he remained a player in Washington. Sometimes, the movie czar was able to do this in relatively innocuous ways. When, for instance, Joseph Moore, Hearst's film adviser, was taken to the hospital for surgery, Hays wrote Coolidge suggesting that he send flowers to Moore, even though the president hardly knew the Hearst executive. An editorial in the Hearst papers calling for an increase in the number of military academies caught Hays's attention in the summer of 1925; he clipped it and sent it to Coolidge with a note attached saying that "it is the one thing the editor is particularly interested." Hays held frequent meetings with Coolidge via telephone and in person, and it was not uncommon for them to talk about Hearst. An *Oneida* yacht trip that Hearst took with Davies and other film personalities off the coast of Florida in the summer of 1927 became the subject of one of their gossipy telephone calls. When that same summer Hearst claimed he had stolen documents in his possession that were evidence that the Mexican president, with Russian financial support, had been the instigator of the Nicaraguan revolution of 1926, he approached Hays to act as a go-between with the president. In late June, while he was vacationing in Rapid City, South Dakota, Coolidge received a telegram from Hays that quoted a message the movie czar had received from Hearst: "Will you please ask the president for me if he will see Edward H. Clark [Hearst's longtime adviser, who had been a party to the pilfering of the documents] the latter part of next week. It is a matter of great governmental importance and not a matter of importance to me except that I want the president to have certain information that I possess. I know that you will know that I would not say it was important if it were not. I will appreciate it if you will take this up for me."

Because he was afraid to open a can of worms he might not be able to contain later or because he simply distrusted Hearst, Coolidge apparently refused to view the documents that were sent to him. Hays was disappointed by the response, and he wrote the president's secretary a week later: "It makes matters difficult in that quarter." Hearst's first batch of stolen documents led to additional stolen documents later that year that prompted even more outrageous claims. Hearst now charged that four U.S. senators had been involved in a Mexican-led, Bolshevik-supported plot to overthrow the U.S. government. In the end, Coolidge's instincts proved to be quite sound. By early 1928 a Senate investigating committee determined that Hearst's sensational documents were fakes.

Some of Hays's intercessions with President Coolidge were not specifically designed to please Hearst but to support the film industry as a whole. The Federal Trade Commission investigation of Adolph Zukor, Jesse L. Lasky, and Paramount Pictures that Hearst had pushed for in 1921 continued well into the decade. Not surprisingly, Hays remained loyal throughout the inquiry to the movie moguls who had elevated him to the role of movie czar. Hays worked vigorously to dilute the impact of the pending FTC decision, although this was not always a simple matter. When in 1924 a commissioner position opened on the FTC, Hays personally lobbied Coolidge to appoint George Christian Jr., knowing that the former secretary to his former boss, Warren Harding, would be soft on his movie friends. On January 17, 1924, Courtland Smith sent a telegram to Hays: "George Christian probable successor of Murdock as chairman of Federal Trade Commission. I have told both our members who are particularly interested in this situation that matters has [sic] been receiving your careful consideration and that a thoroughly responsible person would undoubtedly be appointed. They are both delighted and much relieved." The same day Smith sent his telegram it was reported in the press that Coolidge was considering the nomination of Christian.

An unexpected glitch developed during a committee hearing on Christian's nomination two weeks later. Testifying before the committee, Huston Thompson, former chairman of the FTC, claimed that in May 1921 he had been summoned to the White House for a meeting in Secretary Christian's office. "I understand," Christian reportedly said to Thompson, "you have issued a complaint against the Famous Players–Lasky Corporation. What do you mean by issuing a complaint without giving these people a hearing?" Thompson was dumbfounded by Christian's question and what he believed to be a veiled threat; he told others later that he had never heard of a FTC member being called to the White House. Thompson told Christian that no complaint had yet been issued and asked him repeatedly how he knew that one would be. Later, responding to a questioner at Christian's hearing, Thompson said: "There was an impression in my mind that this action by Christian had some relation to the statements brought to us by our field representatives that this case would never go through." Thompson's testimony caused widespread criticism of Christian in the press, and Coolidge was forced to withdraw the nomination.

Hays was not about to give up. When another opening on the FTC occurred in 1926, he was back again lobbying the White House, this time pushing for the nomination of fellow Hoosier Judge Abram F. Myers. In August 1926 the Hays man became chairman of the FTC, and his position seems to have helped make the difference for Zukor and company. After seventeen thousand pages of testimony and years of deliberation, a weak cease and desist order was issued against Paramount Pictures in July 1927. Zukor continued to assert the legitimacy of the block booking system and boldly declared that he would defy the FTC order. *Variety* found the FTC ruling to be little more than "a gesture." It reported that the stock market had been unfazed by the action and that Paramount stock was still rising. In the film trade journal's opinion, "the optimistic market view was further cheered by the assurance that the findings would be moved for review in the Federal courts." In fact, in 1932 the U.S. Circuit Court of Appeals completely reversed the FTC order concerning block booking. Soon after the ruling, Commissioner Meyers was rewarded with a job in the film industry, signing a three-year contract in 1928 to head the Allied States Association of Motion Picture Exhibitors.

Although Hearst certainly knew that the FTC had issued nothing more than a slap-on-the-wrist ruling, his newspaper coverage made it appear as if

Zukor's power in the industry had been crushed. The Hearst papers found what little satisfaction they could with the news that the Justice Department was still looking into Paramount Pictures' abuses. Nevertheless, it must have been infuriating to Hearst to see his efforts to expose Zukor's monopolistic practices thwarted and to realize the role Hays played in assuring this outcome.

On Courtland Smith's recommendation, William Fox agreed to see a demonstration of Phonofilm in May 1926, and the necessary equipment was shuttled to the movie producer's estate in Woodmere, Long Island. Fox was skeptical of the Phonofilm process at first, but Smith prodded him. Later, Earl Sponable gave Smith much of the credit for paving the way for acceptance of sound films: "The industry is greatly indebted to Courtland Smith for his foresight and aggressiveness in hastening the commercialization of sound-on-film. He did more than anyone else to convince the 'doubting Thomases' of the business that sound motion pictures were a reality and that the days of the silent film were numbered."

Within a few months of the demonstration at Fox's home, the film producer was ready to buy all of Case's patents. There still remained some legal wrangling with De Forest, who owned some patents of his own, but in the end, in an out-of-court settlement, De Forest was eliminated as a factor, and the formation of the Fox-Case Corporation was officially announced. Smith was named general manager of the new company and charged with overseeing sound newsreels.

Fox's closest rival in the late 1920s for a studio experiencing rapid growth was Warner Bros. As late as 1924, Warner was a production company without a distribution unit or a chain of theaters. It was a well-respected studio but clearly a tier below the three big powers of the industry, Paramount, First National, and Loews. Warner's success at bringing its pictures in under budget was impressive to many in the business, and the Wall Street investment company Goldman, Sachs and Company liked what it saw so much it advised Warner to intensify its growth. In 1925 Warner bought control of the old Vitagraph Company, which provided Warner with additional production facilities. A small number of theaters that was part of the deal became the nucleus for Warner's chain of exchanges. Even more significant to Warner's new growth plans was its connection to radio. The studio acquired a radio studio in Los Angeles, which it first used primarily to publicize its motion pictures and later to establish a partnership with Western Electric, the electronics manufacturing subsidiary of American Telephone and Telegraph, the largest private corporation in the world after U.S. Steel.

Warner's association with Western Electric gave the company a foothold in the developing sound film technology, and they dominated experiments in this field for a few years. Warner, however, was primarily focused on a sound system that would not put an end to the silent film but rather enhance it with an accompaniment of relatively cheap synchronized music. The studio envisioned this method of sound films as the ticket into the exhibition market, where all large picture houses and many middle-size theaters relied on costly live orchestras. It was not until its picture *The Jazz Singer* became a smash hit in 1927, in large part because it introduced snippets of dialogue along with the musical talents of Al Jolson, that Warner was forced to readjust its strategy for developing sound films.

Meanwhile, during this same period, William Fox's Fox Film Corporation, a production company with ties to a distribution company, was determined to compete with the big three powers by extending its own theater ownership. Fox's theater expansion began in earnest in 1925 with a one-third interest in the important West Coast Theater chain, followed by theater acquisitions in major cities around the country. Theaters were the key to Fox's very beginnings, a key that opened the doors to Tammany Hall, to his theater partner "Big Tim" Sullivan, and the miniature city of entertainment at the turn of the twentieth century that was Fourteenth Street.

In the 1910s, Fox was still cultivating political connections. A relative of Sullivan in the police department worked for Fox's Gaiety Theater in Brooklyn. Fox befriended John J. Ryan, a Tammany district leader deeply involved in Tammany's system of kickbacks and protection, as well as Johnny White, a onetime prize fight referee known to be a henchman of the Sullivans. White may have been an especially important friend at the time. While Fox was buying and building theaters in New York, White had the position of commissioner of condemnation, the man charged with assessing real estate properties. By the time Fox was producing and distributing films through the Greater New York Film Rental Company, located in Union Square, Winfield Sheehan had become his key executive. Sheehan was a well-known figure in New York City's political and entertainment worlds; he had been a newspaper reporter, a right-hand man to both the fire and police commissioner, and the higher-up that many suspected had ruled over the city's prostitution and police protection system.

In May 1927—one year after the Fox-Case Corporation was formed—the *Fox Movietone* newsreel, organized by Courtland Smith, presented the reverberating sounds of *The Spirit of St. Louis* as it taxied down a makeshift runway preparing to carry aviator Charles Lindbergh across the Atlantic Ocean to Paris. The Lindbergh takeoff film and subsequent films showing the reception in the United States to his success were a major boost for Fox Films, which was soon releasing sound newsreels on a regular basis. Still, as late as 1928 Fox's newsreel distribution was confined to a fledgling chain of motion picture theaters, and his production arm had not fully transferred to sound technology to produce feature films.

Talking features were a natural lure for theater actors who were seeking greater fame and wealth. Likewise, Hollywood producers turned to the stage to meet the new requirements of the sound films that would create greater wealth for their studios. By late 1928 the movement of talent to the West Coast was in full swing, and following close behind the actors was the activist president of the Actors Equity, Frank Gilmore. As the spokesperson for the organization, which had been formed to defend the rights of theater actors, Gilmore now saw an opportunity to extend protection to his newest transplants. Using Equity-sponsored opinion surveys of actors in Hollywood as his guide, Gilmore began to organize the motion picture wing of his organization. Almost immediately, he was met with resistance. A certain number of film actors were not interested in unions, but by far the greatest opposition came from the movie producers. They wanted no organization in their community but their own, either the Motion Picture Producers and Distributors Association (otherwise known as the Hays Office) or the Academy of Motion Pictures Arts and Sciences, which was formed in 1927.

In an editorial published in July 1929, Hearst launched a crusade against what he called "a combination of producers." The attack was made in the form of a defense of Adolphe Menjou. Back in 1927 Menjou had made a number of enemies among industry leaders when he openly supported the formation of a film actors' division of Equity. In 1929 Menjou was still spouting actor's rights—with special emphasis on his own—as he waited through protracted negotiations for his contract with Paramount Pictures to be renewed. Menjou was convinced that his contract was being held up because of his outspoken stands, and matters went from bad to worse when the actor hinted that he might form his own production company or accept work abroad. What had once looked like the runaround to Menjou now looked like a blacklist. He reportedly asked Hearst to intercede. Hearst took to his editorial page, linking the movie trust's scorched-earth policy to its fondness for hiring foreign actors over free-speaking American-born actors:

> If a combination of producers is formed to discipline actors, there will certainly be a combination of actors to protect themselves, and there should be. Mr. Menjou is a good American, and a leading screen actor. His Americanism must not be permitted to injure him. It is possible

that certain moving picture producers are importing into the industry too many foreigners and too many stage actors. . . . The reason that the Actors' Equity has not been successful on the screen is because there has not been much reason for its existence in that field. WHY PROVIDE REASONS?

Four years later, when the Screen Actors' Guild was being formed, Hearst's distrust for the movie moguls was still very much alive. Although he had shown little sympathy for guild or union organizers in the publishing business and in other fields, Hearst sent a directive to the *Los Angeles Examiner* newspaper instructing it to back the Actor's Guild: "It is a singular thing that the attack on the independence of the artists in the film business is being led by the companies who are most guilty of flagrant violation of the laws and ethics in the matter of stock swindling—certain of them more in the business of swindling the public than they are in the business of producing films. . . . The object of the Screen Actors Guild, however, is merely to protect the interest of the actors against this assault upon the independence of the actors and their proper compensation."

In 1929, according to film trade journal accounts, Hearst conducted a private investigation of the film business. Reportedly, several higher-ups in the editorial departments of his publishing empire were dispatched to various sections of the country to gather information from local independent film exhibitors on questionable film practices. One of these prominent editors was Louella Parsons, who also had the distinction in 1929 of making a cameo appearance in Cosmopolitan's "talkie" courtroom drama called *The Bellamy Trial*. Hearst's findings on film industry practices were never reported in detail, but hints of what they contained can be gleaned from stories in the trade papers and editorials related to the film industry that appeared at the same time in Hearst's newspaper chain. In a signed editorial published on June 30, 1929, Hearst made a blistering attack on the major powers of Hollywood:

What has become of the Sherman anti-trust law and the other measures to protect the public from oppressive monopolies? The great interstate public service corporations of the country have become more and more defiant of the provisions of these anti-monopoly measures, more and more defiant of the Government, more and more defiant of the citizenship. . . . The tendency toward monopolization of the moving picture industry has been proceeding for some time. Paramount has bought chain after chain of theatres. Warner Brothers has bought the First National Company and the Vitagraph Company. Fox has lately bought the Metro-Goldwyn-Mayer Company. And the Radio Corporation has entered the moving picture field by securing control of the Keith Corporation and Pathé. The battle is now on between these gigantic spiders of monopoly to see which one will eat up the others.

The editorial focused mostly on RCA, which had recently acquired the Victor Talking Machine Company and the Keith and Orpheum theater circuit, giving the company a foothold in the developing sound film technology as well as the field of film exhibition. With its already tight grip on radio broadcasting and its experiments in television, RCA was poised to be the monarch of the entertainment industry. Always looking for a personalized approach to his crusades, Hearst's editorial zeroed in on two RCA executives, Leon J. Rubinstein and Hiram Brown, the president of the corporation. Hearst mocked the two men as modern-day "Captain Kidds," and he seized on an alleged statement made by Rubinstein to the effect that it might be necessary for RCA to "dynamite" the competition out of the field. "One thing is certain," Hearst wrote, "Mr. Rubinstein and Mr. Hiram Brown, the American people do not like Bolshevism in business, Nihilism in industry. THEY DO NOT LIKE DYNAMITERS." Hearst's need to mention Mr. Brown's first name in the same sentence in which he finds no need to mention Mr. Rubinstein's may have been a subtle form of Jew baiting. Brown responded immediately to the editorial, objecting to the accusation that RCA was swallowing up the competition and declaring that Rubinstein was a low-level employee who had no authority to speak for his company. Most of all, it seemed, Brown was offended by being characterized with words such as "outlaw," "highwayman," and "bolshevist." Hearst reprinted Brown's response, but he had the last word in delivering his intended message; he put Brown's response letter under the headline "Healthy Competition Must Never Be Dynamited Out of Any Field," thus reiterating the viewpoint of Hearst's original editorial.

In a July 12, 1929, article entitled "Mr. Hearst and the Trust Menace," the trade journal *Film Mercury* declared Hearst attacks on movie industry monopolies were exaggerations and distractions. The Hearst editorial allusion to ruthless tactics on the part of movie moguls, it proposed, was a case of the pot calling the kettle black. "For that matter," the journal said, "speaking of the use of high explosives in the removal of competition, who has done more for the dynamite type of journalism in America than William Randolph Hearst himself? Good old T.N.T. used in connection with not only editorial policies, but advertising and circulation has played a big part in building up Mr. Hearst's formidable newspaper chain."

Once the film trade's magazines got wind of Hearst's inquiry into the picture business, they speculated on Hearst's motives and what his findings might yield. *Motion Picture News*, which claimed to have received inside information from an unnamed Hearst executive, said Hearst was chiefly concerned about the effects of the new sound technology on the film industry. If this was true, Hearst wasn't the only one, for 1929 was a nervous year for many in Hollywood. Images of silent film actors fretting over the intrusion of the microphone into their nearly perfected art form and scores of other talents suddenly discarded haunt our memory of the birth of the talkie. But the real problem was the rapid acceptance of talkies by movie audiences; the industry could barely keep up with the demand. Thousands of movie theaters across the country needed to adapt to the new technology, and production companies were forced to revamp their studios and their procedures for marketing films abroad. This urgent situation necessitated huge infusions of capital, a prospect that only further encouraged moves toward consolidation and temptations to engage in unfair business practices.

Motion Picture News opined that Hearst would have a natural inclination to support the independents, because he had always been one himself in the film industry, spending much of his own money and releasing his product though venues he did not control. "His pet screen hobby," the magazine wrote, "has always been his newsreels and any condition within the industry that might threaten the distribution of this particular product would undoubtedly find Mr. Hearst ready to put up a tremendous fight to protect it." Despite *Motion Picture News's* predictions about Hearst's next course of action, however, he seemed suddenly to lose the fighting spirit. As would often happen in his promises to take on the film industry, Hearst was neutralized by his desire to maintain power in a field that required getting along. If the wave was consolidation, Hearst would be able to put aside his anger over movie theater trusts, and he would ride that wave.

In 1929, nearly a decade after his association with Hearst and the Graphic Film Company, Ivan Abramson had not yet recovered from the falling-out that followed his departure and his criticism of Marion Davies's acting ability. Abramson spent most of the 1920s struggling to make and distribute a few forgotten films. His place in the film industry was virtually nonexistent, and his financial situation more bleak than ever. In late 1929, in a last chance for notoriety, Abramson secured the services of Senator Smith W. Brookhart to act as legal counsel in a suit against the Hays Office and its producer and distributor members. Since the summer of 1929 the Iowa senator had been watched closely by the powers of the film industry. It was widely reported in June that he had given a speech before the Senate that threatened federal regulation of the film business. "Never before," Brookhart declared, "was any group of business men so completely subjugated as are the independent theatre owners of the United States." Brookhart proceeded to chronicle the recent monopolistic activities of Warner Bros., Fox, Loews, and others in a manner quite similar to the case laid out by Hearst in his editorial only days later. Whether this similarity of views was merely coincidental is unknown. It is quite likely, however, that Brookhart had already aligned himself with Abramson in the summer of 1929. There were reports that Abramson had gone to Washington to supply information on the trust to the senator and suggestions that he had been interviewed by the Justice Department regarding possible illegal practices in the film business. By the end of the year, Brookhart was officially on Abramson's legal team. The filmmaker's lawsuit focused mostly on the Hays Office, which, he would later write, "claim[s] that my pictures were tasted with too much sex, and that they were never passed by the censors; the result was that the exhibitors had squeezed me out by refusing to buy my pictures." Denying the accusations that had been repeatedly made about his films, Abramson said he was really being targeted because he was an independent filmmaker. Hays was out to destroy him because he was outspoken and out to destroy all independent filmmakers because he had been hired to protect the movie trust. In one interesting charge, Abramson said that movie producers such as Zukor, the Warners, and Fox had been so eager to have the politically connected Hays on their side that they secretly played up the movie scandals of the early 1920s to make it appear to be necessary to call a powerful movie czar to the rescue.

Abramson's suit against the movie trust deteriorated quickly, met with the full force of the Hays organization, which continued to plant stories in the press that characterized Abramson as a film pornographer. By December 1929 Brookhart felt sufficiently threatened by the association to withdraw suddenly from the case. When Abramson was found to be still using the legislator's name on legal documents a few weeks later, Brookhart spoke to reporters and made the astonishing claim that he had never been aware of the type of films made by Abramson. He now joined many others in the press in calling his former client a maker of sex pictures. Brookhart's awkward break with Abramson only weakened the senator's credibility in his calls for an investigation of industry practices. In January 1930 *Variety* reported, "Senator Brookhart sees behind it all an attempt to discredit him and the bill he sponsors for federal regulation of the picture industry."

Abramson's lawsuit languished in the courts for several years and was finally settled with Abramson's receiving a small settlement shortly before his death in 1934. To his dying day, Abramson was convinced that Hearst had been responsible for discrediting a Senate investigation into the practices of the Hays organization, the film trust, and his own crusade for independent filmmakers.

PICTURE AND SOUND AUTOBIOGRAPHY

By 1930—with sound motion pictures achieving nearly universal acceptance—Hearst saw new possibilities for the great storyteller and messenger of the times. He was convinced that so-called serious theater, which had never interested him much anyway, was almost completely irrelevant to the masses. Journalism and literature were still very important to him, but they were poor substitutes for the immediacy of film. Hearst saw film as entertainment, but he was beginning to see it as supplanting publishing in its power to spin his version of current events and history.

Between 1929 and 1937 the majority of films produced by Cosmopolitan Productions, as always, did not star Davies. Still, because of the focus of Hearst's publicity and the deliberate efforts to make the star the trademark of the film company, the general public continued to identify a Hearst film as a Davies film. This impression was made even stronger and the lines between fiction and reality were further blurred by the roles Davies played. In nearly half the sixteen Davies vehicles made during this period, the actress was cast as a professional entertainer or a character whose performing talents were an important element of the picture's narrative. Parallels to Davies's real career, especially in such chorus girl films as *The Florodora Girl* (1930) and *Blondie of the Follies* (1932), are obvious. But these light-hearted often disposable Cosmopolitan films also give us a glimpse into Hearst's own life in entertainment as he would have others see it and have history record it.

The pattern of Davies playing a performer actually began in the silent era. The star played a cabaret singer who did charity work in Manhattan's Tenderloin district in *The Belle of New York* (1919), she takes part in an amateur show in *Enchantment* (1921), and she plays a film actress in *The Cinema Murder* (1919) and *Show People* (1928). Her first appearance in talking pictures was as a performer, among a large cast of MGM stars in the *Hollywood Revue of 1929*. The picture, which premiered in June 1929, was, as its title suggests, a nonstop series of short production acts in the vaudeville tradition. The numbers were strung together by the emcee talents of the actor Conrad Nagel and a young comedian named Jack Benny. The large cast of performers included Laurel and Hardy, Buster Keaton, actress Norma Shearer, a Charleston-dancing Joan Crawford, the comically dour Marie Dressler, and 125 chorus girls. Davies appeared in two acts. In one, she danced with a lineup of male dancers dressed as London bobbies (she appeared in a costume that was a cross between a toy soldier and a Philip Morris cigarette boy). In the film's finale, Davies and many other MGM stars performed "Singing in the Rain" (the film debut of the song) dressed in yellow slickers as Hollywood rain poured on a soundstage, all captured in primitive but still glorious color.

The Hollywood Revue was a hit with audiences and is credited with starting something of a revue craze in film, but it had not been Hearst's first choice as Davies's debut in talking pictures. In the fall of 1928 film trade magazines began writing tidbits about an upcoming Cosmopolitan musical starring Davies (cast again as a performer) in a picture called *Five O'Clock Girl*. In November Davies was busy taking singing lessons, and by early December a week of rehearsals and five days of shooting had been completed. But by mid-December the film was already in deep trouble. The producers—presumably including Hearst—were unhappy with the songs that Davies was slated to perform. Abruptly, a decision was made to proceed with the production as a silent picture, directed by Alfred E. Green. Meanwhile, James Gleason, a prolific screenwriter who would work in Hollywood for decades to come, was commissioned to write a new talkie version of the film. All of this was for naught, since *Five O'Clock Girl* never reached the screen. As no prints of the film have been uncovered, it is uncertain if it was in fact ever completed in either a sound or a silent version.

Davies's costar in the aborted *Five O'Clock Girl* was Charles King, a popular New York stage performer. King did appear in *Broadway Melody*, a Cosmopolitan production of 1929. The idea for *Broadway Melody* was suggested by the Loews executive and Capitol Theater manager Major Edward Bowes in 1928. In a conversation with Irving Thalberg, Bowes pointed out how talking pictures had favored the melodrama over the musical, a genre he believed was more suited to the new cinematic advance. Davies did not appear in the cast of *Broadway Melody*, but Hearst nevertheless took great pride in the picture. "If a musical comedy plot can be improved and made reasonably rational," Hearst wrote his old friend the writer Elinor Glyn in July 1929, "the result is probably the most successful form of talking picture, or shall we say singing picture. Have you seen 'Broadway Melody'? Marion's next picture, 'Marianne,' is a 'talkie' and 'singie' and 'dancie.' I know you will see that, but please see 'Broadway Melody.' " The film was a big box office hit: it cost $379,000 to produce and brought in a profit of over $1.5 million. It was one of the first of the backstage musicals that would soon became a Hollywood cliché. The film was recognized by the Academy of Motion Picture Arts and Sciences as the best picture of 1929.

Still hedging their bets after the fiasco of *Five O'Clock Girl*, MGM produced *Marianne* as both a silent and sound picture. But the silent version was apparently discarded after the talkie version was released to favorable reviews in October 1929. *Marianne* was Davies's first sound film with a plot. While strictly not a musical—it was a love story with music derived from the World War I drama *The Big Parade*—Davies was able to showcase her song and dance talents in the production. "In 'Marianne,' Davies would later recall, "they asked me to do everything but stand on my head. I danced, I sang, did Chevalier imitations in a French accent. I was dramatic and comic at the same time in my first talkie." Three Davies films of the early 1930s, *The Florodora Girl*, *Polly of the Circus* (1931), and *Blondie of the Follies* (1932) followed the successful show business formula of *Broadway Melody* and continued to typecast Davies as a performer. These films also moved into a more obvious autobiographical direction. In all three pictures the lead character is seen not only as a chorus girl or a circus performer with talents but also as something of an outcast in polite society. In *Polly* the drama revolves around the pressures put on the Davies character to conform and on the dangers of excessive censorship. In *The Florodora Girl* (whose working title was *In the Gay 90's* and whose time period more closely resembles Millicent Willson's than Davies's) and in *Blondie* the performer's search for a wealthy and wise suitor is a prominent theme. More often than not, this older man is a benevolent figure—a stage-door Johnny with a heart of gold, as it were.

Davies was reported to have said that playing in *Blondie of the Follies* was like revisiting her past. When the film was in its early stages of production (and was still using the working title *Good Time Girl*), Louella Parsons reported that Davies was contributing "some excellent episodes from her own experience." Another Hearst film critic, Regina Crewe, emphasized the similarities between the fictional Blondie and the real Davies. "All the hopes, the heartaches, the ambitions, triumphs, defeats that Marion, or any girl, experiences in striving earnestly for a career," Crewe wrote, "are portrayed by the star in her Cosmopolitan Production. And in the picture, as in real life, Marion retains the characteristics which finally win the world to her side." The film also had at least one reference to the behind-the-theater world that women like Davies (and Millicent) knew quite well. In a story conference meeting that included producers Irving Thalberg and Paul Bern and writers Frances Marion and Anita Loos, the film's director, Edmund

Goulding, outlined a scene that alludes to the brothel-saloon behind the theater but is carefully constructed to skirt the censors: "Then we come to the 'Rabbit's Foot Club,' the speakeasy, it's a half block from the Follies—or across the back-alley. The Queens, who are the better girls, are the ones that come in when they please and go when they please—they can be early or late—it's the privilege of the Queens. . . . They are the ones that can go down the fire escape from the theatre right into the speakeasy with just a fur coat over their Teddies. They go down between acts for a drink."

The connections between the characters in the light-hearted Cos-mopolitan productions of the early 1930s and Hearst's real-life partners overshadow another more subtle association: the films are a reflection of Hearst's image of himself and his place in the world of entertainment. Because the subject matter of *Blondie of the Follies* seemed to afford Hearst great opportunities to make an autobiographical film, the production spent a long time in development. A character modeled on Hearst's version of himself is played by the Canadian actor Douglass Dumbrille. Dumbrille's role in *Blondie* was the beginning of a long career of character parts that included a memorable but uncredited role as the voice of God in Cecil B. DeMille's *The Ten Commandments* (1956). The actor was handpicked by Hearst to play the role of a kindly, debonair millionaire in *Blondie*. The actor remembered the producer's obsessive attention to detail in the film as well as Davies's generosity to the cast at San Simeon: "Hearst made movies like he did everything else . . . [and] when she [Davies] was working in a picture, she often invited some of the extras to spend a weekend at San Simeon. The cast and crew had great respect for her." Journalist Bob Willett, who wrote an article about Hearst for a Canadian magazine in 1952, noted the contrast between the Dumbrille depiction of Hearst and the later *Citizen Kane* portrait: "The two films, as could be expected, offered completely opposite views. Shown together on a double bill, they might give a true impression of their schizophrenic subject. The 'approved' Hearst was a relaxed figure with a soft voice and courteous manner. As interpreted by Dumbrille, he was a generous and kindly captain of industry. The Wellesian Hearst, on the other hand, was Machiavellian—a frustrated politician with a cold steely eye, a limp handshake and a great yearning for power."

Above the Law

1929–1934

THE WOMEN IN FRONT OF THE MAN

In the spring of 1930, Millicent Hearst sat beside Benito Mussolini in the Italian dictator's Alfa Romeo on a high-speed drive from Rome to the newly excavated town of Ostia. A nervous but excited Millicent pleaded for her driver to slow down. "You're breaking the law," was the only threat she could muster up. "I *am* the law," Mussolini responded. In a more tranquil setting, resting on the steep stone bleachers of a 12 B.C. amphitheater in Ostia, Millicent fell under Il Duce's legendary spell. Unaccompanied by security guards, Mussolini spoke without airs to a group of fawning tourists. One stranger asked if he might take a photograph, and the Italian leader calmly obliged. Another tourist gave Mussolini a bouquet of violets, which he accepted and then gallantly handed to Millicent.

As Millicent informed her readers in an article she subsequently wrote for the Hearst newspapers, she was enthralled by Mussolini's command of his country, and she communicated her thoughts in almost romantic terms. Her view of Mussolini's dramatic flair and his executive skills was one shared by many at the time, including well-known businessmen Otto Kahn and Joseph Kennedy; Nicholas Murray Butler, president of Columbia University; and Amedeo Giannini, of the Bank of America, backer of the Hearst Corporation and Metro-Goldwyn Mayer, among others. "Mussolini is a great executive," Millicent wrote, "a true leader of men and the great works he has accomplished are his genuine fortification to a high place in history and in the hearts of his people." She described Mussolini's office at the Palazzo Venezia, which she had visited earlier, as perfectly suited to his dramatic personality. "As the door opened," she wrote, "I caught a glimpse of the great hall, 18 meters long, 15 wide and 12 in height. . . . At the bottom of the hall, beside a huge fireplace, was a writing table, and behind it stood Mussolini. He bowed slightly and gave me an encouraging smile in my progress up the hall. . . . One does not feel at all overwhelmed in meeting him, although certainly a vague quiver runs through one on encountering his eyes. However, his look is gentle and serene, his voice full and mild."

While Mussolini mesmerized Millicent, she became a source of fascination for him. He wanted her to tell him about the United States. He wondered what the roads were like in America, and he wanted to hear the latest political gossip. Mussolini had a particular interest in Tammany Hall, possibly knowing about Millicent's own connections in that regard. While her husband was spending more and more of his days in California, Millicent had continued to develop her social and political contacts on the East Coast and especially in New York City. In 1921 and 1923, Manhattan's political machine floated Millicent's name as a potential congressional candidate. At the time, the press compared Millicent's charm and political savvy to England's Lady Astor and declared her to be "much more popular with Tammany Hall than is her husband."

As separations became more frequent with her husband, Millicent continued to capitalize on the Hearst name and her own considerable independent charms. Through her unofficial post as consultant to the Hearst publishing empire and her chairmanship of the Free Milk Fund for Babies, she helped to keep her name in her husband's newspapers' society columns. Fund-raisers were held annually in conjunction with the new season of the Metropolitan Opera, but other events, mostly geared toward men, seem to have excited Millicent in particular. The sport of prizefighting, which was directly tied to the mob, was closely associated with the Milk Fund throughout the 1930s and 1940s.

On occasion, the tables were turned, and Millicent was publicly feted for her charity work. In November 1931 a testimonial dinner was held in her honor at the Hotel Commodore, in Manhattan. "Strictly stag," at Millicent's own request, invited guests included Otto Kahn, Senator Royal Copeland, Bernard Gimbel, Condé Nast, FDR confidante James Farley, and an assortment of judges and businessmen. During the entertainment portion of the evening, the men were treated to exhibition bouts set up in a makeshift ring at the center of the hotel's ballroom, showcasing boxers Gene Tunney, Jack Dempsey, Jack Sharkey, and Max Schmeling. At another event, in September 1932, Millicent was honored again for her good deeds and entertained by Jack Benny and Fanny Brice at the Academy of Music, in her old neighborhood of Fourteenth Street.

Encouraged by Hearst, Millicent befriended political and financial leaders in ways that resembled the later activities of diplomat's wife and social-climbing courtesan Pamela Churchill Harriman. Sometimes, however, her flirtations and hobnobbing met with mixed results. When Millicent struck up a friendship with the German ambassador to the United States during World War I, probably in part to gain useful information and influence for her husband, the relationship proved to be one more piece of evidence cited to support the claims that the Hearsts were disloyal Americans. After the First World War, when Hearst's attentions turned to Marion Davies, Millicent began to travel extensively with her own set of friends. In Europe she cultivated relationships with royalty and with heads of state. She was close to the Greek royal family, and she had her fair share of suitors among the British, including Prince Andrew, father of Philip, Duke of Edinburgh, and Lord Castlerosse, a dandy and expert horseman.

Some viewed Millicent's travels through the upper echelons of society as somewhat comical. Hayes Perkins, a Hearst employee who worked at San Simeon for nearly a decade beginning in 1928, observed Millicent during her visits to the castle, which by then were primarily confined to Christmastime and birthday celebrations for the Hearst sons. Perkins thought her manner personified America's nouveau riche. "Mrs. Hearst, whom rumor saith came from a lowly place, has the society bug badly, and with Hearst's wealth and prominence behind her manages to crash the highest in New York. . . . She has such a different crowd here, and among them are some English snobs." The novelist Owen Wister, a close friend of artist Frederic Remington who probably knew of Hearst and Millicent's relationship in its formative years, jotted down the latest gossip in his journal in Great Britain in 1919: "We talked of Hearst! who wants social recognition in London for Mrs. Hearst!! and in exchange promises to be good!!! Dear Dear Dear what things I am hearing."

As early as 1922, Hearst thought Mussolini was someone to keep an eye on. He sent writer Louise Bryant, partner of John Reed, on a mission to Rome to interview the emerging leader and get a feel for his following in Italy. Bryant was probably the first American ever given such an assignment. Millicent had her first meeting with Mussolini a year later, the arrangements made through a mutual friend, Baron Sardi, the Italian undersecretary of state. After Millicent's 1923 visit, Hearst's efforts to court Mussolini escalated. He was motivated by more than one factor, according to a confidential memorandum dictated by his European correspondent Karl von Wiegand:

> In 1924, Hearst sent Bertilli, one of his best correspondents, to Italy for a series of articles designed to appraise accurately the Mussolini movement. After a month or so of work, the first article was sent to Hearst. It was plain enough that [it] was not flattering. It had also been understood that Hearst had no sympathy with dictatorial governments. Strangely enough, Bertilli was recalled and all his work scrapped. Another strange thing, Gianini [sic], President of the Italian Bank System of California, an ardent supporter of Mussolini, agreed to lend Hearst some millions of dollars, Hearst being thought at that time to be in embarrassing financial circumstances. Our friend, and son-in-law of President Wilson, William G. McAdoo, negotiated the deal and the loan was duly made. Hearst then sent me to Rome for an interview with Mussolini, and asked me to engage him to write articles whenever he chose for the Hearst press at $1 a word. Mussolini was greatly pleased and he wrote articles over a number of years, and I delivered to him large checks from time to time. From that time on Hearst was considered by his correspondents as an ally of Mussolini.

Von Wiegand's meeting with Mussolini to negotiate a writing commission occurred in January 1930, a few months before Millicent's third trip to Rome. Mussolini's contributions to the Hearst press continued into the 1930s, and they covered—from a fascist perspective, naturally—subjects ranging from how to deal with the spread of communism to advice on how to deal with gangsters in America.

Millicent's second visit to Rome took place during the summer of 1927, when there was considerable activity on Hearst's part to form partnerships with Mussolini in both publishing and film. In February 1927, with Hearst's concurrence, *Daily Mirror* editor Philip Payne tried to engage Mussolini to write a regularly featured news column. Payne and Hearst thought Mussolini would jump at the offer, because they knew how eager the dictator was to influence public opinion in the United States. For some reason progress on the deal stalled, but Payne was probably still pursuing the matter at the time of his death later that year. In September 1927, when Payne left on a nonstop flight across the Atlantic Ocean that was an aviation experiment and a promotional feat for Hearst's New York tabloid, he was carrying onboard confidential messages for the Italian king and for Mussolini in Rome, his flight's final destination. The voyage ended in disaster when the aircraft went down over the Atlantic, killing Payne and everybody else on board. Only a month after Payne's plane and plans crashed, Moses Koenigsberg, president of International News Service and Universal Service, was in Italy renegotiating a deal with Mussolini to write for the Hearst wire services. On October 15 *Editor and Publisher* magazine published a photograph of Koenigsberg standing side by side with Mussolini, flanked by the I.N.S. correspondent in Rome, Harold J. T. Horan, and Count Capasso Torre, an aide to the dictator. Shortly after his meeting, where an arrangement was concluded, Koenigsberg spoke of Il Duce in the warmest terms, sentiments that were common for years to come in the Hearst press and in many other U.S. publications. "I think that Mussolini is the busiest man in Europe and told him so and he smilingly accepted the designation from me. So far as physical appearances," Koenigsberg added, "Italy has progressed wonderfully under Mussolini."

In negotiating with Mussolini to write articles for his syndicate in 1927, Hearst was also trying to form a film alliance with the man who controlled the film industry in Italy. Through these efforts Hearst could expand his film influence abroad and simultaneously offer the fascist dictator a cinematic platform for propaganda in the United States. Mussolini had been a fan of the movies—especially Hollywood productions—since the early 1920s. He invited movie stars such as child actor Jackie Coogan, from Charles Chaplin's *The Kid*, to visit him at his office at the Palazzo Venezia, and America's most celebrated movie star couple of the 1920s, Douglas Fairbanks and Mary Pickford, visited Mussolini in 1926. In 1923 Mussolini even allowed himself to be pictured in American director George Fitzmaurice's film about Rome called *The Eternal City*. Mussolini began a habit of watching movies nightly in his drawing room at the Villa Torlonia, where he had a projector set up. Often he sat near the back of the room with his household staff, which was as welcome at the screenings as his more celebrated guests.

The program for these ritual movie nights usually included a feature and a newsreel. Mussolini watched the dramas and the comedies (Laurel and Hardy were his favorites) for diversion, but he studied the nonfiction films for their propaganda value. He once told an interviewer that he thought the Soviets were particularly adept at sending messages through films. "The Russians set us a good example there. Soon we shall have more money to spare for the cinemas. To-day the film is the strongest available weapon." Mussolini even had a personal interest in screenwriting, causing *Variety* in

1934 to refer to him as "a disappointed dramatist." After his death, Mussolini's widow concurred with the assessment that her husband had been more than a passive ruler of the film industry in Italy. "He also interested himself in Italian documentaries produced for foreign markets," Rachele Mussolini wrote, "wishing to make certain that his country was given the correct image."

In May Ed Hatrick was dispatched to Europe with E. D. Getlan, European manager of *International Newsreel*, and C. F. Curione, of Metro-Goldwyn-Mayer. The group's itinerary included a trip to Italy. On May 19 Hatrick concluded a news film and photograph exchange agreement with Mussolini. On the day the deal was signed, the Luce Film Company, Italy's largest (and government-controlled) film organization, issued a statement that was published prominently in the Hearst press:

> His Excellency, chief of the Government, received today in Chigi Palace Senator Cremonesi, president of the Luce, and E. B. Hatrick, general manager of the great newsreel and cinematographic organization formed as a result of the alliance of the Hearst film interests, the Metro-Goldwyn-Mayer newsreel and, Europe, of the Gaumont, Metro-Goldwyn Continental newsreel organization.
>
> The Prime Minister has examined, approved and signed the agreement between the Luce and the great American organization, an agreement which provides for the publication of photographs taken by the Luce and the exhibition of films produced by our national institute in the cinematographic halls and theatres served by the powerful American organization of William Randolph Hearst, the great chief of the press of the United States, who is the animator of this reciprocal movement.
>
> This agreement also provides for exchange and diffusion of films education[al] in character as well as great happenings in the news of Italy.
>
> The Prime Minister expressed great pleasure in the realization of this important agreement. Mr. Hatrick expressed to Signor Mussolini, the head of the Government in the name of Mr. Hearst, profound satisfaction with this agreement, which will enable the people in America to understand through cinematographic evidence, better and better, the work achieved in the great spiritual and material renaissance in Italy and to make better and more favorably known in Italy the marvelous progress and development of the American nation.

Mr. Hatrick then expressed to the Prime Minister his admiration for his almost miraculous work in Italy and expressed his firm belief that the agreement signed would strengthen the ties that bind two ever friendly nations.

Hearst's film arrangement with Mussolini was one of the earliest between the Fascist leader and an American producer. By the 1930s independent producer Walter Wanger, Columbia Pictures' Harry Cohn, Nicholas Schenck, and Louis B. Mayer were all admirers of Mussolini and eager to court him as a film collaborator. In 1933 Columbia produced a documentary film called *Mussolini Speaks* that used Italian newsreel footage to propagandize for Italian fascism. The film was highly publicized in the United States, and the Hearst press was at the forefront of the promotion. Following the Hearst party line, editor Arthur Brisbane wrote a review for the chain that praised both the film and the dictator: "Nicholas Schenck said every intelligent man should see the Columbia Pictures film of Mussolini speaking and in action. He is right. In the faces of the crowds and in their frenzied applause you see Mussolini's absolute hold on the people of Italy. This picture should be shown in both houses of Congress, in every school, club and university. It illustrates, as no picture has done, the role that talking pictures are destined to play in education."

In 1934 the Hearst press endorsed another film production boosting Italian fascism, entitled *Man of Courage*. The picture, based on a screenplay written by Mussolini himself, was a narrative that followed the hardships and rising fortunes of Italian peasant families from 1912 on. Mussolini appeared in the film, as did Pope Pius XI, and here again the picture's emphasis was on the public's loyalty to their charismatic leader. The film was screened as a featured attraction in the *New York American*'s annual Christmas Relief Fund, held at the Gaiety Theater, and heavily promoted in articles and editorials. "Is there any wonder," an *American* editorialist wrote on November 20, 1934, "that Mussolini is the idol of the youth of Italy? Youth has the Fourth-of-July complex. Bang! Bang! The more noise the merrier. . . . Keep church bells ringing all day and all night. Fire off cannon at every street corner every half-hour. Let 'er rip! And who knows but that, in other lands, more Mussolinis will rise."

In 1936 Mussolini's adult son, Vittorio, met with Louis B. Mayer while the studio head traveled in Italy, and the two men discussed a production deal that would link the young cinema enthusiast with MGM-affiliated producer Hal Roach (he made the Laurel and Hardy films). One year later Vittorio Mussolini came to the United States as his father's emissary and to study American film methods. In early October he was warmly met by select members of

Hollywood's elite—its most right-wing members—including Hearst, Walt Disney, Will Hays, and Winfield Sheehan, the old Tammany chieftain turned Fox Film executive. Mussolini received a considerably cooler reception from Hollywood liberals, who were outraged over Italy's militarism and its increasingly flagrant anti-Semitic pronouncements. In response to boycott threats and letter-writing campaigns, MGM nixed the Hal Roach deal. Vittorio Mussolini soon retreated to his native Italy. In 1938, after a number of American film companies refused to distribute films in Italy any longer, Mussolini's son lashed out at Hollywood in the press, calling it a "Hebrew Communist center."

At almost precisely the same moment that Millicent and Mussolini sat together in the ruins of a theater in Ostia in 1930, Hearst and Marion Davies sat side by side in their own theater at San Simeon. In 1928 Hearst had decreed the excavation of a deep basement for a theater, followed by the construction of thick earthquake-proof walls. He decided the basement was not deep enough, and a steam shovel dug deeper. The theater was ultimately three stories high over a full basement. In May 1930, two weeks after Hearst's sixty-seventh birthday celebration, the castle staff was treated to a special screening of the most recently completed Cosmopolitan picture, *The Florodora Girl*, along with a color film of the Russian Revolution. Construction on the theater was still in progress at the time; the rich red damask wallpaper had just recently been hung, and fur coats were still being provided for warmth on chilly nights. As Hearst, Davies, and the actress Jean Harlow, a straggler from the birthday bash, sat close to each other up front, a group of groundskeepers, zookeepers, and construction men found their places mostly near the back. Employee Hayes Perkins, who sat directly behind Hearst and Davies, recorded in his diary impressions of the picture on the screen and the picture in the screening room:

> It is a marvel that Hearst allows us to share the pictures with him. He is generous to a fault, but the men don't appreciate it enough to behave when they come in. Just a gang of human hogs. Chewing gum and sticking it under chairs, smoking, though this is forbidden, catcalling and talking, it will be but a little while until we who try to act decently will be barred with them. In this picture [*Florodora Girl*] Marion posed as the innocent country girl who scorned to act as mistress to a wealthy man. I was sitting just behind she and Hearst, and he was petting her while this part was displayed. She was half shot at that, and playfully slapped him as he roughly drew her to him. More from derision than any other reason we cheered her to the echo. Her face

flushed with pleasure, she believed we meant it. I clapped my hands until they were sore, she deserved it after brazening it out in front of a picture like that. . . . Marion and Jean Harlow were on a toot, both of them half seas over, almost maudlin. Hearst is generous to a fault, even if he is a libertine.

Although Hearst eventually saw Davies's drinking as a serious illness and made attempts to keep liquor away from her while he searched for methods of treatment, as late as 1930 he did little to discourage drinking by Davies or their guests at San Simeon. He was even still involved in the bootlegging business that seems to have been a factor in the confusing stories and cover-ups related to the death of director Thomas Ince in 1924. The same employee that observed Davies and Harlow's drunkenness chronicled Hearst's ongoing illegal liquor operation. In October 1928 Perkins noted that liquor acquired overseas was being stockpiled in a deep, underground level of the castle. "Frequent trucks, sedans, coupes, moving vans and what-not," Perkins wrote, "come up the long hill laden with every brand Europe affords." In January 1930 Perkins went into further detail on the extent of the operation, and he opined as to how his employer was able to bypass the law:

> Under the castle is a vault with double doors. The keys to this vault are carefully guarded, for stored there are vast quantities of liquors. . . . I have seen a ship come alongside the pier at San Simeon and unload 14,000 cases, but not much of it came here. Merely an accommoda-tion to big shot bootleggers from San Francisco and Los Angeles. Last year, when I was on my vacation in San Francisco, I saw several coast guard officers with whom I served in that branch of the service. They asked who was running booze down this way, and I told them Hearst. "We don't want anything to do with Hearst!" they declared. "Do you suppose I want to be chased out of the service, or transferred to some cold station up on the New England coast? Tell us something about the smaller fry we can handle." That is the lord of San Simeon. He is so big no one dares touch him.

Dictating Film

On one of his frequent *Oneida* yacht trips in the early 1920s, between screenings of movie rushes, Hearst noticed Marion Davies's costume designer Gretl Urban with her nose buried in a copy of the *New York Daily News*. Like many others, Hearst had been curious about the newspaper since publishers Robert McCormick and Joseph Medill Patterson first introduced it in 1919. Part of the *News*'s attraction was its willingness to cut down on the news to pump up the pictures. In addition to its reliance on photographs, the trim size of the newspaper was about half that of standard newspapers, giving it the name "tabloid." Possibly because he thought this combination of factors took his yellow journalism too far in one direction or because he felt restricted by an already heavy investment in starting up other newspapers at the time, Hearst was initially reluctant to enter the tabloid field. Miss Urban, who was an educated woman in her early twenties in the early 1920s, was amused when she looked up from her paper to see those familiar "penetrating eyes," as Davies called them. Hearst wanted her opinion on every aspect of the new-format newspaper. The fact that her erudite father, Joseph Urban, thought the *News* was garbage seemed to mean little to Hearst. In Gretl Urban's view, Hearst was using her in the same way he sometimes used his mistress: he was keeping his finger on the pulse of the younger generation that he realized would lead the way for the masses.

In 1922 Hearst reduced the size of one of his Boston newspapers, the *Advertiser*, and in the summer of 1924 the wheels were set in motion for a brand-new tabloid, the *New York Mirror*. Walter Howey, Hearst's all-around newspaper fixit man, was brought in from Chicago to get the *Mirror* started, and within two weeks it was up and running. Under the management of Howey, its editors Emile Gauvreau and Philip Payne, and its publisher Albert J. Kobler, the *Mirror* worked quickly to reach its targeted audience and to form the alliances to organized crime and Tammany Hall that were legendary among New York newspapers. Owney "The Killer" Madden, a leading racketeer, became a presence in the newspaper city room. Other hoods were hired to protect the *Mirror*'s printing plant. Editor Gauvreau befriended Tammany boss James J. Hines, accompanying him to prizefights and boosting Tammany benefits with regularly featured newspaper spreads. A rumrunner named Morris "Little Ziggy" Zeig was called in to make sure that newsstand operators were marketing the Hearst product properly. Even more than he did when facing Pulitzer and others in an earlier circulation war, Hearst competed with his rivals by imitating them.

Much like the *News* and Bernarr Macfadden's *New York Evening Graphic* (introduced a few months after the *Mirror*), the *Mirror* was fashioned with eye-catching stories that did not entail in-depth analysis. The tabloid became an ideal format for innocuous movie star news, short-lived scandals, and local crime stories. Even its editorials and opinion columns were concise and jazzy in style (columnist Walter Winchell, formerly of the *Graphic*, would excel at the *Mirror* and become one of the newspaper's most popular attractions). The *Mirror* proudly announced that it would be 90 percent entertainment and 10 percent news.

Despite his best efforts and his rough-neck hired hands, Hearst's *Mirror's* circulation lagged behind the *News*, and the paper suffered what editor Gauvreau later described as "murderous losses." In 1926, one year before he died in an air stunt, the *Mirror's* Phil Payne (formerly of the *News*) pursued a project that had actually been instigated but ultimately abandoned by Gauvreau when he worked on the *Graphic*. The *Mirror* decided to reopen a murder case that had remained unsolved since 1922.

In September 1922 the Reverend Edward Wheeler Hall, a prominent New Brunswick, New Jersey, pastor, was discovered shot to death; his wealthy married companion, Eleanor R. Mills, was also found dead, with three bullet holes in her body and her throat slashed. In what can only be described as a filmmaker's or tabloid writer's dream, the victim's bodies were found together near a crab apple tree on a lover's lane, their arms reaching for each other and covered with a scattering of torn and torrid love letters sent by Mills to Hall. In its first incarnation, the Hall-Mills murder case was followed closely by most New York's newspapers, especially Hearst's *Journal* and the *Daily News*. Newspapers covered the discoverer of the bodies, a woman dubbed the Pig Woman, and Mrs. Mills's daughter, Charlotte, referred to as a flapper. Mostly they focused on Mrs. Hall, whom the Pig Woman had implicated in the crime. In late 1922, in spite of the continuing newspaper coverage, a grand jury found the Pig Woman's testimony wanting and decided against indicting Hall.

By the summer of 1926 the Hall-Mills story appeared destined for a half dozen or more dusty newspaper morgues. But in July the *Mirror* announced that it had new evidence that warranted the reopening of the case. Phil Payne—who reportedly harbored a grudge against the *News* for firing him shortly before he came to the *Mirror*—claimed that a maid in the Hall household had personal knowledge that Mrs. Hall and her brother had demonstrated their intention to kill Mr. Hall and his lover. The maid, Payne said, had been bribed to remain silent in 1922. Soon, the *News* followed the *Mirror* with its own relentless coverage. Within days, Mrs. Hall was arrested.

The arrest and subsequent trial brought even the normally staid *New York Times* into the act, and the newspaper put sixteen reporters and photographers of its own on the case. To appeal to (and increase) its readership, the *Mirror* used everything at its disposal: drawings, photographs—some real and some faked—and a retelling of the case in comic strip form. Hearst's Universal Service, a wire service, hired novelist Fannie Hurst to report on the trial, and the *Mirror* published articles by Charlotte Mills, who claimed to have been in communication with her mother in the spirit world. By one estimate of printed words on the subject of the case, the *Mirror* outcovered the *News* four to one. As in the early days of yellow journalism, a Hearst editorial touted its tabloid sensationalism as nothing short of a religious crusade: "It was not until the independent, fearless, intelligent unpurchasable press began to function according to original principles that the masks were torn away and the majesty of the law tardily rose from the dust in New Jersey."

In late 1926 the Hall-Mills murder trial ended with the credibility of key witnesses being seriously challenged and a jury deciding after a short deliberation to acquit Mrs. Hall. Critics of tabloid journalism were quick to point to the verdict as proof that Hearst and the others had a careless disregard for fact and an insatiable thirst for blood. There were a few calls for the *Mirror* to be banned in certain localities, although these protests against sensationalism fell short of the level of frenzied objections to yellow journalism in the 1890s. Shortly after the verdict, Mrs. Hall told the *New York Times* that she had been violated by the morbid curiosity of newsmen and their intrusive cameramen. "I don't think it is fair." she said, "I think that it is stealing. Just as much stealing as taking one's personal property. I think one's appearance is one's own, and I think that no one has a right to take that appearance in a picture without permission." In 1927 Mrs. Hall instructed her lawyers to issue libel suits against the Public Press Corporation, Hearst's holding company for the *Mirror* and the *New York Evening Journal*, and Hearst himself.

Hearst paid a hefty price for his tabloid venture into murder and scandal. In late 1928 it was reported that Hearst made an out-of-court settlement with Mrs. Hall for upward of $150,000, which was almost the exact cost of Hall's 1926 trial. There was also a considerable loss of advertising revenue for the *Mirror* following the attacks on its methods. Before Hearst and Mrs. Hall reached their settlement, *Mirror* editor Payne became a victim of another one of his reckless publicity campaigns, an attempt to fly nonstop from New York to Rome. Payne's death made sensational headlines in the Hearst press for several days, a strange but fitting coda to the Hall-Mills tabloid story.

Despite outward signs of self-confidence and his years of practicing and publicly defending yellow and tabloid journalism, Hearst was actually rather thin-skinned when it came to criticism, especially when it emanated from Hollywood. Hearst's brand of journalism had been an easy target since the birth of the film medium. Until the 1930s, however, most films that had newspaper characters or used newspapers as a backdrop were likely to poke fun at the yellow journalist's excesses and avoid more serious questions about ethics. The newspaper world was often seen as a comedy or as an adventure closely aligned with the world of show business and the sporting life. Its more notorious connections to political corruption and vice were considerably less visible in movies. Cosmopolitan's production of *The Great White Way* (1924), directed by E. Mason Hopper, was typical of the newspaper-friendly films that dominated the silent era. Based on a short story called "Cain and Mabel" (which became the title of Hearst's 1936 remake), the film's plot follows a love story between a Ziegfeld Follies chorus girl and a prizefighter, set in a newspaper and Broadway milieu. *The Great White Way* was a near-record-breaking $1 million production, with sets by Joseph Urban. In addition to its elaborate studio shots, a climactic fight scene incorporated footage assembled from five thousand feet of film shot by six cameramen from Hearst's *International Newsreel* company at the recent Willard-Johnson fight at Yankee Stadium. The film starred real Follies chorus girls but was most noteworthy for its cast of well-known Hearst employees in rare cameo roles, including writers Damon Runyon, "Bugs" Baer, and Nell Brinkley and cartoonists George McManus, Windsor McCay, and Harry Hershfield. The film's credits also included the name of Arthur Brisbane, who was said to play himself. Reports in *Variety* disputed this claim, however, saying that the Brisbane part was actually performed by an actor with an uncanny resemblance to the editor. "If Brisbane has charge accounts," *Variety* wrote, "he's taking a chance." *Variety* began its positive review of the production by taking note of the motivation and message behind the film: "A glance of the cast above and you get the idea of the picture. It seems to have been made with a view of the glorification of prizefighters and Hearst newspapers. . . . On the screen you see the New York 'American' and on the program it's mentioned the press room is from the Los Angeles 'Examiner.' The newspaper men appeared human in the picture."

The introduction of sound and dialogue to film, coming at the same time as the economic and political turmoil of the Great Depression, brought a greater sense of realism to the newspaper film genre. Newspapermen were still the heroes in many films, but they also appeared as figures with darker shadings, seedy connections, and flexible morals. Where once a movie like Hearst's *Great White Way* might show city editors smiling and greeting their staffs at the start of the workday with a handshake, they were now more often seen as grumpy alcoholics shouting orders with machine gun rapidity. More and more, producers and screenwriters who had come from the publishing profession began to look to real news stories for their film plots. They modeled their fictional characters after real newspaper people, men and women who were celebrities themselves in large part as a result of Hearst's long-standing efforts to romanticize their profession. But their film scenarios were grittier because they reflected the changing tone of the newspapers. As this new journalism genre took hold with audiences but came under increasing attack from moral watchdogs, Hearst felt compelled to defend the institution he had shaped while making symbolic attempts to counteract the trend. He did this by infusing certain myths about journalism into his own films and by doing what he could to influence films that were not produced by his company. He was also not above leveling threats against the film industry when he felt that it was not marching to his tune.

One of the most troubling trends to Hearst in the early 1930s was the number of anti–yellow journalism films, some targeted generally and some aimed specifically at his own news operation. Charles E. Chapin, the tough editor of *New York World* who once referred to his reporters as "cogs," was the model for a character in *Scandal Sheet* (1931). The Paramount film shows an unscrupulous newspaper editor who himself becomes prey to the gossip hounds. Through some laborious plot twists, he is exposed in a scandal and sent to prison; in a final irony he is seen editing a prison newspaper. Characters based on Hearst editor Walter Howey and other lesser-known Chicago newspapermen showed up in *The Front Page* (1931), and Pat O'Brien plays a reporter who is based on *Daily Mirror* editor Philip Payne in Universal's *Scandal for Sale* (1932). On his last assignment for his newspaper, O'Brien's character is killed when his plane plunges into the ocean. The film was based on a novel called *Hot News*, written by *Mirror* editor Emile Gauvreau, who dedicated his book to Payne. Gauvreau was still working for the *Mirror* when the film opened in New York, and although it is unknown what if anything Hearst did to suppress the production, the movie apparently displeased him. "The novel," Gauvreau later wrote, "which told of the idiosyncrasies of tabloidia with thinly veiled characters, one being [Walter] Winchell who I had changed into a female gossip writer, disturbed Hearst who communicated his displeasure to [Hearst publisher Albert] Kobler, who in turn, ordered me never to write another book. To dampen my enthusiasm he remained at my desk, to keep me on the job, brandishing his cane and watching me work on the night that my movie opened on Broadway as 'Scandal for Sale,' with my name in the lights."

Warner Bros., a leader in the field of more realistic and socially conscious films, made *Five Star Final* in 1931, a movie based on a Broadway hit by Louis Weltzenkorn, a onetime editor of the *Evening Graphic*. In the film, actor Edward G. Robinson plays a ruthless tabloid editor who, hungry for circulation, decides to reopen a murder case with the flimsiest bit of evidence to support him. In the end, the editor's unethical behavior, egged on by an even more unethical publisher, winds up causing anguish and even death to a completely innocent family. To anyone with any knowledge of the *Daily Mirror*'s resurrection of the Hall-Mills murder case in 1926, it was plain to see that Hearst's methods were being skewered. The Robinson character seems to be based on Hearst's editor Philip Payne and possibly on Victor Watson, who, like the fictional character, broke into the newspaper business on the old *New York Press*. The film also has a newspaper publisher named Hinchecliffe, played by actor Oscar Apfel, who appears to be a cross between *Mirror* publisher Kobler and Hearst himself. In bits that show the Hearst influence, Hinchecliffe has a penchant for blondes and comes up with the idea of getting ministers to introduce a series of yellow journalism articles, which he much prefers to call "human interest." In another parallel to the *Mirror*, the film has a character named "Ziggie," a gangster type like "Little Ziggy" Zeig, who is hired by the publisher to keep newsstand workers in line.

It is not known when Hearst first learned about *Five Star Final*, but when the film was readied for release in the fall of 1931 his newspaper editor Walter Howey was readying a campaign to sabotage it. In late October or early November, Howey paid Boston mayor James M. Curley a visit, and he made an argument for banning the film. He pointed out the instances where the film was ridiculing Hearst or Hearst journalism and the many instances in the past where Hearst had helped the mayor. Surely and at the very least, Howey told the mayor, help should be given to make sure certain deletions were made. The editor reminded the mayor that similar changes had been made after pressure had been put on the play version of *Five Star Final* when it premiered in Boston in 1930.

Howey was not the only one on the Hearst payroll involved in the *Five Star Final* campaign. By the early 1930s Louella Parsons had taken on responsibilities well beyond those of a typical Hearst columnist. Her friendship with Davies and Hearst and her years in the newspaper business made her an insider and an expert of sorts who freely offered advice to Hearst on everything from San Simeon invitation lists to proper newspaper layout and movie publicity. "Now about the San Francisco Examiner!" she wrote Hearst in November 1931, "One thing I find radically wrong with our Sunday page is that they use too much press matter." What Parsons meant by "press matter" was the endless stream of press releases produced by movie studios that Hearst was more than willing to publish for a fee. "The San Francisco Examiner," she continued, "gives more space to press articles than any one of our papers and while it is not the time now to antagonize our advertisers Mr. Lindner [a newspaper editor] agreed with me it was advisable to cut down the press matter." As Hearst's representative, Parsons regularly hosted elaborate luncheons for individual movie studio heads. She had a long talk with Jack Warner after he became aware of the Hearst organization's activities in Boston and assured the executive that Hearst was not directly involved in trying to ban *Five Star Final*. Soon after their talk, Parsons wrote Hearst that Warner seemed to have accepted the columnist's assurances, but she acknowledged that she had been less than confident going into their meeting. Aware that Warner Bros. was interested in striking a production deal with Davies, Parsons was prepared to remind Warner that any public protests against Hearst would not be useful in developing any future relationships. "It was not necessary for me to mention our star." Parson wrote Hearst with some relief. "Jack Warner asked me when she would be free at Metro-Goldwyn-Mayer. I told him she had one more picture. . . . He reiterated that she had not had the proper vehicles and that she was, in his opinion, one of the greatest comediennes on the screen. If you think it's a good idea why not let me bring Mr. and Mrs. Warner up next weekend so that you can have an informal talk with him."

By the time Hearst received Parsons's letter he had already written letters to both Harry and Jack Warner assuring them that his campaign against *Five Star Final* implied no enmity toward their company. Still, in his letter to Jack Warner Hearst made it clear that he objected to antinewspaper films. He also reminded the movie mogul of his own potential for being objectionable:

I am in no way hostile to you or your enterprises. In fact, as you must know, I am extremely well disposed towards both. I do think, however, that the patience of newspaper people has been very much taxed by the constant attacks upon the newspaper fraternity in films which portray reporters as drunkards and editors as unscrupulous rascals. I am sure the patience of motion picture producers would be similarly outraged under similar circumstances. . . . What would the producers say if there were a succession of such plays, all of which went further in their attacks on the character of the producers, and which represented them as drunkards and degenerates?

Then, driving the point home even further, Hearst added:

All the screen productions have been practically attacks upon the press; and yet the screen producers are continually appealing to the newspapers and the newspaper editors to interfere in behalf of the moving picture business and to prevent legislatures from passing obnoxious laws, and censor boards from banning their productions. These friendly acts the newspapers have almost uniformly performed for the screen producers, and yet all the newspaper folk get in return is a succession of slaps in the face through the production of plays which reflect so disagreeably and so untruthfully upon the newspaper profession. If the newspapers should reverse their attitude toward moving picture producers, I do not think it would be very beneficial for the producers. . . . I believe that it would be good judgement on the part of picture producers not to deprive themselves of the sympathetic cooperation of the press.

Hearst's letter is not likely to have encouraged Warner's thoughts about a production deal with Cosmopolitan. By late 1934, however, any ill feeling that lingered between the principals was overlooked for the sake of business, and Hearst moved his film operation to Burbank.

Hearst's pressure on Mayor Curley did effect a brief ban on *Five Star Final* in Boston. But a compromise was eventually reached when the film's producers agreed to insert a foreword to the film that stressed how most newspapers did not subscribe to the methods employed by the picture's fictional newspaper and that no particular paper or publisher was being targeted in the film. Hearst found little support among his press competitors in his campaign against *Five Star Final*. The Scripps-Howard chain attacked Hearst and Brisbane in its columns, and *Variety* gloated about the fact that Hearst's crusade had actually generated box office interest in the film. But Hearst's threats against Warner, which might easily have been extended to the rest of the industry, seemed to have the desired effect. With the *Five Star Final* campaign behind him, Hearst more fully realized an unparalleled position in Hollywood as a sort of sub–Hays Office that was consulted on films in which he had a vested interest. To placate Hearst, in February 1932 Warner Bros. sent him a script of a newspaper drama called *The Famous Ferguson Case* shortly after the film went into production. According to *Variety*, Hearst made several suggestions that the producers followed. Reviewers noted that the film's indictment of scandal sheets had been somewhat diluted by the introduction of a small-town newspaper editor with high standards of journalism. The high-minded editor works for a newspaper called the *American*, a fact that the *New York Journal-American* made note of three times in its review. At the close of the film, this character delivers a speech (which could easily have been written by Hearst) that offers a somewhat strained defense for yellow journalism by emphasizing its benefits: "We're selling two intangible commodities. One is news and the other is public service. Pretty hard to tell sometimes whether a story's news or just plain snooping into people's private affairs. That's when you get disgusted. Then you go out and do something that's public service. And then we carry on."

It is quite possible that Hearst's warning shot to Warner was meant to bring to mind a film project that had recently caused much anxiety in Hollywood, especially among the movie moguls. At the time of the *Five Star Final* controversy, film trade journals reported that Howard Hughes was trying to produce a film version of *Queer People*, a novel about the film industry that he had recently purchased. Since the novel focused on the dark side of Hollywood, with characters based on Louis B. Mayer and others in the industry, it was not surprising that the film never saw the light of a movie projector. It is unknown how Hughes thought he might translate the property to the screen, but in early 1932 he received an unsigned letter marked "Confidential," probably written by his publicist Lincoln Quarberg, that may reflect the maverick producer's thinking. The letter urges Hughes to revive the *Queer People* project and suggests a course of action to get the film made. Hughes should hold a press conference with great fanfare announcing that he is leaving the Hays organization to produce an independent film that would be a "back-stage lowdown on Hollywood" with "sensations and revelations." While the media waited with anticipation, Hughes would then produce a film that attacked the industry's "Big-Shot Jews," and the "hooey-dispensing" Will Hays. "Only a few chatter-writers like Louella Parsons would be against the idea of filming the story," the overly optimistic writer tells Hughes.

The reference to Parsons may not have been offhand. When *Variety* published reports in April 1931 on the difficulties Hughes faced in getting his film project off the ground, it claimed that a female syndicated columnist was leading the movement to squelch the film. "[The] Columnist has been carrying weekly pans on the proposed picture," the trade paper wrote, "and is known to have directed a number of articles to Will Hays in hope that Hays would officially ban the picture from the screen." In 1931 no "femme columnist," as *Variety* put it, aside from Parsons had the clout to do this. And if *Variety*'s reports were accurate, Parson's campaign against *Queer People* was a prime example of Hearst's working to save the necks of the Hollywood establishment—an example that Hearst was unlikely to forget or let others disrespect.

By late 1931, with his hopes for *Queer People* all but evaporated, Hughes put most of his energies into releasing a film he had already completed. *Scarface,*

directed by Howard Hawks and starring Paul Muni in the role of gangster
Tony Camonte, is now considered a classic of the crime film genre, but for
several months in 1931 it looked like it might not be released. The concept
of the film, as worked out between Hughes and Hawks, was to present what
one historian has called "a violent tragicomedy, and not an indictment" of
crime. Hughes worked hard with screenwriter Ben Hecht to give his film
an air of authenticity. As the lead character was clearly modeled after gang
leader Al Capone, Hughes and Hecht cultivated contacts with the mob that
were both useful research tools and a required courtesy. The film was infused
with other references to real people and real events, like the bloody St. Valentine's Day Massacre, that would be familiar to newsreel audiences and tabloid
readers. Although much of the violence, which was extreme for the period,
remained in the final film, the Hays Office was able to remove some
sequences from a rough cut that tended to make the lead character and his
relationship with his family more complex. Scenes that suggested an inces-
tuous relationship between Camonte and his sister were the first to go, and
some of the comic touches were eliminated to make the gangster harder and
less sympathetic. Another problem for Hays was the relatively minimal
amount of moralizing in the film. For instance, as the film was first shot,
Camonte surrenders to the police at the end of film, but there is nothing
approaching a cathartic execution scene that might have more graphically
demonstrated society's "right" of retribution for murder and other crimes.
The charge was made that with its scenes of gangsters in all their glory and
without the usual heavy-handed moralizing seen in most films, *Scarface* was
merely capitalizing on crime, a criticism that had often been leveled on the
yellow press.

Because Hughes was being pulled in one direction by the Hays Office
and in another by his underworld contacts, who wanted him to soften the
criminal portrayals in his film, months passed with the fate of *Scarface* in
doubt. Worried about getting a green light from Hays but reluctant to make
major changes in his film, Hughes turned for help from the man who may
have blocked his last screen project, *Queer People*. Hearst was not opposed
to offering his services to Hughes on *Scarface*, especially as he believed he
might be able to use the film as a vehicle for expressing his own point of
view on the role of government and journalism in exposing and controlling crime. Sometime in January 1932 Hearst gave Hughes suggestions on
ways he could mollify the Hays Office. Shortly afterward a more confident
Hughes sent a telegram to his publicist, Lincoln Quarberg, with an update
on the film's progress: "For general distribution the picture will carry the
foreward [*sic*] which was on it when shipped to New York the last time

A photographer (with his stereo camera) and his favorite subject tour Europe in 1930.

In 1929, Hearst (*white hat, dark suit*) and camerman Joe Hubbell set up for a newsreel on the MGM lot. In final group shot with Hearst are (*left to right*) Winston Churchill, Louis B. Mayer, and Hubbell.

Cosmopolitan's *The Secret Six* (1931) was inspired by a group of Chicago industrialists who joined together to protect their interests from gangsters.

Hearst rewrote scenes for Howard Hughes's superviolent *Scarface* (1930) to appease film censors.

Cosmopolitan's early talkie *The Bellamy Trial* (1929) featured flashbacks and cameos by noted writers (*left to right*) John Colton, William Dudley Pelley, Louis Browne, Samuel Ornitz, and Louella Parsons. (Regional History Center)

Hearst's *The Big House* (1930) was a sensationalized plea for prison reform. (Regional History Center)

At his Santa Monica beach house in the 1930s, Hearst greets Norma Shearer and Irving Thalberg.

Bing Crosby and Davies star in *Going Hollywood* (1933).

Hearst, out on the town with (*left to right*) Mrs. Harry Crocker, Mrs. Jack Warner, and Jack Warner in 1937.

Shipmates Forever (1935), a hit film musical that Hearst foes called "militaristic."

MOTION-PICTURE
ELECTRICAL-PAGEANT
WORLDS GREATEST

"Lady of the Cameo"

OFFICIAL
PROGRAM
SEPT. 24, 1932

MOTION PICTURE NIGHT

Presented Under the Auspices of the

MOTION PICTURE RELIEF FUND

and

MARION DAVIES FOUNDATION

Olympic Stadium at Night

In 1932, Hearst and Davies were behind a Hollywood gala for candidate Franklin D. Roosevelt.

Hearst meets with coproducer Walter Wanger on the MGM lot during the filming of *Gabriel Over the White House* (1933), a film made to celebrate FDR's election. (Wisconsin Center for Film and Theater Research)

Walter Huston played the dictator-president in *Gabriel*, delivering lines written by Hearst. (Regional History Center)

In 1934, Hearst with two actors from the Passion Play in Oberammergau, Germany. (Germeinde Oberammergau Archiv)

In 1934 one German newspaper reports on Hearst and Davies's visit to Munich. (California Historical Society, San Francisco)

Another newspaper shows Hearst posing with Nazi Alfred Rosenberg. (California Historical Society, San Francisco)

Hearst's International Magazine Building in New York was under siege in the late 1930s when the FTC called *Good Housekeeping*'s Seal of Approval false and misleading. (Regional History Center)

In retaliation, Hearst put J. B. Matthews in charge of an anticommunism crusade against consumer groups and Hollywood. (Courtesy of the Matthews family)

Cosmopolitan's *Oil for the Lamps of China* (1935) was one of the first anti-Communist films.

Anti-hearst Examiner

HEARST IN WAR
HEARST IN PEACE

HEARST IN EVERY
NEWS RELEASE
TO INCREASE NO CIRCULATION

Our country may be in a
bad way, but so long as it
does not go from BAD to
HEARST, it will have some
chance of recovery.
LINDSEY.

VOL. 1, NO. 2   PUBLISHED BY FRIENDS OF THE SOVIET UNION   LOS ANGELES, SEPTEMBER, 1935 — PRICE 1

INTENSIFY DRIVE ON HEARST

EXPOSING LOUELLA PARSONS, HEARST'S HOLLYWOOD STOOGE

CHEER BOYCOTT MEETING

Packed Mason House Condemns Hearst and Yellow Press

On Friday, August 30th, a capacity house at the Mason en-thusiastically greeted individual speakers who urged the boycott of the Hearst press. Each speaker stressed the fascistic, war mongering, anti-labor char-acter of the Hearst yellow jour-nals. Resolutions were adopted condemning the recent Soviet note; for a Hearstless Sunday on September 18th and con-demning the tar and feathering of two Santa Rosa workers.

Speakers introduced by Dr. J. C. Coleman, organizer of the Friends of the Soviet Union, in-cluded Eugene J. Reed of the Abundance Society and founder of the Utopians; Clare Lee Purdy of the Public Works and Unemployed Union; Lou Lorenz of the Friends of Etopiha; Rob-ert Whitaker, arriving from Santa Rosa where he had inves-tigated Vigilante activities; Theodore Bayer, National Or-ganizer of the Friends of the Soviet Union; Assemblyman J. C. Pelletier and Assemblyman

The Wolves Howl –
And Washington Sends a Note!

Americans with a sense of justice are both bewildered and startled by the recent note of protest dispatched by our State Department to the Soviet Union. In essence, the note constitutes an unwarranted slap at a gov-ernment that has tried to main-tain and develop a healthy spirit of friendship with our nation de-spite the ruthless, obstructionist tactics of the Hearsts, Fishes and the Wall Street war mon-gers.

Recognizing the fragile ma-terial of which the note was built, many Americans are keen to learn what is behind the ac-tion of our government. Obvi-ously the note was sent in order to placate the cries of the re-actionary, howling wolves who have been snapping at the heels of the State Department ever since the recognition agreement was signed with the Soviets. Al-though filled with dynamite the protest is sure to gladden the hearts of the potential fascists, the die-hards, profiteering 100 percenters, and other reaction-aries who tremble with fear on witnessing the Soviet march of progress in human relationships.
HEARST LEADS

Leader of the pack, of course, is William Randolph Hearst, the "distinguished" publisher whose yellow press reeks with slander-

document to appease the howls of the flag waving wolves who can never think of profits with-out seeing stars and stripes? Summarizing the charges briefly we find they had no basis in fact. The Soviet Government has never pledged itself to "suppress all communistic activ-ities in the United States," in the words of the note. It is not within its province to make such a pledge. It would have been equally absurd for the Soviet Government to have demanded of Washington that Americans be stopped from speaking En-glish, or wearing grey hats while in Moscow!

If the Communist Internation-al had met in Paris would the French government have been held responsible for the speeches of the American speakers? The answer is definitely NO! The wolves howled and Washington sent its note! And in doing so has created a more likely situa-tion for a new war, a "holy" war, with Hitler as the aggres-sor on the Soviet Union on the one side and Japan on the other.
ANTI-SOVIET BARRAGE

It will be hard for the pack to assume babe-like expressions if presented with other facts. The barrage of anti-Soviet propaganda which grown daily in volume and viciousness is

BOYCOTT STRIKES
Popular Note
IN LOS ANGELES

The Hearst boycott grow by leaps and bounds! So thern California has accep ed the challenge of the n torious yellow journali and is responding to his a tempts to fasci-size Ame ica by curtailing the circ lation of the Examiner, th Herald - Express and oth Hearst publications.

Now comes the big drive. T boycott movement can spre to every home in Los Angel and environs when a Hearstl Sunday is observed on Septe ber 22nd. From now until th day thousands of conscientio workers who recognize Hears fifth for what it is, will carry a house-to-house campaign f the boycott. Revealing in deta to others the filthy lies a slimy manoeuvres of Public E emy Number One, every ind vidual will be urged to drop t Hearst paper on Sept. 22 a continue to boycott it.

From all sides comes enthu sasm for this recent moveme to put the war-monger into t discard. With the present wor crisis shaping itself into a ne World War the danger of An

Joe Hubbell (*short man in straw hat*) with arm around a man believed to be Edwin Stevens, the actor who played a Hearst-like pro-German publisher in the suppressed film *Enemies Within* (1919). The debonair actor Douglass Dumbrille (*top right photo*) was handpicked by Hearst to play a character based on himself in Cosmopolitan's *Blondie of the Follies* (1932). Orson Welles's portrayal of Charles Foster Kane (*bottom photo*) had the most lasting effect.

Isolationist Hearst wrapped himself in the flag after Pearl Harbor and reminded readers that he had warned America about Japanese aggression in 1916 with his film *Patria*.

At one of his last public appearances, in 1942, Hearst was once again in his element. Seated to his left is Rita Hayworth and to his right is Hedy Lamarr. Others stars surrounding Hearst include Jack Benny, Caesar Romero, and George Raft. (Both photos courtesy of Caren Roberts-Frenzel)

which it might interest you to know was written by Mr. Hearst personally furthermore most of the last changes were suggestions Mr. Hearst was kind enough to give me when I showed him the picture and he thinks it vastly improved."

The *Scarface* foreword, which pops up after the opening credits, addresses the concerns of the Hays Office, but it also presents a decidedly Hearstian touch—a jab at the lethargic Herbert Hoover administration accompanied by a suggestion of vigilantism: "This picture is an indictment of gang rule in America and of the callous indifference of the government to this constantly increasing menace to our safety and our liberty. Every incident in this picture is the reproduction of an actual occurrence, and the purpose of this picture is to demand of the government: 'What are you going to do about it?' The government is your government. What are *you* going to do about it?"

Almost certainly the scene added late in production about midway in the film was also conceived and written by Hearst. It takes place in the office of a newspaper publisher, and an assistant director shot it with little preparation on January 12, 1932. Ostensibly the tabloid publisher is having a dialogue with a civic group that has demanded a meeting to discuss the role of newspapers in crime. The scene is really an excuse for Hearst to defend yellow journalism and to expand on his rabble-rousing prologue. Hearst's last-minute producing enabled the film to be released:

MALE CITIZEN: Your paper could be an influence against the gangster. Yet you keep right on playing up his activities as front-page news. Murders, gang wars, killings—that's all we read about. You're glorifying the gangster by giving him all this publicity.

PUBLISHER: You're trying to tell me you can get rid of the gangster by ignoring him—by keeping him off the front page. That's ridiculous. You're playing right into his hands. Show him up! Run him out of the country! That'll keep him off the front page.

FEMALE CITIZEN: In the meantime, you expect our children to read of nothing but outrage and murder?

PUBLISHER: That's better than them being slaughtered! The city is full of machine guns, gang war in the streets, kids aren't even safe to go to school! You want that to go on?

ANOTHER MALE CITIZEN: Certainly not, but what can private citizens do? Even our police force can't stop it.

PUBLISHER: (standing up and speaking directly into the camera) Don't blame the police. They can't stop machine guns from being run back and forth between the state lines. They can't enforce laws that don't exist.

ANOTHER FEMALE CITIZEN: Then it's up to the federal government to do something about it.

PUBLISHER: You're the government—all of you. Instead of trying to hide the facts, get busy and try to see that laws are passed that will do some good. . . . Pass a federal law that puts the gun in the same class as drugs and white slavery. Put teeth in the Deportation Act. These gangsters don't belong in this country—half of them aren't even citizens.

MAN WITH AN ITALIAN ACCENT: That's true, they bring nothing but disgrace to my people.

PUBLISHER: All right, I'll tell you what to do. Make laws and see that they're obeyed—if we have to have martial law to do it. The government of Mexico declared martial law to stop a bullfight, the governor of Oklahoma to regulate oil production. Surely gang rule and wholesale law defiance are more of a menace to the nation than the regulation of oil or a bullfight. The army will help, so will the American Legion. They offered their services over two years ago, and nobody ever called it. Let's get wise to ourselves. We're fighting organized murder!"

Hearst's interest in crime films dates back to his earliest film productions of the 1910s, the cliff-hanging serials that were the precursors of the genre. Four of his most popular serials of this period—*The Perils of Pauline*, *The Exploits of Elaine*, *The Mysteries of Myra*, and *Patria*—involve characters inhabiting a world of sinister forces working outside the law. The films were marked by crimes of kidnapping, smuggling, and illegal drug activities where the gun, the knife, and various other forms of torture were the tangible signs of a formless, looming underworld. In these movie serials—like the morality tales in the Hearst newspapers and other sensational journals—women were principally at risk and in need of rescue. But Hearst's personal views on crime and punishment were more complex than his attention-getting newspaper headlines or his one-, two-, and three-reelers. He was a longtime opponent of the death penalty and a strong advocate for more humane treatment of criminals. He believed that crimes were primarily committed as a result of environmental forces and mental illness and that incarceration, while sometimes necessary, was more often than not a useless exercise.

At some point in the late 1920s or early 1930s, Hearst toyed with the idea of exploring the notion of the criminal as victim of circumstances. He discussed the project with writer and social critic Lincoln Steffens. The two men had known each other since the 1890s, when Hearst was directing Stephen Crane adventures in the Tenderloin for the *New York Journal* and Steffens was a reporter for the *Post* uncovering graft in the police department and in Tammany Hall. Ultimately, the two men were of different temperaments, and they lived by different philosophies, but at one time, as writer Justin Kaplan pointed out in his biography of Steffens, they looked like they might travel the same path. "There was a certain community," Kaplan wrote, "between Hearst and Steffens—they were nearly the same age, both had the air and manners of gentlemen, both had come East from California derisive of conventional heroes, and, in the same way that muckraking and yellow journalism had been lumped together, both of them, rightly or wrongly, were reputed to be radicals."

Hearst was particularly attracted to the psychoanalytical style of journalism Steffens had brought to studies of hypocrisy and corruption in politics and business. In 1906 the writer had even tried to analyze Hearst. In an article titled "William Randolph Hearst: The Man of Mystery," Steffens concluded that his subject used power and money "as a substitute for persuasion, charm, humor, pleadings." Hearst's plan for Steffens now was that he cover a murder trial not so much from the point of view of the evidence in the case or the trial's outcome but from the perspective of an in-depth examination of a particular individual's life. He wanted Steffens to look deeply into the criminal's childhood experiences and family relationships and into anything else that might explain the path someone takes to reach the climactic crossroads of the justice system. How far Hearst and Steffens got in their project is unknown, but there is no evidence it was ever published.

It is unclear whether Hearst honestly believed his newspapers were playing a role in controlling crime by exposing it. He could not have been unaware of the personal benefits he derived from his crime coverage, despite his challenges to the criticism that he was glorifying crime. A typical Hearst response to the criticism was published in an editorial published in his papers in 1931 that linked his newspapers with other forms of entertainment:

> President Hoover complains of the glorification of gangsters. "Instead of the glorification of cowardly gangsters," he said in his recent broadcast to the meeting at St. Petersburg, Florida, of the International Association of Chiefs of Police, "we need the glorification of policemen who do their duty and who give their lives in public protection."

Hoover is quite right, of course. Gangster pictures, particularly, have gone to vicious lengths and have justified such censorship as the country has, and made further censorship desirable. But after all the existence of the gangsters is more important than their portrayal upon the stage or screen, more important than the relation of their performance in books and newspapers. Actual conditions must find some reflection in the drama and in literature and in the press.

Hearst suggested that the best response to crime would be the deportation of illegal aliens. Then he turned his attention to Hoover's failure to combat crime adequately: "Would it not be well if President Hoover, instead of sententiously delivering useless platitudes, would actually do something to rid the country of the gangsters who infest it?"

Hearst's public pronouncements on crime did not always dovetail with his own business practices, where a laissez-faire attitude toward violence and criminal acts carried out in the name of his political aspirations seems to have held sway. From time to time, he spoke out against organized crime and its insidious connections to politics and corruption. But to achieve prominence in Chicago in the early part of the twentieth century, Hearst was an organizer of organized crime. His bloody newspaper wars became the training ground for Al Capone and the Prohibition racketeering boss Dion O'Banion, a former chief of circulation for the Hearst newspapers in Chicago. At times, Hearst's language seemed to be dismissive of society's concerns about gangsters and the mob. He was unfazed by criminals (including those in his employ) who circumvented immoral or foolish laws like Prohibition. As his longtime employee Hayes Perkins wrote in his diary in 1930, "[Hearst] is a law unto himself." In a signed page one editorial published in March 1932 Hearst wrote about what he saw as greater crimes against society than those perpetrated by better-known gangsters:

The income tax system has become the greatest racket in the United States and the Government the biggest racketeer. . . . The tax system has made bullies out of Government agents and a blackmailer out of the Government itself. Crime is compromised for cash and false accusations are made in order to be compromised by payment of blood money. . . . There are two great historical failures and political evils which this country can indelibly engrave on the blackest pages of its record. One is the wholly ineffective and un-American policy of prohibition and the other is the inequitable, tyrannical, Bolshevistic policy of confiscatory income taxation.

In July 1929 the nation was startled by two back-to-back prison disturbances at separate facilities in upstate New York. At a prison in Clinton one
convict was shot dead while trying to murder an officer, and two others
were killed while attempting an escape. A week later, the Auburn prison—
which had the reputation of being the most humane prison in the world—
was the scene of massive fires and unrest. Two inmates were killed, and a
number of guards were seriously wounded. Naturally these prison riots (and
a third one that occurred in Colorado in October) generated big headlines
and big stories in the Hearst newspapers, and the *International Newsreel*
which showed aerial views of smoke billowing from the destruction of cell
blocks and prison yards. The riots also became an opportunity for Hearst to
advocate for an overhauling of the prison system by exposing the problems
of overcrowding and robotlike regimentation. Governor Franklin Roosevelt was quoted as saying that prisons should be modernized "as an act of
simple humanity." In an article entitled "Prison System Held Failure," a psy-
chiatrist articulated Hearst's position on society's dismal response to crime:
"If society continues to use unscientific methods in housing criminals and
treating them en masse, rather than as individuals, jail breaks certainly will
continue. All criminals are psychiatric studies and only from such viewpoint
can rehabilitation be hoped for."

The prison riots of 1929 were the impetus for a Cosmopolitan film that
went into production for MGM later that same year called *The Big House*.
Early on, Hearst's production company recognized that a prison drama
would be a hot film property. It also suspected such a film might be controversial. It sent the Hays Office a summary of *The Big House* in hopes of
averting censorship issues and to put its plans on record should some other
production company swoop in to steal its thunder. James Wingate, of the
Hays Office's Studio Relations Committee, thought the prison problem was
serious and that a film publicizing it might be useful. The screenwriter
Frances Marion, who already had more than a dozen Cosmopolitan films
under her belt, and her husband, director George Hill, were assigned to the
project. The couple studied Hearst newspaper clippings on the New York
and Colorado prison riots, and they personally visited San Quentin Prison.
At the San Francisco facility, Marion observed a brawny but good-natured
inmate nicknamed "Butch" and immediately came up with a character
called "Machine Gun" Butch, casting actor Wallace Beery in the role.

In the *The Big House*, actors Beery, Chester Morris, and Robert Mont-
gomery play three inmates who struggle for their humanity in a cruel and
ineffectual system of justice. The film's climax—a prison break thwarted by
authorities in a merciless assault of machine guns and army tanks—is sug-

gestive of real prison stories recently chronicled in the newspapers. In a transitional sequence near the end of the film, the producers show the convicts in a sympathetic light and make a clear association to their newspaper sources. A brief shot of a newspaper shows a headline announcing that one of the convicts saved the life of a guard during the riot. Above the headline is the masthead of Hearst's *Examiner* (although no specific city is indicated).

The Big House is one of the first talking pictures to be set almost entirely in a prison, and it set the pattern—in its use of language and character types—for many prison films to come. Reviewers noted that the picture was written and acted with surprising restraint. *International Photographer* magazine pointed out that the film's impressive camerawork and lighting helped to propel the drama and deliver its message about the inhumane conditions in prisons: "Here is an effect achieved by contrasting lights and shadows—shadows, cruel, cold hard, overpowering in their intensity; shadows that seem to breathe the grimness of prison. . . . The effects of these shots are highly impressive, due to the lighting treatment, which seems to bring forth more clearly and forcefully than could otherwise be obtained the relentless efficiency, the everlasting constriction of Law wrapping its coils about the criminal."

Under Cedric Gibbons's art direction, the visuals in *The Big House* reinforce a sense of the powerful state overwhelming the individual. In fact, some of Gibbons's sets are reminiscent of an earlier film about conformity versus individuality, Fritz Lang's *Metropolis*, produced in 1926 for Germany's Ufa Company. *The Big House*, which was released to theaters in the summer of 1930, was nominated for an Academy Award for best picture of the year. Beery was nominated for best actor, and Douglas Shearer for the film's sound recording. Frances Marion won her first Oscar for screenwriting. It was a sign of Hearst's achievement with *The Big House* that censorship boards in Ohio sought to ban the film in their state. The *St. Louis Star* newspaper responded to the threat with an editorial praising the film and its message:

> This is a great tribute to the people of Ohio and to motion pictures. It shows that an artistic medium subject to criticism for many vapid and commonplace offerings, for many offenses against good taste and decency, can and sometimes does strike deep into human life and appeal to the highest promptings of the human heart. It shows that the people of Ohio, with plenty to keep them occupied in their daily lives, can be so deeply stirred by the sight of wrongs inflicted through their corporate entity, the state; that the state servants immediately responsible dare not face the consequences of such revelation.

In the late 1920s a group of six Chicago industrialists came together as a response to the growing power of Al Capone and the inability of the police and the government to control his criminal activities. For the most part these men kept their identities a secret from the public, but the local newspapermen they befriended used the covert angle as a romantic tease for their readers and dubbed them the Secret Six. It was generally believed that the Secret Six were motivated by a belief that Capone was a danger to society at large. But it must be assumed that these successful men felt their own business growth and opportunities in Chicago were being threatened by Capone's increasing dominance. The precise nature of the work of the Secret Six remains a mystery, but they were without a doubt one of the most elite vigilante groups in U.S. history. Their members included prominent leaders of the Chicago community such as the chairman of Sears, the president of the Association of Commerce, and the head of the Chicago Bar Association. By some accounts they raised $1 million or more to hire private detectives, conduct wiretaps, and pay informants in the hope of bringing Capone to justice. They apparently worked closely with the Internal Revenue Service and others, including the legendary law officer Elliot Ness and his Untouchables.

The Secret Six were an outgrowth of several public crime-fighting organizations that sprang up in Chicago in the late 1920s. The most widely recognized of these was the Chicago Crime Commission, which gathered reams of information on crime and collected testimony from various experts. An organization less known today but well publicized in Chicago at the time was the American Crime Study Commission. Its membership included the pioneering social activist Jane Addams, former governor Charles Whitman of New York, various judges, and a significant number of Hearst newspapermen from Chicago. Its chairman was Hearst himself. Hearst attended sessions of the organization, and he publicized its work in his papers. The idea for the commission was said to have originated in 1926 with the publication of a Hearst-signed editorial entitled "We Cannot Cure Murder by Murder." In June 1927 Hearst said that his commission had been established to seek the causes and cures for crime. He defended his newspapers' approach to crime reporting, saying that "the duty of a newspaper is to record the events which happen in the world, the good occurrences and the bad occurrences, the achievements of worthy people, the mistakes and failures of the unfortunate and the evil deeds of the unworthy." In July 1927 the *New York American* went to San Francisco's San Quentin prison to find an unusual expert to praise the open-minded work of Hearst's crime study. "Certainly," an inmate named John F. Kelly was quoted as saying, "no field of scientific endeavor ever presented the complications of this most humane undertaking, and Hearst deserves to be highly commended for taking the initiative."

Whether Hearst had any direct involvement with the Secret Six has not been documented. But clearly, as a businessman with significant capital invested in Chicago and as a leading figure in Chicago's crime study organizations, he would have been keenly aware of their efforts. He was sufficiently interested in the Secret Six to produce a film in 1931 that used their activities as a jumping-off point and their mysterious name as a title. Cosmopolitan's *The Secret Six* reunited the team of Frances Marion, George Hill, and Wallace Beery. As before, the actor, writer, and director got their inspiration from Hearst and his newspaper coverage. "We like to work out stories from actualities, so that they echo life itself," Hill would later say. " 'The Big House,' for instance, had its inception in the newspapers, as also did 'The Secret Six.' " Beery, who played a role based on Al Capone, would later describe his character as "real" because "he came right out of police records and the newspapers." Today, *The Secret Six* is mostly remembered as one of the earliest vehicles for superstars of the 1930s Clark Gable and Jean Harlow. The film was also a conduit for expressing a dictatorial streak in Hearst's notions about combating crime.

The Hays Office found surprisingly little in *The Secret Six* that was offensive. A scene of police taking money from gangsters and the film's gloomy approach to life in the city were somewhat objectionable, but the film's message was ultimately praised. "The picture does contain one powerful suggestion," an aide to Hays wrote the movie czar, "namely, that when the people of the community band together it is not difficult to whip the criminals, and in this respect the picture has a rather vital place in these days of gangdom." In Chicago *The Secret Six* passed the usually tough city censorship board unscathed. A prerelease serialization in the Hearst papers had generated enormous public interest in the film that the board was not inclined to disregard. In addition Hearst had a fix-it man in Chicago named Jim Bickett who had previously been called in to smooth things over with local censors. In other parts of the country, the film was not viewed as being so harmless. *The Secret Six* was apparently marketed toward children, and when a twelve-year-old New Jersey boy went home and shot his friend in the head after seeing the film, there was a statewide drive to ban it.

Cosmopolitan's *Beast of the City*, released by MGM in March 1932, was another example of Hearst's forays into the crime genre. The film, directed by Charles Brabin and with a standout performance by a sexy, tough-talking Jean Harlow, tells the story of crime's assault on society, shifting its emphasis from the gangster to the police. The effect of this reallocation of sympathies, however, is somewhat murky, since the police chief, played by Walter Huston, condones methods that are somewhat indistinguishable from those employed by the gangsters. During the production of *Beast of the City*, there was some speculation in the film trade papers that the movie was made after discussions between Herbert Hoover and Louis B. Mayer on how best to glorify the police during the ongoing crime wave. One can imagine Hearst agreeing in principle to a film that boosted law enforcement, but it is doubtful he wanted Hoover to get credit for anything in one of his productions. It was only a year earlier that Hearst had published an editorial attacking a Hoover speech on crime for being filled with vagaries and seemingly glorifying inaction. Surprisingly, a portion of that very same speech was spliced in as the written foreword to *The Beast of the City*.

The decision to open *The Beast of the City* with a Hoover quote indicates Mayer's strong hand in the production. After the film was completed and screened for him, Hearst sent Louis B. Mayer a telegram that outlined in some detail his objections to the film's tone and his suggestions for how to improve the story:

Dear Louis:

I don't like the lesson of Beast of the City, and I don't believe you and Irving do if you analyze it. The police chief swears to do his duty and does it. What is the consequence? He is criticized by the press, repudiated by the public, humiliated by the jury, and finally killed by the gangsters, leaving a lovely family without protection. Under such circumstances, the average policeman or the average person will say, what's the use of trying to be honest? The picture has proved that honesty is the worst policy. It is all right for the boy to be killed. There is no other way out for him. But why murder all the police after making clear that they all have families dependent on them? We establish clearly not that the wages of sin is death, but that the wages of virtue is death, and I guess most policemen will decide when they see the picture that the easiest way is to take the money. I suppose I am all wrong, as usual, but I think that the wholesale slaughter at the end is ludicrous and the dying handclasp a cheap study in strained sentiment. The director even had to shoot poor Jean Harlow in the little belly she had used so effectively in her dancing number earlier in the picture. The only person who wasn't shot was the supervisor, and he should have been. Moreover, why wait till sunrise?

MGM disregarded Hearst's advice. There is no evidence that Hearst pursued the matter and no explanation for why he appears to have been relatively passive about influencing the content of his picture. Possibly, he gave up his challenge for the sake of some greater aim that he had in mind with Mayer. Nevertheless, Hearst's telegram is revealing of his momentary view on how to deal with crime in film and perhaps tells us something about the compromising of ideals in Hollywood. When the film was released, Hearst held nothing back in promoting it. One of his reviewers would call it "exciting melodrama, stirring entertainment with acting powerful and convincing."

ELECTION RESULTS

During the last week of October 1932, practically every female star in the film industry received a telegram from their favorite Hollywood blonde: "Will you be one of 100 motion picture girls joining my committee by donating $100 to Roosevelt campaign fund. If I secure this committee I will give $5,000 myself to Democratic cause. Send contributions to me at Metro Goldwyn Mayer studio. Thank you. Marion Davies."

Davies's generosity to Franklin Roosevelt's campaign for the presidency was coupled with a $25,000 personal check from Hearst, who suggested it be used for radio advertising. Hearst and Davies's financial backing was part of a concerted effort to help Roosevelt, but Hearst had originally been cool to FDR when the New York governor's friends lobbied for support in early 1932. Hearst was not eager to jump on the candidate's bandwagon even after Roosevelt publicly changed his position on the League of Nations and internationalism to one more in line with his own. Hearst's nominal candidate at the time was Speaker of the House John Nance Garner, a cigar-chomping Texan with whom he had had a casual friendship since their days together in Congress at the turn of the century. With Hearst's publicity machine in gear and his political connections in California, Illinois, and Texas put to use, Garner was able to arrive at the Democratic Convention in June with a significant number of delegates. He was far short of the two-thirds required for the nomination, but he had enough strength to influence the choice. Only after Hearst was convinced by Joseph Kennedy and others that denying Roosevelt a victory would result in the convention's turning to former governor Al Smith rather than Garner did Hearst order his candidate's delegates to release their votes.

The prospect of Al Smith getting the nomination of the Democratic Party was no small matter to Hearst. He had long despised the man. As

Davies would later write, Hearst's feelings toward Smith may have been more personal than political:

> The only open attack on living in sin, being a mistress and all that, was from Al Smith when he was campaigning for something or other, president, maybe [1928]. He made a stump speech, and then W.R. wrote an article and said he had no respect for a man who would do that. Then Mr. Smith made another speech. He started in on "the man who attacks me." There was a little bit of a legal thing I guess. He didn't mention my name, but everybody knew who he meant. . . . W.R. wrote a few articles in the paper, and then Mr. Smith figured out that he couldn't get even with a newspaperman, so he tried to attack me, by the grapevine route. When anybody ever said anything to W.R. about me, he would be ready to kill them. He didn't care about himself, but he wouldn't take anything about me.

With Hearst's help, Roosevelt secured the nomination, and Garner was picked to fill the vice presidential slot. Immediately after the convention Hearst was actively engaged in supporting his Democratic candidates. From San Simeon he instructed Millicent, commuting between the Clarendon and her Long Island mansion, to cozy up to FDR and the Democratic National chairman, Jim Farley. In late July she accepted a post as head of the women's division of the Nassau County club for FDR, and later she donated $10,000 as seed money to stimulate the selling of Roosevelt-Garner medallions to bring additional money to the campaign war chest. Using his wife as a go-between, Hearst coached candidate Roosevelt on subjects for speeches and offered other advice on how best to run the campaign (he suggested that FDR follow the methods of the Warren G. Harding campaign, or what would later be called a "rose garden" strategy, and let others run around the country for him). On Hearst's instructions a coordinated plan was followed in the fall of 1932 to boost Roosevelt and Garner at every possible opportunity, using the resources of his newspapers, his newsreels, his chain of radio stations, and the two women closest to him.

As vindictive and ruthless as he might be to others, Hearst still expected an old-fashioned, gentlemen's-agreement form of acceptance of his own place among the power elite. He was not foolish enough to think he would not have his share of enemies, but he expected and practically demanded that his intelligence, his self-proclaimed patriotism, and even his relationship with Davies be respected. In part, Hearst's single-minded desire for acceptance of Davies drove him into the arms of Roosevelt and away from both

Smith and President Herbert Hoover, the Republican nominee. In 1928 Hearst supported Hoover when the alternative was Smith, but they never really trusted each other. Between 1929 and 1932 the two men met only a couple of times and then only briefly for lunch. Apparently a final break occurred when Hoover rejected an invitation to visit San Simeon, which Hearst interpreted as a rejection of his summons to meet and accept his mistress. Roosevelt, as Hearst undoubtedly knew, was no Hoover when it came to the issue of mistresses. If it might help him to win the election in 1932, Roosevelt saw no harm in embracing a man with the kind of lifestyle he himself enjoyed.

The inevitable Washington-Hollywood love feast of 1932 occurred on the night of September 24 at the Olympic Stadium, in Los Angeles. Roosevelt's stop in LA was the climax of a campaign swing through California that started in San Francisco. A special train took the candidate through Santa Barbara, where he addressed a gathering and met privately with Hearst. The campaign train then moved on to Los Angeles. An hour outside LA, the train came to a stop so that Roosevelt could deliver a short speech that was carried over station KFWB, the Hearst-owned *Los Angeles Examiner*–affiliated radio station. At the Hollywood Bowl FDR addressed an overflowing crowd. In the evening a Motion Picture Electrical Parade and Sports Pageant was held at the Coliseum. The event, which was attended by tens of thousands, was advertised as both a rally for FDR and a benefit for the Marion Davies Foundation for Crippled Children. The pageant's official program, which included a full-page photograph of Davies, described the event as "a series of illuminated floats, nationally famed bands and marching organizations with a galaxy of cinema stars riding in decorated motor cars heading the spectacular procession." According to *Variety*, Jack Warner had called up every major motion picture star and asked them to attend. Most did, but a few, like Marie Dressler, loyal Republicans and loyal to both Hoover and Louis B. Mayer, turned Warner down. When the mayor of Los Angeles refused to attend, Will Rogers stepped in as emcee. He was one of two people to introduce FDR to those who had gathered to see and hear him. The other was Marion Davies. There is no record of what Davies said, but Rogers's speech was recalled in a book written by his wife, who attended the event: "There must be a hundred thousand people here tonight. This is the biggest audience in the world that ever paid to see a politician. . . . Now, I don't want you to think that I am overawed by being asked to introduce you. I'm not. I'm broadminded that way and will introduce anybody. And if this introduction lacks enthusiasm or floweriness, you must remember you're only

a candidate yet. Come back as President and I will do right by you. I'm
wasting no oratory on a prospect."

Over the open arena a Goodyear dirigible carrying International News
Service photographers took snapshots of the kaleidoscope below, thousands
of people moving in a spray of klieg lights, a flotilla of floats, and a dust-
kicking celebrity polo match. Hearst's motion picture cameramen captured
the scene from the ground, and his film company released two separate
newsreels over the following week that showed highlights of FDR's entire
campaign through California. Curiously, in the sections devoted to the Coliseum show, neither Hearst nor Davies, the prime movers of the night, can
be seen in any of the surviving footage.

Herbert Hoover campaign staffers referred to the Coliseum event as "the
Hearst–Marion Davies–Roosevelt show" and described it as a strange triumvirate they were convinced would spell disaster for the Democrats and
signal their own success in November. Some of those working for Hoover
who thought they could exploit the event were *Los Angeles Times* publisher
Norman Chandler and Frank Knox, the general manager of the Hearst
newspapers between 1928 and 1931 who, though a Republican, would serve
in FDR's third administration as secretary of the navy. On September 25
Knox received a letter from a Hoover operative in California describing his
observations at the gala event. In his letter, the unnamed campaign worker
can hardly contain his glee:

> I came to Los Angeles last night to witness the Roosevelt–Hearst–
> Marion Davies show. What a reaction it is to follow this unholy exhi-
> bition. Plenty of pictures were taken and the public address by Miss
> Davies before the assembled thousands thanking Governor Roosevelt
> for his part in making the party a big success was a "wow"—Nature
> will do the rest.... In a later letter I wrote [Mark] Reed [national com-
> mitteeman in the state of Washington] and told him that Hearst,
> always inclined to overdoing things, would make a fatal mistake with
> Roosevelt before the campaign ended. I think the Hearst–Marion
> Davies–Roosevelt show here which Hearst promoted (of course) is
> the fatal mistake. The reaction is rolling up like mountains apparently
> everywhere. Will you imagine the fun I am having placing the dyna-
> mite around in strategic spots. When I see you I will give you many a
> laugh in my story of the crazy antics of the frothing, frantic Hearst
> crowd. In my own way I have hung the name William Rasputin Hearst
> on the old man. Up to now the "gang" have had no knowledge of just
> what I am doing. They will undoubtedly before long. Lots of good

luck to you and many thanks for the opportunity of doing work of which I am proud in a cause that will certainly win when the facts are known, and they will be known.

Knox sent the anonymous report on the Hearst-sponsored event to President Hoover, who gave only a brief reply. "Such things," Hoover wrote Knox, "do one good."

Hoover's men were overly optimistic to say the least; on election night Roosevelt achieved a landslide victory. California went solidly for FDR, a triumph that Senator William Gibbs McAdoo attributed in large part to Hearst's Los Angeles rally. When news of Roosevelt's win reached the public, Hearst was with Davies in California, but he had his own ambassador inside the newly elected president's inner sanctum. Gathered around FDR in his Biltmore Hotel suite in New York City was a handful of close friends and advisers, including Jim Farley, the Vincent Astors, and a tireless worker for various causes, Millicent Hearst.

Between election day and inauguration day, in March 1933, Hearst continued to offer advice to Roosevelt. The two men exchanged messages through emissaries and spoke to each other on the telephone about plans for the new administration. During a break in a story conference in the Cosmopolitan bungalow on the MGM lot, where a film project called *Casting Office* was being discussed, among others, Hearst called Roosevelt with his personal choices for the cabinet. When Davies noticed that Sam Marx, an MGM story editor, was eavesdropping as Hearst gave his recommendations, she turned to him and whispered, "The Chief is casting, too!"

Others had advice for FDR on what to do for Hearst in a new administration. *Variety* reported that Hearst's son George was being considered as assistant secretary of the navy. In early 1933 one of FDR's supporters, Colonel Edward House, thought the elder Hearst should be made an official member of the president's team. House suggested that Hearst be appointed ambassador to Germany, because he was a forceful personality who might have some influence on Hitler. Precisely what House thought Hearst could do is unclear. House was apparently of two minds about the Jews in Germany; he was disturbed at the way they were being mistreated by Hitler, but he also believed they "should not be allowed to dominate the economic and intellectual life in Berlin as they have done for a long time."

With his political and motion picture industry ties, Hearst may have been a serious candidate for a diplomatic mission to Germany. In the spring of 1933, the U.S. State Department was anxiously working with contacts in Berlin and representatives of the Hays Office to get a clearer picture of what was happening to the film industry in Hitler's Germany, an important trade partner. There were increasingly troublesome reports coming out of Berlin that American studio representatives headquartered there who were Jewish were being manhandled and forced to leave the country. It was also rumored that Alfred Hugenberg—head of the Ufa film company and minister of economics in Hitler's cabinet—was purging his film operation of Jews and possibly planning to sever all ties to Hollywood.

Gabriel Over the White House was one of several cinematic inauguration gifts that Hearst gave Franklin Roosevelt in gratitude for the courtesy extended toward him and Marion Davies and assistance in elevating his political profile in Hollywood. Between election day and inauguration day—which in 1933 took place on March 4—Roosevelt and his family were shown at their best in several Hearst newsreels. During this period *Hearst Metrotone* began preparing a special two-reel documentary on the life of the new president called *Man of the Hour* that it planned to have ready for movie theaters within days of the inauguration. The minidocumentary would be a companion piece to two MGM feature films with the Cosmopolitan trademark that Hearst hoped would give FDR and his plans for the nation a psychological boost.

No Hearst motion picture—with the possible exception of *Patria*—has been more written about by contemporary critics and film historians than *Gabriel Over the White House*. Ever since its release in March 1933, the film's genesis, its merits, and its impact have been explored. Reviewers at the time called *Gabriel* the first important political film of the sound era and hailed it as the first Hollywood production to acknowledge the Depression openly. Although film historians have not put *Gabriel* in the league of great films, they have generally agreed that it was a defining motion picture that expressed a tendency shared by many during the economic turmoil of the 1930s to gravitate toward totalitarian solutions to society's problems. From the very start, Hearst's involvement in the production of *Gabriel* was seen as a key ingredient of the film's political sensibility, but surprisingly little attention has been paid to how the film fit into the broader picture of Hearst's life in the early 1930s or his views on crime, on dictatorship, and on the uses of film. There are really two *Gabriel Over the White House*s: the film and the novel it is based on. There are some significant differences between the two versions, and a brief exploration of both is necessary, since the film is not as close to the book as Hearst wanted it to be. The *Gabriel* project was on an exceedingly fast track at

MGM. Producers there, including Hearst, became aware of the novel *Gabriel Over the White House* at least one month before it was published. According to more than one account, Walter Wanger, newly hired producer at MGM, got his hands on the book property in early January 1933, and he immediately became interested in making the story his first picture at the studio. At about the same time, Hearst and Wanger held discussions in which Hearst expressed a desire to present *Gabriel* as a Cosmopolitan Production. Within a week or two, the two men were working closely together on the project.

Hearst and Wanger had a number of things in common, including a soft spot for showgirls—Wanger's first wife was Davies's friend and Ziegfeld Follies beauty Justine Johnstone—and a passion for the political possibilities associated with the medium of film. As a maverick filmmaker himself, Wanger must have viewed Hearst's path in Hollywood as both an inspiration and a window on the pitfalls threatening the Hollywood outsider. The two men first met around 1916. At that time, working as a manager for a theater company, Wanger secured the services of actor and dancer Irene Castle to appear in a new serial to be produced by Hearst's International Film Service. With its message of "preparedness" and its anti-Japanese undercurrents, *Patria* gave Wanger his first exposure to film's potential for propaganda; the film's release and the trouble with President Woodrow Wilson demonstrated what controversies might be generated by taking such a direction in the film industry. Wanger got a further idea of what film could do to sway public opinion and what Hearst's influence was all about when he joined the film division of the government's World War I propaganda operation, the Committee on Public Information. In a key position in this unit was at least one Hearst operative with whom Wanger would work in the 1930s, Cosmopolitan Productions' Edgar Hatrick.

Gabriel Over the White House was a natural progression from *Patria* (and the Creel Committee as well), and Hearst was as hands-on with this film as he had been on the previous productions where he encountered Wanger. On February 12 the *New York Times* reviewed the novel, which was published by the New York publishers Farrar and Rinehart. The author of *Gabriel Over the White House* was listed as anonymous. But a couple of weeks later, when the book was published in Great Britain, the author was listed as Thomas Frederick Tweed, a political adviser and chief of staff to the former British prime minister David Lloyd George between 1916 and 1931. Why the book was published anonymously in the United States has never been explained, but an intriguing possibility is that Hearst had something to do with the making of the book as well as the film. According to William Randolph Hearst Jr. and a surviving member of the Rinehart family, the Hearst Corporation had an unpublicized affiliation with the book's U.S. publishers, possibly through the magazine division. There may have also been a connection between Hearst and Tweed. Lloyd George and Hearst were on friendly terms for many years, and they shared a similar point of view on political matters. In fact, between the publication date of the novel *Gabriel Over the White House* and the film release date in late March 1933, the former prime minister was regularly contributing opinion pieces that were syndicated by the Hearst wire service.

The basic narrative structure of the novel is retained in the film version of *Gabriel Over the White House*. The story is set in the near future of the late 1930s. It opens with the inauguration of the fictional president, Judd Hammond (Walter Huston), a Tammany-style politician who approaches governing and the issues of the day with blatant cynicism. Hammond surrounds himself with party bosses and functionaries, and his White House seems more like a backroom saloon than an executive mansion. In the film's early scenes the new president displays the worst characteristics of two recent presidents: the good-old-boy style of Warren G. Harding and the ineffectiveness of Herbert Hoover (in the background of a later scene there is actually a photograph of Harding on a shelf). Hammond is identified as a bachelor, but he has a female secretary who visits him after hours and is clearly his mistress. Everything changes for Hammond and the nation when a car accident results in a severe blow to the president's head. As Hammond lies in a coma in his bedroom at the White House, on the verge of death, a powerful and mystical force hovers over him. As the lacy window curtains rise and the sound of distant trumpets is heard, Hammond is revived and spiritually enlightened. Is it the work of the archangel Gabriel or Cosmopolitan Productions' special effects department?

Looking dazed and disheveled, a truly new new president throws away his old ways and decides to attack the country's economic troubles and social ills full force. As dictatorial behavior replaces his usual indifference, Hammond suddenly has no time for his former party boss cronies. Without blinking, Hammond fires cabinet officials who stand in his way. When he learns that the leader of a group of unemployed men and women has been killed during a march, Hammond usurps the power of Congress, declares martial law, and establishes a far-reaching public works program to help the poor and disenfranchised. Hammond offers no refuge to the film's villain and his nemesis, an Al Capone stand-in named Nick Diamond. Calling the hoodlum to the White House, he pressures him to give up his bootlegging business or risk an unrestrained response from the "federal police." When an unrepentant Diamond has his thugs spray the White House with machine gun bullets, Hammond orders an armed tank assault on Diamond and his followers, who are busy ridiculing Hammond and drinking their bootleg booze in a fortresslike hideout. Although many of the gangsters are killed in the shootout, some survive, and these men are brought before authorities in a Nazilike tribunal (there is no jury present) and quickly sentenced to death before a firing squad. With little fanfare the criminals are executed, the Statue of Liberty standing proudly in the harbor in the background.

With his crime crusade concluded, Hammond turns his attention to international affairs. He is incensed that so many countries have found the money to pursue an arms race but have reneged on their promises to pay off their outstanding war loans to the United States. Using the same bullying approach against the leaders of the world that he used against domestic criminals and Congress, Hammond doesn't threaten prison; he holds the threat of total annihilation over them. To demonstrate that he means business, Hammond gathers scores of foreign diplomats on his yacht to witness a dramatic show of military might. Putting in a phone call to his air force commanders, Hammond orders a dozen or more bombers that are hovering overhead to drop their weapons on two obsolete American battleships stationed in the waters a safe distance from the yacht. "The next war," Hammond tells his fellow world leaders, "will be a terrible story of the terrible failure of antiquated machinery and antiquated methods and of the horrifying destructiveness of modern agencies of war. . . . The next war will depopulate the earth." Hammond's theatrics do the trick, and in the next scene prime ministers, kings, and other leaders gather at the White House for the signing of the "Washington Covenant," a document that will disarm the world and usher in a millennium of peace. At the moment of his greatest triumph, just as he is about to sign his own name to the document, Hammond collapses. Taken to his room, he seems briefly to be reverting to his former state, before the first Gabriel visit. Has everything since that moment been a dream or a near-death experience? Never mind: Hammond closes his eyes, the sound of the trumpets and the lace curtains rises—the president is dead.

It is easy to see why Hearst was attracted to the domestic and international themes in the novel of *Gabriel Over the White House*. Hearst was not only able to translate these themes into the action of the film, he rewrote whole narrative passages and lengthy dialogue sequences to approximate more closely his own views on fighting crime, invigorating the economy, and disarming the nations of the world. Despite Hearst's extensive input, however, he was not satisfied with the end product, which had gone through several editing stages. Probably the least destructive changes, from Hearst's point of view, came from President Roosevelt himself. After requesting a rough cut of the film for viewing in early March, FDR suggested minor changes. (As an example, the climactic scene where Hammond demonstrates the air power of the United States was moved from a battleship to a yacht.) Apparently, all of Roosevelt's suggestions were followed. Numerous other retakes requested by Louis B. Mayer and Will Hays were made throughout March. In fact, more time was spent on retakes than on the original shooting of the film.

While all these cooks were getting involved in the film's production, Hearst found a way to help himself out with Will Hays and other censorship boards by coming to the aid of the motion picture industry just when it needed rescuing. At the time of *Gabriel's* release, William Irving Sirovich, a congressional representative from New York, was pushing for a resolution calling for a broad-based investigation of "financial, operative, and business irregularities and illegal actions by interests inside and outside the motion and sonant pictures industry." Sirovich was particularly vexed by the calculated destruction of the independent motion picture theaters "through devices of interlocking, long-term franchises, preferential zoning, clearances, and protection." A House colleague supporting Sirovich's resolution told Congress that Hollywood was controlled by a "coterie of manipulators and racketeers" who were defrauding stockholders and "who have been allowed to continue their peculations and fraud unmolested, controlling, as they do, some of the highest officials in the several States and even in our own government." Once again, negative publicity about Hollywood and its power structure threatened to affect the financial stability of the industry. The playwright Elmer Rice was quoted in a Missouri newspaper as saying, "I would rather be controlled by Hitler, Mussolini or Stalin than Will Hays."

Hays and his operatives worked hard to minimize news reports of a possible investigation and to counteract the attacks. The little the Hearst press published on the subject was blatantly dismissive of Representative Sirovich. The congressman was charged with being a publicity seeker who would spend a quarter of million dollars of taxpayers' money during the depths of the Depression. There were also editorials in the Hearst press extolling the virtues of the film industry. The *Chicago Herald-Examiner* called the Sirovich investigation "ridiculous" and recommended that everyone "go to the show" because "there is no surer way of getting rid of the blues . . . there is no wiser investment than in good amusement and we need it more when times are dull."

On the eve of a vote on the resolution, John F. Curry, a Tammany Hall leader, and John H. McCooey, a Brooklyn Democratic boss, suddenly showed up in Washington. Curry and McCooey went to the White House and met with Roosevelt's aide, Louis Howe. The *New York Times* speculated they had come to discuss patronage matters. After the meeting they simply told the press that they were "here to pay our respects." Apparently the two Tammany men also saw an unknown number of congressmen during their stay in the capital.

On May 12 the Sirovich resolution was defeated. The Hearst press noted that the Roosevelt administration had taken a "hands-off policy" toward it; however, according to *Variety* the quarter-million-dollar figure that had been used as a scare tactic had originated with the Federal Trade Commission. Meanwhile Sirovich continued to rail against "sinister lobbying" and "financial racketeers masquerading as honest men." On the same day of the defeat, Hays sent Hearst a telegram: "Matter just now concluded two hundred twenty eight to one hundred fifteen the right way. Thanks again and best wishes." Hearst responded to Hays on May 13 with a telegram of his own: "Thanks but do not thank me thank Mr. Curry he did the trick."

It is unknown precisely how much material from the *Gabriel Over the White House* novel or from Hearst's pen wound up on the MGM cutting room floor. On March 25, just days before the film *Gabriel Over the White House* premiered, Hearst wrote Mayer a letter in which he expressed his reluctant acceptance of FDR's input and the disdain he felt toward the MGM chief's intrusion:

> Still there were a lot of alterations in the picture which were not requested by the government and which in my humble opinion were in no way necessary. . . . I think you have impaired the effectiveness of the President's speech to the Congress because you have been afraid to say the things which I wrote and which I say daily in my newspapers and which you commend me for saying, but still do not sufficiently approve to put in your film. . . . I believe the picture will still be considered a good picture and perhaps an unusually good picture. Nevertheless, I think it was a better picture.

One of the novel's most interesting themes that never made it to the screen but must have strongly attracted Hearst and Wanger was President Hammond's use of modern propaganda methods—such as radio, film, and even television—to bypass democratic laws and the traditionally impartial press. The novel has a character (nowhere in the film) named Peale Lindsey who advises Hammond on propaganda matters. Lindsey is identified as a California native who got his start as a media mogul by taking over a newspaper from his father. After heading to New York, Lindsey became the head of a leading publicity firm with strong connections to Hollywood and the fledgling television industry. After holding a private meeting with President Hammond, Lindsey has a discussion with the president's staff about a project he is hatching. The scene seems remarkably like an encapsulated version of what propelled Hearst and Wanger to make their propaganda movie as an aid to FDR. To the somewhat dumbstruck gathering, Lindsey lays out a plan for a film production full of sensationalism and manipulation that would be funded by the president and produced to enhance the president's image with the public. As the book's narrator tells the story:

> Lindsey, whose company controlled one of the more important motion picture production concerns in Hollywood, had been instructed to prepare a film based on the story of the Chicago squatters. In the screen version Bronson [activist leader of the unemployed] was to have a highly melodramatic death with every adventitious aid to stimulate sentimentality and patriotism. Every conceivable artifice of the film industry was to accentuate the viciousness of the gangsters and there were to be passages that were nothing less than undisguised attacks on local officials who had failed to befriend the luckless squatters. It sounded dreadful—the most horrible atrocity ever to be inflicted on the patient and docile American cinemagoer. Before the symbolic Bronson finally fell dead, he was to wrap himself in Old Glory and call upon the President as the only savior of the nation. Before his eyes closed, he was to be granted visions of the future of a happy contented country at work and at play. The President was secretly to pay for this monstrous ballyhoo out of his own pocket. It had to be done quickly and arrangements made for a private subsidy, if necessary, to ensure its being shown in every picture house in the land. I was nauseated. It appeared to be a cheap, tawdry propaganda and absolutely pointless.

Gabriel Over the White House made an impression at the box office and at the real White House. President Roosevelt sent notes to Hearst and to Loews president Nicholas Schenck, thanking them both for their cooperation and their help to the new administration, and he told Walter Wanger that he saw the film three times. Hearst, however, continued to feel that he had been prevented from making the film he really wanted to make. His rift with Mayer would never fully heal, and it was probably a factor in the dissolution of their production partnership in 1934.

There seemed no reason to believe that Hearst and Walter Wanger would not work together again after *Gabriel*. Their collaboration had gone smoothly, and Wanger and his wife, Justine, were guests of Hearst and Davies at a San Simeon gathering in honor of writer George Bernard Shaw just days before the film's opening. For some unknown reason, however, Wanger turned against his friend and collaborator. In late 1934 he began production on a picture he viewed as a kind of sequel to *Gabriel*. *The President Vanishes*, directed by William Wellman and released in January 1935, is the story of a fictional president of the United States who is forced by a group of business moguls to enter the war in Europe (which had not yet actually begun) as a way to stimulate the economy. *The President Vanishes* is a virtual remake of *Gabriel Over the White House*, but it is even more dark and disturbing than that earlier film. In *The President Vanishes*, the disenchanted but orderly marchers of unemployed seen in *Gabriel* are replaced by a vigilante group called the Grey Shirts. They roam the streets beating up pacifists and antiwar demonstrators. The president appears, like Judd Hammond, to be a benevolent leader, but when he fakes his own kidnapping to avoid making a moral decision about declaring war, he proves himself capable of being as manipulative as anyone else. The film's message about political corruption relates directly to Hearst. The president is pressured to abandon his isolationist policy by a group of six mercenary businessmen who are willing to sacrifice peace to fill their own pockets. The conspiratorial group is made up of a judge, a former senator, a banker, a munitions manufacturer, and an oilman based on John D. Rockefeller Sr. The sixth member of this businessmen group is a newspaper publisher with a readership of ten million who plasters the nation with sensationalist propaganda posters to stir up war sentiment. The character is clearly meant to recall Hearst and his jingoist methods during the Spanish-American War.

In *The President Vanishes*, Wanger fashioned his former film partner as a cynical communications mogul exploiting the public. As might be expected, Hearst was not pleased by the characterization, and it was rumored that he worked with the Hays Office to delay the release of the film and force Wanger to cut one whole reel from his original version. Wanger biographer Matthew Bernstein claims that Wanger's Hearst satire caused the producer to lose his entrée to San Simeon temporarily. This is possible, but it is untrue, as some have contended, that the Hearst press had orders to ban any mention of the film. Reviewers in more than one Hearst newspaper praised *The President Vanishes*, albeit without any reference to the publisher character based on Hearst.

Gabriel Over the White House was not the only feature film that Hearst offered FDR as he began his new administration. On March 24, 1933, a studio master print of an MGM picture tentatively titled *Service* was screened for Hearst. The film was based on an English stage play of the same name and dealt with the effects of the economic depression on a bookkeeper and his London department store. Hard times cause the department store owner—an angelic chap appropriately named Gabriel Service—to let a trusted employee go. Despite this sudden turn of events, the bookkeeper is not defeated, and his inner resourcefulness sees him through. When he is able to save Service from the clutches of an unscrupulous businessman seeking to take over the company, he is back on top, and all's well that ends well. Hearst was immediately drawn to the film's sentimentality and its spirit of optimism. When Louis B. Mayer told him that an effort was under way to rename the film *Looking Forward* as a way to take advantage of a book recently published with that title by Franklin Roosevelt, the country's optimist of the hour, Hearst was eager to help.

Hearst told Mayer he was willing to back the film as a Cosmopolitan Production and publicize it through his papers. Since the film's release was imminent, Mayer needed to act fast. He had already inserted a quote from Roosevelt in the film's foreword, but he still needed the president's okay on the title. When Hearst sent Mayer a telegram one day after the screening describing his reaction to the film, Mayer immediately sent a letter to the president's secretary Stephen T. Early, quoting Hearst's telegram in full. Hearst's telegram was so effusive about the film, about Mayer, and about FDR that one suspects it may have been a theater performance, written with the knowledge that Mayer intended to send it to the president. The telegram also seems to anticipate the Production Code of 1934 and the changes forced on film content in its wake.

"*Service*," Hearst's telegram to Mayer began,

> is a glorious picture and inspiring picture it should be of immense value in this depression. I think you are making a most valuable contribution toward the restoration of courage and confidence. This is the kind of picture which reflects credit on the industry and must give you pride in our profession. I wish the picture was a Cosmopolitan production it is the kind of picture I want to make and want to see the industry make. There have been gangster pictures and sex pictures

until the public is sick to death of them and until there is a rising tide of indignation and protest which may imperil the picture business. Why not have more pictures like Service which have an inspiring theme and a high purpose. I don't say that every picture must be serious there is of course need for romance and comedy and the lighter phase of life but occasionally a big picture with a useful helpful message gives dignity to the industry and commands the approval and the respect of the most captious and critical. I like the foreword from Roosevelt's address it is a good thing for the picture and a good thing for the President it is an endorsement of this attitude in picture which is really a fine editorial.

Clearly, Mayer was hoping that word of Hearst's interest would be a sufficient selling point for the president to agree to the title change. It was. On April 6 MGM announced the name change, and the president was sent a check from the studio for $7,500.

In late July 1934, several weeks after its release, the Cosmopolitan film *Manhattan Melodrama* was still playing at theaters around the country. As was their habit with films produced by their boss, the Hearst papers kept the film in front of the public with frequent boosts that had actually begun weeks before its release. On April 29 the *New York American* described the plot of the upcoming gangster picture, directed by W. S. Van Dyke:

"Manhattan Melodrama" [is] a story of life today in the seething metropolis of the nation. . . . Three stars play the leading roles in "Manhattan Melodrama," with Clark Gable and Myrna Loy, first teamed in "Men in White" [another Cosmopolitan film] again sharing the romantic leads. They are joined by William Powell, who plays Jim Wade, Gable's boyhood friend, who rises to the office of Governor of the State while Blackie Gallagher (Gable) becomes a power in the underworld. A thrilling climax is provided when their paths cross, bringing up the problem of loyalty to friendship or to the State on Jim's part. . . . The picture is a reflection of front page events that have amused, shocked and entertained New York for thirty years.

On the evening of July 22 *Manhattan Melodrama* achieved the kind of notoriety no one in the Hearst organization could have anticipated or desired. It happened at the Biograph Theater, in Chicago. In the audience of the 8:30 P.M. screening was John Dillinger, murderer and bank robber wanted by the FBI and dubbed "Public Enemy Number One" after breaking out of prison in March. It was speculated by some that Dillinger went to see the picture on that hot summer night in part because he saw the Gable role as a glamorized depiction of his own life in crime. Others said he was simply a big Myrna Loy fan or that he went to the theater for its "air-cooled" temperature. With Dillinger that night were two female escorts, a prostitute and a madam. Unbeknownst to Dillinger, in exchange for leniency on deportation charges the brothel keeper had tipped off the FBI to the gangster's moviegoing plans. As Dillinger watched *Manhattan Melodrama* the FBI surrounded the Biograph Theater. At 10:30 the lights in the theater went up, and Dillinger exited onto the street. With him were the prostitute and her madam, who was dressed in a bright orange dress (not red, as the myth developed) as a signal to the waiting FBI agents. Noting the suspicious movements of the undercover men outside, Dillinger reached for his pistol, but it was too late for him to escape. As he ran for the alley at the side of the theater, three bullets knocked him to the sidewalk. Dillinger was declared dead within minutes.

Overnight, photographs of the exterior of the Biograph Theater were published in newspapers across the country. Most of the stories about the shooting detailed the last fugitive days of Dillinger's life and the irony of his last "cinematic" moments. To assure the public that the FBI had in fact gotten their man (Dillinger had recently undergone plastic surgery to camouflage his identity), newsreel cameramen were permitted to take graphic footage of the gangster's bullet-ridden body as it was laid out in morgue. Within days, other photographs and news films were taken of the Biograph Theater. In the new pictures the theater's signboard had changed slightly from the night of the shooting: under *Manhattan Melodrama* and the title of a Mickey Mouse cartoon short were reflecting letters announcing a newsreel special called *Dillinger Scoop*.

The image of the Biograph Theater so widely dispersed by the media remained for decades a symbolic marquee hanging over the death of a gangster and marking the end of the gangster era. News of Dillinger's death in front of the theater came while Hearst was traveling in Europe. Reportedly, orders were received by the editors of the Hearst press that any future publicity on *Manhattan Melodrama* should avoid mention of the Cosmopolitan connection. From now on, Hearst's film ventures would be more circumspect in associating themselves with crime.

TRAVELING WITH DICTATORS

In the summer of 1934 Hearst traveled to Europe with a large party. From the brief reminiscences of this trip that he left behind, Hearst seems to have experienced the trip with a certain nostalgia for his past journeys abroad. "I knew Lenbach and Kaulbach and Stuck, and many of Munich's great artists," he wrote. "I also knew the café Luitpold and the Bierkellers quite well. In fact, I may say quite intimately." A visit to a modern art gallery also made him long for earlier times. "But what has become of Munich's art?" He asked rhetorically. "It has gone Communist." Still, Hearst enjoyed playing the role of tourist guide and elder teacher to a group that included his mistress, his sons, their wives, and Gandhi, one of Hearst and Davies's favorite German dachshunds. A staff of drivers, maids, and valets from San Simeon also accompanied Hearst, and according to more than one account among this group were a few rabidly pro-Nazi German-born employees who used the trip as a way to return to their homeland. The Hearst caravan also had its sprinkling of Hollywood's lesser-known luminaries, such as actors Dorothy Mackaill, Mary Carlisle, and Buster Collier and a traveling secretary named Harry Crocker, a relative of the famous California banking family, a sometime Hearst columnist, and a film industry contact.

As Hearst moved from town to town in Europe, he was never far from Hollywood. His motorcade of black sedans drove through the pastoral scenery, to the castles, museums, and the walled cities, as Hearst, in the role of location scout, came up with ideas for film stories, costumes, and set designs. In London in May, at the beginning of his travels, Hearst and Davies spent their evenings in the theater district, shopping for possible film projects. Hearst was in England when he was reminded of one of his very first film star fixations, actress and dancer Irene Castle. The star of 1917's *Patria* sent two cables to Hearst complaining about how a story in his *American Weekly* was claiming that the stylish actress had lambasted Hollywood fashions. To ease the tension, Hearst ordered his Sunday supplement editors to publish two separate complimentary articles about Castle.

In Rome Hearst took in an outdoor theatrical: Mussolini speaking to a crowd. It is not known if Hearst had a private audience with Mussolini at this time, but while the Hearst party was in Venice his secretary, Harry Crocker, apparently paid a call on another visitor to the city, Germany's propaganda minister and film czar Joseph Goebbels. Whether Hearst was in on their meeting or what they may have discussed is unknown, but, according to Crocker, he used the occasion to ask the Nazi leader to sign his autograph book.

In Venice Davies made an unpublicized visit to the Nineteenth International Biennial Art Exhibition, where she was most interested in seeing a portrait of herself that had been painted in 1928. The highly romanticized Davies painting had caused considerable controversy in Venice, since it had arrived at the exhibition a few weeks earlier unannounced and with no connection to any participating exhibitors. When Whitney Museum director Juliana Force learned that the large portrait, which had been painted by a Polish artist, was hanging in an area set aside for her American artist collection, she was outraged. To Mrs. Force and almost everyone else connected with the exhibit, it was plain that Hearst wanted his mistress to be celebrated in Europe during the couple's holiday there and had used his influence with the Italian government to bypass the basic requirements of the art show. Force ordered the painting to be removed and backed up her demand with a threat to pack up all her art work and ship it back to the United States. At first the Italians stalled for time, saying they were considering the Venetian Pavilion as an alternative site for the painting. Apparently this was not a satisfactory solution for Hearst, who ordered his International News Service representative in Italy, Seymour Berkson, to meet with Italian officials and pressure them to keep the Davies painting hanging right where it was. Although Mrs. Force filed a lawsuit against the organizers of the art show, the painting remained in the American art section when Davies arrived for a personal tour, and it stayed there until the show closed.

Davies's moving picture career was very much on Hearst's mind during his European trip. At the time, he and Davies considered tapping her nephew Charles Lederer to write a scenario for a project called *Movie Queen*, discussed at length in Hollywood before their departure for Europe. Other plans were made for MGM producer Lucien Hubbard (he oversaw Davies's last picture at Metro, *Operator 13*) to sail for Europe in late July in order to meet up with the Hearst party in London. The subject of this meeting was a project that never materialized, the film adaptation of "The Transgressor," a short story about a French prison camp, written by Anthony Richardson. Hearst had his eye on at least one other project for Davies during the summer of 1934, an MGM starring vehicle called *Marie Antoinette*.

Besides his preoccupation with motion pictures, Hearst was stimulated by photography during his trip to Europe. A lightweight motion picture camera was brought along on the trip, but Hearst's favorite type of camera was a relic of his youth, a double-lens stereo camera that produced still pictures with an illusion of three dimensions. In Germany Hearst bought actress Mary Carlisle a camera and gave her lessons in how to take artistic photographs. Hearst had long been interested in photography developments in

Germany. When he saw a photograph taken of himself with Davies drinking beer in a dark restaurant successfully reproduced in a German newspaper, he ordered the fast film process cameras for his newspaper operation back home. Hearst particularly admired the use of photographs and the design layout in the Ullstein Company's magazines, such as the illustrated weekly *Berliner Illustrierte*, a hugely popular magazine with a circulation well over one million. Ullstein was Germany's largest book, newspaper, and periodical publisher, but by 1933 the future of the Jewish-owned company was in serious doubt. With increasing demands by the Nazis that they "Aryanize" their corporate structure, the Ullstein family reluctantly decided to find a buyer. In 1934 they sold their company for a song to Max Winkler, a trustee of press agencies and film enterprises who was working on behalf of Propaganda Minister Joseph Goebbels. Hoping to take advantage of Ullstein's dissolution, the Hearst organization, through its magazine division head, Richard Berlin, successfully negotiated to acquire Ullstein's driving creative force. From London on July 17, where he was traveling with the Hearst party, Berlin sent Ullstein's departing managing director, Kurt Safranski, a letter:

Dear Mr. Szafranski [sic]:

Will be looking forward to seeing you [in] the early part of September, as we spoke yesterday. Indeed, I will enjoy having you with us. I am sure that you could contribute liberally to the success of our publications. Do not hesitate to write me in case you are having any difficulty with your visa. I will be able to help you.

A week later Berlin sent Safranski another letter, in which he discussed salary. Hearst was willing to start Safranski at $150 per week, a substantial cut from the $40,000 a year he made at Ullstein. But Safranski, a Jew, obviously did not need money as an incentive to leave the new Germany. Another factor encouraging to Safranski was the chance to work on *Pictorial Review*, a magazine that Dick Berlin was in the process of adding to the Hearst stable of periodicals. Safranski emigrated to the United States on October 1, 1934, and immediately began working for the Hearst magazines.

Also joining the Hearst team in 1934 was Martin Munkacsi, a Hungarian photographer and colleague of Safranski well known in Germany for his work on *Berliner Illustrierte*. Munkacsi had been to the United States a year or more before 1934 and had even photographed Hearst and Davies at San Simeon. In early 1935 Safranski traveled back to Central Europe searching for even more photographers to add to the Hearst organization. Before long, Safranski and Munkacsi's contributions to the look of the Hearst magazines—especially the elegantly produced *Town and Country*—began to get noticed. There was talk of a "German influence" on the magazines, and Hearst told Berlin that he appreciated the "photographic effectiveness" of his new employees.

One project that Safranski and Munkacsi were hoping would excite Hearst was a concept for an entirely new magazine that would mix the visual advances in Germany (including the strong red, black, and white color scheme of the cover of *Berliner Illustrierte*) with the vibrant approach to current events that was being achieved in newsreels. In December 1934 Safranski produced a dummy magazine that Berlin brought out to California for Hearst to see. Hearst was enthusiastic about the magazine concept, telling Berlin, "Well, go ahead—let's make such a book!" But, for some unknown reason, possibly related to paper costs, the project simmered on a back burner for months. In 1935, with Hearst's permission, Safranski brought the dummy to *Fortune* publisher Henry Luce. In November 1936 Hearst witnessed a rare opportunity slip through his fingers when Luce published the century's most famous magazine, simply titled *Life*.

On August 22, 1934, the Hearst party reached Germany and the rural town of Oberammergau. Together with Davies, Harry Crocker, and perhaps others, Hearst attended an outdoor performance of the Passion Play, a theatrical presentation of the last days and crucifixion of Christ. The year 1934 marked the three hundredth anniversary of the production, which was originally launched as a celebration of the town's survival of the plague. Newspapers reported that Adolf Hitler saw the production on August 13. As the *New York Times* put it, Hitler had come to Oberammergau "in the role of a casual tourist." A German newspaper reported that two of President Roosevelt's sons had also seen the play that summer. According to a history of the centuries-old production written by James Shapiro, the script for the Passion Play of 1934 had been rewritten "in part with the Nazi regime in mind." Shapiro says that in one of the play's series of tableaux—the sale of Joseph into slavery, where Jews are portrayed as "money-grubbers and back-stabbers"—a spirit of mercy that had been a part of the 1930 production had been eliminated. In its place a chorus calls for, in Shapiro's words, what can only be interpreted as "revenge and the annihilation of the Jews."

Hearst had long been aware of the Passion Play and may have even seen previous productions during his earlier trips abroad. The presentation had even inspired a pioneering film re-creation that Hearst had promoted as part of a fund-raising event for the building of a *Maine* Memorial in 1898. In

1934, after seeing the production in person, Hearst was photographed standing side by side with two young, longhaired actors from the play. At the nearby Hotel Wittelsbach, Hearst and Davies had a light meal of frankfurters after the show; then, with Crocker, they strolled over to a woodcarving shop where the signature "W. R. Hearst, Los Angeles, Cal." was left behind in a guest book.

After his brief stay in Oberammergau Hearst traveled to Munich. He visited some of city's modern art galleries, but he came away from them disgusted by the exhibitions and by what he saw as a communist influence in the work. During his stopover in Munich, Hearst met with his friend, the Hitler aide Putzi Hanfstaengl, and they made plans for a formal meeting between Hearst and the German dictator in Berlin on September 17. After a German newspaper requested an interview with him, Hearst provided a carefully written account of his observations of Munich and Oberammergau. While carving large slices of a German sausage he kept stored in a food hamper in his car, Hearst described what he saw as a central theme in the Passion Play. The play was about the eternal struggle between a "gentle philosophy" and "the evil characteristics of human nature—treachery, fickleness, infidelity, ignorance, prejudice, cruelty." Then he added that "the production could have been a bit shorter for us Americans—we don't have enough padding."

Also on Hearst's traveling itinerary was another long spectacle, the Nazi Party Congress in Nuremberg, a five-day series of meetings and rallies in early September. The Nazis were anxious to have Hearst and his party as guests, and an invitation was sent to Hearst through Crocker in late August: "The Führer is honored by inviting you to attend the Congress of the NSDAP, which will take place from September 5 until 10, 1934 in Nuremberg. I ask you to reply before August 27, 1934 by sending the card enclosed whether you will accept the invitation. In this case, the tickets for guests of honor, the program and a certificate of accommodation will be transmitted to you." In early September Hearst and his party quietly registered at the Grand Hotel in Nuremberg, the most splendid accommodations in the city and a fifteen-minute walk from the sites of many of the Nazi Congress proceedings. The "Hearst-Familie," as the hotel register described the Hearst traveling party, was a major presence at the hotel, taking over ten separate rooms (all the other guests at the hotel had only one or two rooms).

During the first week of September, Nuremberg's first-class five-story hotel had turned into a headquarters of Nazi conventioneers, packed with the country's most prominent party members. Names on the register included von Ribbentrop, von Papen, and Reich Minister Herman Goering, who had an article boosting Hitler published during the week of the rallies in the *New York American.* On the same ground-floor level as the Hearst party were the hierarchy of the SS; in fact, Heinrich Himmler and SS Führer Reinhard Heydrich had rooms adjacent to some of Hearst's. There appears to have been only a handful of foreigners at the hotel besides Hearst and his group. Of these, the most noteworthy was British publisher Lord Rothermere, a pioneer in tabloid journalism and widely recognized as a Nazi appeaser. Soon after most of the guests had settled into the Grand Hotel, the Party Congress's guest of honor arrived in Nuremberg. For security reasons, Hitler was ushered into a separate hotel from his fans and followers.

German director Leni Riefenstahl captured and memorialized the dictator's public appearances in Nuremberg in her film entitled *Triumph of the Will.* In this classic propaganda documentary, Hitler is portrayed as a divine figure. At first he is unseen but omnipresent, arriving in a plane that mystically sweeps down out of the clouds, casting a shadow that races over the rooftops of Germany. When Hitler is ultimately seen in the flesh and on the ground, he is traveling in a motorcade through the medieval city, through crowds of citizens swelling to ever-increasing size and fanaticism.

Whether Hearst attended any of the public events of the five-day conclave remains unclear. After his trip to Germany Hearst mentioned "stopping at Nuremberg," but he did not discuss the Nazi rallies for publication. Although writer David Nasaw quotes this casual reference in his biography of Hearst, he declares categorically that his subject did not attend the rallies. The main reason for his assertion seems to be Nasaw's belief that Hearst was at the baths of Bad Nauheim at the time. (Hearst may have taken the rest cure during part of September 1934, but according to the Grand Hotel records he was in Nuremberg during the rallies.) Nasaw also acknowledges the existence of a telegram from William Hillman, the International News Service representative in Europe, sent to Hearst editors on August 25 relaying an order from Hearst to "lay off story" of his visit to Nuremberg, because it is "nobody's business whether [or] not he attends Nazi gathering." According to the Hillman telegram, Hearst insists that he has not received an invitation to the rallies. However, the invitation for Hearst—which requests a response by August 27—is in the Harry Crocker papers at the California Historical Society in San Francisco but without the enclosed R.S.V.P. card. Hearst's message through Hillman appears to be an admonishment to those that would tell him what to do; he seems to have had every intention of going to the rallies.

Even if Hearst did not attend the rallies in person, his son certainly did. A local Nuremberg newspaper reported that Hearst's oldest son, George, went to several key events of the Nazi Congress. According to a small article published on page twelve of the September 10, 1934, issue of a Nuremberg newspaper called *Frankischer Küner*, George Hearst attended SA and SS gatherings at the Luitpold-Arena, where a speech by Hitler blamed "Jewish intellectualism" for Germany's "cultural problems." He was also in the audience of the parade before the Führer at Adolf-Hitler-Platz, an outdoor event of colossal proportions staged to meet the visual demands of filmmaker Riefenstahl. George Hearst's activities were reported by the Deutsches Nachrichten-Buro (DNB), a German press agency under complete control of Goebbels's Propaganda Ministry. The DNB provided its readers with the younger Hearst's reaction to the proceedings. "Six years ago I saw Germany for the last time. Since then Adolf Hitler took over Germany. The hours in Nuremberg gave me the chance to gather a deep insight into the German people and the German youth. I will take home a great impression."

George Hearst's visit to the Nazi rallies and the Hearst party's stay at Nuremberg's Grand Hotel do not appear to have been reported in the Hearst press or in any other American publication. In fact, Hearst newspaper reports on the events taking place in Nuremberg during the week of rallies are noticeably sparse, considering the Hearst presence in the city. On the other hand, there appears to have been no effort on Hearst's part to hide the bare facts of a controversial meeting he held with Hitler in Berlin on September 17.

For his part, Hearst claimed that his encounter with Hitler was motivated simply by a journalist's hunger for a good story; a meeting with Hitler, he said, was the same as an interview with FDR or any other head of state. He offered another defense several years later. In early 1941 the usually Hearst-friendly journal *Liberty* published an excerpt from Ambassador Dodd's diary, with its accusations about a secret deal between Hearst and Hitler. Although rumors of some sort of deal had surfaced soon after the meeting took place, fueled primarily by the leftist press, *Liberty* was the first mainstream venue to give the story wide distribution. What *Liberty* seemed to be confirming was a business deal between Hearst's International News Service and the German wire services, whereby the two entities would have an exclusive arrangement to exchange news reports, feature articles, and possibly even photographs. From Hearst's point of view, it was opined, the deal gave him a market on valuable publishable items from one of the most newsworthy countries in the world. Additionally, it was said, the Hearst Corporation received upward of $400,000 from Germany to sweeten the deal. Presumably, Hitler's incentive for making the deal was equally strong; through the Hearst news outlets, he would establish an unfiltered presence in the United States. On February 2 Hearst made the unusual move of writing a letter to the editor of *Liberty* magazine denying Ambassador Dodd's accusations. In order to refute the charges, Hearst made the claim—a false one—that "the full text" of his interview with Hitler had been published in American and English newspapers. "Nothing was said that was not publishable," he said, "and nothing was withheld from publication." He also floated another motivation for the meeting, for the first time injecting into the controversy the name of Hollywood's most famous Jew. "The question of whether I should see Hitler and what I should say to Hitler," Hearst wrote, "was discussed in general with Mr. Louis B. Mayer before the interview took place." Then, in closing, Hearst offered a challenge to *Liberty* magazine: "All the evidence as to the accuracy of this statement of mine is at the disposal of your attorneys. Furthermore, the books of the International News Service are open to your investigation."

Liberty published Hearst's letter, and in the same issue the magazine's editor published his response (dated February 5), which was an apology to Hearst and a retraction stating the magazine's overnight conversion to the belief that Dodd had been wrong in his account. According to *Liberty*, the magazine came to this conclusion after being given the keys to the Hearst warehouse and making an allegedly thorough and unrestricted examination of the records of INS within a period of two or three days.

In 1952 a book was published entitled *William Randolph Hearst: A Portrait in His Own Words*, edited by Hearst newspaper editor Edmund D. Coblentz and compiled with the assistance of Jean Willicombe, the widow of Hearst's longtime secretary. Coblentz's book offered what it claimed was a narrative of Hearst's trip to Germany in 1934 written by Hearst "in his own words." Coblentz cites no specific dates for the account, and for a reason that is not apparent at first it is written in the third person. Nevertheless, according to this published account, Hearst was taking a rest cure at Bad Nauheim, Germany, when he received word that Hitler was "anxious" to meet with him. Hearst's immediate reaction to the news was to contact Louis B. Mayer and consult with him "as to the advisability of any discussion." It is known that Mayer was traveling in Europe at the same time as Hearst, and presumably it was easy for Hearst to track him down. As the narrative continues in the Coblentz book, Mayer urged Hearst to visit with Hitler in the hope that a meeting might "accomplish some good," the implication being that Hearst was being urged to lobby Hitler for an end to the atrocities against the Jews.

This narrative of the Hearst-Hitler meeting and its connection to Louis B. Mayer has been commonly accepted by Hearst biographers and by many Hollywood historians, but it has some significant holes in it. Just before he embarked on his European trip in 1934 Hearst told reporters that he was anxious to meet with Hitler and not the other way around. Clearly, Hearst did not need Mayer's backing if he was already determined to meet Hitler. And while he might want Mayer's backing for publicity purposes, he never used it at a time when it might have been helpful. Furthermore, it is questionable whether anyone could have swayed Hearst to meet with Hitler to "accomplish some good." In 1932, when another movie mogul, Carl Laemmle, had written a letter to Hearst pleading with him to publicly protest Hitler's treatment of the Jews, there is no evidence that Hearst responded to the letter, let alone made any public protest. Neither was this the first correspondence Laemmle had with Hearst regarding Hitler. In 1929 he asked for Hearst's help when Hitler's functionaries threatened to block the release of *All Quiet on the Western Front*, a film perceived in Berlin as being anti-German.

There is no record that Mayer, who died in 1957, ever commented on his alleged role in Hearst's meeting with Hitler. Possibly he saw no need to comment after the story surfaced in *Liberty* in 1941 or in the Coblentz book of 1952. Whether the Coblentz-Hearst version was fabricated or embellished, it still portrayed Mayer as a man concerned about the plight of Jews in Hitler's Germany. If the story is true, one wonders what Hearst may have felt about his MGM friend never publicly coming to his defense.

There is another credibility problem attached to the Coblentz narrative. Although it is attributed to Hearst, it is in fact practically a verbatim transcript of an account by Hearst's traveling secretary and Hollywood publicist, Harry Crocker, apparently written within a few years of the events of 1934. The Crocker account, which was never published, is part of an incomplete manuscript that was eventually donated to the library of the Academy of Motion Pictures Arts and Sciences in Los Angeles. In Crocker's account there is no mention of Hearst's lack of interest in meeting Hitler or his concern about getting "mixed in the Nazi politics," as the Coblentz account asserts. Crocker does say that Mayer urged Hearst to meet Hitler, but he also says that Arthur Brisbane advised him against it (not in the Coblentz account), because "persons in America will not understand." Crocker's reference to Brisbane is reminiscent of advice the newspaper editor once gave others about reporting on Hitler. According to *New York Daily Mirror* editor Emile Gauvreau, Brisbane gave high marks to Hitler, but he also knew the importance of keeping such admiration secret. "Although he gave Hitler an occasional dusting of the jacket," Gauvreau wrote in his autobiography,

> Brisbane's opinions of the Dictator were written with interesting reservations. He admired the upstart's audacity and believed that history justified cruelty, although as he pointed out at the luncheon table,

"such thoughts in print would not be popular with our Jewish population." He was impressed with the murderous Nazi purge of the previous summer [1934]. "On this occasion," he wrote to me in a memorandum, "Hitler did some shooting that needed to be done. There is something admirably decisive about the man. He shot men who were indulging in practices that were just as well interrupted. That was the way to handle it."

There are other details in Harry Crocker's memoir about the meeting between Hearst and Hitler that do not appear in the Coblentz book or anywhere else:

Thereupon we flew from Munich to Berlin on the appointed day, September sixteenth. In an official black Benz limousine, Hearst, [Putzi] Hanfstaengl, and I drove to the Reichs-Konslerei [sic]. I sat up front with Hearst's favorite hardboiled chauffeur Julius Schreck [elsewhere in the manuscript identified as Hitler's driver]. A Bavarian, a Munchener, he was a stout, red-faced, gay fellow. "Germany is much better now," he informed me in German. "No communism—no socialism—order—no unemployment!" The Reichs-Konslerei is a gray stone building crouched behind an impressive black, grille fence. At the entrance and exit hovered groups of S.A. and S.S. guards, Brown Shirts and the elite Black Shirts. Flanking the doorway, in sentry boxes, sentries were carved figures. Field gray uniforms, heavy World War helmets, bayoneted guns, booted feet planted apart. Motionless.

The doors opened to a series of booted heel-clicks. Sharp. Like castanets. "Heil Hitler!" Arms flew out so energetically we fully expected to see hands fly off.

A brown Shirt colonel—huge, apple-cheeked, smiling—presided over us as we washed up, conducted us to a reception room, and left us.

A long, low ceilinged room. More of an enlarged, furnished corridor than a room. All along one side, French windows; outside, a lawn and shade trees. On the opposite wall old tapestries, but throughout the room modern furniture. "Used to be Bismarck's study," explained Putzi.

Outside the only door, the one we had entered, a barrage of heel clicks exploded. The doors, with German precision, flew open. There was no indecision. They flew open so far, no further.

Enter Hitler. In a brown ersatz suit, brown shirt, black tie, and low black shoes.

"Heil Hitler!"

The sharp greeting and the military atmosphere put us all bolt upright, heels together. I'd always heard of the psychological tricks employed by dictators to put persons off balance, but I was unprepared for Hitler's maneuvers. In rapid succession he seized each of us by the hand. One quick forward jerk pulled each of us off balance. A second quick reverse movement thrust each back on his heels, nearly toppling him over backwards. It was enough to disconcert anyone.

Amenities. "Hanfstaengl," said Hearst through Hanfstaengl as interpreter, "has just been telling us that this was once Bismarck's study. One day, future generations may call it Hitler's study!"

I was prepared to see Der Fuehrer take a bow, "No, no," he replied earnestly, "Germany is too young a country to lose even one little tradition. Even Berlin is only three hundred years old. No, this must always be Bismarck's study!"

He waved for us to be seated. Hearst sank deep in a sofa. Hitler sat on Hearst's left in a straight-back chair, Hanfstaengl his right. I sat on Hitler's left. Between us was a low circular table containing a squat vase of flowers.

Much of what follows in Crocker's account is nearly identical to the Coblentz narrative. Hitler says he has been "misrepresented" and "misunderstood" in the American press. Hearst tells him that Americans are "averse to dictatorship" because they have been "inculcated" with democracy since their foundation. Then, Crocker says, Hearst explained that "there is a very large and influential and respected element in the United States who are very resentful of the treatment of their fellows in Germany." Although in his discussion with Hitler, Hearst describes "these subject people" as having the sympathies of all Americans, he is vague about the mounting discriminatory measures, and he never uses the word *Jew* in his exchange. According to both the Crocker account and the account edited by Coblentz, Hitler responded to Hearst by assuring him "that those vigorous measures of the government were due to temporary circumstances, and that all discrimination is disappearing and will soon entirely disappear. . . . You will soon see ample evidence of it."

In one hour, Hearst and Hitler had concluded their meeting. Before departing with Hearst, Crocker asked the dictator for his autograph, which he later described as "the smallest, most insignificant in my book."

In biographer Nasaw's account of the Hearst trip to Germany, he dismisses the idea that a business deal—rumored for years to be a wire service exchange deal—might have motivated Hearst. "The story was without foundation," Nasaw writes, "and on its face ludicrous, as Hearst needed no financial assistance to support Hitler." While hard evidence concerning a wire service deal remains illusive, documentation is available concerning another business arrangement just as significant and formulated at the same time. The summer of 1934 was a period of expansion for the Hearst newsreel operation that culminated in the early fall with a severing of ties with Fox and the incorporation of *Hearst Metrotone News*. While Hearst traveled in Europe, his film executive, Ed Hatrick, was also visiting London and the major capitals of the Continent, reaching a series of agreements that enhanced Hearst's status in the international film market. Hatrick's actions actually began before he left for Europe. On May 1 the International Film Service entered into an exclusive three-year newsreel-printing agreement with the De Luxe Laboratory in New York City. A few days later another deal was concluded with Eastern Service Studios for rerecording (synchronizing of narrator's voice, sound effects, etc.) of newsreels. On May 11 Edwin C. Hill, a prominent radio announcer already working for Hearst, was engaged to do news commentary as the Hearst newsreel "Globe Trotter." Hearst's acquisition of Hill was heavily promoted, and pictures of his debonair face were plastered on newspaper delivery wagons and thousands of billboards. An ad in *Motion Picture Herald* emphasized that Hill "interprets and dramatizes news events giving them an informative and thrilling background." (The use of celebrity Hill was part of long history of Hearst news dramatizations that went back at least as far as the 1890s and Stephen Crane's "novelettes" about the Tenderloin for the *New York Journal*.) During May and June Hatrick was busy hiring cameramen and technicians and making purchases of new cameras, lenses, and trucks, as well as eight film-recording systems costing almost $4,000 each. Before returning from Europe in July 1934, he concluded an agreement with the Gaumont British Distributors to supply Great Britain with a newsreel suitable for its uses in exchange for a British reel to be shown in the United States and Canada. Hatrick made an attempt to establish a similar relationship with Mussolini's Luce Company (much like the 1927 agreement), but for some reason the arrangement did not go into effect until 1935. Meanwhile Hatrick made agreements to beef up the Hearst presence in the Far East: World War I cameraman Ariel Varges was dispatched to Japan, and "Newsreel" Wong was sent to China to work for Hearst.

Hatrick's most consequential foreign newsreel arrangement in 1934 was with the leading film company of a leading European film-producing country—and a deal that the Hearst organization did not publicize. Hearst's connections with the Ufa company of Germany predated 1934. Ufa was born in 1917, founded by the German High Command specifically as a propaganda tool during World War I. Alfred Hugenberg, a media mogul, sometimes referred to as the German William Randolph Hearst, took control of Ufa in 1927, with a specific aim to expand his sphere of influence and to rid the company of Jews and foreigners. By the spring of 1933, Ufa was one of the largest film companies in Europe, and it employed virtually no Jewish actors, directors, or administrators.

Between 1918 and 1931, Ufa's foreign press representative was a man named Albert A. Sander, a former Hearst man, who had been the drama critic for Hearst's German-language newspaper in New York, *Deutsches Journal.* In 1918 the Hearst-owned newspaper suspended its operation in the face of charges that its owner was un–American and pro-German. At about the same time, Sander was embroiled in a controversy of his own, which may or may not have been connected to Hearst. The U.S. Secret Service exposed Sander as a German spy, president of a German propaganda organization called the Central Powers Film Exchange that was involved in a variety of espionage activities including the smuggling of British war films to Germany. Sander and a close ally who had been employed as a publicist for William Jennings Bryan were arrested, tried, and sentenced to a short term in prison. But, as the *New York Times* reported, the resolution of the case did not end rumors that Sander was a patsy for higher-ups. When Sander suddenly pleaded guilty during his trial, the *Times* suggested he had done so "rather than disclose facts that might prove embarrassing to the agents or friends of Germany in the United States." After serving a prison sentence in Atlanta, Georgia, Sander returned to his homeland and joined Ufa. In 1933 he was appointed foreign press chief for the newly formed adjunct to the Reich Culture Chamber, called the Reich Film Chamber, a unit designed to regulate the film industry and bring it under tighter Nazi government control. Sander remained in this prominent position until his death in 1936.

In 1925, as previously discussed, Hearst was a partner in a concerted effort on the part of MGM and Paramount Pictures to provide Ufa with a $4 million loan in order to establish an American film distribution presence in Germany. The joint effort between Ufa and the U.S. film companies faltered in 1931, but in that same year Ufa and Hearst's Cosmopolitan company made an agreement that provided the German film company with an American outlet for the whole spectrum of its film product: comedy and drama features, newsreels, and short subjects. In May, after what were called lengthy negotiations, a contract was signed authorizing "a long term lease" of the Cosmopolitan Theater in Columbus Circle to Ufa. The film company's weekly organ, *Ufa Week*, enthusiastically reported the company's connection with Hearst:

> Ufa opens own theater in New York, the Ufa executives being convinced that it is essential to have their own show window for the presentation of their big productions. . . . The theater will be known as the Ufa-Cosmopolitan. The house has a seating capacity of 1100 and is perhaps one of the most beautiful theaters in the world. The Urban decorations are exquisite works of art and can be claimed as unusually attractive and one of the finest pieces of work in this line. When remodeling this house some time ago for the purpose of showing pictures, Mr. [William] Randolph Hearst had excellent acoustical devices installed. An attractive Neon sign will be erected on the roof displaying Ufa's well-known Trademark in blue and red. This sign is the continental insignia of quality and the guarantee for the finest pictures produced abroad. . . . It shall be remembered that it was in this particular theater that Max Reinhardt, Germany's famous stage director scored great success when presenting German stage plays with his troupe of players. The atmosphere of the house will be strictly continental and a special European style refreshment service bar will be installed.

Martin Huberth, Hearst's real estate executive, kept him informed of the arrangement with Ufa. On May 12 he sent Hearst a copy of *Ufa Week* that included an announcement of the opening picture at the Ufa-Cosmopolitan, *Der Grosse Tenor*. Huberth attached a note to the publication that read in part, "I know you will be interested in their program."

On September 5, 1934 (the opening day of the Nuremberg Congress), a letter of newsreel agreement was signed between Hearst and Ufa. Representing the International Film Service in Berlin was George Schubert, a German actor and film producer of the 1920s. The agreement granted Hearst exclusive access to Ufa news films. Schubert was assigned to make weekly selections of Ufa newsreels to be used in the United States and by Hearst affiliates in Canada. Many of these Ufa reels would be absorbed into the Hearst reels unedited with only minor voice-over translations. On their end of the exchange, Ufa representatives were permitted to make suitable selections from Hearst newsreels to be used in newsreels screened in Germany and its allies, Austria, Poland, the Balkan States, Switzerland, and the Scandinavian countries. As part of the arrangement, Ufa agreed to the use of its films in other countries where Hearst might wish to send his newsreels, with the notable exception of European countries that were not allied with Germany. No charges were made to either side in the deal for the use of footage. A commencement date was set for the first of October for an "indefinite period with the understanding that it can be cancelled by either party by giving two months notice." In many ways the German deal mirrored the one Hearst made with Great Britain, with one major difference: Hearst was affording a totalitarian government's propaganda machine relatively unrestricted access to movie audiences in the United States.

On September 25, a few days before Hearst left Europe for New York, Ufa's board of directors met in Berlin to discuss the new arrangement with his film operation. There is no detailed record of this meeting, but all the key executives of Ufa, including Ludwig Klitzsch, its CEO since 1927, were in attendance. Klitzsch was one of the founders of Ufa, who had a program for selling film propaganda to the United States as early as 1916:

> We will never gain a foothold in foreign movie theaters with films on Germany industry, culture, and transportation. To do that, we will have to take into account the hunger of foreign movie audiences for sensationalism, a hunger that viewed from our German perspective, seems to know no bounds. We have to surround the serious kernel of German propaganda films with the opulent trimmings of drama, comedy, and so forth, so that the foreign audiences will continue to swallow the initially quite alien kernel for the sake of the pleasing husk until they eventually become accustomed to the kernel and until the constantly dripping water has hollowed out the stone.

The Hearst newsreels continued to incorporate Ufa footage throughout the late 1930s and early 1940s. The controversial nature of the arrangement must have been apparent to the Hearst organization, which only discussed it through internal communications. A large archive of Hearst newsreels survives to this day; however, a document that came from Hearst's newsreel organization indicates that some material originating with Ufa was ordered to be destroyed in 1940. No reason was offered for the destruction. There is no record of Hearst's making any public comments on his deal with Ufa or offering any explanation for why he was willing to publicize the Nazi regime by incorporating unfiltered propaganda into American newsreels. The Germans, however, on one occasion attached great weight to having their views represented by Hearst in in the United States. During the Nuremberg Trials of 1946, lawyers for the Nazi Elite Guard and Alfred Rosenberg, who was in charge of the Nazi party's foreign press office and was photographed with Hearst in Bad Nauheim in 1934, tried to justify their clients' crimes by invoking the name of the powerful American media mogul. The lawyers did not allow their statement into the official record of the proceedings, but the *New York Times* reported that the Nazis wanted to say that Hearst and other "prominent American publicists" were responsible for giving credibility to the Nazis, even to the point of causing "otherwise innocently inclined Germans to join the Elite Guard."

By the fall of 1933 Hearst's alliance with Franklin Roosevelt was already showing signs of crumbling. The first major breach occurred over the National Recovery Administration (NRA), which President Roosevelt established as a means of reforming the economy by setting industry guidelines on wages and work hours. Hearst was particularly concerned about what effect the NRA might have on his publishing business, which he had always viewed as a romantic pursuit that should function outside the restrictions of the law. Hearst saw the idea of communal labor standards, even in a time of emergency, as akin to socialism. In November 1933 he sent a telegram to Howard Davis, president of the American Newspaper Publishers Association. In it he declared that "the NRA is simply a program of social betterment . . . a menace to political rights and constitutional liberties, a danger to American ideals and institutions, a handicap to industrial recovery, and a detriment to the public welfare."

Hearst's disdain for NRA restrictions on business did not extend to every field. In an editorial published in his newspaper chain in October 1933, Hearst used the president's recovery program as a leitmotif for an attack on the moral tone of movies. The editorial, which with apparently unintended irony was entitled "A Letter from an American Husband," was one of Hearst's most harshly written tracts:

> Are we going to allow our young people to be educated to admire gangsters and harlots? Are we going to teach them that there is very little in life except evil? . . . Can we not recover our one-time sound and sturdy moral standard, which we proudly maintained before we were debased by the European moral standard, and the Oriental and the African unmoral standards? Can we not have an NRA for the screen and the stage to compel these great influences to do their duty by society? Maintaining the morality of a nation is a proper governmental function. . . . Let government do its duty. Let it enable ourselves and our families to see something else on the screen except harlots in

the morning, strumpets at noon, and courtesans at night. When an American husband takes his family to the theatre, he ought to be certain that he is not taking them to a house of ill fame.

As Hearst became increasingly disenchanted with boosting FDR and his recovery programs, he turned his spotlight of publicity on the Federal Bureau of Investigation. He spoke of the FBI as the only federal agency doing any real work for the country, but as always his motivation was neither simple nor pure. Certainly, he must have recognized that the diligence and daring of government men, when presented in the right light, would prove to be an attractive commodity that boosted circulation and brought audiences into movie theaters far more than FDR's pronouncements on wages and other industry codes. But another important factor probably motivating Hearst was the knowledge of what the FBI might do for him in response to what he did for them. Although Hearst's power was much feared and often attended to, he had very few trusted friends in public office. As Hearst began to fall out of favor with Roosevelt, he saw the immeasurable value of ingratiating himself with John Edgar Hoover and his veritable shadow government.

According to an FBI memorandum, Hearst had "instructed his keymen [sic] to go along with the Bureau 100% and to keep it out in front of the public at all times." Hearst made a coordinated effort to highlight the FBI's work, including laudatory editorials and cartoons, newsreels, and even a feature film. In editorials published after 1933 he applauded law enforcement officials whose efforts had long been thwarted by politicians. "Existing criminal conditions are NOT due to the indifference of the American people," an editorial said in September 1934. "They are due to the inefficiency of American government." One newspaper series published in early 1935 focused on the harsh reality of crime and was accompanied by relatively graphic murder scene photos. It was a sign of the proliferation of crime imagery in the early 1930s that the series met with little hue and cry from religious and civic groups. Even the FBI gave its seal of approval to the photographs. Hoover sent a letter to Hearst thanking him for his "constructive" and "vigorous" crime photo campaign. "I sincerely trust that there will be no cessation," Hoover wrote, "of this fine work which you are now carrying on and which is already giving indications of producing such excellent results."

As early as 1933 Hearst's film company formed an unofficial partnership with the FBI, and his newsreel cameramen became a recognizable presence in the bureau's fingerprint identification division and crime labs. In 1934 a Mr. Sackett, a special agent in the FBI's Los Angeles office who was close to

Arthur Brisbane, suggested that Hearst show photographs of wanted criminals in his newsreel. The Hearst editor may have recalled his involvement in
a similar use of pictorial journalism at the turn of the century when the *Journal* plastered the city of New York with pictures of baby Marion Clark in the
hopes of capturing her kidnapper. Shortly after his meeting with Brisbane,
agent Sackett reported to Hoover. "Mr. Brisbane was very enthusiastic," Sackett wrote. "He stated in addition to the fact that news reels would be securing a feature of current value and such a procedure would result in this Division securing numerous leads of inestimable value, it would also give the
Division good wholesome publicity." Hoover quickly approved the idea, and
he wrote a memorandum on the subject to his colleague Clyde Tolson:

> Mr. Sackett suggested the desirability of having the photographs of
> some of the most notorious fugitives which we are seeking placed in
> the Hearst Metrotone News Reel which appears weekly on all news
> screens. I stated that this would be a very practical idea.... It did seem
> to me that the filming of the photographs of some of the most noto-
> rious criminals in the news reel with a description of their outstand-
> ing characteristics might result in their apprehension, as it was a fact
> that the photographs of criminals appearing in some of the detective
> magazines had resulted in the apprehension of these individuals, and
> certainly it would be applicable to the news reel which reaches a much
> larger public.

In early 1936 an executive of *Hearst Metrotone News* sent Hoover a synopsis
sheet for a just-released newsreel highlighting the important stories of 1935.
Included in the special reel was a sequence on the FBI's efforts to capture
"public enemies." On January 14 Hoover sent a letter to the Hearst newsreel company thanking it for the courtesy. "If this Bureau can be of service
to you at any time" Hoover said in closing, "please feel free to call upon me."

Although he was initially reluctant to publicize the FBI through film,
with persistent courting by the Hearst organization Hoover eventually recognized the value of the medium and even saw the special attraction his
own persona might convey. But before Hoover fully consented to becoming a star of the newsreel, he sent the Hearst outfit a quotation to use in its
reels, a statement that seemed to be more a boost of the film medium than
the FBI: "I like the movies because they are educational or diverting, affording instruction or pleasurable release from the cares of the day. They are the
modern era's artistic gift to the multitude. The movies to me mean mental
exhilaration and recreation. They afford color, zest, and at times inspiration

to those of us who are so deeply immersed in the realism of current difficulties and problems."

In May 1935, less than a year after Hearst broke with MGM, Warner Bros. released a Cosmopolitan feature film celebrating the work of J. Edgar Hoover's men that was recognized by *Variety* as "a tie-in" with the Hearst newspapers' anticrime campaign. *G-Men*, which Warners later dubbed "the daddy of all FBI pictures," was at once seen as a turning point for the crime film genre. No longer, it was predicted, would the focus be on the criminal; now the law enforcer would be the star.

G-Men was said to be based on a novel by one Gregory Rogers, but no such publication or author has been discovered. According to recent sources, Rogers was a pseudonym for Warner Bros.'s onetime production head, Darryl F. Zanuck. True or not, the film was likely to have originated with its producers and given a high priority at the Warner studio. A major theme in the film is how criminals and law enforcement live in a shadowy existence where the differences in their behavior patters are often blurred. Emblematic of the film's shifting moral views on methods and motives for crime was the casting of the film's star and the trajectory of the character he plays. For the part James "Brick" Davis, a young mob lawyer turned FBI agent, the producers chose James Cagney, an actor who had previously established himself in Hollywood playing gangster roles and had most recently been seen in Cosmopolitan's military preparedness film *Devil Dogs of the Air* (1935). With the Davis character's career track somewhat paralleling Cagney's real career transformation, producers found themselves a clever hook with which to publicize their film.

In fact, much of *G-Men* involves character conversions and flip-flopping situations, some less credible than others. In the film's opening scene we find Davis in his office practicing a speech to a jury that he has no prospect of ever addressing. Then we see him idly reading a newspaper and swatting flies. The audience is led to believe that Davis is a well-respected attorney. But we quickly learn that he is a lawyer with only one client, a big-time bootlegger named McKay, the man responsible for taking Davis from "the gutter" of the East Side and putting him through law school. After Davis sees a friend killed in a gangland shooting, he decides to completely sever his frayed connections to the law profession and join the FBI. When Davis tells McKay of his decision, the bootlegging mentor tells him that he too is switching careers and will soon be starting a legitimate hotel business. A series of typical FBI training scenes follows, with predictable friction ensuing between Davis and his boss, Jeff McCord, who resents the fact that his young recruit is resistant to playing cops and robbers by the book. Meanwhile we discover that Davis's old girlfriend at the bootlegger's nightclub, Jean Morgan (played by *Scarface* lead Ann Dvorak), who seemed street-smart but sweet when we first met her, is now married to a big-time gangster wanted by the FBI. In one of the many transformations in the film, Morgan eventually betrays her husband so that she can help her real love, Davis. With Morgan's help and Davis's street smarts, the gangsters are nabbed. But in a twisted moral tie-up, both Morgan and McKay are killed in the film's excessively violent climax (fortunately for Davis, his boss has a beautiful sister). When Davis realizes that he is the one who has accidentally shot McKay—now a Wisconsin lodge owner being held hostage by his former hoodlum employees—he holds him in his arms in his last dying moments. Just before he dies, McKay whispers his forgiveness to Davis, and—as if the audience still needed proof—tells him he is an "okay" guy. Even Davis's boss, McCord, must now acknowledge that his brash recruit's "criminal instincts" were a boon to his new law enforcement position. He too tells Davis, and the audience, that the onetime mob lawyer is now a "good guy."

According to film historian Andrew Bergman, the solutions to crime and the Great Depression offered by *G-Men* and other films following in its wake resemble moral themes in the movie western and even in the earlier cliff-hanging serials that Hearst pioneered: "Along with the renaissance of the western hero and the elevation of the federal government into a virtual leading man in Warner Bros.'s topical films, it brought that law and that government into a strong position in the culture. The grim policeman of the early thirties had become an expansive but watchful guardian of everyone's interests. Hoodlums would turn craven at his approach, social problems would slink away like the villains of 'Perils of Pauline,' and bad men would be driven from the West."

Contemporary reviews of *G-Men* focused mostly on the film's action-packed scenes and the excitement of what seemed like a fresh approach to the crime film genre. *Variety* called the film "the first of a new cycle of gangster pictures" but also warned that a continuing trend of obscuring the distinctions between the criminal and the law enforcer might lead to both a moral and cinematic ambiguity:

"Little Caesar," "Scarface," and "Public Enemy," were more than portrayals of gangster tactics; they were biographies of curious mentalities. They were photographic and realistic analysis of mentality and character (or lack of it). But in the new idea of glorifying the government gunners who wipe out the killers there is no chance for that kind of character development and build-up. . . . By understressing the various gangsters and by using a whole string of them in one episode after another, producers manage to avoid giving them any buildup from a sentimental standpoint. But at the same time the cops don't come out any too well.

Although Cagney's work in *G-Men* was heralded in publicity ads as a great departure from his previous roles, a critic in the *New Republic* saw "few changes" between the two types of characters he played. Cagney the former gangster and Cagney the lawman are driven by feelings of revenge. The problem and ultimate dishonesty of the picture was a result of the producers' indifference to confronting the crime issue seriously. In the view of the *New Republic*, filmmakers had taken it on themselves to be "the keepers of national morals" and had compelled the film's writers

> to wriggle around and show the underworld from the top looking down. . . . The big-time gangster as a sort of inverted public hero (not enemy), a lonely, possessed and terrible figure . . . is not shown here. In "G-Men" he [the gangster] is simply a dangerous bad man who would have gone on nefariously forever if the government had not come along, with the aid of love and that delightful man Cagney put a stop to him for good. All gone now, all better. It not only makes a flabby evasion of the rather cruel truth, but it makes a flabby picture, and a disappointment.

G-Men was given the usual Cosmopolitan production publicity, but Hearst's role in the production remains a mystery. *Variety* called the picture, "red hot off the front page," and the film makes numerous allusions to newspaper work and frequent use of the now-cliché newspaper headline transitional sequence. The film's title itself comes from the gangsters' term for FBI agents, a term introduced to the public in newspapers and newsreels. One scene in *G-Men* seems especially reminiscent of Hearst's contribution to *Scarface*. Standing before a group of passive congressional leaders, a fictional FBI bureau chief gives an impassioned speech that calls for tough (though vague) measures to put "teeth" in their fight against criminals. His underlying message, like that of the publisher in *Scarface*, is that his warnings about crime carry a threat of undemocratic solutions. The rallying cry of the chief government man and the ambiguous moral tone throughout the film seem to descend from Hearst's hilltop view of the world in the early 1930s. When FBI agent Davis uses his links to the underworld and his still valuable street instincts, he displays a kinship with other beasts of the city who have felt at times that the law was a hindrance or something that applied only to others. Like the vigilante Secret Six businessmen of Chicago, the six business-men of *The President Vanishes*, and the president-dictator of *Gabriel Over the White House*, the G-man of the movies stands with one foot on the side of the law and the other in the shadows. He can be transformed, in the movies and in real life, into a well-tailored respectable man of the community, but he is still shielded by his secret pacts, his bulletproof black sedans, his machine guns, and all the darker accoutrements that once differentiated the criminal from the citizen living under the law.

15

Remote Control
1934–1940

COMING HOME TO ROOST

Thirteen years before screenwriter Ring Lardner Jr. was jailed for refusing to cooperate with a House committee investigating Communism in the film industry and became known as one of the Hollywood Ten, he was traveling between countries that appeared to him to be worlds apart. Lardner was nineteen years old and fresh out of college in 1934, beginning his trip with an eye-opening tour of the Soviet Union. No doubt Lardner was an idealist during his summer abroad—he had joined a socialist club at Princeton University before he went to Russia—but the belief that Communism could improve the lives of people outlasted his youthful impressions. To Lardner, this faraway country was a land of economic growth; there was building construction everywhere. Contrary to reports back home—especially in the Hearst press—people actually smiled in Russia.

The young traveler's father, Ring Lardner Sr., was a nationally well-known author whose satirical writings on sports subjects appeared frequently in Hearst's magazines and newspapers; he died shortly before his son's trip abroad. The senior Lardner's name and fame created both a shadow and a guiding light over his son. His life was a great influence on the son's decision to pursue writing, but his death seemed to have hastened his son's desire to explore new ideas and make it on his own. Lardner remembered his father as being apolitical and sometimes willing to compromise principles to further his career. He thoroughly enjoyed the wealth and notoriety that came with employment with Hearst, but he "disliked Hearst, not because of anything political, but because he thought his papers were cheap or sensational." Even Ring Lardner Jr. found connecting with Hearst hard to resist: for his first job right out of college he joined his brother as a cub reporter for Hearst's *New York Daily Mirror*.

By early August 1934 Lardner had completed his tour of Russia and traveled to Germany, where he stayed with an architect family friend for about six weeks. "The contrast of the trips to the Soviet Union and Germany," Lardner remembered, "had a big impact on me." Men dressed in imposing uniforms seemed to be everywhere he went in Munich and Berlin. "Some of this existed in the Soviet Union," he would later recall, "but it was less noticeable." What modest construction work he saw in Germany was "in the context of a militaristic atmosphere."

One day that summer, standing on a street corner, Lardner was startled when the police or storm troopers suddenly cleared the streets of traffic. All eyes turned in the direction of what appeared from a distance to be an advancing parade. As the attraction approached, however, Lardner realized it was only a short motorcade heading toward him. When a big closed limousine passed directly in front of him, Lardner looked into the backseat to see the faces of two men who were quite familiar to him. Only days before, Lardner had seen both of these men pictured separately in local German newspapers. Adolf Hitler of course had just seized dictatorial power in Germany, and William Randolph Hearst was his father's boss and his own on the *Daily Mirror*. Viewing the close-up image of these two men sitting side by side was almost a transcendental experience for Lardner and one that would haunt him and his comrades on the left over the next decade.

After Hearst's return to the United States on the S.S. *Bremen* on September 30, 1934, he and Marion Davies stayed in his New York apartment building, the Ritz Tower, for about two weeks. Momentarily at least he was alerted to the controversy over his travels in Germany when he received a letter from Adrian J. Berkowitz, a reporter for the Jewish Telegraphic Agency, who for some unknown reason had been denied an interview with Hearst when he arrived in port. In his letter, written on October 9, Berkowitz stressed his concern as a representative of Jewish publications that in his opinion there was a growing movement in the country to stir up prejudice and racial agitation. He asked Hearst to comment on former mayor John Hylan's solicitation of support for a possible run for governor from German-American groups "dominated by men closely allied with the Hitler regime in Germany." Hearst, obviously angered by the attack on his loyal friend, which was implicitly an attack on himself, sent a letter to Berkowitz the following day. In his response, Hearst ignores the question about Hylan and seems to imply that it is Berkowitz who is "arousing class feeling." The close of his letter contains what appears to be a veiled warning about the reporter's outspoken Jewishness. Hearst tells Berkowitz that he has never found it wise to discuss politics from the standpoint of being a hyphenated American, "[and] I respectfully recommend that you proceed in the same manner. I am sure that any other course is likely to bring down disaster not only upon the nation but upon the promoters of an unwise and un-American policy."

Hearst was eager to resume his role as movie producer and powerbroker while he was in New York in early October. He and Davies spent their evenings with friends seeing the latest Broadway shows and looking for suitable film properties for Cosmopolitan Productions. On October 4, while still at the Ritz, Hearst received a letter from Will Hays, who was also in New York at the East Coast headquarters of the Motion Picture Producers Association. The letter was a welcome-home greeting, in which Hays emphasized how Hearst had truly never been out of reach: "We hear much these days in scientific circles of 'remote control'—airplanes being run by it, ships piloted by it, etc., etc. The most outstanding example of 'remote control' that ever happened is your own experience this summer. I wonder if you have any idea of the far-reaching influence exercised in this country by your messages sent home."

One area of Hearst's "far-reaching influence" that Hays apparently had in mind referred to the Legion of Decency, a religious-based film censorship movement whose efforts had mushroomed over the summer of 1934. A few days after sending his October 4 letter, Hays met with Hearst in person. Apparently one area of discussion was the recent activities of the legion, as Hays followed up the meeting with another letter to Hearst attached to material on that very subject. The attachment was a written exchange between Hays and Cincinnati's archbishop, John T. McNicholas, in August that formalized a film industry agreement to accept the demands of the Legion of Decency.

From his earliest forays into the issue of film morality, when he launched a campaign against picture peep shows in the 1890s, Hearst had a fluid approach to film censorship. Publicly Hearst was often a vocal critic of film censorship, arguing that restrictions on freedom of expression in film would bring a chill to other U.S. institutions, especially the press. But increasingly he felt that movie producers were going too far and taking advantage of the guarantees of freedom of expression that he seemed to cherish. In 1926

Hearst expressed his belief that movie producers would never fully adhere to a system of self-regulation unless they considered government censorship a real possibility. He signed his name to an editorial that appeared in his newspapers on December 30, 1926, offering his advice on treating issues of morality on the stage and screen equally by opposing censorship in practice but welcoming it as a threat:

> There are certain inconveniences in censorship, certain injustices, in fact, certain dangers, if the censorship should be misused. But there is nothing in censorship which carries so great a menace to the life of the nation, to the moral standards of the American people, as the appalling degeneracy of the present-day drama. The actual process of censorship may not have done so much to make moving pictures cleaner than they were, but the fear of censorship, the dread of what censorship would do to the picture, if the producer transgressed, has been almost entirely responsible for the redemption of moving pictures. That fear has made the efforts of Mr. Will Hays toward higher standards in moving picture effective. It has made the producers submit to his rulings and proceed in accordance with his very wise judgment.

Censorship historians have speculated that as early as 1929 Hearst considered joining forces with other Protestant-owned news organizations to lobby for government censorship. Certainly by the start of the 1930s Hearst was on the side of those who saw films as being cheapened by appealing primarily to the public's interest in sensationalism. Many critics often linked the crime film and the sex film in their discussions about salacious films, but this was not exactly Hearst's approach. He thought films about crime, if done properly, could actually reduce crime in society. He compared crime films to the crime stories his newspapers had published to educate the public on a serious social issue and to warn criminals about the consequences of their actions. Sex was another matter, however. Although his newspapers were still fond of printing tantalizing images of the female form and stories about love triangles, messy divorces, and even murders with a sex angle, Hearst did not believe films were an appropriate medium for the same approach. Exactly why Hearst felt this way is unknown; he may have feared that graphic depictions of prostitution, brothels, and other related subjects would open his own life to such investigations. Possibly he simply felt the film medium was incapable of any degree of subtlety with such sensational material. In March 1931 Hearst wrote a letter to Louella Parsons, saying that the proliferation of sex films was a Pandora's box that would encourage the public to call for extreme measures: "I think it is a moral duty to try to keep the morals of the public from being corrupted by these rotten sex pictures. ... Everybody knows that this has been a bad thing for the stage, and yet the moving picture people have not taken the lesson to heart and are apparently proceeding to make the same mistake."

Since the day in 1922 when the two had sat near each other on a dais before an audience of movie people welcoming the movie czar, Hearst had generally been publicly supportive of Will Hays. But in private he was often mistrustful and disappointed. In 1931 he told columnist Parsons that Hays efforts toward "internal censorship" were a failure, and he predicted that "soon we will have a revolt against indecency on the screen."

As with his position on film monopoly and other issues, Hearst was capable of changing his views on Hays and censorship to adapt to his changing financial situation and the climate of public opinion. Sometimes he reevaluated his position after careful deliberations, and sometimes he seemed to be swayed more by some relatively unrelated personal grudge or perceived offense. Perhaps Hearst's greatest motivation concerning film censorship was neither principle nor greed but an incessant need to be recognized as an important industry player.

Before departing for California from New York, Hearst and Davies caught up with the latest Hollywood news in the daily newspapers and film trade journals that had accumulated while they were away. Old wounds were apparently reopened when they read about the box office success of Norma Shearer in MGM's *The Barretts of Wimpole Street.* A year earlier Hearst had lobbied for Davies in the lead role of this film project, but Irving Thalberg had other casting ideas, and Louis B. Mayer backed up his award-winning prodigy.

Barretts was one more disappointment in a year that included what Hearst perceived as Mayer's meddling in *Gabriel Over the White House* and his growing disenchantment with Cosmopolitan Productions in general. The trouble over *Gabriel* pointed out the different approaches that Mayer and Hearst took to the new president, Franklin Roosevelt, and the outgoing president, Herbert Hoover. By 1934 Mayer and Hearst were still cordial with each other and able to work together, but a festering distrust had settled into their relationship as well. No doubt Mayer was pleased by Hearst's newsreel deal with Ufa, which promised to make the MGM-distributed newsreel a unique source for international news. But possibly he was becoming concerned about the lengths to which Hearst would be willing to go with German leaders for business purposes. Disagreements over domestic politics also continued to gnaw at their relationship. While Hearst was in Europe and Mayer was vacationing there as well, for some unknown reason the MGM studio head sent a wire soliciting Hearst's support for Hoover in what Mayer hoped would be a rematch with Roosevelt in 1936. By 1934 Hearst had soured on FDR, but he had no nostalgia for Hoover. In a blunt response to Mayer, Hearst declared that another Hoover administration would be disastrous and only serve to strengthen the cause of radicalism. Hearst seemed to be mocking Mayer's judgment. "If you don't suppress this hoodoo," he wrote Mayer, "your party will lose its chance, too of electing a Congress as well as a President. His name is an anathema to the American public."

In October Davies telephoned Irving Thalberg from New York to discuss the possibility of starring in *Marie Antoinette*, a costume drama percolating at MGM. Hearst and Davies had been excited about the film project for months and were especially eager to discuss their ideas about tapping Davies's unique comedic flair in the development of the lead character. Thalberg, who had been awakened by the call, told Davies he had no problem casting her but that he had already promised the part to his wife. When he woke Shearer up to join in on the conversation, she reportedly told her fellow MGM star, "Marion, I'll be delighted to give it to you if you want it." Shearer handed the phone back to Thalberg, went back to bed, and the matter seemed to be settled. But just minutes after Davies and Thalberg had hung up, the phone rang at the Hearst-Davies Ritz Tower suite. The call was from Louis B. Mayer; Thalberg was obviously passing off the dirty work to his boss. Rather bluntly the MGM head told Davies he wanted Shearer for the role. "I won't do it with you," Davies remembered Mayer saying, "because I wouldn't spend that much money on a production—with that idea—because—this would be a comedienne—strictly—and you'd be no good for Marie Antoinette." Insulted, Davies told Mayer, "I'll be no good for your studio then—goodbye." That night Hearst and Davies put in a call to Jack Warner and Ed Hatrick. Working quickly with Warner representatives in New York, Hatrick drafted a contract for Cosmopolitan Productions that broke the ten-year feature film relationship with Mayer's MGM and established a new five-year association with Warner Bros.

On the eve of the public announcement of the Cosmopolitan-Warner alliance, Louella Parsons devoted her column to Marion Davies. The columnist pointed out that Davies had replaced Mary Pickford as tinsel town host, even referring to her Santa Monica beach home, modeled after Mount Vernon, as "a white house on the beach." In case there was any doubt about it,

Parsons wanted everyone in Hollywood to know the importance of being associated with Marion Davies: "I doubt if Marion realized her popularity all over the world before she went to Europe. London feted her and hailed her as a great artist. Her beauty, her wit, and her gift for making friends were the talk of the town. She was entertained by all the social leaders and the same was true in every country she visited. She is not simply Marion Davies of Hollywood, she is Marion Davies of the big world."

Actress Louise Brooks, who was close to Marion Davies's niece Pepi Lederer, heard a different interpretation of Cosmopolitan Productions' break with MGM and subsequent merger with Warner Bros. In an essay she wrote about Pepi, Brooks pointed to "the stigma of failure [at MGM] rather than the hope of success" as a factor that made Hearst and Davies leave MGM. Hearst must have thought he would have better opportunities with Warner Bros., but he continued to be wary. "As for Mr. Hearst," Brooks wrote,

> Pepi told me, he privately said that the reason Louis B. Mayer was blocking his efforts to make Marion the biggest star in Hollywood was that Mayer was afraid that Hearst might usurp his production throne at MGM. The Jewish control of the film industry, Mr. Hearst thought, had worked against Marion's success. . . . Hollywood Jews had been indignant over his visit to Hitler at a time when the Gestapo and the storm troopers were in full operation, when the free press and the film studios had been seized by decree, and the Jewish journalists and actors had been dismissed from their jobs and deprived of their German citizenship. But now the full import of his gesture was coming home to them.

AMERICANISM VERSUS COMMUNISM

While Hearst was on his European tour in 1934, San Francisco was paralyzed by a general workers' strike that had been called in sympathy with longshoremen, who were dissatisfied with working conditions on the docks. From overseas, in another act of "remote control," Hearst kept in close contact with his representatives in the city, on his newspapers, and in the government. He had long opposed unionism and had not objected to strong tactics—even violence—to break strikes, but this latest trouble seemed to be particularly ominous. Hearst feared the labor outbursts in San Francisco were the warning shots of a Communist-inspired revolution. If they went unchecked, he thought, they would lead to nothing but further chaos. For

Hearst, there was only one saving grace to the strike, and it was not insignif-icant: events seemed to be proving that San Francisco and the country still needed his leadership, strong-armed and otherwise. From his European van-tage point Hearst directed his attorney and newspaper executive, John Fran-cis Neylan, to break the strike. Using behind-the-scenes political maneu-vering coupled with the threat of National Guardsmen and the tacit approval of vigilante groups as a weapon, Hearst's man on the scene united the entrenched powers of the city. Emotionally and often physically beaten, the strikers called off their struggle.

Another grave situation, from Hearst's point of view, occurred in the summer of 1934: the End Poverty in California (EPIC) campaign for gov-ernor of California of writer and activist Upton Sinclair. Like other pow-erful businessmen, Hearst saw Sinclair as the vanguard of an anticapitalist and antiestablishment movement whose ultimate goal was institutionalized socialism. Sinclair was particularly troubling to the Hollywood establish-ment, which saw his advocacy for special taxes on the film industry and the institution of a state-run program to hire the unemployed to produce films in underutilized studios as a usurpation of their power. An added factor causing consternation to moguls like Mayer and Thalberg was Sinclair's close relationship with odd-man-out producer William Fox, the two men having recently collaborated on *Upton Sinclair Presents William Fox*, a book that was particularly critical of MGM. It was rumored that Fox was actually financ-ing Sinclair's campaign. Working closely with the leading producers and even rival newspapers such as the *Los Angeles Times*, Hearst did everything he could do to defeat Sinclair.

Historians have documented a host of orchestrated assaults on Sinclair's candidacy, including a steady drumbeat of disinformation about the EPIC candidate spewed out primarily by Hearst's California newspapers and behind-the-scenes chicanery by the leaders of the film industry. In Septem-ber, two months before the election, Sinclair opponents spread the word through the *Hollywood Reporter*, widely considered the mouthpiece of the film industry, that as many as six major studios would close up and move out of California if voters picked Sinclair. Nicholas Schenck and the Warner brothers said they would transfer their operations to Florida, and other reports had MGM reopening Hearst's old Cosmopolitan studios in upper Manhattan. In October photographs appeared in the *Los Angeles Examiner* and the *Los Angeles Times* purporting to show homeless men and women arriving in Los Angeles by the trainload, eager to receive Sinclair's alleged handouts. *Variety* reported that one of the pictures was actually a still from a 1932 feature called *Wild Boys of the Road* and the other was a staged photograph of extras from Central Casting. On the day before the phony photograph appeared in the *Examiner*, the opinion page of the same newspaper published an editorial titled "Five Million Extras." In a strong warning against a Sinclair election, the Hearst paper compared the predicted influx of unemployed into the state of California to the hopeful but hungry extras who lined up day after day outside the film studios.

The most infamous slight used against Sinclair was a series of movie shorts that hit theaters just in time for the election. Produced by Irving Thalberg in conjunction with the Hearst newsreel organization and titled *The Inquiring Reporter*, the films were cast with actors playing wild-eyed, gruff-looking revolutionaries or foreigners who gave an unseen interviewer their reasons for supporting Sinclair. Felix Feist Jr., a Hearst newsreel executive, was in charge of the anti-Sinclair camera crew, and when the movie shorts were completed they were tagged on to regular Hearst newsreels and distributed to exhibitors, who were forced to take the combined package or nothing at all. In November the *New York American* reported that movie financier A. P. Giannini had declared Republican Frank F. Merriam his candidate and that Sinclair's plan for California was a "hazardous experiment which would seriously hamper the progress of our state."

The Sinclair campaign was a prime example of Hollywood's ability to close ranks when it perceived its very existence was at risk. On the eve of the election, the *Hollywood Reporter* voiced enthusiasm over the conflagration set off against Sinclair, favorably comparing Hollywood's methods to those bread-and-circus voter manipulation extravaganzas perfected at the turn of the twentieth century: "This campaign against Upton Sinclair has been and is DYNAMITE. It is the most effective piece of political humdingery that has ever been effected, and this is said in full recognition of that master-machine that used to be Tammany. . . . And this activity may reach much farther than the ultimate defeat of Mr. Sinclair. It will undoubtedly give the big wigs in Washington and politicians all over the country an idea of the real POWER that is in the hands of the picture industry."

The reference to Tammany Hall was not incidental. Not only had the political headquarters been a model for the film industry and for Hearst's synergistic methods, but even Irving Thalberg would later point to Tammany Hall as justification for his participation in producing the fake interview newsreels. "Nothing is unfair in politics," Thalberg told a private gathering in Hollywood years later, during a discussion about the Sinclair campaign. "We could sit down here and figure dirty things out all night, and every one of them would be all right in a political campaign. . . . I used to be a boy orator for the Socialist party on the East Side in New York. Do you think Tammany ever gave me a chance to be heard? They broke up our meetings, and we tried to break up their meetings. If there had been any chance that we might beat them in our ward, they would simply have thrown the ballot boxes into the East River, as they did against Hearst."

Sinclair was narrowly defeated by Merriam. It was speculated that the campaign against the EPIC candidate had extended right up to election day. *Variety* reported that an "anti-Sinclairite" had gotten the assistance of Republican and Democratic leaders to have photographers with tiny Leica cameras (coined "candid cameras") stationed at six precincts considered strongly pro-EPIC. The operation was touted as a precautionary measure to discourage floaters and repeaters, but it seems more likely that the tactic was used to intimidate potential Sinclair voters. When Merriam had been declared the winner, Hearst sent a telegram to editor Brisbane: "Sinclair is handsomely beaten by over two hundred and twenty thousand. People of California do not have to try the small pox in order to realize that they do not like it. I think the actual experience with Sinclairism would not merely have been expensive but would have been ruinous. As it is, we are well rid of him, thank Heaven."

On the next day, November 8, Brisbane responded to Hearst with a humorous compliment to his boss's hard work in defeating Sinclair: "I have your telegram about Sinclair. I think there was a considerable chance of his being elected if one of my grandsons had not owned several newspapers in the State of California, and used them discreetly and effectively." In early December, Brisbane was still reminding Hearst of his central role in the anti-Sinclair crusade. "Skit on California election at Gridiron dinner," Brisbane wrote Hearst in a telegram, "giving you credit for defeating Sinclair was much applauded."

Despite his ultimate defeat, Sinclair's strength in the polls aroused the left to the possibilities of radical change and in turn caused great concern to the right. Coinciding as it did with the unrest among workers in San Francisco, the campaign of 1934 became a rocket that propelled Hearst's last great political crusade. Fresh from his European travels and his flirtations with dictators, Hearst was raring to fight what he perceived to be the enemies of capitalism and the way of life he enjoyed, wherever they might be. Although later his crusade would be called anti-Communism, in 1934 he called it "Americanism."

In November 1934 Hearst was settled back at San Simeon, ready to launch an attack on the Communist influence on the nation's education system. To provide the proper cinematic touch, Hearst added Philip Kellogg, a production man working with Irving Thalberg at MGM, to his newspaper staff and instructed his news film team to produce an anti-Communism crusade with drama. With increasingly broader stokes, Hearst's campaign painted a number of major universities, including Harvard and Columbia, as citadels of communistic thought. Leftist professors were the main targets, but radical youth groups were also attacked. When Hearst was unable to produce hard evidence to back up accusations, he shifted the focus of his attack, claiming that universities were encouraging an epidemic of "free love."

Presumably, there were greater numbers of Communists or Communist sympathizers on the campuses than in other areas of American life. In the 1930s, as in other periods of history, the university had led the way opposing war and fascism, flirting with and sometimes embracing radical ideologies. But Hearst, as was his habit, had overstated his case and perhaps not counted on the fact that these champions of academic freedom were also some of the more articulate, vocal, and committed critics he had ever encountered. With his college attacks coming on the heels of his controversial meeting with Hitler, Hearst galvanized his opponents to a degree unseen since his pro-German troubles during World War I. Although his tactics for creating stories and fighting crusades had changed little since he began in publishing, the times had. Hearst's methods were now being compared with the Nazis', and he was accused of distributing disinformation and using secret-police methods by hiring undercover reporters to pose as students for the purpose of exposing Communists. Educator Charles Beard warned his colleagues that "unless those who represent American scholarship, science, and the right of a free people to discuss public questions freely stand together against his insidious influences he will assassinate them individually by every method known to yellow journalism."

In 1935 feature film releases with an anti-Communist theme were extremely rare. Only three films, *Together We Live* (Columbia), *Fighting Youth* (Universal), and *Red Salute* (UA), connected radicalism with the college campus and with youth in general. Just one film, *Oil for the Lamps of China* (Warner Bros.), made an unequivocal attack on foreign Communism. All the films dealing with Communism at home show the influence of Hearst's highly publicized crusades against radicalism that were launched in 1934. *Oil for the Lamps of China* was actually a Cosmopolitan Production. *Together We Live* was a low-budget Columbia Pictures film that gave its anti-Communist message an added dimension by using a general strike as the catalyst that tears apart a San Francisco family. Audiences at the time would likely have been aware of the inspiration for the fictional strike. Although the picture's release was delayed until 1935 because of the death of its director, writer, and star,

Willard Mack, it had gone into production shortly after the real San Francisco strike of 1934 that had been unashamedly suppressed by Hearst operatives. Two other films of 1935 exploring the theme of radicalism were set on American college campuses and were in production at the height of Hearst's college red-baiting campaign. In *Fighting Youth*, a Universal film directed by Hamilton Macfadden, a college becomes the target of young radicals, who devise ways to subvert the campus football hero, played by Charles Farrell, and generally spread wild communistic thought among the student body. *Red Salute*, a United Artist picture released in September 1935, was a screwball comedy that followed the exploits of a college girl, played by Barbara Stanwyck, who falls for a student activist. The girl's family, mortified by their daughter's interest in a radical, sends her away to Mexico, only to find out that she has enlisted a young soldier, played by Robert Young, to help reunite her with her campus sweetheart. In the course of events, against her better judgment but to everyone's satisfaction, the Stanwyck character falls in love with the soldier. As the *New York Evening Journal's* glowing review put it, the young girl's military man talks her out of "her Communist theories." Hearst's *New York Daily Mirror*, which also gave the movie a positive review, said the soldier and his girlfriend's "hair [sic] brained escapade results in merry complications, cures her of her juvenile infatuation, arouses her real Americanism." One of the complications of the story, which Hearst's newspaper characterized as "merry," involved the girl's father working in cahoots with an immigration official to remove the radical student from the campus by trumping up a false charge against him of inciting a riot. An article in the *New York Times*, which called the film "simple-minded and actively dangerous," saw the film as an extension of Hearst's anti-Communism campaigns:

> When Hollywood embroils itself in the drama of controversy and ideas, it is well for the judicious to get out of the way. Like the small boy with an air rifle, the studios are likely to hit almost anything but the target. Americanism, for example, means little enough that is admirable now that it has become the private property of the sage of San Simeon. . . . It has come to represent the glorification of war as an outlet for the nervous energy of our young men, the suppression of political thought in our universities, the abolition of the Bill of Rights with the connivance of the United States Army, and several other doctrines which are less than completely democratic.

Several thousand high school and college students protested *Red Salute* at its evening premiere at the Rivoli Theater on September 28, and the police charged the picket line, arresting eighteen protesters for unlawful assembly. During the afternoon showing, two men in their early twenties were arrested for booing the picture and refusing to leave the theater. One of the men, Joseph Lash, identified himself as the executive secretary of the Student League for Industrial Democracy, an organization that was Communist controlled. Lash was not a Communist Party member, but he once dubbed himself "a non-Party Communist." Following the Nazi-Soviet pact in August 1939, Lash attacked Communism and became a trusted friend and biographer of Eleanor Roosevelt. During the week following *Red Salute*'s opening, student protests and arrests continued outside the theater. The protests drew little notice in the Hearst press, which seemed content to let the Hearst-inspired motion picture speak for itself.

Oil for the Lamps of China, Hearst's first major dramatic film for Warner Bros., was directed by Mervyn LeRoy and based on a 1933 novel written by Alice Tisdale Hobart. The film focuses on an American businessman named Stephen Chase who is sent to the Far East as an employee of a large oil company. The oil corporation is obviously based on the Standard Oil Company, but in the film it is called the Atlantis Oil Company (in an earlier draft of the script it was the American Oil Company). While working in Manchuria, Chase invents a kerosene lamp that works more cheaply than anything else on the market. He convinces his bosses they should distribute his lamp free to the Chinese so that before long they will have millions of loyal customers. When Chase's previously announced marriage plans fall through and he is confronted with the possibility of "losing face" with his future clients, he finds a quick solution by forming a partnership with Hester Adams, a woman he meets in a bar. Chase and Adams marry and eventually fall in love. Chase is a fully committed company man. He sticks with his oil company even after they give credit to another employee for his invention, his immediate boss kills himself after being passed over for a promotion, and his wife loses their baby in childbirth while he is off fighting an oil well fire.

For more than three-quarters of its running time, the film paints a picture of a corporation that is more concerned with money than life and an employee more concerned with his company than his wife. The character of Chase is the embodiment of the work ethic, telling his wife in one of the film's more dramatic scenes that work is his only identity. But while actor Pat O'Brien's portrayal of Chase often strains credibility, it is generally sympathetic, with touches of pathos. The mood and direction of the film changes with a sudden sequence of bold newspaper headlines announcing the spread of Communism in China. In the very next scene a car driven by Communists rebels on their way to see Chase callously rams into a horse-driven carriage, causing it to throw local peasants into the street. The message is clear: the Communists are literally bulldozing their way through the villages of China. When one of the Communist officials bursts into Chase's office, he mocks the American slogan "the customer is always right" and demands that the oil company representative hand over all the gold in his safe. Chase stalls the rebels and devises an escape plan. Although he is injured in the process, he manages to survive and to save the company's money. From a hospital bed, Chase learns that despite his heroism, he too has been passed over for a top position in the company. But while Chase is again working as a clerk for his beloved company, his wife holds a secret blackmail session with a company executive. When she sees that reasoning is getting nowhere, she makes a threat to file a lawsuit on her husband's behalf for the royalty payments owed on his kerosene lamp patents. In one of the film's final scenes the president of the oil company is seen on the telephone calling the threatened executive, demanding to know why Chase was not given the important position he so deserves. The oil company president seems to represent all the good that Chase always saw in his company, since there is no indication that he was motivated by any threat from Chase's wife. In the film's happy ending, Chase and his wife are seen locked in a sweet embrace, the wife believing that her behind-the-scenes maneuvering has saved the day, and the company man holding strong to his belief in the ultimate good of the corporation.

Oil for the Lamps of China took a long time to reach the screen. Warner Bros. purchased the novel on January 3, 1934, nine months before Hearst became associated with the studio and a year before filming began. A Warner Bros. camera crew under the direction of Robert Florey was sent to China and Japan for several weeks in the summer of 1934, returning with twenty thousand feet of film that the producers planned to use for Oil (only snippets of this footage wound up in the picture) and other Warner productions. The film's director, Mervyn LeRoy, also traveled in China for several months, and he worked with writer Laird Doyle to develop a script. By the time the film was slated as a Cosmopolitan production, the script had already been revised a number of times. LeRoy cast his film almost entirely with stage-trained actors, including Pat O'Brien, Josephine Hutchinson, Jean Muir, and Donald Crisp and two Asian-Americans, Tetu Komai and Willie Fung, who were selected for prominent roles. Filming took place between January and March 1935—some exterior scenes were shot in the Mojave Desert—and several weeks of editing followed. The film cost $366,000 to make, a figure slightly above average for Warner Bros. productions in 1935.

The slow pace of the Oil production is related to several factors, includ-

ing the touchy subject matter of the novel, the desire of the film's producers to be topical, and the involvement of Hearst in the later stages of production. As early as December 1934, Joe Breen's censorship office questioned the wisdom of even embarking on such a project. In a letter sent to
Jack Warner a month later that accepted the film's revised final script but
offered some additional cuts, Breen reminded the studio head of his earlier
letter: "As I suggested to you in our letter of December 4, 1934, our chief
concern with regard to this proposed production is from the general standpoint of industry policy. The book, as you know, has been accepted as a
vicious attack upon the Standard Oil Company. . . . You ought to take serious counsel before actually putting this picture into production in order to
escape any possible serious criticism from some of the oil companies, if not
actual litigation."

During the preproduction and filming of *Oil*, China was very much in
news. In the fall of 1934, under attack from the Nationalist armies of
Chiang Kai-shek, eighty-seven thousand Chinese Communist troops
began a journey of six thousand miles from southern China to northern
China. When the Long March reached the northern province of Shanxi
in the fall of 1935, only one-tenth of the original retreating army had survived. The Long March was a yearlong trek of tragedy for thousands of
Chinese, but it strengthened the true believers and brought forth countless stories of courage and heroism that galvanized a revolutionary movement. From defeat rose a distinctly Chinese Communism led by Mao
Tse-tung. These dramatic events, which could not have been included in
the novel *Oil for the Lamps of China*, found their way into the film version. In the Hollywood production, the battle between Communism and
capitalism is reduced to a few sensationalized episodes that use the political struggles in China as a backdrop to a confused message about an individual's place in a corporate world. In a sequence that typifies the Hearstian exploration of the Communism issue in the film, newspapers are
thrown on the screen with direct and frightening headlines such as "COM-
MUNIST REVOLT THREATENS IN SOUTHERN PROVINCES"
and "COMMUNISTS ACTIVE IN CHOW YANG DISTRICT."

Exactly why Hearst chose *Oil for the Lamps of China* as a Cosmopolitan
production is unknown. The novelist's thinly veiled attack on Standard Oil
might have interested him, since he had done the same thing himself
through his newspapers in the 1920s. By the mid-1930s, however, Hearst's
trust-busting days were far behind him, and he rarely took on crusades
against big business. Quite possibly Hearst was not terribly involved in the
early stages of production, being distracted by a search to find a suitable

vehicle for Davies at Warner Bros. At the time, he was considering several films for the actress, including a remake of *Little Old New York*, a film version of the musical *Rosalie*, and *Captain Blood*, which ended up being a box office hit for Cosmopolitan in 1935, teaming Errol Flynn with Olivia de Havilland, not Davies. Still, despite his focus on Davies's career, it is doubtful that Hearst was completely unaware of such a high-visibility project as *Oil*. Cosmopolitan chief Ed Hatrick was certainly involved in the production and in regular contact with the film's producer, Hal Wallis. And it was Hatrick's pattern to kept his boss informed of all Cosmopolitan productions. Hearst may have been less than hands-on in the early stages of the production, but the anti-Communist messages and the flip-flop view of corporations in the film's later sequences more than suggest his direct influence.

Shortly after Breen's letter to Warner in January 1935, the filming of *Oil for Lamps of China* began. In late April 1935 a two-hour version was previewed before moviegoers in Hollywood. In response to audience reactions, Jack Warner and Hal Wallis immediately called for nearly two thousand feet to be cut from the film. Soon afterward Wallis gave a private screening of a trimmed version of the film to Harry Bercovich, a Canadian exhibitor friend, who seems to have had some relationship with Hearst as well. The following day, from the Ambassador Hotel, Bercovich wrote Wallis a two-page letter, calling the film "anti-corporation propaganda" that was straight out of the writings of Upton Sinclair. "Thus we also feel," Bercovich wrote, "that it is not only contradictory to the work which Mr. Hearst is so ably doing, but adds further impetus to dangerous corporate legislation, and to those who are urging new economic and social systems upon business. . . . There are no two sides to this story—only one. This is especially focused in the present ending. Here the heroine triumphs—but only by trickery. The oppressor is outwitted by the oppressed. Nothing gracious about it. Downright blackmail is depicted as necessary." Interestingly, Bercovich's letter to Wallis makes no mention of the anti-Communist themes in the film's final reels.

According to press reports, Hearst saw a version of the film around the first of May. He was so upset about the film's anticorporation message that he briefly considered removing the name Cosmopolitan from the credits. During the first week of May, the *Oil* production team was called back and put to work following Hearst's orders to fix the film. On May 8 *Daily Variety* reported: "To soften what some previewers and Warner's executives regarded as unsympathetic treatment of a fictitious but typical corporation in the production of 'Oil for the Lamps of China,' a few added scenes have been inserted in the final reel. New takes are designed to show corporation in less callous attitude toward its outpost employees than was the case in the first assembly of film made from Alice Tisdale Hobart's story." It is all but certain that the major change made to the film was the inclusion of the scene featuring the kindly oil company president at the film's ending. Quite possibly the film was also edited to pump up the anti-Communism propaganda in hopes of offsetting the film's anticorporation messages. On May 12 Hatrick saw the film at a private screening with Harry Warner in New York; he thought it was improved but still too long. Eventually, the film would be cut to approximately ninety-six minutes.

The press analysis of *Oil for the Lamps of China* was often as baffling as the message of the film itself, but it did highlight the political polarization existing in the United States in the mid-1930s. Most of the mainstream press ignored the film's anti-Communism propaganda, but they were divided over whether the film was pro- or anticorporation. The *New York Times* thought the film was a dishonest version of the novel that "tries to be a glowing tribute to the Atlantis Oil Company and its high-minded crusade to bring light to the Chinese barbarians." The *New York Herald Tribune* found the film to be ultimately anticorporation. It was perplexed by Hearst's ending and suggested the possibility that it was meant to be tongue-in-cheek. The *Daily Worker* review left the impression that Hearst's clumsy attempt to defend corporations at the end of the film was a constant theme throughout the film: "Mr. Hearst's feverish pleas in favor of big business heroically mouthed by Hollywood's best, are in the vein of 'The company will never fail you.' What if it lets you down once in a while? But that's only because here and there you will find an inefficient official, not corrupt mind you, but merely inefficient, who will spoil your chances for advancement. But, the company will find out and you shall be rewarded."

The *Worker* thought the film's message on Communism was as phony as the one on corporations:

> The real reasons for the rising revolutionary movement are not even mentioned. Instead the only solution for all these ills, according to Hearst, is that "China is not only ready but anxious for American business!" Even were the chauvinism, the ballyhoo for big business, removed, the film would still be nil. A distortion of the story, the picture is a slow-moving tale of little interest. Hearst may be able to foist his rotten lies on the public in print, but when he attempts to put them on the screen, before the eyes of millions of workers who day in and day out are exploited by big business, the falseness is too glaring, however coated with sweet love and happiness!

The left and the right saw what they wanted to see in the film to measure their loyalty or loathing toward the issues of Capitalism, Communism, and Hearst. The level of intensity from both sides seemed to unite both sides in a belief that Hearst was a real force in Hollywood who had the power or the potential to produce film propaganda. How much the public seemed to care about the undercurrents of the film is uncertain. Despite the *Daily Worker*'s assessment, audiences seemed to be attracted to the love story and the action—and maybe even the political potpourri as well—for they made it one of Warner Bros.'s box office successes of 1935.

In early June, as *Oil* opened around the country, most Hearst newspapers carried glowing reviews, written by Rose Pelswick and Louella Parsons, that focused on the love story and the evils of Communism and ignored the still discernible anticorporation messages. The film's director, Mervyn LeRoy, who happened to be spending the weekend at San Simeon at the time of the film's premiere, was surprised to find a less than enthusiastic review in Hearst's *San Francisco Examiner*. In the morning he found Marion Davies in the second-floor library and expressed his disappointment. "Why, that's awful," she told the director. "Let me go upstairs and get Poppy." Hearst, who was still dressed in a long nightgown, returned with Davies but was unruffled by LeRoy's concerns. "I want to tell you something, Mervyn," Hearst said. "Just remember this—the newspaper of today is the toilet paper of tomorrow."

Hearst seems to have been in a generally fatalistic frame of mind during this period. On June 11, 1935, Davies's niece Pepi Lederer committed suicide by jumping from the window of a hospital where she had been under observation. News of Pepi's death came as a serious blow to Davies. Hearst, who was close to the young woman as well, tried to comfort Davies by offering the hope of reincarnation. "We should not fear death." Hearst told her on the way home from the funeral. "We [have] all died and returned so often that there is really nothing to fear. Indeed, if we did not have a fear instilled in us on earth, our knowledge of the delights of the far beyond would lead us to suicide to attain them."

Writer and journalist Lincoln Steffens, Hearst's longtime friendly nemesis, closely watched the ever-widening, often reckless crusade against Communism carried on by the Hearst films and press. To the old-time muckraker, Hearst still had enormous talents, but he was morally adrift and a man who had traveled far afield of his early promise:

William Randolph Hearst begins to sound sincere, and that's too bad. He is intelligent, you know. Not many careers have been so planned, so intelligent, so firmly managed as his. A work of art, that man's life has been, and conscious. . . . But lately this wise man has been writing articles under his own name and they sound as if he believed them, every word. He seems to think, really, that communism is a menace here and that it is an evil dictatorship in Soviet Russia. It's all right to say this when you're fighting as he always was and always is, but how can he believe it? . . . Why doesn't he send a reporter, like me, for instance, over into Asia and see what is really happening there. He knows perfectly well that I believe in Russia and that I could still report the facts, if facts would be news to the editor of Hearst's chain of newspapers. Might be news even to me. . . . I certainly would get some news there. I would find out, for instance, what substitutes they have for our profit motive; whether there is in human nature a substitute for individual gain that really works. I would not be sincere, you know, not as Mr. Hearst is. I would see the whole thing, as I do Mr. Hearst's fight against free thought, free speech, free learning in the University. I certainly would not be blind to anything but my rather humorous convictions. I wish Mr. Hearst would be again an artist journalist.

In February 1935 the film journal *Motion Picture Herald* published a history of cinema in the Soviet Union and a long detailed report on the current state of Russian film imports to the United States. In its look at present conditions, the *Herald* concluded that although propaganda was evident in many of the current Soviet films being presented in the United States, their influence on American culture was negligible. In its investigation, the *Herald* found that approximately 152 independently owned theaters in the United States, or less than 1 percent of the total number of theaters in the country, were screening Soviet films. In addition, 94 percent of those theaters were located in a handful of eastern states. "There is only one theatre steadily showing Soviet product for every 829,000 inhabitants in this country," the *Herald* wrote, "and one seat for each 1,360 persons, whereas regular motion picture theatres provide a seat for each 13 inhabitants and there is one theatre for every 8,590 persons."

Facts and figures had never been an obstacle to Hearst, who used the *Herald* article as a jumping-off point and began an editorial crusade that exaggerated the influence of Soviet films. "Moscow Films Poison U.S. Screens!" and "Red Octopus Grabs Control of 152 Theatres to Widen Spread of Propaganda" were typical Hearst headlines. Hearst's over-the-top attack galvanized the left, which heretofore had been unable to sustain an effective protest. In May 1935 it was reported that undergraduates at Princeton University and Amherst College were demonstrating against *Hearst Metrotone News*, collecting petitions and protesting outside local theaters, asking for the cancellation of the newsreels. *Newsweek* reported that they "called the features offensively militaristic and Fascist propaganda."

In June some twenty-five anti–Hearst picketers were arrested in Manhattan and Brooklyn for causing disturbances in theaters and on picket lines, but most of those arrested were reportedly released within a few hours or punished with suspended sentences. Still, the publicity over the arrests and other activities of the boycott movement was causing concern for the Loews theater circuit, exhibitors of the Hearst newsreels. Movie executives were worried about the effect of the demonstrations on some of the more liberal neighborhoods where their sixty theaters in Greater New York were located and where they hoped to maintain friendly community relations. Quietly and unofficially they ordered the *Hearst Metrotone News* to be dropped from the bill of seven movie houses, and they ordered deletions of sequences in the reels that might be deemed militaristic by the protesters. The move did not satisfy the American League Against War and Fascism. When they got wind of Loews' actions, they demanded that the Hearst newsreels be stricken from the circuit's remaining theaters.

Evidence suggests that Loews was preparing to accept the protesters' objections when on July 8 Ed Hatrick flew from California to New York to meet with its top executives. Shortly afterward the film company became more aggressive, announcing that it would no longer act alone in attempting to dissuade the protesters. From now on it would be "cooperating with the authorities to stamp out the menace." After the Loews statement there was a marked increase in the number of protesters arrested (twenty-five within one week in August). The so-called Radical Squad of the New York City police department, under Captain Thomas F. Dugan, was called in to dispatch private detectives to investigate boycott organizers and empowered to prevent disorder in and around the theaters. A spokesman for Hearst's film ventures let it be known that they were contemplating taking up the matter of the boycott with the U.S. postal authorities, since many of the threats against them and the Loews theaters had been distributed by the mails. In some college towns, where boycotts of Hearst newsreels were particularly popular, it was reported that local American Legion posts were forming their own patriotic youth organizations to counteract the leftist groups.

Motion Picture Herald, which only months earlier had ridiculed Hearst's crusade, now chose to defend one of its own and the industry it now claimed faced a real threat:

Those who have regarded with no special or practical concern the drive of the Reds against the newsreel issued by and bearing the name of Mr. William Randolph Hearst may now be discovered themselves discovering that next, in inevitable sequel, comes a drive aimed at dictation of the whole theatre program. . . . There is a Red press in this country. There are also, all imported, many Red pictures. They have both been permitted circulation among their followers. That it seems is not enough. The Reds would now decide what all America must see.

The left was particularly threatened by Hearst's newsreels because it too understood that the film medium was a powerful tool for propaganda and recognized that Hearst's power in the film industry was multiplied by his domination of the publishing field. Andrea Marin Kalas, who has studied the surviving *Hearst Metrotone News* films extensively, has argued that Hearst infused his point of view into his news films and that the brand of progressivism that marked his entrance into journalism is also evident there:

Underlying "liberal" Progressivism was a commitment to the maintenance of the status quo. The American system of free enterprise was lauded in populist terms—portraying heart-wrenching hardships as creative entrepreneurship. American values were also upheld by ethnocentric mockery of other cultures. This same isolationism was used to color ideological threats to capitalism—socialism and communism—as foreign intervention. In this way, any oppositional protest was equated with subversion. . . . It was a movement which developed as a reformist reaction to the inhumane effects of urban industrialism while tied strongly to the established order of government and free enterprise.

One example of Hearst progressivism in the *Hearst Metrotone News* that must have been especially worrisome to the left was a sequence in a newsreel released on May 5, 1934, just weeks before Hearst went on his European trip. The focus of the reel is the traditional socialist May Day celebrations in New York. In Hearst's presentation the event becomes a propaganda piece that sends its audience messages about law-and-order values and subtly advocates the suppression of forces it perceives to be subversive. As Hearst cameramen capture scenes of large crowds, there is a glaring omission of the gathering's purpose and only vague reference to troubles in Europe. A narration declares: "Record crowds hail May Day—Disorders reported abroad but cops in full control as 125,000 celebrate in New York." Only in a slow-motion viewing of the film—undetectable to a contemporary newsreel audience—can one protester at the rally be seen holding a sign that reads "Stop the Nazi Butchers."

By the summer of 1935 calls for a boycott of Hearst publications, newsreels, and feature films were continuing to spread. While the anti-Hearst movement was centered in New York, there was considerable activity in Los Angeles as well. Parker Sercombe, a former magazine publisher who had been attacking Hearst's brand of journalism since the early 1900s and had recently worked for Sinclair's election, was part of the organized opposition on the West Coast. Through the auspices of the Friends of the Soviet Union—a Communist front organization since 1921—Sercombe and others put out a mock Hearst newspaper titled the *Anti-Hearst Examiner*. Within a drawing of octopus tentacles encircling the masthead title was a parody of Hearst and his yellow journalism methods: "Hearst in War, Hearst in Peace, Hearst in Every News Release, Spreads His Filth and Desolation to Increase His Circulation." The satirical newspaper—which was really more like a broadside, being only two pages long—lasted for only two issues, August and September 1935. The August issue focused mostly on Hearst's alleged falsehoods about economic conditions in the Soviet Union. It also had a takeoff on the banality of Arthur Brisbane's "Today" column (called "Any Day"), ample mentions of Hearst's 1934 visit with Hitler, and allusions to the Hearst and Davies relationship and the mysterious death of director Thomas Ince in 1924. The second issue brought more attention to Hearst's influence in the film industry. A large caricature showed Hearst as an overweight ogre with both Marion Davies and Louella Parsons nestled in his lap. The illustration was borrowed from the August issue of the leftist *New Theatre* magazine, but the original version is even more devastating, showing Hearst and his paramours surrounded by dozens of miniature swastikas. The article under the picture is also from *New Theatre*, a partial reprint of a piece entitled "Exposing Louella Parsons, Hearst's Hollywood Stooge."

Taking aim at Hearst's film ventures, the American League Against War and Fascism and some two hundred other leftist or Communist front organizations guaranteed that their cause would get attention in the mainstream press. On August 9 the *Daily Worker* put out an "anti-labor" and "pro-war" movie list that was topped by the Hearst newsreels and three Cosmopolitan–Warner Bros. films: *Oil for the Lamps of China* and two pictures with military themes, *Shipmates Forever*, and *Special Agent*. A fourth Warner Bros. picture on the *Daily Worker* list, called *Stranded*, was erroneously identified as a Cosmopolitan production. "Organizations are urged," the *Daily Worker* wrote, "to take prompt measures to prevent the appearance in neighborhood movie houses of the current anti-working class films mentioned in the list, as well as to send protests to the producers in Hollywood to help defer or stop production of some of the forthcoming ones."

As the decade of the 1930s came to a close, Hearst remained obsessed about the proliferation of anti-American propaganda in films. In 1937, shortly after the Paramount picture *John Meade's Woman* (written by future *Citizen Kane* screenwriter Herman Mankiewicz) was released, Hearst sent a directive to Tom White, the general manager of his newspaper division. The letter makes references to past crusades and is a blueprint that Hearst would follow in future battles with the film industry:

> There is a picture called "John Meade's Woman" which is very communistic. It is produced by [B. P.] Shulberg, who makes a habit of producing such pictures. I would like our papers to give it one initial roast as a poor picture, and also a communistic one. Then ignore it. However, I think something should be done to arouse the churches and patriotic societies against communistic pictures. The moral elements of the community, after long suffering, aroused against prurient pictures and stopped them in ten days. The moral and patriotic people of the land could stop these anarchistic pictures just as quickly if they chose to. The communists have banded together to boycott pictures they do not like. Please see if we cannot arouse true American sentiment against subversive films.

In the midst of his intense anti-Communism drive and the equally intense backlash it caused, Hearst was still able to remain engaged by less overtly political film efforts. He continued to micromanage Marion Davies's career as he had always done, focusing in 1936 on a frivolous vehicle for his star and the actor Clark Gable called *Cain and Mabel*. The Warner Bros. production was a remake of Hearst's successful silent film *The Great White Way*, and the plot once again revolved around the sport of prizefighting and the world of show business. Hearst was prepared to make *Cain and Mabel* a big budget musical and was especially upset over signs that Warners was scrimping on its end of the production deal. During a rehearsal for one of the film's musical numbers in late July, Davies showed up at the studio to find only a dozen or so musicians on hand to accompany her. She stormed off the set only to return a short time later after a call came in for the director from the film's ultimate decision maker. From New York, where he was taking his annual break from California and its state taxes, Hearst demanded that Davies have at her disposal a full orchestra of one hundred musicians. To make sure that the film's final rehearsals and takes went smoothly thereafter, Hearst kept an open telephone line between his Ritz Tower apartment and the Burbank studio to listen in on his favorite actress's production number.

Hearst's promotion of *Cain and Mabel* extended beyond his interest in Davies. According to an article in *Variety*, Hearst came up with the idea of exploiting a story about Clark Gable knocking out his sparring partner during the filming. He personally penned a press release that exaggerated the incident to make Gable look like a he-man. When the generally modest Gable learned about the story, which had been picked up by the non-Hearst newspapers, he gently asked for it to be toned down in future releases. Despite this request from the film's star, Hearst's Universal Service continued to distribute the story to its wire service clients just as its boss had written it.

During the summer of 1936, production was wrapped up on the film *San Francisco*, starring Clark Gable and Spencer Tracy. Since the picture was a product of his former studio, MGM, it was of no particular interest to Hearst. When it was learned that the film's climax was a chilling reenactment of the 1906 earthquake, however, Hearst's organizer of the 1934 strike suppression, John Neylan, hopped into action. Neylan convinced Louis B. Mayer that motion pictures of modern-day San Francisco, showing the city in a more positive light, needed to be made to offset the damaging special effects in his feature film. Neylan sent cameraman Clyde DeVinna (photographer for Cosmopolitan's *White Shadows in the South Seas*) and a small crew to San Francisco for three days, where they shot several hundred feet of appealing film of the Golden Gate Bridge and other attractions. The footage was then incorporated into *Hearst Metrotone* newsreels and tacked on to the ending of MGM's *San Francisco* as an uplifting coda.

In late 1936 Hearst found time to do what he could to assist his film partner Jack Warner, who was in a sticky battle with Bette Davis. Following a heated argument in his office, Warner had suspended the actress. Unable to work for Warner Bros. but still under a stultifying contract, Davis left the country for London to follow up on an offer to make two pictures for the British producer Alexander Korda. Between August and November Hearst was traveling in Italy and Germany when he received word that Warner Bros. was planning to start legal proceedings against Davis while the actress was in England. Suddenly Hearst showed up in London at Davis's trial, where he served as Jack Warner's surrogate, holding what the English courts call a watching brief. At the same time, Hearst directed his newspaper editors back home to treat Davis as a disloyal, naughty, and temperamental actress. In the end the court found in favor of Warner Bros., and the actress was forced to resume work for the studio at the end of her suspension.

Hearst's working relationship with Warner Bros. proved to be short-lived. In January 1937 Hearst accepted a script for *Ever Since Eve*, a film that would be Marion Davies's last picture for Warner and her last film acting role. After picking the property, Hearst went to work casting the film and developing a final draft of the script. Shooting and reshooting on the film dragged on throughout the spring. In April Hearst was clearly dissatisfied with the progress on *Ever Since Eve*, convinced that the film was part of a pattern of disrespect and disregard toward Davies. He had Ella Williams, his longtime Cosmopolitan studio manager, send Jack Warner a letter on April 13: "Mr. Hearst has asked me to tell you how he feels about material that Marion has had to date at Warners. He said one thing that Metro did was to get stories for Marion, realizing that she was a star and the stories were about and for her, and he would much prefer not to do any pictures until some such story is obtained for her. If it would make it easier, he would like a release from you so she could feel free to negotiate on the outside."

Hearst was not the only one dissatisfied with the film; it found few sympathetic reviewers when it was released in the summer of 1937. Hearst's time with Warner Bros. was clearly at an end.

It Pays to Defend Advertising

The rise and fall of a movie mogul's power in Hollywood was usually closely related to the box office success of his films at any given point in time. Often, depending on the extent of the investment and/or the pre-publicity hype, a single film can make or break a producer. Because Hearst's involvement in the film industry was measured by different standards—his films in combination with his political and publishing power—his influence was also more mercurial than most. Although they have evoked surprisingly little interest among Hearst biographers, Hearst's magazines were as important in their own way as his newspapers, and Hearst used them too to promote Hollywood and help him prevail as a film industry leader.

Good Housekeeping magazine, purchased by Hearst in 1911, was by the late 1930s fourth in circulation among women's magazines and first in advertising. With its growing success, *Good Housekeeping* fashioned itself as a bellwether of public opinion, especially women's opinions. Like other Hearst venues, it also engaged in swaying the public whenever possible to support issues of importance to its publisher. Ultimately *Good Housekeeping* used its success and the connections it fostered with women to better tap into lucrative advertising markets and maintain its supremacy in the magazine field.

Being a national magazine, *Good Housekeeping* found it necessary to reach out to readers in the communities where they lived and the places where they generally congregated. In the 1930s and 1940s the place to find educated women with a certain level of buying power was the socially, religiously, politically, and educationally based club. For the most part *Good Housekeeping's* Club Service acted as a consumer information bureau that issued publications and suggested discussion groups on subjects ranging from color decisions for home furnishings to guidance in shopping for silk hosiery. The Club Service was an umbrella for other departments, and in August 1939 it introduced a branch it referred to as a motion picture "clearing house." Theresa Wells, executive secretary of the all-encompassing Club Service, ran the Motion Picture Club Service. In the motion picture division Wells was assisted by Mary Hamman, who wrote a monthly column for *Good Housekeeping* called "Movie Forum." Hamman's column became a sort of jumping-off point for an interactive program tied in with women's clubs across the country. Hamman discussed various subjects of interest to moviegoers and followed up these articles with large mailings to women's clubs that suggested programs for discussion groups and courses of action to publicize their opinions.

Hamman's articles were generally innocuous; there were pieces on character actors and starlets, and from time to time a feature film was singled out for praise. An article on Greta Garbo in the film *Ninotchka*, for instance, seemed to anticipate Hearst's own "In the News" piece on the movie star but without the red-baiting. "Movie Forum" sometimes touched on more serious subjects, such as film censorship, regarding which Hamman's attitude was more rosy than confrontational. In Hamman's view, the Hays Office had been far less oppressive than similar watchdogs abroad, and she pointed to a number of films produced over the preceding decade—among them, *Black Legion* and *Fury*—that were critical of American culture and institutions. "Aren't you pleased that our pictures are free to admit we have failings," she wrote in an April 1940 article, "that Hollywood suffers from few restrictions, and that producers can present facts?"

Even when Hamman's articles championed various film causes, they remained faithful to the Hollywood establishment. One example was a November 1939 "Movie Forum" that focused on the practice of showing double features at movie theaters that had become common after 1931, started in hopes of attracting moviegoers during the Depression. In Hamman's opinion audiences had long tired of double bills, and she encouraged her readers to work through their clubs and demand a return to the single-feature presentation. The campaign against the double-feature bill appears to be a crusade against an established film practice, but a subtext of the criticism actually reveals a subtle allegiance to the industry. "Movie Forum" points out that the elimination of the double feature would make room for the return of the two-reel movie short, a genre that included the travelogue, the animated cartoon, and the scientific or educational film. As it turns out, movie studios in 1939 had extensive plans for producing shorts during the coming season. Still pushing the matter, the December issue of *Good Housekeeping* was devoted entirely to the subject of shorts. Hamman chronicled their long history, pointing out that shorts were the earliest films, and provided minireviews of recent releases. "We believe that you can use shorts as a real weapon against the double bill." Hamman wrote. "Suppose instead of saying, 'Down with doubles,' you shout, 'Up with shorts.' That gives you a positive program. It's all very well to be *against* something; but you're in a stronger position if you are fighting *for* something!"

Movie shorts were deemed so important to *Good Housekeeping* that they symbolically extended their Seal of Approval to the genre, creating a Shorts Preview Board to select outstanding examples each month for readers to urge their local theaters to screen. On the board of twenty-six men and women were a treasurer from a New York branch of the American Legion and a managing editor from *Good Housekeeping*, but the group also included a number of academics as well as the distinguished curator of the Museum of Modern Art's Film Library, Iris Barry.

"Movie Forum" followed up its monthly column by distributing pamphlets with discussion topic suggestions to club members. Film reviews written by the "Movie Forum" staff, accompanied by still reproductions from films, were mailed to members. These club packages also included comments on films from more official movie critics such as the National Board of Review. The movie service solicited feedback on a variety of film subjects and encouraged club members to actively promote particular pictures that *Good Housekeeping* favored. "Put your club's telephone chain to work on the picture," urged one pamphlet, "each member telephoning 10 people, asking them in turn to phone 10, and so on." In another group mailing to women's clubs, Hamman wrote: "This is where the clubwomen of America can be of untold aid to the makers of pictures and to far flung audiences. Hollywood rarely hears a word from an intelligent nation as a whole.... We are turning especially to clubwomen to help us shape this new department and in return, we shall make every effort to pass on to your club valuable and useful information in conducting your club and community motion picture activities."

Hearst's movie clearinghouse remained active throughout the 1940s as the magazine continued cultivating relationships with various movie associations such as the Motion Picture Producers and Distributors of America, the National Motion Picture Council, and the motion picture divisions of various other national and local organizations. These organizations were eager to assist the industry-friendly Hearst service, providing it with movie publicity packages including stills, cast lists, and other materials. The movie club service claimed that it was "maintained for the sole purpose of meeting the demands of club and club members" as "an unadvertised and unsolicited division of 'Good Housekeeping' magazine." Whether movie associations and film studios may have had monetary arrangements with Hearst is not known. There is little doubt, however, that "Movie Forum" as well as other aspects of the Club Service were advertisements in and of themselves for Hearst's magazine and for the industry. The *Good Housekeeping* logo was displayed prominently on all literature sent out to club members, who were encouraged to express their opinions to the editor of the magazine. Comments from readers were generally favorable to the film industry. Even if the film studios were not literally paying to having their films plugged, it seems likely that there was a financial quid pro quo. Payments may have been channeled back into *Good Housekeeping* itself, where it was not unusual to find advertisements for films that had been praised in Hamman's column or in the program package sent to club members.

During the same period that *Good Housekeeping* was launching its movie club service, it was undergoing a crisis that threatened the backbone of the magazine. In August 1939, after numerous complaints from consumers, the Federal Trade Commission issued a indictment charging the Hearst Corporation and *Good Housekeeping* with "misleading and deceptive acts." The FTC claimed that *Good Housekeeping*'s famous and coveted Seal of Approval was essentially up for sale to manufacturers who paid for advertisements in the pages of the magazine and that its specified or implied guaranties of product performance or reliability were exaggerated or patently false. To those familiar with Hearst's advertising methods over the years, such a good-play-for-good-pay policy was reminiscent of a number of previous schemes, including the one in the 1910s when theatrical producers bought ads in the Hearst papers in exchange for positive reviews.

By the time the FTC made its charges against Hearst public, Richard Berlin, executive vice president of Hearst Magazines, was well prepared for a forceful response. For two years leading up to the August 1939 complaint, there had been rumors that the government agency was gathering personal accounts of *Good Housekeeping*'s abuses in its Seal of Approval contract with consumers. Months before the complaint looked imminent, Berlin began lobbying any official he thought could be useful to the Hearst cause. Assisting Berlin in his efforts were Sidney Boehm, a *New York Journal* reporter who later became a Hollywood screenwriter, and John Aloysius Clements, another reporter who had worked for Walter Howey, the legendary Hearst editor in Chicago. In addition to their more official duties, Boehm and Clements had worked on various personal assignments for Hearst over the years. According to Boehm, in the early 1930s, when Hearst suspected Marion Davies of carrying on an affair with a New Jersey political boss, he hired the reporter to investigate the rumors and put him in charge of mounting a newspaper crusade against vice in Atlantic City. Davies's biographer, Fred Guiles, has written that Hearst once hired Clements to assist in locating the daughter of Marion's sister Rose, who was kidnapped by her father in a bitter divorce battle with Rose. In the late 1930s Clements gained further entry into Hearst's inner circle of star reporters when he became engaged to marry Elaine St. Johns, the only daughter of the longtime Hearst reporter Adela Rogers St. Johns. Herbert R. Mayes, a longtime editor of *Good House-keeping*, remembered Jack Clements as more of an undercover man for the Hearst magazines than a reporter, kept on the Hearst payroll to spy on employees and gather dirt for his bosses. Hearst employees sarcastically dubbed him "Honest John," because "there wasn't an honest bone in his body."

According to Boehm, by early 1939 Berlin had moved his part-time lobbyists into Washington's Willard Hotel (ironically, the landmark hotel is credited with coining the term *lobbyist* in the nineteenth century). Berlin himself would often commute to the nation's capital from his New York office. Apparently, during this period Berlin authorized Hearst lawyers to offer more than one stipulation to forestall more serious impending legal trouble. The government, however, felt these offers would let Hearst off the hook too easily. Negotiations broke down, and the investigation continued. As the months dragged on into the summer of 1939, Berlin's secretive but still legal maneuvering appeared futile. In his autobiography Mayes wrote that with increasing pressure to avert action against Hearst, Clements "undertook one night to break into the offices of the [Federal Trade] Commission in Washington to discover what its plans in connection with the magazine might be. He was caught in the preposterous act." Mayes suggests that Clements's actions were authorized by someone high up in the Hearst organization. "After Clements' Washington misadventure I felt," Mayes wrote, "like others, he should be thrown out of the company. He wasn't." While no newspaper accounts of a Hearst break-in at the FTC have been located and the agency itself cannot find any information on the alleged incident, this does not exclude the possibility that the break-in attempt was aborted or that it occurred and was successfully covered up. The skullduggery described by Mayes, a highly placed employee, was not out of character for the Hearst organization, which had overseen the hiring of gangsters to win circulation wars and the theft of private letters and secret treaty documents to blackmail opponents.

In the early 1950s, during a meeting between Herbert Mayes and Martin Huberth, the longtime Hearst real estate executive, the discussion turned to Dick Berlin. The two men had known Berlin for years and had heard him openly voice his support for fellow Catholic and pro-fascist radio preacher Father Charles Coughlin and watched as he became a close friend and admirer of Wisconsin senator Joseph McCarthy. Both men were loyal to their employers, but Mayes in particular had grown weary of Berlin's political obsessions. Huberth, who had been with the Hearst organization considerably longer than Mayes, turned to his colleague and said with resignation, "You know as well as I do that Dick is irrational about Communism." While Huberth and Mayes's talk focused on Berlin, they must have known that his attitude was a mirror image of Hearst's. It is not known who at Hearst first thought of using the anti-Communism movement as a shield against the mounting attacks on the corporation. Once it found allies with a zeal to match its own, however, the Hearst group was well prepared to do battle to protect everything it had established, from the sanctity of the *Good Housekeeping* Seal of Approval to claims of entitlement in Hollywood. It only needed a spark, and it found it in someone as politically changeable as Hearst himself.

Joseph Brown Matthews (more commonly called J. B. Matthews) had been, according to his third wife, Ruth Inglis, an activist since his childhood in Kentucky. He began his career as a Methodist missionary, a calling that ushered in a lifetime of fiery crusades. "In line with my religious upbringing," Matthews acknowledged in 1938, "I am afraid that I envisioned the whole world's becoming something very much like a Kentucky Methodist meeting house, with resounding hallelujahs." As a teacher and a preacher, he traveled to Java in the late 1910s, and he studied theology at various American universities after his return.

The First World War left Matthews disheartened by politics, and he began to speak out on human rights issues and pacifism. A break with church hierarchy in the 1920s did not soften his religious zeal, however. As a white man in the South, Matthews became a controversial figure, urging racial justice from his position at the African-American Howard University, where he joined the faculty of the School of Religion in 1928. Over a relatively short period, between about 1932 and 1934, Matthews skyrocketed to prominence in a number of radical organizations. He took a leadership role in at least two groups during this period, being appointed chairman of both the American League Against War and Fascism and the Revolutionary Policy Committee of the Socialist Party. He made half a dozen trips to Russia between 1928 and 1935 and was so enraptured by the social and political system there that even witnessing the great famine in the Ukraine during one of his final visits could not elicit a single critical word from him. Matthews's Russian trips and an extensive lecture tour speaking before radical groups around the United States brought him into close contact with many leading Communists, but apparently he never became an official Communist Party member. Still, with his links to almost every other radical organization and a growing list of highly regarded articles in left-wing publications on his résumé, Matthew was most certainly, in the phrase he helped make famous, a "Communist fellow traveler."

Matthews's radicalism began shifting around 1934, as he found himself in an increasingly fractured Socialist Party, caught in the middle of the conservative old guard and a far left faction that promoted a united front with the Communists. Increasingly, Matthews saw the Communists as being more interested in seizing control than righting the wrongs he observed in society. Several disturbing events that he saw firsthand, including a Communist Party power play to take over the Furrier's Union in 1933 and an incident in 1934 when a group of Communists disrupted an American League Against War and Fascism rally at Madison Square Garden, further disillusioned Matthews. For reasons that are not entirely clear, he rapidly began losing support in the Socialist Party, and his membership was suspended in 1934. That same year, needing steady employment to provide for his growing family, Matthews took a position as vice president in the New Jersey–based consumer watchdog organization run by Fred J. Schlink called Consumer Research, where he had already been a board member. Matthews's young son and namesake also worked at Consumer Research.

During the first year or so at his new job, Matthews's politics were still considerably left of center. With help from Ruth Shallcross, soon to be his second wife, he wrote *Partners in Plunder: The Cost of Business Dictatorship*, a severe critique of capitalism that declared modern advertising methods to be one of the causes of fascism's rise in the United States. While researching his book, Matthews was able to utilize the archives of Schlink's organization, a consumer clearinghouse that held a sizable collection of books, pamphlets, clipping files, and correspondence. Although he became close to Matthews, Schlink never had as great an enthusiasm for radicalism as his new friend did; he preferred to see himself as a progressive, advocating for consumer protection by making legislative changes within the capitalist system. Nevertheless, Schlink was disturbed by a number of right-wing organizations. He maintained files on groups and individuals he perceived to be a threat to consumers, including William Randolph Hearst and the Hearst Corporation. Schlink was more than willing to share his Hearst file with anyone he felt was sympathetic to his beliefs. He corresponded with Parker Sercombe, the radical publisher and anti-Hearst activist in California, and with the author Ferdinand Lundberg, who in 1935 was putting together a critical biography that was published the following year under the title *Imperial Hearst*.

In the summer of 1935, soon after Matthews's attack on U.S. business was published, a strike occurred at Consumer Research pitting Matthews, Schlink, and the rest of the management team against a handful of employees and a union led by Arthur Kallet. The strike propelled Kallet—whom Matthews had always accused of being a Communist—into forming a more leftist consumer organization in 1936, the Consumer Union, which still exists today. It also set in motion a chain of events with more far-reaching consequences. Shortly before the strike at Consumer Research, however, Schlink still relished his reputation as a left-winger. In a letter written at the time, he joked about the rumor that the Hearst press had put the freeze on the MGM film *The President Vanishes* because its villain looked and acted like Hearst. Apparently, Schlink wrote, "the resemblance was so obvious that the Hearst papers did the natural thing in spite of the fact, as I understand it, that the picture itself was highly favorable to Mr. Hearst's general cause of fascism." After the strike at Consumer Research, the formerly warm relationships that had been maintained with leftist associations were suddenly severed, and Schlink's politics shifted accordingly.

For many activists on the left and on the right during the 1930s, proximity to Hearst became the gauge for where they stood. Shortly after leaving Consumer Research, Kallet went out of his way to position himself as an enemy of Hearst. With two colleagues in Chicago—one was the son of the prominent rabbi Stephen S. Wise—Kallet published a weekly tabloid called the *People's Press*. One issue included a story about Hearst's "California love nest, his movie queen and their children." In a subsequent issue Kallet and his partners reported that their Hearst exposé had resulted in a variety of "gangdom threats," including at least one distribution manager's being slugged and several editors' being followed and continuously harassed with anonymous telephone calls and letters. Soon after reporting this, copies of Kallet's paper disappeared from many newsstands in Chicago, and the publication folded two years later.

One particularly violent incident during the Consumer Research strike has been cited by those close to Matthews as the catalyst that hastened his conversion to anti-Communism and brought him close to Congressman Martin Dies and Hearst. According to several reports, a group of Consumer Research employees who were not striking were traveling on a bus to the company's nearby plant when they suddenly noticed the road was being blocked by strikers. The bus managed to get through the demonstrators, who suddenly ran to their waiting cars, those who had none hanging on to their fellows' running boards. As cars followed the bus in hot pursuit, rocks were thrown through the bus windows, injuring some of the employees. It looked as though the bus might escape the attackers when one of the cars pulled in front of it, causing it to come to a full stop. An avalanche of rocks rained on the employees as glass shattered all around them. Witnesses saw at least one employee, a seventeen-year-old boy, dragged out of the bus to the street, where he was severely beaten up. His name was Joseph Matthews Jr. The boy survived the attack. (In 1959, in what may have been a completely unrelated incident, the grown-up boy took a baseball bat, clubbed his three children to death at their breakfast table, attempted to kill wife in the same manner, and then took his own life with a butcher knife.)

The strikers at Consumer Research had cast J. B. Matthews as a traitor to workers. Matthews in turn felt betrayed and alienated by his former ideological comrades. In his own words, the aftermath of the strike left him with "awful spells of blues over the dastardliness of these incredible hypocrites in the labor and radical world." Weeks before the strike Matthews had made his last trip to Moscow. While he was there he bought an assortment of consumer products for later testing. After the strike he wrote a book devoted to consumer issues in which fraudulent practices in the Soviet Union came in for special scrutiny. Over the next few years his growing flirtation with anti-Communism hardened into a permanent philosophy. The far right was more than happy to welcome him into its camp.

By 1938 Schlink felt it necessary to respond to rumors that Hearst was actually dictating his policies. In a letter to a man who had been told about a Hearst connection, Schlink said "the notion that our 'policies are controlled by William Randolph Hearst' is a brand new one to us and quite amusing." In a long denial of the accusation, Schlink was eager to provide evidence that he had often been critical of Hearst, but he was equally anxious to know where the rumor had started. Schlink urged his correspondent to challenge those who were spreading the rumor and asked that he be kept informed "if anything further develops." Despite his denials, however, as the 1930s came to a close Schlink was becoming noticeably less critical of Hearst. The splintering of his organization had significantly lessened his importance as a leader in the consumer movement, and as he struggled to regain his former role he found himself sometimes ardently anti-Stalinist and sometimes anti–New Deal. According to J. B. Matthews's third wife, Schlink went through a long period of bitterness after the strike of 1935 and eventually settled into a more consistent conservatism. By the middle of 1939, his pragmatic passage would take him further from his origins than he cared to admit.

Matthews remained a vice president of Consumer Research until 1938, spending most of his time writing, traveling, and reevaluating his politics. As his disillusionment with Communism grew, his small circle of influential friends became more conservative. One of his closest friends was George Sokolsky, a *New York Herald Tribune* columnist who had made a similar conversion from socialism to anti-Communism. In his youth, Sokolsky had stumped for William Randolph Hearst when he ran for mayor of New York City, because the candidate was then considered a radical. In time Sokolsky grew to believe that Marxists had "perverted an ideal of human progress into the enslavement of man to the state."

Matthews and Sokolsky had a common interest in the politics of consumer issues. Sokolsky focused on what he perceived to be a left-wing consumer movement that was threatening to big business. He infused his concerns into his newspaper columns and into *Liberty* magazine, a Macfadden publication, to which he became a contributing writer. It was later discovered that at the same time that he was presenting himself as an objective reporter he was being paid by Japanese and Chinese interests and employed—for a salary of $1,000 a month—as a propagandist for the National Association of Manufacturers (NAM), a powerful pressure group. NAM, which was investigated by a congressional committee for antilabor practices, was a sophisticated organization that tapped into a host of media, including the press, radio, and short-subject films, to influence public opinion and government leaders. Investigative journalist George Seldes said that Sokolsky's eagerness to recoup financial losses that his earlier idealism may have created caused him to lose whatever credibility he once had. Seldes claimed that in 1938 Sokolsky was quite boastful to him about his amoral approach to journalism. "Be a crook, Seldes; but don't be a little crook. Be a big crook. I've made a lot of money. Be a big crook, Seldes." A long series of articles for *Liberty* published in late 1938 lends credence to Seldes's accusation about Sokolsky's work ethic or lack thereof. In one article after another, Sokolsky glorifies advertising in the United States. While "reporting" on all the good done by corporations, he manages to drop the names of numerous name-brand products. In one article, he shows his disdain for critics of his corporation boosting: "The left-wingers—Communists, Socialists, and social workers—will say that I am doing propaganda for the big companies and for advertising. All right. Believe that if you want to. Maybe I'm doing propaganda for something bigger than all the big companies—for the American way of life."

With its frequent trumpeting for the advertising business and big business in general, NAM became a natural ally of the Hearst Corporation. Both Hearst and Berlin were friendly with many of its key leaders, which included conservative businessmen such as Alfred E. Sloan of General Motors and members of the Du Pont family. Sloan and the Du Ponts were also founders of the American Liberty League, another lobby group, which was formed in 1934. The Liberty League claimed that it was nonpartisan and only interested in protecting the Constitution. But it was decidedly anti–New Deal and often asserted its conviction that members of the wealthy elite in the United States were rightfully entitled to special privileges and destined for positions of leadership.

At first the Liberty League was given laissez-faire treatment by the mainstream press, but gradually the public tired of its haughty attitude toward wealth and property. Meanwhile the left began to make accusations that the league's membership harbored significant numbers of racists, anti-Semites, and profascists. Hearst's direct association with this group remains unclear, although he came out strongly in support of the organization when it was revealed that its activities were being secretly monitored by government agencies. He may have been connected in less public ways. The Liberty League was apparently an umbrella organization over a number of other, smaller groups, all financed primarily by the Du Pont family and associates and with money from J. P. Morgan and Andrew W. Mellon associates. Two of these satellite lobby groups, the Crusaders and the American Taxpayers League, both anti–FDR administration outfits, may have received financial support surreptitiously from Hearst. In one instance, according to author Kenneth G. Crawford in his book *The Pressure Boys*, Hearst gave the head of the American Taxpayers League free air time on WINS, his New York radio station, to broadcast some seventy-five speeches. The Liberty League also had a strong presence in Los Angeles, where its southern California branch was located. Key leaders of the Los Angeles branch included local industrialists, the president of the chamber of commerce, and Henry S. MacKay Jr., Hearst's longtime personal attorney, later named by Hearst as executor of his will.

In their book about the origins of the blacklist in Hollywood, Larry Ceplair and Steven Englund claim that progressives in the film community in the 1930s were as fearful of the elitist movement of the Liberty League as they were of the populist movement of Louisiana politician Huey Long: "The rich, corporate face of homegrown fascism was the American Liberty League. . . . The League spent vast sums of money, published lavishly designed pamphlets depicting a country on the brink of communism and bankruptcy, and generally displayed a furious level of activity."

Hearst's campaign against Communism was the underpinning of the House Un-American Activities Committee (HUAC), and his media empire engaged in a relationship with its chairman, Representative Martin Dies, and his operatives that crossed the line between support and collaboration. Despite his own troubling experience during World War I as a target of government surveillance, Hearst was an early advocate for an investigating arm of Congress, and he applauded efforts to root out Bolshevik, anarchist, and Communist groups as well as (to a lesser degree) organizations that were friendly to fascist causes. Hearst generally supported Dies's predecessor, New York City representative Samuel Dickstein, not so much because he offered a resolution in 1934 to investigate Nazis in America but because the hot-tempered HUAC chairman held views on restricting immigration. Even in 1932, when Will Hays sent a letter to Hearst urging him to oppose a Dickstein bill that would bar all but "exceptional" foreign actors from entering the United States, there is no evidence to suggest that Hearst could be persuaded that such legislation would be harmful to the film industry. In 1938 Hearst was pleased that John Nance Garner, the Texan he had handpicked to be the vice president of the United States, had in turn handpicked Dies, a young Texas congressman on the committee, to be the new chairman. Dies had even harsher views on immigration than Dickstein did, and he was persistent in equating aliens with Communist sympathies. In addition, Dies's opposition to sitdown strikes as a form of protest in labor disputes was completely in line with Hearst's own views.

Hearst had been drawn to Dies before he saw him become HUAC chairman. By the mid-1930s the two men had strong contempt for the policies of Franklin Roosevelt, and Dies's speeches criticizing the president and his administration often mirrored Hearst's editorials. Remarks Dies made in 1935 in particular must have been sweet music to Hearst's ears. Dies accused the president of controlling the media "through a well-organized and highly developed plan employing hundreds of newspapermen as press agents." In 1936 Hearst used his newsreels to subtly communicate his anti–New Deal message. A summer issue of *Hearst Metrotone* had a sequence showing FDR enjoying a picnic while on vacation, followed by shots of "hunger marchers" in Pennsylvania demanding better treatment for the poor and ill fed. A few years later, Hearst newspaper editors were told to make Roosevelt look too old to seek a third term. They instructed staff artists to retouch photographs of the president, adding wrinkles and jowls to his face and drawing a pair of crutches in the background of a shot where none had been visible.

On August 20, 1938, fellow traveler turned anti-Communist J. B. Matthews was back in the spotlight again, sworn in before Martin Dies and his committee. Throughout the day, before an audience gathered in a large caucus room of the Capitol and a row of newsreel cameras, Matthews named several Communist fronts in the United States, organizations that he had known from personal experience were linked financially to Moscow. Matthews's appearance before the committee—part lecture, part confessional—was a tour de force. Overnight, his testimony was set in type for Sunday newspapers in cities across the country. As one Hearst columnist would later describe it, Matthews became "the sparkplug of the Dies Committee." He certainly became a darling of the Hearst press, which had been championing the Communism issue for years but had always lacked a sensational human-interest angle to advance its cause. Hearst reporters and newsreel men were immediately dispatched to cover Matthews, and they followed him with almost religious devotion for years to come. On the night of his testimony in Washington, an ebullient Matthews wrote a letter from the Mayflower Hotel to his friend Fred Schlink of Consumer Research: "My first appearance on the stand was much more of a bombshell than was anticipated. Dies tells me tonight that I made page one of every newspaper in the U.S. . . . . All the newsreels are making shorts of me and parts of my testimony Monday. The Journal-American says it is going to use its entire front page in a box for some of my testimony in its Monday edition. Dies says that it is the most sensational and competent testimony he has heard during his years in the House."

Actually, Hearst's *New York Journal-American* did not wait until Monday or even Sunday to print its first story on Matthews: it had a page one story on newsstands on the night of his testimony. In its initial reports, the Hearst press paired Matthews's testimony with the ongoing Dies investigation of the Federal Theatre Project of the Works Progress Administration, which it had been covering since July. The story was a natural for Hearst; there were daily reports on HUAC's charges that the Theatre Project was "infested" with Communists and a continuous refrain that the government-sponsored performing arts answer to the Depression was really a propaganda machine linking the Soviet Union to FDR's New Deal administration. While searching for radicals in the Theatre Project, Dies was not at all averse to linking radicalism with immorality. And naturally the Hearst press knew this line of interrogation was guaranteed to get its audience salivating. When a friendly witness appearing before Dies suggested that the Workers' Alliance, a Communist-controlled pressure group working with the Theatre Project, was encouraging sexual relations between the races, his eyes lit up. "Is that the policy of the Communist Party?" Dies asked the witness. "Yes," she replied, "social equality and merging of the races."

Coverage of Matthews's testimony continued into the following week, with the focus turning to the influence of Communism in the press and in Hollywood. Matthews claimed that many newspapers were employing Communists. The *New York Times*, he asserted, had so many Communists on its staff that they felt empowered to put out their own Red pamphlet, which was called *Better Times*. In reporting Matthews's claim, the Hearst press was quick to mention that its own papers and the Scripps-Howard chain had rid themselves of any such subversives who may have traveled in their midst. Directing attention to the film industry, Matthews maintained that a significant number of film actors had been duped into supporting Communist front organizations. Although he was careful not to accuse anyone of being a card-carrying member of Communist Party, he did submit a list of Hollywood celebrities who had recently sent greetings to *Ce Soir*, a French Communist-controlled newspaper. It was obvious, Matthews said, that this list was evidence of Hollywood's naïveté. The sweeping suggestion backfired, however, when it was revealed that the list of actors and screenwriters included the name of the child actress Shirley Temple.

A Hearst editorial published on August 25, 1938, focused again on Matthews and the WPA Theatre. Matthews's testimony was called "direct and unequivocal." Pointing to the theater, Hearst asserted that "nobody can any longer seriously deny that the stage is prostituted to Communism." Hearst was particularly enraged by a dramatic genre put forth by the Federal Theater called "The Living Newspaper." In these plays subjects that might be read about in the daily newspaper—such as strikes, droughts in the farm belt, or unemployment—were placed in the context of a left wing–right wing conflict. Aside from their social content, the productions were especially noteworthy for their special visual and audio effects, bold attempts to break away from traditional stage presentations. The most talked-about Living Newspaper, *Triple-A Plowed Under* (1936), had some actors reading lines from the audience while others onstage wore masks. Hidden microphones were used to amplify voices, and stereopticon slides were projected on scrims. As author Morgan Y. Himelstein has written: "The rapid flow of stage pictures was a combination of the agitprop, the motion picture—especially 'short subjects' like the 'March of Time'—and the musical revue." One imagines Hearst's being more than a little disturbed to see the combining of various media devices that he had perfected for his own yellow journalism being put on a stage for what he was convinced was Communist propaganda. The Living Newspaper plays were some of the most controversial works produced by the Theatre Project and prime examples for Hearst and the Dies committee to use in their complaint that taxpayer's money was being used to promote the New Deal and Communism. The pressure was kept up until June 1939, when Congress decided to cut off funds for the Theatre Project.

Although the Hearst editorial of 1938 applauded Matthews, it found his statements regarding individuals being innocent dupes of the Communists less than compelling. "We can understand how that might be true of persons of meager intelligence and limited information. But how can it be true of highly educated persons?" Hearst advised Matthews and Dies to dig deeper, and despite the misstep on Shirley Temple he urged further investigations of Hollywood. "Nobody," the editorial declared, "can any longer seriously deny that the screen is tainted with Communism." Funding problems caused delays in following Hearst's advice on Hollywood, but within a year or so Matthews, now director of research for the Dies committee, had two investigators, George F. Hurley and James Steedman, plus an assistant on the East Coast named Benjamin Mendel scouring the film industry for Communists.

Perhaps the only thing as inevitable as Matthews's odyssey to Martin Dies and anti-Communism was his journey to Hearst. Although no personal correspondence between Hearst and Dies or between Hearst and Matthews has surfaced, in December 1938 Hearst received a copy of Matthews's book, *Odyssey of a Fellow Traveler*, from Edmond Coblentz. In a letter accompanying the book, the loyal Hearst editor wrote: "Here is a very interesting book written by J. B. Matthews, the 'Fellow Traveler' who gave such sensational testimony at the Dies hearing. It is beautifully written. This is one of the first copies off the press. I am sending one to Connolly [in charge of both International News Service and King Features Syndicate]. You may want to use it in large part as a serial."

At about the same time that Hearst received Matthews's book, Dick Berlin was becoming increasingly interested in using the former "fellow traveler" for his own purposes. Matthews was being tailor-made to suit the Hearst Corporation's needs, a man who would march to their tune of Americanism, on the way to wage war over *Good Housekeeping*'s Seal of Approval. Berlin had already assembled the foundation for an effective team in reporters Sydney Boehm and Jack Clement. But Matthews was a jewel who was also linked to two other valuable allies: Fred Schlink, the Consumer Research head who ironically had once urged the FTC to investigate *Good Housekeeping*, and George Sokolsky, a more recent Matthews friend.

Berlin's counteroffensive against the FTC was probably in place by the summer of 1939. According to Boehm, at about this time Matthews was authorized to arrange a meeting with Martin Dies at the Hotel Carlton in Washington, D.C., and a plan was hatched to have Matthews make a spectacular return appearance before Dies's committee timed to coincide with an anticipated FTC complaint. The second coming of Matthews would not be under the hot lights of the newsreel cameras or in front of a large audience; indeed, no other committee members would be in attendance. Matthews would testify in private, to a committee of one, and the report to Dies would be distributed through the auspices of the Hearst organization. At the Hotel Carlton, as Boehm recalled, Dies was given further inducement to assist the Hearst team with a considerable payment of $40,000, or four times his salary as a congressman. In a profile of the HUAC chairman that appeared in the October 3, 1942, issue of the *Nation*, writer Willson Whitman discussed Dies's talent for making money: "Martin Dies is economically shrewd. Anybody is smart who can rise from a $1,500-a-year small-town law practice to a $10,000-a-year job, and hold the job. But really smart people learn how to get along without spending their own money, and Representative Dies has learned this. . . . Representative Dies is, presumably, too smart to take checks or stock or any other form of emolument from the corporations whose interests his policies serve, and which have supported him ever since he started his political career."

To sweeten Berlin's financial deal with Dies or possibly to give it an aboveboard appearance, the congressman was commissioned to write a series of articles for *Cosmopolitan* or one of the other Hearst magazines. Over the following months there appear to have been no articles authored by Dies in *Cosmopolitan* or any publications at all generally known as Hearst's. However, a series of seven articles entitled "More Snakes than I Can Kill" did appear in *Liberty* magazine, a Macfadden publication, between January and February 1940. Evidence suggests that these were the articles commissioned by Hearst and that *Liberty* magazine was acting as what might be called a sub-Hearst publication. There are two theories about how the arrangement occurred. According to Hearst biographer Ferdinand Lundberg, around 1934 Hearst secretly acquired a financial interest in Macfadden Publications. Lundberg claimed that Hearst's involvement was substantial enough to influence editorial content and move the magazine chain in a more conservative direction. By late 1934 Macfadden's publications included some of the most popular magazines in the field, including *True Stories, Physical Culture, Radio Mirror*, and two film journals, *Photoplay* and *Shadowland*. The most influential magazine in Macfadden's stable was *Liberty*, a journal that contained both fiction and nonfiction with a heavy emphasis on current affairs and Hollywood. Lundberg's book is chock-full of financial information about Hearst that has proven to be quite accurate; however, he offers no documentation to support his claim about Hearst's interest in Macfadden.

The idea that Hearst used a surrogate in the magazine field to shield a financial interest or his true ownership is quite reasonable since he did this sort of thing in the newspaper field with men like Arthur Brisbane and Paul Block. Over the years Hearst surrogates technically owned some newspapers that had every earmark of being Hearst publications. Sometimes the publisher of record sold his paper to Hearst. In the magazine field Hearst may have had connections with non-Hearst magazines through shared printers. One in particular was close to both Hearst and Macfadden. Early in the twentieth century John F. Cuneo considered a career in the film industry. He was a financial backer of the pioneering Chicago-based Essanay Film Company and a pro-German film made on the eve of World War I entitled *The German Side of the War* (1915). But Cuneo soon found his real success in magazine and book printing. His clients were many and diverse, publications running the gamut from Sears and Roebuck catalogs to Father Charles Coughlin's *Social Justice* magazine. His biggest client was Hearst. Cuneo became a trusted adviser to Hearst, and they also met socially in New York and Chicago and at San Simeon.

Cuneo's relationship by marriage to the Gianninis of the Bank of America must have been an added value to Hearst. Theodore Peterson writes in *Magazines in the Twentieth Century* that Cuneo's involvement with Hearst and other publishers went beyond the technical operation of magazine production: "Not uncommonly printers and suppliers found themselves owners of a magazine to which they had overextended credit; and in the hope of recovering their losses and keeping the magazine's business, they sometimes staked a new publisher, even to the extent of plowing new capital into the magazine." Peterson points out that as a result of overdue debts Cuneo had a significant stake in at least two publications: *Screenland Magazine* and Macfadden's *Liberty*. According to George d'Utassy, who was a key player at the birth of the Hearst magazine empire, Hearst was always financially interconnected with printers. In 1904 Hearst gave d'Utassy ten thousand dollars to start up *Motor*, his first magazine. "That ten thousand," d'Utassy would later recall, "was the only cash put into the magazines during the years I was connected with them. I mean literally. By using credit with printers and paper makers, and by giving bonds and redeeming them out of the profits when other magazines were bought, the Hearst magazine system was built up."

In a piece written for his *In Fact* magazine, journalist George Seldes claimed that Dies was paid a large fee to write articles that were published in *Liberty* as a payoff for helping Hearst. Apparently unaware of any possible Hearst-Macfadden business relationship, Seldes attributed the arrangement to a common Hearst practice of placing controversial articles in friendly, non-Hearst publications as a way to advance his causes while avoiding the glare of the spotlight. Seldes believed that the arrangement to place the Dies articles in *Liberty* had been made by George Sokolsky, who had been working closely with Matthews and Berlin in the months preceding their publication. Seldes's scenario resembles Sydney Boehm's recollection of the events as told to Hearst biographer William Swanberg. According to Boehm, *Cosmopolitan* magazine bought eight articles from Dies for his help in the FTC matter, but they were never used by the Hearst publication. Boehm makes no mention of *Liberty* magazine using these same articles, but in fact the number they did publish—seven—comes close to Boehm's recollection of the original offer.

The *Liberty* articles supposedly authored by Dies (by the early 1940s, Dies's lectures and articles were reportedly ghostwritten by J. B. Matthews) did not focus on Communism in the consumer movement. That subject must have been considered something less than exciting to the average reader. Instead Dies aroused the public (and helped to keep his House Committee on Un-American Activities alive and well funded) by exposing "fearlessly and fully the truth about Communism in the Hollywood colony." The *Liberty* articles, which apparently evolved from Hearst's battle for advertisers, turned out to be decisive documents for the anti-Communist movement and its focus on the film industry. Dies's first article, "The Reds in Hollywood," appeared on February 17, 1940, and it focused on the beginnings of the congressman's investigation of Communism in Hollywood. In August 1938, within days of J. B. Matthews's testimony before HUAC and a Hearst editorial urging the committee to look into Communism in motion pictures, Dies announced that he would be bringing his committee to Hollywood later in the year. As the film trades reported, Dies was going to allow members of the industry the opportunity to respond to charges of communistic activities. Although it was not widely publicized at the time, Dies had actually made an unofficial visit to Hollywood a few months earlier. In May he went to Los Angeles at the invitation of the American Legion, which had arranged a luncheon for film producers who were reportedly anxious to meet with the committee chairman. As he told it, Dies attended the luncheon and left "with a strong impression" that a majority of film producers were Communist sympathizers. In explaining the situation he encountered, Dies presented himself as a reasonable man who understood why the producers might be "duped by the Communists." Below the surface he was sending out another message, which he and others would deliver over the next several years with varying degrees of subtlety: the movie producers were a powerful cabal most interested in protecting their power and whose real loyalties were more toward their fellow Jews than their fellow Americans:

> The Hollywood film producers are naturally and properly opposed to Nazi activities and fearful of the growth of any anti-Semitic feeling throughout the country. Being sensitive on this point, they naturally sympathize with any group or organization which professes strong opposition to Nazi or Fascist ideologies. Most of the producers are Jews who have made a remarkable success in the building of the film industry from an insignificant beginning to one of the greatest industries in the world. . . . They are therefore anxious to do everything within their power to prevent the spread of Nazism and Fascism in America. In my judgment, every professional liberal, racketeer, and Communist group has sought, often successfully, to take advantage of this situation.

In another passage, Dies declared that over forty prominent members of the film industry were Communists or fellow travelers, contributing money to the Communist Party and influencing film productions. He pointed to *Juarez* (1939), *Blockade* (1938), and *Fury* (1936) as prime examples of recent pro-Communist films. Few individuals were named in the article, but Dies seemed to relish ridiculing a head of one of the few studios that occasionally produced films that showed concern for world affairs. Watching the screening of the Warner Bros. feature *Confessions of a Nazi Spy* following the Hollywood luncheon, Dies couldn't help turning from the melodrama on

the screen to the one on producer Harry Warner's face. "I was more interested in watching him," Dies wrote, "than the show because his attitude
demonstrated to me how deeply the Hollywood producers felt about the
Nazi threat. It also explained to me how easy it was for the Communists and
fellow travelers to use Hollywood to promote their program in America."

A second article on Hollywood appeared one week later, on February 24.
In "Is Communism Invading the Movies?" Dies chronicled the systematic
growth of Communism in Los Angeles since the early 1930s, the party's
infiltration of unions, and its strong reliance on Hollywood moviemakers
for money and sympathy. This time Dies made no mention of specific films,
but he declared with absolute certainty that the Communists had already
succeeded in spreading subtle propaganda in films by "continually stressing
the weak points of the American system without giving due credit to its
marvelous accomplishments."

16

Hollywood Isolationist

1940–1947

> The evidence before us leads inevitably to the conclusion that the film *Citizen Kane* is nothing more than an extension of the Communist Party's campaign to smear one of its most effective and consistent opponents in the United States.
>
> —*FBI report on Orson Welles*

SCAPEGOATS

Indications of Hearst's omnipresence in Hollywood at the start of the 1940s can be found in two of the most famous novels of the period, Aldous Huxley's *After Many a Summer Dies the Swan* (1939) and F. Scott Fitzgerald's *The Last Tycoon*, which was written in 1939 and published posthumously in 1941. Jo Stoyte, a central character in Huxley's book, is a dour millionaire who owns a myriad of corporations and properties, including a cemetery in Beverly Hills that resembles an amusement park. High on the bluff is Stoyte's skyscraper castle, constructed "out of pure fun and wantonness" and housing a zoo, a chapel, an indoor swimming pool, secret vaults, and artwork by Rubens, Vermeer, and El Greco. Like Hearst, Stoyte is fascinated by experiments in longevity and the promise of reincarnation, often telling others that "God is love; there is no death." Stoyte's mistress, Virginia Maunciple, is some forty years his junior. She is a Catholic, like Marion Davies, who regularly attends mass, and she is also fond of "getting tight with the boys." Her Hollywood girlfriends work at a Germanic-sounding film company called "Cosmopolis-Perlmutter Studios."

References to Hearst surface only two paragraphs into Fitzgerald's *The Last Tycoon*, considered by many to be one of the most insightful works about Hollywood. The novel's narrator, Cecelia Brady, the daughter of a movie producer, describes her decision to forsake the writing of her memoirs about growing up in the film industry. "It's just as well," Cecelia tells the reader, "it would have been as flat as an old column of Lolly Parsons." The Hearst columnist acts as a sort of bookend to the published manuscript. "That's how the two weeks started that he and I went around together," the narrative says in closing the novel. "It only took one of them for Louella to have us married." Fitzgerald's only direct reference to Hearst occurs about midway in the story. As *The Last Tycoon*'s main character, Monroe Stahr (a film producer modeled after Irving Thalberg), is stopped at a red light, he is startled by a newsboy shouting out a yellow journalism headline like an actor from a Living Newspaper production: "Mickey Mouse Murdered! Randolph Hearst declares war on China!"

Fitzgerald's comic putdowns of Hearst's brand of journalism give an incomplete picture of the author's recognition of Hearst's influence in Hollywood. Having written short stories for the Hearst magazines and observed Hearst and Davies up close at San Simeon and in the beach house in Santa Monica in the 1920s and early 1930s, the writer certainly knew better than to laugh Hearst off. In fact, during one of his screenwriting stints at Metro-Goldwyn-Mayer—at a time when Cosmopolitan Productions was associated with the studio—Fitzgerald may have even been personally stung by Hearst's prickly power. In December 1931, as a momentary member of the MGM family, Fitzgerald was invited to attend a party at Irving Thalberg and Norma Shearer's beach house in Malibu. As was his pattern, Fitzgerald began drinking soon after arriving, and after the second or third round he began to bring the gathering of Hollywood swells to a deadly stop by reciting a meandering sophomoric poem about a dog. One week later the writer, who was already being approached cautiously by the powers that be because of his reputation for drinking, was summarily fired by MGM. Never one to turn a blind eye to good story material, Fitzgerald used the Thalberg party and his embarrassment as the centerpiece of a short story called "Crazy Sundays." This tale of Hollywood inhabitants (including an Irving Thalberg character) living in a heightened, altered state of existence has been seen as a prelude to *The Last Tycoon*. In "Crazy Sundays" Fitzgerald disguises the names of the Thalbergs and their guests, but he does make a rather blatant reference to the "Marion Davies crowd" being in attendance at the party. For several months after being fired by MGM, Fitzgerald tried without success to get his "Crazy Sundays" published in a popular magazine. In October 1932 the story finally found a home in H. L. Mencken's monthly journal *American Mercury*. In a letter written to Mencken at the time of publication, Fitzgerald gave a clue to the story behind the troubled history of his "Crazy Sundays." He had written the story specifically for Hearst's *Cosmopolitan* magazine, he said, but the magazine's editor had rejected it "on the ground that it discusses well-known figures at Metro which Hearst controls."

In March 1940 Ed Hatrick announced to the press that Hearst's production contract with Twentieth Century–Fox would not be renewed. Coinciding with the announcement, Marion Davies's Cosmopolitan bungalow, which in one form or another had followed the actress from the United Studios in Hollywood to the MGM and Warner Bros. lots and finally to Fox, was on the move again. The bungalow has come to represent the extent of Hearst's film involvement, when in fact it was more a symbol of Hearst's importance to his studio associates: he provided the film factories with a three-dimensional advertisement for movie glamour. Now the two-story structure was unceremoniously being trucked over to Beverly Hills to begin its final Hollywood incarnation, as an addition to Davies's home at 910 Benedict Canyon Road.

In the weeks preceding Hatrick's announcement, there was talk in Hollywood that other studios were interested in making a film deal with Hearst, if only to take advantage of the provision of first refusal rights on Hearst publications that had been a staple of previous agreements. But Hatrick refuted the rumor. Hearst, it seemed, had taken the advice that Joseph P. Kennedy had been giving him since the late 1930s. After Hearst called in the banker turned movie producer, industrialist, and ambassador to England to be his financial adviser, Kennedy told his old friend to get out of filmmaking. Hearst took Kennedy's advice, but only to a point. As he began his final decade in Hollywood, he fashioned himself as an elder statesman of the film industry, apparently seeing himself as someone whose long career in the service of Hollywood and its institutions had guaranteed him respect. He may have been confusing respect with fear. Critics, as they always had, saw Hearst in a different light; to them, Hearst was Hollywood's version of the old-time political boss who struggled to change with the times merely to maintain his power. In some ways Hearst's last years in Hollywood resembled his earliest years, when he was closer to Tammany politics and yellow journalism was his main vehicle for creating picture stories. Hearst was still a force behind the scenes in Hollywood at the start of the 1940s, but his advancing age, his hardening views, and the changes occurring within the industry made him more vulnerable than ever before.

Even as his involvement in feature filmmaking declined in the late 1930s, Hearst continued to exert influence through his news film operation, his political connections, and his publishing empire. In 1937 Hearst's Cosmopolitan Corporation was elected a member of the Motion Picture Producers and Distributors of America (an organization to which Hearst had never belonged before despite his longtime relationship with Will Hays). That same year Edgar Hatrick began to represent Hearst's interests as a board member on the MPPDA, and he was reelected to that position into the 1940s. Meanwhile Hearst's MGM *News of the Day* remained a strong force in news film.

Hatrick's health began to deteriorate by the early 1940s, and newsreel executive Caleb Stratton took up many of his responsibilities. In the 1920s Stratton had juggled a number of duties at Cosmopolitan Productions. Officially, he was the film company's treasurer, but he was also in charge of organizing Hearst's *Oneida* yacht parties, inviting guests and making arrangements to hire Ziegfeld's showgirls for entertainment. Stratton was a good friend of Marion Davies, and when efforts were being made to pay off Hearst's crippling debts in 1937, Stratton helped liquidate the actress's stock in the Anaconda mine of Montana and facilitated loans from the Gianninis of the Bank of America. In early 1948, a little more than a year before Hatrick died in a tuberculosis sanitarium, he and Stratton purchased television station WBAL-TV in Baltimore for Hearst, and they negotiated a deal between the International News Service and a preexisting company called Telenews Productions, Inc. (the Hearst Corporation acquired Telenews completely in 1954).

The Telenews partnership was formed to supply news films for the Dumont television network. The *New York Journal-American* reported that the new twenty-minute news program "presented 12 different news events in swiftly paced sequence." Another news program with Hearst participation, called the *INS-INP Camera Headlines*, was also running on television simultaneously. The utilization of newsreel footage on television was not exactly new to Hearst: films were part of the program for a television station he ran briefly out of New York in 1930. By 1935 a Berlin television station was broadcasting regularly scheduled newsreel films three nights a week. As Hearst's newsreel exchange arrangement with Germany was in place at this point, it is conceivable that some of those Berlin TV broadcasts included foreign footage originating with Hearst.

When NBC television made a deal in 1948 to have its news provided by Fox Movietone News, CBS made a similar arrangement with Hearst. Ironically, journalist Edward R. Murrow's *See It Now* television program—most famed for its exposé on Senator Joseph McCarthy—was produced in conjunction with the Hearst newsreel team. (The Hearst press had attempted to smear Murrow as a Communist sympathizer in 1935 and had done much to bolster McCarthy's career as a rabid anti-Communist.) Hearst's newsreels ended their long run—domestic and foreign—in January 1968. According to a former top executive of the United States Information Agency, the Hearst newsreel outlived its competitors by striking a lucrative deal in its last years. Nicknamed "Kingfish," the secret Hearst-USIA operation created newsreels with subtle pro-American propaganda for the government to distribute abroad.

Although Hearst would never again stand on a balcony in a film studio overlooking a soundstage, he was still captivated by the world of movie stars, stories, and gossip. In March 1940 he started writing, for the first time in his publishing career, a regularly featured column that was syndicated on the front page of his chain of newspapers. The columns were a combination of news commentary, gossip, and Hearst-style autobiography. Frequently, Hearst opened his column for readers' letters, which were occasionally used to supply pleasant anecdotes about Hearst's life and career. One example of this method of memoir writing was a letter that Hearst published with some relish in his September 21, 1940, column. A reader from Chicago told Hearst a story he had heard when he enrolled at Harvard University only a few years after Hearst had been there. A Mrs. Buckman, proprietress of his dormitory, had held the same position when Hearst was at the university. She remembered Hearst as a "very learned Harvard man" who had made quite a show of himself on campus. During a Democratic election victory celebration, Mrs. Buckman recalled, Hearst bought a number of gamecocks that he put in a cage and swung from one of the dormitory windows. This was the straw that broke the undergraduate's back, and although Mrs. Buckman tried to intercede on Hearst's behalf, she was rebuffed by university president Elliot. "Madam," he told her, "if the offenses of this young man were catalogued the list would begin within a few hours after he first appeared in Cambridge."

In addition to carrying his autobiographical writings, Hearst's column became a vehicle for crusades such as anti-Communism and an opportunity for him to engage in Hollywood chitchat. In one column, Hearst acted like movie columnist Louella Parsons, plugging the Twentieth Century–Fox film *Swanee River*, which was actually produced in late 1939. *Swanee River* does not appear to have had any association with Hearst's last production company deal, but it did star Don Ameche, the lead in the Fox-Cosmopolitan film *The Story of Alexander Graham Bell*. Calling *Swanee River* a "marvelous moving picture," Hearst wrote that he found it especially moving because it followed the story of one of his favorite composers, Stephen Foster, and reminded him of his childhood, when his father had often sung to him the melancholy miners' song "Oh, Susanna." In describing the real life of Foster, Hearst alluded to the fact that Hollywood had sanitized the songwriter's biography. "He reached the heights of success and happiness," Hearst wrote, "but died in squalor and misery, his ending as sad as the ending of the song ["Oh, Susanna"]." The film had softened the focus on Foster's life, avoiding even a mention of his last song, the haunting "Beautiful Dreamer," because it was composed as Foster lay dying. Hearst was still dreaming of Stephen Foster in November 1940. When the composer was elected to a songwriter's hall of fame, he published an editorial in the *New York Journal-American*. Foster, Hearst wrote, had "put the American way to music—lilting ideology that will never perish."

Hearst's columns about the film industry were frequently little more than puffs for Hollywood friends such as Carole Lombard and Clark Gable. He gave more than one boost to Shirley Temple, the child actress that one frequent guest at San Simeon described as Hearst's last favorite actress. Hearst lavished praise on "the beautiful and talented" Greta Garbo in one column, relaying an anecdote about the actress that was probably overheard at one of his San Simeon get-togethers. Garbo, Hearst wrote, had recently been traveling in Italy, when she telephoned a movie star friend back in America (perhaps Davies) for advice on how to avoid the persistent reporters who challenged her desire "to be let alone." Garbo's friend in the States had recognized that the actress's studied silences were only whetting the public's curiosity. In a simple, no-nonsense cable message she advised Garbo: "Answer their questions."

Shortly after Louis B. Mayer paid Hearst a visit at San Simeon in May 1940, Hearst wrote another column about Garbo. Mayer had told Hearst that although Garbo's latest film, *Ninotchka*, was a hit, the actress's great successes were usually abroad, because in the United States, "the money is mainly in those films which appeal to the American home and family." Once again in the role of producer and coyly reminding readers that Garbo's first American films, *The Torrent* (1925) and *The Temptress* (1926), were adapted by his own film company from *Cosmopolitan* magazine stories, Hearst wrote: "She appealed to everybody then. She swept American audiences off their feet in big theaters in the largest cities, and in the little theaters in the smallest country towns. . . . Give this lovely lady happy, wholesome plays like 'Ninotchka,' which Mr. Brackett so cleverly created, and she will appeal intensely to all classes. And why should she not? She has every kind of talent. She has power; she has pathos; she has a keen sense of comedy; she has the highest dramatic ability; she has beauty; she has charm." What Hearst didn't include in his praise for Garbo's performance in *Ninotchka* was what he had written elsewhere about the film's message. When the film was first released in 1939, Hearst hailed *Ninotchka* as a perfect spoof of Communism. "Nothing else has appeared on the screen," he wrote, "which equaled the effectiveness of that ridicule or offered more devastating exposure of the impractical operation of that particular form of lunacy."

Hearst told reporter Adela Rogers St. Johns that he considered using his column to deny the still-circulating rumor that he had murdered director Thomas Ince during a yachting trip in 1924. But in the end he decided against it, feeling it would not be "tactful" to bring up the subject in a column whose Hollywood observations were meant to be primarily entertaining. Perhaps, Hearst told St. Johns, it was best to "leave it alone."

By the summer of 1940 Representative Martin Dies had several investigators searching for leads in Hollywood, and he was in Texas hearing private testimony on Communist infiltration from former Communist Party sympathizers. One of his key witnesses was John L. Leech, whom some activists in Hollywood believed was a paid police agent from the time he joined the Communist Party in 1931 until he was expelled in 1937. The authors of *The Inquisition in Hollywood*, a book about the blacklist period, concluded that Leech was one of "the most notorious of a large group of police undercover agents who infiltrated the Los Angeles branches of the Communist Party." Informants like Leech would be the mainstay of anti-Communist inquiries from Dies's early Hollywood sortie through the movie investigations of California legislator Jack Tenney in the mid-1940s and the House Un-American Activities Committee hearings a few years later.

In August 1940, a few weeks after his meeting with Dies, Leech appeared before a grand jury in Los Angeles, repeating the assertions he had made in private regarding Communist influence in Hollywood. His testimony included a list with dozens of names of film actors and screenwriters who were alleged to be Communist or Communist sympathizers. Although the well-respected dean of the Harvard Law School had denounced Leech as a "pathological liar" only six months prior to this testimony, a number of newspapers carried Leech's charges without challenging their accuracy. Even the *New York Times* printed the grand jury accusations in a manner that gave them added credibility. The thrust of the story appeared on page one of the newspaper, while the denials of actors Fredric March, James Cagney, Humphrey Bogart and others did not show up until page twenty-two.

In its coverage the next day, the *Times* published what was more or less a retraction of its previous report. An editorial acknowledged that Leech's accusations lacked credibility and suggested that his actions were part of a "sinister" smear campaign. George Seldes's *In Fact* magazine of August 26, 1940, claimed that Hearst was chiefly responsible for promoting Leech. "The story was a typical smear," Seldes wrote, "it was concocted by Hearst's 'Herald Express' in cahoots with [Buron] Fitts, running for district attorney. Hearst can now afford to smear Hollywood stars since he is no longer financially interested in boosting the producing company employing his protégé Marion Davies."

Hearst's International News Service syndicated a story on the grand jury proceedings one day before Leech appeared with his attack on Hollywood. The story ran in the Hearst press one day before the *New York Times* and other papers picked up on it. In its preview of Leech's testimony (the informant was not named in the piece), the INS predicted "the greatest fifth-column expose yet unearthed in the United States." Hearst's wire service said that grand jury witnesses would soon disclose "ramifications of the Communist element throughout Southern California and possibly the Pacific Coast." The scoop, it said, had come from Los Angeles District Attorney Buron Fitts.

In his August 8, 1940, "In the News" column, Hearst addressed what he considered to be the important work of Leech and Representative Dies (he called Dies "a most able and earnest gentleman"), but he expressed impatience with the slowness to act against Communism in Hollywood:

> It is not only fashionable to be pink, but profitable too. The screen is almost wholly Technicolor these days, and the favorite Technicolor is rosy red. There the propaganda is not so popular but even more persistent. Sensible people are bored by so much propaganda, but if disposed to stay away from the theatres are lured there by double bills and bank nights and dish distributions. . . . Five years ago—in fact now nearly six years ago—the writer of this column revealed in a series of signed editorials and of radio addresses the menace of Communism. . . . But still there is lacking ACTION. Every healthy American movement to expose Communism and to preserve the essential character of the American Government dies when it reaches Washington.

Later in the same column, Hearst repeated Leech's charge that Hollywood was a "hot bed of Communism," and he quoted his *Los Angeles Examiner*'s report on Leech's testimony: "Beautiful young girls members of the

Young Communist League are used to recruit United States sailors into the party by any means, and that the Communist party, through the Young Communist League, sought membership among boys and girls as young as 13." If the language about beautiful girls and young children suggested the accusations of prostitution and pedophilia that were laid at the doorsteps of the early nickelodeons, it also reminded readers of Hearst's previous attacks on Communism's infiltration of American youth.

Throughout his associations with Warner Bros. and with Twentieth Century–Fox, Hearst had maintained a generally cordial relationship with Louis B. Mayer, and his newsreel, *News of the Day*, continued to be released by Metro-Goldwyn-Mayer. According to *Newsweek*, late in 1940 Hearst was holding meetings with Mayer, hoping to reenter the film industry by renegotiating a deal with his old production ally. The magazine speculated that Hearst was no longer interested in picking properties or casting pictures; there was no mention of Marion Davies or any other hands-on production involvement. Hearst was now looking to reunite with MGM strictly as a film promoter. A deal with MGM, it was said, would mean a release of four to six films a year labeled as Cosmopolitan productions, with Hearst putting his publicity machine behind the pictures for a cut of the films' profits. Just how far the negotiations went is unknown, and the rumor about a possible deal vanished as quickly as it had surfaced.

By 1940 Marion Davies had not worked in a film studio for nearly three years. With two decades of film acting behind her, and three years having passed since she last faced a camera, there was little evidence that she missed the life of a film star. The transition was far from sudden. Her final years in the business were vastly different from her first, when she was in production for one movie or another most months of the year and the novelty of her craft and the glamour attached to her rise to fame made for heady times. By the late 1930s there were long stretches of time between her films, which by most accounts were mostly box office failures. The youthful movie star role that she had cherished as much as Hearst was becoming increasingly impossible to pull off as each passing year dimmed the spark that was so evident in her earlier performances on the screen. Once the decision to quit was made, whatever pangs Davies may have felt were no match for the overwhelming sadness she experience at the news that came to her by telephone from Los Angeles in late July 1940. Her sister Ethel had died choking on a piece of steak. For the rest of the summer and the rest of the year, there were attempts at distraction: the nightly film screening ritual continued, friends were still invited for the weekends, and small dinner parties and picnics were organized in the wooded seclusion of the Wyntoon estate. But the death of her favorite sister, coming at the moment of her retirement, seems to have been especially unsettling; her alcoholism, which had begun early in her career but was little noticed by most for long periods, was now most apparent, most of the time.

In describing the end of her film career, Davies told the writer Margaret Ettinger, a cousin of Louella Parsons, that it was Joe Kennedy who had "knocked sense" into Hearst's head about quitting the movie business. When she found out that Hearst had reluctantly agreed with Kennedy's assessment of his future in the film industry, she said, "I was almost glad—in fact I was glad." Kennedy had been a friend and adviser of both Hearst and Davies since at least the early 1920s, when all three were involved in making films, Kennedy first as an investor and later as a producer. In the late 1930s, when the Hearst Corporation was in dire financial straits, Kennedy offered a myriad of suggestions for cost cutting, many of which Hearst followed. According to author Lawrence Quirk, Walter Howey, Hearst's newspaper editor, who first met Kennedy in 1922, said it was Kennedy who was single-handedly responsible for saving the Hearst empire. But according to William Randolph Hearst Jr., the empire was saved by not taking Kennedy's advice in one crucial area. In 1939 Hearst's magazine *Pictorial Review* folded, the largest magazine up to that point to close. In the end its circulation had reached three million, but the magazine's profits had been on a downward spiral ever since it was bought in 1934. The news caused widespread fear in the Hearst organization that the bottom was about to fall out of the entire empire. Kennedy seized the opportunity and offered $14 million for all the Hearst magazines. Despite pressure from a number of executives over him, the magazine division's vice president, Richard E. Berlin, strongly resisted the offer. Simultaneously Berlin negotiated a bank loan of $8 million from A. P. Giannini, president of the Bank of America, that brought a financial stability to the organization that was made even stronger with the onset of the Second World War.

According to William Randolph Hearst Jr., Kennedy's sole interest in becoming a Hearst consultant was self-interest; he wanted an inside track so that he could get the first grab at pieces of the corporation that might be offered for sale. Bill Hearst believed his father never forgot how Kennedy acted when the chips were down. "When Pop was informed about what Joe tried to pull," Hearst Jr. wrote in his autobiography, "he was shocked. I don't think I ever saw him so taken aback. He looked on Joe not only as a trusted friend but also as a gentleman. Kennedy's attempted manipulation so dismayed the old man that the two were never close again." Kennedy had made a similarly manipulative move in the 1930s when he was called on by Paramount Pictures to offer advice to improve its financial situation. After studying the film company's assets and liabilities, Kennedy reported to the board of directors that he had arrived at a unique answer to their problems: he would buy the company himself. With a gentile at the company's helm, Kennedy hypothesized, the financial establishment's discomfort over the belief that the film industry was run by Jews would be eased at least somewhat.

If Hearst was less trusting of Kennedy after the attempted magazine takeover, the two men were still able to enjoy each other's company and offer each other advice on various subjects of mutual interest. Such contradictions were not out of character for either Hearst or Kennedy; trust was a malleable commodity in their world. Both men were charismatic and narcissistic, original and enormously controversial figures in politics and Hollywood. Like Hearst, Kennedy fell madly in love with the movies and became passionately involved in film production in the early 1920s. Both men developed serious relationships with glamorous movie stars while remaining legally married to women with their own considerable charms (Gloria Swanson wrote that Hollywood saw her relationship with Kennedy as "a modified version" of Hearst and Davies). What especially endeared Kennedy to Hearst in later years was the interest he showed in Davies's financial security, especially as it might be affected after Hearst's death. Despite a friendly flirtation between Kennedy and Davies and rumors of a brief affair—not to mention the ambassador's history of insider trading with the Hearst magazines and the attempted Paramount takeover—there is no evidence to suggest that Hearst viewed Kennedy's concerns for Davies as anything but aboveboard. And Hearst had no problem flattering Kennedy's ego, which was a close match to his own. When Kennedy took over as ambassador to England and found his London residence in something less than a luxurious state, Hearst suggested he go to St. Donat's, Hearst's rarely visited eight-hundred-year-old castle in Wales, and borrow whatever he wanted.

Politically, Hearst continued to have a high regard for Kennedy's advocacy of isolationism, a view that had also garnered the support of others, including Father Charles E. Coughlin, whose *Social Justice* magazine once featured the photogenic Kennedy on its cover. In February 1940 Hearst was delighted by reports that Kennedy believed "there are no justifiable circumstances for America's entry into the current European war." At around the same time, stories that Kennedy might be interested in seeking the presidency must also have caught Hearst's attention. He wrote an editorial in his newspapers in March that, without mentioning Kennedy by name, floated the merits of the election of a Catholic president. Kennedy's controversial public remarks in early July, to the effect that England was likely to be defeated by Germany within a month, proved no obstacle for Hearst. A few days later the Hearst papers published an editorial entitled "Qualified and Available" that boosted Kennedy for president. Ambassador Kennedy, the Hearst press claimed, had sound fiscal ideas and a better understanding of foreign affairs than did FDR, but his chief qualification was his unflinching opposition to U.S. entry into the war. Kennedy made no public comment on Hearst's endorsement, and he did not declare himself a candidate. One week later Roosevelt was nominated to run for an unprecedented third term. Hearst announced his support for FDR's opponent, Wendell L. Willkie, the dark horse candidate of the Republican Party.

Kennedy returned to the United States from his post in London in late October convinced of the political practicality of throwing his support over to Roosevelt. On October 27 he met with the president at the White House and agreed to deliver an endorsement speech over the radio two days later. Kennedy reportedly told others that his meeting at the White House elicited a promise from FDR that when the time came for Joseph Kennedy Jr. to run for governor of Massachusetts, Roosevelt would repay the favor. At the same conference the future of Kennedy's role as ambassador was also discussed, and Kennedy voluntarily agreed to resign officially around the first of the year. In the meanwhile he continued speaking out for isolationism and held a meeting in November with another figure of the period with similar opinions, the aviator Charles Lindbergh. On November 9 Kennedy told a reporter that he would soon travel to the West Coast for a trip that would include visits with his second oldest son and Hearst.

By late 1940 John F. Kennedy, the second oldest son of the ambassador to England, was fast becoming more famous than any actor or actress his father had nurtured in Hollywood. Joe Kennedy, the guiding force behind Jack Kennedy's ascent, received some backstage help from Hearst, something of a specialist himself in celebrity creation. Ironically, considering his good looks and charisma, the Harvard graduate did not first make his mark in the movies or even politics. His outward, nonintellectual attributes were first put to use in the next best arena: the Hearstian or Hollywood version of journalism. In the spring of 1940, with the urging of his father, Kennedy transformed a 150-page college thesis into a book entitled *Why England Slept*. The whole process, from writing to publishing, took only four months, but it was a team effort. By most accounts, it was Joe Kennedy's cronies, including *New York Times* writer Arthur Krock and a speechwriter, who had pulled the book together and his own fame that hastened a publishing contract.

Critics of *Why England Slept* have found the book's message—ostensibly a plea for American military preparedness—mixed at best. The book offers a defense of Neville Chamberlain's appeasement of Hitler by making the case that the British public was psychologically unprepared for war and needed to buy time. There are passages (some copied verbatim from Joe Kennedy statements) that seem to espouse isolationism, while others express ambiguity over issues of war and peace (JFK's echoing of his father's opinions was further demonstrated a year later when he personally sent a small contribution to the isolationist organization the America First Committee). Some historians have found Kennedy's writing hackneyed and his analysis faulty. But others have called the book mature and timely. Contemporary reviews were almost uniformly glowing, and sales were good (it was reported that the ambassador personally bought thousands of copies to enhance sales figures).

In the end, the book's merits seemed destined to be linked to the pseudoevent surrounding it, a well-orchestrated promotional campaign of Hollywood-style image making for the debut of John F. Kennedy on the American stage. One historian, John Hellmann, thinks that the book's "pattern of inertia and arousal" reflects the author's inner struggle to make his own way in the world. Hellmann called the book "the crucial first text in the production of John F. Kennedy, in terms of both Jack's projection of his own ideal image and his father's and others' collaborative presentation of that image as an idealized representation of its reader."

With his book on bestseller lists around the nation, Jack Kennedy set off for California in late 1940 to take a no-credit course at Stanford University's School of Business Administration in Palo Alto and to enjoy the sun and stars in Hollywood. With the backseat of his Buick convertible piled high with copies of his hardcover book, JFK was much in demand on the Stanford campus and in Los Angeles, where he befriended the actor Robert Stack and met Spencer Tracy and Clark Gable at Hollywood parties. At the Universal Studio, he got a glimpse of filmmaking and was photographed with the actress Margaret Sullavan. In November, while still attending classes at Stanford, Jack Kennedy took time off see his parents, who were spending a week in California. Shortly before this visit, Kennedy made one of two or three visits to Hollywood. Harriet Price Fullerton, Kennedy's closest Stanford University girlfriend, says he told her that he had taken a drive down the Pacific coast from Palo Alto to Hollywood with a midway stopover at Hearst's San Simeon estate. Kennedy said he had dinner in the Refectory at San Simeon, but he ate alone, as Hearst and Davies were at their Wyntoon estate at the time.

The Kennedys and Hearst and Davies had a friendly relationship for years. In 1941 the Hearst press syndicated "Why England Slept," pumping up the publicity for the already skyrocketing author. Following his service in the war and the well-publicized events of his PT 109, Kennedy got his first civilian job when Hearst, at the request of Joe Kennedy, personally offered the war hero a post as a Hearst correspondent reporting on the first United Nations meetings in San Francisco. When Kennedy ran for his first elective office in 1946, Hearst's *Boston American* enforced a virtual news blackout on his congressional opponent, failing even to mention his name during long stretches of the campaign. When Jack Kennedy married Jacqueline Bouvier in 1953, two years after Hearst's death, Davies attended the wedding and later turned over her Beverly Hills home for the newlyweds to use during their honeymoon. In a thank-you note to Davies sent afterward, Jacqueline Kennedy said she and her new husband had particularly enjoyed seeing their first movie as a married couple, the Hearst and Davies film *Little Old New York*, which had been offered to them at the mansion as a diversion. Davies's Beverly Hills home was loaned again, this time to the growing Kennedy family, during the Democratic presidential convention of 1960, in Los Angeles. At the swearing-in ceremony in front of the Capitol Building in Washington, D.C., in 1961, Davies can be seen in film footage taken of Kennedy as he gives his inaugural address. Looking frail but still recognizable, she sits a few rows behind the new president, bundled up against the bitter cold and wearing what appears to be a dark bonnet from another era.

A male friend of Jack Kennedy remembers being with him when he greeted his father at a San Francisco airport, probably on November 14, 1940, and he saw the two Kennedys off as they drove further north to Wyntoon. In comments he made to reporters in New York on November 9, Joe Kennedy had indicated a desire to meet with Hearst to discuss a way to organize a newspaper campaign to keep the United States out of the war in Europe. During his trip west in November, Kennedy would not focus solely on a combination of newspapers to propel his isolationist views; he was eager to enlist Hollywood in his cause as well. Apparently Hearst and Kennedy discussed their compatible stands on isolationism at Wyntoon. Gossip columnist Hedda Hopper, staying with Hearst and Davies at the time, remembered Kennedy's visit and her own expressions of support for his views. Hopper recalled suggesting to Kennedy that he hold a public debate over the issue of isolationism with Bernard Baruch. Considering their mutual histories, it is not unlikely that Hearst and Kennedy also discussed Hollywood. Even as ambassador to England Kennedy had paid close attention to developments in the film industry. He was intimately involved in negotiations related to foreign film distribution, for instance, trying to find a solution to ease the burden on American film studios that had gone unpaid for films sent to war-torn and financially unstable Britain. In fact, shortly after he returned to the United States, his days as ambassador numbered, Kennedy held a number of long conferences with Will Hays presumably on just that subject.

Immediately after Kennedy's visit with Hearst, he traveled to Los Angeles, where Davies and Hearst had given him the loan of their Santa Monica beach house. In Hollywood the ambassador gave a speech to a gathering of movie executives that proved to be one of his most controversial. Although the speech was not delivered for public consumption and no contemporary press accounts have been discovered, a sense of what transpired is found in a letter the actor Douglas Fairbanks Jr. wrote to President Roosevelt. Fairbanks, an acquaintance of the FDR family, was not in attendance at the Kennedy gathering, but he claimed to have close contacts with those who were. In his letter, dated November 19 and probably written within a day of the event, Fairbanks admitted to the president that he was acting somewhat like a "tattle-tale":

> As you know, Ambassador Kennedy has been out here and has been visiting with Mr. Hearst. He phoned me before he went north, telling me that he planned to meet with me on his return. This, however, did not transpire.
>
> Because of some pressing business of my own I was unable to attend a meeting which took place here at one of the studios, over which Ambassador Kennedy presided. He spoke to the gathering for about three hours, and it was another "off the record" talk. I have checked on my information as to the points he covered and the attitude he took from about four different people who attended the meeting and their reports were identical. . . . He stated that although he did not think that Britain would lose the war, still, she had not won it yet. He repeated forcefully that there was no reason for our ever becoming involved in *any way*. According to reports, he suggested that the Lindbergh appeasement groups are not so far off the mark when they suggest that this country can reconcile itself to whomever wins the war and adjust our trade and lives accordingly. He did maintain, however, that we should continue aiding Britain, but not at the expense of getting ourselves into trouble.

Fairbanks's reference to "another 'off the record' talk" was the interview Kennedy gave to reporters in Boston in early November that wound up in print and was broadly characterized as defeatist and by some even treasona-ble. As Fairbanks continued his letter, the most troubling aspect of Kennedy's speech became apparent:

> He [Kennedy] apparently threw the fear of God into many of our producers and executives by telling them that the Jews were on the spot, and that they should stop making anti-Nazi pictures or using the film medium to promote or show sympathy to the cause of the "democracies" versus the "dictators." He said that anti-Semiticism [sic] was growing in Britain and that the Jews were being blamed for the war. . . . He continued to underline the fact that the film business was using its power to influence the public dangerously and that we all, and the Jews in particular, would be in jeopardy, if they continued to abuse that power.

In his letter to FDR, Fairbanks speculated that Kennedy had a hidden agenda. The ambassador, he said, was working behind the scenes with Will Hays to push for "clean-ups" and "clean-outs" that would put Kennedy and Hays in greater positions of power in the film business. Fairbanks also expressed his belief that Kennedy had been "violently influenced" by Catholic appeasement groups, the Legion of Decency, and the America First Committee, an organization formed to oppose U.S. entry into the war in Europe. Although Fairbanks does not mention him in this context, Hearst too had come out strong for the Catholic hierarchy's positions on issues of war and peace and had been a vocal supporter of the Legion of Decency and its calls for movie censorship. Less clear is the depth of Hearst's rela-tionship to the isolationist America First Committee.

Hearst used the phrase "America First" often and long before its later association. In a 1908 editorial he explained what he meant by the slogan: America should be most proud of its own achievements and indebted to no other country. He said that Americans were strong and self-reliant people who "have blessed all civilization," and he went on to provide a list of Amer-ican inventions—including the typewriter, the telegraph, and the kineto-scope—that had benefited the world.

In the years between the two world wars, Hearst championed his philos-ophy of America First. In late 1932 Hearst began a newspaper and newsreel campaign that he called "Buy American," which linked prosperity to isola-tionism and the crisis of the Great Depression to gambling internationalists. To spread his "Buy American" message, Hearst was filmed by the *Hearst Metrotone News* cameras outside the main doorway of San Simeon, and he teamed his own scene with a talk by California senator Hiram W. Johnson called "Europe Must Pay." The promotion of American-made products seems to have been related to Hearst's resentments over European war debts and to an incident in 1930, when the government of France expelled the vacationing Hearst from the country for publishing a secret Anglo-French naval treaty.

In early 1933, reporting on Hearst's campaign, *Variety* claimed that Paramount Pictures, busy filming Maurice Chevalier pictures, and Fox, about to start a picture with French actor Henry Garat, were worried that Hearst was chiefly targeting France in his campaign. The journal also reported that the "Buy American" campaign was sparking interest among filmmakers and that the production company Radio Pictures would soon start work on a film based on the subject (there is no evidence that such a film was made). There was concern that the "Buy American" slogan might have a chilling effect on Hollywood. "A feeling of discomfort is evident at the studios," *Variety* noted on January 17, "in connection with name players of several nationalities." When the British-made film *Woman in Bondage* was previewed at a theater on New Year's Eve, an audience member shouted, "Give us an American picture," and the picture was pulled from the double bill, the magazine reported. Right up to the Second World War, Hearst continued his Americanism drive, maintaining his assertion that he had no desire for a political or economic retreat from the world but only that the United States should be "wisely self-devoted."

Although no documentary evidence has been located to tie Hearst directly to the America First Committee, his son William Randolph Hearst Jr. claimed his father was the mastermind behind the organization, which was formed in 1940. In a memoir he wrote that his father "helped found the America First movement to protect U.S. international interests." The closest contemporary account of Hearst's involvement in the origins of America First comes from J. Edgar Hoover, who wrote Hearst a letter on April 8, 1940, shortly before America First was officially organized. The letter is essentially a thank-you note from Hoover to Hearst for his generous newsreel and newspaper publicity for the FBI. Almost in passing, Hoover also seems to be acknowledging Hearst's secret role as America First's angel. "I, of course, know that the policy of preaching 'America First' emanates from you," Hoover writes, "and, so, to you, I want to express my thanks, both personally and officially." Whether or not Hearst played a role in the origins of America First, he certainly was one of its most enthusiastic supporters.

Joe Kennedy's threat to the movie moguls, inspired if not instigated by Hearst, was not the only trouble plaguing Jews in Hollywood in 1940. Concern over European refugees finding work in the film industry at the expense of native-born Americans became an issue that was often used to stir currents of anti-Semitism. There was a special interest among some studios in hiring writers and other creative personnel with progressive sensibilities in the hopes of bringing a greater sense of artistry and reality to film situations and characters. A European writer or artist also brought along a hint of exoticism to what might otherwise have been moviemaking's fairly provincial, factorylike routine. For just these reasons, Hearst himself had sought out Joseph Urban in the late 1910s, and other producers had encouraged a whole wave of foreign migration to Hollywood throughout the twenties. Many of these immigrants brought along their socialist beliefs. No doubt some were even in sympathy with Communist Party solutions to war, hunger, and discrimination.

In reality, the number of refugees in Hollywood who might be accused of taking jobs from Americans was minuscule. An article in *Variety* on October 9, 1940, reported the Screen Actors Guild as claiming that refugee actors were hardly overrunning the Hollywood studios. According to SAG, out of forty-five hundred employees at MGM only five might be considered refugees. There were three refugees out of four thousand employees at Warner Bros., and three out of twenty-seven hundred at Twentieth Century-Fox. Back in August Variety also pointed out that those unknown numbers of refugee screenwriters who had made their way to Hollywood were mostly without work and many were destitute.

The backlash against refugees was mostly confined to those escaping persecution in Germany and other neighboring countries. but as conditions continued to deteriorate in Great Britain in the late 1930s, there were fears expressed in the mainstream press that an English invasion of Hollywood might displace or replace native-born American talent. In late 1939 Hedda Hopper made a subtle comment about the refugee issue and what she perceived as favoritism to foreigners. In a column that was largely a plug for the "boy genius" from the East Coast whose recent highly trumpeted arrival at RKO studios was meeting some resistance and would soon meet with a great deal more, she wrote: "Too bad Orson Welles isn't an Englishman. If he had been, Hollywood would never have given him such a run-around. We reserve that for our own citizens."

In the summer of 1940 the refugee issue had put Hollywood, in the words of Louella Parsons, "in the throes of one of the greatest discussions that ever rocked the industry." A good deal of the trouble was being stirred up by a controversial and somewhat mysterious local radio broadcaster named G. Allison Phelps who had latched on to Hollywood's refugee issue with a vengeance and was not prepared to let go. He gave daily broadcasts on the subject and often laced his attacks on aliens with threats to expose immorality among prominent members of the film community. According to the *New York Times*, Phelps was not averse to breaking into studio files to search for dirt, and he was armed with "a well organized movement afoot to provide him with other trade information." By the late summer of 1940, Hearst newspapers had begun to focus more specifically on the influx of refugees into Hollywood. In her August 5 column Parsons wrote: "Famous refugees have been pouring into this country by the boatload ever since Herr Hitler marched into Paris—and right or wrong, mark my word, plenty of Hollywood's best jobs will go to them . . . and while it is swell that so many artists are coming to Hollywood—let's not forget our own American talent."

A few days later Parsons was back on the subject again in a short article for the *American Weekly* entitled "Refugee Issue Divides Hollywood." The piece was generally balanced, airing the voices of those who were pro-immigration (Darryl Zanuck and MGM executive Eddie Mannix) and those opposed (Frank Freeman, president of the Motion Picture Producers Association, and the transplanted Ufa producer Erich Pommer). Meanwhile another Hearst writer seemed to harden the attack on aliens in an August 9 editorial that linked the refugee issue to two other pet crusades. The writer deplored the fact that "the screen has teemed with Communist propaganda, war propaganda and alien propaganda of all kinds."

One Hollywood figure who became particularly vocal about the issue of refugees in 1940 was an out-of-work screenwriter named Paul Schofield (no relation to the actor with a similar name). Schofield, whose last writing credit had been the 1939 film *Mystery Plane*, organized a writing campaign to warn anyone willing to listen that real Americans would not stand by and give up their livelihoods for writers who "are AWOL from concentration camps." In a letter he sent to Will Hays on August 30, Schofield took up the issue of anti-Semitism without flinching. The letter is also instructive in revealing the vulnerable state of mind of Jewish movie executives who were eager to assimilate:

> It is commonly supposed to be almost fatal to mention the word Jew in the picture business, but I'll take the chance, in order to say that the heads of major studios, predominantly Jewish, are understandable in their desire to help these unfortunate people. But I believe they entirely under-estimate the temper of this country, and it is time someone has the guts to warn them. Are these producers Americans or

are they Jews? If they are going to give contracts to refugee Jews while denying them to equally or even more capable Americans, the question is answered.

A copy of Schofield's letter to Hays was sent to President Roosevelt, various magazine editors, and members of Congress, including Martin Dies. A similar letter was mailed to the Screenwriters' Guild, along with a cover letter, to Westbrook Pegler, a Scripps-Howard syndicated columnist who later work for King Features. In the closing of his letter to Pegler, Schofield makes a provocative aside: he tells the columnist that his refugee crusade has an ally in his neighbor in Pacific Palisades, the Hearst reporter Adela Rogers St. Johns.

Schofield's views resurfaced in 1945 in a fifty-six-page edition of *G. Allison's American Voice: A Journal of Truth* called *Hollywood, the Filth Column of America*, authored by the radio broadcaster G. Allison Phelps. In the course of this anti-Semitic assault on Hollywood, Phelps alludes to a screenwriter who has been of assistance to him. He does not mention Schofield by name, but he includes quotes from this unnamed screenwriter that are taken verbatim from Schofield's 1940 letter to Hays and others. Phelps's self-published diatribe also provides some interesting information on the broadcaster's background. For several years, beginning in 1908, Phelps worked on Hearst's *Los Angeles Examiner*. In the late 1920s, after becoming a radio broadcaster, he went to work for another Hearst newspaper, the *Los Angeles Evening Express*, where he wrote a radio column called "Behind the Microphone."

MAKING THE YELLOW FILM

Almost from the moment *Citizen Kane* was released in 1941, debate has raged over the film's true authorship. A battle between the screenwriters themselves, Orson Welles and Herman Mankiewicz, began early on, with Welles attempting to take all the credit for the production, as had been his practice in his radio career. Ultimately Mankiewicz, who wrote the film's first bare-boned script and made contributions to subsequent drafts, would share screen credit with Welles. Critics and historians weighed in next; sometimes Welles was in favor, and at others it was Mankiewicz. Over the years *Kane* was subjected to analysis sometimes so intense as to obscure the collaborative art inherent in all film undertakings and the political and cultural context specific to *Kane*'s production. A natural starting point for a student of a film is the viewing of that film followed by a study of its screenplay. But, like any film of significance, *Kane* is much more than the sum of its visual and audio parts and the path of its narrative. It should be viewed in its context. Even its useful screenplay (or the several versions written before the final shooting script) is somewhat incomplete without a look into the background of its screenwriters, especially, in the case of *Kane*, as they relate to Hearst.

In addition to making major contributions to the film's dialogue and the overall cinematic structure, Mankiewicz deserves most of the credit for the film's journalistic approach, a story-driven portrait of a man's rise and fall, presented through a series of highly charged flashback, flashbulb memories. Long before he met Welles, Mankiewicz had toyed with this many-sided biography concept. For a while he thought of writing a film about the gangster John Dillinger; at other times, his favored subject was Howard Hughes. In the mid-1930s he even wanted to make a film about Hitler.

Mankiewicz was interested in exploring a character's psychological makeup and his or her impact on the surrounding culture. He was drawn to the sweeping stylization of a novelist and a great admirer of the work of F. Scott Fitzgerald. Mankiewicz and Fitzgerald first met in the 1920s, and they renewed their friendship in the early 1930s when they found themselves working together in Hollywood. The two writers soon discovered that in addition to their mutual interest in writing and their love-hate relationship with Hollywood they shared an attraction to alcohol and fatalism. One Mankiewicz friend described him as "a kind of German Jewish Scott Fitzgerald," and the screenwriter Donald Ogden Stewart said that "Scott had a bit of a death instinct. I think Mank and he [Fitzgerald] were closer to each other than any of that generation."

Notwithstanding his Fitzgeraldian aspirations, Mankiewicz's primary instincts were those of a newspaperman who learned his craft during the era of fast-talking, fast-paced picture journalism. Naturally, as a newspaperman Mankiewicz knew of Hearst early on. While he was working for the *Chicago Tribune* in the early 1920s, Mankiewicz was stationed in Berlin, where he befriended a number of Hearst reporters, including the enigmatic Karl von Wiegand, a later sometime champion and sometime critic of the Hearst papers' contributing writer Adolf Hitler. In California in the 1930s Mankiewicz and his wife, Sara, often crossed paths with Hearst and Marion Davies at various Hollywood functions. One photograph shows the Mankiewicz couple among partygoers at a 1931 Mayfair Ball in honor of Marion Davies. In a group shot, seated near the middle of the first row, are Davies, Louella Parsons, and Sara Mankiewicz. Herman Mankiewicz is standing behind his wife. Ironically, standing next to the screenwriter is

George Fitzmaurice, the director who had made the first film about Hearst, in 1919, and who died the year *Citizen Kane* was filmed.

Herman and Sara Mankiewicz were part of the Hollywood crowd that occasionally made the drive to Hearst and Davies's beach house in Santa Monica and traveled by train and limousine for overnight or weekend stays at San Simeon. When they stayed at Hearst's ranch they always occupied the La Casa del Monte cottage. Mankiewicz spent his days playing tennis, sometimes matched against Davies and Harry Crocker, Hearst's confidant and social secretary, who had accompanied him on his trip to Europe in 1934. Mankiewicz would later admit that he had used some of his visits to San Simeon as an opportunity to trade stories about his host with Hearst's majordomo, Joe Willicombe. Crocker, another fan of Hearst and Hollywood gossip, was also a source for Mankiewicz. It is not known if Fitzmaurice, who was at San Simeon at least once with Mankiewicz, also passed along any valuable tidbits to the screenwriter.

Mankiewicz created nearly every character in *Citizen Kane* in his very first draft. Even so, considerable credit must go to Orson Welles for transforming the character of Charles Foster Kane into much more than a thinly veiled portrait of Hearst. Today, *Kane* is clearly the most famous Hearst satire ever created, but the concept was far from original; before 1941 there had been a number of literary works, stage productions, and at least one other film that had tackled the same subject. The 1930s were particularly ripe for Hearst lampoons on the stage. A 1933 theatrical production by the Workers' Laboratory Theater, called *Newsboy*, included a Hearst character who appears in a spotlight shouting out war headlines to his staff. A theater piece called *Parade* produced in 1935 had two skits related to Hearst. In one, a Hearst photographer takes pictures of a starving American family and tries to palm them off as evidence of widespread famine in Russia; the other, entitled "The Tabloid Reds," is a parody of Hearst's obsession with bomb-throwing Reds.

Five years before his film work in *Kane*, Welles himself starred in a theatrical production called *Ten Million Ghosts* that used a Hearst character to drive home playwright Sidney Kingsley's anti-Fascist themes. In the play (which made use of motion pictures projected on screens) munitions manufacturers are attacked and blamed for war. According to a review in the *Daily Worker*, "The play exposes the international ramifications of the munitions gang, links them with an American chain newspaper publisher, obviously Hearst, and adds that they backed Hitler in his meteoric rise to power, so that his brutal methods might aid them in suppressing the rising tide of antagonism to war, to capitalism and equally, to themselves."

In February 1940 Herman Mankiewicz began working for Orson Welles on a script he titled *American* (like so many Hearst newspapers and possibly suggesting Hearst's current Americanism campaign). By May Welles was deeply involved in the writing process himself, editing Mankiewicz's work or, as the Welles biographer Simon Callow has put it, "smudging" some of the Hearst references. The similarities between Hearst and Charles Foster Kane have been explored in numerous articles, books, and film documentaries. Notwithstanding the protests of Welles and Mankiewicz in interviews and legal documents, along with some recent revisionist studies, there is little doubt that the screenwriters had had their sights on Hearst for a long time and that they set out to make a film that would illuminate his character and his meaning.

By the time Welles was actively working on *American*, the name of the main character had been changed from Craig to Kane, and the script was being renamed *Citizen Kane*. Precisely how the filmmakers came up with the name Kane is unclear, but everything from Cain and Abel, to an old Welles colleague named Whitford Kane, to a San Simeon regular named Eddie Kane has been suggested. There was also a film producer named (Robert) Kane, who took over the Cosmopolitan studios in New York when Hearst moved his operation to the West Coast. Another source, perhaps subliminal, also exists. Charles Foster Kane's principal political enemy in most versions of the film script is "Boss" Jim Gettys, a Tammany-style politician modeled after Hearst's real-life opponent in the early 1900s, Charles F. Murphy. "Boss" Murphy's bodyguard during those days was a man who later became a well-known New York City police detective. In February 1940 the detective was found dead on the floor of a hotel bathroom. His death prompted prominent obituaries in a number of newspapers, in which he was identified as Charles F. Kane. In an early draft of *American*, the Kane character dies shortly after being found unconscious on a hotel's bathroom floor.

Kane's obsession over the career of his blonde, boozy former shop girl is copied from the commonly accepted view of Hearst's micromanagement of Davies's career. Less known are the references to Hearst and others close to him that appear in the earlier versions of the script, some of which did not make it to the final shooting script. In one draft the character of *Enquirer* writer Jed Leland, played by Joseph Cotton, leaves Kane because he is morally repulsed by Kane's advertising scheme of giving theatrical productions good play for good pay. This was a direct lifting of real events that were revealed to the public in the 1910s and were later repeated with slight variations in the newsreel deals with Hitler and Mussolini, as well as the *Good Housekeeping* Seal of Approval irregularities exposed by the Federal Trade Commission in

1939. Welles and Mankiewicz could easily have known about Hearst's various advertising schemes by reading newspaper and magazine reports over the years and studying Ferdinand Lundberg's biography of 1936.

The filmmakers may have also heard a firsthand account of the Hearst advertising policy. During the writing of *Kane*, Welles consulted with Ashton Stevens, the Hearst drama critic and a longtime friend of the director. One of their meeting places was a hotel in downtown Los Angeles called the Town House. Welles would later tell film producer George Stevens Jr., a nephew of Ashton, that the Hearst drama critic was a great friend who was especially helpful. George Stevens Jr. thought his uncle was really a mentor to Welles. In *Kane*, the newspaper writer who leaves in protest is obviously based in part on Ashton Stevens. Welles came as close as he could to actually putting the Hearst drama critic in *Kane*: he cast Ashton's brother, Landers Stevens, an old-time San Francisco theater actor, for a bit part in the film.

Two other references to Hearst that didn't make it into the film except in a veiled fashion are related to Hearst's courtship of Millicent Hearst and the political connotations of their relationship. At first glance, aside from a certain similarity in their names—Emily Norton and Millie Willson—Mrs. Kane (played by Ruth Warwick) and Millicent Hearst seem to have little in common. But possibly there is a reference to Millicent Hearst in a scene that was filmed but never included in the final version of *Kane*. One of the very first scenes that Welles filmed took place in a brothel called Georgie's. It falls at a point in the film's narrative that corresponds with the meeting between Kane and Emily and also with the meeting between Hearst and Millicent and Hearst and Mr. and Mrs. *George* Willson. There are few traces of the projected brothel scene in the final film. But later, when a political opponent exposes Kane's adulterous relationship to Susan Alexander on the eve of his election for governor, causing him to lose the race, there are shades of Hearst's own political downfall at the hands of those who disapproved of his relationship to Millicent and the Willsons. The characterization of Kane's political rival, "Boss" Gettys, in addition to owing much to Charles F. Murphy and any number of Tammany Hall bosses, may suggest President Theodore Roosevelt, who in the closing days of Hearst's 1906 race for governor of New York disseminated information about Hearst and Millicent, whom he called "a chorus girl or something like that."

Although some of the Hearst-Kane parallels in various versions of the script may seem isolated and insignificant, collectively and in conjunction with broader themes they form a design that works brilliantly to achieve the filmmakers' dual goals. They create a psychological portrait of Hearst, and they send what film historians call "a contraband message" to audiences, a cinematic diatribe against Hearst's yellow journalism and his embrace of capitalism, isolationism, and fascism. Kane's Xanadu, with its enormous fireplace and its jumbled mix of classical styles, is obviously meant to suggest San Simeon, but it is a decidedly sinister version of Hearst's California home that the filmmakers chose to emphasize. There are echoes of other overpowering sets like this in the films of D.W. Griffith and Cecil B. DeMille, as well as in the great Hollywood horror films of the 1930s. There are even hints of the Gothic designs created by Joseph Urban for Hearst's own films. Lighting is used effectively and efficiently in *Kane* to produce a relatively low-budget sense of power and foreboding. Here, Welles and his cinematographer, Gregg Toland, drew on the film work of John Ford and the expressionist theater lighting that been the hallmark of Welles's theater career. The evocative, minimalist use of light and shadow in American film can also be traced to Joseph Urban, who used the German expressionist film *The Cabinet of Doctor Caligari* (1920) for inspiration.

The sets, the lighting, and even the sound in *Kane* are all combined to communicate a sense of Hearst as a man, but they also express the political themes of isolationism and fascism so closely associated with Hearst in 1940. Elements of this left-wing/right-wing polarization are apparent in the early lightning-fast newsreel sequence that summarizes the recently ended life of Charles Foster Kane, a preview of the narrative of the remaining film and a subliminal political manifesto. In a quick shot of Kane's once vibrant, now decaying *Enquirer* newspaper building, a seemingly incongruous hammer and sickle, symbol of the Communist Party, can be perceived stenciled on a brick wall. In another sequence, Kane is seen in Germany with Hitler. In one episode in an early script that does not end up in the final film, the filmmakers actually have Charles Foster Kane connected through his son to a homegrown fascist group.

In the decades since its release, *Citizen Kane*'s heightened visual qualities and its sensationalized portrayal of one man's public power haunted by private passions and a foreshadowed loss have attracted countless filmgoers. Part of the film's attraction—especially when it was first released—almost certainly comes from its larger-than-life subject matter, William Randolph Hearst. But what makes this connection stronger still is how the filmmakers treat their subject with many of the same methods of yellow journalism employed by their subject. Like Hearst's journalism, *Kane* uses methods of inquiry that alternate between superficiality and penetration, between psychobabble and psychoanalysis. Even the optical illusions in *Kane* owe a debt to composite illustrations and other trickery perfected by the yellow journals over the previous half-century.

An early version of the script suggests that the filmmakers may have intended to present Kane as someone even more closely resembling Hearst: a Hollywood showman. The character is said to have had a passion for watching movies at home after dinner, and he has a Hearstian flair for spontaneous soft-shoe dancing. In the final film only the newsreel sequence—called "the single most impressive, most spoken-of element in the movie" by Welles biographer Simon Callow—seems to relate directly to Hearst the filmmaker. Entitled *News on the March*, it appears to be a reference to both Henry Luce's newsreel, *March of Time*, and Hearst's own *News of the Day*. Significantly, the sequence begins a narrative thread that is maintained throughout *Kane* in the form of the film's persistent reporter. Jerry Thompson, as played by William Alland, is a shadowy figure whose questions serve to spark the memories of the film's key characters. Thompson has not been dispatched by a respectable newspaper. In pursuit of the sensational and superficial meaning in Kane's last dying words, this is a yellow journalism film reporter, exemplifying all the drama and gaudiness of Hearst's long career. In the end, Hearst becomes more than the mere subject of the film. He is in the shadows of the film's sometimes shallow, sometimes probing, but always sensationalist approach. He is in the long, multimirrored view of reality, an incomplete picture with many angles. *Kane* from inception through production, and to release becomes far more than a Hollywood version of Hearst's life—it is the essence of a Hollywood life.

The more obvious and even the more subtle similarities between Hearst and his movie counterpart play no small role in allowing the film to enter the viewer's subconscious. The film's staying power is closely related to an understanding that Hearst had come to before the turn of the twentieth century: yellow journalism and cinema are intrinsically connected. It was the genius of Orson Welles and Herman Mankiewicz to make not only a psychological study that captures Hearst better than many nonfiction studies but to absorb Hearst's own vision of communication into the making of their film. In the end, *Citizen Kane* endures as a reluctant homage to Hearst's significance, done so well that it has become both a reflection and a reflector of a man and his meaning.

The Yellow Reprisal

As a backdrop to the making and release of *Citizen Kane*, in the winter of 1940–1941 a quarterly magazine called *Unbelievable* (that folded after one issue) carried a pictorial story on Hearst that attempted to tie him to fascist causes at home and abroad. Soon after it was published, in February 1941, Hearst and his King Features Syndicate filed a lawsuit against Friday, Inc., the parent company of *Unbelievable* and a separate magazine called *Friday*. The Mankiewicz-Welles script—now retitled *Citizen Kane*—was shot during the late summer of 1940. *Friday* was the first magazine to view the film in a political context and to make allusions to Hearst. In its September 13 issue, an article called "Wellesapoppin'" previewed *Kane* and reproduced six film stills taken from the production. With an understated commentary on capitalism, *Friday* described the central character of the film as "a typical American business man." A caption under a photograph of actress Dorothy Comingore in the role of Susan Alexander described her as "a ringer for Marion Davies."

One of the first mentions of the film and its use of Hearst as a model to appear in a mainstream publication was in *Newsweek*'s September 16, 1940, issue. The magazine reported that certain unnamed columnists were already gossiping about the similarities between Kane and Hearst, causing the script to be sent to Hearst for his perusal. "Hearst," wrote *Newsweek*, "approved it without comment." It is uncertain who *Newsweek*'s alleged gossipers were, but the frequently anti-Hearst magazine called *Friday* may have been one source. Even if *Newsweek*'s assertion about the sending of the Kane script was made in error—as most historians agree—one imagines a story about a film on Hearst's life appearing in such a prominent mainstream magazine would raise a red flag with someone in the Hearst organization. As late as late December 1940, however, Louella Parsons's Hollywood column was still offering friendly blurbs about Orson Welles, praising his talent, and gossiping about his romance with Dolores Del Rio. Years later, in her memoirs, Parsons wrote that she had been troubled by the rumors about *Kane* as early as August 1940, soon after shooting began. She claimed that during an interview over lunch and during subsequent meetings with Welles, she asked the director directly about the rumors. As she later discovered, he continuously lied to her. Assuming Parsons's account is true, and she was not simply making this after-the-fact claim to prop up her sullied reputation as an effective Hearstling, it is still curious that she would ever have completely believed Welles. More curious still is the apparent nonreaction of Hearst. It is inconceivable that with all his interests and connections in Hollywood he was either unaware of or unfazed by the increasingly frequent hints that he was the film's subject.

Hearst once told his reporter Adela Rogers St. Johns that he believed that responding publicly to critics was a surefire way of increasing the public's interest in the criticism. He seems to have held to this principle during a number of controversies, from the rumors about his romantic alliances to the death of Thomas Ince and the questions about his being pro-German during World War I and in the 1930s. What Hearst did in private to respond to criticism is difficult to discern, but in the case of *Citizen Kane* there is ample evidence to suggest that he was anything but passive in the face of the cinematic attack.

According to Herman Mankiewicz, anti-Semitism was a prime weapon Hearst used against *Citizen Kane*. Sometime after the events took place, Mankiewicz wrote a description of Hearst's retaliation that conjures up the image of a gangster or a powerful Tammany boss who uses the heavy hand of intimidation but is careful not to leave his own fingerprints at the scene of the crime. "Mr. Hearst casually gave them [the movie moguls] a hundred examples of unfavorable news—rape by executives, drunkenness, miscegenation and allied sports—which on direct appeal from Hollywood he had kept out of his papers in the last fifteen years. General observations were made—not by Mr. Hearst but by high-placed Hearst subordinates—that the portion of Jews in the industry was a bit high and it might not always be possible to conceal this fact from the American public." According to author Neal Gabler, whose book *An Empire of Their Own* explores the history of Jews in Hollywood, *Kane*'s producer, George Schaefer, believed Hearst had an ally in Louis B. Mayer in his use of anti-Semitism to suppress his film. After the controversy over *Kane* died down, Schaefer discovered that in order to unite the Jewish movie moguls against him, a close but unnamed associate of Mayer had orchestrated a "whispering campaign" accusing Schaefer himself of being anti-Semitic.

Apparently Orson Welles, too, was convinced that Hearst was responding to *Kane* by threatening the Jews in Hollywood. On the afternoon of Sunday, April 6, 1941, a half-hour radio play written and narrated by Welles and entitled *His Honor the Mayor* was broadcast under the auspices of a theatrical troupe that called itself the Free Company. James Boyd, chairman of the Free Company, introduced the play and described his group as "writers, actors and radio workers who have come together voluntarily to present a series of plays about our basic liberties." Before handing over the microphone to Welles, he reminded radio listeners that the play's author and most of its cast would be appearing in the forthcoming production of *Citizen Kane*. A subtle reference to Kane's model and the film's political message was introduced through the play's dialogue minutes later:

JERRY: These here Reds . . .
KNAGGS: You mean Communists?
JERRY: Yeah.

KNAGGS: We only got one Communist in town, Jerry. Joe Enochan, and he can't hurt anybody—He's eighty-seven years old. Besides, there's nothin' illegal about bein' a Communist.

JERRY: That's what *you* say, Bill.

KNAGGS: That's what I say. There's no law in this country against havin' opinions.

JERRY: What about them labor organizers that come into town? They're Reds, ain't they?

KNAGGS: I don't think so. They're just tryin' to get the hands over at the factory to form a union.

JERRY: Yeah—Unions!

KNAGGS: If the hands get paid more for their work, they're going to spend more. Maybe buy some new tires for their cars from you. Maybe buy some new cars. Woudja object to that?

What was most startling about the Welles radio play was not the naïve expressions about Communism or even the homespun plot, which has a small-town mayor defending the rights of an extreme right-wing group called the White Crusaders to assemble. In the middle of the controversy over the film *Citizen Kane*, Welles created for radio another character based on Hearst. Colonel Egenhorn, who is a financial backer of the White Crusaders, is described by the mayor as a semiretired millionaire publisher who got rich on patent medicines (the medical fakery often compared to yellow journalism by muckrakers) who moved to the county and "built that big ranch."

In a confrontation with Egenhorn, the mayor blasts him for distributing "anti-Semitic garbage" in his publications throughout the country. When the mayor informs a crowd about the real objectives of the White Crusaders, his dialogue includes an amusing wink at Welles's writing partner on *Kane* and a more ominous allusion to Hearst's threats of retaliation against the film and the movie moguls of Hollywood: "They're talkin' about hating the Jews. We only got one Jewish family in the county—the Mankiewicz's—Anybody hate the Mankiewicz's? (Silence)."

Hearst saw nothing amusing about the Welles radio play, and he was quick to respond. His papers began to call Welles a Communist, and his friend J. Edgar Hoover began his own investigation of the director. Like many other FBI files generated by Hoover and his loyalists, the Welles files are informant reports filled with unsubstantiated or hearsay allegations. Mostly, however, the files are clippings or copies of clippings scraped from the Hearst papers.

Hearst did not stop with rallying his newspapers and his friends at the FBI. To add some cachet to his political attack on the *Kane* director, he exploited the American Legion, the nation's most prominent patriotic association, which had from time to time lent its services as a film industry watchdog. By 1941 the American Legion was decidedly right of center on most political issues, and this was reflected in its approach to films. The local branches of the legion, however, had not always been inclined in this political direction. In 1921 for instance, only a few years after the post–World War One formation of the national organization, the legion's Hollywood post created a division it called the American Film League whose sole purpose was the suppression of Universal's *Foolish Wives*, directed by Erich von Stroheim. According to a letter to a Universal executive by Irving Thalberg, the movie's young producer, the legion post opposed *Foolish Wives* because it said the film was being made by a German director (although von Stroheim was actually Austrian), financed by German money, and intended as pro-German propaganda. Thalberg, who had spent most of the production time on the overbudget film tearing his hair out over his director, whom he called a "crazy bird," now had other worries. Thalberg felt threatened that his film might be destroyed by boycotts and demonstrations mounted by "a gang of Bolshevik extra men who are out of jobs" and running the Hollywood American Legion.

It was anti-Communism that occupied the more activist segments of the American Legion in 1941. According to reports in *Variety*, shortly after the Free Company radio program was broadcast Hearst began to use his influence with the American Legion to publicize Welles's Communist affiliations. Heading Hearst's latest attack on Welles was a fellow name Kent Hunter, oddly described in the press as both a Hearst reporter and a publicity director for the Legion. Hunter's dual role is made clearer in the charter records of the American Legion. In November 1938 Legion Post No. 1197 was formally chartered and named the Phoebe Apperson Hearst Memorial, in honor of Hearst's mother. The Hearst legion post, which is still active today, rented space in the Hearst-owned Hotel Warwick in Manhattan, providing programs on Americanism and legal and financial aid for its members and regularly issuing pamphlets concerning its activities. It included some 280 members, who were all employees of Hearst's New York newspaper and syndication enterprises. Hunter was one of the founding members of the post.

Although he appears to have been primarily attached to the local chapter of the legion, Hunter was prominent enough to author at least two articles in 1940 that appeared in the widely circulated *American Legion Magazine*. Both pieces closely resemble Hearst editorials, touching on aspects of

Hearst's Americanism campaign and the claims that refugees were taking jobs away from "real" Americans. Hunter also uses the articles to applaud the work of Congressman Martin Dies. In addition to his regular duties as a reporter for the *New York Journal,* Hunter seems to have played a more covert role in Hearst's anti-Communist crusades of the late 1930s and early 1940s. *New Masses* on June 13, 1939, said that Hunter was known among Hearst employees as a "Patriot Expert," the key man Hearst used to coordinate his campaign of exposing Communist infiltration of the nation's schools. According to *New Masses,* Hunter boasted about having one of the biggest files on Reds anywhere. Hearst's new role for Hunter, as crusader against Welles and *Kane,* was the logical extension of his earlier attacks on aliens and Communism.

As early as January 1941, when the controversy over *Kane* was just breaking, the *New York Times* saw a link between Hearst's threat of retaliation and the threats of the Senate's most vocal alien baiter and isolationist. "Other representatives of the publisher," the *Times* observed, "began an investigation of the alien situation in Hollywood, something about which the industry is most sensitive. In making their inquiries, they explained that the information was being gathered for Mr. Hearst's private use. . . . Hollywood's apprehension is based upon the knowledge of its vulnerability. A rip-snorting newspaper Americanization campaign could prove embarrassing. A Congressional investigation, hinted at by Senator Burton K. Wheeler on Monday, might be disastrous."

Outwardly, Hearst seemed to be little concerned over *Kane.* In February 1941 he traveled to Mexico with a party that included Marion Davies, his sons, and the wife of film director Raoul Walsh. His private life was coming under increasing scrutiny, but during a visit with President Manuel Avila Camacho he allowed himself to be photographed seated next to Davies. The rare picture was published in the Hearst chain of newspapers apparently without any concern.

Throughout most of 1941, Hearst and Davies were in residence at Wyntoon. Their most prominent guests during this period were Charles Lindbergh and his wife, Anne, who arrived for a three-day visit in late June. Although Lindbergh was impressed with the beauty of the natural surroundings, writing in his diary about the redwoods and pines and the "rushing water outside the windows," he was also full of complaints about Hearst's controlling nature. Lindbergh described the atmosphere at Wyntoon as "too much Hollywood, too much efficiency, too much organization." He thought the arrangement of painted cottages resembled a movie set. He called the nightly movies "very stupid," and he balked at Hearst's meal regimen—breakfast was served promptly at 11 A.M., lunch at 2:30 P.M. and supper at 9 P.M. Even though he was aware of the routine, Lindbergh arrived for breakfast at 10:45 A.M. and fumed for fifteen minutes as he waited to be joined by others.

These little things were not the real problem. Lindbergh held Hearst and his yellow journalism methods responsible for his inability to lead a private life. After Lindbergh's triumphant crossing of the Atlantic Ocean in 1927, Hearst courted the aviator with lavish gifts (a pair of silver globes worth $50,000) and an extravagant offer (a guarantee of at least $500,000) to appear in a Hearst-produced movie. He took the gifts but refused to be Hearst's actor. The kidnapping of Lindbergh's baby in 1932 let loose the worst aspects of Hearst's operation; reporters and photographers hounded the grieving couple until they found it necessary to leave the country in 1935 for the sanctuary of England.

By 1941 Lindbergh was working hard to reconcile his emotions with the practical necessity of having a relationship with Hearst. Lindbergh knew that Hearst could be his most powerful ally in his increasingly visible role as the country's most famous isolationist. "The Hearst press has done things to me in the past which I cannot forgive from a personal standpoint," Lindbergh wrote in his diary, a few weeks after his visit, "but the issue of war or peace for America at this time is far above personal issues. Hearst has been assisting us, and I intend to assist him as far as this war issue is concerned. I cannot forget the past, but I have put it in the background, at least for the time being. . . . Experience warns me that the principles his papers follow may be only as stable as the popularity of his stand and the circulation figure which results."

Lindbergh used his visit with Hearst as an opportunity to discuss their shared views on keeping the United States out of war. Quite likely they also discussed the America First Committee and the role they believed Hollywood was playing as an advocate for intervention. In the days preceding his arrival at Hearst's estate, Lindbergh held several meetings in Hollywood with key boosters of America First, including the organization's Los Angeles chief John L. Wheeler (son of Senator Burton Wheeler) and Senator D. Worth Clark of Idaho. A speech Lindbergh delivered before a large crowd at the Hollywood Bowl on June 20 was under the auspices of the isolationist group and warmly reviewed by the Hearst press. In the weeks following his stay at Wyntoon, Lindbergh held conferences with other isolationists including Senator Gerald P. Nye of North Dakota and John T. Flynn, a *Collier's* magazine and newspaper writer with an interest in film. After a meeting with Flynn on August 8 in New York, Lindbergh wrote in his diary:

"Flynn says the investigation he has been carrying on is 'bringing amazing results,' and that he thinks he will be able to show clearly that a strong undercover movement for war exists. He says it is most obvious in the motion-picture industry. Flynn says the Administration has made direct requests that the motion-picture producers run a certain percentage of 'war films.' Flynn feels certain that this situation can be exposed in a congressional investigation."

On September 11 Lindbergh addressed an America First rally in Des Moines, Iowa. As Lindbergh alerted the crowd to the "other" forces in society that he believed were pulling the nation into a European conflict, he created for himself a controversy that would forever mark his life: "Instead of agitating for war, the Jewish groups in this country should be opposing it in every possible way, for they will be among the first to feel its consequences. Their greatest danger to this country lies in their large ownership and influence in our motion pictures, our press, our radio and our government."

On September 13 the *New York Times* reported widespread condemnation of the Lindbergh speech. Except for a brief report that FDR's press secretary had criticized Lindbergh, the Hearst papers on that same day paid little attention to the speech. Then on the following day, September 14, in what reads like an attempt to make up for lost time, an editorial entitled "An Un-American Address" appeared on page one of most of the Hearst newspapers: "The raising of the racial issue by Charles A. Lindbergh in his Des Moines, Iowa, speech is the most unfortunate happening that has occurred in the United States since the present tense international situation developed. . . . The assertion that the Jews are pressing this country into war is UNWISE, UNPATRIOTIC and UN-AMERICAN. . . . Mr. Lindbergh makes a still graver charge when he says that the 'greatest danger' to this country lies in the 'ownership' and 'influence' of the Jews in radio, motion pictures and 'our government.' "

On September 15 the Hearst press published comments from various political and religious leaders criticizing Lindbergh and another editorial entitled "Racial Prejudices Have No Place in America." In this second editorial, Hearst is clearly putting distance between himself and Lindbergh and between Lindbergh and the America First Committee, which Hearst was loath to criticize. Lindbergh, the editorial says, "most fortunately represents no other American. . . . He most certainly represents no organization worthy of having loyal Americans affiliated with its activities."

Hearst does not appear to have arrived at his decision to criticize Lindbergh without receiving heavy pressure from someone of particular importance to him at the time. John Wesley Hanes, of the handkerchief and underwear family, was a close adviser to Joseph Kennedy and a former undersecretary of the Treasury before joining the Hearst Corporation as a financial consultant in the summer of 1940. By most accounts, Hanes, working in conjunction with Joseph Kennedy, was largely responsible for restructuring the Hearst Corporation and putting it on the road to solvency. While Hanes was working for Hearst he was secretly employed by the British Security Coordination (BSC), an agency in charge of British covert operations that used propaganda techniques in an attempt to cripple the isolationist movement in the United States in the years just before World War II. Hanes's efforts to exert influence inside the Hearst Corporation were not known by the general public and presumably never discovered by Hearst (who continued to employ Hanes as late as 1947). According to correspondence between operatives of the BSC, immediately after Lindbergh's Des Moines address, Hearst was pressured by his adviser to respond in a dramatic manner that would leave no one doubting that Hearst believed the anti-Semitism in the speech was more than a simple mistake. Hanes also advised Hearst to serve notice on the America First Committee that they too should distance themselves from such sentiments.

While many of Hearst's critics were satisfied with his anti-Lindbergh editorials, the *Daily Worker* took a more cynical view of the sudden turnabout. In an editorial entitled "Hearst's Frantic Try at Covering Up," the Communist paper took note of the capitalized words in the first anti-Lindbergh editorial. "It is the 'unwise' character of Lindbergh's tirade," the *Worker* wrote, "which causes Hearst all the concern. . . . Hearst and his fellow-conspirators of the America First Committee had hoped that Lindbergh's treasonable assault upon Americanism would go over with the people. Hearst has ballyhooed every seditious utterance of Lindbergh's and had even given him a special interview recently in which to expound Hitlerite doctrines, although Lindbergh more than a year ago had given vent to 'racial' theories which fitted in with his anti-Semitic venom." The article the *Worker* mentions was an interview Lindbergh gave to Larry Kelly, a Hearst newspaperman from Chicago who was given the assignment of publicizing the aviator's views. Always wary about the prospect of speaking to a Hearst reporter, Lindbergh was ultimately satisfied to find the subsequent newspaper article was "fairly accurate in meaning." He later noted that "he [Kelly] did the best he could, and on Hearst standards of journalism it was not a bad piece of work."

Hearst never really severed his private relationship with the man he had publicly raked over the coals. After Pearl Harbor Lindbergh (like Hearst) completely abandoned his public stand against intervention. He even tried to reenlist in the army, but President Roosevelt denied him that opportunity. In 1942 Lindbergh went to work for Henry Ford, another American icon widely considered to be an anti-Semite, as a technical adviser in the automobile magnate's efforts to convert his factory operation to bomber production. In the winter of 1943–44, Lindbergh was once again a guest at Wyntoon, asking for Hearst's help to get him reinstated in the service. It is unknown whether Hearst played a decisive role in changing the administration's position, but a few months after the meeting at Wyntoon Lindbergh was put on active duty as a combat pilot in the Pacific.

For several decades now, most film critics and historians have awarded *Citizen Kane* their highest accolades. Nearly every all-time top ten list starts with *Kane*. At the Academy Awards ceremony in 1942, however, the film only received one Oscar for screenwriting, a prize that Welles and Mankiewicz shared. Some have said the film was simply too experimental or too dark or maybe even too controversial to win a popularity contest with Academy voters. According to *Variety*, after Welles was nominated in multiple categories by writers, directors, and actors who disliked the way he had been "treated and maligned by the Hearst papers," an even greater force had somehow united against him to leave the film director "scuttled":

> Just why "[How Green Was My] Valley" accounted for six statuettes, or "Okies" as Wendell Eilkie described them, was not as difficult to explain as the biz to Welles. . . . Into the voting picture, as in divisions, must be drawn the 6,000 extras, who held the balance of power. These supes [supernumeraries] must have been influenced, it is generally agreed, by the terrific advertising and publicity campaign given the film by the studio. . . . As for Welles, there is no dissent to the prevailing opinion that the extra vote scuttled him. It was patent that the mob didn't like the guy personally and took it out on him at the polls.

Although *Variety*'s accusations are intriguing, they have not been documented. On the surface the claim seems more like a diversion than a signpost to another plausible scenario. If in fact some forces were working behind the scenes to deny *Kane* its well-deserved Oscars, wouldn't they more likely have been the same forces that nearly suppressed the film before it was released?

Although Herman Mankiewicz had received the highest honor of the film industry for his work on *Citizen Kane*, he was not exactly out of the woods as far as Hearst was concerned. During the evening of March 11, 1943, Mankiewicz was driving home after having a few drinks at Los Angeles's Romanoff's restaurant when his car collided head-on with a station wagon. The screenwriter was unhurt, but one of the three passengers of the station wagon, Lee Gershwin, wife of the composer Ira Gershwin, suffered a cut on the forehead and bruised knees. A drunk-driving accident involving Hollywood celebrities of note was something that rarely made it to the newspapers, especially the pro–film industry Hearst papers. But this accident involved one of the Academy Award–winning authors of *Citizen Kane*, and it occurred at a most inconvenient location. At the sound of the car crash, a man came out the front door of the nearest house. The man was William Curley, publisher of the *New York Journal-American*, and the nearby house was the former Marion Davies bungalow that was now an addition to her Benedict Canyon estate. This wing of the estate was used as an office, and according to Mankiewicz's biographer, Hearst was with Curley in his office when Mankiewicz slammed into Gershwin's car. The accident and Mankiewicz's subsequent arrest became headlines in the Hearst newspapers. Photomontages were published just in case readers were unable to imagine what a typical car accident looked like. In a series of repetitious articles on the incident, there were no mentions of Hearst or Curley or the fact that the screenwriter had been held for five hours before he could see a lawyer, but there were frequent references to Mankiewicz's drinking problem. With some reluctance it seemed the Hearst press reported that the case against Mankiewicz had been dismissed after a hung jury decision. Hearst was more than making up for all the years he had happily buried news concerning countless celebrity misadventures. And he was giving an author of *Citizen Kane* some of his own yellow journalism treatment.

MISSIONS AND ALLIANCES

Since the mid-1930s Hearst had made it his mission to alert the public to what he saw as a growing infusion of Communist propaganda in motion pictures. As early as 1937 the attacks had become part of a full-fledged campaign, personally orchestrated by Hearst through his newspapers but extending beyond the confines of the editorial page. In a letter written in April 1937 by his editor Edmond Coblentz, Hearst was informed that other prominent organizations were already working hand-in-glove with his operatives and awaiting further instructions:

> In order to make our campaign against Communistic film effective, there must be close cooperation between all of our papers. Our papers

in Los Angeles and New York must be particularly on the alert, because most of the releases of Communistic films originate in these two cities. Films that are produced abroad, particularly in Russia, are released in New York through Amkino. We shall watch these releases here, and take immediate steps to apprise the religious, fraternal and patriotic organizations that are making the fight. This will enable them to take action before the film gets wide circulation. I think the same procedure should be followed by Los Angeles, where it is possible Communistic films may be produced. If Los Angeles will notify us if and when such films are being produced or released, we can in turn set the machinery of the Knights of Columbus in motion here and throughout the country. . . . Shall I write to all of our papers, telling them of your wishes, and giving them information as to what we are doing in the way of organization of this campaign.

Throughout the late 1930s and into the 1940s, Hearst's editorial response to Coblentz's suggestions was persistent, and his language was uncompromising, but there was a certain vagueness in his arguments, because he generally refrained from singling out specific motion pictures, studios, or producers. The tactic was the same one he had taken in his earliest criticisms of films at the turn of the century: threatening filmmakers with his power to mold public opinion and rallying Washington politicians without rupturing the bonds with producers and studios that were needed to do business. In 1943, however, Hearst changed his strategy, vigorously attacking two specific motion pictures and their producers. Hearst's new approach was likely to have been influenced by the fact that he was no longer making feature films. *Citizen Kane* may have also been a factor since the two producers Hearst zeroed in on—Jack Warner and Samuel Goldwyn—were known to be lukewarm in their support for him during the controversy over that film's release.

The release of the film *Mission to Moscow* in May 1943 gave Hearst a golden opportunity to kill two birds with one stone: he could attack the producers, the Warner Bros., and the Roosevelt administration as well. The Warner production, based in part on the memoirs of U.S. ambassador to Russia Joseph Davies, was a sympathetic portrait of life in the Soviet Union that seemed to be designed to act as an adjunct to the Roosevelt administration's call for public support for a military alliance with the Soviet Union against Nazi Germany. Hearst was not the only one to view the film as propaganda; published criticisms by such liberals as Dorothy Thompson, Edmund Wilson, and Max Eastman actually preceded his own.

Hearst's first newspaper attack on May 16 was in the form of a reprint of a long letter in the *New York Times* authored by Professor John Dewey and Suzanne La Follette, chairman and secretary of the International Commission of Inquiry into the Moscow trials. Dewey and La Follette called *Mission to Moscow* "the first instance in our country of totalitarian propaganda for mass consumption." On the same day the Hearst papers published the Dewey and La Follette attack, the *Times* made an attempt at balance by publishing a defense of the film by an American expert on Russian affairs. This profilm point of view was not reprinted in the Hearst papers.

The controversy over the film might not have reached such wide proportions or been so closely associated with Hearst had Jack Warner chosen to ignore Hearst's troublemaking. Instead, possibly because he knew troublemaking would draw more attention to his film, Warner dashed off a telegram to Hearst on May 17:

Dear W.R.—

Your papers displayed yesterday complete reprint of three column letter by John Dewey and Suzanne Lafollette which appeared Sunday before in New York Times denouncing picture Mission to Moscow from Trotskyist point of view. Yesterday in Times was letter of similar length by Dr. Arthur Upham Pope, eminent authority, defending film from American viewpoint. In view of our long friendship am submitting to you that reproduction of the Pope letter in your papers would be only fair to all concerned. . . . I know you will give this your serious consideration and that the articles on the other side will also be reprinted in your valuable papers. Every good wish to Marion and yourself.

Sincerely,
Jack Warner

Not only did Hearst choose not to publish any expert's defense of the film, he decided to reprint Warner's letter (deleting the Marion Davies reference) along with his own telegram response to Warner. The act of publishing their confidential correspondence was devious to say the least:

Dear Jack:

I certainly do not wish anything to impair our friendship and I hope that criticism of any screen product offered for public patronage and customarily subject to public criticism will not be considered an unwarranted or an unfriendly act....You say our papers "should state the other side of the case in reply to such attacks as Dewey and La Follette." Your film, Mr. Warner, gives "the other side of the case" — the Communist side—quite completely. . . . I think it is quite as much the duty of the American press to defend democracy against Bolshevism as against Fascism or Nazism or any other form of totalitarian tyranny. I am sorry that we disagree on the proper function of the press,—and of the moving picture.

Twenty years after the release of his film, Jack Warner's autobiography recalls his fury over the publication of his correspondence with Hearst. He still seemed particularly stung by Hearst's saccharine use of "Mr. Warner" in the telegram. Regretfully, he writes, the controversy put an end to their friendship.

Warner's postmortem on his confrontation with Hearst was somewhat duplicitous, since he was as responsible as Hearst for creating a storm over the film. His lamenting the loss of Hearst's friendship is suspect as well. On May 22, 1943, just days after Hearst published their letters, Warner wrote an associate at his studio: "You are right, not only did we stir up a hornet's nest with MISSION we have stirred up every Red baiting and Facist [sic] element and everything else. . . . So we will go by MISSION TO MOSCOW and let the chips fly where they may. For every Red-baiter and Facist [sic] who does not see the picture there are ten thousand people who will."

Warner had been dishonest to Hearst about his motives for making *Mission*: the film was indeed propaganda. As he reveals in his autobiography, in early 1943 Warner was summoned to the White House for an unpublicized meeting with the president. "The problem is Stalin," FDR confided to Warner. "I know that if he loses at Stalingrad or on any other major front because he hasn't got the guns and tanks and other things—then he'll make a deal with Hitler again. That would be disastrous. We simply can't lose Russia at this stage, and we have to get the stuff to them. We have to keep Stalin fighting—and your picture can make a case for him with the American people."

Apparently, Roosevelt was satisfied with Warner's picture—and so was the Kremlin. Shortly after *Mission* premiered in the United States, Ambassador Davies flew to Moscow with prints of the film that had been purchased by the U.S. government especially for Stalin's personal viewing and for distribution in the Soviet Union.

Hearst's argument against Sam Goldwyn's *North Star*, released late in 1943, was much the same as it had been against the Warner Bros. picture. Lee Mortimer's review in the *Daily Mirror* on November 6, headlined " 'North Star' Is Red Propaganda," was typical of the Hearst chain's tact. The film was a "fraud" according to Mortimer, who also managed to mention Goldwyn's name four times in his review. To Mortimer, the scenes of schools and hospitals in Russian collectives resembled "the swankiest endowed institution in Mr. Goldwyn's Beverly Hills."

Goldwyn tried to prepare Hearst for the release of *North Star* by sending a copy to Wyntoon a month before the premiere. Not surprisingly, Hearst's telegram reaction to a screening of the film did not mince any words: "You are a very great producer Sam but I think a good American like yourself ought to be producing pro-American propaganda instead of pro-Russian propaganda." Goldwyn responded a day later, defending his film with a disingenuous claim that it had been made "purely as entertainment." While Goldwyn may not have been instructed by President Roosevelt to make his film, as Warner claimed for *Mission to Moscow*, he could not have been unaware that his film was propaganda that supported the administration's program of reconciliation with the Soviet Union. Later he even boasted that his film had become one of Stalin's favorites. Of course, Goldwyn knew it would be foolhardy to mention any of this to Hearst, whose hatred for Russia was being compared to Adolf Hitler's by Secretary of the Interior Harold Ickes during the same week that *North Star* premiered.

In late 1943 meetings were held in Los Angeles leading to the formation of the Motion Picture Alliance for the Preservation of American Ideals. During a meeting at the Beverly Wilshire Hotel on the evening of February 4, 1944, the establishment of the alliance was officially announced to the press. The Hearst chain devoted extensive coverage to the event on the following day. Buried in the body of the many articles published on the subject in the Hearst papers was the group's stated commitment to fight "Fascism and kindred beliefs." This phrase seems more like an afterthought and is vastly overshadowed by the more frequently mentioned and Hearst-popularized term *Americanism* and the oversize headlines about the alliance's war on Reds. Explaining the reasons for the alliance, the Hearst papers first called attention to a recent "Communist-inspired" writers' congress at the Los Angeles campus of the University of California. "Also sparking the [alliance] movement," the *Los Angeles Examiner* said, "were the recent bold attempts to infiltrate Communist propaganda, through the ranks of screen writers, into movie plays and to give the public the impression that the small group of left-wingers, pinks and Reds actually represented the great bulk of the people who make up the film industry." Hearst newspapers reprinted the alliance's "statement of principles," which subsequently appeared as well in a full-page ad in the *Hollywood Reporter*. In part the alliance's statement read: "In our special field of motion pictures, we resent the growing impression that this industry is made up of, and dominated by, Communists, radicals and crack-pots. We believe we represent the vast majority of the people who serve this great medium of expression. But unfortunately it has been an unorganized majority."

In a series of investigative reports on Hollywood written for the *Chicago Daily News* in May 1944, a reporter named Edwin A. Lahey was quoted as saying "it is interesting to note that this 'growing impression' is largely the result of crusades by Mr. Hearst and other newspaper publishers who have terrorized producers for turning out 'propaganda' pictures." Lahey pointed to the example of Sam Goldwyn, whom he said had incurred "the wrath of the Hearst newspaper system" for producing *North Star*.

More recent historians—perhaps reflecting the views of leftists in the 1940s and 1950s—suspect that Hearst was not only an inspiration for the alliance but the group's primary financial backer. It may be more difficult to disprove that such an arrangement existed than to prove it did. According to a later alliance member, Roy Brewer, the financial needs of the organization were not great; members were generally men and women of means, and facilities for meetings were often supplied quite willingly by local posts of the American Legion. The only major expenses were research and advertising. In this sense Hearst did bankroll the alliance: his anti-Communist investigators supplied alliance members with research material, and his newspapers' relentless and uncritical pieces on the alliance were more positive publicity than money could buy.

Some of the most prominent members of the Motion Picture Alliance—including chairman Sam Wood, vice president Walt Disney, Rupert Hughes and James K. McGuinness of the group's executive committee, and actor Adolphe Menjou—had long-standing connections to Hearst. The only actor among the group's founders, Menjou had been a loyal Hearstman since the late 1920s, when the Hearst press defended him when he was facing a movie producer blacklist for attempting to organize his profession. The actor and his wife were frequent guests of Hearst and Davies at San Simeon and were also close to Millicent. In August 1936 Menjou and his wife, Katherine, joined Millicent and a female friend at the closing day ceremonies of the Berlin Olympic Games. The American tourists seemed as interested in getting a good view of Hitler as seeing the athletes, so Hearst reporter William L. Shirer prevailed upon S.S. guards to provide prime seating in the diplomatic section of the reviewing stands.

Later, Shirer recorded in his diary, "Afterwards, they seemed quite thrilled at the experience."

James McGuiness was a former newsman turned filmed producer and screenwriter. He arrived in Hollywood in the late 1920s and was Irving Thalberg's production assistant and script doctor when the producer was overseeing Hearst's Cosmopolitan films at MGM. He was even associated with at least one of Hearst's Warner Bros. productions in the 1930s: in 1936, ten days after shooting began on the Marion Davies film *Hearts Divided*, Hearst halted the production until McGuiness and Davies's nephew, Charles Lederer, could rewrite the script. McGuiness was chummy with a number of Hearst reporters and columnists. He became a friend to Louella Parsons when the two worked together on the *Morning Telegraph* newspaper. And he was also close to writers Westbrook Pegler, Frank Conniff, J. B. Matthews, and other Hearst employees, who were always happy to share their own sources and information on Communism. Pegler's files contain letters and clippings concerning McGuiness, including one item that offered the producer's view on what motivated the Alliance. According to McGuiness, the organization had more value as a publicity machine than as an agent for action. He had personally formed the Alliance to serve as a "better public relations" organization established for motion pictures than the one represented by people like Charlie Chaplin and Orson Welles.

Although his rich and eccentric nephew Howard would later overshadow Rupert Hughes, he was an extremely well known author and screenwriter in his own day. He began his career in the 1890s with a brief stint as a reporter on the *New York Journal* shortly before Hearst bought the newspaper. In the early decades of the twentieth century, Hughes became a successful author of short stories, books, and plays. He was one of the first authors to make a smooth transition into moviemaking. In 1914 Hughes's stage version of the novel *Tess of the Storm Country* was bought by Famous Players–Lasky and produced as a Mary Pickford film; a few years later a short story written under an exclusive contract with *Hearst's Magazine* generated another Pickford vehicle, called *Johanna Enlists*. Several other works by Hughes were turned into films in the 1920s and 1930s, and he also worked as a director. By the early 1940s Hughes had a well-paying career as a lecturer on political subjects. He became a regularly featured radio commentator for the National Broadcasting Company, and his speeches opposing foreign entanglements and issuing warnings about the threat of Communism were often reprinted in full in the Hearst newspapers.

Beginning in the late 1920s the comic strip version of Walt Disney's *Mickey Mouse* was syndicated by King Features. The extensive Hearst distribution helped give the artist and his character a wide audience in both the United States and abroad. Disney was also a visitor to San Simeon from the 1920s through the 1940s, and elements of the recreational atmosphere at the castle—Hearst's History through a Hollywood lens—seem to have found their way into the Disneyland theme parks.

Hearst and film director Sam Wood met in the 1920s, when the director was assigned to the Cosmopolitan production *The Fair Co-Ed* (1927), which starred Marion Davies. Although Hearst was unimpressed with Wood's talents at the time (he preferred the director Sidney Franklin for the assignment), he liked the director personally, and the feeling was mutual. Two years later Wood was picked to direct a proposed film that would star a winner in a screen-test contest run by the *Los Angeles Examiner*. Wood benefited from the ensuing publicity, but there is no record that the MGM film, called *Behind the Screen*, was ever produced. During a European vacation in 1934, Wood and his wife and two daughters were invited to join the Hearst party at a hotel in Amsterdam where a large outdoor dinner party was being thrown for press representatives. One of Wood's daughters, Jean—who, incidentally, was cast as an extra in Hearst's film *Florodora Girl* (1930)—remembered her father and many others being spellbound listening to Hearst giving a welcoming speech to those gathered around his table. Hearst would soon leave Holland and eventually make his way to Germany for his meeting with Hitler. That summer, Wood also had a rendezvous of sorts with the dictator. By chance, the Wood family arrived in Berlin during the funeral of Von Hindenburg. When an open limousine began to pass before him, Wood reached for his hand-held camera, but he was prevented from filming Hitler by storm troopers.

By the mid-1930s Wood's views were following the editorial positions of the Hearst press closely; he broke with President Roosevelt at the same time as Hearst, and their stances on the Communist threat were remarkably similar. Like Hearst, Wood eventually referred even to FDR as a Communist. In early 1944 *Variety* called Wood Hollywood's biggest moneymaking director; he had scored hits with two of Gary Cooper's box office hits, *Pride of the Yankees* (1942) and *For Whom the Bell Tolls* (1943). Despite this accolade and the critical acclaim he received for such films as *A Night at the Opera* (1935) and *Goodbye, Mr. Chips* (1939), Wood's daughter Jean believes her father was an embittered man by the early 1940s. She thinks her father's wounds—he was particular disappointed about never having received an Academy Award for directing—were entirely self-inflicted. She saw her once apolitical, kind, and generous father change into an abrasive and irrational man who was spurred by the Hearst press to intolerant militancy on the issue of Communism. Increasingly the director brought his strong opinions to the studio, his workplace, where he carried a little black book around with him and went out of his way to harangue actors and production personnel. He began to lose friends, and even his longtime secretary left him to join the armed services just to get away from the stress. Jean Wood, who considers herself a liberal, acknowledges that things had gotten so bad that when her father lay dying from a heart attack in 1949, she made an anguished and silent prayer over his body that God might take him away from his misery.

If Wood's behavior had made him a pariah in Hollywood's more progressive circles, he was welcomed by others who felt underappreciated and were determined to protect both their principles and what they perceived were their endangered positions in the industry. As historians Larry Ceplair and Steven Englund point out in their book *The Inquisition in Hollywood*, the members of the Motion Picture Alliance were outsiders in Hollywood with no particular devotion to the art of film or the established film community. "On the contrary," they write, "as almost every political person in the film industry, liberal and conservative alike, perceived, the MPA exemplified a new genus—one which was out for blood and which exhibited an anti-Communist zeal and tenacity greatly overshadowing its members' loyalty to the film industry."

While the Alliance was on the rise, Martin Dies, the man who had been at the forefront of attacks on Communism in Hollywood in the late 1930s and early 1940s, was on the decline. His last hurrah occurred in the spring of 1944, in a pubic battle with an unlikely opponent. As a King Features Syndicated columnist, Walter Winchell was a Hearst man, but he was decidedly independent as well. His views on Roosevelt and other political matters were at odds with Hearst's but usually tolerated because they were delivered in the pictorial, sometimes vitriolic style that embodied yellow journalism. Clearly, as troubled as Hearst was by Winchell's politics—and he was forced to rein him in from time to time—he recognized the circulation value of having an inside agitator over an outside agitator. For years, Winchell had been fairly close to Martin Dies, apparently to the point of supplying the congressman with information on homegrown groups with Nazi sympathies. Their relationship was strained, however, as Winchell came to believe that Dies himself was an anti-Semite, sympathetic to fascism, and only seriously aroused by Communism.

In early March 1944 Dies gave a speech in Congress followed by a press conference suggesting that Winchell was a subversive and part of a Communist-led conspiracy aimed at discrediting Congress. He made this move after some of Winchell's columns criticized Congress for its lukewarm

investigation of right-wing hate groups. In what must have been at least partially motivated by each man's egocentric need for the spotlight, Winchell
and Dies agreed to address each other in consecutive radio broadcasts on
NBC, on which station the columnist had a radio program. Despite a big
buildup, the radio "debates" lacked any real excitement, both men having
decided on a strategy of relatively cool detachment. It was the press consensus that Winchell's steady, high-minded approach to Dies—that he was
being accused of disloyal activities without a shred of evidence—had won
the day. Although Hearst did not stop Winchell's radio debate with Dies,
shortly before it occurred he let it be known through his subordinates that
he was not pleased with the columnist and exactly whose side he was on.
Jack Lait, editor of Hearst's *Daily Mirror*, was quoted as saying, "the Winchell
columns should not be used to attack the figures in American life who agree
with the policy of the *Mirror*." In the month ahead Hearst struggled to tol-
erate Winchell's various affronts to his papers' policies. Increasingly, however,
he took control away from Winchell, cutting undesirable items. After one
particularly violent editing job, one of Hearst's secretaries, H. O. Hunter,
wired a Hearst editor: "Chief thinks it would be better to leave Winchell out
entirely than to chop the column to pieces . . . and that when you feel it necessary to make such drastic deletions you better leave the column out that
day in its entirety." Later that same year, Hearst got reports that Winchell was
not only using his column to attack what he called "jackassolationists" but
also calling up his editor and heaping verbal abuse on him for slashing his
column. Another politically impolite statement in a Winchell column one
week later pushed Hearst to be more blunt. Hunter told his editor: "Chief
instructs—'Kill it everywhere.' " The moment passed, however: Winchell's
contract was renewed, and he was back to making enemies and being one
of Hearst's biggest newspaper stars.

Dies's initial attacks on Winchell, before their radio debate, had closely
followed the anti-Winchell sentiments espoused by fellow congressman
John Rankin of Mississippi, a virulent anti-Semite who in 1938 lobbied for
the appointment of Dies to head the House Un-American Activities Committee, rather than Representative Samuel Dickstein, because Dickstein was
a Jew. When Dies announced in May 1944 that he would not seek reelec-
tion to Congress for health reasons, Rankin moved front and center in the
congressional anti-Communist movement. On the opening day of Congress in January 1945, he introduced an amendment to make the committee
a more autonomous and more permanent investigating body. In arguing for
the amendment, Rankin invoked the name of an American who had
worked so hard to route out Communists. He pointed out that J. B.

Matthews, in his capacity as an investigator for Dies, had produced in late 1944 a seven-volume tome that came to be called "Appendix 9." Reportedly the document contained the names of somewhere between twenty-two and one hundred thousand individuals whom Matthews claimed were associated with Communist organizations. Rankin reminded Congress of the importance of Matthews's work and how their commitment to a standing House Un-American Activities Committee would prevent such valuable information from being forever lost. The Rules Committee defeated Rankin's amendment, but it passed a House roll call. Rankin was not interested in the chairmanship of the new permanent HUAC, so that honor went to a rather malleable Jersey City congressman named Edward J. Hart. Meanwhile Matthews continued to do work for the new HUAC, but he also took copies of Appendix 9 with him to an office at Fifty-eighth Street and Fifth Avenue where he was officially hired as a consultant in Jack Clements's public relations wing of the Hearst Corporation. Matthews's files became Hearst's files in the coming years, shared with fellow yellow journalists and with fellow anti-Communists from J. Edgar Hoover to Senator Joseph McCarthy.

Under Congressman Hart's brief stewardship of the committee (he was replaced by John S. Wood of Georgia in the summer of 1945) but without his authorization, Representative Rankin reopened the Communists-in-Hollywood crusade. Rankin called the film community "the greatest hotbed of subversive activities in the United States." According to Walter Goodman's *The Committee*, Rankin had a specific bias against the film industry. "The source of Rankin's animus against Hollywood—and he made no particular effort to conceal it," writes Goodman, "was the large number of Jews eminent in the film industry." Rankin equated Communism with Jewry. "Communism," Rankin said in one speech, "is older than Christianity. It hounded and persecuted the Savior during his earthly ministry, inspired his crucifixion, derided him in his dying agony, and then gambled for his garments at the foot of the cross."

According to an FBI informant, prominent Los Angeles Communist Party members were quick to respond to the Motion Picture Alliance. Within two days of the Alliance's debut announcement, meetings were being held that would lead to the formation of the Council of Hollywood Guilds and Unions, an organization to respond to the Alliance's charges. Over the following weeks more meetings were held, some in Sardi's restaurant and others at the home of screenwriter Albert Maltz. Screenwriter Dalton Trumbo was also involved in organizing this response group, and together, according to an FBI file, they conspired to make false claims against

Alliance members, using buzz words such as "Fascism, anti-Democracy, anti-Semitism, anti-Catholicism, anti-Negro, anti-labor, anti-British, anti-Soviet, etc." Alliance members were quick to respond, rejecting the accusations as nothing more than a smear campaign to discredit their organization's objectives. In one convoluted statement, James McGuiness said it was impossible for the Alliance to be anti-Semitic since Jews were the most active opponents of Communism in the United States. Neal Gabler's *Empire of their Own*, however, argues forcefully that Jews were indeed a special target of the Alliance's attacks on Communism and that at least two of the group's key figures, Walt Disney and McGuiness, were anti-Semites. Jean Wood believes her father too was an anti-Semite, his friendship with Irving Thalberg and other Jews notwithstanding. According to Ms. Wood, there was significant self-loathing among her father's Jewish friends in Hollywood. "They were Jewish," she said, "but they were anti-Semites sometimes."

More than any other group, the Motion Picture Alliance was responsible for drawing HUAC to Hollywood. Over a two-day period in May 1947, HUAC chairman John Parnell Thomas, Representative John McDowell of Pennsylvania, chief investigator Robert Stripling, and several others held private meetings in Los Angeles's Biltmore Hotel. Except for the government officials, participants of the sessions were almost exclusively Alliance members. By the fall of 1947 HUAC was being readied for hearings in Washington, and forty-three individual subpoenas were issued. Slightly more than half of those subpoenas were issued to so-called friendly witnesses, Alliance members, and movie moguls. The remaining subpoenas went to those considered Communist or those actively engaged in promoting Communism. A battle was set to begin that at least one participant believed had as much to do with prejudice as with politics. Writer Ring Lardner Jr., one of the unfriendly witnesses to be called (and eventually jailed for contempt of Congress), thought it was a salient point that except for the movie moguls the friendly witnesses were nearly all gentiles and that ten of the nineteen on his side were Jewish. Although Lardner was not Jewish himself, he said, "There was considerable feeling that this was a force in which anti-Semitism played a strong part."

Inevitably, the Motion Picture Alliance moved to the forefront of the HUAC hearings that took place in October 1947. And while other segments of the right-wing press covered the hearings with a bias toward the committee, in his papers Hearst went well beyond most because he saw himself as indistinguishable from the committee. In many ways Hearst and the committee were indeed one and the same. Hearst used the Alliance, his widely read columnists and editorialists, and other operatives such as J. B. Matthews to support the committee, and the committee in turn used its channels to Hearst as sources of information and as a machinery of publicity. A symbiotic relationship was created between Hearst and the committee that advanced Hearst's decades-old crusade against Communism. Championing HUAC became another variation on Hearst's earlier film censorship crusades: he would exert influence in the film industry by holding the threat of a government crackdown over the heads of the Jews in Hollywood.

On November 24, 1947, the House of Representatives voted contempt citations against one director, Edward Dmytryk; a producer, Adrian Scott; and eight screenwriters, including John Howard Lawson, Dalton Trumbo, and Ring Lardner Jr. On the same day a meeting was held in New York City, called by Loews' chief Nicholas Schenck and Motion Picture Association of America president Eric Johnston. Along with Schenck, producers Louis B. Mayer, Samuel Goldwyn, Jack Warner, and about sixteen other representatives of the major film studios came together to launch the Hollywood blacklist. After the meeting, an International News photograph was sent out over the wires; it showed Mayer and Schenck in conference and arrived with a suggested caption: "At a meeting of leaders in the motion picture industry at the Waldorf-Astoria Hotel, New York, the nation's film magnates acted today to purge the industry of known communists, and ordered the suspension or discharge of 10 Hollywood figures under citation for contempt of Congress, pending outcome of their trials."

Historian Neal Gabler argues that the decision of the moguls to issue their so-called Waldorf Statement was "stupid and reactionary" but one made in an atmosphere of justifiable fear. "To save themselves from the wrath of the anti-Semites," Gabler writes, "that is what they did." A shadow blacklist that extended beyond the Hollywood Ten also went into effect on November 24. This list included a number of Hollywood figures who had every intention of refusing to answer questions before HUAC were they called and another group of entertainers who had formed the Committee for the First Amendment and flown to Washington to protest the hearings.

HUAC continued to name Communists over the next several years, and by 1954 the blacklist was well over three hundred names long. J. B. Matthews, still working for the Hearst organization, kept an active role in prodding film studios and right-wing groups to clean house in Hollywood. In response to a Matthews article on the continuing problem of Communism in Hollywood, published in 1951 in its own house organ, the American Legion appointed Hearst columnist George Sokolsky to oversee a clearinghouse aimed at ridding Hollywood once and forever of Reds. The

Hearst columnist, who little more than a decade earlier had helped save the *Good Housekeeping* magazine from Communism and paved the way for Martin Dies's assault on Hollywood, was now in another powerful position; whomever Sokolsky deemed unrepentant would be blacklisted and whoever renounced Communism might be "rehabilitated."

There was truth in the assertions of Hearst and HUAC that Communists had long been interested in the film industry. In fact, through various channels, some quite public, like the *Daily Worker*, the Communist Party did not hide its desire to effect changes in society through the use of propaganda films. A prime example of the Communists' determination to use films to further their causes was seen in the response to *Citizen Kane*, which some leftists saw as being too soft on capitalism. But the argument put forth by Hearst and others that the Communist Party came close to dominating the production or messages of films in Hollywood remains unconvincing. Those factions in the Hollywood community that identified themselves as socialists or Communists were never large or persistent enough to dominate the industry and its core interests. Rarely did the public ever see an image or hear a word written by anyone approaching the status of subversive. Hollywood remained relatively unscathed by attacks from the left, and the movie industry continued to be a mirror of its makers. The capital of film was a billboard for capitalism, underwritten by conservative Wall Street backers and propelled by a press that was certainly more reactionary than revolutionary. The danger from Soviet propagandists in the United States was hardly comparable to the repressive tactics of Hearst's agents, members of Congress, the FBI, and grassroots organizations such as the American Legion and the Knights of Columbus. In their relentless pursuit of Communism in Hollywood and their defense of capitalism, Hearst and his loyal subjects in HUAC and Hollywood seem to have overlooked a final irony: the intersection and commonality of yellow journalism, politics, and cinema raised some Hollywood "communists" to celebrity status and afforded them a public forum far greater than the one the film industry had previously offered.

17

No Trespassing

1947–1951

THEIR HOUSE

On an afternoon in 1948 Laura and Sean Brady drove their car around a corner in Beverly Hills, approaching the gated entrance of 1007 North Beverly Drive. The arrival of the young couple had been expected—Sean was escorting Laura on a job interview for a position as a personal secretary— and they were ushered onto the grounds of the estate by two plainclothesmen standing watch. The Bradys were directed down a long driveway that was divided by a reflecting pool and lined by the prerequisite California palm trees that pointed to a house not yet visible. Gradually, beyond the manicured lawns, the mechanical water sprinklers, and the statues and columns of varying degrees of authenticity, "the Beverly house," as Hearst and Davies's home was called, emerged. Their final home together was a sprawling two-story Spanish-styled structure, configured in such a way that from the sky it looked like the letter *H* drawn in terra-cotta tiles. As Laura entered the front door of the house, her husband, waiting outside in his car, caught a brief glimpse of a man or his shadow peering through the curtains of an upstairs window.

Only a few days before coming to meet Davies and Hearst, twenty-year-old Laura Brady had been working at Twentieth Century–Fox, employed as a fill-in secretary to producer Darryl F. Zanuck, director Otto Preminger, and various other studio executives. On what started as a typical workday,

Laura was spotted by a reporter from Hearst's *Los Angeles Examiner* newspaper, who made it his business to prowl studio offices looking for attractive girls to be photographed for the Sunday edition of the newspaper's rotogravure section. The *Examiner* man was surprised by Laura's response when he suggested taking her photograph and mentioned the possibility that the exposure might lead to a movie contract down the line. Although Laura was not immune to the allure of Hollywood—her husband, Sean, was actually a struggling actor—she had no particular interest in movies or photography herself. The Hearst reporter was about to leave when he remembered someone at the paper saying that the Chief's longtime live-in mistress was looking for an assistant to work at the Beverly house.

"Would you be interested in working as Marion Davies's personal secretary?"

"Who's she?" Laura asked.

That night Laura talked over the offer with Sean, who had only a vague knowledge of the retired actress. As for Hearst, he knew he owned a bunch of newspapers and had something to do with the movies.

Laura enjoyed working at the Beverly house. Hearst was kind to his household employees, always referring to them as staff and not servants and pleasantly old-fashioned, often acting like one of the characters in the comic strip *Alphonse and Gaston*, begging for others to go through a doorway ahead of him. Davies was more emotionally effusive and clearly appreciative to be in the company of a young person. The two women spent many long mornings together, gossiping at the kitchen table. Typically Hearst would arrive after noon as they were clearing their dishes. He would grab a jelly doughnut or one of his favorite cream éclairs, pausing to turn his attention toward Davies's eyes and into her coffee cup. "Let me see what's in your cup" was Hearst's constant refrain. Davies and Laura knew Hearst's routine well, and the sounds of his slowly approaching footsteps always gave them time to stash Davies's alcohol and replace her drink with a cup of coffee.

A longtime insomniac, Hearst usually began his workday in the early afternoon. One of his editors, William Curley, having had his own share of sleepless nights, wondered after all these years why his boss didn't try Nembutal. "But they are habit forming," Hearst answered, recalling his unswerving newspaper editorials against narcotics. When Curley reminded Hearst that such a habit at his age was quite excusable, Hearst laughed at himself and called his doctor for a prescription. Davies was convinced that jealousy and paranoia had added to Hearst's restlessness, and she told Laura Brady that Hearst stayed awake at night thinking she might sneak away for a romantic rendezvous. Laura and Sean Brady believed that Davies was unhappy with her life but that her only vice was her drinking. "She was a woman who had it all," Sean would later say, "but she was a prisoner."

Hearst and Davies had been living at the Beverly house for about a year when Laura Brady first came to work for them. Hearst had every intention of spending his last years at San Simeon, but in the spring of 1947 he suffered a mild heart attack. A decision was quickly made to move to Beverly Hills so that Hearst could be nearer to the heart specialists he now required. The couple had purchased the Beverly house as a replacement for their Santa Monica beach house, which had been sold as an economizing measure. By early December 1945 the contents of the beach house had been shipped to New York, and the Park Bernet Galleries divided them into 429 lots of Early American furniture, Old English china, Georgian silver, and other assorted baubles "as big as the Ritz."

In early May 1947 some of the San Simeon staff gathered outside, as they usually did when Hearst and Davies left on an extended excursion. As the group waved their good-byes, everyone was dry-eyed, sure that their employers would soon return. Hearst was not the type to discuss his health with his staff, and he always projected optimism. Alone with Davies, driving down the hill, Hearst cried like a baby. It was one sign of Hearst's awareness of his old age; another was that he would even consider living full-time in Los Angeles. The city was not his favorite place. On one occasion, before the couple left San Simeon permanently, Davies wrote a friend, "We did not stay long in LA as W.R. really detests the place and is miserable every minute he is there." Although he enjoyed the closer proximity to the studios and the stars, and his luxurious home was even situated on a small hill, in Beverly Hills he was just one among a crowd of wealthy movie types.

The Beverly house was one of the few houses where Hearst lived that was neither built from scratch nor entirely made over. Still, he did make changes—such as the installation of ornately carved wooden portals—and he moved in antiques, which were arranged alongside contemporary department store furnishings. Hanging on the walls of a hallway that led to an office and an intimate movie projection room were gold-framed floor-to-ceiling paintings of Davies costumed in her virginal screen roles from the 1920s, the same paintings that Hearst had commissioned to hang in Hearst's Cosmopolitan Theater in Columbus Circle. Now, some twenty-five years later, Hearst would make his way to his own private theater shuffling past romanticized paintings of romanticized movies like *Little Old New York* and *Yolanda*.

Except for a few secret passageways and doorframes fashioned from Gothic architectural fragments, the eighteen-room house at 1011 Beverly

Drive did not resemble the haunted spaces in *Citizen Kane*'s Xanadu anymore than San Simeon had. Surrounded by lush grounds, set far back from the street, and situated next door to the Sam Goldwyns, the Beverly house was a Hollywood retirement home, the perfect resting place for a former star and her mostly forgotten movie mogul. When Hearst took solitary walks on the grounds of his Beverly Hills estate, security men on loan from the *Los Angeles Examiner* were always nearby, strategically stationed, hidden by the manicured shrubbery. The couple had some reason to be on the alert. Hearst had been a polarizing force throughout his life. His yellow papers and his propaganda films had brought on controversies not to mention innumerable process servers and extortionists. In his early days it was said he hired a double and carried a gun for protection. During the Depression even Davies was threatened, receiving a small bomb in the mail, gift-wrapped for Christmas. Many years before the widely covered drama of Hearst's yet-to-be-born granddaughter named Patty, the FBI, on a tip from someone in Hearst's advertising department, quietly investigated a plot to kidnap his own young sons.

Although Hearst's physical health steadily declined during his last years, he was not bedridden or mentally disengaged until the very end. He never returned to San Simeon or Wyntoon, but he took long drives along the coast from time to time. Small groups of friends were invited over for dinner, and he and Davies occasionally dined out in town at Romanoff's restaurant. Visitors noticed little change in Hearst's mental abilities in his last years, and his interests in publishing, film, and politics stayed strong. There are no accounts of Hearst personally visiting film studios during this period, but he did continue to inject himself into the Hollywood scene. In May 1949 Hearst and countless fans were captured by the sexy Cinderella story of actress Rita Hayworth, who announced plans to marry international playboy-prince Ali Khan. When Hearst learned the news, he tracked down Louella Parsons, who was in Paris, and sent her a telegram with instructions for a fourteen-part series of articles on Hayworth to appear in the Hearst chain. Working round the clock with her substitute columnist Dorothy Manners, Parsons put together two articles within a day, which were quickly shipped to the *New York Journal-American* office. Two days later Parsons had five more articles ready for delivery when she received another cable from Hearst canceling the series. Parsons, who knew her boss's changeable nature, was still perplexed: the first two parts of her "Cinderella Princess—The Life of Rita Hayworth" were already running on page one of the Hearst papers and apparently a big success. Hearst told Parsons that he had soured on the romance between Hayworth and Khan because the prince had disrespected the news media. Apparently as the newlyweds were leaving their French villa at the start of their honeymoon, they were spotted by three wire service photographers, and the paparazzi-weary Khan took a cane and his fists to all three, yelling "You annoy me! Get out! You're a bunch of bores!" It was also reported that after the scuffle Khan's car deliberately swerved toward the group of photographers but without causing any injuries. One of the three targeted photographers was a woman, but, more important, all three were employed by Hearst's International News Service. Hearst's response was to discard the Parsons series and direct his society columnist, Cholly Knicker-bocker (a.k.a. Igor Cassini, brother of the fashion designer, Oleg), to play up Khan's violent behavior. As the heavily promoted series on Hayworth suddenly vanished without explanation from the front pages of the Hearst papers, an editorial appeared inside entitled "A Spoiled Prince." The editorial stand against Khan's actions looked like a nasty excuse for airing bigotry: "The egotism and vanity of the dark colors which were demonstrated are the petulance of a spoiled Oriental prince. . . . Cholly Knickerbocker related what usually happens to American girls who marry Orientals. Although we hope that nothing unpleasant will happen to Rita, the indications are that it might."

In his last years Hearst seemed to have a particular fondness for Twenti-eth Century–Fox, although his own production company was only briefly associated with the studio. Richard Stanley, Hearst's last personal secretary, had been employed by Fox before coming to the Beverly house. Harry Brand, head of Fox's all-important publicity department, like Howard Strickling, his counterpart at MGM, was a friend of Hearst and Davies. Fox provided Louella Parsons with an office at the studio, although she mostly worked out of her home on Maple Drive. In 1944 Fox announced that it had optioned her autobiography, *The Gay Illiterate*, although a film was never produced. Parsons's husband, Dr. Harry Martin, affectionately known as "Dockie," was a urologist and a venereal disease specialist with an office at the Fox studio as well. Some referred to him as the abortionist to the stars, but at Fox he was officially known as a technical adviser on films with medical themes.

By the late 1940s Hearst's early connections to film production were fading fast. In New York, the Godfrey Building at 729 Seventh Avenue, early home of his International Film Service, was still standing. United Artists was headquartered there by 1947, and UA film executives were able to enjoy Hearst's rooftop apartment, once used to hatch plans for Cosmopolitan Productions and to rendezvous with Davies. The building was still intact when Times Square underwent a renewal at the turn of the twenty-first century;

its rooftop garden was long gone, but a paneled office once used by Mary Pickford remained as petite and private as the star herself. Hearst's second film headquarters, at Second Avenue and 127th Street, did not fair as well as the Godfrey Building. When Hearst moved his production operations to the West Coast in 1925, he rented the space out to various film companies, including the producer named Robert Kane. By the late 1930s the building was no longer in use as a film studio. It made one last stand as a fantasy factory in 1939, however, when the General Motors Corporation leased the space from Hearst and cleared out the dusty medieval wardrobes and tin suits of armor used for Hearst's costume adventures. The giant stages became work spaces to build an elaborate miniature "World of Tomorrow" pavilion for the New York World's Fair. Finally the building was torn down to make way for the Triborough Bridge. Hearst's Tammany connections pulled the proper strings to make his property the bridge's point of entry in Manhattan and enabled the absentee landlord to make a small bundle of money in the process. It was a fitting ending to the Cosmopolitan studios, since the property where his film studio stood had previously been a summer playground for Tammany leaders and their constituents.

Holding Their Own

Until 1947 Hearst remained nearly as active as he had been for a decade. But that fall he suffered a severe heart attack. Within a few months a palsy in his hands became more visible, and he was noticeably thinner (by some accounts over the next few years he lost nearly half his typical body weight of 250 pounds). A young doctor named Frank Nolan came by from time to time to check on the octogenarian's irregular heart rhythms. After Hearst's second heart attack, his more frequent visiting physician was Myron Prinzmetal, who came to Hearst's attention at the suggestion of Louella Parsons's husband. In the spring of 1949 Hearst learned that Dr. Prinzmetal had assisted in the making of a pioneering film that showed for the first time in color and in slow motion completely exposed hearts. With his old producer instincts still intact, Hearst immediately sent orders to his chain of newspapers to give Prinzmetal's films the highest visibility. Still photographs appeared in all the Hearst papers, and the *Los Angeles Examiner* published an eight-column box on the heart film. Strangely, Prinzmetal refused to be interviewed for the article. He claimed that lay publicity was unethical, but perhaps he had other reasons for lying low. It seemed that everyone but Hearst was aware that it was a medical impossibility for the beating heart in the film to belong to a human being; in fact, it was a dog's heart. Hearst meanwhile was the country's most famous antivivisectionist. On the rolling acres of San Simeon, signs warned drivers that animals had the right of way. Dr. Prinzmetal had witnessed the affection Hearst had for animals on more than one occasion; as he listened to his patient's irregular heartbeat, several dachshunds always scurried underfoot. Spurred by the work of his friend the dancer and actress Irene Castle, who had set up an "orphanage" for stray animals, Hearst, through his editorials, became an outspoken crusader against cruelty to animals in films. Unbeknownst to Hearst he was now financing a doctor—at a cost of approximately $60,000 a year—who was doing medical experiments on dogs when he wasn't working on keeping his human patient alive.

In 1950 a group of Hearst's Hollywood cronies, among them producer James McGuiness and actor Adolphe Menjou, as well as company employee loyalists and anti-Communists such as Adela Rogers St. Johns, J. B. Matthews, and John Clements, went to work for Richard Nixon in his campaign to defeat Helen Mary Gahagan Douglas. Historians have seen this California Senate race as a defining event for Nixon, one that set him on his trajectory toward the White House and established his reputation for dirty tricks. Whether Hearst had any specific role in the Nixon campaign awaits further research, but his decades-long campaign against Communism was certainly a driving spirit behind the Hollywood Nixon supporters.

The rise of the nation's last great anti-Communist leader and its first official Hollywood president is certainly traceable to Hearst. Louella Parsons was famous for her misspellings and factual errors, but in the fall of 1949 Hearst's gossip queen was called on to correct a mistake made by someone else. A Hollywood trade paper reported that a certain woman, named Nancy Davis, was a Communist sympathizer. With her doe eyes set far apart but nevertheless focused on becoming a movie star and with several films already on her résumé, a different brunette actress of the same common name was horrified. She immediately turned for help to Mervyn LeRoy, her producer at MGM and a friend of Hearst's. LeRoy called up Louella Parsons. Within days the columnist had inserted a single line that stated categorically that the promising wide-eyed Metro contract player was not now and never had been a Communist. Although this mention in Parson's widely syndicated column was generally considered a press agent's dream, Nancy Davis was not appeased. She made it her business to get in touch with the president of the Screen Actors' Guild, who was one of Warner Bros.'s most popular actors, Ronald Reagan.

In those days Reagan happened to be a protégé of Parsons; she had taken him under her wing when she learned that the photogenic Reagan was from her hometown of Dixon, Illinois. The columnist okayed Reagan's getting a role in *Hollywood Hotel* (1937), a film version of her popular radio program, and although the former radio announcer had a minor role in the film, Parsons welcomed him into her inner circle. It was also no small advantage to Reagan that during his first years in Hollywood he was contracted to Warner Bros., where Hearst was making pictures between 1934 and 1939. Reagan made two Cosmopolitan films at Warner: *Cowboy from Brooklyn* (1938) and the aptly titled *Going Places* (1939). Throughout this period Reagan received nothing but positive publicity from the Hearst press.

Parsons took it upon herself to be something of a guardian angel over Reagan's love life as well as his career. In the forties she propelled his so-called all-American romance with actress Jane Wyman into a borderline national obsession. When Reagan proposed, Parsons broke the story of the engagement on her radio show and in her column. After a wedding ceremony in a romantic patch of Forest Lawn Cemetery, she hosted a reception for the newlyweds at her Maple Drive home in Beverly Hills. Parsons became a frequent guest at the young married couple's home, and their daughter Maureen called her Aunt Lolly. The Reagans' breakup a few years later was a surprise to moviegoers, but for Parsons, who had played the roles of their matchmaker, overprotective chaperon, matron of honor, and press agent, the news was devastating. She spoke out in her column once again, this time pleading—without success—for the couple to work things out. "Jane and Ronnie," Parsons wrote, "have always stood for so much that is right in Hollywood. . . . That's why this hurts so much. That's why we are fighting so hard to make them realize that what seems to have come between them is not important enough to make their break final."

Single again, Reagan began devoting more time to the Screen Actors' Guild and what he saw as its mission to fight Communism. (Although Jane Wyman would later blame Reagan's obsession with politics and union affairs for their divorce, she was no passive witness to the cause. For a time she was, like her husband, an FBI informant.) While Reagan had already been involved in the work of clearing actors of false accusations, according to her own account, at least initially he considered trivial Nancy Davis's concerns about being tainted as a Red. Reagan sent word to Davis that if she wasn't satisfied with Louella Parsons's work on her behalf she should either change her name or contact the guild in the future if she found the situation was really damaging her career. The ambitious Davis demanded a face-to-face meeting with Reagan. As she would later recall, one sight of Reagan made her forget about any possible career obstacles. After dinner and a night on the town, Ronnie and Nancy discovered that they had a lot in common. Not only were they both interested in history (Civil War buffs), but they found they had a mutual concern for current events. Within two years the name problem was totally solved when Nancy Davis became Mrs. Ronald Reagan.

Ingrid Bergman's real-life saga in 1949 reads like an archetypal movie love story. A beautiful, almost saintly actress married to a cold, dominating neurosurgeon meets an Italian film artist and finds real passion for the first time in her life. Infidelity and divorce among movie people was as old as the movie business itself, but in the spring of 1949 such behind-the-scenes stories were still mostly reserved for the movies, not the newspapers. It was Hearst who changed this, turning the story of Bergman, her husband, Dr. Lindstrom, and her lover, director Roberto Rossellini, into Hollywood's first modern scandal. On April 13, 1949, the Hearst society columnist Igor Cassini revealed news that he said had been delivered to him from an "undiplomatic pouch." According to Cassini, writing under his nom de plume, Cholly Knickerbocker, "Rumors of a romance between Ingrid Bergman, Sweden's greatest gift to Hollywood since Greta Garbo, and Roberto Rossellini, Italy's foremost director, have been rampant ever since Ingrid flew to Rome to star in a new Rossellini picture. But the rumors were only repeated in discreet whispers, since both Miss Bergman and Signor Rossellini are married. Finally, however, the bombshell had to explode." Cassini went on to report that the two lovers would "shed" their spouses and "marry immediately."

In 1949 there were few actresses in Hollywood of Bergman's stature with a more pristine image. At the time of Cassini's revelation, Bergman's film *Joan of Arc* was in movie theaters across the country. Many moviegoers saw this role as something of an extension of her similarly spiritual role as a nun in the previously released *The Bells of St. Mary's* (1945). Throughout 1949 readers—especially Hearst readers—were able to follow the real-life adventures of Ingrid Bergman as they happened and as they contrasted with her screen life. On May 2 Dr. Lindstrom held a six-hour meeting with his wife in Italy. Two days later he issued a statement that Bergman would soon be returning to Hollywood. But by August the actress was in Rome giving her lawyer in California, Gregson Bautzer, instructions to start divorce proceedings. With the world press closing in on the lovers' hideaway, it was decided that her publicist would reveal Bergman's divorce announcement on August 4 during a press conference in Rome. Although rumors had already reached

Hollywood by then, no newspaper had printed Bergman's decision. Once again the prize would fall in the lap of the Hearst press. Apparently Bergman's publicist in Italy, Joseph Henry Steele, had succumbed to the pleading of Perry Lieber, publicity director for Howard Hughes, whose RKO studio was producing Bergman's yet-to-be-released Rossellini-directed film *Stromboli*, named after the Mediterranean island where their romance began. According to publicist Lieber's message to publicist Steele, Hughes was anxious for the Hearst press to get the scoop on the divorce decision.

Steele had a release about Bergman's divorce announcement prepared and ready to be distributed to the press who were gathering in his hotel room. As the reporters read the brief copy of the release and began to ask questions of Steele, one reporter, Mike Chinigo, Hearst's Rome correspondent for the International News Service, was already on the telephone. Steele had given the release to Chinigo a half-hour before the press conference, with Chinigo giving his word that he would not call in the story until the conference began. It was enough lead time for Parsons, anxiously waiting by her phone, to scoop every other paper by at least two hours. Over the next few months, Bergman's announcement, Lindstrom's subsequent refusals, and the estranged couple's torturous battle over their young daughter, Pia, were stiff competition to the news of the atomic test in Russia. But on December 12 the Hearst papers wiped every other story off page one with the headline: "Louella Parsons Hears: Ingrid Expects Stork in 3 Mos."

How Parsons got this scoop has never been fully documented. Parsons would later say that her source was "a man of great importance, not only in Hollywood, but throughout the United States . . . who had connections in many other parts of the world—including Italy." In publicist Steele's biography of Bergman, published in 1959, he revealed that he had told Howard Hughes about the actress's pregnancy only twenty-four hours before Parson's story appeared. He was convinced that Hughes, believing that any publicity was good publicity, called Parsons with the scoop. Two Hearst journalists told Louella Parsons biographer George Eells they were certain that the "man of great importance" was actually Hearst. According to their version, Chinigo, the Chief's INS man, sent his boss the report on Bergman, and Hearst gave the gossip to Parsons.

There are other possibilities. Hearst and Hughes had been friends for years, even before their collaboration to avert censorship problems for the film *Scarface*. It may have been at Hughes's suggestion that Hearst took a day trip by plane to the burgeoning resort area of Las Vegas in 1946. In the summer of 1947, when Trans World Airlines faced accusations of influence peddling through expensive gifts and sexual favors from Hollywood actresses, Hearst published counterattacks that claimed Hughes was being crucified for breaking the Pan American Airlines monopoly. With Hearst's publicity backing him, Hughes turned the table on the investigators and accused Maine senator Ralph O. Brewster of being on the take himself. In December 1949 the millionaire film producer and hero aviator was living in a secluded bungalow set among pink hibiscus and huge Mexican fan palms on the grounds of the Beverly Hills Hotel. The small house was next door to Hearst and Davies's estate. He was one of the few visitors who was welcomed when he dropped by on the spur of the moment.

Parsons's cryptic words about the source of her scoop appear to be a description of both Hearst and Hughes, and perhaps the scoop did come from both men. Surprisingly, there was virtually no criticism of Bergman by the Hearst press throughout the ordeal of her infidelity and the birth of her child in February 1950. While Senator Edwin Johnson of Colorado took to the Senate floor denouncing Bergman as "evil" and proposing the licensing of movie actors by the Department of Commerce (for the sole purpose of revoking the license of someone guilty of moral turpitude), the Hearst papers recognized Bergman's courage. Walter Winchell, Hearst's New York–based columnist, would later write that the actress was "the victim of a lynch mob." And while he received bags of negative Bergman mail, Winchell maintained: "This reporter was among the lonely few who urged compassion." Winchell was not alone in the Hearst press. Igor Cassini, who broke the story, often took Bergman's side and was particularly cutting about her doctor husband's refusal to compromise. Parsons was rarely judgmental. She preferred to see the romantic qualities of the story and compared Bergman and Rossellini to Lady Hamilton and Lord Nelson and King Edward VIII and Wallis Simpson. Later, the strain of constant attention caused Bergman to view all the media as the enemy, but at the time she in fact allowed the Hearst press preferential treatment. She even gave Hearst the exclusive rights to the first pictures of her love child, little Robertino Rossellini. And Bergman was particularly moved by the very first wire and basket of flowers she received following her much-anticipated delivery. A note simply said: "I love and admire you." It was signed by Marion Davies.

POSTPRODUCTION AND PRERELEASE

Nearly every night at eight o'clock two men, who had been picked out of a stable of projectionists at the always-eager-to-please Twentieth Century–Fox studio, arrived at the Beverly house servants' entrance. Although only one man was necessary to run the theater's movie projector, two were always sent, thus ensuring an uninterrupted evening's entertainment. Richard Fenton, one of the regular operators, had royal Hollywood lineage. His father, Albert, had been the projectionist at the first Academy Awards ceremony in 1928. And during the thirties the senior Fenton was Hearst and Davies's chief projectionist at their Santa Monica beach house. Young Dick Fenton was often teamed with a veteran newsreel cameraman named Gus Boswell, who had first met Hearst in the twenties when he ran films for the producer's movie friends on the luxury yacht *Oneida*.

After setting up the film reels in the cramped projection room, the two young men were ushered into another room, where they were provided with pinochle cards and club sandwiches. Around midnight Davies and Hearst would enter the theater and find their favorite sofa. The room was not unusually appointed, but a huge marble table near the center of the room was eye-catching: it had swastikas prominently carved in each of its four legs. Fenton wondered if the symbols stamped it as a mystic Indian relic or a Nazi souvenir. Perhaps it had been picked up as bounty by Hearst Corporation president Richard Berlin, who was one of the first U.S. journalists to enter defeated Germany in April 1945. Berlin's daughter Brigid remembered her father's keeping a piece of Hitler's wooden bed and Eva Braun's hairbrush, which had been snatched from their mountain retreat at Berchtesgaden, under glass on a wall of their country house. Hearst and Berlin would certainly not have been the only ones to find Nazi memorabilia memorable enough to put on view. Even movie mogul Jack Warner kept some captured Hitler stationery displayed on a desk near his Oscars.

More often than not Hearst and Davies watched their movies alone or with a housekeeper, a valet, or a gardener. Sometimes the couple was joined by Arthur and Patricia Lake and Davies's nephew, screenwriter Charlie Lederer. Arthur Lake became famous playing Dagwood Bumstead, the unlikely hero of some three dozen *Blondie* movies based on the King Features comic strip. When the young actor married Patricia Van Cleve in one of several wedding ceremonies that took place at San Simeon, he became a member of Davies and Hearst's extended family. Davies always introduced Pat Lake as her favorite niece. It was widely believed but never documented that the tall, long-faced blonde was actually her daughter with Hearst. When Pat Lake died an old woman in the late 1990s, her survivors told reporters that the rumors about her being a child of Hearst and Davies were true; simultaneously, in true Hollywood fashion, they feverishly tried to sell her life to the movies.

Although Hearst's doctors allowed him to take short automobile drives—even up to the last week of his life—any extended trips to San Simeon or Wyntoon were out of the question. At one point Hearst was almost desperate to visit his former homes again. Reawakening his skills as a film producer, he contacted Eddie Hubbell, the head of MGM's still photography department, and Norman Alley, his famed WWII newsreel cameraman, with instructions to take photographs and color motion pictures of both San Simeon and Wyntoon. Later the two men spliced the photographs and the film footage together for Hearst's nostalgic viewing pleasure.

Hubbell had been assigned to Hearst's most northern estate, and he remembered thinking that Wyntoon without Hearst looked like a ghost town or, more precisely, a film studio re-creation of a ghost town. He was particularly amazed to see a number of artificial-looking structures in the quasi-Bavarian village, similar to those buildings on a movie set that look real only from one side. Hubbell was not entirely unfamiliar with false fronts fabricated by Hearst. The MGM executive was the son of Joe Hubbell, the West Coast head of Hearst's newsreel operation who had been involved in a number of well-publicized news assignments and a few picture-taking jobs that were of a more personal nature. At Hearst's direction Joe Hubbell was sent to San Diego to take motion pictures of the temporary building structures of the Mediterranean-style Panama California Exposition before they were taken down in 1917. Later some elements of these structures—especially the twin towers of the Varied Industries Building—were incorporated into the main building of Hearst's castle at San Simeon. In the 1920s a picture of Hubbell's son, Edwin, had received wide distribution when the boy was announced as the "surprise" winner in a *New York American* contest to discover a child movie star.

Occasionally some of Davies's pals from her acting days, such as Clark Gable or Tyrone Power, would drop by without entourage through the back entrance, but it was a far cry from the weeklong parties and picnics at San Simeon. Writer George Sokolsky came by in 1950. In January the columnist had become an official member of the Hearst team, signing a contract to write for King Features Syndicate. Unofficially Sokolsky had been connected to Hearst since at least as early as the *Good Housekeeping* magazine–Federal Trade Commission–Martin Dies connections of the late 1930s. The writer implied as much in a letter he sent to Westbrook Pegler on January 10, 1950. "Thanks for your welcome." Sokolsky wrote. "I had my nose in the tent but my foot never got inside. Now that I am all in, it will be more fun than ever. I like the gang and I like the atmosphere and I like you." Shortly after Sokolsky signed with King, he paid Hearst a visit in Beverly Hills. The two men had never before met in person, at least as adults. When Hearst showed an interest in the story of Sokolsky's transformation from Socialist to ardent anti-Communist, the columnist reminded Hearst of his own earlier political leanings and how as a boy Sokolsky had campaigned on the Lower East Side for Hearst the radical candidate for mayor. "Sokolsky," Hearst told the columnist, "the reason you and I really understand the evils of Communism is that we were once familiar with the nature of Socialism."

The Hearst sons, George, Bill, Jack, David, and Randy, were middle-aged playboys and highly paid figureheads in the Hearst organization in the 1940s and infrequent visitors to the Beverly Hills house. Bill Hearst was probably there the most, asking for advice and sending notes and presents until the very end of his father's life. Years later he was convinced that Davies had gotten to most of the gifts first, hiding them in a closet. All the Hearst sons, except George, who treated her like an older sister, blamed Davies for their strained relationship with their father. During one of Bill's last visits, knowing of his father's enthusiasm for photography, he made certain that one of his presents got through. Weak, hoarse, and confined to his upstairs bedroom, Hearst was revived by the gift of a relatively new invention, the Polaroid camera. Hearst, who had seen the photographic advances of two centuries and had his own darkroom as early as the 1880s, suddenly had that old twinkle of imagination in his eyes. "He was," Hearst Jr. said "like a kid again."

Quite naturally Millicent, still entitled Mrs. William Randolph Hearst, was never a guest of Hearst and Davies. She held court on the Upper East Side of Manhattan or at the Sandy Point, Long Island, mansion Hearst had bought for her in the late 1920s. In the late 1940s she was still running the Milk Fund and throwing society balls from her swanky Park Avenue apartment or her moated castle on Manhasset Bay. Sometimes she was escorted to functions by Herbert Hoover, a man her estranged husband once called "selfish and stupid," or Dick Berlin, the Hearst magazines chief whom she had personally groomed for power since the 1920s. On special occasions she wore one of her favorite jewelry pieces, a diamond tiara.

On April 5, 1950, the Brand Names Foundation, a merchandiser organization, sponsored a luncheon at New York's Waldorf-Astoria, in cooperation with the Hearst Advertising Service. Louis B. Mayer spoke before an audience of one thousand business and civic leaders, praising the film industry for playing a role promoting American products on the screen. He reminded those gathered that U.S. industries should be fortified with "new cement and steel," because one industry helps another. To Mayer there were only two obstacles in the way of progress in America: complacency and Communism. In concluding his remarks Mayer thanked his political mentor for showing him the way. "And I am mindful of the indifference," the mogul said, "that greeted the first warnings against Communism sounded by my dear friend, a truly great American, William Randolph Hearst. He had the foresight, the courage, the patriotism. Most people thought him an alarmist, didn't pay much attention to what he had to say about this menace to our freedom. There are many today who wish they had given more heed."

Because of his declining health, Hearst was unable to be by Mayer's side to hear his warm if somewhat melancholy remarks. A week later Hearst missed another party at the Waldorf-Astoria, this one thrown by the Jewish Veterans of the United States especially in Mayer's honor. Mayer again used the occasion to attack Communism, and he returned to the issue of indifference among the public. He told his audience that years ago he had complained to Hearst about how little people seemed to care about the best interests of the country. "Son," Hearst told Mayer, "let me tell you what I have discovered through the years. I admit there are periods in which our people coast along, cease to think, enjoy happy times. Then something very important happens and they begin to think. And when they begin to think, Louis, don't worry—they always think it through."

After he returned to California, Mayer visited with his "dear friend," sometimes even dropping by with a bowl of matzo ball soup. In the last months of their friendship, Mayer may have seen his own future in the face of the man who called him son. The studio system was cracking, and the old vanguard was being discarded. After decades of near misses, cover-ups, and arm-twisting on the part of both Mayer and Hearst, movie monopolies were really breaking up. Television, which Hearst had flirted with in its infancy, was further eroding the profits from movie ticket sales. The sacred family audience for which Mayer and Hearst had made their entertainments was spending its leisure time at home. Movie executives eventually employed such shabby gimmicks as "Smell-O-Vision" and dinnerware giveaways to lure customers back to the theaters. In the summer of 1951, after a showdown with producer Dore Schary, MGM's latest Irving Thalberg, Mayer announced to the press that he had decided to leave his post as the most powerful studio head in film history. In reality Nick Schenck and the New York office had forced him out. His grand throne room would be cleaned out by the end of August. Mayer's departure was assured, according to his biographer Bosley Crowther, "because his ideas of screen entertainment and his ways of operating were obsolete." But the old mogul was a brawler; before fading from the scene he would make one brief comeback, in 1952, as a spokesman for Cinerama.

Histories

Around 1950 Laura Brady made plans to give up her job with Hearst and Davies. She and Sean were expecting a child. Davies threw a baby shower for her assistant and was thrilled to learn later that the Brady girl was named Marion. Often short of breath, Hearst now spent most of his days in an upstairs bedroom. On the wall he faced from his bed was a somber painting of an Antwerp cathedral. As a boy of ten, in that Belgium city Hearst had found some refuge from his mother's exhaustive tours of museums and churches by sneaking down a side street into a photographer's studio. He convinced Mother Phoebe to have a portrait taken of her son. She mailed it home to Papa George in California, who was making money in part to help support his wife's extravagances. On another wall of the bedroom was a dark painting of the interior of a Spanish church. On his night table was an airbrushed 1930s' publicity photograph of Davies. The only visible incongruity in his room was a child's small windup toy perched on a stand: a four-piece band of monkeys in tuxedos ready to clank out a popular song.

In January 1950 the press reported that Davies's nephew, Charles Lederer, had been commissioned to write a six-part series for *Cosmopolitan* magazine. The articles would tell the story of the film industry by profiling some of its top leaders, starting with Darryl F. Zanuck of Twentieth Century–Fox and Dore Schary of MGM. The Hearst magazine was an appropriate venue for a human-interest story on film since it was filled with ads for movies featuring movie stars hawking products and regularly featured a column written by Louella Parsons. It was expected that Lederer's close connections to Hearst and Davies would be a valuable source of inside information, but for some reason the series never materialized. Another version of Hollywood's history did.

Adela Rogers St. Johns was one of Hearst's most versatile reporters, and since 1913 she had covered everything in his papers from crime to sports to society. Her writing was often gushy but rarely boring. Her enthusiasm for motion pictures and their stars was genuine, and it endeared her to Hearst. In her writings, Hollywood is a land where dreams and *Star Is Born* myths far outshine reality.

St. Johns had once tried to tell a more honest tale about the movie business. In the 1930s she wrote a short story (with the real names changed) that was based on the meteoric rise of her friend, flapper actress Colleen Moore, and the contrasting decline of Moore's husband, an alcoholic producer named John McCormick. Like St. Johns's character, Moore had come to Hollywood with no experience and great dreams of fame. St. Johns called her movie story "The Truth About Hollywood," and producer David O. Selznick hired Gene Fowler—another Hearst writer—and several other screenwriters to translate St. Johns's scenario into *What Price Hollywood?* (1932). The picture became the inspiration for three successive *A Star Is Born* films.

Despite St. Johns's original intention to use darker touches to tell her story, it was the stronger myth of instant success, the rags-to-riches story of Hollywood, that really resonated with movie audiences. Glimpses of harsh reality were no competition for the dreams created by studio factories, and their work was enhanced by St. Johns and others in the Hearst press, who rarely found a film contest they could not run and rerun. "Is your little boy or girl pretty enough to be a child star?" and "Do you know what Pauline's next peril will be?" were two of the more popular Hearst come-ons. In the late 1940s the *New York Journal-American* launched a promotional campaign that gave its readers a chance to vote on the city's "Dearest Secretary." The first prize winner would receive an all-expense-paid trip to Hollywood and the possibility of being screen tested. Day after day photographs of the finalists appeared, as frequently as the stories about the hunts for Communists in the government and Hollywood. Finally, the judges—model agency representatives and film publicists from the West Coast—announced their decisions at the Stork Club. Before long a pretty but ultimately forgotten bank secretary flew off for sunny California via TWA. With the real chances for success in Hollywood a long shot at best, the contestants might have been better off with one of the consolation prizes: a brushup course in the Royal Business School of New York.

Soon after the Charlie Lederer series on Hollywood was abandoned, Hearst called St. Johns and suggested his idea for another Hollywood series. In typical fashion Hearst told St. Johns that only she could write the series. It would not be long, Hearst said, before people who had never been there would be writing the histories of Hollywood. St. Johns had been a witness to it all, and "the coming of the motion picture was as important as that of the printing press." St. Johns did not need much convincing; she quickly got ready to work on the series. Together, she and Hearst made plans for a series of twenty-five installments to appear in Hearst's Sunday supplement, *The*

American Weekly, a string of human-interest stories that together would make "one grand picture" of Hollywood.

Most of the articles reached back to the early days of the movie business, but there were installments with more up-to-date themes. On April 29, 1951—Hearst's eighty-eighth birthday—the second of a two-part piece entitled "The Rebellion of Ingrid Bergman" appeared. It had been over a year since Bergman had given birth to her out-of-wedlock child, but she was still big news. Once again, in the name of the Hearst press, St. Johns was asking the public for understanding of what she called "a grave dilemma regarding Ingrid Bergman." In a plea that could have been made by Hearst himself, St. Johns asked the American public to withhold their judgment of the actress. "It is wrong for a wife to fall in love with another man," she wrote, "but it has been happening since Bathsheba, the wife of Uriah, the Hittite, first caught the eye of King David." Moving on from biblical references, St. Johns argued that movie people were different and should be allowed to live by different standards. Their human frailties should not be judged so harshly as their purpose is so noble.

Some days, when she was up to it, Davies would join St. Johns and Hearst, contributing anecdotes of her own, and the three would laugh together as in the old days. St. Johns's son Mac, who had been a crime reporter for Hearst's *New York Daily Mirror* in the thirties and a campaign worker for Nixon in his Senate race, helped his mother on the series by interviewing some of the surviving legends of the Silent Era, such as comedy producer Mack Sennett, and scouring the *Los Angeles Examiner* newspaper morgue for photographs and anecdotes. The *American Weekly* series went over so well that it ran for over a year, continuing past Hearst's death, like a swan song he just might have envisioned.

On a late Monday afternoon, following the usual procedure, St. Johns was invited to Hearst and Davies's house to have dinner and go over plans for the next installment in the series. St. Johns brought along Mac. That afternoon, the Hollywood collaborators got very little work done. Davies nestled close to Hearst and encouraged him to recollect their early days making movies, but he drifted in and out of sleep. Davies and Adela and Mac St. Johns eventually moved to the dining room, where Mac noticed something strange in an otherwise unremarkable setting. Propped up in one of the dining-room chairs was a life-size cardboard cutout of Gen. Douglas MacArthur. Apparently a discarded advertisement (MacArthur was the last in a long line of Hearst-sponsored candidates for president) had found a happy home in the Beverly house. It was a seriocomic moment in a darker scene. Davies was drinking now and talking incessantly. Hearst's will seems to have been her main concern. Adela, who had struggled with alcoholism herself, felt unusually embarrassed, perhaps because her son was present or because she felt uneasy discussing codicils and other legal terms with Hearst still hovering one story above them. She decided it was time to leave. Adela said her good-byes to Davies, and sitting in her car she turned to her son. "I didn't want to hear about that will" was all the original snooping sob sister could say. They drove down the driveway, under the palm tree leaves in the flickering light and shadows, and out through the gates to the street.

GOING, HOLLYWOOD STYLE

Even in his final days Hearst was still drawn to Hollywood. Screenwriter Frances Marion paid him a visit on August 12, 1951, and on the same day film director Raoul Walsh came by to see his old friend. Marion Davies, who had starred in Walsh's Cosmopolitan film *Going Hollywood*, greeted the director at the door of the Beverly house. Tearfully she confided the news that doctors were likely to amputate Hearst's leg because of the onset of gangrene. Upstairs, on the second floor, Walsh found the wasting Hearst in his bedroom, "lost in an overstuffed chair." Together with Davies Walsh tried to be cheerful, and Hearst was grateful for the company. "The only visitors I've had," he told Walsh, "have been doctors with needles which they stick in me." When the two men were alone, Walsh told Hearst how concerned Davies was about a possible amputation. "Not a chance. Not a chance." Hearst whispered. "As soon as I get some of my strength back, it's up to San Simeon again. Down here, I can't breathe." Two days later Hearst was dead.

When the eighty-eight-year-old body of William Randolph Hearst was carried out of San Francisco's Grace Cathedral after the funeral service on August 16, 1951, it was followed through high open doors, down steps, and into the midday sun by the widow walking arm in arm with a man the general public would not easily recognize. Millicent's escort was not a Hearst family member in the usual sense, but he was a hallowed member of Hollywood's family. He was Howard Strickling, Metro-Goldwyn-Mayer's public relations chief.

It was no accident that Strickling stood in such a prominent place at Hearst's funeral procession. Strickling and Hearst had known each other since the 1920s and shared a fascination with celebrity and a talent for imparting that fascination to the public. Strickling was a master of publicity and a proverbial keeper of Hollywood secrets who knew where all the bod-

ies were buried. More important, at the hour of Hearst's death he knew precisely how one very famous body was about to be buried. Strickling and
Richard Berlin, who was now the Hearst Corporation's chief executive
officer, had been in on the funeral plans for weeks. Timing was important in
a Hollywood production, and when the publisher-producer's last breath
came, there would be no awkward hesitation. In the early morning hours of
August 14, Hearst's body was taken from the Beverly Hills house to a local
undertaker. No one had tried to awaken Davies, who slept in another room,
sedated by drugs administered by one of the doctors or nurses who were
keeping the death vigil for Hearst. As Hearst was flown north to San Francisco, Millicent was in position at a New York airport for a flight west.

After the Hearst family gathered in a San Francisco hotel, someone suggested that a proper mourning photograph be taken and given out to the
press. A picture showing one of the sons with an inappropriate smile was
quickly retouched in classic Hearst tradition. Meanwhile several meetings
were held in anticipation of Hearst's funeral. Charles Mayer, business manager of the *San Francisco Examiner* and Millicent's cousin, worked with the
police on crowd control issues, and Strickling took charge of a guest list and
the transportation of Hearst's body. Working with Hearst's son George and
Dick Sarno, the director of photography for the Hearst papers, Strickling
and Mayer considered options on a procession leading from Grace Cathedral. Sarno was particularly anxious to make Hearst's funeral a picture-per-
fect affair. As he later told a reporter for *Editor and Publisher* magazine,
"[Hearst] was our severest critic up until the last few weeks. He knew more
about pictures than anyone in the whole organization. He not only knew
more about pictures, he invented them." Typically a side exit of Grace
Cathedral leading to a narrow alley was the preferred route chosen by family members, but George Hearst suggested that photographs of all the
church exits be taken. To help Millicent make the final decision, an *Examiner* cameraman took five shots of the alley and one photograph of the main
entrance. After studying the pictures in her hotel room, Millicent decided to
accompany George on an unpublicized visit to the church. Squeezing
through the alley with her son by her side, Millicent quickly decided on the
larger, more prominent front exit.

Strickling put together an appropriate list of honorary pallbearers for the
Hearst funeral, and the lineup along the steps of Grace Cathedral was a cross
section personifying Hearst's lifelong interests. From the world of power and
propaganda stood J. Edgar Hoover, Bank of America executive L. M. Giannini, and former Committee on Public Information chief George Creel.
Hollywood was well represented by such figures as Louis B. Mayer, Joseph

Schenck, Will Hays, and Hearst film columnists Louella Parsons and Harrison Carroll. The widow of Ashton Stevens was also in attendance; her husband, the independent-minded Hearst writer and secret source of information for the filmmakers of *Citizen Kane*, had died only weeks before his boss.

Beyond the gestures of those who attended Hearst's funeral, numerous tributes filled the pages of the Hearst papers. From overseas accolades came from Britain's Lord Beaverbrook; from Carlos Romulo, foreign minister of the Philippines, who called Hearst a patriot; and from the president of Korea, who recalled Hearst's long battle against Communist aggression. Local and national politicians, judges, and figures in publishing and Hollywood spoke about Hearst's greatness and expressed the depth of their personal loss at his passing. Former president Herbert Hoover, who had not always been a champion of Hearst, gave out a dry statement praising his "positive views, his trenchant expression and his enormous circulation." Colonel Robert R. McCormick, publisher of the *Chicago Tribune*, called Hearst a man "devoted to the interests of his country and of humanity." Evangelist Billy Graham, who had benefited greatly from boosts in the Hearst press when he first launched his ministry, asked his congregation to pray that Hearst's successors would carry on his good work. State senator Jack B. Tenney, the anti-Semitic chairman of the California branch of the Un-American Activities Committee, gave credit to Hearst for keeping alive the issue of Communism in Hollywood and elsewhere. "Much of the success attained by the California Legislative Committee on Un-American Activities," Tenney said, "was due to his efforts to place the facts before the public."

Film industry leaders were particularly effusive about Hearst's place in Hollywood history. Darryl F. Zanuck called him "one of the pioneers of our industry" and "one of the first to perceive the importance and future of the screen." Sam Goldwyn, who had quietly supported Orson Welles during the *Citizen Kane* controversy, said he "admired and respected and loved him not only for his great stature and accomplishment, but for his wonderful personal qualities as a human being and a friend." Also weighing in on Hearst's impact on the movie business were Cecil B. DeMille, Dore Schary, Joseph Schenck, theater executive Charles Skouras, and Frank Freeman, head of Paramount. Jack Warner, who had had practically no contact with Hearst in the five years since their battle over the film *Mission to Moscow*, said he would miss "a warm personal friend." Ida Mayer Cummings, sister of Louis B. Mayer and president of the Jewish Home for the Aged in Los Angeles, said she was shocked to hear of Hearst's death, and she thanked him profusely for the financial support he gave to her organization. The Motion Picture Industry Council, which represented studio unions and producer groups such as the Screen Actors' Guild and the Screen Writers' Guild, said that Hearst would be remembered for "his boundless enthusiasm and his honest devotion to the Hollywood scene."

One wonders what Hearst would have made of the outpouring of love and affection. Could it be that so many sincerely believed in Hearst's greatness, or did his power, still alive and well in his publishing empire, make them fear him even in death? Was the praise for Hearst's methods simply a sign that what Hearst practiced was now thoroughly and widely engrained in the collective world of entertainment, politics, and news? Hearst's cynical side would certainly have been aware that his employees had a history of feverishly soliciting tributes to their publisher and were never caught downplaying Hearst's accomplishments in print or in the newsreels in which he appeared. On the other hand, Hearst's enthusiasm for his methods, based in an obsessive need to convince the world that his communications empire was an honest reflection of public opinion, would probably overshadow any of his personal doubts.

In its August 27, 1951, issue, Henry Luce's *Life* magazine published no less than three dozen photographs and illustrations to tell the story of Hearst's cinematic life, but in an accompanying editorial the magazine was considerably more somber and skeptical. *Life* thought the glowing endorsements of the passing legend were a product of Hearst manipulation and a result of fearful times. Hearst, they said, had made even his memory immune to criticism by cultivating alliances with the American Legion and the Catholic Church and helping to create the mid-twentieth century's cold climate of fear: "It is easy to be intimidated by an opponent who stands wrapped in the American flag, particularly when he stands in a church—and this is one reason so many people, in recent days, have rallied to the praise of Hearst Journalism. To do less would have been to run the risk of sounding unpatriotic, or even irreligious. Few public figures, in times like these, care to take that kind of risk."

"Hollywood Loses Great Champion in Passing of W. R. Hearst" was the headline of Harrison Carroll's King Features syndicated column on August 15. An article authored by Terry Ramsaye in the August 18, 1951, issue of *Motion Picture Herald* was the most extensive piece on Hearst's passing published in a film journal. Although Ramsaye gave some credit to Hearst for his work in serials, newsreels, and features, he virtually ignored his role as a film industry powerbroker. Many of Hearst's movies for Cosmopolitan were competent, Ramsaye wrote begrudgingly, but "none to command memory today." Ramsaye devoted considerably more space in his article to Hearst's management of Marion Davies's career and to the controversy over *Citizen Kane*, calling the episode "the last flare of attention for Mr. Hearst in the land of cinema." Ramsaye seems to have come a long way from his earlier assessment in *One Million and One Nights* (1926), a book that called Hearst and his motion picture journalism a singular inspiration to the medium. What caused the change is a mystery, but absent any serious studies of Hearst's relationship to film, the Ramsaye article of 1951 would remain the prevailing view of Hearst for decades to come.

Although the Hearst Corporation retained the name of its founder after his death, it did not seem to relish the association. The corporation seemed to be particularly disinclined to highlight Hearst's involvement in the film industry. When in the mid-1960s the company began the task of cataloging its voluminous collection of Hearst papers, it put Paul Schoenstein in charge. The Pulitzer Prize–winning journalist who had been city editor of the *New York Journal-American* was given specific instructions to search for and destroy correspondence related to Marion Davies. Although the editor's efforts were not entirely successful and Davies material survives, it is unknown how much more might have existed and whether material related to Hearst's other ventures in film might have been lost in the process. A similar purging of film records may also have occurred as the Hearst Corporation donated its Hearst newsreel collection to the University of California at Los Angeles in installments over a period of several years. Few paper records related to the newsreels exist, and there are gaps in reels of film that originally included footage of Davies and other shots related to Cosmopolitan Productions. Even material related to Hearst's comic strips and animation studio was tossed into dumpsters in the 1970s. Hearst's corporate descendants tried hard to reshape his image, thinking it was best to focus on his merits as a journalist, when they focused on him at all. But by taking this track they found themselves in a no-win situation, since they found few supporters of Hearst's brand of journalism outside their own organization. As they ran away from Hearst's unique role in film, they lost an opportunity to reveal Hearst as he really was and did a disservice to film history as well.

When the Hearst Corporation headquarters building on Eighth Avenue and Fifty-eighth Street came up for landmark designation in the 1980s, Hearst executives fought hard to retain their rights. They said that this work by Hearst film-set designer Joseph Urban—one of only a handful of Urban designs still standing—was unworthy of such consideration. But one suspects they saw the six-story Urban building set on prime New York real estate as far less remarkable than an income-generating skyscraper might be on the same site.

In the days following Hearst's death, there was passing talk that New York City's Union Square—onetime center of politics, vice, and entertainment—might be renamed William Randolph Hearst Square. A local patriotic group pushed the plan, but whether the City Council seriously considered the matter is unknown; in any case, it came to nothing. There would be no Hearst Squares built in Manhattan or in Los Angeles, where Hearst died. In the end, Hearst was memorialized by nothing equivalent to the Irving Thalberg Award, the Pulitzer Prizes, or Times Square. His name lived on in film, television, and news, but never to the same extent as Fox, Goldwyn, Mayer, or Warner.

Today only San Simeon survives as an entity inseparable from its onetime owner. But even Hearst Castle does not resonate as a testament to a great journalist. Instead it is a monument to Hollywood and a cenotaph to the man who once sat nightly in its miniature movie palace theater. In fact, as the whole of Hearst Castle resembles a film set more than a home, it is a reminder of Hearst's unparalleled role in the triumph of entertainment over art and news. Even at the beginning of the twenty-first century, the castle on the hill remains an oddly powerful attraction for countless sightseers. Over and above its stone sculptures and tapestries, it is a sign that points to Hollywood under Hearst.

$\mathcal{Notes}$

Unless otherwise specified, all interviews were conducted by the author.

PREFACE

Page ix. **Bernays**: Interview with Edward Bernays; Larry Tye, *The Father of Spin: Edward L. Bernays and the Birth of Public Relations* (New York: Crown, 1998); Edward L. Bernays, *Biography of an Idea: Memoirs of Corporate Public Relations Counsel Edward L. Bernays* (New York: Simon and Schuster, 1965).

Page ix. **"publicity a play received**: Bernays, *Biography of an Idea*.

Page x. **through the black peepholes of a darkly stained stereopticon**: Ludwig Bemelmans, *To the One I Love the Best* (New York: Viking, 1955).

Page xi. **not how Hearst's relationship to Hollywood was always perceived**: *The Lantern*, Mar. 1916; Terry Ramsaye, *A Million and One Nights* (New York: Simon and Schuster, Touchstone, 1926).

Page xii. **Hearst hired Alexander Black**: Alexander Black, *Time and Chance* (New York: Farrar Rinehart, 1937); interviews with Alexander Black family, Apr. 18, 1995; correspondence with Black family, 1995.

Page xiii. **"always acutely concerned [with] clearness**: Black, *Time and Chance*.

Page xiii. **"Black . . . is the yellowist of them all"**: Ibid.

1. BEHIND THE SCENES

Page 1. **a writer described Hollywood**: George P. West, "Hearst: A Psychological Note," *American Mercury*, Nov. 1930, 298–308.

Page 1. **A gaslight rialto**: John Warren Frick Jr., *The Rialto: A Study of Union Square, the Center of New York's First Theatre District, 1870–1900* (Ph.D. diss., New York University, Mar. 1983); Leslie Fiedler, "What Shining Phantom: Writers and the Movies," in *Man and the Movies*, ed. W. R. Robinson (Baton Rouge: Louisiana State University Press, 1967),

304–23. Fiedler points out that the name *Hollywood* has long had a negative connotation and that in this regard associations with prostitution have been "not incidental but essential to Hollywood."

Page 2. **William Fox:** *Chicago News,* Nov. 5, 1912; William Fox clipping file, Performing Arts Library, New York Public Library; *Variety,* July 4 and 11, 1908, Aug. 8 and 15, 1908, Dec. 19, 1908.

Page 2. **This legend about Pastor:** Albert E. Smith, *Two Reels and a Crank* (Garden City, N.Y: Doubleday, 1952), 46.

Page 3. **Photographs of Tammany Hall:** M. R. Werner, *Tammany Hall* (Garden City, N.Y.: Doubleday, Doran, 1928); Timothy J. Gilfoyle, *City of Eros: New York City, Prostitution, and the Commercialization of Sex, 1790–1920* (New York: Norton, 1992), 87–88, 256–58, 298–302.

Page 3. **"organization of crime":** Gilfoyle, *City of Eros,* 300. In 1928, waging a campaign against Democrat Al Smith, Hearst himself would write, "Tammany is a political mafia, an organization of graft and political blackmail" ("Why Smith Can't Win," a pamphlet published by the Republican State Committee, San Francisco, in the Herbert Hoover Presidential Library, West Branch, Iowa).

Page 4. **Tammany, he declared, is a business enterprise:** Various NYC newspapers, Feb. 15, 1892; Charles P. Parkhurst, *Our Fight with Tammany* (New York: Scribner's, 1895); Charles P. Parkhurst, *My Forty Years in New York* (New York, 1923).

Page 5. **Everything is business:** Justin Kaplan, *Lincoln Steffens* (New York: Simon and Schuster, 1974), 64.

Page 5. **Sullivan actively courted press coverage:** Alvin F. Harlow, *Old Bowery Days* (New York: Appleton, 1931); Daniel Czitrom, "Underworlds and Underdogs: Big Tim Sullivan and Metropolitan Politics in New York, 1889–1913," *Journal of American History,* Sept. 1991; Werner, *Tammany Hall.*

Page 6. **future site of Hearst's Cosmopolitan motion picture studio:** The Consumers Brewing Company owned the property in 1919 when Hearst purchased it to use as a film studio. Hearst made only minor changes to the building's exterior, which had been rebuilt following a fire in 1908. A large *S* that was carved into the cement of the building's front signifying "Sulzer's" remained after Hearst took it over. NYC Building Records, Municipal Archives. NYC. For Sullivan's use of Sulzer's, see *New York Times* (hereafter, *NYT*), Aug. 2, 1892, and Sept. 14, 1897.

Page 6. **recognizable scent of sassafras:** *Commercial Advertiser,* Nov. 6, 1894, 3.

Page 7. **Gerard personally delivered bags of cash:** James W. Gerard, *My First Eighty-Three Years in America* (Garden City, N.Y.: Doubleday, 1951).

Page 8. **a miniature theater:** Inventory of Chestnut Street house, Phoebe Apperson Hearst Papers, Bancroft Library, University of California, Berkeley.

Page 8. **The San Francisco where Hearst was born:** William A. Bullough, *The Blind Boss and His City: Christopher Augustine Buckley and Nineteenth-Century San Francisco* (Berkeley: University of California Press, 1979); Bruce Blivin, "The Boodling Boss," *American Heritage,* Dec. 1959; Buckley obituary, *New York Tribune,* Apr. 22, 1922; Alexander Callow Jr., "San Francisco's Blind Boss," *Pacific Historical Review,* Aug. 1956; Werner, *Tammany Hall.*

Page 10. **"Churches have to compass their ends"**: Grace Church Archives.

Page 10. **irreligious Fourteenth Street**: For Theiss's music hall, Huber's, and other 14th Street resorts, see building records, Municipal Archives, NYC; *The Sun,* June 1, 1895; *New York Tribune,* June 26, 1895.

Page 11. **Thirteenth Street wasn't any better**: *NYT,* May 23, 1897, 5; *New York Evening Post,* June 8, 1901. The Clarendon was located on a narrow street directly across from the Willson resort. The manager of the Clarendon, Tony Gartner, also managed another music hall located at 112 Third Avenue between Thirteenth Street and Fourteenth streets considered questionable in character because its audience comprised mostly women without escorts (Report on Concert Saloons, Mayor's Papers, Aug. 19, 1893, 89GTF-15, Municipal Archives, NYC). For William Fox at the Clarendon, see *Chicago News,* Nov. 5, 1912.

Page 11. **Maggie Brown**: Police records, Municipal Archives, NYC.

Page 11. **Martin Huberth, a young agent**: Huberth's commission book, courtesy of Huberth family.

Page 11. **Volks Garden**: *New York Dramatic Mirror,* Nov. 28, 1896.

Page 12. **George Leslie**: George C. D. O'Dell, *Annals of the New York Stage,* vol. 2, *1892–96* (New York: Columbia University Press).

Page 12. **Millicent Willson Hearst**: NYC Directory, 1890s, NY Public Library; Billy Bitzer, *His Story: The Autobiography of D. W. Griffith's Master Cameraman* (New York: Farrar, Straus, 1973); Irving Bacheller, *Coming up the Road* (New York: Bobbs-Merrill, 1928); Luc Sante, *Low Life: Lures and Snares of Old New York* (New York: Farrar, Straus, 1991); Gilfoyle, *City of Eros;* Hannah Murray birth records, Portland Historical Society, Portland, Maine; "Hollywood and Vice," *Newsweek,* Aug. 23, 1993, 47–51.

Page 13. **The Girl from Paris**: *New York Press,* Dec. 9, 1896.

Page 13. **1913 one-sheet broadside**: James Gerard Papers, Mansfield Library, University of Montana, Missoula.

Page 14. **the Dewey Theater had a reputation**: " 'Wide-Open' New York," *Harpers Weekly,* Oct. 22, 1898, p. 1045; *New York Tribune,* Oct. 4, 1898, June 3, 1899; *NYT,* Nov. 1, 1898, 1, May 2, 1900, 5, Jan. 27, 1901; *New York Dramatic Mirror,* Oct. 1, 1898; *New York Morning Telegraph,* Jan. 5, 1911.

Page 14. **Meanwhile Martin Huberth**: Huberth commission book, Huberth family. The only previous Hearst study to link Huberth and the Willsons was John Winkler's revised biography of Hearst (*William Randolph Hearst: A New Appraisal* [New York: Hastings House, 1955]). According to Winkler, "Mrs. Willson possessed a keen business instinct and had invested shrewdly in properties lining fast-growing Harlem's leading thoroughfare, 125th Street. The Willsons lived on Gramercy Park. A neighborhood real estate agent whom Mrs. Willson took a liking to and often consulted, was an engaging young man named Martin Huberth." The reference to 125th Street suggests that the Willsons may have had connections to enterprises on the city's other entertainment rialto, in Harlem. Hannah Wilson had another important municipal connection. Her nephew, August Mayer, was a high-ranking detective with the New York City police department (Mayer obituary, *NYT,* Sept. 20, 1958, 19). See also Marion Davies's memoirs for her awareness of the Willson connection to the police (Marion Davies transcripts, Fred Lawrence Guiles Collection).

Page 14. **even the mayor suspected**: Mayor Gaynor to Commissioner Waldo, Oct. 3, 1912, Papers of William Jay Gaynor, Mayor's Papers, Municipal Archives, NYC.

Page 14. **"decided penchant for chirpies"**: *Tenderloin*, Nov. 2, 1898.

Page 15. **an unplanned pregnancy**: Interview with Gretl Urban, Oct. 24, 1991.

Page 15. **News of Hearst's marriage**: *New Yorker*, May 6, 1903.

Page 15. **Potter was a friend of the Willson family**: *Atlanta Constitution*, May 29, 1904, Millicent Willson Hearst clipping, New York Public Library for the Performing Arts, NYC. Potter was not the only religious leader to have a seemingly contradictory relationship with Hearst. In 1909 Rev. Charles Parkhurst urged Hearst to run for mayor. In 1913 he wrote op-ed pieces for the Hearst papers. And in 1916 he appeared along with "representatives" of the *New York American* in the prologue of *Is Any Girl Safe?* an inflammatory film about white slavery that apparently had some Hearst financial backing (*New York American*, Sept. 3).

Page 16. **"Big Tim" Sullivan played a prominent role**: "W. R. Hearst Mentioned as a Candidate for President in 1904," *Tammany Times*, Nov. 29, 1902, 1–2; "William Randolph Hearst," *Outlook*, Oct. 20, 1906, 403.

2. THE ARTIST-JOURNALIST

Page 17. **"dramatic form"** . . . **"novelettes"**: These quotations recur in the Hearst-Crane correspondence: WRH to SC, Aug. 11, 1896, HRH to SC, Sept. 10, 1896, HRH to SC, Sept. 13, 1896, Stephen Crane Papers, Rare Book and Manuscript Library, Columbia University.

Page 17. **Henry Haxton**: Over the years numerous Crane scholars unfamiliar with Hearst and his associates have misspelled the surname of the *Journal* editor as "Huxton." Columbia University, the repository for the Crane Papers, makes the same mistake. For the correct spelling, see New York City directories and articles in the *Journal* for the period; John Winkler, *Hearst: An American Phenomenon* (New York: Simon and Schuster, 1928); Oliver Carlson and Ernest Sutherland Bates, *Hearst: Lord of San Simeon* (New York: Viking, 1937).

Page 18. **"adventure squad"**: *William Randolph Hearst: A Portrait in His Own Words*, ed. Edmond D. Coblentz (New York: Simon and Schuster, 1952), 46.

Page 19. **"a regular self-praise sheet**: "Sunday Journal," *Tammany Times*, Apr. 20, 1896.

Page 19. **Those who knew Crane**: Correspondence with Willis Abbot and Arthur Brisbane in Crane Papers. For biographies of Stephen Crane, see Bill Brown, *The Material Unconscious* (Cambridge: Harvard University Press, 1997); R. W. Stallman, *Stephen Crane: A Biography* (New York: Braziller, 1968); Christopher Ben Fey, *The Double Life of Stephen Crane* (New York: Knopf, 1992); John Berryman, *Stephen Crane* (New York: Farrar, Straus, 1977).

Page 20. **"effect of a photographic revelation"**: *NYT*, Jan. 26, 1896, 22.

Page 20. **"shown with such vivid and terrible accuracy**: *NYT*, May 31, 1896, 31.

Page 20. "scores and scores of tiny flashlight photographs: *San Francisco Wave*, July 4, 1896.

Page 20. a "confidential" letter: WRH to Stephen Crane, Sept. 10, 1896, Crane Papers.

Page 20. The Tenderloin: For Crane and the Tenderloin, see "Stephen Crane and the Police," *American Quarterly* 48, no. 2 (June 1996).

Page 21. entertainment with a message: As sociologist Robert E. Park wrote, Hearst's "appeal was frankly not to the intellect but to the heart. The newspaper was for him first and last a form of entertainment" ("The Yellow Press," *Sociology and Social Research* 12 [Sept.–Oct. 1927]: 10). A prostitution and police corruption story (similar to the one featuring Crane and Clark) involving a Mrs. Lizzie Sommers became a page one story in the Hearst papers in early 1897; see *New York Evening Journal*, Jan. 9, 1897, 1. For the theme of rescuing prostitutes and its connection to film, see Orrin G. Cocks, "Applying Standards to Motion Picture Films," *The Survey*, June 27, 1914.

Page 22. A fictional character modeled on Hearst: Stephen Crane, *Active Service* (New York: Frederick A. Stokes Co., 1899).

Page 23. Hearst met George Pancoast: W. A. Swanberg, *Citizen Hearst* (New York: Scribner's, 1961); Cora Older, *William Randolph Hearst, American* (New York: Appleton Century, 1936); Pancoast clipping file, Regional History Center, Los Angeles.

Page 23. he converted the entire second floor: Architect A. C. Schweinfurth made a rendering for a greatly expanded Sausalito mansion; however, it is unknown what if anything was built (correspondence with Richard Longstreth, Nov. 26, 1996).

Page 24. sent out to lucky readers was a photograph: See various issues of the *San Francisco Examiner* for 1892.

Page 24. Once the locals found out: clippings, Sausalito Historical Society, Sausalito, Calif.

Page 25. Hoffman House: Building records, 1894, Municipal Archives, NYC; *New York Tribune*, Aug. 17, 1897; 1890 census, New York Public Library; WRH to Phoebe Hearst on Hoffman House stationery, ca. 1889, Phoebe Apperson Hearst Papers.

Page 25. George Thompson: WRH to PH, ca. 1895, Phoebe Apperson Hearst Papers.

Page 26. Nymphs and Satyr: The onetime Hoffman House attraction now hangs in the Sterling and Francine Clark Art Institute in Williamstown, Massachusetts.

Page 26. The Worth House: John Tebbel, *The Life and Good Times of William Randolph Hearst* (New York: Dutton, 1952); Swanberg, *Citizen Hearst*.

Page 26. He hired the prominent California architect A. C. Schweinfurth: Correspondence between WRH and Schweinfurth, ca. 1895, WRH Papers, Bancroft Library. Renovation plans for the Powers's Lexington Avenue townhouse are in the Building Records department of the Municipal Archives of the City of New York.

Page 27. Powers's whereabouts: New York State Census Records, 1900 and 1920, New York Public Library.

Page 27. Hanfstaengl opened a branch shop: Author's correspondence with Egon Hanfstaengl.

Page 28. **paintings and drawings by Frederic Remington**: Remington Papers, St. Lawrence University, Canton, N.Y.

Page 28. **inspired by the medium of photograph**: Edward Buscombe, "Painting the Legend: Frederic Remington and the Western," *Cinema Journal* 23, no. 4 (summer 1984): 12–27.

Page 28. **"a taste for dramatic narrative**: Ibid.

Page 28. **"I tried to get his color**: Ibid.

Page 29. **the types Stephen Crane called**: Stallman, *Stephen Crane.*

Page 29. **Remington once said**: Peggy Samuels and Harold Samuels, *Frederic Remington: A Biography* (Garden City, N.Y.: Doubleday, 1982), 418.

Page 29. **a marriage of journalism and art**: John Osborn, "The Dramaturgy of the Tabloid: Climax and Novelty in a Theory of Condensed Forms," *Theatre Journal*, Dec. 1994, 519–22.

Page 29. **"more truthful as 'human'**: Sergei Eisenstein, *Nonindifferent Nature* (Cambridge: Cambridge University Press, 1987), 309–10.

Page 29. **"If a sensation is true**: "Pacific Coast Journalism," *Overland Monthly*, Apr. 1888.

Page 30. **"I am a yellow journalist**: "Brisbane Addresses College Newspapers," *New York American*, Jan. 20, 1910. See *Editor and Publisher*, Feb. 5 and 12, 1910.

Page 31. **the adjectives freak, fake, and vaudeville**: For freak journalism, see "Ethics of 'Freak Journalism,' " *NYT*, Sept. 24, 1896; "The Sorrows of Freak Journalism," *NYT*, Dec. 25, 1896.

Page 31. **The use of the word yellow**: *Oxford English Dictionary*, 2d ed. (Oxford: Oxford University Press, Clarendon, 1989); Committee of Fifteen Papers, New York Public Library; Richard Ellmann, *Oscar Wilde* (New York: Vintage, 1987); Katherine Lyon Mix, *A Study in Yellow: The Yellow Book and Its Contributors* (Lawrence: University of Kansas Press, 1960).

Page 31. **"New Journalism indeed!**: "New Journalism and Vice," *NYT*, Mar. 3, 1897. The *New York Mail and Express* reported on the Society for the Suppression of Vice's attack on "new journalism" on March 3, 1897. On March 5, 1897, the same newspaper attacked both the *Journal* and the *World* for what it claimed were "fake pictures" of the inauguration of McKinley. The paper said the lies were perpetrated by "yellow journalism's reporters."

Page 33. **The period leading up to the fight**: Daniel J. Boorstin, *The Image* (New York: Vintage, 1961); *San Francisco Examiner*, various issues, Mar. 1897; Fred S. Mathias, *The Amazing Bob Davis* (New York: Longmans, Green, 1944). On February 24, 1897, the *New York Tribune* used the term *yellow journals* in connection with the Corbett-Fitzsimmons fight. On March 5, 1897, the same newspaper used the term *yellow journalism* in discussing the election of 1896 and the competition between Hearst and Pulitzer over the Yellow Kid cartoon. This is the only mention of the Yellow Kid in connection with Hearst's journalism to be found in scores of issues of a half-dozen New York newspapers for the period from September 1896 through June 1897.

Page 34. "scandals of all sorts in high life and low life: *New York Tribune*, Feb. 9, 1897.

Page 34. "art of presenting": See illustration above article entitled "The New Journalism," which features a banner saying "The Business of Getting the News and the Art of Presenting It" (*San Francisco Examiner*, Feb. 21, 1897).

Page 34. these two mediums of entertainment: On film as a communication medium, see Sol Worth, "Film as a Non-Art: An Approach to the Study of Film," in *Perspectives on the Study of Film*, ed. John Stuart Katz (Boston: Little, Brown, 1971), 180.

Page 35. "Living Pictures" to describe moving pictures: Benjamin B. Hampton, *A History of the American Film Industry, From Its Beginnings to 1931* (reprint, New York: Dover, 1970); "Kinetography: The Production of 'Living Pictures,' " *Knowledge: An Illustrated Magazine of Science, Literature and Art* (London), Sept. 1, 1897.

Page 36. Hearst made an unpublicized debut as a movie cameraman: John Winkler, *William Randolph Hearst: A New Appraisal* (New York: Hastings House, 1955), 88. For more on the McKinley footage, see "Movie Archives to Preserve Historic Scenes," *Literary Digest*, Nov. 27, 1926, which states that the International Newsreel had in its possession film footage of Grover Cleveland riding with McKinley on the way to the Capitol and reproduces a still from a film of McKinley delivering his inauguration speech, also said to be in the possession of Hearst's newsreel company.

Page 37. L. Edson Raff: *New York City Directory*, 1890s, New York Public Library; correspondence with Col. Edson D. Raff; unpublished memoirs of Frank Nankivell, Nankivell family; "The New Journalism at 106 Miles an Hour," *New York Journal*, Mar. 7, 1897, 31.

Page 37. "it proved that the principle of the vitascope: *New York Journal*, Mar. 7, 1897.

Page 37. John Grierson visited the United States: "Briton Addresses Paramount Theatre Managers School," *Exhibitors Herald*, Sept. 26, 1925; Forsyth Hardy, ed., *Grierson on the Movies* (London: Faber and Faber, 1980); James Beveridge, *John Grierson, Film Master* (New York: Macmillan, 1978).

Page 38. "popular appeal": This and all subsequent Grierson quotations are from "Briton Addresses Paramount Theatre Managers School."

Page 38. "kinetic, motion-pictorial journalism": Terry Ramsaye, *A Million and One Nights* (New York: Simon and Schuster, Touchstone, 1986), xlvii.

Page 38. visual newspaper: Ramsaye, *A Million and One Nights*; W. I. Thomas, "The Psychology of the Yellow Journal," *American Magazine*, Mar. 1908; Warren Francke, "An Argument in Defense of Sensationalism: Probing the Popular and Historiographical Concept," *Journalism History* (autumn 1978): 70–73.

3. FILM NEWS

Page 40. The Mystery of the Maine: "Raising the *Maine* in Moving Pictures," *NYT*, Nov. 9, 1911; *Variety*, Nov. 11, 1911; *Billboard*, Nov. 18, 1911; Terry Ramsaye, *A Million and One Nights* (New York: Simon and Schuster, Touchstone, 1986).

Page 40. what historians today call an actuality: In 1911 Hearst published a long editorial that called film "the great educator of the future" ("Show Children the Real

World," *New York Journal*, Nov. 10, 1911). The film journal *Motography* thought the editorial was so noteworthy that it reproduced it in full in its December 1911 issue. "The chain of newspapers published by William R. Hearst's company are [*sic*] chiefly remarkable for their free use of illustration," the journal wrote in their introduction to the editorial. "No story of action is considered complete by the Hearst editors unless it carries at least one photographic reproduction. . . . It follows naturally, then, that the Hearst editors must recognize the enormous potential force of the motion picture."

Page 40. **the battleship U.S.** *Maine*: Oliver Carlson and Ernest Sutherland Bates, *Hearst: Lord of San Simeon* (New York: Viking, 1937); "*Maine* Sold in Europe," *Billboard*, Apr. 6, 1912. A 1912 film titled *Last Rites of the* Maine, which shows the raising of the battleship on February 2, 1912, is held by the Motion Picture, Sound, and Video Branch of the National Archives at College Park, Maryland.

Page 41. **Hearst was exceedingly impatient:** Articles about the *Journal's* monument fund appeared frequently beginning on February 20, 1898. Typical of these articles was "Patriots Eager to Subscribe to the *Maine* Fund," *New York Evening Journal*, Feb. 24, 1898. See Ben Procter, *William Randolph Hearst: The Early Years, 1863–1910* (New York: Oxford University Press, 1998).

Page 42. **"I might as well now confess:** *NYT*, Sept. 2, 1912, 3.

Page 42. **America's tropical playground:** Carlson and Bates, *Hearst*, 94, 104.

Page 43. **exhibited as an adjunct to Hearst's fund-raising efforts:** *NYT*, Nov. 9, 1911.

Page 43. **after considerable haggling with city officials:** *New York American*, Oct. 17, 1905. In 1911 Ernest Harvier, a political adviser to Mayor William Gaynor, complained that on Hearst's orders "fine shade trees" were being chopped down for a "shaft and gateway" to bridge the new headquarters of the *New York American* at Fifty-ninth Street, Eighth Avenue, and Broadway and the proposed *Maine* Monument. He suggested that this was in violation of the city charter (EH to Gaynor, July 24, 1911, Mayor's Papers, Municipal Archive, NYC). Hearst was attracted to Columbus Circle and the area surrounding it as an alternative to Fourteenth Street, an amusement center for publishing and theatrical enterprises. Among the many properties he eventually owned or leased in this vicinity were the Cosmopolitan Theater and the Ziegfeld Theater. See " 'Build Circle Express Stop Now' Is Plea," *New York Journal*, Dec. 16, 1913; "Theatres of Future Will Be Housed in Big Buildings Around the 'Circle,' " *New York American*, Sept. 20, 1925.

Page 44. **The truth about Cisneros:** Charles Johnson Post, *The Little War of Private Post* (Boston: Little, Brown, 1960), 131. See *New York Journal*, Oct. 12, 1897, for a two-page "film strip" illustration of the Cisneros story. See *New York Journal*, Oct. 17, 1897, for Cisneros posing for *Journal* photographer at Hotel Waldorf wearing "the same dress she wore in the prison."

Page 44. **"They make motion pictures:** *Morning Telegraph*, Sept. 2, 1923.

Page 45. **"Here . . . like one of those dissolving views of a stereopticon:** *New York Journal*, Oct. 17, 1898.

Page 45. **David Belasco—described by one writer**: Nicholas Vardac, *Stage to Screen: Theatrical Origins of Early Film* (Cambridge: Harvard University Press, 1949), 248.

Page 46. **"the star of the night"**: *New York Journal*, Oct. 17, 1898.

Page 47. **"so much to the health and wealth**: William Randolph Hearst, *Selections from the Writings and Speeches of William Randolph Hearst* (San Francisco: published privately, 1948), 56.

Page 48. **"stage fright"**: Cora Older, *William Randolph Hearst, American* (New York: Appleton Century, 1936).

Page 48. **Hearst's air flight**: Older, *William Randolph Hearst.*

Page 48. **Hearst and Edison did manage to share**: Edward Marshall of the *New York Journal* to Thomas Edison, Feb. 26, 1896; WRH to Thomas Alva Edison, Feb. 5, 1896; WRH to TAE, Feb. 15, 1896; TAE to WRH, Feb. 17, 1896. The Hearst-Edison correspondence is in the Thomas A. Edison Papers, Edison Archives, microfilmed and stored at New York University, NYC, and at the Edison National Historical Site, West Orange, New Jersey. See Allen Koenigsberg, "Edison's Brain: An Inside Look at the Discovery of X-Rays and Recorded Sound," *Antique Phonograph Monthly* 9, no. 2 (1992): 2–7.

Page 49. **an account that appeared later in the** *New York Journal*: "To Send Pictures by Telegraph," *New York Journal*, Oct. 18, 1896.

Page 49. **a Journal reporter told Edison**: Ibid.

Page 49. **a letter of agreement**: See unsigned letter from Edison laboratory to Paul Latzke, a Hearst representative, Apr. 24, 1896, Thomas A. Edison Papers.

Page 54. **the Lathams**: Terry Ramsaye, *A Million and One Nights* (New York: Simon and Schuster, Touchstone, 1986).

Page 55. **Crusading for William Jennings Bryan**: Willis J. Abbot, *Watching the World Go By* (Boston: Little, Brown, 1933).

Page 55. **"Bryan was Punch**: Ferdinand Lundberg, *Imperial Hearst: A Social Biography* (New York: Equinox Cooperative, 1936), 83.

Page 56. **Yellow Kid character made a mockery**: See various Sunday issues of the *New York Journal* leading up to the November 1896 election.

Page 56. **"marvellous Election Day display**: "Journal Bulletins," *New York Journal*, Nov. 4, 1896. See also "The *Journal's* Star Will Tell the News . . . with Bands of Music, Stereopticons and Moving Picture Machines," *New York Journal*, Nov. 3, 1896.

Page 56. **"enthusiastic, up-to-date women"**: "Journal Bulletins."

Page 56. **"The success of the Journal's**: Ibid.

Page 57. **"violation of divine law"**: "Ministers on Newspapers," *New York Daily Tribune*, Dec. 8, 1896.

Page 57. **he embraced the nonthreatening association**: Walter McDougall, *This Is the Life!* (New York: Knopf, 1926), 245.

Page 57. **"Nobody understands the popular mind**: John Winkler, *William Randolph Hearst: A New Appraisal* (New York: Hastings House, 1955), 68.

Page 57. **The Journal Kinetoscope**: *New York Evening Journal*, Sept. 28, 1897.

Page 58. **"an American internal policy"**: *New York Morning Journal*, Feb. 5, 1899, 24.

Page 58. **vaudeville show as a benefit concert**: *New York Journal*, Feb. 5–10, 1897. Years later, in a special Christmas issue, the *Evening Journal* boasted that it was "the first [news-paper] to give serious attention to vaudeville, and it stirred the other newspapers to do what they have since done" (Dec. 24, 1913).

Page 58. **A "monster operatic, dramatic and vaudeville performance":** *New York Journal*, Feb. 10, 1897. See W. A. Swanberg, *Citizen Hearst* (New York: Scribner's, 1961).

Page 59. **"the paper . . . temporarily making their lives worth living":** *New York Journal*, July 9, 1897.

Page 59. **Beginning in June:** *New York Journal*, June 23, 1897; see also Aug. 25, 1897.

Page 59. **"pictures will be the best proof:** "Journal Outings to Be Shown in Pictures," *New York Journal*, Sept. 6, 1900.

Page 59. **The fame of the Journal Junior Republic:** *New York Journal*, July 28, 1897, as it appears in Kemp Niver, comp., *Biograph Bulletins: 1896–1908* (Los Angeles: Locare Research Group, 1971). See advertisement for benefit for Junior Republic Fund, *New York Evening Journal*, July 24, 1897. See also Charles Musser, *The Emergence of Cinema: The American Screen to 1907*, vol. 1 of *History of the American Cinema* (New York: Scribner's, 1990).

Page 60. **"Illustrations of the news":** *New York Evening Journal*, Sept. 28, 1897.

Page 60. **running guns:** Abbot, *Watching the World.* Three days after the *Maine* exploded, the *Buccaneer* was in Havana Harbor, where it was searched and then seized by the police after several pieces of artillery were found onboard. See Joyce Milton, *The Yellow Kids* (New York: Harper and Row, 1989).

Page 60. **"a pleasure trip":** Stanley Wertheim and Paul Sorrentino, eds., *The Crane Log: A Documentary Life of Stephen Crane, 1871–1900* (New York: Hall, 1994), 243–45.

Page 61. **Hearst's reputation was being discussed openly:** Swanberg, *Citizen Hearst.*

Page 61. **dispatch boats to Cuba:** Joseph E. Wisan, *The Cuban Crisis as Reflected in the New York Press* (New York: Columbia University Press, 1934); Charles H. Brown, *The Correspondent's War* (New York: Scribner's, 1967).

Page 63. **"Journal Pictures":** Musser, *The Emergence of Cinema.*

Page 64. **In his memoirs:** Billy Bitzer, *Billy Bitzer, His Story: The Autobiography of D. W. Griffith's Master Cameraman* (New York: Farrar Straus, 1973).

Page 65. **"The thing to do with a dirty sheet:** Edwin Emerson, *Pepys's Ghost* (Boston: Richard G. Badger, 1900).

Page 65. **Hemment later recalled:** John C. Hemment, *Cannon and Camera* (New York: Appleton, 1898). *Leslie's Weekly* published a large number of war photographs that were copyrighted by Hearst and taken by either Hearst or Hemment. See, for example, the issues of Aug. 11 and 18, 1898.

Page 66. **The detail about "the . . . ladies:** Notes to interview with Anne Flint, research notes for *Citizen Hearst*, William S. Swanberg Papers, Columbia University.

Page 67. **A history of the Vitagraph Company:** *Motion Picture News*, Feb. 14, 1925.

Page 67. **An article in the George Eastman house journal:** *Image* 2, no. 6 (Sept. 1953): 39–40. For more on American Vitagraph, see Charles Musser, "The American Vitagraph, 1897–1901: Survival and Success in a Competitive Industry," in *Film Before Griffith*, ed. John L. Fell (Berkeley: University of California Press, 1983).

Page 67. **Slide has written of an interview:** Anthony Slide, *The Big V: A History of the Vitagraph Company* (Metuchen, N.J.: Scarecrow, 1987).

Page 68. **A Spanish-American War veteran's memoir:** Post, *The Little War.*

Page 69. **letter written to his mother:** Judith Robinson, *The Hearsts: An American Dynasty* (Newark: University of Delaware Press, 1991).

Page 69. **Emerson remembered Paley:** Emerson, *Pepys's Ghost.*

Page 70. **A Journal article that gave a synopsis:** "Passion Play for the Journal's Maine Fund," *New York Journal,* June 26, 1898.

Page 70. **"The Big Store":** *New York Journal,* Sept. 13, 1896; June 27–28, 1898.

Page 70. **A Journal advertisement:** *New York Journal,* June 26, 1898.

Page 71. **Another Journal ad:** *New York Journal,* June 26, 1898.

Page 71. **His prominent obituary:** *New York Journal,* Aug. 26, 1898. See also obituary in *New York Dramatic Mirror,* Sept. 3, 1898.

4. MEDIUM FOR A NEW CENTURY

Page 73. **"from loathsome disease:** W. A. Swanberg, *Citizen Hearst* (New York: Scribner's, 1961).

Page 73. **"nervousness":** WRH to Phoebe Apperson Hearst, in Judith Robinson, *The Hearsts: An American Dynasty* (Newark: University of Delaware Press, 1991).

Page 73. **In court records:** *William Fox, Plaintiff, Against Lawrence Mulligan and Patrick H. Sullivan, as Executors Under the Last Will and Testament of Timothy D. Sullivan, Deceased, Defendants,* Dec. 1920, Supreme Court, New York County. Municipal Archives, NYC.

Page 74. **the Mazet Committee:** The report issued by the investigative committee does not mention the Willsons, but it does contain several lengthy passages related to the Dewey Theater. It establishes its connection to Sullivan and Tammany Hall and also points out its numerous fire and safety violations. "The theater has a backing on Thirteenth Street," one witness said. "I am sure of that. Runs right through the block, a dressing-room in the rear" (Documents of the Assembly of the State of New York, 124 sess., 1901. no. 78, pt. 2, vol. 2, New York Public Library).

Page 74. **"Mr. Croker, the City Looks to You":** *New York Journal,* Nov. 24, 1899.

Page 74. **"All the time; the same as you":** M. R. Werner, *Tammany Hall* (Garden City, N.Y.: Doubleday, Doran, 1928).

Page 75. **three consecutive page-one theater reviews:** "Worst Plays on New York's Immoral Stage," Oct. 18–20, 1899. For an overview of Hearst's concerns about stage morality, also see "Concerning Stage Indecency" (editorial), *New York Evening Journal,* Oct. 17, 1899; "Mothers Hear Praise for Journal," Oct. 18, 1899; "Why Do Jews Ridicule Their Race for Profit?" (editorial), *New York Evening Journal,* Oct. 6, 1899, 12; "The Indecency of the New York Stage" (editorial), *New York Evening Journal,* Oct. 14, 1899, 10; "Crusade Against Dancers," *New York Evening Journal,* Oct. 18, 1899, 2.

Page 75. **the Hearst press had widened its stage crusade:** Kaier Curtin, *We Can Always Call Them Bulgarians* (Boston: Alyson, 1987), 17. See "*Sapho* Denounced by Many

Ministers," *New York Evening Journal*, Feb. 2, 1900, and other attacks in this same newspaper from February to April 1900.

Page 76. **Hearst launched his own "picture crusade":** See the following articles in the *New York Evening Journal*: "Picture Dives Close in Panic," Nov. 28, 1899; "Evening Journal Puts Dives Out of Business," Nov. 28, 1899; "Two Arrests in Slot Machine Crusade," Nov. 29, 1899; "Devery Fights the Slot Dives," Nov. 30, 1899; "Evening Journal Wins for Decency After Quickest Crusade on Record," Dec. 1, 1899. This final issue has a cartoon illustrating a "proprietor" of a "moving pictures" establishment running for his life under the glare of a searchlight being held by the police. In his rush to escape he is seen knocking over two peepshow machines.

Page 78. **"The evil results:** *New York Evening Journal*, Dec. 1, 1899.

Page 78. **"Laws may make gambling legal:** *New York Evening Journal*, Apr. 27, 1900.

Page 78. **Only weeks before the crusade:** "Jeffries Fights for the Pictures," *New York Evening Journal*, Oct. 30, 1899.

Page 79. **"expensive scheme":** Richard H. Peterson, "The Philanthropist and the Artist: The Letters of Phoebe A. Hearst to Orrin M. Peck," *California History* (Dec. 1987): 278–85.

Page 79. **"The city was a hub:** M. Koenigsberg, *King News* (Philadelphia: Stokes, 1941), 256.

Page 79. **"an army of thugs":** Quoted in "Mr. Hearst's New Chicago Paper," *New York Herald*, July 24, 1900.

Page 80. **"ultra-yellow methods":** Ibid.

Page 80. **"to congregate about the polling places:** Werner, *Tammany Hall*, 438.

Page 80. **remained a a crowd-pleasing public figure:** Kevin Brownlow, *Behind the Mask of Innocence* (New York: Knopf, 1990), 129–30. As late as 1917 director J. Stuart Blackton thought Bryan had star appeal. He cast the charismatic presidential hopeful in a temperance film he was making, but Bryan dropped out of the project at the last moment.

Page 81. **Augustus Thomas:** Arthur Lubow, *The Reporter Who Would Be King: A Biography of Richard Harding Davis* (New York: Scribners, 1992), 282; Craig Timberlake, *The Bishop of Broadway* (New York: Library, 1954), 302; Cora Older, *William Randolph Hearst, American* (New York: Appleton Century, 1936), 219.

Page 81. **Homer Davenport:** M. Hickman, *Homer: The Country Boy* (Portland: Binford and Mort, 1986), 69.

Page 82. **the childish nature of the publisher's war exploits:** Interview with Michael Hall. Mr. Hall was a child actor in the 1940s when he befriended Hearst and Marion Davies. He is in possession of the famous Davenport portrait of Hearst.

Page 82. **"Just as movement was the element:** John L. Fell, *Film and the Narrative Tradition* (Norman: University of Oklahoma, 1974), 90.

Page 82. **magic of film and cartoons:** Biograph Production records for Oct. through Nov. 1903, Museum of Modern Art; Charles Musser, *The Emergence of Cinema: The American Screen to 1907*, vol. 1 of *History of the American Cinema* (New York: Scribner's, 1990).

Page 82. **Hearst advertised the sale:** *New York Evening Journal*, Nov. 7, 1903.

Page 83. **baby writings**: Charles Musser, *Before the Nickelodeon: Edwin S. Porter and the Edison Manufacturing Company* (Berkeley: University of California Press, 1991).

Page 83. **Marion Clark**: On the use of a photograph of Marion Clark in the Hearst newspaper coverage, see "Baby Marion Clark Kidnapped for Ransom," *New York Evening Journal*, May 22, 1899. A photograph of the child holding a doll was published in the *Evening Journal* on June 3, 1899. In the same day's paper, five illustrations of "Baby Clark's First Day at Home since Her Restoration" were spread like a filmstrip across the top of an inside page. The child is seen in various poses; waving to a crowd from a window, eating breakfast, and playing with her toys. A Biograph film called *Childhood's Happy Days* and sometimes called *Baby Marion Clark at Play* was filmed by cameraman F. S. Armitage. Its listing in the American Film Institute Catalog reads "A little girl seated in a big armchair amusing herself with a drum and horn." The following appeared in the the 1899 *Biograph Bulletin*: "Since the issue of the last press sheet about 300 new views have been added to our stock, many of them of sensational interest. One of the most talked of pictures is that of the Kidnapped Baby Marion Clark and her Mother. The *Mail and Express* of June 6 said: The biggest hit at Keith's yesterday was made by Baby Marion Clark. She was shown by the Biograph" (Kemp Niver, comp., *Biograph Bulletins: 1896–1908* [Los Angeles: Locare Research Group, 1971], 47).

Page 84. **journalism and film could work "hand in hand"**: *Leslie's Weekly*, July 6, 1899.

Page 84. **"a safety valve for public indignation"**: Arthur Brisbane, "The American Newspaper: Yellow Journalism," *The Bookman*, June 1904, 402.

Page 84. **Opper cartoon**: *New York Journal*, Oct. 19, 1901.

Page 85. **"This may be a wake**: *New York Herald*, Aug. 31, 1900.

Page 85. **Hearst was in Chicago**: William L. Crosthwait, M.D., and Ernest G. Fischer, *The Last Stitch* (Philadelphia: Lippincott, 1956).

Page 86. **McCutcheon assigned Billy Bitzer**: Billy Bitzer, *Billy Bitzer, His Story: The Autobiography of D. W. Griffith's Master Cameraman* (New York: Farrar Straus, 1973); Crosthwait and Fischer, *The Last Stitch*; "Monster Benefit for Journal Flood Fund To-Night," *New York Evening Journal*, Sept. 21, 1900. The Galveston films are advertised in *New York Clipper*, Sept. 29, 1900.

Page 86. **"You see, Mr. Hearst is giving a lot of valuable space**: William Salisbury, *The Career of a Journalist* (New York: Dodge, 1908), 180.

Page 86. **a number of films appear to have been made**: Musser, *Before the Nickelodeon*. Porter's Hearst-inspired film on the Biddles was the premiere attraction of Thomas L. Tally's Electric Theater, located at South Main and Third Street in Los Angeles. In 1902 filmgoers at the Electric—one of the most important of the early storefront theaters—would not have been aware of Porter's film model, for there was no Hearst newspaper in Los Angeles until a year later.

Page 87. **William Travers Jerome**: Paul Baker, *Stanny: The Life of Stanford White* (New York: Free Press, 1989), 285, 393.

Page 88. **Parker H. Sercombe**: *To-morrow*, Mar. and May 1907, courtesy of Romanie Sercombe.

Page 88. **Bitzer inserts an extreme close-up**: Musser, *Emergence of Cinema*.

Page 89. **The Unwritten Law**: *Variety*, Mar. 30, 1907; Brownlow, *Behind the Mask*, 143–51.

Page 89. **Chaplin film for Mack Sennett**: Mack Sennett, *King of Comedy* (Garden City, N.Y.: Doubleday, 1954), 182.

Page 89. **"Our wedding was cheerful"**: Ben Proctor, *William Randolph Hearst: The Early Years, 1863–1910* (New York: Oxford University Press, 1998), 180.

Page 90. **I certainly think that a journalism**: *Editor and Publisher*, May 30, 1903, 2.

Page 90. **"damned picture**: Quoted in *Collier's*, Oct. 6, 1906.

Page 90. **he would not seek office again**: Clipping, *Editor and Publisher*, ca. Nov. 1904.

Page 91. **"the exploitation of himself**: *Collier's*, Oct. 6, 1906.

Page 91. **"defamatory" comments about Hearst's character**: Ibid.

Page 92. **Hearst turned to Arthur Brisbane**: *NYT*, Oct. 10, 1906; and *New York Herald*, Oct. 10, 1906. Possibly more than one location was used for the Hearst films. The *Times* reported that Hearst was filmed inside the recording shop, and the *Herald* reported that films were made of Hearst delivering a speech "on the village green."

Page 92. **"graphophone" cylinders**: For information on the recording techniques of the period, I am indebted to the recording historian Allen Koenigsberg (correspondence, 1999).

Page 92. **"By utilizing these agencies**: *NYT*, Oct. 10, 1906.

Page 93. **"Hearst's vaudeville show"**: *New York Sun*, Nov. 1, 1906.

Page 93. **"political self-seeker**: *Indianapolis Morning Star*, Oct. 11, 1906.

5. IT PAYS TO ADVERTISE

Page 95. **his new drama department policy**: Will Irwin, "The American Newspaper: Vol. X, the Unhealthy Alliance," *Collier's*, June 3, 1911, 17; Ashton Stevens obituary, *Los Angeles Evening Herald*, July 12, 1951; Alan Dale obituary, *Editor and Publisher*, May 26, 1928, 38; "Motion Picture Notes," *New York American*, Feb. 4, 1917; *NYT*, Jan. 27, 1922; Charles H. Meltzer clippings, New York Public Library for the Performing Arts, NYC; *Variety*, July 10 and Oct. 3, 1914, 1; Robert Grau, "The Theatre and the Newspaper," *Editor and Publisher*, Apr. 10, 1915, 912; J. Wesley Hamer obituary, *NYT*, Oct. 23, 1944. See Gertrude Jobes, *Motion Picture Empire* (Hamden, Conn.: Archon, 1966), 108. Jobes contends that Hearst's use of movie advertising in the 1910s broke "the fear of the newspapers for motion pictures," but I believe Hearst embraced film much earlier, because he saw its potential for generating revenue and had a personal passion for the medium.

Page 95. **"We made it pay**: *Moving Picture World*, July 20, 1918, 332. All Zittel quotations in the text are from this source unless otherwise indicated.

Page 95. **The sporting-life concept**: James Wyman Barrett, *Joseph Pulitzer and His World* (New York: Vanguard, 1941).

Page 96. **"constructive criticism"**: *New York Evening Journal*, Jan. 8, 1908, editorial page.

Page 97. **As you know I am wholly averse:** WRH to Dent H. Robert, Jan. 15, 1915, WRH Papers, Bancroft Library, University of California, Berkeley.

Page 97. **"While Mr. Loew was never:** Will Gordon, "Broadway Wings, His Last Press Notice, C. F. Zittel, 'Zit,' " *New York Morning Telegraph*, ca. 1943, Carl Zittel clipping file, New York Public Library for the Performing Arts, NYC.

Page 98. **he wrote the first advertisement for Corn Flakes**: *Editor and Publisher*, Jan. 27, 1917.

Page 99. **"the undertakers"**: *Moving Picture World*, July 20, 1918.

Page 99. **Victor Watson**: Interview with Victor Watson family; Watson clipping file, New York Public Library for the Performing Arts, NYC.

Page 99. **"Though I regard Watson:** Watson obituary, Watson clipping file.

Page 99. **Schenck hired Zittel**: Gordon, "Broadway Wings."

Page 100. **In a 1914 newspaper column**: Quoted in ibid.

Page 100. **Zittel later recalled that**: Ibid.

Page 100. **Hearst's first full-scale film production**: Interview with Dewitt Goddard, June 5, 1992; John Winkler, *Hearst: An American Phenomenon* (New York: Simon and Schuster, 1928); Robert Watters, "Chasing Goddard: Episodes in Genesis of Biography," *Journalism Quarterly* (spring 1966): 231–38; Charles Goddard clipping file, New York Public Library for the Performing Arts, NYC.

Page 100. **"a background of wealth**: Charles Goddard clipping file.

Page 101. **As early as 1905 Koenigsberg had toyed**: Terry Ramsaye, *A Million and One Nights* (New York: Simon and Schuster, Touchstone, 1986), 652–69.

Page 101. **At Hearst's direction, Edgar Hatrick**: Norman Alley, *I Witness* (New York: Funk, 1941), 55–57. No information related to the filming of the Wilson inauguration has been found among the papers of either Wilson or Hearst. There is documentation of Hatrick's early involvement with Hearst's photographic enterprises in the William Howard Taft Presidential Papers. Hatrick sought approval to have a Hearst photographer attached to the Taft party during a trip to Panama in late 1912. Ariel Varges and A. E. Wallace were two photographers engaged by Hatrick at the time. Whether Varges and Wallace were making films as well as taking photographs is unknown, but certainly by 1914 they were both motion picture cameramen, sent by Hearst to Mexico to document the revolution. International Film Service was incorporated in New York on November 30, 1914 (IFS incorporation records in Municipal Archives, NYC). See Raymond Fielding, *The American Newsreel, 1911–1967* (Norman: University of Oklahoma Press, 1972).

Page 102. **Hearst went to Pathé . . .** *The Perils of Pauline*: "Boosting Pathé Pictures," *Moving Picture World*, Mar. 14, 1914; *Moving Picture World*, Feb. 28 (advertisement) and Aug. 11, 1914; *Variety*, Feb. 27, Mar. 6, and July 3, 1914; *New York American*, Mar. 1, 1914; Raymond Fielding, *The American Newsreel, 1911–1967* (Oklahoma: University of Oklahoma Press, 1972); Ramsaye, *A Million and One Nights*; Richard Abel, *The Ciné Goes to Town: French Cinema, 1896–1914* (Berkeley: University of California Press, 1994). Hearst's arrangement with Pathé apparently gave him a financial interest in several Pathé productions, including *Pearl of the Army*, *The Girl Philippa*, *The Secret Kingdom*, *The Scarlet*

Runner, and *When My Ship Comes In*. For a short period he also produced one or two political cartoons for the Bray animation studio, then affiliated with Pathé. See International Film Service–Pathé agreement, 1917, Municipal Archive, NYC.

Page 103. **she had been a circus performer**: Pearl White notes, Victor Shapiro Papers, Department of Special Collections, University Research Library, University of California, Los Angeles.

Page 103. **"that starry effect**: Charles Goddard clipping file.

Page 104. **" 'A girl's best friend was herself'**: Pearl White notes, Victor Shapiro Papers.

Page 105. **"[Hearst] was projecting crude**: John Winkler, *Hearst: An American Phenomenon* (New York: Simon and Schuster, 1928), 255. Charles Chaplin came to the United States in 1910; see David Robinson, *Chaplin: His Life and Art* (New York: McGraw-Hill, 1985).

Page 105. **The Lighthouse Keeper's Daughter**: Although some scenes of the home movie were not filmed until 1920, the project apparently started in 1914. In a letter written to Phoebe Hearst, a friend of the Hearst family described watching "the moving pictures of the play at San Simeon. . . . W.R. didn't like some of the parts of the San Simeon play because Miss Bliss and Miss Goodrich made up too much." Ethel Whitmore to Phoebe Hearst, Oct. 5, 1914, Phoebe Hearst Papers, Bancroft Library, UC, Berkeley.

Page 106. **"Live well, dress well**: Zittel clipping file.

Page 106. **"was one of the very first newspapers**: Robert Grau, *Theatre of Science: A Volume of Progress and Achievement in the Motion Picture Industry* (New York, 1914). Grau could also be critical of Hearst, albeit in a covert fashion. In 1915 he wrote about an unnamed publisher (Hearst) who "inaugurated a policy which brought about a more intimate relationship between the publishers and the producers and amusement managers generally. The policy was the result of the large financial returns from advertising of a theatrical nature" ("The Theatre and the Newspaper," *Editor and Publisher and Journalist*, Apr. 10, 1915, 912).

Page 106. **[The war] played havoc**: Joseph Wyman Barrett, *Joseph Pulitzer and His World* (New York: Vanguard, 1941).

Page 107. **"the whole shooting match**: Alan Dale clipping file, New York Public Library for the Performing Arts, NYC.

Page 108. **"Dale accounts as his**: Ibid.

Page 108. **"It seems to me that an era**: "Alan Dale Quits as Hearst's Critic," *NYT*, Oct. 8, 1914.

Page 108. **He issued a statement**: Ibid.

Page 108. **he never completely retired the system**: In 1942 *Daily Mirror* editor Jack Lait, who knew the value of advertisers, gave orders to his movie and theater critics that headlines to reviews should be "innocuous." When writing unfavorable reviews, Lait instructed his staff, "the headline may announce that such and such a production has opened, or that this is a review of such and such a production, etc., etc" (*In Fact*, Aug. 24, 1942, 3). The "good play for good pay" policy was apparently used in other ways. In 1910 an adviser to New York City mayor William Gaynor complained that money was being paid to Hearst in exchange for publicity for city employees. "I observe from the minutes that as late as June 14 there was audited a bill for $667 for the *N.Y. American*—almost coincident with the appearance of an illustrated article in its columns extolling the work of the present Commissioners. At the present rate of progress the funds of the Water Commission will soon be exhausted" (Ernest Harvier to William Gaynor, July 6, 1910, General Correspondence, 1910, Mayor's Papers, Municipal Archives, NYC).

Page 109. **"the distribution of this pictorial**: "First Hearst-Vitagraph Goes Big," *Motography*, Jan. 22, 1916, 169.

Page 110. **The Goddess**: Released in May 1915, *The Goddess* was an unusual serial according to trade reviews, a movie with "a definite theme behind it." It concerned a triumvirate of monopolists who find their power slipping as the public clamors for control of utilities. These three industrialists decide to hypnotize a radiant woman (the Goddess) and send her out into the world in hopes of "winning the public by some semispiritual means" (*Moving Picture World*, May 15, 1915, 1089).

Page 110. **"By using my friendship**: Affidavit of Albert E. Smith, *Vitagraph Company of America Against Anita Stewart and Louis B. Mayer*, New York Supreme Court Appellate Division, First Department, 1917, Municipal Archives, NYC.

Page 110. **Virtuous Wives**: Mayer gave credit to Hearst publicity for his first success as a film producer. He pointed out that the publication of *Virtuous Wives* in *Cosmopolitan* magazine before his film's release had reached "an approximate total equivalent to three-quarters of the entire population of the United States" ("Film Story Credited with Wide Circulation," *Motion Picture News*, Nov. 16, 1918, 2956).

6. WHEN MEN BETRAY

Page 111. **Ivan Abramson, a cousin of the deserter**: Interview with Walter Gould, Nov. 2, 1993; interview with Milton Gould, Nov. 5, 1993; Ivan Abramson, *Mother of Truth* (New York: Graphic Literary, 1929).

Page 113 **"almost everything [the Hearst Press]**: Ferdinand Lundberg, *Imperial Hearst: A Social Biography* (New York: Equinox Cooperative, 1936), 226.

Page 113. **Bankhead was close to the War Department's secretary**: Interviews with Walter and Milton Gould; "Baker Admits Ban on Papers' Critics," *NYT*, June 26, 1918.

Page 114. **One critic complained**: "Baker Admits Ban." All quotations in this paragraph are from this source.

Page 114. **Teddy Roosevelt**: Teddy Roosevelt to George Walbridge Perkins, Dec. 21, 1917, and to Miles Poindexter, May 22, 1918, in Elting E. Morison, ed., *The Letters of Theodore Roosevelt* (Cambridge: Harvard University Press, 1954), 1265, 1320–35.

Page 115. **"I think she's nuts**: Interviews with Walter and Milton Gould.

Page 115. **Years later, Bankhead did remember**: Tallulah Bankhead, *Tallulah: My Autobiography* (New York: Harper, 1952).

Page 116. **Abramson owned and managed the Teglikhe Presse**: Jewish Division, New York Public Library; Abramson, *Mother of Truth*.

Page 116. **"We must bring down to a minimum**: Abramson, *Mother of Truth*.

Page 117. **American grand opera**: Ivan Abramson clipping file, New York Public Library for the Performing Arts, NYC.

Page 119. **"although the corporation**: Benjamin Hampton, *A History of the American Film Industry: From Its Beginnings to 1931* (1931; reprint, New York: Dover, 1970), 67.

Page 119. **Ivan Productions**: Ivan Abramson file in National Board of Review Papers, Rare Books and Manuscripts Division, New York Public Library.

Page 119. **"point out an evil in life**: Abramson clipping file.

Page 119. **Sex Lure**: Edward De Grazia and Roger K. Newman, *Banned Films: Movies, Censors, and the First Amendment* (New York: Bowker, 1982).

Page 120. **"was inviting the public**: Ibid.

Page 120. **film as an "extension" of publishing**: Four-page advertisement for International Film Service, *Motion Picture News*, Apr. 29, 1916; "Modern Publishing Extends to Film," *Motography*, May 13, 1916, 1079. Between 1916 and 1917 Hearst made arrangements with several different film companies to release pictures that seemed to be "extensions" of his newspapers' Sunday supplement. These included a fashion reel called *The Adventures of Dorothy Dare*, an Italian adventure import called *The Jockey of Death*, and a series of films called Golden Eagle Features: *When My Ship Comes In, Jaffrey, Flower of Faith*, and *Ocean Waif*, a film directed by Alice Guy-Blaché, considered to be the first woman director. A film about eugenics called *The Black Stork*, written by Jack Lait, a columnist at Hearst's *Chicago Herald*, was produced by the Whartons for IFS in 1916. The film, which argues for selective mating, starred Dr. Harry J. Haiselden, a surgeon widely promoted in the Hearst press for his advocacy of a perfect race. Details about Hearst's involvement in the film's production are unknown, but he visited the Wharton studio at the time the film was being edited. Author Martin S. Pernick has written: "The issue [of eugenics] certainly lent itself to the type of sensational 'yellow journalism' at which the Hearst organization excelled. Haiselden's German-American connections and his concern about Japanese power might have played some role as well" (*The Black Stork: Eugenics and the Death of "Defective" Babies in American Medicine and Motion Pictures since 1915* [New York: Oxford University Press, 1996], 143–58).

Page 120. **"noble by heritage"**: Abramson, *Mother of Truth*, 153.

Page 121. **"[Hearst was] a man**: Ibid.

Page 121. **"to save my business**: Ibid.

Page 121. **Hatrick's career started in advertising**: Interview with Gloria Hatrick Stewart, Apr. 24, 1989.

Page 121. **a string of alliteratively titled cliff-hangers**: Wharton Studio Collection, Cornell University Libraries, Ithaca, N.Y.; "International Presents New Ideas," *Motography*, May 6, 1916, 1021; "International Innovation," June 3, 1916, 1269.

Page 122. **"master of light and shade**: *New York American*, Sept. 8, 1916. See *New York American*, Nov. 19, 1916.

Page 122. **"split reel"**: The Hearst press reported that Curtis film scenes had been secured "at great expense" and that the "series" of films would begin appearing in split reels on September 25 (*New York American*, Sept. 8 and Nov. 19, 1916). See "Pathé and

International Join Forces," *Moving Picture World*, Jan. 13, 1917, 202, 235; *Wid's*, Sept. 1916, 892; *Motion Picture News*, Dec. 9, 1916, 11.

Page 122. **The Hearst Animation Studio**: Interview with Gregory LaCava family, 1991; clippings courtesy of Suzanne LaCava. Walter Lantz, who worked first as a copy boy for the *New York American* and then as an animator for the Hearst cartoon studio, credits LaCava with being a pioneer in the use of storyboards to illustrate an entire film (interview with Walter Lantz, June 1, 1992). See Donald Crafton, *Before Mickey: The Animated Film, 1898–1928* (Cambridge, Mass.: MIT Press, 1984), 178–84.

Page 122. **Godfrey Building**: *Moving Picture World*, July 29, 1916, 799; *Motion Picture News*, Oct. 21, 1916, 2547; Godfrey blueprints in building records, Municipal Archives, NYC; photographs, microfilm series on NYC, New York Public Library. As the twentieth century came to a close, the Godfrey Building was still standing near the recently reinvented Times Square district. The basic structure of Hearst's penthouse apartment remained intact on the building's rooftop, but its interior had been significantly altered for use as a film-processing facility.

Page 124. **Clara Kimball Young**: Interviews with Walter and Milton Gould.

Page 124. **Isaac E. Chadwick**: Ibid.

Page 125. **"He was so enthused**: Abramson, *Mother of Truth*, 154.

Page 125. **"created a great demand**: Ibid.

7. PERILS OF PASSION

Page 126. **The town is plastered with Lithos**: *Town Topics* clipping in Joseph A. Moore Papers, Manuscripts Division, Library of Congress, Washington, D.C.

Page 127. **Marion's grandparents**: Marion Davies, *The Times We Had: Life with William Randolph Hearst*, ed. Pamela Pfau and Kenneth S. Marx (Indianapolis: Bobbs-Merrill, 1975); Fred Lawrence Guiles, *Marion Davies* (New York: McGraw-Hill, 1972).

Page 128. **"I have a laugh**: Charles Dillingham, unpublished memoir, portions of which are in the Charles Bancroft Dillingham Papers, Rare Books and Manuscripts Division, New York Public Library.

Page 128. **Hearst remembered feeling**: *William Randolph Hearst: A Portrait in His Own Words*, ed. Edmond D. Coblentz (New York: Simon and Schuster, 1952).

Page 129. **"Paderwiski's [sic] long hair**: Charles Dillingham to Millicent Hearst, Nov. 23, 1915, Dillingham Papers.

Page 129. **put her on her dancing slippers and return**: Ibid.

Page 129. **"The Hesitating Hearst"**: Millicent Hearst to Charles Dillingham, Feb. 6, 1915, Dillingham Papers. Millicent's last New York stage performance was apparently in 1898, when she appeared with her sister in the operetta called *The Telephone Girl* at the Casino Theater. According to William Randolph Hearst Jr., for a brief period of time Millicent and Anita toured the vaudeville circuit with their father, George Willson (interview with William Randolph Hearst Jr., Apr. 6, 1989).

Page 129. **Dillingham was forced to file for bankruptcy**: "Dillingham Fails; $7,337,703 in Debt," *NYT*, July 9, 1933.

Page 129. on Halloween, when Davies: Davies, *The Times We Had*; Guiles, *Marion Davies*.

Page 130. Hearst met his mistress: Hedda Hopper, *The Whole Truth and Nothing But* (Garden City, N.Y.: Doubleday, 1963).

Page 130. "Will it be possible for me: Victor Watson to Charles Dillingham, Jan. 7, 1914, Dillingham Papers.

Page 131. slight variations: For Taub and Zittel, see interview with Eugene Zukor, Jan. 13, 1994; for Davies and Block, see Marion Davies transcripts, Fred Lawrence Guiles Collection; Guiles, *Marion Davies*; Davies, *The Times We Had*; Anita Loos, *Kiss Hollywood Good-by* (New York: Viking, 1974).

Page 131. Block, Davies, and Hearst: Guiles, *Marion Davies*; private source.

Page 132. Harry Crosby: Marion Davies's fan letters, New York Public Library for the Performing Arts, NYC; Geoffrey Wolff, *Black Sun: The Brief Life and Violent Eclipse of Harry Crosby* (New York: Random House, 1976).

Page 132. Runaway Romany: Guiles, *Marion Davies*.

Page 133. Ella "Bill" Williams: Interview with Gretl Urban, Oct. 24, 1991.

Page 133. Davies and Zittel: Guiles, *Marion Davies*.

Page 133. I went over—I think it: Interview with Milton Gould, Nov. 5, 1993.

Page 134. "much involved sex mess: *Ashes of Love* reviews, New York Public Library for the Performing Arts, NYC.

Page 134. "from then on they were enemies: Interview with Walter Gould, Nov. 2, 1993; interview with Milton Gould, Nov. 5, 1993. Despite the rift with his Graphic partner, in the summer of 1920 Abramson paid International Film Service $8,000 for the rental of the Cosmopolitan studios in New York and the loan of the film plant's carpenters and technicians while Hearst was shooting a picture in California. Hearst considered this "found money" since the studio was idle at the time. Subsequently, Abramson sued IFS, claiming that the company had not provided him with the level of studio assistance it had promised in their verbal agreement.

8. TRADER

Page 135. George Allison: George F. Allison, *Allison Calling* (London: Staples, 1948); interview with Jana Allison, Oct. 12, 1990; George Allison Papers, courtesy of Jana Allison.

Page 135. "There was a wild scramble: Allison, *Allison Calling*.

Page 136. Roger Casement: Various Hearst newspapers, Aug. 4–5, 1916.

Page 136. England boycotted the Hearst wire services: *Editor and Publisher*, Oct. 14, 1916, 7, and Oct. 21, 1916, 3.

Page 137. "ownership" of news: *International News Service vs. Associated Press*, 248 U.S. 215, 39 S. Ct. 68, Supreme Court of the United States, decided Dec. 23, 1918.

Page 137. a much wider arrangement: "War Gives U.S. $1,600,000 Trade Chance Says Maxim," *New York American*, Aug. 10, 1914; "The War, Sad as It Is, Means Marvelous Business Opportunity for the United States," signed editorial by WRH, *New York Evening*

Journal, Aug. 22, 1914. A 1918 Senate inquiry into German propaganda in the United States turned its attention to Hearst activities and disclosed correspondence between the publisher and Hale and others. These disclosures were widely reported by the press between October and December 1918. The December 14, 1918, issues of the *New York Sun* and the *New York Tribune* and the December 11, 1918, issue of the *New York Times* are particularly useful sources of information on this subject.

Page 137. "**View British news blockade**: *New York Tribune*, Dec. 14, 1918.

Page 137. "**Can perfect arrangements International News Service**: Ibid.

Page 137. **Ariel Varges**: "Around the World with an American Newsreel Camera Hero," *American Weekly* magazine, *New York American*, Jan. 27, 1924. The Imperial War Museum catalog lists Varges as the likely cameraman on twenty-nine films in their archive, ranging in length from a few minutes to nearly one hour. These films were produced by the International Film Service for the War Office Cinema Committee, Lord Beaverbrook's Ministry of Information, and the Topical Film Company. Roger Smither, of the Imperial War Museum (London, England) believes that it is unlikely that as an American Varges would have been given anything more than an honorary commission in the British Army. Nicholas Hiley, a writer on British intelligence and the British media during World War One, doubts that Varges was a captain in the British Army but acknowledges that he was engaged as the British Official Kinematographer. See Smither and Hiley to author, June 16, 1994; Terry Ramsaye, *A Million and One Nights* (New York: Simon and Schuster, Touchstone, 1986), 691; S. D. Badsey, "Battle of the Somme: British War-Propaganda," *Historical Journal of Film, Radio and Television* 3, no. 2 (1983): 111–12.

Page 138. **Thomas Lipton**: *NYT*, June 29, 1915; obituary, *NYT*, Oct. 3, 1931.

Page 138. **After "covering" the earthquake**: Edgar Hatrick, *New York American*, n.d.; newsreel clipping file, New York Public Library for the Performing Arts, NYC.

Page 138. "**I had to break**: Allison correspondence, Allison Papers.

Page 139. **The propaganda pictures**: Allison, *Allison Calling*.

Page 139. "**old faked-up junk**: "All War Pictures Fakes," *Moving Picture World*, Oct. 3, 1914, 50.

Page 140. "**We saw him no more**: Allison, *Allison Calling*.

Page 140. "**a crime against civilization**: *New York Evening Journal*, Aug. 22, 1914.

Page 140. **Maxim echoed Hearst's repeated calls**: "Germany Will Triumph, Is Belief of Hudson Maxim," *New York American*, Aug. 23, 1914; see also Aug. 10, 1914.

Page 141. "**Never before in the history**: *Moving Picture World*, Sept. 26, 1914, 1751.

Page 141. "**The men on the other side**: "Europe Hungry for Quality," *Moving Picture World*, July 27, 1914, 583.

Page 141. **The meeting was no secret**: Comments on the meeting between Hearst and Albert and correspondence between Hearst and von Bernstorff are in U.S. Senate, 66th Cong., 1st sess., doc. no. 62, *Brewing and Liquor Interests and German and Bolshevik Propaganda: Report and Hearings of the Subcommittee on the Judiciary, United States Senate*, vol. 2, 1919. Justice Department files on Hearst claim that his newsreel cameraman, A. E. Wallace, stayed with a contributing writer for the Hearst press named August F. Beach in Germany in 1917. According to the government's investigators, Beach was strongly pro-

German. Wallace reportedly left Hearst's employ in late 1917 (Bureau of Investigation files, Record Group 65, National Archives, Washington, D.C.). The Hearst papers reported that Hearst News Pictorial cameraman Nelson E. Edwards returned to the United States from Germany with "many thousands of feet of film" in early October 1916 after spending the past year on the German, Balkan, and French battlefields (*New York American*, Oct. 9, 1916).

Page 143. **A March 2 telegram**: U.S. Senate, *Brewing and Liquor Interests and German and Bolshevik Propaganda.*

Page 144. **rooftop swimming pool**: Interview with Robert and Spencer Samuels, July 8, 1993.

Page 144. **Deutschland Library**: *New York Tribune*, Dec. 14, 1918.

Page 145. **American Correspondent Film Company**: Ron van Dopperen, "Shooting the Great War: Albert Dawson and the American Correspondent Film Company, 1914–1918," *Film History* 4 (1990): 123–29; *New York World*, Aug. 15, 1915; *NYT*, July 16, 1918, 1; *The American Film Institute Catalog of Motion Pictures Produced in the United States: Feature Films, 1911–1920* (Berkeley: University of California Press, 1989). Edward Lytell Fox, in 1915 considered "a valued special contributor of war articles to the *New York American*" by that paper's publisher, was at the same time employed by the American Correspondent Film Company as a screenwriter and lecturer (*New York Tribune*, Dec. 14, 1918).

Page 145. **"As propaganda through pictures**: *New York Tribune*, Dec. 14, 1918.

Page 145. **an affinity with German propagandists**: Report of Dr. Karl Fuehr, Nov. 14, 1915, Military Intelligence Division, National Archives, Washington, D.C. Hearst appeared on the cover of *The Fatherland: Fair Play for Germany and Austria-Hungary* on July 14, 1915. The weekly was published in New York and edited by George Sylvester Viereck. Under Hearst's portrait appears this quote: "He led this country into one war— He has helped to keep us out of another." One of Hearst's correspondents with strong ties with Germany was Karl von Wiegand, who worked for the International News Service for several decades. According to ambassador to Berlin William Dodd, in the spring of 1918, anticipating a possible defeat to Germany, the U.S. State Department sent von Wiegand to Sweden and prepared him to negotiate for better terms with the high German officials that he knew well. The mission was canceled when the war took a turn in favor of the Allies (William E. Dodd to Franklin D. Roosevelt, Mar. 20, 1935, Dodd File, FDR Papers, Hyde Park, N.Y.). In his autobiography, Ambassador von Bernstorff wrote that he was close to Hearst because of his "neutral attitude throughout the war." He also acknowledged that he had "often visited Mr. Hearst" and that Dr. Fuehr wrote at least one article for the Hearst press (*My Three Years in America* [New York: Scribner's, 1920], 56, 195–96, 260–61).

Page 146. **A film rivalry**: John Wheeler, *I've Got News for You* (New York: Dutton, 1961), 197–98.

Page 146. **As the Senate investigation**: "Bielaski Says No Prosecution of Pro-Germans," *Buffalo Times*, ca. 1918.

Page 147. **Hearst was eagerly watching developments in Germany**: "America's

Returns Sent 200 Miles by Wireless Telephone," *New York American*, Nov. 8, 1916, 5; "Radio Shows How British Distort News," Nov. 15, 1916, 1.

Page 147. **"first Wireless Telephone Newspaper"**: *New York American*, Nov. 9, 1916, 4.

9. THE PERILS OF PROPAGANDA

Page 148. **The Yanks Are Coming**: *NYT*, June 24, 1918, 1; June 25, 1918, 24; June 26, 1918, 7; June 28, 1918, 6; June 29, 1918, 6; *New York American*, June 24, 1918.

Page 148. **James M. Sheen**: *NYT*, June 24, 1918.

Page 148. **"Creel Committee"**: Stephen Vaughn, *Holding Fast the Inner Lines* (Chapel Hill: University of North Carolina Press, 1980); George Creel, *How We Advertised America* (New York: Harper, 1920); Cedric Larson, *Words that Won the War: The Story of the Committee on Public Information, 1917–1919* (Princeton: Princeton University Press, 1939); Raymond Fielding, *The American Newsreel, 1911–1967* (Norman: University of Oklahoma, 1972); Charles Hart obituary, *NYT*, Jan. 26, 1951; Roy L. McCardell, "George Creel, the Story of a Live Wire," *New York Morning Telegraph*, May 1, 1921; Woodrow Wilson Papers, Library of Congress, Washington, D.C.; Timothy J. Lyons, "Hollywood and World War I, 1914–1918," *Journal of Popular Film* (winter 1972): 15; Joe Hubbell taped memoirs, author's collection.

Page 149. **"very Western in his**: George Creel, *Rebel at Large: Recollections of Fifty Crowded Years* (New York: Putnam, 1947).

Page 150. **he oversaw the film division's reorganization**: Hubbell memoirs.

Page 151. **"Our idea was to make up**: Hubbell memoirs.

Page 152. **"Out of the entire industry**: *NYT*, June 19, 1918, 9.

Page 152. **Hearst describes himself as "greatly disturbed"**: WRH to George Creel, Mar. 13, 1918, CPI Records, National Archives. See Larry Wayne Ward, *The Motion Picture Goes to War: The U.S. Government Effort During World War I* (Ann Arbor, Mich.: UMI Research, 1985).

Page 153. **[Creel] is so completely under Hearst's control**: *NYT*, June 24, 1918. In 1931 movie moguls Samuel Goldwyn, Irving Thalberg, Benjamin P. Schulberg, Winfield Sheehan, and Jesse Lasky proposed that movie czar Will Hays oversee what Thalberg called a "bureau of public information" in Hollywood. Their purpose was to coordinate contacts with government officials and to respond effectively to bad publicity. The movie men wanted "to clean up or sweeten up" the press so that it would be more inclined to create "constructive publicity." Hays had made public relations a top priority from the start, but it is unknown whether such a specific bureau was organized or what direct role Hearst might have played. See memorandum from Maurice McKenzie to Will H. Hays, Sept. 3, 1931, Will Hays Papers, Indiana State Library, Indianapolis.

Page 153. **the most modern form of presentation**: "Beatrice Fairfax to Be Serial," *Motion Picture Mail*, July 30, 1916.

Page 154. **"the Japanese stuff"**: *NYT*, Dec. 14, 1918; *New York Tribune*, Dec. 14, 1918; Howard Hall, "Hearst: War Maker," *Harper's Weekly*, Nov. 6, 1915, 436; "Jap-German Alliance to Build New Yellow Empire Is Advocated," *New York American*, Aug. 6, 1916.

Page 154. **Fox wrote a memorandum to Captain Fritz von Papen:** U.S. Senate, 66th Cong., 1st sess., doc. no. 62, *Brewing and Liquor Interests and German and Bolshevik Propaganda: Report and Hearings of the Subcommittee on the Judiciary, United States Senate,* vol. 2, 1919.

Page 155. **Production on Patria commenced:** Hearst traveled West to oversee the production of *Patria* during its shoot in Los Angeles. See *Moving Picture World,* Dec. 30, 1916, 1948; *Patria* and Irene Castle clipping files, New York Public Library for the Performing Arts, NYC.

Page 155. **A 1917 magazine article:** Samuel Hopkins Adams, "Invaded America," *Everybody's Magazine,* Dec. 1917, 9–16, 86.

Page 155. **"the film we consider most essential":** WRH to Will Bradley, n.d. (ca. late 1916), Will Bradley Papers, Archives of American Art, New York City Research Center.

Page 155. **According to William Randolph Hearst Jr.:** Interview with William Randolph Hearst Jr., Apr. 6, 1989.

Page 156. **"Fortunately," Castle would write:** Irene Castle, *Castles in the Air* (New York: Da Capo/Plenum, 1980).

Page 156. **a young business manager named Walter Wanger:** Bernard Rosenberg and Harry Silverstein, *The Real Tinsel* (New York: Macmillan, 1970), 82.

Page 156. **footage of the Ziegfeld Follies:** On Hearst's specific instructions, the Follies sequence was filmed at the New Amsterdam Theatre's roof garden in late November 1916. See Leonard Wharton to E. A. McManus, Nov. 17, 1916. Wharton Brothers Collection, Cornell University Libraries, Ithaca, N.Y.

Page 156. **"retakes and improvements":** WRH to Will Bradley, n.d., Bradley Papers.

Page 158. **In the foreword:** *New York Evening Journal,* Nov. 21, 1916.

Page 158. **Possibly your attention:** William Redfield to Woodrow Wilson, June 1, 1917, Woodrow Wilson Papers (hereafter, WW Papers), Library of Congress, Washington, D.C.

Page 158. **Several times in attending:** WW to J. A. Berst, June 4, 1917, WW Papers.

Page 159. **"several scenes portraying Japanese:** J. A. Berst to WW, June 8, 1917, WW Papers.

Page 159. **Polk claimed that he:** Frank L. Polk to WW, June 12, 1917, WW Papers.

Page 159. **modifications were still "inadequate":** Polk to WW, Aug. 11, 1917, WW Papers.

Page 160. **International Film Service had called a conference:** Berst to WW, Aug. 16, 1917, WW Papers.

Page 160. **We make these changes at any cost:** Grenville MacFarland to WW, Aug. 23, 1917, WW Papers.

Page 160. **"engenders ill feeling:** Robert Lansing to Joseph P. Tumulty, Sept. 1, 1917, WW Papers.

Page 161. **"Apropos our recent conversation:** MacFarland to WW, Sept. 21, 1917, WW Papers.

Page 161. **"I confess myself very much mixed up:** WW to Tumulty, n.d. (ca. late Sept. 1917), WW Papers.

Page161. **"Please intimate to the Department of State:** WW to Tumulty, Oct. 1, 1917, WW Papers.

Page 161. **"I hate substituting nationalities:** Hatrick's reference to *Patria* was made during negotiations with novelist Peter Kyne concerning the "talking rights" for *Pride of Palomar* (E. B. Hatrick to Peter B. Kyne, Feb. 16, 1937, Peter Kyne Papers, University of Oregon, Eugene). Hearst's animosity toward Japan continued over the years. According to a January 20, 1920, memo in the War Department file on Hearst, representatives of Japanese interests in the United States approached the publisher in October or November 1919, offering him $3 million to carry pro-Japanese propaganda in his newspapers. The memorandum indicates that Hearst refused the offer (165 War Department, MID, National Archives). After Pearl Harbor was attacked, Hearst reminded his readers of *Patria*'s early warning about Japanese aggression; see "Japs Failed to Stop This Prophetic Movie," *San Francisco Examiner,* May 17, 1942.

10. FITS AND STARTS

Page 162. **It may only have been:** Confidential report, Nov. 30, 1917, and letter from Robert Goldstein to M. F. Ihmsen, Apr. 19, 1917, in letter from Assistant U.S. Attorney Palmer to U.S. Attorney J. Robert O'Connor, June 17, 1918; *The Spirit of '76* photoplay, Robert Goldstein, MID File, Record Group 165, National Archives.

Page 164. **Despite the fact that Hearst's actions:** *NYT,* May 16, 13; May 26, 1918, 26; May 27, 1918, 22.

Page 164. **Liberty Loan posters:** *New York Evening Journal,* Apr. 10, 1918.

Page 164. **America's Answer:** *Wid's Daily,* July 31, 1918.

Page 164. **films of soldier's families:** *Wid's Daily,* Oct. 16 and 23, 1918.

Page 165. **"We note by the HEARST:** James Gerard Papers, Mansfield Library, University of Montana, Missoula.

Page 165. **"the foundation of our success:** Harry Warner to James Gerard, Jan. 7, 1924, Gerard Papers.

Page 166. **"desperately in love":** Interview with Mrs. Anne Flint, research notes for *Citizen Hearst,* William S. Swanberg Papers, Columbia University.

Page 166. **"May I be a mother:** Marion Davies, *The Times We Had: Life with William Randolph Hearst,* ed. Pamela Pfau and Kenneth S. Marx (Indianapolis: Bobbs-Merrill, 1975).

Page 166. **Anita Loos:** Anita Loos, *Kiss Hollywood Good-by* (New York: Viking, 1974), 142.

Page 166. **chaperones:** Gretl Urban to author, Oct. 24, 1991.

Page 167. **"Phoebe said she felt:** Interview with Anne Flint.

Page 169. **Burden of Proof:** Clipping file, New York Public Library for the Performing Arts, NYC; Fred Lawrence Guiles, *Marion Davies* (New York: McGraw-Hill, 1972); *Wid's Daily,* Sept. 8, 1918.

Page 169. **Hearst treated his newsreels:** *New York American,* Sept. 13, 1916; Sept. 5, 1916; Dec. 2, 1916; Aug. 13, 1916.

Page 170. "**This letter will be presented**: *New York American,* Aug. 13, 1916.

Page 170. **The Belle of New York**: *Wid's Daily,* Nov. 1, 1918.

Page 171. **Knowing of Hearst's king complex**: Terry Ramsaye, *A Million and One Nights* (New York: Simon and Schuster, Touchstone, 1986); *Wid's Daily,* Nov. 6, 1918.

Page 172. **[They] conceived the idea of combining**: Ivan Abramson, *Mother of Truth* (New York: Graphic Literary, 1929).

Page 173. **His point man in this inquiry**: Walter W. Irwin testimony before Federal Trade Commission investigation of Famous Players–Lasky, FTC, Washington, D.C.; "Mrs. Tovey Is Bride of Walter W. Irwin," *New York American,* Feb. 22, 1914, 3; *Motography,* Jan. 22, 1916, 178.

Page 173. **Paramount could destroy**: Irwin testimony before FTC.

Page 174. **lead counsel to the Thomas A. Edison Company**: *Wid's Daily,* Nov. 10, 1918; Gertrude Jobes, *Motion Picture Empire* (Hamden, Conn.: Archon, 1966).

Page 174. **"It seemed to me that something**: Adolph Zukor clipping file, New York Public Library for the Performing Arts, NYC.

Page 175. **Zukor sent Walter Irwin**: *Variety,* Apr. 18, 1919; *Moving Picture World,* Feb. 1, 1919.

Page 175. **Zit Jr.**: On April 16, 1919, Carl Zittel Jr. died suddenly. He was nineteen years old. In the 1930s, long after Zittel Sr. had severed his ties to Hearst's film company, he ran a theatrical newspaper called *Zit's* that was said to be partially financed by Hearst. For the anniversary of his son's death, Zittel published a large page one "memoriam" photograph of Zit Jr. See Will Gordon, "Broadway Wings, His Last Press Notice, C. F. Zittel, 'Zit,' " *New York Morning Telegraph,* ca. 1943, Carl Zittel clipping file, New York Public Library for the Performing Arts, NYC; *Zit's,* Apr. 19, 1930, 1.

Page 175. **"Hearst was very fond**: Interview with Eugene Zukor, Jan. 13, 1994.

Page 176. **"pornographer"**: Ibid.

Page 176. **Soon after the turn of 1919**: *Wid's Daily,* Jan. 23, 1919. The quotations from Zukor and Zittel Sr. are found in this source.

Page 176. **"Naturally have heard**: Ibid., 1.

Page 177. **formed United Artists**: *Variety,* Feb. 7, 1919; Benjamin Hampton, *A History of the American Film Industry: From Its Beginnings to 1931* (1931; reprint, New York: Dover, 1970); Richard Koszarski, *An Evening's Entertainment: The Age of the Silent Feature Picture, 1915–1928,* vol. 3 of *History of the American Cinema* (New York: Charles Scribner's Sons, 1990), 77–78.

Page 177. **"The lunatics**: Attributed to Richard Rowland, head of Metro Pictures Corporation, in Ramsaye, *A Million and One Nights,* 795.

Page 177. **"determined not to permit**: *Variety,* Feb. 7, 1919.

Page 177. **"Ivan Abramson is so**: *Wid's Daily,* Feb. 2, 1919.

Page 177. **After much persuasion**: Abramson, *Mother of Truth.*

Page 178. **"The specials produced**: *Variety,* Mar. 12, 1919.

Page 178. **The deal between Hearst and Zukor**: *Wid's Daily,* Mar. 13 and 15, 1919; *Variety,* Mar. 14, 1919, 53; Mar. 21, 1919, 57.

Page 178. **Personally, I am**: *Variety,* June 6, 1919, 57.

11. OVER PRODUCTION

Page 179. "**What would I get**: Interview with Mrs. Anne Flint, research notes for *Citizen Hearst*, W. S. Swanberg Papers, Columbia University.

Page 180. **the end was coming**: Judith Robinson, *The Hearsts: An American Dynasty* (Newark: University of Delaware Press, 1991).

Page 181. "**closer to her**: Vonnie Eastham interview, 1977, Oral History, California State University, Chico.

Page 181. "**Rosebud**": Ibid.

Page 182. **The biographical motion picture**: Kevin Brownlow, *Behind the Mask of Innocence* (New York: Knopf, 1990).

Page 182. "**the enthusiastic patronage**: Broadside in James Gerard Papers, Mansfield Library, University of Montana, Missoula.

Page 183. "**practically motion pictures**: Brooks McNamara, "Owen Davis and the Shubert Brothers," *The Passing Show: Newsletter of the Shubert Archive* (spring 1995): 2–6.

Page 183. "**plenty of things**: Owen Davis, *My First Fifty Years in the Theatre* (Boston: Baker, 1950), 36–37.

Page 183. "**a genuine political melodrama**: *New York Dramatic Mirror*, Sept. 1, 1906.

Page 184. **The Pathé release, "Enemies Within"**: "Hearst Objection Prevails," *Variety*, Feb. 7, 1919, 64.

Page 185. **The story is laid Washington**: Review, possibly Hartford, Conn., newspapers, n.d. (ca. Aug. 20, 1918), clippings, New York Public Library for the Performing Arts, NYC.

Page 185. **a financial backer**: *Variety*, Mar. 12, 1915.

Page 186. "**Glorifying the American Girl**": On the Follies as icon, see Linda Mizejewski, *Ziegfeld Girl* (Durham, N.C.: Duke University Press, 1999); Fred Lawrence Guiles, *Marion Davies* (New York: McGraw-Hill, 1972).

Page 186. **Anna Held**: John Winkler, *Hearst: An American Phenomenon* (New York: Simon and Schuster, 1928), 108.

Page 186. "**Yellow Fellow**" **race**: *New York Journal*, Sept. 3–25, 1896.

Page 187. **Hearst hired Joseph Urban**: Interviews with Gretl Urban; Randolph Carter and Robert Cole, *Joseph Urban: Architecture, Theater, Opera, Film* (New York: Abbeville, 1992).

Page 187. **The Cabinet of Dr. Caligari**: Interview with Gretl Urban.

Page 189. **River's End**: *New York American*, Feb. 22–25, 1920; James Oliver Curwood Papers, 1918–1920, Bentley Historical Library, University of Michigan, Ann Arbor.

Page 189. "**We are, as Brisbane**: WRH to Carl Zittel, May 31, 1919, Joseph A. Moore Papers, Manuscripts Division, Library of Congress, Washington, D.C.

Page 190. "**to make sure that**: Moore Papers.

Page 190. **International Story Company**: Incorporation records, Municipal Archives, NYC; *Variety*, Feb. 18, 1921, 45; Raymond Gardner to William Swanberg, Nov. 23, 1967, Swanberg Papers.

Page 191. "**the inventory was**: Gardner to Swanberg, Nov. 23, 1967.

Page 191. **Authors' League of America**: On the Authors' League controversy, see *New York Tribune*, Feb. 26, 1921; *NYT*, Feb. 26, 1921, 14; Feb. 27, 1921, 5; Feb. 28, 1921, 10; Mar. 1, 1921, 7; Mar. 2, 1921, 8.

Page 191. **William Randolph Hearst, being duly assembled**: *NYT*, Feb. 27, 1921, clipping, Authors' Guild archives, NYC.

Page 192. **Editor Long sent the league**: Various clippings from the *Authors' League Bulletin*, July 1921, Authors' Guild archives.

Page 192. **Allan Dwan**: William Randolph Hearst to Joseph Moore, Apr. 23, 1919; Apr. 26, 1919; Apr. 27, 1919; JAM to WRH, Apr. 24, 1919, Moore Papers.

Page 193. **"sleight-of-hand"**: WRH to JAM, June 30, 1921, Moore Papers.

Page 194. **massive theater expansion**: For a firsthand account of this expansion, see Walter W. Irwin's testimony in Federal Trade Commission complaint against Famous Players–Lasky, Aug. 30, 1921, FTC Archives, Washington, D.C.

Page 194. **"to create for said organization**: FTC complaint against FPL.

Page 195. **Curiosity is existent**: *Variety*, Sept. 23, 1921, 45.

Page 195. **Variety seemed to be implying**: *Variety*, Feb. 1, 1923, 47.

Page 196. **Humoresque**: Brownlow, *Behind the Mask*; Frances Marion, *Off with Their Heads!* (New York: Macmillan, 1972).

Page 196. **"to prove to the exhibitor**: WRH to George Van Cleve, June 17, 1921, WRH Papers, Bancroft Library, University of California, Berkeley.

Page 196. **Zukor placed a plea for support**: *Exhibitors Herald*, June 18, 1921, 6–7.

Page 198. **the prostitutes at Kennedy's place**: David A. Yallop, *The Day the Laughter Stopped: The True Story of Fatty Arbuckle* (London: Hodder and Stoughton, 1976).

Page 198. **Herbert Hoover as head of a proposed organization**: *NYT*, Dec. 9, 1921, 17.

Page 198. **Zukor and Hays would continue to meet**: Hays diary, courtesy of Will Hays Jr.; Kenneth Crawford, *The Pressure Boys* (New York: Julian Messner, 1939); Janet Wasko, *Movies and Money: Financing the American Film Industry* (Norwood: Ablex, 1982); Ivan Abramson, *Mother of Truth* (New York: Graphic Literary, 1929).

Page 198. **"finance king of films"**: "H. B. Rosen, Finance King of Films, Dies," *Variety*, Jan. 12, 1923.

Page 199. **I called today on Lewis J. Selznick**: Robert G. Tucker to Will Hays, Aug. 17, 1920, Will Hays Papers, Indiana State Library, Indianapolis.

Page 200. **Hays's life had been insured**: *NYT*, Jan. 16, 1922.

Page 200. **a late dinner at Delmonico's**: *NYT*, Jan. 19, 1922.

Page 200. **"love feast"**: Will H. Hays, *The Memoirs of Will H. Hays* (Garden City, N.Y.: Doubleday, 1955).

Page 201. **the dinner for Hays**: Hays, *Memoirs*; *New York American*, Mar. 17, 1922.

Page 202. **Hearst made a series of telephone calls**: *Variety*, Oct. 13, 1922.

Page 203. **"Battle of the Hoods"**: *Variety*, Sept. 29, 1922.

Page 203. **"the opening of the 'Knighthood'**: *Variety*, Oct. 20, 1922.

Page 203. **"the best bet**: *Variety*, Sept. 22, 1922.

Page 203. **the total cost of the film**: Linda Arvidson, *When the Movies Were Young*

(New York: Dutton, 1925). D. W. Griffith was apparently fond of Hearst and his methods. He once wrote that "the moving picture is simply the pictorial press" ("The Rise and Fall of Free Speech," 1916 pamphlet in response to criticism of *Birth of a Nation*). He visited San Simeon on at least one occasion in 1936. Griffith home movies taken at Hearst's castle are at the Museum of Modern Art.

Page 203. **"is figured to top:** *Variety*, Nov. 3, 1922.

Page 204. **Exhibitors who had balked at Zukor:** *Variety*, Nov. 17, 1922.

Page 204. **A Hearst paper in Boston:** *Variety*, Oct. 20, 1922.

Page 204. **When Electric Light Was in Power:** *Variety*, Nov. 24, 1922.

Page 204. **"about special publicity:** WRH to JAM, Oct. 6, 1921, Moore Papers.

Page 205. **"to comply with Paramount's:** WRH to JAM, Oct. 14, 1921, Moore Papers.

Page 205. **Moore suggested that Hearst allow Paramount:** JAM to WRH, Oct. 14, 1921, Moore Papers.

Page 205. **"vehemently opposed and unwilling:** WRH to JAM, Oct. 15. 1921, Moore Papers.

Page 205. **"Advertising in our paper:** WRH to JAM, Oct. 21, 1921, Moore Papers.

Page 205. **"I thought I made clear:** WRH to JAM, Nov. 7, 1921, Moore Papers.

Page 206. **"utterly emasculated":** WRH to JAM, Nov. 12, 1921, Moore Papers.

Page 206. **Hearst told Moore to retain:** WRH to JAM, Nov. 12, 1921, Moore Papers.

Page 206. **"interference from anyone":** Ibid.

12. FIRE AND SMOKE

Page 207. **"Your January 24 letter:** John Eastman to Will Hays, John Eastman, Jan. 27, 1923, Will Hays Papers, Indiana State Library, Indianapolis.

Page 207. **Davies was forced to halt work:** *Variety*, Feb. 8, 1923.

Page 208. **The film was ready for release:** *Moving Picture World*, June 9, 1923.

Page 208. **"or some such concern:** William Randolph Hearst to Joseph Moore, Dec. 22, 1922; see also WRH to JAM, Jan. 7, 1923; Goldwyn contract draft, ca. Dec. 1922, Joseph A. Moore Papers, Manuscripts Division, Library of Congress, Washington, D.C.

Page 208. **Lord Beaverbrook:** Scott A. Berg, *Goldwyn* (New York: Knopf, 1989); John Tebbel, *The Life and Good Times of William Randolph Hearst* (New York: Dutton, 1952); Piers Breddon, *The Life and Death of the Press Barons* (New York: Atheneum, 1983).

Page 209. **"one of the great American:** *NYT*, Aug. 15, 1951.

Page 209. **According to Arthur Brisbane:** Brisbane-Beaverbrook correspondence in Beaverbrook Papers, House of Lords, London.

Page 209. **During the last year:** *Variety*, Feb. 22, 1923, 47.

Page 209. **"Understand 'Yolanda':** WRH to JAM, July 25, 1923, Moore Papers.

Page 210. **I was thrilled:** Unpublished manuscript by Everett Shinn, Archives of American Art, Smithsonian Institute, NYC.

Page 211. **an entire American film troupe:** *New York American*, Nov. 5, 1922. See *New York American*, Mar. 25, 28, and 29, 1923.

Page 211. **in the Wiener Werkstätte style**: "One Thousand Viennese Artists Show Their Work," *NYT*, June 14, 1922. Gretl Urban believed that Hearst was helpful to her father in setting up a branch of the Wiener Werkstätte in New York, greatly influencing the spread of the design movement to the United States (interviews with Urban).

Page 211. **Hearst planned to spend $25,000**: *Variety*, Mar. 22, 1923, 22.

Page 211. **"Urban will use**: *New York American*, Mar. 25, 1923.

Page 211. **Unseeing Eyes**: Capitol Theater program, Dec. 1923, author's collection.

Page 211. **the only trouble on the shoot**: Interview with Urban.

Page 212. **"Motion picture fans**: *Nth Commandment* press book, New York Public Library for the Performing Arts, NYC.

Page 212. **constructed with a ceiling**: *New York American*, Mar. 11, 1923.

Page 213. **"The public has been played**: *Moving Picture World*, June 2, 1923.

Page 213. **"No phase of tense interest"**: *Moving Picture World*, June 16, 1923.

Page 213. **The three-page document**: Godsol statement, ca. Oct. 1923, Hays Papers.

Page 214. **In his correspondence with Joseph Moore**: Moore Papers.

Page 215. **luncheon at the Hotel Astor**: *New York American*, Jan. 30, 1924.

Page 216. **"Too Much Hearst"**: *Variety*, Feb. 28, 1924, 16.

Page 216. **"Negotiations for the purchase**: Nicholas Schenck to Bosley Crowther, n.d., Bosley Crowther Papers, Brigham Young University, Provo, Utah.

Page 217. **"There is an enormous advantage**: *Exhibitors Herald*, Jan. 26, 1924.

Page 217. **Hearst was an unofficial board member**: Charles Higham, *Merchant of Dreams: Louis B. Mayer, M.G.M., and the Secret Hollywood* (New York: Fine, 1993).

Page 218. **To publicize Janice Meredith**: *Variety*, Apr. 16, 1924, 18.

Page 218. **"actresses or others"**: *Variety*, June 4, 1924, 25.

Page 218. **keeping Hearst's involvement with MGM unofficial**: Higham, *Merchant of Dreams*; Bosley Crowther, *Hollywood Rajah* (New York: Holt, 1960); David Nasaw, *The Chief* (New York: Houghton Mifflin, 1999); Samuel Marx, *Mayer and Thalberg: The Make-Believe Saints* (New York: French, 1988). Gertrude Jobes writes that Marcus Loew was particularly eager to have Hearst as a partner in the MGM deal, because he hoped the publisher would editorialize against monopolies and thereby aid the FTC and Justice Department in their attempt to break up Zukor's Paramount (Jobes, *Motion Picture Empire* [Hamden, Conn.: Archon, 1966], 248).

Page 219. **an adobe-style camp house**: *Variety*, June 25, 1924, 1; interview with Gretl Urban.

Page 219. **We fade out on Mamie**: WRH to Marion Davies, Sept. 8, 1924, Fred Lawrence Guiles Collection.

Page 219. **"Just waded through**: WRH to MD, Nov. 6, 1924, Guiles Collection.

Page 220. **"You're running around**: WRH to MD, n.d. (ca. Nov. 1924), Guiles Collection.

Page 220. **"I had a talk**: WRH to MD, n.d. (ca. Nov. 1924), Guiles Collection.

Page 220. **"So, they planned**: Elinor Ince to George Pratt, reprinted in *The Silent Picture*, no. 6 (spring 1970).

Page 220. **the Oneida spelled luxury**: Interview with Mrs. Dean Goodsell, Oct. 10,

1996. Mrs. Goodsell was the daughter-in-law of the man who purchased the *Oneida* from Hearst. In the early 1930s she took many trips on the yacht, and today she still possesses china and furniture from the *Oneida* dating back to Hearst's time.

Page 222. **a legend of Hollywood's "unsolved mysteries"**: interview with Gretl Urban; *NewYork Daily News*, Nov. 20–21, 1924; *Morning Telegraph*, Nov. 20, 1924; telegram, WRH to MD, circa Nov. 22, 1924, private collection.

Page 223. **demands that Hearst be charged**: Hearst FBI files; interview with children of Aimee McPherson, Aug. 3, 1993.

Page 223. **at least two medical personnel**: *NYT*, Dec. 11, 1924, 6.

Page 223. **alleged to have been rum-running**: U.S. Department of Justice, Classified Subject Case File 23–11–57 for *United States vs. the* Skedaddle; Dorothy M. Brown, *Mabel Walker Willebrandt: A Study of Power, Loyalty, and Law* (Knoxville: University of Tennessee Press, 1984); Higham, *Merchant of Dreams*; interview with Mrs. Joseph Willicombe, Sept. 23, 1993.

Page 224. **"Have considered matter**: WRH to MD, Nov. 28, 1924, private collection.

Page 224. **FBO**: Colleen Moore interview, 1972, edited by Robert C. Pavlik, Hearst San Simeon State Historical Monument, oral history project, California Department of Parks and Recreation, San Simeon Region, San Simeon, Calif.

Page 224. **Hearst fired director Clarence Badger**: *Variety*, Nov. 26, 1924.

Page 225. **he cut some 140,000 feet**: *Variety*, Dec. 3, 1924.

Page 225. **"W. R. Hearst Quits Movies"**: *Variety*, Dec. 17, 1924; see also Mar. 4, 1925.

Page 225. **permanent move to Hollywood**: *Variety*, Mar. 18, 1925.

Page 226. **Chickie**: *Variety*, Mar. 25, 1925.

Page 226. **a lavish dinner party**: Gardner to Swanberg, Nov. 23, 1967.

Page 226. **the $20,000 bungalow**: *Variety*, Mar. 4 and Apr. 1, 1925.

Page 226. **When Hearst got his first newspapers**: Quoted in Gary Carey, *All the Stars in Heaven* (New York: Dutton, 1981).

Page 227. **I had a long talk**: Arthur Brisbane to WRH, Nov. 19, 1926, WRH Papers, Bancroft Library, University of California, Berkeley.

Page 227. **"Of all my father's friends**: Irene Mayer Selznick, *A Private View* (New York: Knopf, 1983).

Page 228. **"Received your interesting wire**: Louis B. Mayer to WRH, Oct. 1, 1927, WRH Papers.

Page 228. **"Gosh man don't you realize**: WRH to Louis B. Mayer, Oct. 7, 1927, WRH Papers.

Page 228. **"I didn't select this story**: WRH to MD, n.d., in Marx, *Mayer and Thalberg*, 90.

Page 228. **"The play had been a failure**: Ibid.

Page 228. **"Mayer moved quickly**: Ibid.

Page 229. **Cosmopolitan productions were at the forefront**: Donald Crafton, *The Talkies: American Cinema's Transition to Sound, 1926–1931* (Berkeley: University of California Press, 1999).

Page 229. **"unless he was permitted**: *Variety*, Mar. 4, 1925.

13. INDUSTRY

Page 230. **The grainy photographic image of Davies:** *New York American,* Apr. 19, 1925.

Page 230. **"inexpensive information:** *New York American,* May 8, 1925.

Page 231. **He had worked tirelessly with Nick Schenck:** Valeria Belletti to "Irma," Apr. 23, 1925, Belletti Papers, Academy of Motion Picture Arts and Sciences Library, Los Angeles.

Page 231. **"all of the reliable bootleggers:** Ibid.

Page 231. **"Sunday the New York 'Graphic':** *Variety,* Aug. 19, 1925.

Page 232. **"a series of exquisitely:** Sara Holmes Boutelle, *Julia Morgan, Architect* (New York, Abbeville, 1988); see also Victoria Kastner, *Hearst Castle* (New York: Abrams, 2000). In addition to its recreational attractions, San Simeon was a center of film business. When the actor Charles Bickford complained to Irving Thalberg about having to travel to San Simeon in order to be considered for a Cosmopolitan picture in 1930, the MGM producer warned him about insulting Hearst. "It happens to be the way Hearst operates," Thalberg said. "And it's a pleasant way of doing business." Bickford went to San Simeon, but after he dismissed a film story Hearst was interested in producing, he was escorted from the estate by two pistol-carrying roughnecks. See Charles Bickford, *Bulls, Balls, Bicycles, and Actors* (New York: Ericksson, 1965), 241.

Page 232. **"in a respectable neighborhood":** Will H. Hays, *The Memoirs of Will H. Hays* (Garden City, N.Y.: Doubleday, 1955). See correspondence with Georganne Scheiner, Nov. 11, 2000. For the history of the Hollywood Studio Club, see Registration for Historical Places, U.S. Department of the Interior.

Page 232. **"Coast-to-Coast party":** *New York American,* Apr. 19, 1925.

Page 232. **appeared as extras in the Hearst film:** *New York American,* July 26, 1925.

Page 233. **"Movie Star Spoon":** *New York American,* Sept. 24, 1925.

Page 233. **"nationality is no bar:** Bosley Crowther, *Hollywood Rajah: The Life and Times of Louis B. Mayer* (New York: Holt, 1960), 126.

Page 233. **Davies was enlisted to hold a private screening:** *New York American,* Sept. 20, 1925.

Page 234. **"Mount Vernon by the sea":** Helen Hayes, quoted in Aaron Latham, *Crazy Sundays* (New York: Viking, 1971).

Page 234. **"a newspaper of the screen":** *Moving Picture World,* Mar. 13, 1927.

Page 234. **The eclipse special:** *Moving Picture World,* Feb. 7, 1925.

Page 235. **"Impressed by the remarkable:** *New York American,* July 26, 1925.

Page 236. **Pommer immediately began:** Oscar Solbert to Will Hays, June 4, 1925, and July 2, 1925, Will Hays Papers, Indiana State Library, Indianapolis.

Page 237. **"What astonishes me most:** Oscar Solbert to Will Hays, July 2, 1925, Hays Papers.

Page 237. **As I recall it:** Nicholas Schenck to Bosley Crowther, Bosley Crowther Papers, Brigham Young University, Provo, Utah.

Page 238. **he was intimidating:** *Variety,* Aug. 26, 1925, 1; *NYT,* July 15, 1925; Jane Ardmore, *The Self-Enchanted* (New York: McGraw-Hill, 1959), 162–64.

Page 238. **During dinner:** Ardmore, *The Self-Enchanted*, 162–64.

Page 239. **Hollywood's deference to Germany:** *Daily Worker*, Jan. 1, 1941; Charles Higham, *Merchant of Dreams: Louis B. Mayer, M.G.M., and the Secret Hollywood* (New York: Fine, 1993); Andrew Bergman, *We're In the Money: Depression America and Its Films* (New York: Harper Colophon, 1971); *Motion Picture Herald*, Aug. 8 and Sept. 12, 1936.

Page 240. **"Have following cable:** Than Vanneman Rank to William Randolph Hearst, box 4, folder 57, Than Vanneman Rank Papers, Sterling Memorial Library, Yale University.

Page 240. **the first motion picture to cross the ocean by air:** Lion's Share Research files, ca. Oct. 1928, Crowther Papers.

Page 241. **Hartman has been on the huge dirigible:** *Exhibitors' Herald-World*, Sept. 7, 1929. See also John Tebbel, *The Life and Good Times of William Randolph Hearst* (New York: Dutton, 1952); Cora Older, *William Randolph Hearst, American* (New York: Appleton Century, 1936).

Page 242. **Homer Watters:** Interview with Homer Watters, research notes for William S. Swanberg Papers, Columbia University.

Page 242. **"father of radio":** Robert W. Desmond, *Windows on the World: World News Reporting, 1900–1920* (Ames: Iowa State University Press, 1981).

Page 243. **businessmen such as Martin Egan:** Martin Egan papers (including those related to Phonofilm), Pierpont Morgan Library, NYC.

Page 243. **To enhance prospects for Phonofilm:** "King Guests to Hear Talk by Coolidge," *New York American*, Apr. 19, 1925; "Coolidge Speaks in Talking Picture," *NYT*, Apr. 22, 1925; " 'Talking Film' Radios Coolidge's Address," *New York American*, Apr. 22, 1925; "Shade and Voice of Coolidge at Annual 'Lark,' " *Editor and Publisher*, Apr. 25, 1925; "Garden Lark Loads of Fun for 500 Visiting Editors," *New York American*, Apr. 26, 1927. John Grierson, the critic and filmmaker who had kind words to say about Hearst's pictorial journalism in 1925 (see chapter 2), was less enthusiastic about Phonofilm. "But even though the phonofilm progresses beyond the empty metallic tone of its present-day stage . . . it is doubtful if the future will look for the thin voice of Chaplin or the presumable bass of Wallace Beery. The screen has a value of its own art, and that value would disappear if its silence were violated" (John Grierson, "An Appreciation of the Silence of the Silent Drama," *New York Sun*, Sept. 22, 1925).

Page 244. **"The address you will hear:** *Editor and Publisher*, Apr. 25, 1925.

Page 244. **he came in for public ridicule:** "Talking Pictures Speak Their Praise," advertisement for Phonofilm, *New York American*, Mar. 8, 1925; Lee De Forest to E. T. Clark, May 7, 1925, Calvin Coolidge Papers, Library of Congress, Washington, D.C.; Department of Justice memorandum regarding use of Coolidge Phonofilm to promote sale of stock, J. Edgar Hoover to Attorney General, May 9, 1925, Coolidge Papers.

Page 245. **Smith was also keenly aware of developments:** Courtland Smith obituary, *NYT*, Aug. 13, 1970; correspondence with Rita McCaffrey, Courtland Smith clipping file, New York Public Library for the Performing Arts, NYC.

Page 245. **"If Fiction is Truth's:** Motion Picture Producers and Distributors of America press release, July 24, 1926, Hays Papers.

Page 246. **"In our news reels**: Lucius Beebe, "The Man Who Edits the News Reels," n.d., Smith clipping file.

Page 246. **Smith sent Hays a memorandum**: Courtland Smith to Will Hays, Jan. 27, 1926, Hays Papers.

Page 246. **"it is the one thing**: Coolidge Papers.

Page 246. **An Oneida yacht trip**: *NYT*, July 3, 1927; Calvin Coolidge to Will Hays, June 28, 1927, Coolidge Papers.

Page 247. **"Will you please ask**: Will Hays to Calvin Coolidge's secretary, June 28, 1927, Coolidge Papers.

Page 247. **"It makes matters difficult**: Will Hays to Everett Sanders (President Coolidge's secretary), July 5, 1927, Coolidge Papers.

Page 247. **"George Christian probable successor**: Courtland Smith to Will Hays, Jan. 17, 1924, Hays Papers. See *NYT*, Jan. 17, 1924, 5; Jan. 22, 1924, 32; Feb. 17, 1924, 1; Feb. 21, 1924, 1.

Page 248. **"I understand," Christian**: *NYT*, Feb. 17, 1924, 1.

Page 248. **"There was an impression**: Ibid.

Page 248. **little more than "a gesture"**: "Paramount Stock, Ignoring Trade Commission, Scores Gain," *Variety*, July 13, 1927.

Page 249. **"The industry is greatly indebted**: *Society of Motion Picture Engineers Journal*, April–May 1947, Case Research Lab, Auburn, N.Y.

Page 250. **a foothold in the developing sound film technology**: John Izod, *Hollywood and the Box Office, 1895–1986* (Houndmill, Basingstoke: Macmillan, 1988); Douglas Gomery, "The Coming of Sound: Technological Change in the American Film Industry," in *The American Film Industry*, ed. Tino Balio (Madison: University of Wisconsin Press, 1985); Douglas Gomery, "Problems in Film History: How Fox Innovated Sound," *Quarterly Review of Film Studies* (Aug. 1976): 315–30.

Page 250. **Winfield Sheehan**: Private source. After a stint as a newspaper reporter, Sheehan became secretary to NYC Fire Commissioner Rhinelander Waldo (see *Editor and Publisher*, Jan. 15, 1910). A year later, Sheehan was appointed Waldo's secretary when Waldo became police commissioner. In his role as secretary to Waldo, Sheehan was responsible for issuing movie theater licenses, and he consequently became friendly with William Fox, Timothy Sullivan, and others. In 1914 Sheehan became involved in a Tammany-graft-prostitution scandal and was apparently rescued from further trouble when Fox tapped him to work in his movie company. See "Calls W. R. Sheehan the Man Higher Up," *NYT*, Apr. 30, 1914; Edwin C. Hill, "Mr. Sheehan, Genius Extraordinary," *American Weekly* magazine, *New York Journal-American*, Feb. 10, 1946; Andy Logan, *Against the Evidence: The Becker-Rosenthal Affair* (New York: Avon, 1970).

Page 251. **Adolphe Menjou**: Alexander Walker, *The Shattered Silents* (New York: Morrow, 1979), 145–47.

Page 251. **"a combination of producers"**: *New York American*, July 17, 1929.

Page 252. **"It is a singular thing**: WRH to City Editor, *Los Angeles Examiner*, Oct. 16, 1933, WRH Papers, Bancroft Library, University of California at Berkeley.

Page 252. **The Bellamy Trial**: Also making cameo appearances in the film were screenwriters Samuel Ornitz and William Dudley Pelley. Ornitz would go on to become one of the Hollywood Ten, and Pelley became one of the most notorious American Nazis of the 1930s.

Page 252. **"What has become of the Sherman anti-trust law**: *New York American*, June 30, 1929.

Page 253. **Brown responded immediately**: Brown letter to WRH, *New York American*, July 2, 1929.

Page 254. **"His pet screen hobby"**: *Motion Picture News*, July 27, 1929.

Page 254. **Brookhart to act as legal counsel**: *Ivan Abramson and Graphic Film Corporation vs. Motion Picture Producers and Distributors Of America, Inc., et al.*, Feb. 1930, National Archives, NYC.

Page 255. **"Never before," Brookhart declared**: "Film Company Sues Hays Body as Trust," *NYT*, Jan. 1, 1930.

Page 255. **"claim[s] that my**: Ivan Abramson, *Mother of Truth* (New York: Graphic Literary, 1929).

Page 255. **"Senator Brookhart sees behind it all**: *Variety*, Jan. 8, 1930, 79.

Page 256. **To his dying day**: Interview with Milton Gould, Nov. 5, 1993.

Page 256. **supplanting publishing**: *Editor and Publisher*, June 14, 1924.

Page 257. **Five O'Clock Girl**: Fred Lawrence Guiles, *Marion Davies* (New York: McGraw-Hill, 1972); Samuel Marx, *Mayer and Thalberg: The Make-Believe Saints* (New York: French, 1988).

Page 257. **Bowes pointed out**: Marx, *Mayer and Thalberg*.

Page 257. **"If a musical comedy plot**: WRH to Elinor Glyn, July 31, 1929, WRH Papers.

Page 258. **"In 'Marianne'**: Marion Davies, *The Times We Had: Life with William Randolph Hearst*, ed. Pamela Pfau and Kenneth S. Marx (Indianapolis: Bobbs-Merrill, 1975).

Page 258. **"some excellent episodes**: *New York American*, Apr. 26, 1932.

Page 258. **"All the hopes, the heartaches**: *New York American*, Sept. 4, 1932.

Page 259. **"Then we come to the 'Rabbit's Foot Club'**: *Blondie* story conference notes, May 7, 1932, MGM script files, USC Cinema-Television Library, University of Southern California, Los Angeles.

Page 259. **"Hearst made movies like he did everything else**: Quoted in Bob Willett, "Hearst—The Man," *New Liberty*, Feb. 1952.

Page 259. **"The two films**: Willett, "Hearst—The Man." See interview with Anne Dumbrille Murray, 1999.

14. ABOVE THE LAW

Page 260. **Millicent Hearst sat beside Benito Mussolini**: "Millicent Hearst Describes Her Chat with Mussolini," *New York American*, May 11, 1930. See Elsa Maxwell, *RSVP* (Boston: Little, Brown, 1954).

Page 261. **Mussolini had a particular interest**: *New York American*, Sept. 4, 1932.

Page 261. **"much more popular with Tammany Hall**: *NYT*, July 3, 1921, 18. For more on Millicent Hearst and Tammany, see *New York American*, July 1, 1922; July 27, 1923.

Page 261. **a testimonial dinner was held**: Invitation, Nov. 18, 1931, James Gerard Papers, Mansfield Library, University of Montana, Missoula.

Page 262. **Academy of Music**: *New York Daily Mirror*, Sept. 19, 1932.

Page 262. **Pamela Churchill Harriman**: Sally Bedell Smith, *Reflected Glory: The Life of Pamela Churchill Harriman* (New York: Simon and Schuster, Touchstone, 1997).

Page 262. **"Mrs. Hearst, whom rumor**: Hayes Perkins diary, Feb. 10, 1929, private source.

Page 262. **"We talked of Hearst**: Darwin Payne, *Owen Wister* (Dallas: Southern Methodist University, 1985), 301.

Page 263. **In 1924, Hearst**: Von Weigand–dictated memorandum, William Dodd to FDR, Mar. 20, 1935, FDR Papers, FDR Library, Hyde Park, N.Y.

Page 263. **Mussolini's contributions**: Many articles were actually written by Margherita Sarfatti, Mussolini's Jewish mistress. See Phillip V. Cannistraro and Brian R. Sullivan, *Il Duce's Other Woman* (New York: Morrow, 1993).

Page 263. **how to deal with gangsters**: "Highest-Placed Criminals Must Be Mercilessly Suppressed," *New York American*, Oct. 23, 1932.

Page 264. **"I think that Mussolini is the**: *Editor and Publisher*, Oct. 15, 1927.

Page 264. **Mussolini had been a fan of the movies**: Rachele Mussolini, *Mussolini* (New York: Morrow, 1974).

Page 264. **"The Russians set us a good example**: Emil Ludwig, *Talks with Mussolini* (Boston: Little, Brown, 1933). See Mussolini, *Mussolini*.

Page 265. **"a disappointed dramatist"**: *Man of Courage* clipping file, n.d., New York Public Library for the Performing Arts, NYC.

Page 265. **"He also interested**: Mussolini, *Mussolini*.

Page 265. **His Excellency, chief**: *New York American*, May 20, 1927.

Page 266. **"Nicholas Schenck said**: Scott Allen Nollen, "Mussolini Speaks," *Films in Review*, June/July 1989.

Page 266. **Man of Courage**: *New York American*, Nov. 7, 19, and 20, 1934.

Page 266. **Mussolini's adult son, Vittorio**: Charles Higham, *Merchant of Dreams: Louis B. Mayer, M.G.M., and the Secret Hollywood* (New York: Fine, 1993); *Variety*, Oct. 13, 1937, 5.

Page 267. **"Hebrew Communist center"**: *New York Post*, Nov. 26, 1938.

Page 267. **It is a marvel**: Perkins diary, May 11, 1930.

Page 268. **"Frequent trucks**: Perkins diary, Oct. 1928.

Page 268. **Under the castle**: Perkins diary, 1930.

Page 269. **Miss Urban, who was**: Interview with Gretl Urban, Oct. 24, 1991.

Page 269. **"penetrating eyes"**: Marion Davies, *The Times We Had: Life with William Randolph Hearst*, ed. Pamela Pfau and Kenneth S. Marx (Indianapolis: Bobbs-Merrill, 1975).

Page 269. **New York Mirror**: Oliver Carlson, *Brisbane: A Candid Biography* (New York: Stackpole Sons, 1937); Emile Gauvreau, *My Last Million Readers* (New York: Dutton, 1941).

Page 269. **to form the alliances to organized crime**: Gauvreau, *My Last Million Readers*.

Page 270. **"murderous losses"**: Ibid.

Page 270. **Hall-Mills murder case:** William M. Kunstler, *The Minister and the Choir Singer* (New York: Morrow, 1964).

Page 270. **"the case in comic strip form":** *New York Daily Mirror,* Nov. 12, 1926.

Page 271. **a Hearst editorial touted:** *New York Daily Mirror,* July 2, 1926, in John D. Stevens, *Sensationalism and the New York Press* (New York: Columbia University Press, 1991).

Page 271. **"I don't think it is fair:** *NYT,* Feb. 9, 1927.

Page 271. **out-of-court settlement:** *NYT,* Mar. 16, 1927, 25; Aug. 16, 1927, 28; Kunstler, *The Minister.*

Page 271. **the attacks on its methods:** *NYT,* Feb. 9, 1927, 11; Mar. 5, 1927, 32; Mar. 26, 1927, 20.

Page 272. **"If Brisbane has charge accounts:** *Variety,* n.d. (ca. Jan. 1924), *The Great White Way* clipping file, New York Public Library for the Performing Arts, NYC.

Page 273. **Scandal for Sale:** Gauvreau, *My Last Million Readers; Variety,* Nov. 10, 1931.

Page 273. **"The novel":** Gauvreau, *My Last Million Readers,* 163.

Page 274. **The editor reminded the mayor:** *Variety,* Nov. 10, 1931. See Jay Robert Nash and Stanley Ralph Ross, *The Motion Picture Guide* (Chicago: Cinebooks, 1986), 865–66.

Page 274. **"Now about the San Francisco:** Louella Parsons to William Randolph Hearst, Nov. 6, 1931, WRH Papers, Bancroft Library, University of California at Berkeley.

Page 275. **I am in no way:** WRH to Jack Warner, Nov. 6, 1931, WRH Papers.

Page 276. **Variety gloated:** *Variety,* Nov. 17, 1931.

Page 276. **The Famous Ferguson Case:** *Variety,* Feb. 23, 1932; Apr. 26, 1932; *NYT,* Apr. 25, 1932, 18; *New York Journal-American,* Apr. 25, 1932; Richard R. Ness, *From Headline Hunter to Superman: A Journalism Filmography* (Lanham, Md.: Scarecrow, 1997).

Page 277. **an unsigned letter marked "Confidential":** Confidential letter to Howard Hughes, Jan. 30, 1932, Lincoln Quarberg Collection, Academy of Motion Picture Arts and Sciences Library, Los Angeles.

Page 277. **"[The] Columnist has been:** *Variety,* Apr. 15, 1931.

Page 278. **"a violent tragicomedy:** Carlos Clarens, *Crime Movies* (New York: Da Capo, 1997), 89.

Page 278. **"For general distribution:** Howard Hughes to Lincoln Quarberg, Jan. 21, 1932, Quarberg Collection.

Page 281. **Lincoln Steffens:** Justin Kaplan, *Lincoln Steffens* (New York: Simon and Schuster, 1974); Lincoln Steffens, *American Magazine,* Nov. 1906. In another attempt to "psychoanalyze" criminals, Hearst invited Sigmund Freud to cover the trial of murderers Leopold and Loeb in 1924, but for health reasons the father of psychoanalysis turned down the invitation. See George Seldes, *Tell the Truth and Run* (New York: Greenberg, 1953), 107–8.

Page 281. **"There was a certain community:** Kaplan, *Lincoln Steffens.*

Page 281. **"as a substitute:** Steffens, *American Magazine.*

Page 281. **President Hoover complains:** Editorial, *New York American,* Oct. 22, 1931.

Page 282. **an organizer of organized crime**: Frank Browning and John Ferassi, *The American Way of Crime* (Toronto: Academic, 1980); Alan A. Block, *Organizing Crime* (New York: Elsevier North Holland, 1981); Perkins diary.

Page 282. **"[Hearst] is a law unto himself"**: Perkins diary, Jan. 4, 1930.

Page 282. **The income tax system**: *New York American*, Mar. 13, 1932.

Page 283. **"as an act of simple humanity"**: *New York American*, July 31, 1929.

Page 283. **"If society continues**: "Prison System Held Failure," *New York American*, Aug. 1, 1929.

Page 283. **the impetus for a Cosmopolitan film**: Lamar Trotti to Will H. Hays, Apr. 14, 1931, Will H. Hays Papers, Indiana State Library, Indianapolis; Frances Marion, *Off with Their Heads* (New York: Macmillan, 1972).

Page 284. **"Here is an effect**: *International Photographer*, Sept. 1930, 45.

Page 284. **This is a great tribute**: *St. Louis Star* editorial, quoted in *The Film Mercury*, Sept. 5, 1930, 16.

Page 285. **"We Cannot Cure Murder by Murder**: Hearst editorial distributed in pamphlet form by Hearst Corporation.

Page 285. **"the duty of a newspaper**: *Editor and Publisher*, June 11, 1927.

Page 285. **"Certainly," an inmate**: *New York American*, July 13, 1927.

Page 286. **"We like to work**: Press book, New York Public Library for the Performing Arts, NYC.

Page 286. **"he came right out**: Ibid.

Page 286. **"The picture does**: August Vollmer to Will Hays, Apr. 30, 1931, Hays Papers.

Page 286. **Hearst had a fix-it man**: Ed Hatrick to WRH, Dec. 17, 1930, WRH Papers; Carlos Clarens, *Crime Movies* (New York: Da Capo, 1997).

Page 286. **marketed toward children**: Andrew Bergman, *We're In the Money: Depression America and Its Films* (New York: Harper Colophon, 1971).

Page 287. **Dear Louis**: WRH to Louis B. Mayer, n.d., E. D. Coblentz Papers, Bancroft Library.

Page 288. **"exciting melodrama**: *New York Daily Mirror* review, in *New York American* ad, Mar. 14, 1932.

Page 288. **"Will you be one**: *Variety*, Nov. 1, 1932.

Page 289. **The only open attack**: Davies, *The Times We Had*.

Page 289. **later she donated**: *NYT*, Sept. 30, 1932, 11; July 28, 1932, 3.

Page 290. **Motion Picture Electrical Parade**: Official program, author's collection.

Page 290. **"a series of illuminated**: Quoted in *NYT*, Sept. 26, 1932.

Page 290. **Jack Warner had called up**: *Variety*, Sept. 27, 1932, 2.

Page 290. **"There must be a hundred**: Betty Rogers, *Will Rogers: His Wife's Story* (Indianapolis: Bobbs-Merrill, 1941.

Page 291. **"the Hearst–Marion Davies–Roosevelt show"**: Anonymous to Frank Knox, Sept. 25, 1932, President's Personal File, Herbert Hoover Presidential Library, West Branch, Iowa. For more on the "show," see Frank Knox to Herbert Hoover, Oct. 1, 1932, President's Personal File, Herbert Hoover Presidential Library; Herbert Hoover to Frank

Knox, Oct. 3, 1932, President's Personal File, Herbert Hoover Presidential Library; and the Perkins diary.

Page 291. I came to Los Angeles: Anonymous to Knox, Sept. 25, 1932.

Page 292. "Such things": Hoover to Knox, Oct. 3, 1932.

Page 292. California went solidly for FDR: Jack Warner, *My First Hundred Years in Hollywood* (New York: Random House, 1965).

Page 292. Gathered around FDR; Maxwell, *RSVP.*

Page 292. Casting Office: *Variety*, Mar. 28, 1933.

Page 292. "The Chief is casting: Samuel Marx, *Mayer and Thalberg: The Make-Believe Saints* (New York: French, 1988).

Page 292. Hearst's son George was being considered: *Variety*, Mar. 7, 1933.

Page 292. Colonel Edward House: Karl von Wiegand to WRH, May 17, 1933, WRH Papers; Charles Callan Tansill, *The Back Door to War* (Chicago: Henry Regnery, 1952).

Page 292. "should not be allowed to dominate: Quoted in Charles Callan Tansill, *The Back Door to War* (Chicago: Regnery, 1952).

Page 293. troublesome reports coming out of Berlin: *Variety*, numerous articles, April–May 1933.

Page 293. the film's genesis, its merits, and its impact: *Nation*, Apr. 26, 1933; Matthew Bernstein, *Walter Wanger* (Berkeley: University of California Press, 1994); Bergman, *We're In the Money*; Robert L. McConnell, "The Genesis and Ideology of *Gabriel Over the White House*," *Cinema Journal* (spring 1976).

Page 295. Lloyd George and Hearst: *New York American*, Feb. 12, 1933; Apr. 2, 1933.

Page 297. "financial, operative, and: House Resolution 95, Report No. 33, *Congressional Record*, 73d Cong., 1st sess., Hays Papers.

Page 297. "through devices of interlocking: Ibid.

Page 297. "coterie of manipulators: Ibid.

Page 297. "I would rather be controlled by Hitler: Elmer Rice, quoted in *Lewiston Missouri Journal*, Apr. 8, 1933, in report to Will Hays, Apr. 19, 1933, Hays Papers.

Page 297. The congressman was charged: *Chicago Herald-Examiner*, Apr. 12, 1933, in report to Will Hays.

Page 297. "ridiculous": *Chicago Herald-Examiner*, Apr. 11, 1933, in report to Will Hays.

Page 298. The New York Times speculated: *NYT*, May 10, 1933.

Page 298. "here to pay our respects": Ibid., 12.

Page 298. "hands–off policy": *New York American*, May 13, 1933.

Page 298. scare tactic: *Variety*, May 23, 1933.

Page 298. "sinister lobbying" and "financial racketeers: *NYT*, May 13, 1933.

Page 298. "Matter just now concluded: Will Hays to WRH, May 12, 1933, Hays Papers.

Page 298. "Thanks but do not thank me: WRH to Will Hays, May 13, 1933, Hays Papers.

Page 298. Still there were a lot: WRH to Louis B. Mayer, Mar. 25, 1933, WRH Papers.

Page 299. Lindsey, whose company: *Gabriel Over the White House* (New York: Farrar and Rinehart, 1933).

Page 299. **President Roosevelt sent notes to Hearst and . . . Schenck**: Hearst–FDR and Schenck–FDR correspondence in FDR Papers; *New York American*, Dec. 9, 1934.

Page 299. **he had been prevented from making the film he really wanted to make**: Hearst was apparently in demand after his speech writing for *Gabriel* star Walter Huston. When a feature film called *March of Time* went into production at MGM in the spring of 1933 and Huston was cast once again as the president of the United States, Hearst was called on to write speeches and dialogue for the actor. The results of this encore effort are unknown, since the Huston part was cut from the final film when it was released in September 1933, retitled *Broadway to Hollywood*.

Page 300. **The President Vanishes**: Oliver Carlson and Ernest Sutherland Bates, *Hearst: Lord of San Simeon* (New York: Viking, 1937); *Variety*, Nov. 27 and Dec. 4, 1934; *NYT*, Dec. 8 and Dec. 16, 1934; *New York American*, Dec. 8 and 9, 1934; clippings, New York Public Library for the Performing Arts, NYC.

Page 300. **Wanger biographer**: Bernstein, *Walter Wanger*.

Page 301. **Louis B. Mayer told him**: Louis B. Mayer to Stephen T. Early, including Hearst telegram, Mar. 25, 1933, FDR Papers, FDR Library. For more on *Looking Forward*, see *NYT*, Apr. 7, 1933, *Looking Forward* clipping file, New York Public Library for the Performing Arts, NYC; *NYT*, May 1, 1933, 10.

Page 301. **"Service," Hearst's telegram**: The telegram is included with Mayer to Early, Mar. 25, 1933, FDR Papers.

Page 303. **The image of the Biograph Theater**: The iconography of Dillinger's death under the *Manhattan Melodrama* marquee resonated so strongly for screenwriter Herman Mankiewicz that he considered using it as the opening scene for a film script idea he worked on between 1935 and 1940. It was his intention to use this opening to introduce various characters who would provide a psychological portrait of the dead man. Mankiewicz abandoned the idea of using Dillinger as a subject when he hit upon Hearst in *Citizen Kane*. Mankiewicz discussed his ideas for a Dillinger film in testimony for *Lundberg vs. Orson Welles, et al.*, Nov. 30, 1950, National Archives, NYC.

Page 304. **"I knew Lenbach**: "A Newspaper King Who Likes to Stay in Munich," *Stadt-Nachrichten*, Aug. 23, 1934 (translation by Alison Bond).

Page 304. **a few rabidly pro-Nazi German-born employees**: Hearst FBI files, Freedom of Information Files; Perkins diary.

Page 304. **Harry Crocker, apparently paid**: Unpublished Harry Crocker manuscript, Academy of Motion Picture Arts and Sciences Library, Los Angeles.

Page 305. **In Venice Davies**: Fred Lawrence Guiles, *Marion Davies* (New York: McGraw-Hill, 1972); interview with Eleanor Lambert Berkson, Sept. 12, 1993.

Page 305. **Davies's moving picture career**: "Hearst, Davies Fete MG Producer Abroad," *Variety*, June 26, 1934, 6; *Variety*, May 29, 1934, 15; July 24, 1934, 51.

Page 305. **Hearst bought actress Mary Carlisle**: Interview with Mary Carlisle, Nov. 1993.

Page 306. **fast film process cameras**: Edgar "Scoop" Gleeson interview notes, William S. Swanberg Papers, Columbia University. A Hearst interview was published in the *Berliner Illustrierte* on September 18, 1934, just as the Hearst party ended its stay in Germany. Hearst told the interviewer that his group had stayed in several German "medieval towns," including Nuremberg, Rothenburg, and Dinkelsbuhl. Germany provides "wonderful opportunities" for a photographer, Hearst told his interviewer. "My whole family takes photos, and I think we used up all our films in Germany" (translation by Alison Bond).

Page 306. **Kurt Safranski**: Safranski correspondence, courtesy of Tina Friedrich.

Page 306. **Martin Munkacsi**: Exhibition catalog, "Spontaneity and Style: Munkacsi, A Retrospective," Mar. 22 to Apr. 30, 1978, International Center of Photography, NYC.

Page 307. **"German influence"**: Kurt Safranski to Richard E. Berlin, Feb. 28, 1936, Safranski correspondence.

Page 307. **"photographic effectiveness"**: Richard E. Berlin to Kurt Safranski, Jan. 9, 1935, Safranski correspondence.

Page 307. **"Well, go ahead—let's make such a book!"**: Kurt Safranski to Richard E. Berlin, Feb. 28, 1936, Safranski correspondence.

Page 307. **Passion Play**: *NYT*, May 16, 1934, 10; Aug. 14, 1934, 13; clippings and photographs, Gemeinde Oberammergau, Archiv.

Page 307. **"in the role of**: *NYT*, Aug. 14, 1934, 13.

Page 307. **A German newspaper reported**: *Hannover Anzeiger*, Sept. 28, 1934, Gemeinde Oberammergau, Archiv.

Page 307. **"in part with the Nazi**: James Shapiro, *The Troubling Story of the World's Most Famous Passion Play* (New York: Pantheon, 2000).

Page 308. **a carefully written account**: "A Newspaper King"; *William Randolph Hearst: A Portrait in His Own Words*, ed. Edmond D. Coblentz (New York: Simon and Schuster, 1952).

Page 308. **"The Führer is honored**: Scrapbook in Harry Crocker papers, California Historical Society, San Francisco. This small collection of letters and items belonging to Harry Crocker also includes German newspapers from September 1934. The *Stadt-Nachrichten* for August 23, 1934, features page one photographs of Hearst and Davies taken at a Munich beer garden. In the accompanying article, Hearst was quoted as calling Communism an "epidemic [that] will spread not by rational thinking but by hysteria" (translation by Alison Bond).

Page 308. **a headquarters of Nazi conventioneers**: Nuremberg Grand Hotel guest list for week of Nuremberg Rally, 1934, Stadtarchiv, Nuremberg.

Page 308. **an article boosting Hitler**: Gen. Hermann Wilhelm Goering, "Hitler Has Greater Popular Backing than Any Other Statesman—Goering," *New York American*, Sept. 9, 1934.

Page 309. **"stopping at Nuremberg"**: *New York American*, Sept. 24, 1934.

Page 310. **"Six years ago I**: *Frankischer Küner* (Nuremberg), Sept. 10, 1934, 12.

Page 310. **the usually Hearst-friendly journal**: *Liberty*, Feb. 1941.

Page 311. **"was discussed in general with Mr. Louis B. Mayer**: In researching *Citizen Hearst*, biographer William Swanberg interviewed Ella "Bill" Williams, a former executive at Cosmopolitan Productions. On the question of Hearst's visit with Hitler, Swan-

484 * 14. ABOVE THE LAW

berg recorded a shorthand account of her response: "Bill says it was LB Mayer who suggested Hst visit Hitler, try to get better treatmt for Jews. Did Hst lot of harm, but Hst wud never contradict public reports. Bill says this is in diary of Harry Crocker, Hst man along on trip" (interview with Williams, Nov. 1, 1959, Swanberg Papers). A thorough analysis of Mayer's views on Hitler, Nazism, and anti-Semitism awaits further research. In the most recent exploration, author Neal Gabler paints a contradictory but incomplete portrait of Mayer. He does offer examples of Mayer's behavior that suggest elements of self-loathing. See Neal Gabler, *Empire of Their Own* (New York: Crown, 1988), 272–73, 279–80. Gabler does not mention that in the late 1930s and early 1940s Mayer was a prominent supporter of the Oxford Group, later called the Moral Re-Armament Movement, that claimed to seek world peace and end global disputes through spiritual means. Critics of the movement said that the Oxford Group was mostly interested in attacking Communism and boosting big business. The Oxford Group received generally favorable publicity from the American press, especially the Hearst press. Its leader, Dr. Frank N. D. Buchman, was said to have been close to Heinrich Himmler, and he was quoted in 1936 as saying, "I thank Heaven for a man like Adolf Hitler, who built up a front line defense against the anti-Christ of Communism" (*Time*, Sept. 7, 1936, quoted in *In Fact*, Jan. 19, 1948, 1–4).

Page 311. **a book was published:** *William Randolph Hearst: A Portrait.*

Page 312. **swayed Hearst to meet with Hitler:** According to Jack Warner, Hearst considered another meeting with Hitler in 1936, during his annual European trip, but was talked out of it by the producer. Marion Davies recalled that during this same trip Hearst met with Mussolini in Rome for the first time. Hearst was apparently impressed with the dictator's huge office, saying it reminded him of Louis B. Mayer's on the MGM lot. See Warner, *My First Hundred Years*; Davies, *The Times We Had.*

Page 312. **Carl Laemmle:** Carl Laemmle to WRH, Dec. 10, 1929; Jan. 18, 1932, WRH Papers.

Page 312. **another credibility problem:** *William Randolph Hearst*, ed. Coblentz, 103–5; Harry Crocker, unpublished manuscript, Academy of Motion Picture Arts and Sciences Library, Los Angeles. The Crocker account was written at least as early as 1940, because screenwriter Herman Mankiewicz was aware of it when he worked on the script for *Citizen Kane.*

Page 312. **"Although he gave Hitler:** Gauvreau, *My Last Million Readers*, 210.

Page 315. **"The story was without:** David Nasaw, *The Chief: The Life of William Randolph Hearst* (New York: Houghton Mifflin, 2000), 510–11. For more on the wire service exchange deal, see Frederick T. Birchall, "Personal Liberty Vanishes in Reich," *NYT*, Dec. 31, 1934. The *Times* reported that "some Nazi papers are now buying American news services," but it did not mention Hearst's International News Service by name. In response to a libel suit initiated by Hearst in 1941, lawyers for *Friday* magazine provided an amended answer that contained what they claimed was the truth about the INS deal with Germany, including details about a large payment of cash from Germany to Hearst in exchange for uncritical reports on Germany. Hearst did not pursue the suit after *Friday* made these charges, and the case was dismissed in 1942. See *William Randolph Hearst Against Friday, Inc.*, Index number 3576, Amended Answer, July 12, 1941, Judgment, Oct.

6, 1942, Supreme Court of the State of New York County of New York, Municipal Archives, NYC; see also William Dodd file, WRH file, Karl von Wiegand Papers, Hoover Institute for War and Peace, Stanford University, Palo Alto, Calif.

Page 315. **Hill "interprets and dramatizes news events**: "Adding Star Value," advertisement for Edwin C. Hill and Hearst Metrotone News, *Motion Picture Herald*, Sept. 22, 1934. See also "Newsreels Give Speedy Coverage of Lindbergh Kidnapping Arrest," *Motion Picture Herald*, Sept. 29, 1934; "Newsreel Scene Changes, with New Companies and New Faces," *Motion Picture Herald*, Oct. 6, 1934.

Page 316. **Albert A. Sander**: Sanders obituary, *Variety*, July 29, 1936; *NYT*, Feb. 20, 1917, 1; Mar. 3, 1917, 3; *New York American*, Feb. 21, 1917.

Page 316. **As the New York Times reported**: "Spies Plead Guilty and Keep Their Secrets," *NYT*, Mar. 22, 1917.

Page 316. **"a long term lease"**: *Ufa Week*, May 12, 1931.

Page 317. **Ufa opens own theater**: Ibid.

Page 317. **"I know you will**: Martin Huberth to WRH, May 12, 1931, WRH Papers.

Page 317. **a letter of newsreel agreement was signed**: Hearst newsreel records, UCLA; Ufa Records, Bundesarchiv, Berlin.

Page 318. **We will never gain**: Klaus Kreimerier, *The UFA Story* (New York: Hill and Wang, 1996).

Page 319. **"prominent American publicists"**: *NYT*, July 23, 1946. In the January 10, 1946, issue of the *New York Times* Rosenberg was quoted as saying that Hearst personally told him that his articles on German foreign policy "represented well-founded arguments." See also *NYT*, July 10, 1946. George Seldes reported in 1945 that "about 50% of the Americans now facing trial for treason in Berlin were at one time or another Hearst employees." As examples, Seldes named Jane Anderson, Donald Day, Douglas Chandler, and Charles Flick (Flicksteger), an assistant to INS correspondent Karl von Wiegand, "who escaped a treason indictment by becoming a Nazi" (*In Fact*, Oct. 8, 1945, 1).

Page 319. **"the NRA is simply**: *Newsweek*, Nov. 4, 1933.

Page 319. **Are we going to**: *New York American*, Oct. 6, 1933.

Page 320. **According to an FBI memorandum**: All information and quotations relating to Hoover, the FBI, and Hearst are from FBI Freedom of Information Files on Hearst, 1933–1936.

Page 322. **"a tie-in"**: *Variety*, May 15, 1935.

Page 322. **"the daddy of all**: Ibid.

Page 323. **"Along with the renaissance**: Bergman, *We're in the Money*.

Page 323. **"the first of a new**: *Variety*, May 8, 1935.

Page 324. **"few changes"**: *New Republic*, May 15, 1935.

Page 324. **"red hot off**: *Variety*, May 8, 1935, 16.

15. REMOTE CONTROL

Page 326. **screenwriter Ring Lardner Jr.**: In an interview with me and in a previous interview with Barry Strugatz and Pat McGilligan, Lardner was clear that he had seen

Hearst and Hitler together in Munich in 1934. If Lardner's account is accurate, then Hearst had more than one encounter with Hitler in 1934, the publicly acknowledged meeting taking place in Berlin. See interview with Ring Lardner Jr., Apr. 27, 1999; Pat McGilligan, ed., *Backstory 3: Interviews with Screenwriters of the 1960s* (Berkeley: University of California Press, 1997), 197–98.

Page 327. "disliked Hearst, not because of anything political: This and subsequent quotations from interview with Ring Lardner Jr., Apr. 27, 1999.

Page 327. "dominated by men: Adrian J. Berkowitz to WRH, Oct. 9, 1934, WRH Papers, Bancroft Library, University of California at Berkeley.

Page 328. "arousing class feeling": WRH to Adrian J. Berkowitz, Oct. 10, 1934, WRH Papers.

Page 328. "We hear much these days: Will Hays to WRH, Oct. 4, 1934, Hays Papers, Indiana State Library, Indianapolis.

Page 328. another letter to Hearst attached to material: Will Hays to WRH, Oct. 15, 1934, Hays Papers. See "Exchange of Letters," *Variety*, Aug. 21, 1934. See also Frank Walsh, *Sin and Censorship: The Catholic Church and the Motion Picture Industry* (New Haven: Yale University Press, 1996). During the summer when the Legion of Decency was formed, Hays traveled to Detroit to meet and consult with the Catholic radio priest Charles Coughlin. According to Hays's notes on the meeting, Father Coughlin told him that "producers should become captains in the Legion of Decency." He suggested that Hays get the press to "publicize the good that motion pictures do." He also volunteered to offer his services, possibly on a committee headed by Walt Disney, to make movies that would be a positive influence on children. In the meeting Coughlin alluded to the rumors that he was anti-Semitic and about to launch an attack on Jewish control of the movie industry, but Hays told him he wasn't concerned about the rumors. Coughlin also suggested that someone investigate actors' "communistic tendencies" (notes on meeting between Hays and Coughlin on Aug. 18, 1934, Hays Papers). In 1936 it was reported that Coughlin had suggested that Hays "better manage Hollywood news," and that shortly thereafter, Hays hired Kenneth Clark of Hearst's Universal News Service to supervise press relations. See *Pacific Weekly*, July 13, 1936.

Page 330. "I think it is a: WRH to Louella Parsons, Mar. 24, 1931, WRH Papers.

Page 330. internal censorship: Ibid.

Page 331. a wire soliciting Hearst's support: Bosley Crowther, *Hollywood Rajah: The Life and Times of Louis B. Mayer* (New York: Holt, 1960), 196–97.

Page 331. "If you don't suppress: WRH to Louis B. Mayer, quoted in Crowther, *Hollywood Rajah*, 197.

Page 331. Marie Antoinette: Marion Davies transcripts, Fred Lawrence Guiles Collection.

Page 331. Parsons devoted her column: *Los Angeles Examiner*, Oct. 28, 1934; Nov. 17, 1934, clipping files, Regional History Center, University Library, University of Southern California.

Page 332. "the stigma of failure: Louise Brooks, "Marion Davies' Niece," in *Lu Lu in Hollywood* (New York: Knopf, 1983).

Page 333. a host of orchestrated assaults: *Los Angeles Examiner,* Oct. 24 and 25, 1934; *New York American,* Nov. 5, 1934; *Hollywood Reporter* article quoted in *New Theatre,* Sept. 1935; *Motion Picture Herald,* Nov. 3, 1934; *Hollywood Reporter,* Sept. 17, 1934; *Variety,* Oct. 30, 1934, 1.

Page 334. The most infamous slight: Greg Mitchell, "How Hollywood Fixed an Election," *American Film,* Nov. 1988.

Page 334. "hazardous experiment: *New York American,* Nov. 5, 1934.

Page 334. "This campaign against: *Hollywood Reporter,* Nov. 1934, quoted in *New Theatre,* Sept. 1935.

Page 334. "Nothing is unfair: Quoted in Kyle Crichton, *Total Recoil* (Garden City, N.Y.: Doubleday, 1960). See Greg Mitchell, *The Campaign of the Century* (New York: Random House, 1992); Upton Sinclair, *I, Candidate for Governor* (self-published, 1934).

Page 335. "anti-Sinclairite": *Variety,* Nov. 6, 1934.

Page 335. "Sinclair is handsomely: WRH to Arthur Brisbane, Nov. 7, 1934, WRH Papers.

Page 335. "I have your telegram: Arthur Brisbane to WRH, Nov. 8, 1934, WRH Papers.

Page 335. "Skit on California: Arthur Brisbane to WRH, Dec. 9, 1934, WRH Papers.

Page 336. anti-Communism crusade with drama: WRH to Jack Warner, June 26, 1936, Jack Warner Papers, USC Cinema-Television Library, University of Southern California, Los Angeles.

Page 336. "unless those who represent: *NYT,* Feb. 25, 1935.

Page 337. in production at the height of Hearst's college red-baiting: *New York Journal,* Sept. 28, 1935; Oct. 5, 1935; *New York Daily Mirror,* Sept. 28, 1935; *Variety,* Oct. 2, 1935; *NYT,* Sept. 29, 1935, 24; Oct. 5, 1935, 8; Oct. 6, 1935, sec. 11, 5; Michael S. Shull and David Edward Wilt, *Hollywood War Films, 1937–1945* (Jefferson, N.C.: McFarland, 1996); "College Communism" (editorial), *Los Angeles Examiner,* Nov. 11, 1934.

Page 337. "her Communist theories": *New York Evening Journal,* Sept. 30, 1935. See *New York Evening Journal,* Sept. 28, 1935; "125 Reds Stage Film Protest," *New York Evening Journal,* Oct. 5, 1935.

Page 337. "hair [sic] brained escapade: *New York Daily Mirror,* Sept. 28, 1935.

Page 337. "simple-minded and actively: *NYT,* Oct. 6, 1935; see Sept. 29 and Oct. 5, 1935.

Page 338. "a non–Party Communist": Quoted in Harvey Klehr, *The Heyday of American Communism: The Depression Decade* (New York: Basic, 1984), 319.

Page 340. "As I suggested: Joe Breen to Jack Warner, Jan. 21, 1935, Warner Bros. Archives, USC Cinema-Television Library, University of Southern California, Los Angeles.

Page 340. a search to find a suitable vehicle for Davies: Jack Warner to WRH, Feb. 20, 1935, Warner Papers.

Page 341. a two-hour version was previewed: *Variety,* May 1, 1935, 4.

Page 341. "anti-corporation propaganda": Harry Bercovich to Hal Wallis, Apr. 30, 1935, Warner Bros. Archives.

Page 341. Hearst saw a version of the film: *Daily Variety,* quoted in *New Theater,* June 1935.

Page 341. "To soften what some previewers: Ibid.

Page 342. The press analysis of Oil: *Oil* clipping file, New York Public Library for the Performing Arts, NYC; *NYT,* June 6, 1935, 25; *New York Herald Tribune* (review), June 10(?), 1935, *Oil* clipping file, New York Public Library for the Performing Arts, NYC; *Daily Worker,* June 11, 1935; *Los Angeles Examiner,* June 7, 1935, *Oil* clipping file, University of Southern California.

Page 343. One of Warner Bros.'s box office successes: Box office figures for 1935, Warner Bros. Archives.

Page 343. "Why, that's awful": Mervyn LeRoy, *Take One* (New York: Hawthorn, 1974).

Page 343. "We should not fear death: Notes on Hearst, Harry Crocker papers, Academy of Motion Picture Arts and Sciences Library, Los Angeles.

Page 343. William Randolph Hearst begins to sound: Lincoln Steffens, *Pacific Weekly,* Jan. 11, 1935, Lincoln Steffens Papers, Columbia University.

Page 344. Motion Picture Herald published a history of cinema: *Motion Picture Herald,* Feb. 23, 1935.

Page 344. "Moscow Films Poison: Quoted in *Motion Picture Herald,* Mar. 16, 1935. At the same time that Hearst was attacking Soviet films in America, *Five Star Final,* the American play that annoyed Hearst so much when it was produced as a film, was having a strong run at the Moscow Theater. It was reportedly a big hit in Moscow, because of its attack on yellow journalism. See *Variety,* May 22, 1935, 56.

Page 345. "called the features offensively:"Amherst: Hearst's Newsreels Can't Compete with Popeye," *Newsweek,* May 18, 1935, 22.

Page 345. When they got wind of Loews' actions: *Newsweek,* May 18, 1935; *Variety,* May 22, 1935, 1; July 10, 1935; *New Republic,* June 26, 1935; *Motion Picture Herald,* Aug. 24, 1935; Aug. 31, 1935.

Page 345. "cooperating with the authorities: *Variety,* July 10, 1935.

Page 346. Those who have regarded: *Motion Picture Herald,* Aug. 31, 1935.

Page 346. Underlying "liberal" Progressivism: Andrea Marin Kalas, "Hearst Metrotone News, 1929–1934," M.A. thesis, UCLA, 1990.

Page 347. Anti-Hearst Examiner: two issues of mock newspaper, Aug. and Sept. 1935, author's collection; interview with Sercombe family, 1995.

Page 347. an "anti-labor" and "pro-war" movie list: *Daily Worker,* Aug. 9, 1935.

Page 348. There is a picture called "John Meade's Woman": WRH to Tom White, 1937, in "Motion Pictures—Communism," 1937, E. D. Coblentz Papers, Bancroft Library.

Page 348. From New York where he was taking his annual break: *Pacific Weekly,* July 27, 1936, Steffens Papers; *Variety,* June 24, 1936, 5.

Page 349. the idea of exploiting a story: *Variety,* June 24, 1936, 5.

Page 349. production was wrapped up on the film *San Francisco:* John Neylan Papers, box 72, Bancroft Library.

Page 349. sticky battle with Bette Davis: Michael Freedland, *The Warner Brothers* (London: Harrap, 1983). Bette Davis was the star of the Cosmopolitan film *Special Agent* (1935).

Page 350. **"Mr. Hearst has asked**: Ella Williams to Jack Warner, Apr. 13, 1937, Warner Bros. Archives.

Page 351. **Good Housekeeping's Club Service**: National Board of Review clippings and correspondence, National Board of Review of Motion Pictures, Manuscripts and Archives Division, New York Public Library.

Page 352. **'Up with shorts'**: Margaret V. Barns to National Motion Picture League, Sept. 5, 1946, box 110, National Board of Review Collection; *Good Housekeeping*, various issues, Sept. 1939–June 1940.

Page 352. **symbolically extended their Seal of Approval**: *Newsweek*, Nov. 13, 1939, 10.

Page 352. **distributing pamphlets**: National Board of Review of Motion Pictures, Manuscripts and Archives Division, New York Public Library. Of particular interest is a pro-HUAC article entitled "Consumer Officials Cited by Rep. Dies" in *Consumers Information Service*, Dec. 1941.

Page 353. **after numerous complaints from consumers**: *Consumers Union Report*, Sept. 1939.

Page 353. **"misleading and deceptive acts"**: For FTC complaint against Hearst, see "Good Housekeeping Seal 'Deceptive' FTC Charges," *Editor and Publisher*, Aug. 26, 1939, 6; "Hearst Called on Carpet Over Ad Guarantees," *New York Post*, Aug. 21, 1939; FTC press release issued Aug. 21, 1939, in box 174, Consumer Research Archives, Rutgers University, New Brunswick, N.J.

Page 354. **Berlin began lobbying any official**: Interview notes with Sidney Boehm in William S. Swanberg Papers, Columbia University; Herbert R. Mayes, *The Magazine Maze* (Garden City, N.Y.: Doubleday, 1980); interview with Elaine St. Johns, 1995. The advertising journal *Space and Time* wrote: "The case was in the works for years. Dick Berlin didn't worry about it. . . . When it got really hot, he came down to Washington to fix it up" (*Space and Time*, Jan. 31, 1940, 3–4).

Page 355. **"You know as well as I do**: Mayes, *The Magazine Maze.*

Page 355. **He began his career as a Methodist missionary**: J. B. Matthews, *Odyssey of a Fellow Traveler* (New York: Mount Vernon, 1938), 46; Nelson L. Dawson, "From Fellow Traveler to Anticommunist: The Odyssey of J. B. Matthews," *Register of the Kentucky Historical Society* (summer 1986): 280–306.

Page 355. **"In line with my**: Matthews, *Odyssey of a Fellow Traveler.*

Page 357. **"the resemblance was so obvious**: Fred Schlink to Crosby, May 22, 1935, Consumer Research archives, Rutgers University.

Page 357. **"California love nest**: *People's Press*, Nov. 9, 1935, quoted in Ferdinand Lundberg, *Imperial Hearst: A Social Biography* (New York: Equinox Cooperative, 1936), 301.

Page 357. **In a subsequent issue**: *People's Press*, cited in Lundberg, *Imperial Hearst.*

Page 358. **One particularly violent**: Affidavit of Irma Albright in Consumer Research complaint against A.F. of L., Federal Union, copy in Consumer Research archives.

Page 358. **clubbed his three children to death**: *Washington Post*, Apr. 12, 1959.

Page 358. **"awful spells**: Ruth Inglis Matthews, unpublished memoirs, courtesy of Martin Matthews.

Page 358. "the notion that our 'policies are controlled: Fred Schlink to Mamolen, Feb. 25, 1938, Consumer Research archives.

Page 359. Schlink went through a long period of bitterness: Ruth Inglis Matthews, unpublished memoirs. During the period when Schlink was anti-Hearst, he helped writer Ferdinand Lundberg with research on Hearst by inviting him to the New Jersey headquarters of Consumer Research and opening his Hearst files to the biographer (F. Lundberg testimony, *Lundberg vs. Welles, et al.*, Aug. 18, 1950, Transcripts Civil 44-62, Southern District of New York, National Archives, NYC).

Page 359. One of his closest friends: Ruth Inglis Matthews, unpublished memoirs.

Page 359. "perverted an ideal of human progress: John Winkler, *William Randolph Hearst: A New Appraisal* (New York: Hastings House, 1955), 293.

Page 359. National Association of Manufacturers: George Seldes, *Witness to a Century* (New York: Ballantine Books, 1987), 331; *In Fact* magazine, various issues during early 1940s; Seldes, *Facts and Fascism* (New York: In Fact, 1943).

Page 359. "Be a crook, Seldes: George Seldes, *Witness to a Century: Encounters with the Noted, the Notorious, and the Three SOBs* (New York: Ballantine, 1987), 370.

Page 360. "The left-wingers—Communists: *Liberty*, Dec. 10, 1938, 38.

Page 360. American Taxpayers League: Kenneth Gale Crawford, *The Pressure Boys: The Inside Story of Lobbying in America* (New York: Messner, 1939), 160–71.

Page 361. Henry S. MacKay Jr.: *Los Angeles Examiner*, Nov. 14, 1934.

Page 361. "The rich, corporate face of homegrown fascism: Larry Ceplair and Steven Englund, *The Inquisition in Hollywood: Politics in the Film Community, 1930–1960* (Berkeley: University of California Press, 1983).

Page 361. urging him to oppose a Dickstein bill: Will Hays to WRH, Feb. 18, 1932, Hays Papers. See *Variety*, Apr. 26, 1932.

Page 361. handpicked Dies: *Los Angeles Examiner*, Sept. 16, 1947.

Page 361. sweet music to Hearst's ears: Kenneth Heineman, "Media Bias Coverage of the Dies Committee on Un-American Activities, 1938–1940," *The Historian* (autumn 1992): 37.

Page 362. followed by shots of "hunger marchers": *Motion Picture Herald*, Aug. 29, 1936, 24.

Page 362. drawing a pair of crutches in the background: Correspondence with Frederic Arnold, Apr. 14, 2000.

Page 362. "the sparkplug: *Los Angeles Examiner*, July 14, 1953, clippings, J. B. Matthews Collection, Duke University.

Page 362. "My first appearance: J. B. Matthews to Fred Schlink, Aug. 20, 1939, Ruth Inglis Matthews, unpublished memoirs.

Page 363. "Is that the policy: *New York Journal-American*, Aug. 20, 1938.

Page 363. "direct and unequivocal": *New York Journal-American*, Aug. 25, 1938.

Page 364. "The rapid flow of stage pictures: Morgan Y. Himelstein, *Drama Was a Weapon: The Left-Wing Theatre in New York, 1929–1941* (Westport, Conn.: Greenwood, 1963).

Page 364. two investigators: *Liberty*, Feb. 17, 1940; Benjamin Mendel to J. B.

Matthews, Mar. 2, 1940, box 692, J. B. Matthews Collection, Duke University, Durham, N.C.

Page 364. **"Here is a very interesting**: Edmond Coblentz to WRH, Dec. 13, 1938, E. D. Coblentz Papers. I have been unable to locate any information about Mount Vernon Publishers, the book's publisher, in the incorporation records for New York City held in the Municipal Archives.

Page 365. **had once urged the FTC**: Lundberg, *Imperial Hearst.*

Page 366. **a financial interest in Macfadden Publications**: Lundberg, *Imperial Hearst.*

Page 366. **Photoplay and Shadowland**: *NYT*, Oct. 24, 1934, 21.

Page 366. **Cuneo**: Correspondence with John F. Cuneo Jr., June 12, 2000; Theodore Peterson, *Magazines in the Twentieth Century* (Urbana: University of Illinois Press, 1956); Mayes, *The Magazine Maze.*

Page 367. **"That ten thousand"**: Quoted in Cora Older, *William Randolph Hearst, American* (New York: Appleton Century, 1936)

Page 367. **In a piece written for**: George Seldes, *In Fact*, Feb. 23, 1942, with quotations from David Munro article in the weekly advertising newsletter *Space and Time*, Feb. 2, 1942, that focused on secret Dies-Sokolsky-Liberty-Hearst relationship.

Page 367. **Sydney Boehm's recollection**: Notes on interview with Sidney Boehm in Swanberg Papers (*Citizen Hearst*). Boehm told Swanberg that Hearst commissioned eight articles from Dies in exchange for his help on the FTC complaint. Seven articles authored by Dies appeared in *Liberty* in early 1940, on Jan. 13, Jan. 20, Feb. 3, Feb. 10, Feb. 17, Feb. 24, and Mar. 30. Also of interest is an early reference to the *Liberty* attack on Hollywood that appeared in the Hearst press; see "Hollywood Hit in Dies Story," *New York Journal-American*, Feb. 9, 1940. *Variety* ridiculed Dies's *Liberty* articles, saying that the congressman's performance suggested a new category for Academy Award winners: "For Best Original Melodrama by a Non-Professional" ("An Oscar for Dies!" *Variety*, Feb. 21, 1940).

Page 367. **ghostwritten by J. B. Matthews**: *Nation*, Oct. 3, 1942, clippings, J. B. Matthews Collection.

Page 367. **"fearlessly and fully**: "The Reds in Hollywood," *Liberty*, Feb. 17, 1940.

Page 368. **an unofficial visit to Hollywood**: Ceplair and Englund, *The Inquisition in Hollywood.*

16. HOLLYWOOD ISOLATIONIST

Page 370. **She is a Catholic, like Marion Davies**: Aldous Huxley, *After Many a Summer Dies the Swan* (New York: Harper Colophon, 1983). In the book's first draft the Davies character was actually named Douras. See David King Dunaway, *Huxley in Hollywood* (New York: Harper and Row, 1989).

Page 371. **"it would have been as flat as an old column**: F. Scott Fitzgerald, *The Love of The Last Tycoon* (New York: Scribner Paperback Fiction, 1993). See Sara Mayfield, *Exiles from Paradise* (New York: Delacorte, 1971); *Correspondence of F. Scott Fitzgerald*, ed. Matthew J. Bruccoli and Margaret M. Duggan (New York: Random House, 1980).

Page 371. **"Crazy Sundays"**: Dwight Taylor, "Scott Fitzgerald in Hollywood," *Harpers,*

Mar. 1959; Jeffrey Meyers, *Scott Fitzgerald* (New York: HarperCollins, 1994); Matthew J. Bruccoli, ed., *The Short Stories of F. Scott Fitzgerald* (New York: Scribner's, 1989).

Page 372. **"on the ground that:** F. Scott Fitzgerald to H. L. Mencken, July 1932, in *Correspondence of F. Scott Fitzgerald.*

Page 372. **Ed Hatrick announced to the press:** *Variety*, Mar. 27, 1940.

Page 372. **Kennedy told his old friend:** Lawrence J. Quirk, *The Kennedys in Hollywood* (Dallas: Taylor, 1996), 116–17.

Page 373. **Hatrick began to represent Hearst's interests:** Clippings, Hatrick file, New York Public Library for the Performing Arts, NYC: *Los Angeles Examiner*, Apr. 3, 1937; *Variety*, Mar. 29, 1939; *NYT*, Apr. 4, 1940; *New York Morning Telegraph*, Dec. 21, 1941.

Page 373. **Caleb Stratton:** Interview with Edward Stratton, Aug. 19, 1990.

Page 373. **Telenews Productions:** Minutes of meeting concerning Telenews purchase, Dec. 31, 1953, UCLA Film Archives; clipping files, New York Public Library for the Performing Arts, NYC: *Television Weekly*, Jan. 26, 1948; *Los Angeles Examiner*, Apr. 2, 1948; *Variety*, Jan. 28, 1948. In 1949 *In Fact* magazine published sample daily script sheets from Telenews, attempting to demonstrate the close ties between the newsreel and the State Department in their negative depictions of the Soviet Union and their smears of a recent peace congress in Paris (*In Fact*, June 6, 1949, 1–4).

Page 373. **"presented 12:** *New York Journal-American*, Jan. 21, 1948. For a review of the debut of the Telenews newsreel, see *Variety*, Jan. 28, 1948.

Page 373. **Edward R. Murrow's:** Raymond Fielding, *The American Newsreel, 1911–1967* (Norman: University of Oklahoma Press, 1972).

Page 374. **"Kingfish":** Fielding, *The American Newsreel*; Thomas C. Sorenson, *The Word War: The Story of American Propaganda* (New York: Harper and Row, 1968); private source.

Page 374. **"marvelous moving picture":** *New York Journal-American*, Mar. 27, 1940.

Page 375. **"put the American way to music:** "Stephen Foster's Fame," *New York Journal-American*, Nov. 18, 1940.

Page 375. **"the beautiful and talented" Greta Garbo:** New York Journal-American, Mar. 10, 1940, 1.

Page 375. **"the money is mainly in those films:** Typescript for Hearst column, May 22, 1940, in E. D. Coblentz Papers, Bancroft Library, University of California at Berkeley.

Page 375. **"She appealed to everybody then:** Typescript for Hearst column, May 22, 1940, E. D Coblentz Papers, Bancroft Library, University of California, Berkeley.

Page 376. **"Nothing else has appeared on the screen:** Quoted in Louis B. Mayer obituary, *Los Angeles Examiner*, Oct. 30, 1957, Mayer clipping file, Regional History Center, Los Angeles.

Page 376. **"leave it alone":** Adela Rogers St. Johns, *Honeycomb* (Garden City, N.Y.: Doubleday, 1969), 205.

Page 376. **John L. Leech:** *Los Angeles Herald Express*, Aug. 5–21, 1940.

Page 376. **"the most notorious of a large group:** Larry Ceplair and Steven Englund, *The Inquisition in Hollywood: Politics in the Film Community, 1930–1960* (Berkeley: University of California Press, 1983), 156–57.

Page 376. **Leech appeared before a grand jury**: *Los Angeles Herald Express*, Aug. 5–21, 1940.

Page 376. **"pathological liar"**: *In Fact* magazine, Aug. 26, 1940.

Page 376. **the grand jury accusations**: *NYT*, Aug. 6, 1940.

Page 377. **a retraction of its previous report**: *NYT*, Aug. 15, 1940.

Page 377. **a "sinister" smear campaign**: *NYT* (editorial), Aug. 15, 1940.

Page 377. **"the greatest fifth-column**: *Los Angeles Herald-Express*, Aug. 5, 1940.

Page 377. **It is not only fashionable**: *New York Journal-American*, Aug. 8, 1940.

Page 378. **A deal with MGM**: *Newsweek*, Sept. 23, 1940.

Page 379. **"knocked sense" into Hearst's head**: Quirk, *The Kennedys in Hollywood*.

Page 379. **"I was almost glad**: Ibid.

Page 379. **saved by not taking Kennedy's advice**: William Randolph Hearst Jr., *The Hearsts: Father and Son* (Niwot, Colo.: Roberts Rinehart, 1991).

Page 379. **Kennedy . . . Berlin**: Lindsey Chaney and Michael Cieply, *The Hearsts: Family and Empire, the Later Years* (New York: Simon and Schuster, 1981), 110–14.

Page 380. **similarly manipulative move in the movie industry**: Axel Madsen, *Gloria and Joe* (New York: Arbor House, 1988).

Page 380. **"a modified version"**: Gloria Swanson, *Swanson on Swanson: An Autobiography* (New York: Pocket Books, 1980), 396.

Page 380. **the photogenic Kennedy on its cover**: *Social Justice*, Apr. 11, 1938.

Page 380. **"there are no justifiable circumstances**: Feb. statement quoted in *New York American* (editorial), July 9, 1940.

Page 381. **the election of a Catholic president**: March editorial quoted in *New York American* (editorial), July 9, 1940.

Page 381. **"Qualified and Available"**: *New York American* (editorial), July 9, 1940.

Page 382. **"pattern of inertia and arousal"**: John Hellmann, *The Kennedy Obsession* (New York: Oxford University Press, 1997).

Page 382. **Kennedy's closest Stanford University girlfriend**: Interview with Harriet Price Fullerton, Apr. 2000.

Page 383. **a thank-you note to Davies**: Jacqueline Kennedy to Marion Davies, n.d. (ca. Oct. 1953), Marion Davies Collection, Academy of Motion Picture Arts and Sciences Library, Los Angeles.

Page 383. **Hedda Hopper, staying with Hearst**: George Eells, *Hedda and Louella* (New York: Putnam, 1972), 223.

Page 384. **As you know, Ambassador Kennedy**: Douglas Fairbanks Jr. to FDR, n.d. (ca. Nov. 1940), FDR Papers, Hyde Park, N.Y. See *Hostage to Fortune: The Letters of Joseph P. Kennedy*, ed. Amanda Smith (New York: Viking, 2001). Smith claims that no surviving correspondence or memorandums relate to Kennedy's threats to Jews in Hollywood and makes only passing references to the incident in her chapter introductions. She does reproduce a Kennedy letter to Hearst written on November 26, 1940, that suggests the ambassador visited Wyntoon immediately before he went to Hollywood to speak to the moguls. For a story about Kennedy's links to Senator Wheeler and their possible scheme to return Kennedy to power in Hollywood, see *In Fact*, Oct. 27, 1941, 1–2.

Page 385. **"America First"**: Ian Mugridge, *The View from Xanadu: William Randolph Hearst and United States Foreign Policy* (Montreal: McGill-Queen's University Press, 1995), 138–39; Hearst, *The Hearsts*, 53; J. Edgar Hoover to WRH, Apr. 8, 1940, WRH FBI files.

Page 385. **he explained what he meant by the slogan**: *San Francisco Examiner*, Sept. 11, 1908.

Page 385. **"Buy American"**: *Variety*, Jan. 17, 1933. One magazine found Hearst's "Buy American" campaign a "remarkable exhibition of mass idiocy" that was having an "unexpected aspect" of making Hollywood studios fearful of producing films with immigrant actors (*New Republic*, Feb. 1, 1933).

Page 386. **the production company Radio Pictures**: *Variety*, Jan. 10, 1933.

Page 386. **"wisely self-devoted"**: Mugridge, *The View from Xanadu*.

Page 386. **"helped found the America First movement**: Hearst, *The Hearsts*, 53.

Page 386. **"I, of course, know**: J. Edgar Hoover to WRH, Apr. 8, 1940.

Page 387. **European refugees**: Neal Gabler, *An Empire of Their Own: How the Jews Invented Hollywood* (New York: Crown, 1988), 323.

Page 387. **Back in August**: *Variety*, Aug. 21, 1940.

Page 387. **"Too bad Orson Welles isn't an Englishman**: Quoted in Harlan Lebo, *Citizen Kane* (New York: Doubleday, 1990), 136.

Page 387. **"in the throes of one of the greatest discussions**: "Refugee Issue Divides Hollywood," *New York Journal-American*, Aug. 11, 1940.

Page 388. **"a well organized movement afoot**: *NYT*, Sept. 22, 1940, sec. 9, p. 3.

Page 388. **"Famous refugees have been pouring**: *New York Journal-American*, Aug. 5, 1940.

Page 388. **"Refugee Issue Divides Hollywood"**: *American Weekly* magazine, *New York Journal-American*, Aug. 11, 1940.

Page 388. **"the screen has teemed with Communist propaganda**: *New York Journal-American*, Aug. 9, 1940.

Page 388. **"are AWOL from concentration camps**: Paul Schofield to Will Hays, Aug. 30, 1940, Westbrook Pegler Papers, Herbert Hoover Presidential Library, Hoover Institute for War and Peace, Stanford University, Palo Alto, Calif. The Nazis first established a concentration camp in Dachau in 1933. In April 1940 Heinrich Himmler ordered the establishment of the Auschwitz concentration camp in Nazi-occupied Poland, and over seven hundred Polish political prisoners arrived there in June.

Page 389. **Phelps worked on Hearst's Los Angeles Examiner**: *Hollywood, the Filth Column of America*, G. Allison's *American Voice: A Journal of Truth*, Pegler Papers.

Page 390. **a film about Hitler**: Richard Meryman, *Mank: The Wit, World, and Life of Herman Mankiewicz* (New York: Morrow, 1978).

Page 390. **"a kind of German Jewish Scott Fitzgerald"**: Ibid.

Page 390. **"Scott had a bit of a death instinct**: Ibid.

Page 390. **One photograph shows the Mankiewicz couple**: Ibid.

Page 391. **Mankiewicz would later admit**: Mankiewicz testimony, *Ferdinand Lundberg vs. Orson Welles, Herman J. Mankiewicz, and RKO Radio Pictures, Inc.*, Nov. 30, 1950, National Archives, NYC.

Page 391. **"The play exposes the international ramifications:** *Daily Worker,* Oct. 26, 1936, Orson Welles file, Pegler Papers. See Morgan Himelstein, *Drama Was a Weapon: The Left Wing Theater in New York, 1929–1941* (New Brunswick, N.J.: Rutgers University Press, 1963), 15–16, 135–36; *Ten Million Ghosts* clipping file, New York Public Library for the Performing Arts, NYC.

Page 392. **"smudging" some of the Hearst references:** Simon Callow, *Orson Welles: The Road to Xanadu* (New York: Viking, 1996).

Page 392. **dead on the floor of a hotel bathroom:** Charles F. Kane obituaries, *New York Journal-American,* Feb. 7, 1940; *New York Herald Tribune,* Feb. 8, 1940; *NYT,* Feb. 11, 1940, 48.

Page 392. **In an early draft of American:** Robert L. Carringer, "The Scripts of Citizen Kane," *Critical Inquiry* (winter 1978): 378.

Page 393. **"a chorus girl or:** Theodore Roosevelt to John St. Loe Strachey, Oct. 25, 1906, quoted in David Nasaw, *The Chief* (New York: Houghton Mifflin, 1999).

Page 393. **Hearst-Kane parallels:** Sometimes, Charles Foster Kane seems to be based simultaneously on Hearst and Welles, and Susan Alexander is based on both Davies and Millicent Hearst. Like Kane (and Welles) Hearst enjoyed parlor magic, picking up the talent when his children were young. Through her Milk Fund charity work, Millicent was closely associated with New York's Metropolitan Opera, and for many years she even took singing lessons, possibly at Hearst's urging. See "Teach Children to Play, Says Mrs. William Randolph Hearst," *Sun,* May 3, 1914, 10.

Page 393. **"a contraband message":** Michael S. Shull and David Edward Wilt, *Hollywood War Films, 1937–1945* (Jefferson, N.C.: McFarland, 1996), 19–22, 125. The authors describe *Citizen Kane* as having an anti-Fascist contraband message.

Page 394. **optical illusions:** Robert L. Carringer, *The Making of Citizen Kane* (Berkeley: University of California Press, 1985).

Page 395. **Closely resembling Hearst: a Hollywood showman:** Apparently Welles saw the worlds inhabited by Kane and Hearst as being somewhat interchangeable. "Such men as Kane," Welles said, "always tend towards the newspaper and entertainment world. They combine a morbid preoccupation with the public with a devastatingly low opinion of the public mentality and moral character" (quoted in Callow, *Orson Welles,* 497).

Page 396. **"a typical American business man":** *Friday,* Sept. 13, 1941, 20. See *Friday,* Feb. 14, 1941, 8–9.

Page 396. **she had been troubled by the rumors:** Louella Parsons, *Tell It to Louella* (New York: Putnam, 1961). See Callow, *Orson Welles,* 493.

Page 397. **"Mr. Hearst casually gave:** Meryman, *Mank.* For more on Hearst's retaliation, see *Variety,* Jan. 15, 1941, 1; interview with Dorothy Mackaill, June 24, 1989; Michael Sage, "Hearst Over Hollywood," *New Republic,* Feb. 24, 1941, 270–71.

Page 397. **Hearst had an ally in Louis B. Mayer:** Gabler, *An Empire of Their Own.*

Page 397. **His Honor the Mayor:** Radio script in Pegler Papers.

Page 399. **a letter to a Universal executive by Irving Thalberg:** Irving Thalberg to R. H. Cochrane, June 20, 1921, Lion's Share Research files, Bosley Crowther Papers, Brigham Young University, Provo, Utah.

Page 399. **Kent Hunter:** *Variety,* Apr. 16, 1941, 3; Apr. 23, 1941; Phoebe Apperson Hearst American Legion Post incorporation records, American Legion National Headquarters, Indianapolis; Robert Terrall, "Hearst Is Still Alive," *New Masses,* June 13, 1939.

Page 399. **to author at least two articles:** *American Legion Magazine,* Aug. 1940 and Oct. 1940.

Page 400. **"Other representatives of the publisher:** *NYT,* Jan. 19, 1941, sec. 9, p. 5. Isolationist senator Wheeler was a member of the subcommittee that began hearings on September 9, 1941, regarding alleged film propaganda aimed at influencing the public toward participating in the European war. Early in the proceedings Senator Gerald P. Nye, who was leading the investigation, put forward a list of films he considered to be pro-war propaganda. Nine out of the eleven American pictures on the list were also on a list of "propaganda pictures" prepared by Hearst's syndicated entertainment columnist, Harrison Carroll, and sent to his boss at Wyntoon just as the Nye Committee was about to commence its hearings. See Shull and Wilt, *Hollywood War Films;* "Harrison Carroll's List of Propaganda Films," H. O. Hunter to Joseph Willicombe, Sept. 5, 1941, WRH Papers, Bancroft Library, UC, Berkeley.

Page 400. **writing in his diary:** Charles A. Lindbergh, *The Wartime Journals of Charles A. Lindbergh* (New York: Harcourt Brace Jovanovich, 1970).

Page 402. **"Instead of agitating for war:** "Lindbergh Sees a 'Plot' for War," *NYT,* Sept. 12, 1941. See Scott A. Berg, *Lindbergh* (New York: Putnam's, 1998).

Page 402. **"An Un-American Address":** *New York Journal-American,* Sept. 14, 1941.

Page 402. **"Racial Prejudices Have No Place in America":** *New York Journal-American,* Sept. 15, 1941.

Page 402. **John Wesley Hanes:** Thomas E. Mahl, *Desperate Deception: British Covert Operations in the United States, 1939–44* (Dulles, Va.: Brassey's, 1999); British Security Coordination Document, courtesy of Thomas Mahl; John Wesley Hanes Papers, American Heritage Center, University of Wyoming, Laramie.

Page 403. **"Hearst's Frantic Try at Covering Up":** *Daily Worker,* Sept. 16, 1941.

Page 403. **"fairly accurate in meaning":** Lindbergh, *Wartime Journals.*

Page 404. **a guest at Wyntoon:** Marion Davies, *The Times We Had: Life with William Randolph Hearst,* ed. Pamela Pfau and Kenneth S. Marx (Indianapolis: Bobbs-Merrill, 1975); Nasaw, *The Chief.*

Page 404. **"treated and maligned by the Hearst papers":** *Variety,* Mar. 4, 1942.

Page 405. **frequent references to Mankiewicz's drinking problem:** Between March 13 and July 18, 1943, the *Los Angeles Examiner* published no fewer than twenty articles about the screenwriter's accident and arrest (Regional History Center, Los Angeles).

Page 405. **In order to make our campaign:** E. D. Coblentz to WRH, Apr. 19, 1937, Coblentz Papers.

Page 407. **"the first instance:** *NYT,* reprinted in " 'Mission to Moscow' Film Attacked," *New York Journal-American,* May 16, 1943; see also "Chaplain Attacks 'Mission' Film As Propaganda," *New York Journal-American,* May 17, 1943.

Page 407. **Your papers displayed yesterday:** Jack Warner to WRH, May 17, 1943, Jack

Warner Collection, USC Cinema-Television Library, University of Southern California, Los Angeles.

Page 407. **I certainly do not wish anything:** WRH to Jack Warner, May 20, 1943; see also Jack Warner to WRH, May 21, 1943, Jack Warner Collection.

Page 408. **an end to their friendship:** Jack Warner, *My First Hundred Years in Hollywood* (New York: Random House, 1965).

Page 408. **"You are right:** Jack Warner to Robert Buckner, May 22, 1943, Warner Bros. Archive.

Page 408. **Warner was summoned to the White House:** Warner, *My First Hundred Years.*

Page 409. **Hearst's telegram reaction:** This and subsequent related Hearst and Goldwyn quotations are drawn from Scott A. Berg, *Goldwyn* (New York: Knopf, 1989).

Page 409. **Harold Ickes:** *New York Journal-American,* Nov. 9, 1943.

Page 409. **"Also sparking the [Alliance] movement":** *Los Angeles Examiner,* Feb. 5, 1944.

Page 410. **"statement of principles":** "Film Leaders Form Anti-Red Organization," *Los Angeles Examiner,* Feb. 5, 1944. See also "Americanize the Movies" (editorial), *Los Angeles Examiner,* Feb. 9, 1944.

Page 410. **"it is interesting to note:** Edwin A. Lahey, "Hollywood, I Love You. II. Political Winds Blow a Gale," *Chicago Daily News,* May 9, 1944.

Page 411. **"Afterwards, they seemed quite thrilled:** William Shirer, *Berlin Diary, 1934–1941* (New York: Galahad, 1995).

Page 411. **James McGuiness . . . Westbrook Pegler:** *American Film Institute Catalog* (Berkeley: University of California Press, 1993); Pegler Papers; Ronald Brownstein, *The Power and the Glitter: Hollywood-Washington Connection* (New York: Vintage, 1993).

Page 411. **Rupert Hughes:** James O. Klemm, *Rupert Hughes: A Hollywood Legend* (Beverly Hills: Pomegranate, 1997).

Page 411. **radio commentator:** *Daily Worker,* May 21, 1944.

Page 412. **Sam Wood:** *Los Angeles Examiner,* Sept. 8 and Oct. 17, 1929; interview with Jean Wood, Mar. 19, 1993.

Page 412. **Hollywood's biggest moneymaking director:** *Variety,* Jan. 5, 1944, 1.

Page 413. **"On the contrary":** Ceplair and Englund, *The Inquisition in Hollywood,* 211.

Page 413. **Walter Winchell:** Walter Goodman, *The Committee* (New York: Farrar, Strauss and Giroux, 1968); Neal Gabler, *Winchell* (New York: Random House, 1995).

Page 413. **"The Winchell columns:** Quoted in Gabler, *Winkler.*

Page 414. **"Chief thinks it:** H. O. Hunter to John B. T. Campbell, Nov. 27, 1944, Dec. 7, 1944, Swanberg Papers.

Page 414. **"Chief instructs—'Kill it everywhere' ":** Hunter to Campbell, Dec. 18, 1944, Swanberg Papers.

Page 415. **"Appendix 9":** Goodman, *The Committee;* Chaney and Cieply, *The Hearsts.*

Page 415. **"the greatest hotbed:** Rankin is quoted in Goodman, *The Committee,* 172–74.

Page 415. **According to an FBI informant:** FBI Files on Communism in the film industry.

Page 416. **James McGuiness said it was impossible:** *(Jefferson City, Mo.) Sunday News and Tribune,* Apr. 30, 1944.

Page 416. **Jews were indeed a special target:** Gabler, *Empire of Their Own*; Ceplair and Englund, *The Inquisition in Hollywood*; interview with Jean Wood; Alliance clipping file, Regional History Center, Los Angeles.

Page 416. **"There was considerable feeling:** Quoted in Gabler, *Empire of Their Own*, 366.

Page 417. **"At a meeting of leaders:** INP photo, clipping file, Regional History Center, Los Angeles.

Page 417. **"stupid and reactionary":** Gabler, *Empire of Their Own.* See also Goodman, *The Committee.*

Page 417. **Sokolsky to oversee a clearinghouse:** Richard Gid Powers, *Not Without Power: The History of American Communism* (New York: Free, 1996).

17. NO TRESPASSING

Page 419. **Laura and Sean Brady:** Interview with Sean Brady, Oct. 10, 1991.

Page 420. **William Curley;** notes for *Citizen Hearst,* William S. Swanberg Papers, Columbia University.

Page 421. **the contents of the beach house:** Park Bernet Galleries catalog, Dec. 7–8, 1945.

Page 421. **everyone was dry-eyed:** Interview with San Simeon housekeeper, Anne Miller Lopez, Jan. 6, 1992.

Page 421. **"We did not stay:** Marion Davies to Lolita Coblentz, n.d., E. D. Coblentz Papers, Bancroft Library, University of California, Berkeley.

Page 422. **bomb:** Fred Lawrence Guiles, *Marion Davies* (New York: McGraw-Hill, 1972); Hearst FBI files.

Page 422. **Rita Hayworth:** Louella Parsons, *Tell It to Louella* (New York: Putnam's, 1961); *New York Journal-American,* May 31, 1949, June 1, 1949.

Page 423. **although a film was never produced:** *Daily Worker,* Apr. 17, 1944, in FBI file.

Page 424. **Triborough Bridge:** Gregory F. Gilmartin, *Shaping the City* (New York: Clarkson Potter, 1995).

Page 424. **Myron Prinzmetal:** "Mr. Hearst's MD," *New York Post,* Mar. 16, 1949; "Opposes Pounds' Aid to Vivisection," *New York Journal-American,* Feb. 24, 1949.

Page 426. **"Jane and Ronnie":** "Ronald Reagan, 'Going Places'—but Fast," *New York Journal-American,* Dec. 24, 1938.

Page 427. **Ingrid Bergman's real-life saga:** *New York Journal-American,* Apr. 13, 1949; Parsons, *Tell It to Louella,* 67–81; Joseph Henry Steele, *Ingrid Bergman: An Intimate Portrait* (New York: McKay, 1959), 168–225, 260–78; *New York Herald Tribune,* Mar. 15, 1950.

Page 428. **"a man of great importance:** Quoted in George Eells, *Hedda and Louella* (New York: Putnam, 1972), 249–50.

Page 428. **It may have been at Hughes's suggestion:** Interview with Anne Miller Lopez, Jan. 6, 1992. See William Randolph Hearst Jr., *The Hearsts: Father and Son* (Niwot, Colo.: Roberts Rinehart, 1991).

Page 429. **"the victim of a lynch mob"**: Walter Winchell column, *New York Daily Mirror*, Dec. 20, 1956.

Page 429. **the very first wire and basket of flowers**: Steele. *Ingrid Bergman*, 277; Ingrid Bergman, *My Story* (New York: Delacorte, 1972).

Page 431. **Eddie Hubbell**: Interview with Eddie Hubbell, June 12, 1992.

Page 431. **Panama California Exposition**: Joe Hubbell taped memoirs, author's collection. Hearst and Julia Morgan would eventually decide to depart from a literal interpretation of the exposition's architectural style.

Page 431. **"Thanks for your welcome"**: George Sokolsky to Westbrook Pegler, Jan. 10, 1950, Westbrook Pegler Papers, Herbert Hoover Presidential Library, Hoover Institute for War and Peace, Stanford University, Palo Alto, Calif.

Page 432. **"Sokolsky," Hearst told**: John Winkler, *William Randolph Hearst: A New Appraisal* (New York: Hastings House, 1955).

Page 432. **strained relationship with their father**: In 1952 Davies wrote her attorney: "[Hearst] wanted a committee, not an individual in this position [head of corporation] . . . large enough to out vote the boys because the one person in particular that he did not want to take over was Bill Hearst, Jr. and the very thing he thought he had prevented has happened" (Marion Davies to Gregory Bautzer, Oct. 16, 1952, Marion Davies Collection, Academy of Motion Picture Arts and Sciences Library, Los Angeles.

Page 432. **"He was . . . like a kid again"**: Interview with William Randolph Hearst Jr., Swanberg Papers. See Hearst, *The Hearsts.*

Page 432. **still entitled Mrs. William Randolph Hearst**: Lindsay Chaney and Michael Cieply, *The Hearsts, Family and Empire: The Later Years* (New York: Simon and Schuster, 1981).

Page 433. **"new cement and steel"**: *Los Angeles Examiner*, Apr. 6, 1950.

Page 433. **"Son," Hearst told Mayer**: *Los Angeles Examiner*, Apr. 13, 1950, Regional History Center, Los Angeles.

Page 433. **"because his ideas of screen**: Bosley Crowther, *Hollywood Rajah* (New York: Holt, 1960).

Page 434. **baby shower**: Interview with Sean Brady, Oct. 10, 1991.

Page 434. **windup toy**: Interview with Joanne Hearst, in Chaney and Cieply research papers, Bancroft Library.

Page 434. **Lederer, had been commissioned**: Charles Lederer clipping file, Regional History Center, Los Angeles.

Page 435. **"Dearest Secretary"**: *New York Journal-American*, Feb. 4, 1949.

Page 435. **another Hollywood series**: Interview with Mac St. Johns, 1991; interview with Elaine St. Johns, 1995; Adela Rogers St. Johns, *Love, Laughter, and Tears: My Hollywood Story* (Garden City, N.Y.: Doubleday, 1978).

Page 437. **"lost in an overstuffed chair"**: Raoul Walsh, *Every Man in His Time* (New York: Farrar, 1974).

Page 437. **When the eighty-eight-year-old body**: On the Hearst funeral, see *San Francisco Examiner* and *New York Journal-American*, Aug. 16 and 17, 1951; *Editor and Publisher*, Sept. 1, 1951.

Page 439. **numerous tributes filled the pages**: *New York Journal-American* and *New York Mirror,* Aug. 15–16, 1951.

Page 441. **it did not seem to relish the association**: On the loss of records, see interview with Ralph Schoenstein, 1990; Ralph Schoenstein, *Citizen Paul* (New York: Farrar, 1978); UCLA film archive; interview with Frank A. Bennack Jr.

Page 442. **Union Square**: *Editor and Publisher,* Aug. 25, 1951.

Index

Note: Some Hearst newspapers and some other periodicals that appear frequently in the text have been omitted from the index; also, listings within main entries follow a generally chronological (rather than alphabetical) sequence.